e state of your marriage, says TV shrink Dr Raj Persaud

present, your wife is telling you that she finds you physically repulsive and can't bear the thought of ever having sex with you again. The tools are a coded message that say: "From now on, you'll have to DIY - Do It Yourself!" The heartless cow's also implying that you're a wanker.

Real meaning: Sex with you makes me physically sick.

𝔒... my missus gave to me...

B...

• ... shiny pair of binoculars on Christmas m... at your missus might be seeking her pl... reet. Binoculars are only ever used fo... is your wife trying to hide the fact that she's on the lookout for birds too ... and not of the feathered variety!

Real meaning: I've gone lesbian.

On the eighth day of Christmas, my missus gave to me...

HANDKERCHIEFS..........................

• A SET of handkerchiefs embroidered with your initials seems innocuous enough... but what does that monogram in the corner really signify? Letters on a handkerchief are an absolute giveaway that letters play a big part in your wife's life. It's certain that she is cheating on you right under your nose - with the postman! That's right, while you're hard at work, she's getting a delivery of first class male every morning... on the kitchen table!

Real meaning: I'm fucking the postie every day.

On the ninth day of Christmas, my missus gave to me...

GOLF CLUBS..................................

• MORE men die on British golf courses each year than on the roads. In buying you a stylish new set of clubs, your wife is really expressing her dearest wish that you were six feet under, so she could get her hands on your insurance money. In fact, she's probably already made a number of attempts on your life without you realising it. Chances are she's tried to cut the brake cables on your car, slipped rat poison into your tea and attempted to smother you with a pillow in the night. For your own safety, you must get out of the house as quickly as possible.

Real meaning: I'm going to kill you for the insurance.

On the tenth day of Christmas, my missus gave to me...

NICE JUMPER..............................

• A SMART new pullover always makes a smashing Christmas present. And when it's been knitted for you by your wife, surely it must be an extra special token of her love. But you'd be wrong, because it actually represents a tangled web of deceit that she has been deftly weaving around you for years. She is almost certainly a bigamist, with a second husband and family living in another house on the other side of town. Don't let her pull the wool over your eyes any longer. Call the police immediately and let them know what she's been up to.

Real meaning: I'm married to someone else.

On the eleventh day of Christmas, my missus gave to me...

SHIRT...

• WE SEE shirts every day, as we walk about in the streets - the same streets where prostitutes ply the oldest trade in the world, peddling their bodies to strangers. The gift of a shirt is a tacit confession from your wife that while you're out of the house, she's whoring herself, engaging in cold, anonymous sex with strangers ... in your marital bed. Even worse, all your friends know what she's up to. Indeed, many of them regularly avail themselves of her seedy services, often paying extra for unprotected anal.

Real meaning: I'm a hooker and you're the only one who doesn't know.

On the twelfth day of Christmas, my missus gave to me...

CHOCOLATES..............................

• THE tempting, foil-wrapped chocolates in an expensive selection box conceal a variety of delicious surprise centres. Some contain delicious montelimar, pralines or fruity nougat, whilst others delight you with coffee, chewy caramel or nuts. And in buying you these chocs your wife is trying to tell you you've got another surprise in store ... For SHE is actually a HE - complete with a set of fully-functioning male genitals! Unless you can live with the fact that your wife has been concealing his true gender from you for all these years, your marriage is over.

Real meaning: I'm a pre-op transexual.

NEXT ISSUE: What your wife buys in the January Sales says a lot about her sexual fantasies

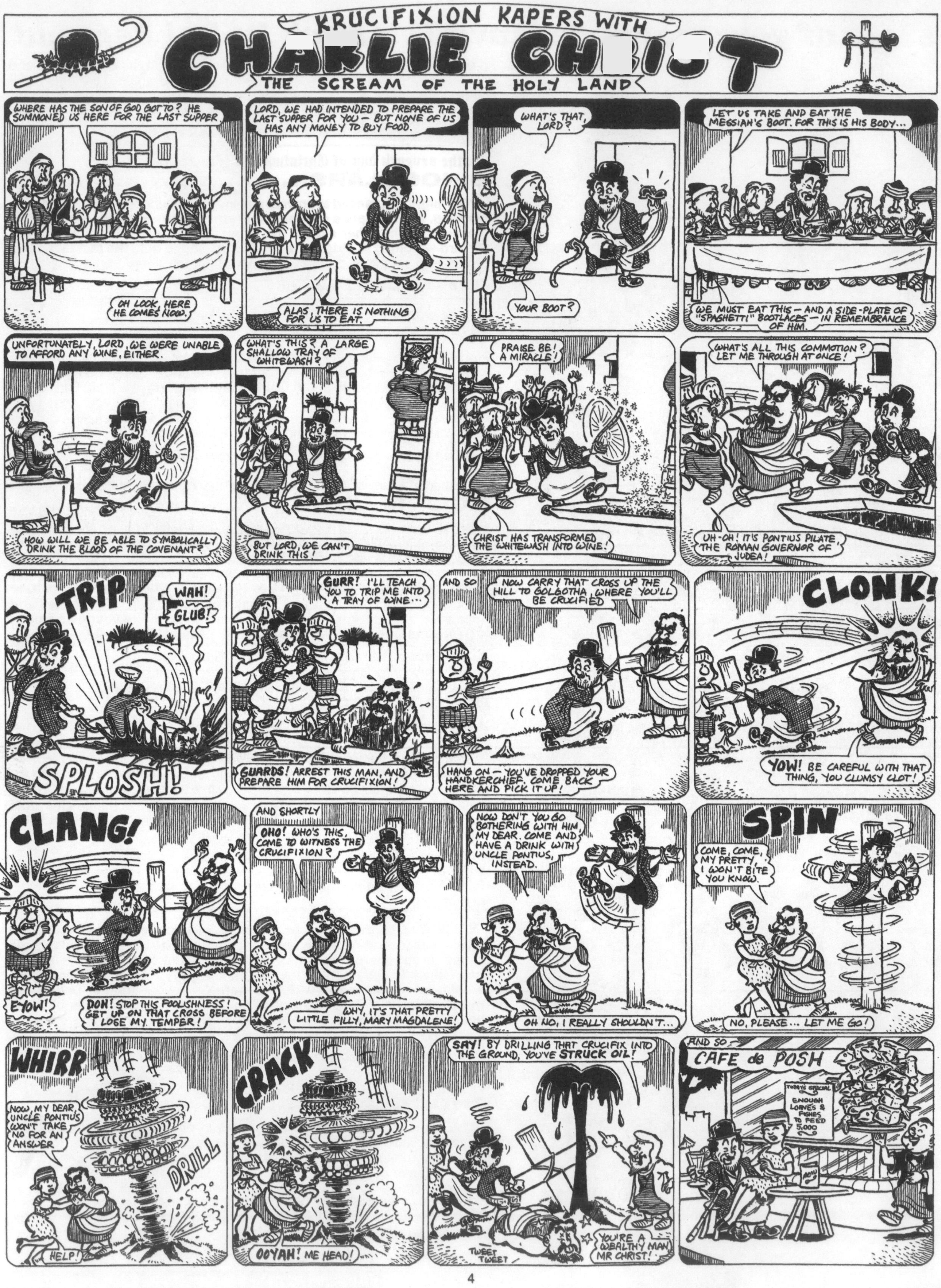
KRUCIFIXION KAPERS WITH
CHARLIE CHRIST
THE SCREAM OF THE HOLY LAND
WHERE HAS THE SON OF GOD GOT TO? HE SUMMONED US HERE FOR THE LAST SUPPER.
OH LOOK, HERE HE COMES NOW.
LORD, WE HAD INTENDED TO PREPARE THE LAST SUPPER FOR YOU — BUT NONE OF US HAS ANY MONEY TO BUY FOOD.
ALAS, THERE IS NOTHING FOR US TO EAT.
WHAT'S THAT, LORD?
YOUR BOOT?
LET US TAKE AND EAT THE MESSIAH'S BOOT. FOR THIS IS HIS BODY...
WE MUST EAT THIS — AND A SIDE-PLATE OF "SPAGHETTI" BOOTLACES — IN REMEMBRANCE OF HIM.
UNFORTUNATELY, LORD, WE WERE UNABLE TO AFFORD ANY WINE, EITHER.
HOW WILL WE BE ABLE TO SYMBOLICALLY DRINK THE BLOOD OF THE COVENANT?
WHAT'S THIS? A LARGE SHALLOW TRAY OF WHITEWASH?
BUT LORD, WE CAN'T DRINK THIS!
PRAISE BE! A MIRACLE!
CHRIST HAS TRANSFORMED THE WHITEWASH INTO WINE!
WHAT'S ALL THIS COMMOTION? LET ME THROUGH AT ONCE!
UH-OH! IT'S PONTIUS PILATE, THE ROMAN GOVERNOR OF JUDEA!
TRIP
WAH!
GLUB!
SPLOSH!
GURR! I'LL TEACH YOU TO TRIP ME INTO A TRAY OF WINE...
GUARDS! ARREST THIS MAN, AND PREPARE HIM FOR CRUCIFIXION!
AND SO
NOW CARRY THAT CROSS UP THE HILL TO GOLGOTHA, WHERE YOU'LL BE CRUCIFIED
HANG ON — YOU'VE DROPPED YOUR HANDKERCHIEF. COME BACK HERE AND PICK IT UP!
CLONK!
YOW! BE CAREFUL WITH THAT THING, YOU CLUMSY CLOT!
CLANG!
EYOW!
OOH! STOP THIS FOOLISHNESS! GET UP ON THAT CROSS BEFORE I LOSE MY TEMPER!
AND SHORTLY
OHO! WHO'S THIS, COME TO WITNESS THE CRUCIFIXION?
WHY, IT'S THAT PRETTY LITTLE FILLY, MARY MAGDALENE!
NOW DON'T YOU GO BOTHERING WITH HIM, MY DEAR. COME AND HAVE A DRINK WITH UNCLE PONTIUS, INSTEAD.
OH NO, I REALLY SHOULDN'T...
SPIN
COME, COME, MY PRETTY, I WON'T BITE YOU KNOW.
NO, PLEASE... LET ME GO!
WHIRR
NOW, MY DEAR, UNCLE PONTIUS WON'T TAKE NO FOR AN ANSWER
DRILL
HELP!
CRACK
OOYAH! ME HEAD!
SAY! BY DRILLING THAT CRUCIFIX INTO THE GROUND, YOU'VE STRUCK OIL!
TWEET TWEET
YOU'RE A WEALTHY MAN, MR CHRIST!
AND SO
CAFE de POSH
TODAY'S SPECIAL
ENOUGH LOAVES & FISHES TO FEED 5,000

THE CLEVELAND STEAMER

A Muddy Cargo of Bottom Sediment Dredged up from the Backwaters of Issues 182 to 191

CAPTAIN'S LOGS

Graham Dury, Wayne Gamble, Stevie Glover, Davey Jones and Simon Thorp

NAVY CAKES

Tony Coffey, Alex Collier, Simon Ecob, Barney Farmer and Lee Healey, Robin Halstead,
Jason Hazeley, Hobnob, Christina Martin and James MacDougall, Alex Morris,
Joel Morris, Paul Palmer, Lew Stringer, Cat Sullivan, Biscuit Tin and Nick Tolson

SAILOR'S FAVOURITE

Russell Blackman

Dennis Publishing Ltd., 30 Cleveland Street, London W1T 4JD

ISBN 1-907779-90-6

First Printing Autumn 2011

Prinited in Grate Britian

SUBSCRIBE TO **VIZ** ONLINE AT www.viz.co.uk

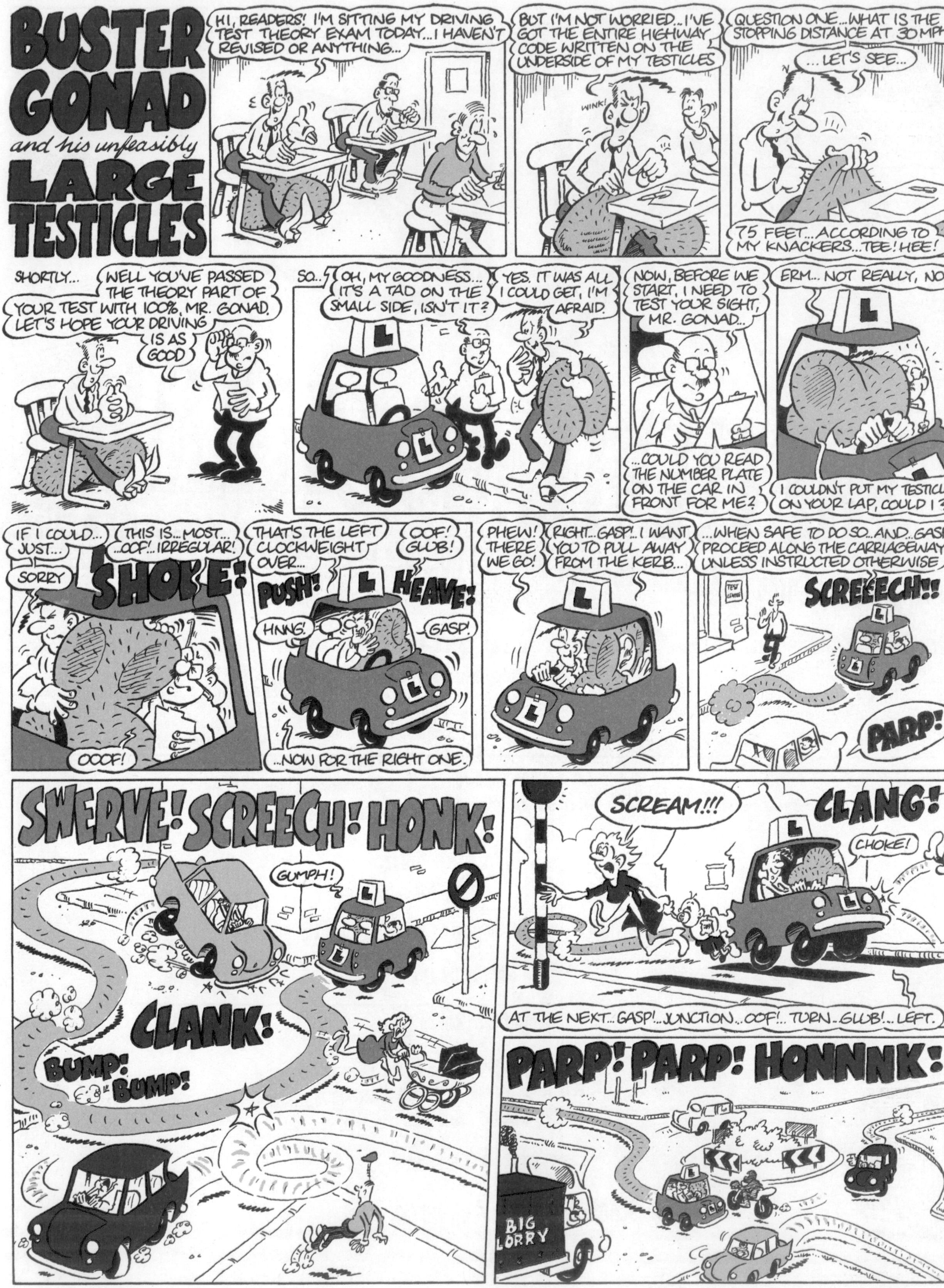
BUSTER GONAD
and his unfeasibly
LARGE TESTICLES
HI, READERS! I'M SITTING MY DRIVING TEST THEORY EXAM TODAY... I HAVEN'T REVISED OR ANYTHING...
BUT I'M NOT WORRIED... I'VE GOT THE ENTIRE HIGHWAY CODE WRITTEN ON THE UNDERSIDE OF MY TESTICLES
WINK!
QUESTION ONE... WHAT IS THE STOPPING DISTANCE AT 30 MPH?
... LET'S SEE...
75 FEET... ACCORDING TO MY KNACKERS... TEE! HEE!
SHORTLY...
WELL YOU'VE PASSED THE THEORY PART OF YOUR TEST WITH 100%, MR. GONAD. LET'S HOPE YOUR DRIVING IS AS GOOD
SO...
OH, MY GOODNESS... IT'S A TAD ON THE SMALL SIDE, ISN'T IT?
YES. IT WAS ALL I COULD GET, I'M AFRAID.
NOW, BEFORE WE START, I NEED TO TEST YOUR SIGHT, MR. GONAD...
...COULD YOU READ THE NUMBER PLATE ON THE CAR IN FRONT FOR ME?
ERM... NOT REALLY, NO.
I COULDN'T PUT MY TESTICLES ON YOUR LAP, COULD I?
IF I COULD... JUST...
THIS IS... MOST... ...OOF!... IRREGULAR!
SORRY
SHOVE!
OOOF!
THAT'S THE LEFT CLOCKWEIGHT OVER...
OOF! GLUB!
PUSH!
HEAVE!
HNNG!
GASP!
...NOW FOR THE RIGHT ONE.
PHEW! THERE WE GO!
RIGHT... GASP!... I WANT YOU TO PULL AWAY FROM THE KERB...
...WHEN SAFE TO DO SO... AND... GASP! PROCEED ALONG THE CARRIAGEWAY UNLESS INSTRUCTED OTHERWISE
SCREEECH!!!
PARP!
SWERVE! SCREECH! HONK!
GUMPH!
CLANK!
BUMP! BUMP!
SCREAM!!!
CLANG!
CHOKE!
AT THE NEXT... GASP!... JUNCTION... OOF!... TURN... GLUB!... LEFT.
PARP! PARP! HONNNK!
BIG LORRY

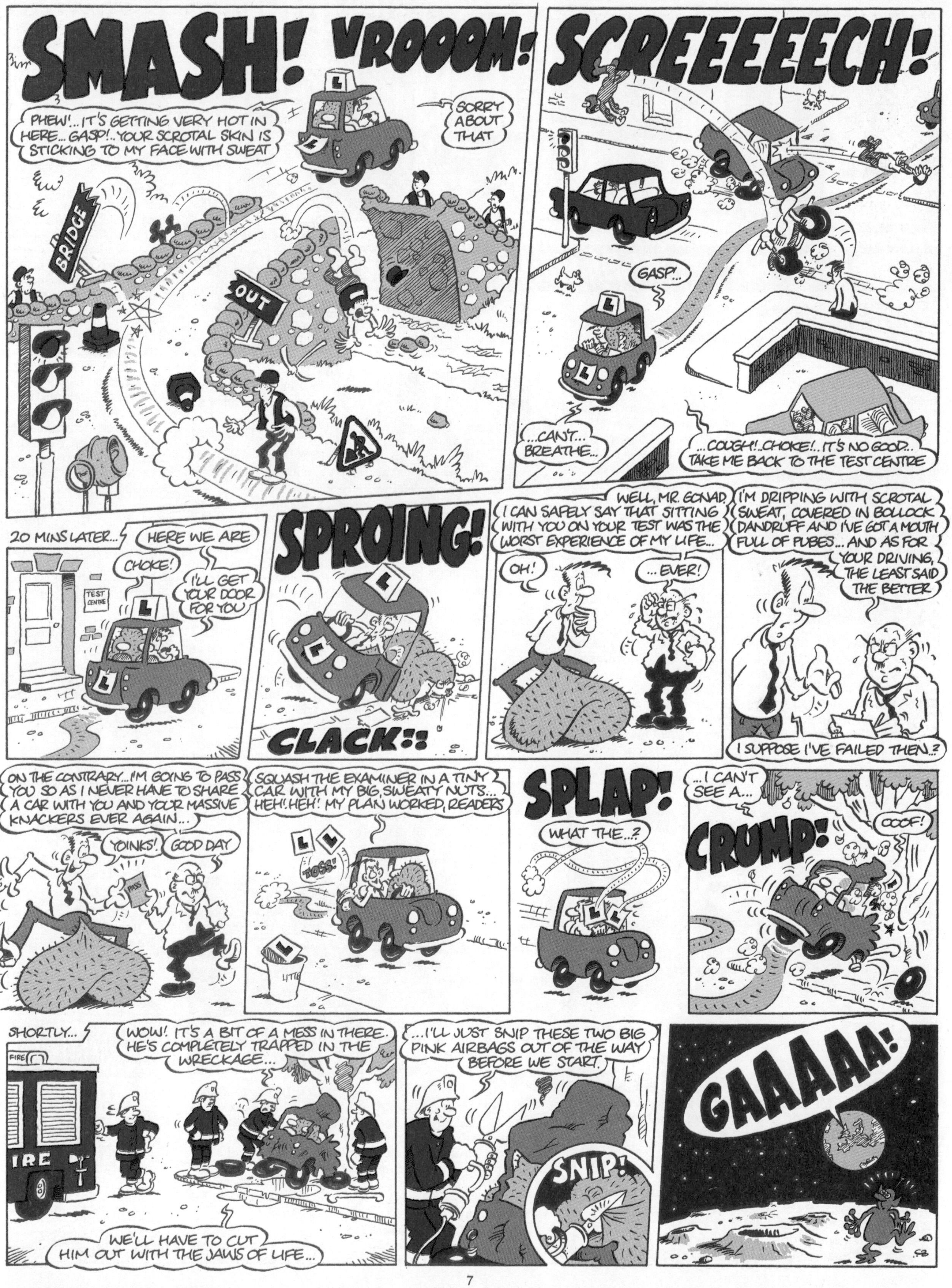

SMASH!
VROOOM!
PHEW!.. IT'S GETTING VERY HOT IN HERE... GASP!.. YOUR SCROTAL SKIN IS STICKING TO MY FACE WITH SWEAT
SORRY ABOUT THAT
BRIDGE
OUT
SCREEEEEECH!
GASP!..
...CAN'T... BREATHE...
...COUGH!..CHOKE!.. IT'S NO GOOD... TAKE ME BACK TO THE TEST CENTRE
20 MINS LATER...
HERE WE ARE
CHOKE!
I'LL GET YOUR DOOR FOR YOU
TEST CENTRE
SPROING!
CLACK!!
WELL, MR. GONAD. I CAN SAFELY SAY THAT SITTING WITH YOU ON YOUR TEST WAS THE WORST EXPERIENCE OF MY LIFE...
OH!
...EVER!
I'M DRIPPING WITH SCROTAL SWEAT, COVERED IN BOLLOCK DANDRUFF AND I'VE GOT A MOUTH FULL OF PUBES... AND AS FOR YOUR DRIVING, THE LEAST SAID THE BETTER
I SUPPOSE I'VE FAILED THEN..?
ON THE CONTRARY...I'M GOING TO PASS YOU SO AS I NEVER HAVE TO SHARE A CAR WITH YOU AND YOUR MASSIVE KNACKERS EVER AGAIN...
YOINKS!
GOOD DAY
PASS
SQUASH THE EXAMINER IN A TINY CAR WITH MY BIG, SWEATY NUTS... HEH! HEH! MY PLAN WORKED, READERS
TOSS!
SPLAP!
WHAT THE...?
...I CAN'T SEE A...
CRUMP!
OOOF!
SHORTLY...
FIRE
WOW! IT'S A BIT OF A MESS IN THERE. HE'S COMPLETELY TRAPPED IN THE WRECKAGE...
WE'LL HAVE TO CUT HIM OUT WITH THE JAWS OF LIFE...
...I'LL JUST SNIP THESE TWO BIG PINK AIRBAGS OUT OF THE WAY BEFORE WE START.
SNIP!
GAAAAA!

LETTERBOCKS

Viz Comic, PO Box 656, North Shields NE30 4XX

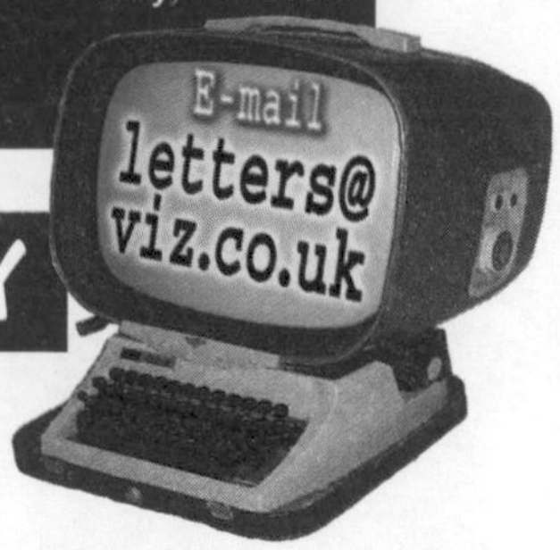
E-mail
letters@
viz.co.uk

STAR LETTER

I DON'T know why everyone is so pleased about America getting a black president. Zimbabwe have had one for years and he's shit.

Billy, Preston

❑ **I THINK** Barry George is a bit like Jesus, because he was punished for the sins of another. And like Jesus, he rose again from prison, only it wasn't after three days, it was nearer 8 and a half years.

Frank Cromarty
Luton

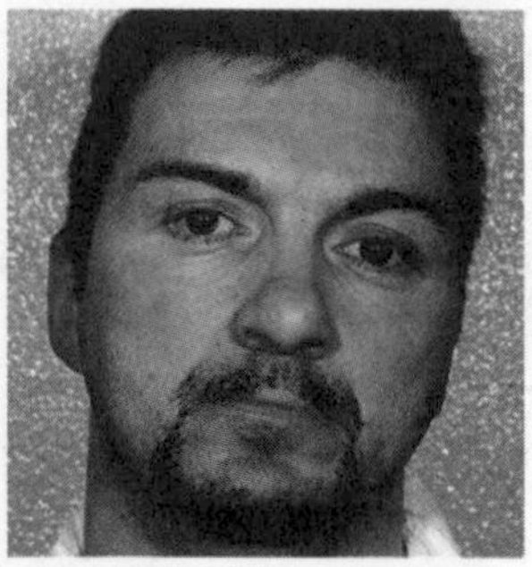

❑ **I DISAGREE** with the above writer who likens Barry George to Jesus. Jesus performed miracles such as walking on water and raising the dead. Admittedly, Barry George once jumped over three double decker busses on roller skates, but whilst this is a fantastic achievement, it does not technically constitute a miracle in the eyes of the church.

Dr Rowan Williams
Canterbury

❑ **COULD** I use your pages to send a message to the high-street retailers FastFrame? Whilst three days could be described as fast in geological terms, perhaps when describing the erosion of a mountain or the formation of an ox bow lake, when it comes to framing a picture, it's not particularly speedy.

Hector Fastnet
Newcastle

❑ **YOU** don't get many songs about bicycles these days. You used to get them all the time - *The Pushbike Song* by The Mixtures, *My White Bicycle* by Tomorrow, *Riding on My Bike* by Madness to name but a few. I think the last bike related song was by Queen some 30 years ago. So come on the likes of Coldplay, Ting Tings and the Arctic Monkeys, get on your bikes and start writing some bike themed songs.

Tim Rusling
e-mail

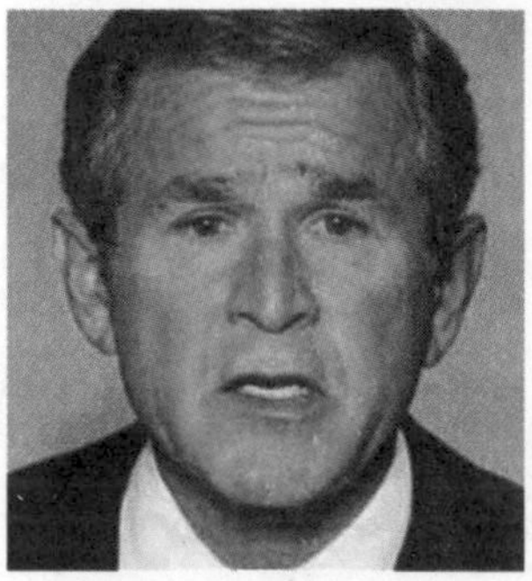

❑ **FOLLOWING** George Bush's hostile reception at a press conference in Iraq - where he had someone chuck their shoes at him - the *Metro* paper reported that the throwing of such an item is a sign of contempt in Iraqi culture. Surely taking off your shoes and throwing them at someone's head doesn't have positive connotations in any culture.

Humphrey Malin
Tekesbury

❑ **YESTERDAY** my 3-year-old son pointed to my bald head and said my head looked like a lightbulb. I was so annoyed I was incandescent with rage.

Chris Allen
Peterborough

❑ **RECENTLY,** Thames Water gave me a free water-saver bag which goes into the toilet cistern and saves a whopping one litre per flush. The trouble is, instead of one flush, it now takes three to shift my morning deposit.

Charlie B
e-mail

❑ **WHAT** a crazy world we live in. Scientists in one laboratory are curing mice of cancer, whilst in another they are devising deadlier mousetraps. Come on scientists, make your minds up what you want to do.

Norman Fletcher
e-mail

❑ **HAVE** you ever had a letter from someone who lives in Angmering, West Sussex?

Gav
Chelmsford

❑ **WHEN** your wife says "Don't bother getting me anything for Christmas," she actually means "Spend six months' wages at H Samuel." But when she says "Leave my arse alone and just do me normally," she means what she says. Honestly, I will never understand women.

Mike Woods
Redhill

❑ **IT WAS** fair enough that Richard Hammond had a best-selling book when he'd almost died, but I see that he has another one out this Christmas despite remaining in good health throughout the year. I'm sorry, but if he wants another best seller he ought to fire himself out of a cannon into a wall or something. Then I'd be happy to see it in Asda.

Tom Wheatley
e-mail

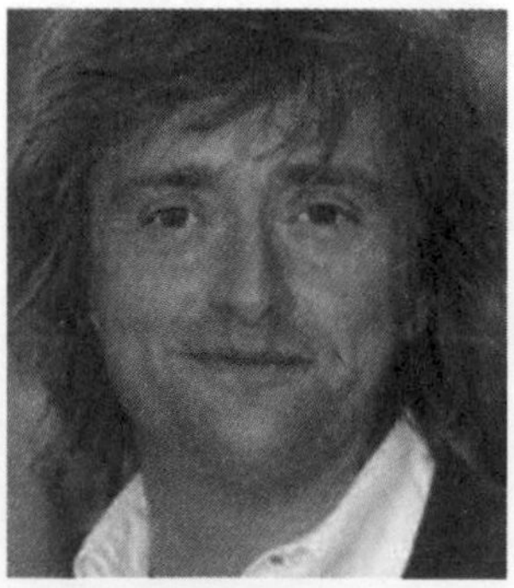

❑ **ACCORDING** to Radio 5, cash-in-hand work costs the Treasury more than 2 billion pounds each year. What a disgrace. You would think the government would set a better example and pay the full price including VAT for their building jobs.

T Dogger
London

❑ **I SEE** the launch issue of Jamie Oliver's magazine 'JAMIE' begins with the editorial 'Hi guys. Well what can I say?' Perhaps he should have thought of that before starting his own magazine.

Edna Carstairs
Nottingham

❑ **THERE** are signs on my local train that say 'In emergency break glass.' I would have thought that any emergency situation could only be made worse by having broken glass all over the place.

Edna Humber
Lewes

❑ **I WAS** pleased to see Felix hosting the Czech Republic UEFA Champions League highlights in his amazing underpants recently. Hopefully this isn't an isolated example and we will soon be treated to other, largely forgotten, almost funny, *Viz* characters on prime time TV.

Pete Wright
Prague

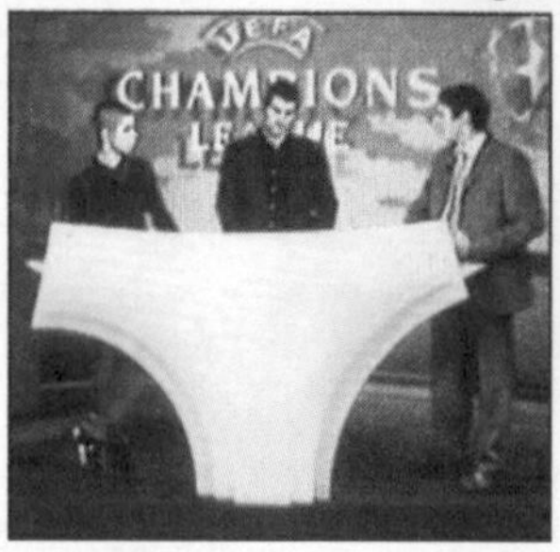

❑ **I HATE** the way the French dip those stale cakes into coffee. Bunch of pigs.

T Portland
Halesowen

Ask the Bish!

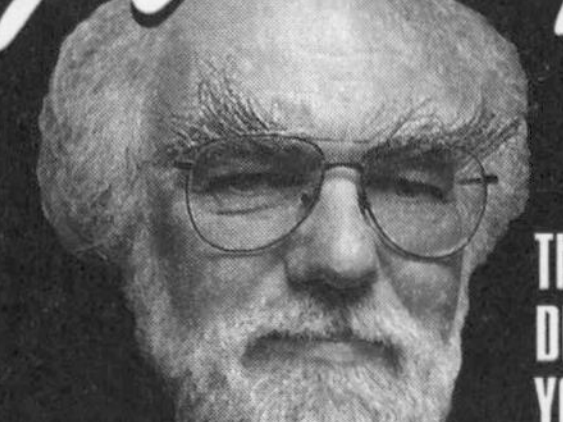

The Archbishop of Canterbury DR ROWAN WILLIAMS answers YOUR queries...

Dear Bish

• I ONCE wanked into a hat in church. Will I be going to hell as a result?

H Fastbender, Luton

The Bish says...

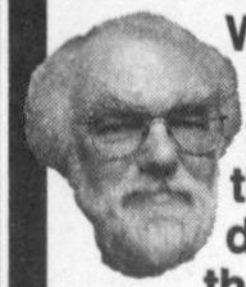

WANKING into a hat in church is indeed a sin, Mr Fastbender, (but at least you took your hat off in the church, and that is one thing that will go in your favour come the day of judgement). It all depends on when the action took place. The Christian Church officially abolished the idea of Hell in 1983, so if you wanked into the hat after that date, you are safe. However, if the deed took place before then, I'm afraid you will be cast into the Lake of Fire for all eternity, and probably even longer.

PSYCHIC Weather Tips

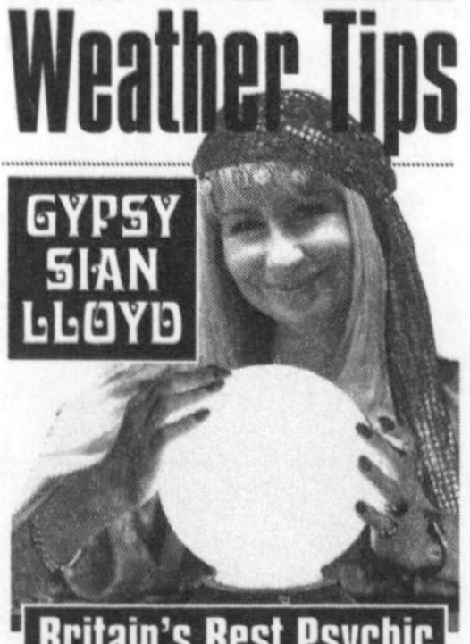

GYPSY SIAN LLOYD

Britain's Best Psychic • Weather Tipster •

RAIN
0890 000 001

SUN
0890 000 002

WIND
0890 000 003

CLOUD
0890 000 004

7TH METEOROLOGIST OF A 7TH METEOROLOGIST

Ed Stewpot Stewart's

MYSTERY NOISE COMPETITION

IDENTIFY this sound and win an exotic dream holiday home of your own in Redcar.

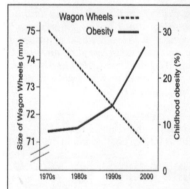

Here it comes now, so read carefully...

"Brrrrrrrmp! Brrrrrrrrrrmp! Schloo-ooo-ooop! Dug-a-dug-a-duga-a-dug-a. B-Dunk! B-Dunk! Ting!"

Do you know what that sound is? Here it is once more...

"Brrrrrrrmp! Brrrrrrrrrrmp! Schloo-ooo-ooop! Dug-a-dug-a-duga-a-dug-a. B-Dunk! B-Dunk! Ting!"

If you think you can identify the mystery noise, write your answer on a postcard and send it to: *Ed Stewpot Stewart's Mystery Noise Competition, Junior Choice, BBC Radio 1, Thirty years ago, London.*

Last week's winner was Helvetica Medium of Windsor, who correctly identified the sound of a man in a kagoule operating a platen printing press near a beehive.

WHERE ARE THEY NOW?

With Top Espionage Expert **"MR SMITH"**

Dear "Mr Smith",

HAVING recently found myself highly entertained by the eccentric antics of David Van Day on *I'm A Celebrity In The Jungle*, I couldn't help but wonder what became of his onetime Dollar band mate Thereza Bazar. Could you let me know if Thereza is still in the music industry and, if not, what is she up to nowadays?

Dave Pinder, London

"MR SMITH" REPORTS................

AFTER my initial research revealed that the subject has permanently relocated to Australia, I quickly set about assigning one of my most trusted Antipodean contacts to the case. They have been following Ms Bazar for seven months using an impressive array of advanced Track n' Trail techniques and so far there has been nothing significant to report in terms of Ms Bazar's possible involvement in the music industry. However, in answer to your other question, our most recent intelligence reports place Ms Bazar in the frozen food section of a Safeway's in central Adelaide, where she appears to be examining a 'two for one' value offer on Goodfella's pizza's.

Dear "Mr Smith",

I USED to very much enjoy the work of comedian John Sessions who seemed to be all over our screens in the early nineties with his quick fire humour and improvisational talents. However, since the turn of the new millennium he is nowhere to be seen! What's the story?

Alan Williamson, Maidstone

"MR SMITH" REPORTS................

I WENT undercover to ascertain the whereabouts of Mr Sessions, my dramatis personae (disclosed on a 'need to know basis' only) unimportant. Investigations revealed him to be living as himself in a Kensington flat. After spending more than a week concealed in one of Mr Session's bins at the rear end of the flat, I have nothing of much significance to report other than the subject's apparent fondness off Beef and Tomato Pot Noodles. I'll keep him under surveillance for another month or so and report back any intelligence.

Dear "Mr Smith",

ONE of my favourite TV shows of all time is *Eldorado*, in my opinion a vastly underrated TV soap which began with much fanfare in 1992 but was sadly axed less than a year later due to poor viewing figures. I'd love to know where the shows various cast members are nowadays and how they are all getting on - any ideas?

Ken Tusk, Hull

"MR SMITH" REPORTS................

THIS is a difficult investigation due to the large numbers of subjects involved. However several agents, including a number of double agents and a mole have been assigned to the case and their diligence and fortitude is already paying off. Without wanting to give too much away at this early stage of the investigation, one of my contacts would appear to have gained the trust of a prominent former cast member whilst posing as a Ukrainian prostitute, and has already fed back some potentially devastating information on his present activities. Another agent managed to break into the house of one of the show's producers yesterday evening and has obtained some highly confidential data including the contact details of several former cast members. I cannot say any more at present, Mr Tusk, but you will shortly be contacted by a man calling himself The Professor who will give you further information.

Do YOU have any queries regarding your favourite stars of yesteryear? If so, sit on the park bench near the statue of Peter Pan in Kensington Gardens and ask your question to a man in his late fifties who sits next to you, raises his hat and says "Spring comes early in Berlin."

Wagon Wheels
Obesity
Size of Wagon Wheels (mm)
Childhood obesity (%)
75
74
73
72
71
30
20
10
0
1970s
1980s
1990s
2000

❑ **HAS** anyone noticed a correlation between childhood obesity and the size of Burton's Wagon Wheels? Graphs don't lie. So come on Burton's Foods, save our podgy bairns and bring back the 1970s-sized Wagon Wheels.

Chris Murgatroyd
e-mail

❑ **37-YEAR-OLD** David Tennant plays Hamlet at the Royal Shakespeare Therare for a couple of weeks and has to have a month off with a bad back. Meanwhile, 60-year-old Jeanette Krankie falls 20 feet out of a pantomime tree and she's back at work the next day. They don't make stars like they used to.

George Fisher
Dunbarton

❑ **IN** response to the challenge laid down by the letter published in your 'First Words' feature (*Roger's Profanisaurus* issue 181), I am proud to report that at his third birthday party, my son expressed his frustration at his new Bob the Builder DVD not loading properly by exclaiming "For fuck's sake!" The fact that he did this in front of two grandmothers, his grandfather, two aunts and an uncle as well as assorted cousins I think not only qualifies him for an honourable mention as the world's sweariest toddler, but also perhaps having the largest audience.

Madgerald
Purley

TOP TIPS

AIR TRAVELLERS. Make your suitcase easy to spot at the luggage carousel by fastening an extremely long-lasting sparkler to it and lighting it before you hand it over at the check-in desk.

Peregrine Fadge
Jedburgh

WHEN NAILING your scrotum to a kitchen table for the purposes of sexual gratification, always ensure that you leave the pliers within arms' reach, not in your toolbox in the shed.

J Paxman
London

ALWAYS STROKE tigers and lions in the direction in which their fur lies. Never stroke against the nap of the fur, as it can make them extremely angry.

Chorlton Cumhardy
Kenilworth

CATCH MOTHS using a mousetrap baited with a jumper.

A Lloyd-Webber
Middlesbrough

HOMEOWNERS. Count your roof-tiles each time you leave the house, so you will know if any of them have been stolen since the last time you counted them.

Alan Fistula
Penmaenmawr

OLD LINGERIE from the Ann Summers shop can be reused around the house as sexually-arousing dusters.

Lambert O'Butler
Devizes

YAKETY YAK
..SO ANYWAY SHE TURNS AROUND BOLD AS BRASS AND SAYS TO JANICE "WELL IT'S A NICE DRESS BUT IT'S A BIT YOUNG FOR YOU ISN'T IT?"
JUST LIKE THAT RIGHT TO HER FACE WELL YOU CAN IMAGINE SO ANYWAY JANICE JUST GIVES HER THIS LOOK LIKE THAT AND SHE SAYS TO HER SHE SAYS...
LOOK, DO YOU MIND?
IT'S JUST THAT I'M TRYING TO WATCH THE END OF THIS PROGRAMME.
OH, WELL I DO BEG YOUR PARDON I'M SURE. I'M SORRY I SPOKE.
PARDON ME FOR TRYING TO MAKE A BIT OF CONVERSATION. I WOULDN'T WANT YOU TO MISS ANY OF YOUR PROGRAMME.
I'LL JUST STAND HERE IN ABSOLUTE SILENCE THEN. I'LL NOT SAY ANOTHER WORD.
GOD FORBID I SHOULD INTERRUPT YOUR PRECIOUS TELLY. YOU'LL NOT HEAR ANOTHER PEEP OUT OF ME. MY LIPS ARE SEALED..

Kettering Man's Appeal to Space Aliens...

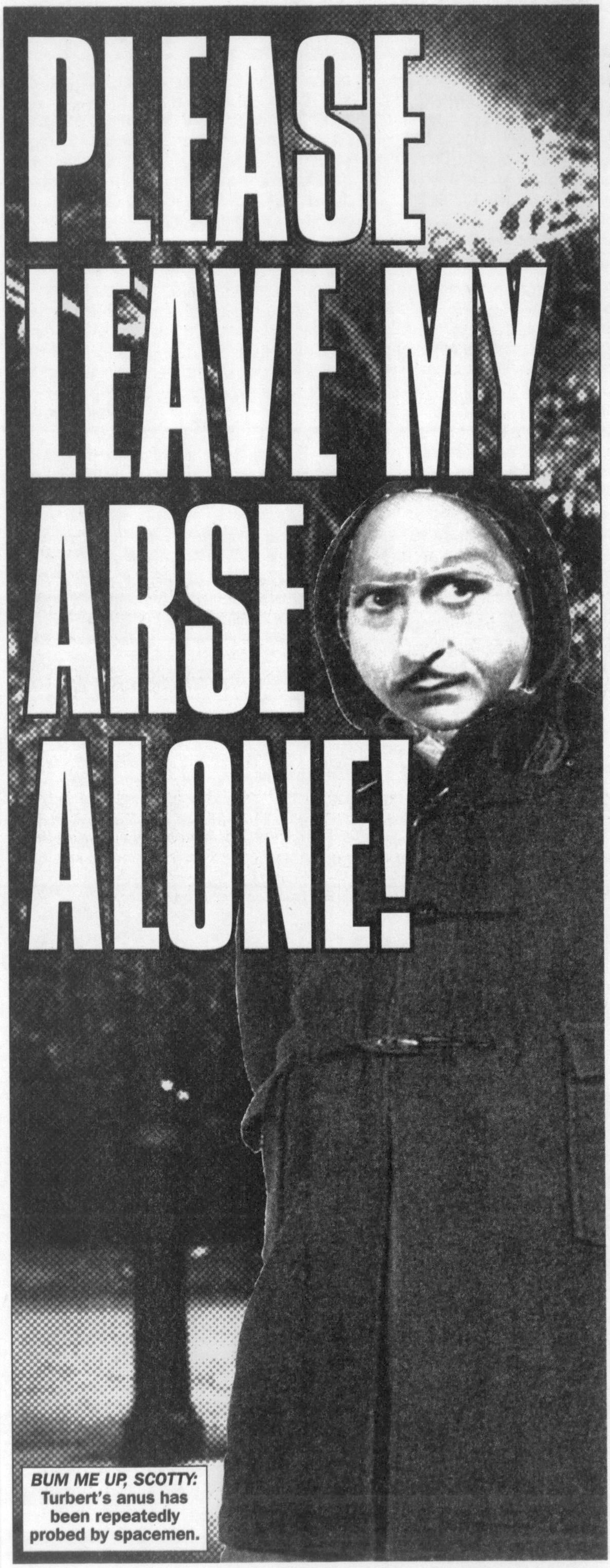
PLEASE LEAVE MY ARSE ALONE!

BUM ME UP, SCOTTY: Turbert's anus has been repeatedly probed by spacemen.

A Northamptonshire man has issued a desperate plea to be left alone after suffering years of medical experiments at the hands of denizens from other worlds. Shoe factory worker TURBERT SCOTT says that the UFO abductions are becoming more frequent, and the repeated experiments performed on his rectum by little green men are making his life a misery.

"My nerves, and my bottom, can't take much more," he told a reporter from his local newspaper, *The Kettering Trombone*.

"They're abducting me up to three and four times a week now. My wife was sympathetic at first, but it's now putting a strain on my marriage," he added.

Scott has been beamed up literally thousands of times over the last 30 years. But he still vividly remembers his first encounter with extra terrestrials.

TOILET

"It was 1987 and me and my wife Marjorie were on holiday in Blackpool. We'd had a bit of a row about something whilst walking on the Golden Mile, and she'd went back to the guest house in a huff. I decided to go into a nearby pub to drown my sorrows. I had a pint or two and eventually needed to nip to the toilet.

"I remember standing chatting to a big man with a bushy moustache at the next urinal. We exchanged a few pleasantries, passing the time of day. He asked me if I was local, and if I came to this pub very often. Then the oddest thing happened.

"Time seemed to freeze. There was a loud throbbing noise and a blinding light lit up the window of the gents. Suddenly I felt myself being lifted up off the ground and floating through the air. Somehow I was being beamed up into an enormous flying saucer hovering above the pub. I was terrified, but at the same time strangely excited."

Within no time, Scott found himself inside the spaceship, strapped face down on a silver operating table. He was surrounded by strange beings, the like of which he had never seen before.

"I knew they were aliens, because they were just like the ones I'd seen on the telly. They were grey with big heads, expressionless black eyes and

EXCLUSIVE!

three fingers on each hand. They didn't speak, but they communicated with me telepathically. They told me that they had come from Mars and they needed to find out out how the earthling body worked.

TOOTH

"Then, one of the Martians produced a shiny probe, about the size of a banana with big glowing end. It was made of some bizarre substance not found on this planet.

"The next thing I knew, he had introduced the probe into a very personal part of my anatomy. It was an unusual sensation that I hadn't felt before and I winced as the galactic being pushed it in and out, taking reading after reading. My ordeal seemed to last a lifetime, but was in reality probably about a minute and a half.

"I must of passed out, because when I came round I found that they aliens had deposited me in one of the cubicles of the pub toilet. My trousers were round my ankles and my backside was really sore. I was frightened and confused."

"When I came round I found that they aliens had deposited me in one of the cubicles of the pub toilet. My trousers were round my ankles and my backside was really sore."

When Scott got back to the guest house, his wife Marjorie could see that he was distressed and asked him what was wrong.

"I didn't tell her what had happened because I was scared she would of thought I must of been going mad."

Turbert put the event to the back of his mind and decided to get on with his life. "I was pretty sure that it wouldn't happen again. I knew the odds of being abducted by aliens was a million to one, so the chance of being abducted twice was two million to one."

YARD

But Scott's faith in statistics were shaken three weeks later, when he was once again subject to an intrusive medical procedure onboard a UFO.

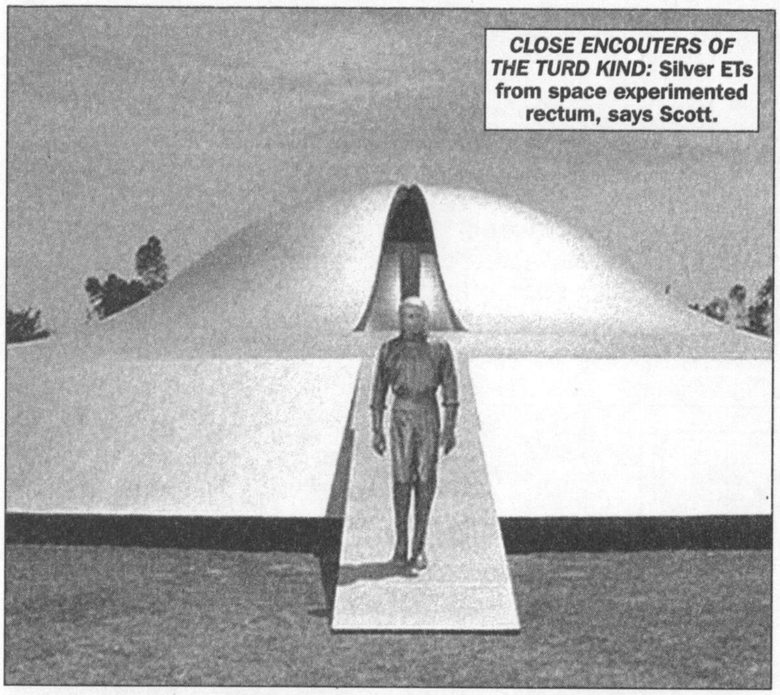

CLOSE ENCOUTERS OF THE TURD KIND: Silver ETs from space experimented rectum, says Scott.

"It was a Friday night, and me and Marjorie had just had a barney over something and nothing, but I remember storming out of the house and slamming the door. I decided to go for a walk in some nearby woods until I'd simmered down a bit."

Turbert followed a narrow path to a secluded area of undergrowth. There he bumped into a couple of men who were out looking for badgers, and the three of them got chatting.

"I was telling them about how things had't been going too well between me and the missus and they were very understanding and sympathetic. Then, suddenly, a huge shadow fell over us. I looked up and saw that the sky was being obliterated by an enormous space craft, covered in aerials and rows of flashing neon lamps. A little hatch opened up in the bottom of it and a bright green shaft of light shot out and caught me.

PAINT

"I desperately wanted to run, but I couldn't move. As I watched, my outline went all glittery and I vanished. The next thing I knew, I had reappeared inside the flying saucer.

"In front of me stood a dozen or so strange beings. Each one was green and slimy with all tentacles and one giant eye in the middle of his head. There was glass dome in the middle of the room with a glowing brain in it which seemed to be controlling them. They spoke in English, but with an electronic voice a bit like a Dalek or the Cadbury's Smash men.

"They explained that they were from the outer sector of Nebulus 3 and they were studying the different life forms of the galaxy. They said that they were not going to harm me, but they needed some data about human physiology. Then one of them opened a box and removed a silver probe about the size of a large courgette.

For the second time in three weeks, Turbert was strapped to an alien operating table and subjected to intimate probing by alien scientists.

"This alien had one of the largest probes I'd ever been experimented on with. It was like a tin of Vim with an apple on the top."

"It wasn't as uncomfortable this time and it lasted a bit longer, but it was still pretty frightening. Once again, I blacked out at the trauma of it all.

"They must of beamed me back down to the woods once they had their information, because I remember waking up in a bush with no trousers or underpants on. A woman out walking her dog saw me and screamed. I was going to explain what had happened, but my story was so fantastic I thought she might of not of believed me. So I picked up my kegs and ran off.

SCRUBBING

Over the next few years, Scott found himself targeted on a regular basis by extra terrestrial beings armed with anal probes, usually at weekends. The abductions usually took place on board the ETs' spacecraft, but Scott recalls one occasion where they travelled a little further afield.

"I remember I was out in my car. I'd just had a blazing row with my wife and I'd gone for a little drive in the country to cool off. Foolishly, I had forgotten to check the fuel gauge before I set out and I ran out of petrol, coasting to a halt in a secluded layby miles from anywhere. I wasn't on my own, there was a biker there. We got chatting and I was just admiring his leathers when the whole scene was suddenly illuminated by a blinding light.

"'Here we go again,' I thought.

"A metallic, cigar-shaped craft appeared from nowhere and landed in a nearby field. It was clearly of intergalactic origin, because it was made of a strange element unknown to human science. A door in the belly of the ship opened downwards, forming a ramp. Brilliant white light flooded out.

"The space creatures in the UFO must of taken over my nervous system, as I was unable to resist. Even though every fibre of my being wanted to run in the other direction, I walked up the ramp towards the light. I couldn't help myself. The door closed behind me, and I immediately felt the vessel rising vertically into the night sky, leaving all crop circles behind it. The creatures controlling it were invisible, like clouds of spangly gas.

"I was strapped naked onto a glowing operating table. I knew what was coming next."

BASIL

"The acceleration was like nothing I'd ever felt before. Within moments, we were travelling at warp speed and the solar system was a mere speck on the horizon. Just parsecs later, the spacecraft arrived at its home planet of Regulo 4, the largest asteroid in Sector 7 of Orion's Belt, over 100 million light years away on the other side of the Milky Way.

"A floating robot ushered me out onto the crater-filled planet surface and into a room, where my clothes were removed by bendy metal arms and I was strapped naked onto a glowing operating table. I knew what was coming next. One of the invisible aliens produced a rectal sensor and began carrying out the usual procedure on my back passage.

"This particular alien had one of the largest probes I'd ever been experimented on with. I'm not exaggerating when I say it was like a tin of Vim with an apple on the top. It really made my eyes water. The aliens must of transported me back to the layby, because I was in the back seat of my car and my trousers and pants were nowhere to be seen. I assumed I had left them in the experimental chamber on Regulo 4 but I later found them under the passenger seat.

"When I got home, my wife noticed that I was uncomfortable and reluctant to sit down. She asked me what was wrong, but I knew she wouldn't believe me if I told her, so I just said I'd got piles."

A sore bottom is usually the worst after-effect of Turbert's space visitors' unwanted attentions. But he well remembers one time when, after carrying out their experiments, their aggressive instincts came to the fore.

"As usual, I'd been abducted from a public lavatory in the park by some galactic beings from a black hole in the Horsehead Nebula. Three or four of them had taken turns to gather information about human anatomy from me in the usual alien way. When they were finished, I fully expected them to beam me back down into the toilets where they'd picked me up.

"However, they must of come from a particularly warlike planet because they decided to beat me up, punching me in the face and stamping on my fingers. The park keeper eventually found me in a pool of blood with my trousers round my ankles in the corner of the lavs. I had a black eye, a split lip, I'd lost two teeth and I had cracked ribs and broken fingers. The aliens had even taken my wallet and watch, though for what reason I'll never know. Earth money is no use on their planet and time stands still in black holes anyway, so the watch would just look like it was broken.

"The park keeper offered to call the police, but I explained that my assailants would be billions of light years away by now. The cops would stand no chance of catching them.

SYBIL

"When I got home I was in a terrible state and my wife had gone to stay with her sister. Again."

And Scott doesn't believe his two decade-long ordeal will be coming to an end in the near future. He said: "Astronomers say there are an infinite number of planets in the Universe that are capable of supporting life. Every one of those alien life forms may decide to carry out anatomical experiments of human beings. This regular anal probing could go on week in, week out for the rest of my life."

NEXT WEEK: **The time Turbert got experimented upon by voyagers from Metabilis 3 after going for a 2am stroll round the dunes at Blyth in a pair of arseless chaps.**

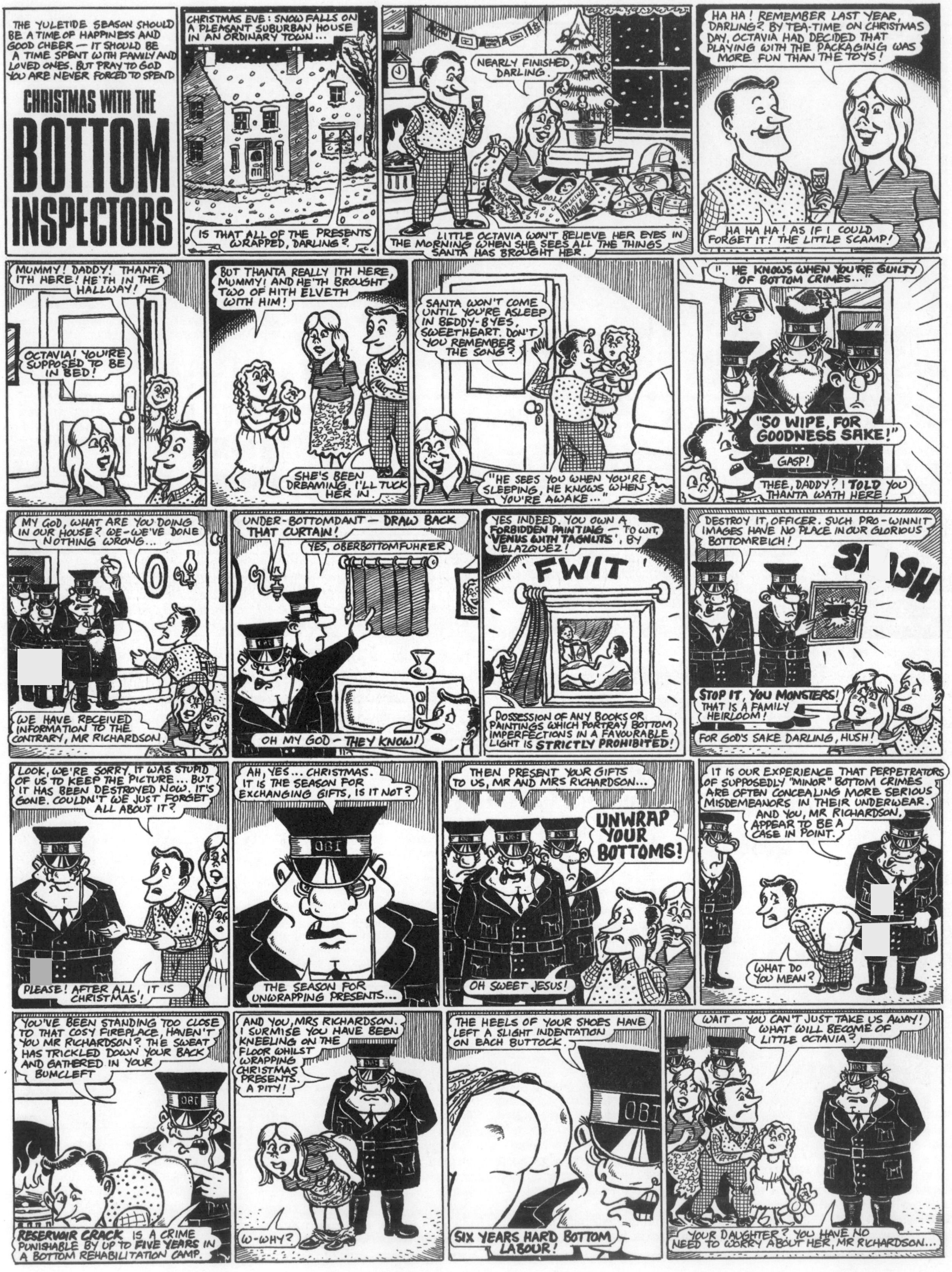
THE YULETIDE SEASON SHOULD BE A TIME OF HAPPINESS AND GOOD CHEER — IT SHOULD BE A TIME SPENT WITH FAMILY AND LOVED ONES. BUT PRAY TO GOD YOU ARE NEVER FORCED TO SPEND
CHRISTMAS WITH THE BOTTOM INSPECTORS
CHRISTMAS EVE: SNOW FALLS ON A PLEASANT SUBURBAN HOUSE IN AN ORDINARY TOWN...
IS THAT ALL OF THE PRESENTS WRAPPED, DARLING?
NEARLY FINISHED, DARLING.
LITTLE OCTAVIA WON'T BELIEVE HER EYES IN THE MORNING WHEN SHE SEES ALL THE THINGS SANTA HAS BROUGHT HER.
HA HA! REMEMBER LAST YEAR, DARLING? BY TEA-TIME ON CHRISTMAS DAY, OCTAVIA HAD DECIDED THAT PLAYING WITH THE PACKAGING WAS MORE FUN THAN THE TOYS!
HA HA HA! AS IF I COULD FORGET IT! THE LITTLE SCAMP!
MUMMY! DADDY! THANTA ITH HERE! HE'TH IN THE HALLWAY!
OCTAVIA! YOU'RE SUPPOSED TO BE IN BED!
BUT THANTA REALLY ITH HERE, MUMMY! AND HE'TH BROUGHT TWO OF HITH ELVETH WITH HIM!
SHE'S BEEN DREAMING. I'LL TUCK HER IN.
SANTA WON'T COME UNTIL YOU'RE ASLEEP IN BEDDY-BYES, SWEETHEART. DON'T YOU REMEMBER THE SONG?
"HE SEES YOU WHEN YOU'RE SLEEPING, HE KNOWS WHEN YOU'RE AWAKE..."
"...HE KNOWS WHEN YOU'RE GUILTY OF BOTTOM CRIMES..."
"SO WIPE, FOR GOODNESS SAKE!"
GASP!
THEE, DADDY? I TOLD YOU THANTA WATH HERE!
MY GOD, WHAT ARE YOU DOING IN OUR HOUSE? WE-WE'VE DONE NOTHING WRONG...
WE HAVE RECEIVED INFORMATION TO THE CONTRARY, MR RICHARDSON.
UNDER-BOTTOMDANT — DRAW BACK THAT CURTAIN!
YES, OBERBOTTOMFUHRER.
OH MY GOD — THEY KNOW!
YES INDEED. YOU OWN A FORBIDDEN PAINTING — TO WIT, 'VENUS WITH TAGNUTS', BY VELAZQUEZ!
FWIT
POSSESSION OF ANY BOOKS OR PAINTINGS WHICH PORTRAY BOTTOM IMPERFECTIONS IN A FAVOURABLE LIGHT IS STRICTLY PROHIBITED!
DESTROY IT, OFFICER. SUCH PRO-WINNIT IMAGES HAVE NO PLACE IN OUR GLORIOUS BOTTOMREICH!
STOP IT, YOU MONSTERS! THAT IS A FAMILY HEIRLOOM!
FOR GOD'S SAKE DARLING, HUSH!
LOOK, WE'RE SORRY. IT WAS STUPID OF US TO KEEP THE PICTURE... BUT IT HAS BEEN DESTROYED NOW. IT'S GONE. COULDN'T WE JUST FORGET ALL ABOUT IT?
PLEASE! AFTER ALL, IT IS CHRISTMAS!
AH, YES... CHRISTMAS. IT IS THE SEASON FOR EXCHANGING GIFTS, IS IT NOT?
OBI
THE SEASON FOR UNWRAPPING PRESENTS...
THEN PRESENT YOUR GIFTS TO US, MR AND MRS RICHARDSON...
UNWRAP YOUR BOTTOMS!
OH SWEET JESUS!
IT IS OUR EXPERIENCE THAT PERPETRATORS OF SUPPOSEDLY "MINOR" BOTTOM CRIMES ARE OFTEN CONCEALING MORE SERIOUS MISDEMEANORS IN THEIR UNDERWEAR.
AND YOU, MR RICHARDSON, APPEAR TO BE A CASE IN POINT.
WHAT DO YOU MEAN?
YOU'VE BEEN STANDING TOO CLOSE TO THAT COSY FIREPLACE, HAVEN'T YOU MR RICHARDSON? THE SWEAT HAS TRICKLED DOWN YOUR BACK AND GATHERED IN YOUR BUMCLEFT
RESERVOIR CRACK IS A CRIME PUNISHABLE BY UP TO FIVE YEARS IN A BOTTOM REHABILITATION CAMP.
AND YOU, MRS RICHARDSON. I SURMISE YOU HAVE BEEN KNEELING ON THE FLOOR WHILST WRAPPING CHRISTMAS PRESENTS. A PITY!
W-WHY?
THE HEELS OF YOUR SHOES HAVE LEFT A SLIGHT INDENTATION ON EACH BUTTOCK.
SIX YEARS HARD BOTTOM LABOUR!
WAIT — YOU CAN'T JUST TAKE US AWAY! WHAT WILL BECOME OF LITTLE OCTAVIA?
YOUR DAUGHTER? YOU HAVE NO NEED TO WORRY ABOUT HER, MR RICHARDSON...

YOUR DAUGHTER IS A GOOD CITIZEN. IT WAS SHE WHO INFORMED US OF THE FORBIDDEN PICTURE IN YOUR LIVING ROOM.
OCTAVIA? IMPOSSIBLE! SHE WOULD NEVER...
OH, BUT SHE DID!
CLICK!
PERHAPS YOU SHOULD HAVE PAID MORE ATTENTION TO THE PROGRAMMES YOUR DAUGHTER WATCHES ON TELEVISION, MR RICHARDSON.
THE MINISTRY OF BOTTAGANDA BROADCASTS CHILDREN'S TV SHOWS 24 HOURS A DAY. THEY ARE MOST.... EDUCATIONAL.
MOB TV
HELLO AGAIN CHILDREN, IT'S SANTA HERE! HO HO HO! AND WHO IS THIS? WHY, IT'S OUR OLD FRIEND RUDOLPH THE REINDEER!
WHAT'S THAT, RUDOLPH? YOU THINK YOUR MUMMY AND DADDY ARE GUILTY OF A BOTTOM CRIME? WELL, WHY DON'T YOU PHONE ME UP AND TELL ME ALL ABOUT IT ON THIS NUMBER...
MOB TV
GASP!
PHONE SANTA: 018118055
IF YOU DO, I'LL BRING YOU LOTS OF EXTRA PRESENTS AT CHRISTMAS.
CHILDREN ARE SO TRUSTING, AREN'T THEY, MR RICHARDSON?
YOU.. YOU ABSOLUTE FIENDS!
OH, OCTAVIA >SOB<
YOUR DAUGHTER WILL BE WELL CARED FOR IN ONE OF OUR BOTTLER YOUTH BOARDING ACADEMIES WHILST THE TWO OF YOU ARE.... INDISPOSED.
BYE BYE MUMMY AND DADDY! I'M GOING TO LIVE WIV THANTA AND HITH ELVETH.
NO! NO! DON'T TAKE OUR BABY FROM US..!
SILENCE!
THE VAN IS WAITING FOR YOU OUTSIDE — YOU HAVE AN APPOINTMENT AT THE BOTTOM REHABILITATION CAMP!
SNOW CONTINUES TO FALL ON THE PLEASANT SUBURBAN HOUSE IN THE ORDINARY TOWN. BUT FOR MR AND MRS RICHARDSON, THE SEASON OF GOOD CHEER IS OVER...
..AND THE SEASON OF HELL HAS JUST BEGUN!

TITMARSH CLOSER TO NUCLEAR CAPABILITY

By our War Correspondent
■ *FENTON SOUPSPOON*

FEARS THAT global peace could be compromised grew last night after it was revealed that *ALAN TITMARSH* had been taking steps to further enrich his stocks of uranium.

Despite international opposition, reports have emerged that Titmarsh has been amassing the ingredients to build weapons of mass destruction in his garden at Foggy Bottom. There were calls for him to abandon his project after Titmarsh launched an unprecedented attack on his former *Ground Force* labourer Tommy Walsh.

devil-dog

In an angry speech, Titmarsh told viewers of his early afternoon ITV chatshow: "The devil-dog Tommy Walsh must die. I will not rest until I have wiped the devil-dog Tommy Walsh off the face of the earth.

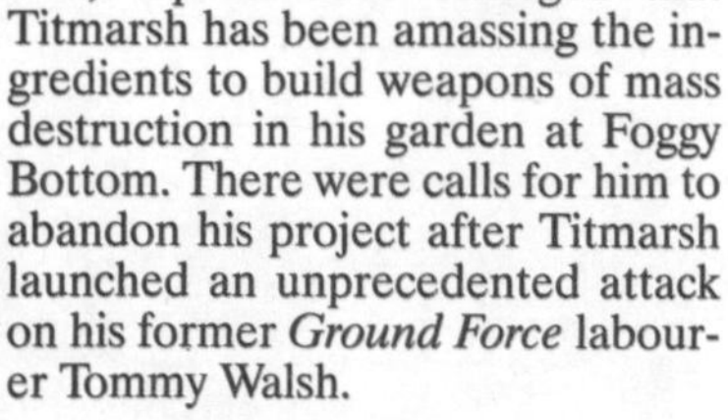

WALSH MUST D.I.Y.: **Handyman Tommy.**

"The rivers of Basildon will run red with the blood of the devil-dog Tommy Walsh. So shall perish all the enemies of Alan Tichmarch who are no more than a poisonous nest of wasps," he added. The inflammatory outburst was accompanied by blurry video footage apparently showing a missile being launched from behind a greenhouse on Titmarsh's allotment.

ballistic

This latest development in the long running saga of the lightweight presenter's development of an atomic warhead has sparked alarm amongst the anti-nuclear lobby. "If Titmarsh has developed the ballistic capability to deliver an atomic warhead, the consequences do not bear thinking about," said CND president Beardsley Weirdsworth. "It's not just sabre rattling any more. This time, he means business," he added.

Meanwhile, a team of UN weapons inspectors led by Dr Hans Blix failed to gain access to Titmarsh's potting shed. Dr Blix, whose glasses arms don't reach his ears, told reporters: "Unfortunately, the shed was locked and Mr Titmarsh told us that he had left the key in his other trousers."

"Our inspection was further impeded by sheets of newspaper which had been sellotaped to the inside of the windows. But we will return at a later date," Blix continued.

However, fears were growing that the situation could escalate out of hand after spy planes spotted what appeared to be a 200-foot stainless steel gun barrel being delivered to Tommy Walsh's Basildon workshop.

CAPABILITY TWAT: **Titmarsh.**

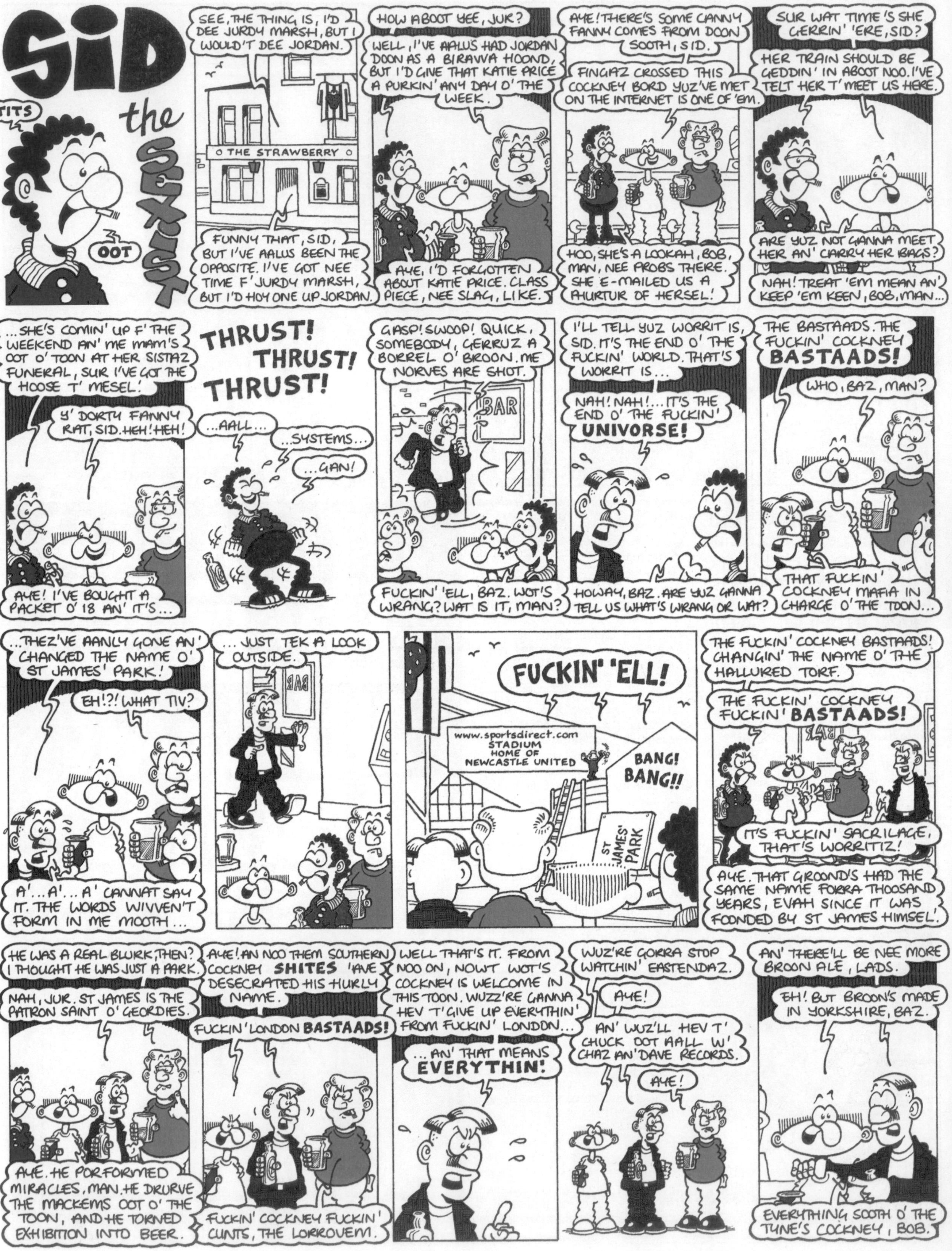
SID
TITS
OOT
the SEXIST
SEE, THE THING IS, I'D DEE JURDY MARSH, BUT I WOULD'T DEE JORDAN.
THE STRAWBERRY
FUNNY THAT, SID, BUT I'VE AALUS BEEN THE OPPOSITE. I'VE GOT NEE TIME F' JURDY MARSH, BUT I'D HOY ONE UP JORDAN.
HOW ABOOT YEE, JUR?
WELL, I'VE AALUS HAD JORDAN DOON AS A BIRAWA HOOND, BUT I'D GIVE THAT KATIE PRICE A PURKIN' ANY DAY O' THE WEEK.
AYE, I'D FORGOTTEN ABOUT KATIE PRICE. CLASS PIECE, NEE SLAG, LIKE.
AYE! THERE'S SOME CANNY FANNY COMES FROM DOON SOOTH, SID.
FINGAZ CROSSED THIS COCKNEY BORD YUZ'VE MET ON THE INTERNET IS ONE OF 'EM.
HOO, SHE'S A LOOKAH, BOB, MAN, NEE PROBS THERE. SHE E-MAILED US A PHURTUR OF HERSEL!
SUR WAT TIME 'S SHE GERRIN' 'ERE, SID?
HER TRAIN SHOULD BE GEDDIN' IN ABOOT NOO. I'VE TELT HER T' MEET US HERE.
ARE YUZ NOT GANNA MEET HER AN' CARRY HER BAGS?
NAH! TREAT 'EM MEAN AN' KEEP 'EM KEEN, BOB, MAN...
...SHE'S COMIN' UP F' THE WEEKEND AN' ME MAM'S OOT O' TOON AT HER SISTAZ FUNERAL, SUR I'VE GOT THE HOOSE T' MESEL!
Y' DORTY FANNY RAT, SID. HEH! HEH!
AYE! I'VE BOUGHT A PACKET O' 18 AN' IT'S...
THRUST! THRUST! THRUST!
...AALL...
...SYSTEMS...
...GAN!
GASP! SWOOP! QUICK, SOMEBODY, GERRUZ A BORREL O' BROON. ME NORVES ARE SHOT.
BAR
FUCKIN' 'ELL, BAZ. WOT'S WRANG? WAT IS IT, MAN?
I'LL TELL YUZ WORRIT IS, SID. IT'S THE END O' THE FUCKIN' WORLD. THAT'S WORRIT IS...
NAH! NAH!... IT'S THE END O' THE FUCKIN' UNIVERSE!
HOWAY, BAZ. ARE YUZ GANNA TELL US WHAT'S WRANG OR WAT?
THE BASTAADS. THE FUCKIN' COCKNEY BASTAADS!
WHO, BAZ, MAN?
THAT FUCKIN' COCKNEY MAFIA IN CHARGE O' THE TOON...
...THEZ'VE AANLY GONE AN' CHANGED THE NAME O' ST JAMES' PARK!
EH!?! WHAT TIV?
A'...A'...A' CANNAT SAY IT. THE WORDS WIVVEN'T FORM IN ME MOOTH...
... JUST TEK A LOOK OUTSIDE.
BAR
FUCKIN' 'ELL!
www.sportsdirect.com STADIUM HOME OF NEWCASTLE UNITED
BANG! BANG!!
ST JAMES' PARK
THE FUCKIN' COCKNEY BASTAADS! CHANGIN' THE NAME O' THE HALLURED TORF.
THE FUCKIN' COCKNEY FUCKIN' BASTAADS!
IT'S FUCKIN' SACRILAGE, THAT'S WORRITIZ!
AYE. THAT GROOND'S HAD THE SAME NAME FORRA THOOSAND YEARS, EVAH SINCE IT WAS FOONDED BY ST JAMES HIMSEL'.
HE WAS A REAL BLURK, THEN? I THOUGHT HE WAS JUST A PARK.
NAH, JUR. ST JAMES IS THE PATRON SAINT O' GEORDIES.
AYE. HE PORFORMED MIRACLES, MAN. HE DRURVE THE MACKEMS OOT O' THE TOON, AND HE TORNED EXHIBITION INTO BEER.
AYE! AN NOO THEM SOUTHERN COCKNEY SHITES 'AVE DESECRATED HIS HURLY NAME.
FUCKIN' LONDON BASTAADS!
FUCKIN' COCKNEY FUCKIN' CUNTS, THE LORROVEM.
WELL THAT'S IT. FROM NOO ON, NOWT WOT'S COCKNEY IS WELCOME IN THIS TOON. WUZZ'RE GANNA HEV T' GIVE UP EVERYTHIN' FROM FUCKIN' LONDON...
...AN' THAT MEANS EVERYTHIN'!
WUZ'RE GORRA STOP WATCHIN' EASTENDAZ.
AYE!
AN' WUZ'LL HEV T' CHUCK OOT AALL W' CHAZ AN' DAVE RECORDS.
AYE!
AN' THERE'LL BE NEE MORE BROON ALE, LADS.
EH! BUT BROON'S MADE IN YORKSHIRE, BAZ.
EVERYTHING SOOTH O' THE TUNE'S COCKNEY, BOB.

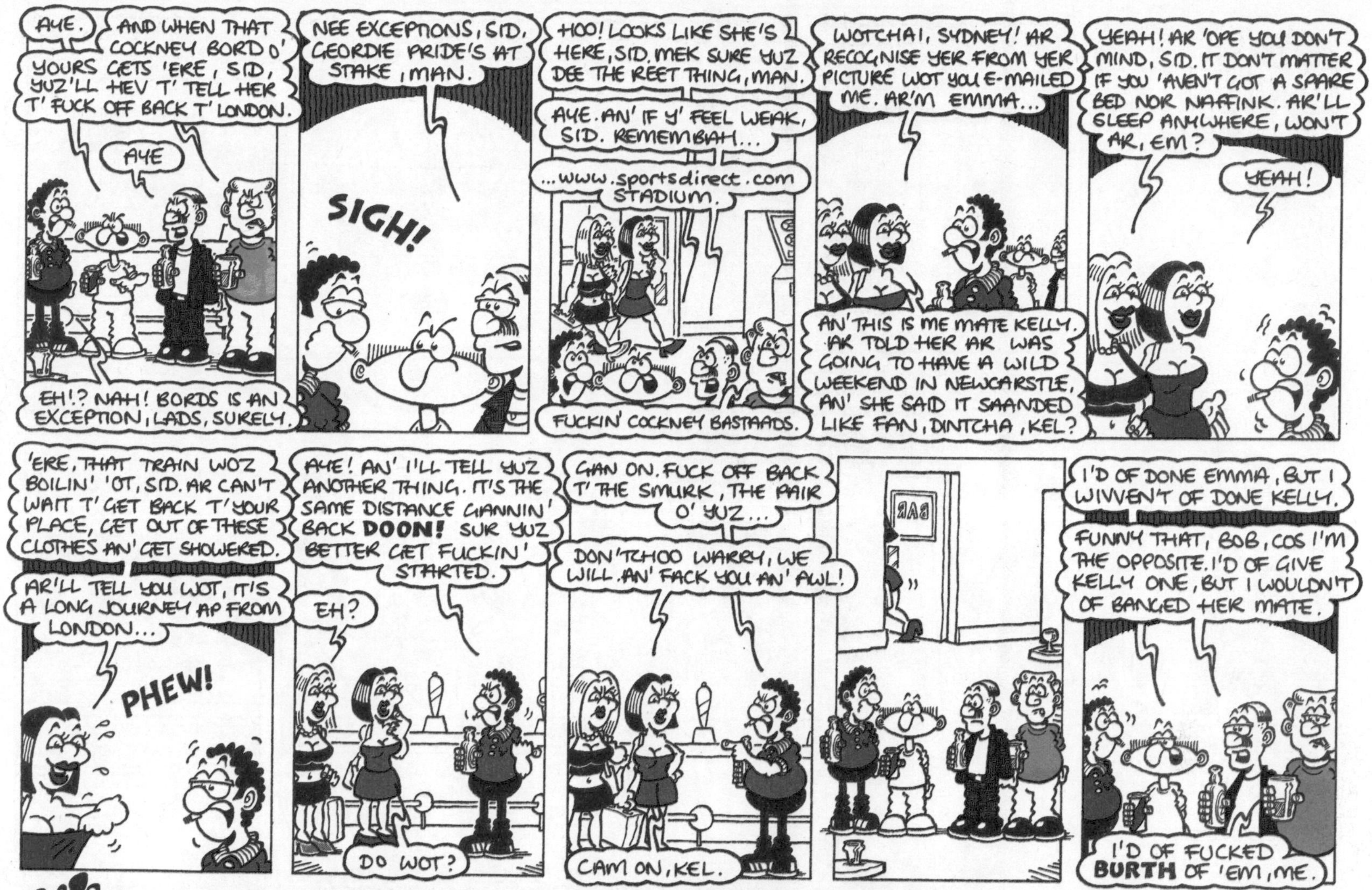
AYE.
AND WHEN THAT COCKNEY BORD O' YOURS GETS 'ERE, SID, YUZ'LL HEV T' TELL HER T' FUCK OFF BACK T' LONDON.
AYE
EH!? NAH! BORDS IS AN EXCEPTION, LADS, SURELY.
NEE EXCEPTIONS, SID. GEORDIE PRIDE'S AT STAKE, MAN.
SIGH!
HOO! LOOKS LIKE SHE'S HERE, SID. MEK SURE YUZ DEE THE REET THING, MAN.
AYE. AN' IF Y' FEEL WEAK, SID. REMEMBAH...
...www.sportsdirect.com STADIUM.
FUCKIN' COCKNEY BASTAADS.
WOTCHA!, SYDNEY! AR RECOGNISE YER FROM YER PICTURE WOT YOU E-MAILED ME. AR'M EMMA...
AN' THIS IS ME MATE KELLY. AR TOLD HER AR WAS GOING TO HAVE A WILD WEEKEND IN NEWCARSTLE, AN' SHE SAID IT SAANDED LIKE FAN, DINTCHA, KEL?
YEAH! AR 'OPE YOU DON'T MIND, SID. IT DON'T MATTER IF YOU 'AVEN'T GOT A SPARE BED NOR NAFFINK. AR'LL SLEEP ANYWHERE, WON'T AR, EM?
YEAH!
'ERE, THAT TRAIN WOZ BOILIN' 'OT, SID. AR CAN'T WAIT T' GET BACK T' YOUR PLACE, GET OUT OF THESE CLOTHES AN' GET SHOWERED.
AR'LL TELL YOU WOT, IT'S A LONG JOURNEY AP FROM LONDON...
PHEW!
AYE! AN' I'LL TELL YUZ ANOTHER THING. IT'S THE SAME DISTANCE GANNIN' BACK **DOON!** SUR YUZ BETTER GET FUCKIN' STARTED.
EH?
DO WOT?
GAN ON. FUCK OFF BACK T' THE SMURK, THE PAIR O' YUZ...
DON'T CHOO WARRY, WE WILL. AN' FACK YOU AN' AWL!
CAM ON, KEL.
I'D OF DONE EMMA, BUT I WIVVEN'T OF DONE KELLY.
FUNNY THAT, BOB, COS I'M THE OPPOSITE. I'D OF GIVE KELLY ONE, BUT I WOULDN'T OF BANGED HER MATE.
I'D OF FUCKED **BURTH** OF 'EM, ME.

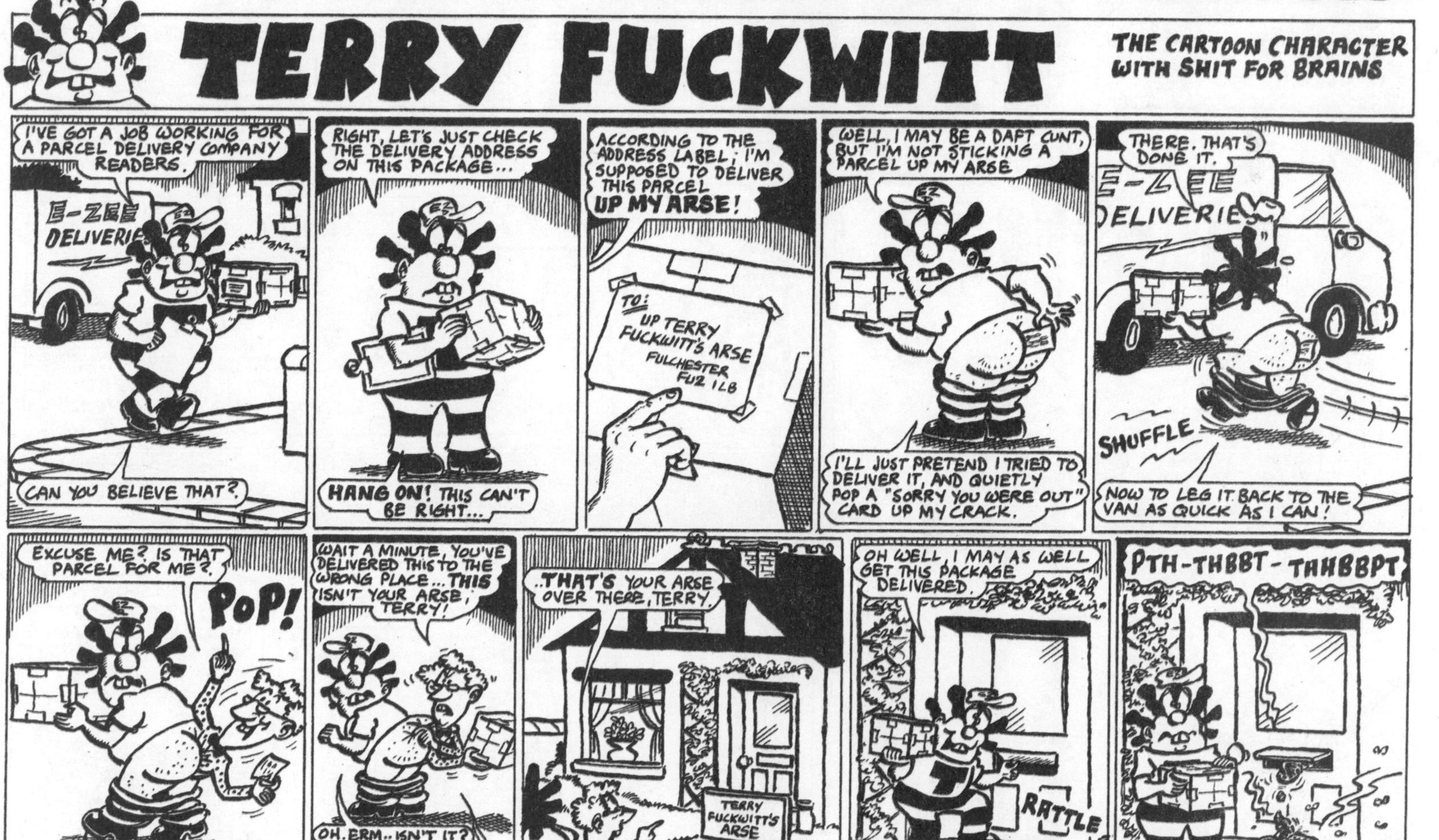
TERRY FUCKWITT
THE CARTOON CHARACTER WITH SHIT FOR BRAINS
I'VE GOT A JOB WORKING FOR A PARCEL DELIVERY COMPANY READERS.
E-ZEE DELIVERIE
CAN YOU BELIEVE THAT?
RIGHT, LET'S JUST CHECK THE DELIVERY ADDRESS ON THIS PACKAGE...
HANG ON! THIS CAN'T BE RIGHT...
ACCORDING TO THE ADDRESS LABEL, I'M SUPPOSED TO DELIVER THIS PARCEL **UP MY ARSE!**
TO: UP TERRY FUCKWITT'S ARSE FULCHESTER FU2 1LB
WELL, I MAY BE A DAFT CUNT, BUT I'M NOT STICKING A PARCEL UP MY ARSE
I'LL JUST PRETEND I TRIED TO DELIVER IT, AND QUIETLY POP A "SORRY YOU WERE OUT" CARD UP MY CRACK.
THERE. THAT'S DONE IT.
E-ZEE DELIVERIE
SHUFFLE
NOW TO LEG IT BACK TO THE VAN AS QUICK AS I CAN!
EXCUSE ME? IS THAT PARCEL FOR ME?
POP!
BAH! I WASN'T QUICK ENOUGH — I'VE BEEN SPOTTED!
WAIT A MINUTE, YOU'VE DELIVERED THIS TO THE WRONG PLACE... **THIS** ISN'T YOUR ARSE, TERRY!
OH. ERM.. ISN'T IT?
OF COURSE NOT! THIS IS **MY HOUSE** — NUMBER TWENTY ONE PONDICHERRY CRESCENT
..**THAT'S** YOUR ARSE OVER THERE, TERRY.
TERRY FUCKWITT'S ARSE
BUGGER ME! I NEVER REALISED MY ARSE WAS SO PICTURESQUE
OH WELL, I MAY AS WELL GET THIS PACKAGE DELIVERED.
RATTLE
YOO-HOO! HELLO? IS THERE ANYONE AT HOME, IN MY ARSE?
PTH-THBBT-TAHBBPT
FUCK ME.

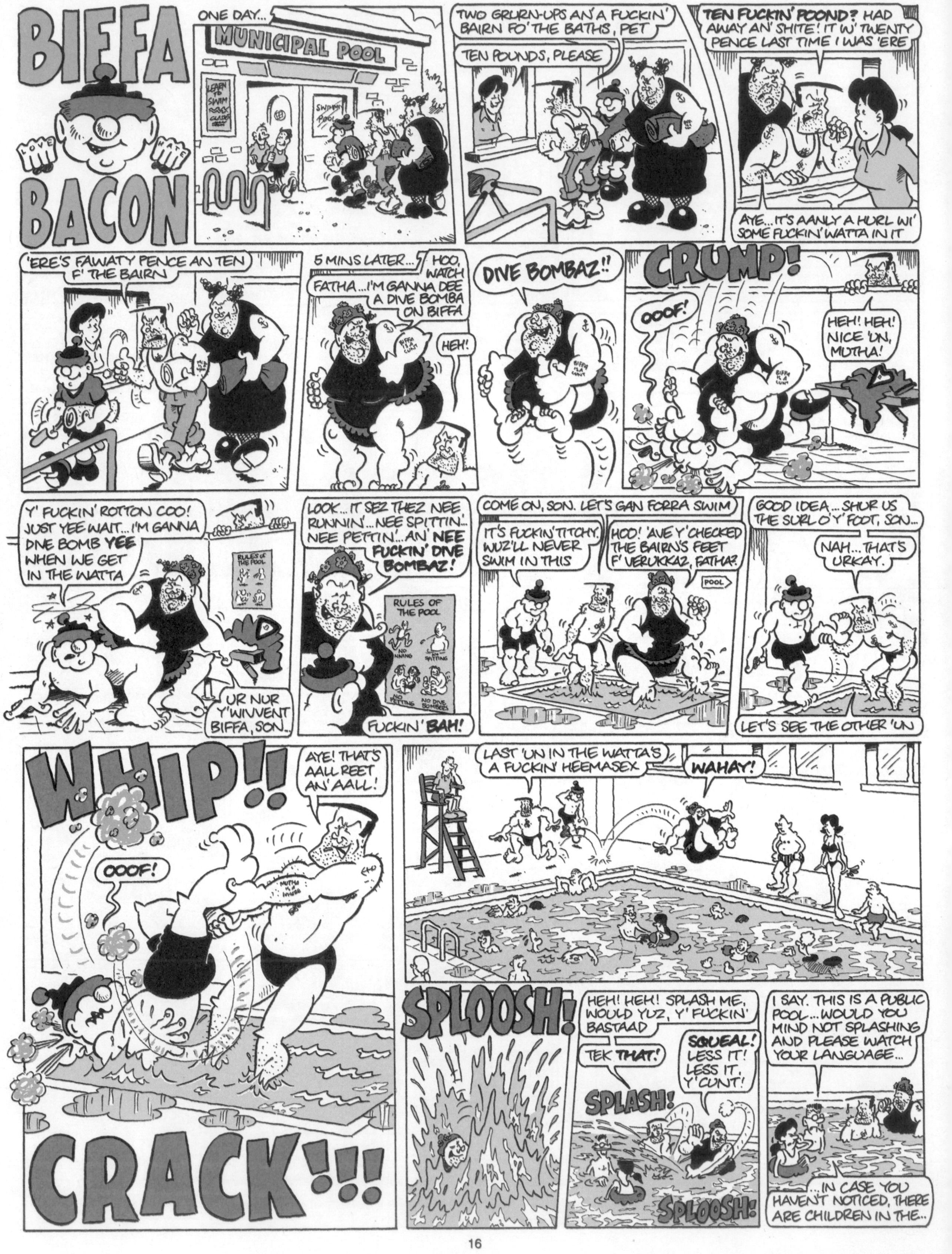
BIFFA BACON
LOVE
HATE
ONE DAY...
MUNICIPAL POOL
TWO GRURN-UPS AN' A FUCKIN' BAIRN FO' THE BATHS, PET
TEN POUNDS, PLEASE
TEN FUCKIN' POOND? HAD AWAY AN' SHITE! IT W' TWENTY PENCE LAST TIME I WAS 'ERE
AYE... IT'S AANLY A HURL WI' SOME FUCKIN' WATTA IN IT
'ERE'S FAWATY PENCE AN TEN F' THE BAIRN
5 MINS LATER...
HOO, WATCH
FATHA... I'M GANNA DEE A DIVE BOMBA ON BIFFA
HEH!
DIVE BOMBAZ!!
CRUMP!
OOOF!
HEH! HEH! NICE 'UN, MUTHA!
Y' FUCKIN' ROTTON COO! JUST YEE WAIT... I'M GANNA DIVE BOMB YEE WHEN WE GET IN THE WATTA
RULES OF THE POOL
UR NUR Y'WIVVENT BIFFA, SON...
LOOK... IT SEZ THEZ NEE RUNNIN'... NEE SPITTIN'... NEE PETTIN'... AN' NEE FUCKIN' DIVE BOMBAZ!
RULES OF THE POOL
FUCKIN' BAH!
COME ON, SON. LET'S GAN FORRA SWIM
IT'S FUCKIN' TITCHY. WUZ'LL NEVER SWIM IN THIS
HOO! 'AVE Y' CHECKED THE BAIRN'S FEET F' VERUKKAZ, FATHA?
POOL
GOOD IDEA... SHUR US THE SURL O' Y' FOOT, SON...
NAH... THAT'S URKAY.
LET'S SEE THE OTHER 'UN
WHIP!!
AYE! THAT'S AALL REET AN' AALL!
OOOF!
CRACK!!!
LAST 'UN IN THE WATTA'S A FUCKIN' HEEMASEX
WAHAY!
SPLOOSH!
HEH! HEH! SPLASH ME, WOULD YUZ, Y' FUCKIN' BASTAAD
TEK THAT!
SQUEAL! LESS IT! LESS IT, Y' CUNT!
SPLASH!
SPLOOSH!
I SAY. THIS IS A PUBLIC POOL... WOULD YOU MIND NOT SPLASHING AND PLEASE WATCH YOUR LANGUAGE...
...IN CASE YOU HAVEN'T NOTICED, THERE ARE CHILDREN IN THE...

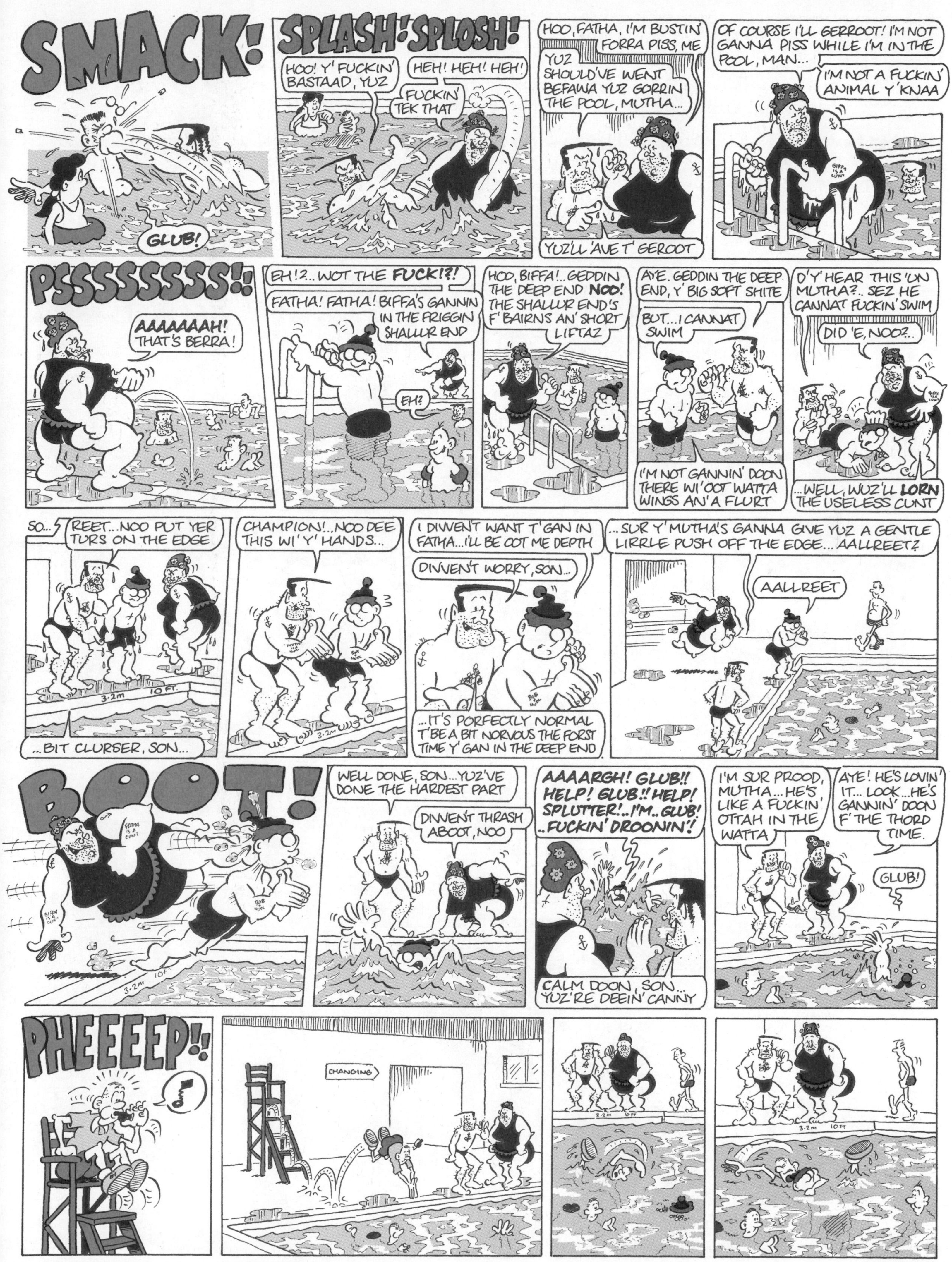
SMACK!
GLUB!
SPLASH! SPLOSH!
HOO! Y' FUCKIN' BASTAAD, YUZ
HEH! HEH! HEH!
FUCKIN' TEK THAT
HOO, FATHA, I'M BUSTIN' FORRA PISS, ME
YUZ SHOULD'VE WENT BEFAWA YUZ GORRIN THE POOL, MUTHA...
YUZ'LL 'AVE T' GEROOT
OF COURSE I'LL GERROOT! I'M NOT GANNA PISS WHILE I'M IN THE POOL, MAN...
I'M NOT A FUCKIN' ANIMAL Y' KNAA
PSSSSSSSS!!
AAAAAAAH! THAT'S BERRA!
EH!?... WOT THE **FUCK!?!**
FATHA! FATHA! BIFFA'S GANNIN IN THE FRIGGIN SHALLUR END
EH?
HOO, BIFFA!... GEDDIN THE DEEP END **NOO!** THE SHALLUR END'S F' BAIRNS AN' SHORT LIFTAZ
AYE. GEDDIN THE DEEP END, Y' BIG SOFT SHITE
BUT... I CANNAT SWIM
I'M NOT GANNIN' DOON THERE WI' OOT WATTA WINGS AN' A FLURT
D'Y' HEAR THIS 'UN MUTHA?.. SEZ HE CANNAT FUCKIN' SWIM
DID 'E, NOO?..
...WELL, WUZ'LL **LORN** THE USELESS CUNT
SO...
REET... NOO PUT YER TURS ON THE EDGE
...BIT CLURSER, SON...
CHAMPION!... NOO DEE THIS WI' Y' HANDS...
I DIVVEN'T WANT T' GAN IN FATHA... I'LL BE OOT ME DEPTH
DIVVEN'T WORRY, SON...
...IT'S PORFECTLY NORMAL T' BE A BIT NORVOUS THE FORST TIME Y' GAN IN THE DEEP END
...SUR Y' MUTHA'S GANNA GIVE YUZ A GENTLE LIRRLE PUSH OFF THE EDGE... AALLREET?
AALLREET
BOOT!
WELL DONE, SON... YUZ'VE DONE THE HARDEST PART
DIVVEN'T THRASH ABOOT, NOO
AAAARGH! GLUB!! HELP! GLUB!! HELP! SPLUTTER!.. I'M.. GLUB! ..FUCKIN' DROONIN'!
CALM DOON, SON... YUZ'RE DEEIN' CANNY
I'M SUR PROOD, MUTHA... HE'S LIKE A FUCKIN' OTTAH IN THE WATTA
AYE! HE'S LOVIN' IT... LOOK... HE'S GANNIN' DOON F' THE THORD TIME.
GLUB!
PHEEEEP!!
CHANGING

CONTINUED OVER

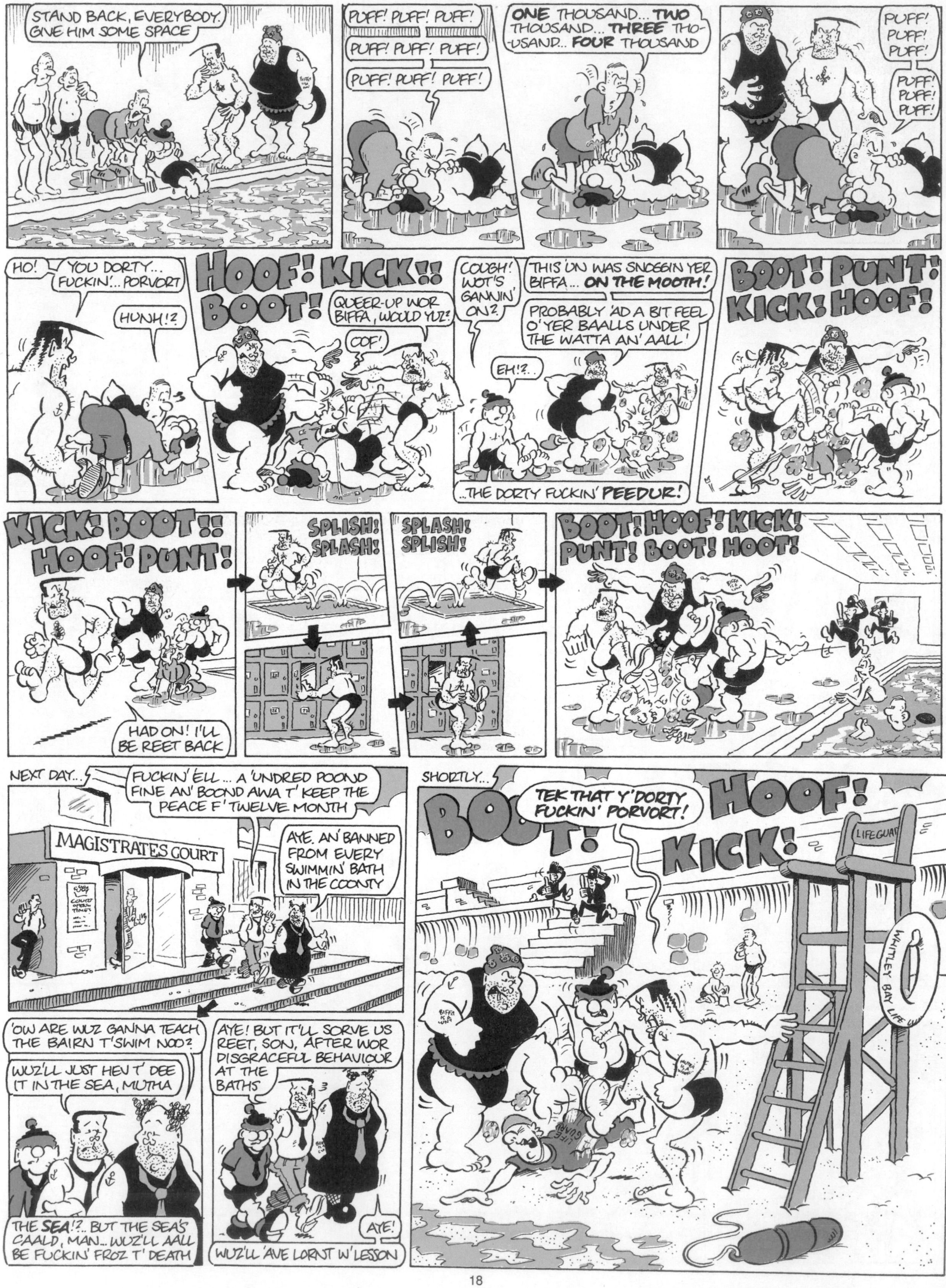
STAND BACK, EVERYBODY. GIVE HIM SOME SPACE
PUFF! PUFF! PUFF!
PUFF! PUFF! PUFF!
PUFF! PUFF! PUFF!
ONE THOUSAND... TWO THOUSAND... THREE THO-USAND... FOUR THOUSAND
PUFF! PUFF! PUFF!
PUFF! PUFF! PUFF!
HO!
YOU DORTY... FUCKIN'... PORVORT
HUNH!?
HOOF! KICK!! BOOT!
QUEER-UP WOR BIFFA, WOULD YUZ?
COF!
COUGH! WOT'S GANNIN' ON?
THIS 'UN WAS SNOGGIN YER BIFFA... ON THE MOOTH!
PROBABLY 'AD A BIT FEEL O' YER BAALLS UNDER THE WATTA AN' AALL
EH!?
...THE DORTY FUCKIN' PEEDUR!
BOOT! PUNT! KICK! HOOF!
KICK! BOOT!! HOOF! PUNT!
HAD ON! I'LL BE REET BACK
SPLISH! SPLASH!
SPLASH! SPLISH!
BOOT! HOOF! KICK! PUNT! BOOT! HOOT!
NEXT DAY...
FUCKIN' 'ELL ... A 'UNDRED POOND FINE AN' BOOND AWA T' KEEP THE PEACE F' TWELVE MONTH
MAGISTRATES COURT
AYE. AN' BANNED FROM EVERY SWIMMIN' BATH IN THE COONTY
'OW ARE WUZ GANNA TEACH THE BAIRN T'SWIM NOO?
WUZ'LL JUST HEV T' DEE IT IN THE SEA, MUTHA
THE SEA!?.. BUT THE SEA'S CAALD, MAN... WUZ'LL AALL BE FUCKIN' FROZ T' DEATH
AYE! BUT IT'LL SORVE US REET, SON, AFTER WOR DISGRACEFUL BEHAVIOUR AT THE BATHS
AYE!
WUZ'LL 'AVE LORNT W' LESSON
SHORTLY...
BOOT!
TEK THAT Y' DORTY FUCKIN' PORVORT!
HOOF!
KICK!
LIFEGUARD

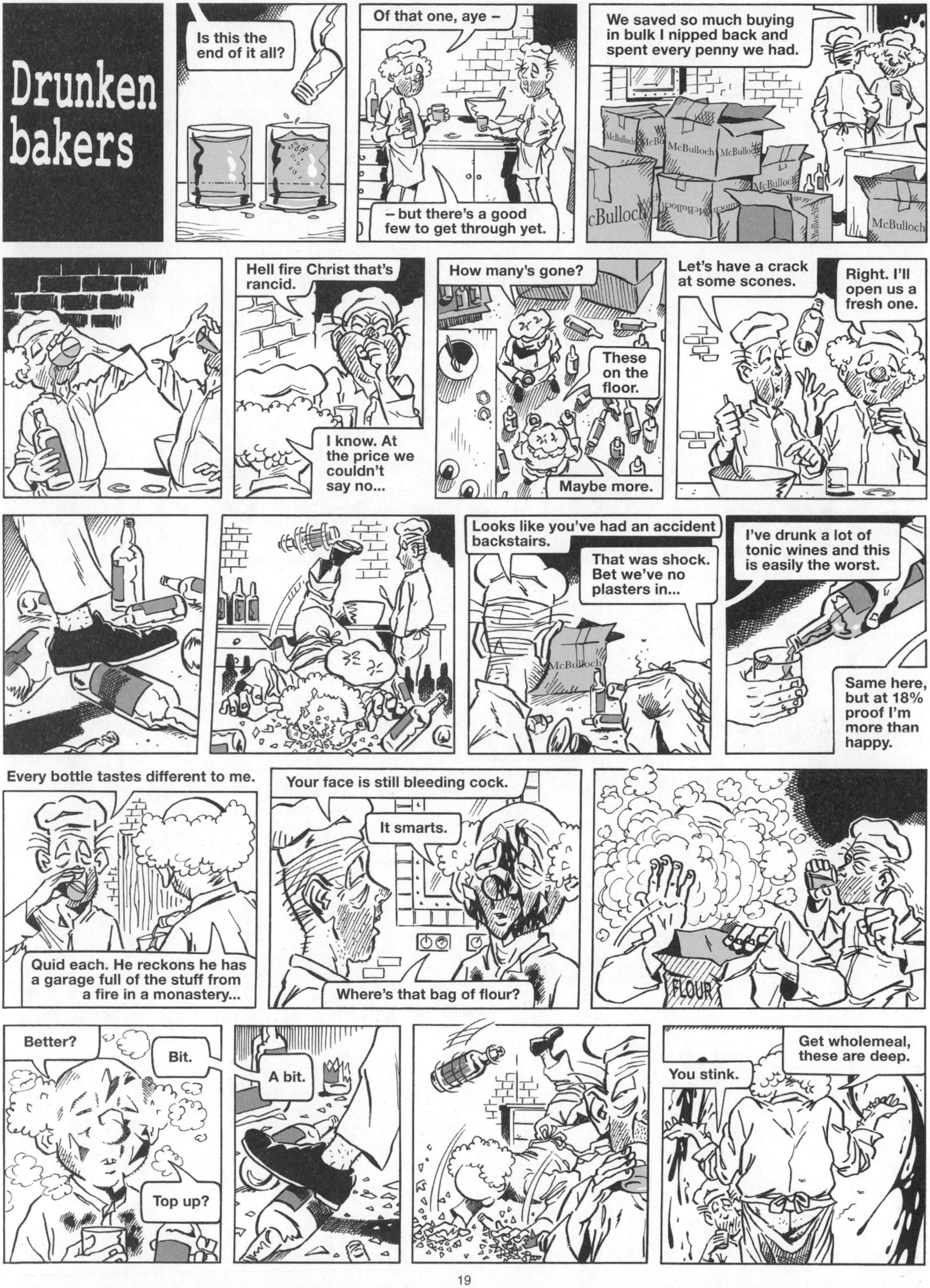

Drunken bakers
Is this the end of it all?
Of that one, aye –
– but there's a good few to get through yet.
We saved so much buying in bulk I nipped back and spent every penny we had.
McBulloch
Hell fire Christ that's rancid.
I know. At the price we couldn't say no...
How many's gone?
These on the floor.
Maybe more.
Let's have a crack at some scones.
Right. I'll open us a fresh one.
Looks like you've had an accident backstairs.
That was shock. Bet we've no plasters in...
I've drunk a lot of tonic wines and this is easily the worst.
Same here, but at 18% proof I'm more than happy.
Every bottle tastes different to me.
Quid each. He reckons he has a garage full of the stuff from a fire in a monastery...
Your face is still bleeding cock.
It smarts.
Where's that bag of flour?
FLOUR
Better?
Bit.
Top up?
A bit.
You stink.
Get wholemeal, these are deep.

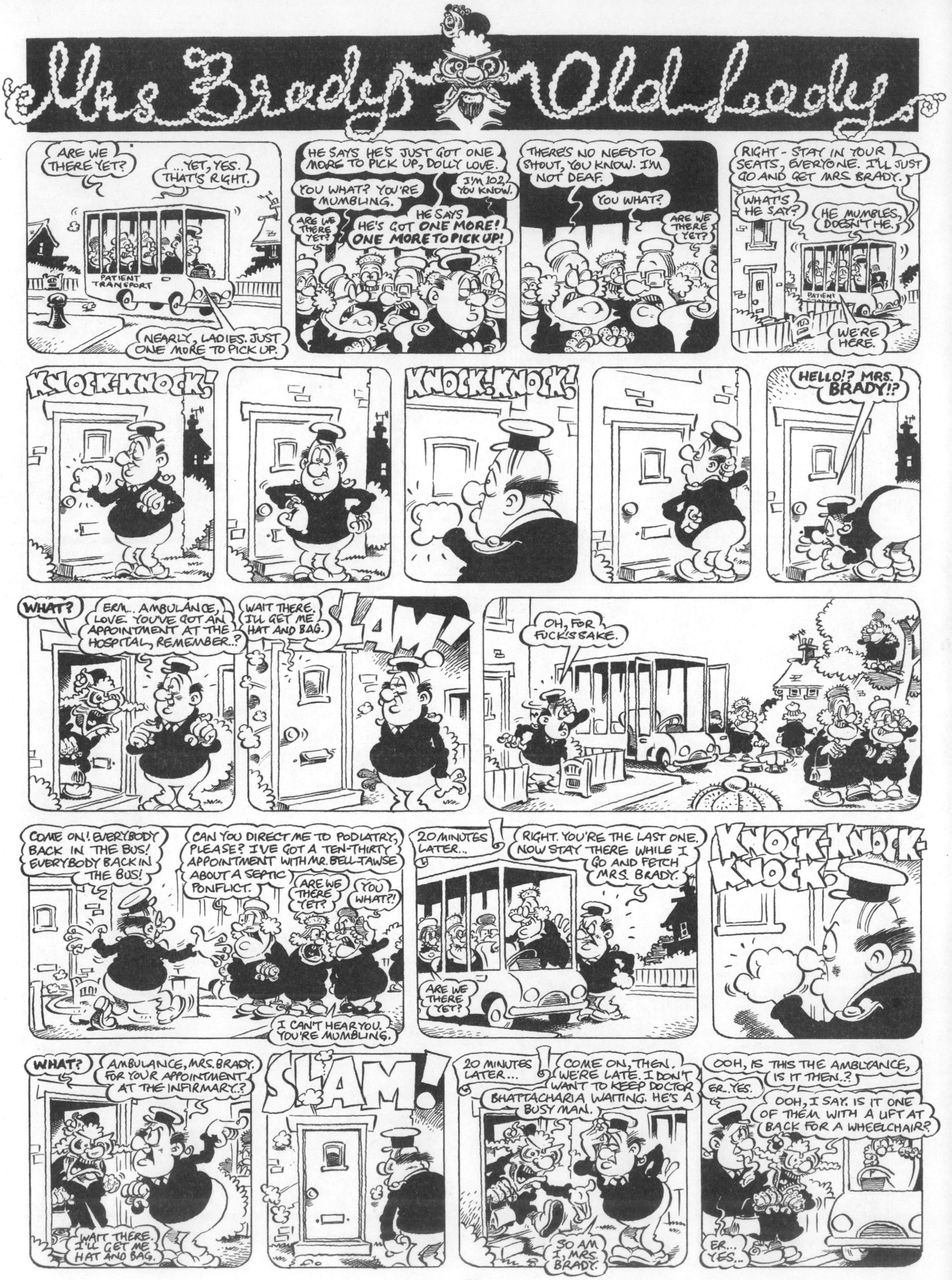
Mrs Brady Old Lady
ARE WE THERE YET?
...YET, YES. THAT'S RIGHT.
PATIENT TRANSPORT
NEARLY, LADIES. JUST ONE MORE TO PICK UP.
HE SAYS HE'S JUST GOT ONE MORE TO PICK UP, DOLLY LOVE.
YOU WHAT? YOU'RE MUMBLING.
I'M 102, YOU KNOW.
ARE WE THERE YET?
HE SAYS HE'S GOT ONE MORE! ONE MORE TO PICK UP!
THERE'S NO NEED TO SHOUT, YOU KNOW. I'M NOT DEAF.
YOU WHAT?
ARE WE THERE YET?
RIGHT - STAY IN YOUR SEATS, EVERYONE. I'LL JUST GO AND GET MRS. BRADY.
WHAT'S HE SAY?
HE MUMBLES, DOESN'T HE.
PATIENT
WE'RE HERE.
KNOCK-KNOCK!
KNOCK-KNOCK!
HELLO!? MRS. BRADY!?
WHAT?
ERM... AMBULANCE, LOVE. YOU'VE GOT AN APPOINTMENT AT THE HOSPITAL, REMEMBER..?
WAIT THERE. I'LL GET ME HAT AND BAG.
SLAM!
OH, FOR FUCK'S SAKE.
COME ON! EVERYBODY BACK IN THE BUS! EVERYBODY BACK IN THE BUS!
CAN YOU DIRECT ME TO PODIATRY, PLEASE? I'VE GOT A TEN-THIRTY APPOINTMENT WITH MR. BELL-TAWSE ABOUT A SEPTIC PONFLICT.
ARE WE THERE YET?
YOU WHAT?!
I CAN'T HEAR YOU. YOU'RE MUMBLING.
20 MINUTES LATER...
RIGHT. YOU'RE THE LAST ONE. NOW STAY THERE WHILE I GO AND FETCH MRS. BRADY.
ARE WE THERE YET?
KNOCK-KNOCK-KNOCK!
WHAT?
AMBULANCE, MRS. BRADY. FOR YOUR APPOINTMENT AT THE INFIRMARY..?
WAIT THERE. I'LL GET ME HAT AND BAG.
SLAM!
20 MINUTES LATER...
COME ON, THEN. WE'RE LATE. I DON'T WANT TO KEEP DOCTOR BHATTACHARIA WAITING. HE'S A BUSY MAN.
SO AM I, MRS. BRADY.
OOH, IS THIS THE AMBLYANCE, IS IT THEN..?
ER.. YES.
OOH, I SAY. IS IT ONE OF THEM WITH A LIFT AT BACK FOR A WHEELCHAIR?
ER... YES...

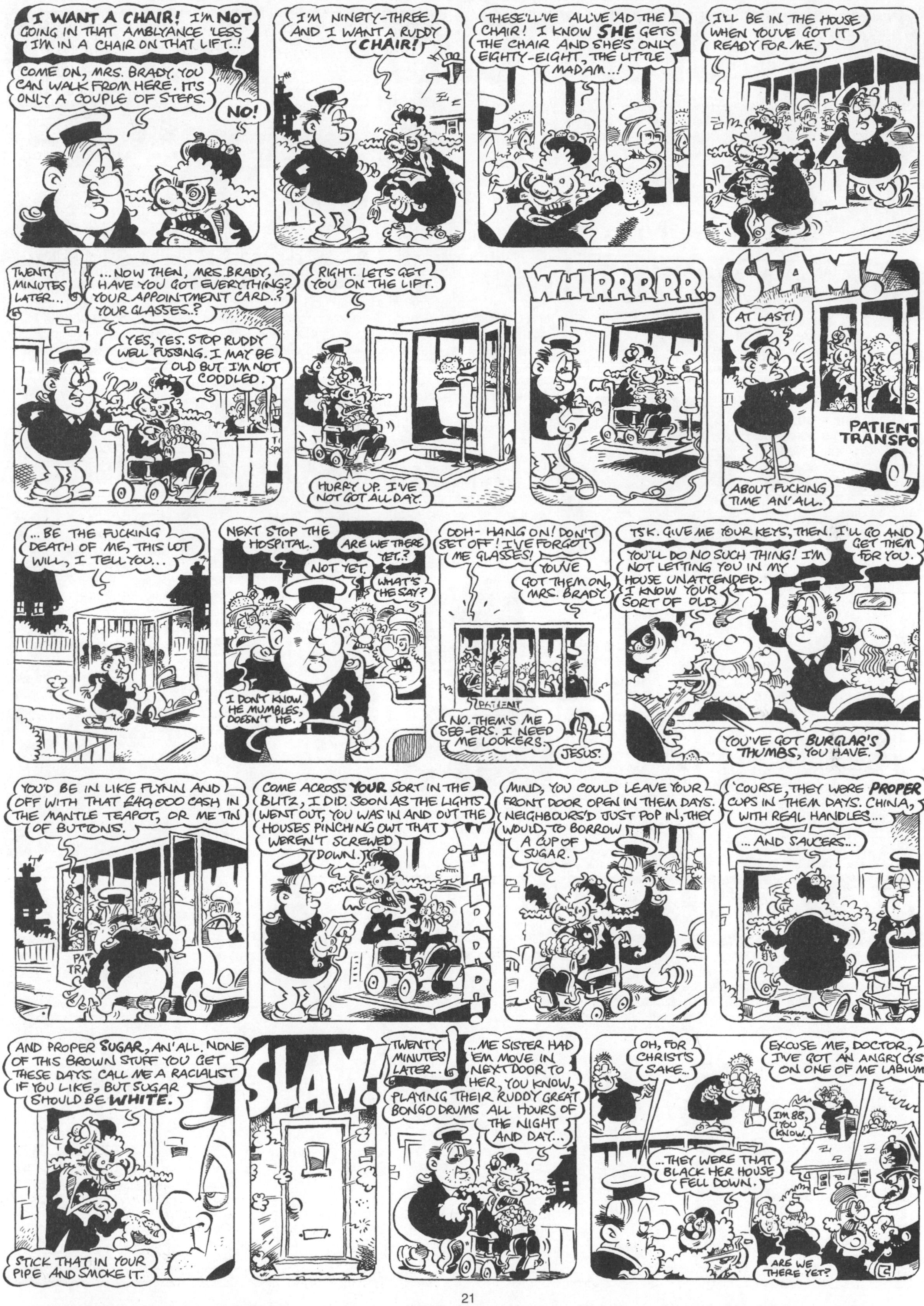
I WANT A CHAIR! I'M NOT GOING IN THAT AMBLYANCE 'LESS I'M IN A CHAIR ON THAT LIFT..!
COME ON, MRS. BRADY. YOU CAN WALK FROM HERE. IT'S ONLY A COUPLE OF STEPS.
NO!
I'M NINETY-THREE AND I WANT A RUDDY CHAIR!
THESE'LL'VE ALL'VE 'AD THE CHAIR! I KNOW SHE GETS THE CHAIR AND SHE'S ONLY EIGHTY-EIGHT, THE LITTLE MADAM..!
I'LL BE IN THE HOUSE WHEN YOU'VE GOT IT READY FOR ME.
TWENTY MINUTES LATER...
...NOW THEN, MRS. BRADY, HAVE YOU GOT EVERYTHING? YOUR APPOINTMENT CARD..? YOUR GLASSES..?
YES, YES. STOP RUDDY WELL FUSSING. I MAY BE OLD BUT I'M NOT CODDLED.
RIGHT. LET'S GET YOU ON THE LIFT.
HURRY UP. I'VE NOT GOT ALL DAY.
WHIRRRRR..
SLAM!
AT LAST!
PATIENT TRANSPO
ABOUT FUCKING TIME AN' ALL.
...BE THE FUCKING DEATH OF ME, THIS LOT WILL, I TELL YOU...
NEXT STOP THE HOSPITAL.
ARE WE THERE YET..?
NOT YET.
WHAT'S HE SAY?
I DON'T KNOW. HE MUMBLES, DOESN'T HE.
OOH- HANG ON! DON'T SET OFF! I'VE FORGOT ME GLASSES!
YOU'VE GOT THEM ON, MRS. BRADY.
PATIENT
NO. THEM'S ME SEE-ERS. I NEED ME LOOKERS.
JESUS!
TSK. GIVE ME YOUR KEYS, THEN. I'LL GO AND GET THEM FOR YOU.
YOU'LL DO NO SUCH THING! I'M NOT LETTING YOU IN MY HOUSE UNATTENDED. I KNOW YOUR SORT OF OLD.
YOU'VE GOT BURGLAR'S THUMBS, YOU HAVE.
YOU'D BE IN LIKE FLYNN AND OFF WITH THAT £49,000 CASH IN THE MANTLE TEAPOT, OR ME TIN OF BUTTONS.
PAT TRA
COME ACROSS YOUR SORT IN THE BLITZ, I DID. SOON AS THE LIGHTS WENT OUT, YOU WAS IN AND OUT THE HOUSES PINCHING OWT THAT WEREN'T SCREWED DOWN.
WHIRRR!
MIND, YOU COULD LEAVE YOUR FRONT DOOR OPEN IN THEM DAYS. NEIGHBOURS'D JUST POP IN, THEY WOULD, TO BORROW A CUP OF SUGAR.
'COURSE, THEY WERE PROPER CUPS IN THEM DAYS. CHINA, WITH REAL HANDLES...
...AND SAUCERS...
AND PROPER SUGAR, AN' ALL. NONE OF THIS BROWN STUFF YOU GET THESE DAYS. CALL ME A RACIALIST IF YOU LIKE, BUT SUGAR SHOULD BE WHITE.
STICK THAT IN YOUR PIPE AND SMOKE IT.
SLAM!
TWENTY MINUTES LATER...
...ME SISTER HAD 'EM MOVE IN NEXT DOOR TO HER, YOU KNOW, PLAYING THEIR RUDDY GREAT BONGO DRUMS ALL HOURS OF THE NIGHT AND DAY...
OH, FOR CHRIST'S SAKE...
EXCUSE ME, DOCTOR, I'VE GOT AN ANGRY CYST ON ONE OF ME LABIUMS...
I'M 88, YOU KNOW.
...THEY WERE THAT BLACK HER HOUSE FELL DOWN.
ARE WE THERE YET?

Letterbocks

PO Box 656,
North Shields,
NE30 4XX

letters@viz.co.uk

WHY are goalkeepers allowed to use their hands in football? It hardly seems fair on the other players in the team.

Angie O'Plasty, Crewe

STAR LETTER

I USED to love cheese until I found out that it was just milk that had gone off. It seems to me that dairy farmers have got themselves a tidy little scam going there.

Edna Trevelyn, Cornwall

I LOVE my wife enormously and I was going to buy her some red roses for Valentines day... until I saw the price of them, that is. £50 a dozen! I could get 2 prostitutes for that. So I did.

Frank Plasterboard London

THESE people who go on about being underpaid really get my goat. If they don't like doing what they do for the amount they get paid, they should get another ruddy job where they do.

Sue Pernoodle Oxford

I'VE just bought a king-sized Dorma duvet reduced from £225 to £50. There was nothing wrong with it, it simply had the Queen Mother's Crest on the packaging, and they are not allowed to use

it after she died. A hundred and seventy five quid saved. Who says the old bat's death was a tragedy?

Hector Cretis North Shields

I NOTICED the role of 'Domestic Violence Co-ordinator' advertised on a job website today. Surely this type of thing should be stopped, not choreographed?

Franklyn Branspeth Goole

AFTER a recent flurry we had snow all over our street. This made the road surface slippery causing difficult driving conditions. To make matters worse some wallies came along in a van and started throwing grit everywhere. Honestly, where are the parents?

Christian Blofeld London

I HOPE singer Eartha Kitt was wearing her make-up when she died, as it would have saved her family a lot of money at the embalmers.

Hampton Doubleday Peebles

THEY say that it's a little worrying when all the policemen look younger

than you. I disagree. I'm 99 and I wouldn't feel safe if I thought all our police officers were centegenarians.

Edith Mucus Peterborough

IF Dale Winton would spend less time camping it up and more time campaigning on green issues, then we might be able to avert global warming.

Dot Braithwaite London

WHEN Sir Patrick Moore sadly, but inevitably shuffles off his mortal coil, I for one will be bitterly disappointed if not a single tabloid newspaper uses the headline 'No More Mr Night Sky'.

Grant Allenby-Hurton e-mail

I HAVE long wondered who has found the most dead bodies. Is it joggers, or people out walking their dogs?

Phill Drolls Glasgow

IS it just me, or has anyone else noticed that money has been a bit tight lately?

Darren Conway e-mail

I DON'T know what the fuss is about over Carol Thatcher's remarks in the green room at the BBC. It was clearly an innocent misunderstanding and nothing more. Carol simply though it was okay to say something racist in private and nobody else did.

Roland Plywood Sheffield

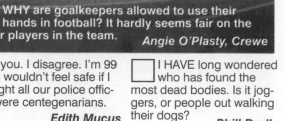

YOU are the BENT REF!

Q: You are officiating at a Premier League match at Old Trafford when, in the second minute of the game, you award a free kick against the home team. As usual, Wayne Rooney runs up to you and calls you a 'stupid fucking wanker'. This is unquestionable dissent and under the new 'Respect' campaign warrants an instant red card. What course of action do you take?

A: You take no action, as you know full well that sending him off would mean the following Saturday you'd find yourself running the line at Blyth Spartans v Hucknall Town in the Blue Square Conference North.

Q: You are refereeing a match in the fourth round of the FA Cup. The score is 0-0 and in the 90th minute, an attacker is clearly brought down inside the penalty area by a defender. He has to be carried off the field by stretcher, a process which takes five minutes. What do you do?

A: As he is being carried off, you caution the attacker for simulating a foul and award an indirect free kick to the offending team. You then spend the five minutes injury time denying goal scoring opportunities by killing play in the midfield, thereby ensuring your fee for the replay.

Q: An attacking team has been awarded a free kick 30 yards from goal. Before you blow the whistle, the kick is taken and the ball strikes a defender who is in the process of retreating ten yards. The ball is deflected into the goal. Do you award the goal or insist the kick is re-taken?

A: There is nothing in the rules of football to say that an attacker has to wait for the defenders to retreat the full ten yards before taking a free kick. However, if you deem the kick to be 'ceremonial', the attacker must wait for your whistle. In this instance you should quickly phone your contact at the Filipino betting syndicate to see if he wants the goal to stand.

LAND a plane safely at an airport and nobody bats an eyelid, but crash it into the Hudson river scaring seven shades of shit out of your passengers and you're a hero. I can't help thinking that the prerequisite for hero status is not what it once was.

Doris Clodge
e-mail

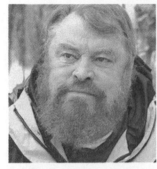

I ONCE saw Brian Blessed eating a scotch egg whilst sitting on Ainsdale beach. However,I wasn't that surprised as I am married to him and we'd gone there for a picnic.

Hildegarde Blessed
e-mail

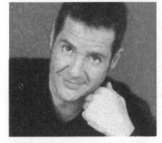

IF Dale Winton would spend less time camping it up and more time acting in the capacity of a diplomat then we might not have all these problems in the Middle East.

Dot Braithwaite
London

I SEE that a £1bn stealth boat the Royal Navy has developed has got the radar signal of a rowing boat. Fantastic. I'm sure our ememies won't raise an eyebrow when their radar screens show a small rowing boat 3000 miles from land travelling in excess of 32 knots.

Willy McWilliams
e-mail

A JUDGE in a recent paedophile case remarked that the defendant's child porn collection was the worst he had ever seen. It sounds to me like the wrong person was in the dock.

Martin Fibreglass
Rhyll

FOR someone who doesn't approve of alternative sexualities, I think the Pope spends an awful lot of his time in a dress.

Frank Gaul
Kent

I NOTICED that on the wall outside the McDonald's drivethough in Newcastle there is a sign reading 'Please Check Your Order Carefully'. Perhaps it would be better if they put it inside.

Hubert Nobacon
Newcastle

ON being given a knighthood, cyclist Chris Hoy said he was delighted with the honour as it was something money can't buy. Top marks top the man, he didn't laugh or anything when he said it.

Hector Littlejohn
Luton

I'm Too Sexy for my Lease

~ Fairbrass on the street after run-in with landlord

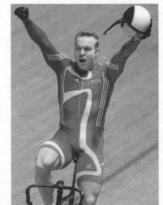

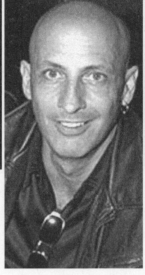

Fairbrass (above) ~ Too Sexy, yesterday and (left) band members who sub-let flat

RIGHT SAID FRED front man *Richard Fairbrass* was last night sleeping in his car after he was sensationally evicted from his West Midlands flat - *for being TOO SEXY!*

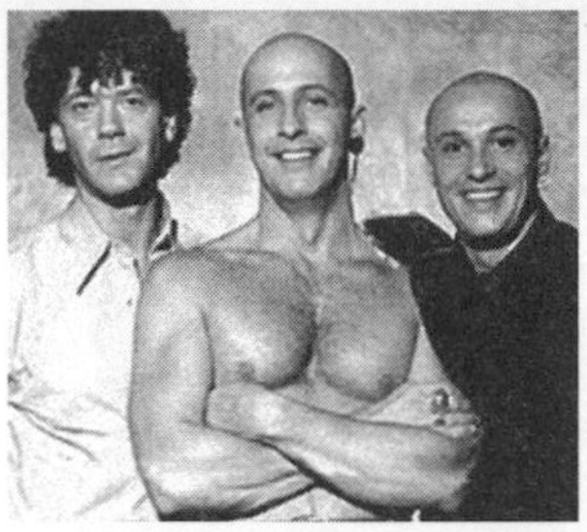

The slap-headed singer was asked to leave the rented property in Droitwich by his landlord who had apparently pointed out that Fairbrass's sultryness and erotic desirability was in breach of the terms of his lease.

problems

"This is outright discrimination and quite frankly I'm sick of it," said the singer, whose hits include *Deeply Dippy* and *Don't Talk, Just Kiss*. "As fans of my band will probably remember I suffered similar problems in Milan, New York and Japan back in the early nineties, but I had hoped that it would be a different story in Droitwich in 2009."

tissue

"It's ridiculous that the atypically high degree of sexual magnetism that I happen to radiate should prevent me from living wherever I want," the novelty song writer and detergent advert actor added.

dysfunction

But landlord Rob Lumb, who penned the fateful eviction notice, dismissed Fairbrass's claims of unfair treatment and flatly denied accusations that he was being sexyist.

"This is nothing to do with Mr Fairbrass's foxyness or beddability," he told reporters. "The fact of the matter is that he is nine months in arrears with his rent and has ignored my verbal and written requests for payment. Not only that, but he has been keeping two dogs in the flat, contrary to the tennancy agreement, and he has been sub-letting a room to other members of Right Said Fred."

warehouse

Speaking from his E-reg Vauxhall Senator, Fairbrass said he would fight the decision, although he admitted he was not hopeful of overturning his eviction notice. "I suspect that if the case ever came before a judge, I may be too sexy for his court, and asked to leave," he told us.

I'M football mad, but I have to work weekends, so I never get to go to any matches. Could I use the pages of your magazine to ask the FA if they could change their regular fixtures from Saturdays to another time. Thursday mornings would be best for me.

Crawford Bartram
London

UP THE ARTS CORNER

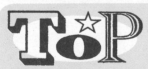

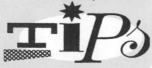

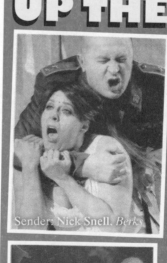

Sender: Nick Snell, *Berks*

Sender: Martin Gibbs, *Tavistock*

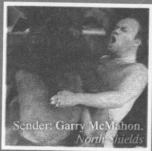

Sender: Garry McMahon, *North Shields*

TOP TIPS

KEEP confusing Sonny and Cher with Sunnis and Shias? Just remember that the former two are an American husband and wife pop duo, the latter are denominations of Islam who have been waring since the death of the prophet Mohammed over which group has the rightful claim to his sucession. Simple.

Alan Cardboard, e-mail

BUTCHERS. Make a mockery of the phrase 'as fit as a butcher's dog' by neglecting your dog horribly.

Big Tom, London

ACTRESSES. Next time you do an advert for a constipation remedy, spend some of your fee on a pair of dark sunglasses. That way, when you are in the supermarket you won't have people pointing at you saying "there's the woman with the painful stools."

Gerry Paton, e-mail

PEOPLE ON 'Eastenders' - don't talk to stall owners or they will make you mind said stall while they go off and settle a score of some sort.

Martin Christian, e-mail

GEOGRAPHY teachers. Attach pitta bread to the elbows of your tweed jacket for a tasty alternative to leather patches.

Chris Miller, e-mail

A PEAR makes an ideal chicken leg substitute for vegetarians.

W Gamble, Newcastle

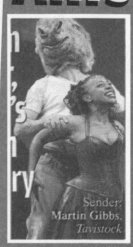

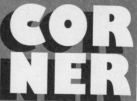

Sugden: "Killed by Showbiz"

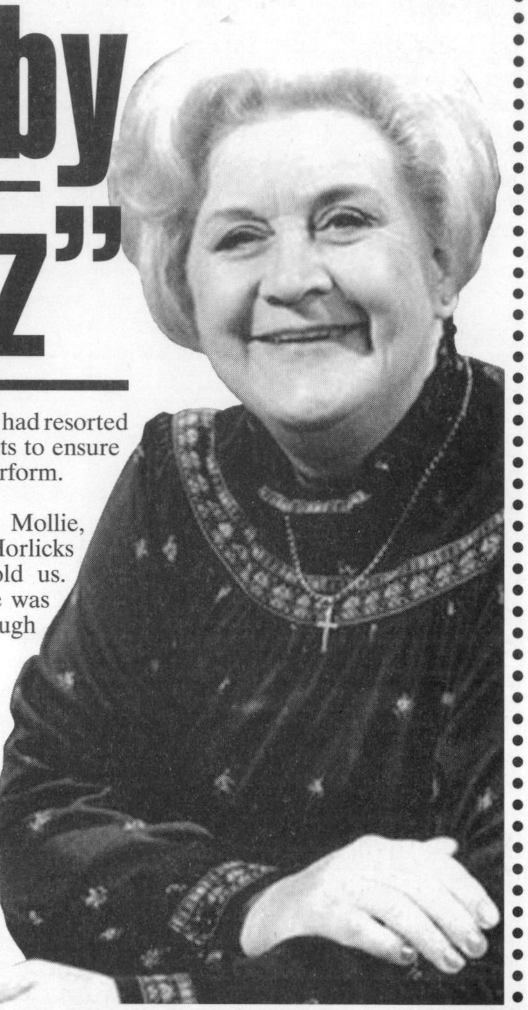

URI GELLER fears that the death of his friend Mollie Sugden may have been caused by the stress of preparing for a record-breaking series of comeback gigs.

The fifty sell out shows at London's O2 Arena had demanded a punishing rehearsal regime, and Geller claims the 86-year-old comic actress had 'pushed herself to the limit' preparing to perform favourites such as *Are You Being Served, That's My Boy* and *Come Back Mrs Noah.*

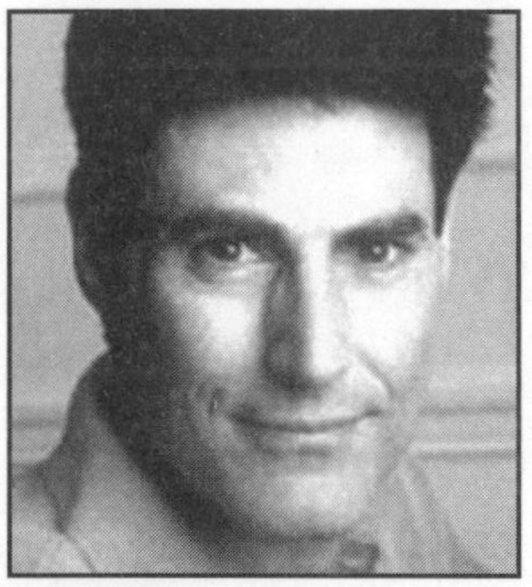

BENDER: *Cutlery manipulator Uri Geller yesterday*

By our showbiz death correspondent
THE LATE CLEMENT FREUD

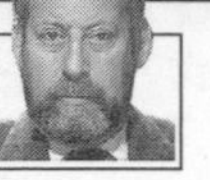

CONDITION

Geller told Sky News, ' I think it was a mistake to schedule fifty shows. I saw the setlist, and she was doing all the hits, and a few surprises. But even someone in peak condition would struggle to deliver twenty or so high-energy sitcom episodes in a night.

'Mollie was in good shape, but pressure can break anyone. Just look what slight pressure, very gentle, can do to this spoon. There.'

PRACTICE

Sugden's attorney, Ingledew Botterill, agrees the star was stressed, revealing that the actress had resorted to a cocktail of stimulants to ensure she was fit enough to perform.

"The last time I saw Mollie, she was strung out on Horlicks and Sanatogen," he told us. "There was no way she was going to make it through fifty gigs."

DISTRICT

Fans who have bought any of the £120 tickets to the cancelled shows will be able to obtain a refund, or swap their ticket for a commemorative limited edition email from the concert organisers, or some magic beans.

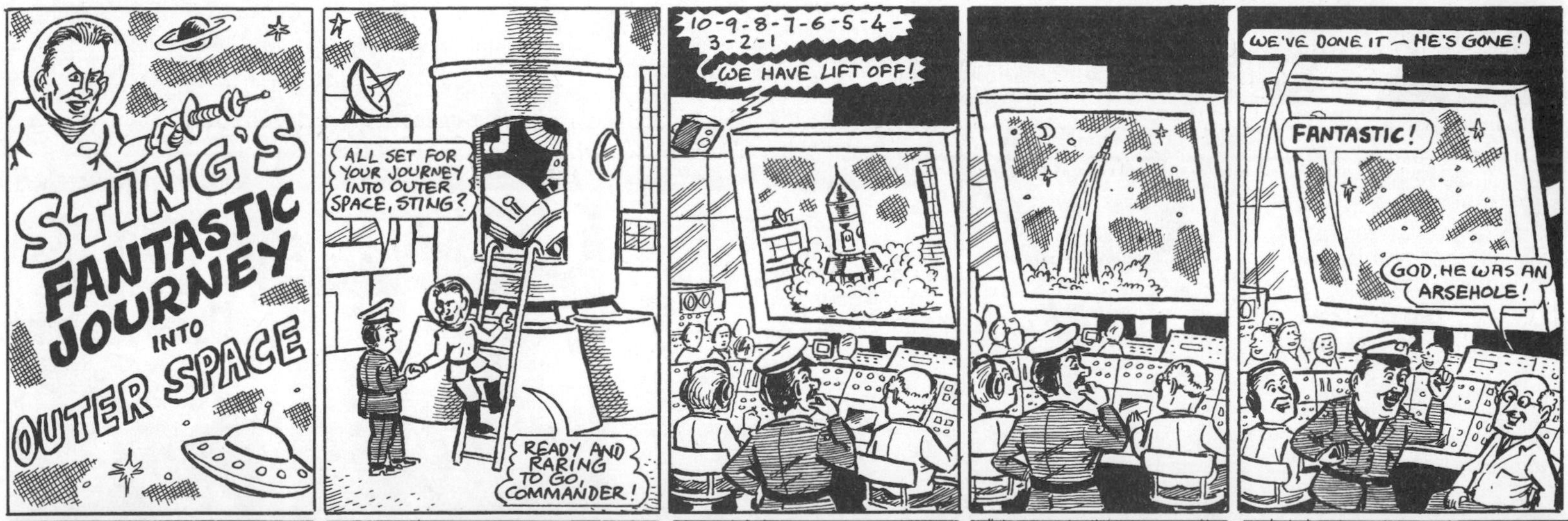

STING'S FANTASTIC JOURNEY INTO OUTER SPACE
ALL SET FOR YOUR JOURNEY INTO OUTER SPACE, STING?
READY AND RARING TO GO, COMMANDER!
10-9-8-7-6-5-4-3-2-1
WE HAVE LIFT OFF!
WE'VE DONE IT — HE'S GONE!
FANTASTIC!
GOD, HE WAS AN ARSEHOLE!

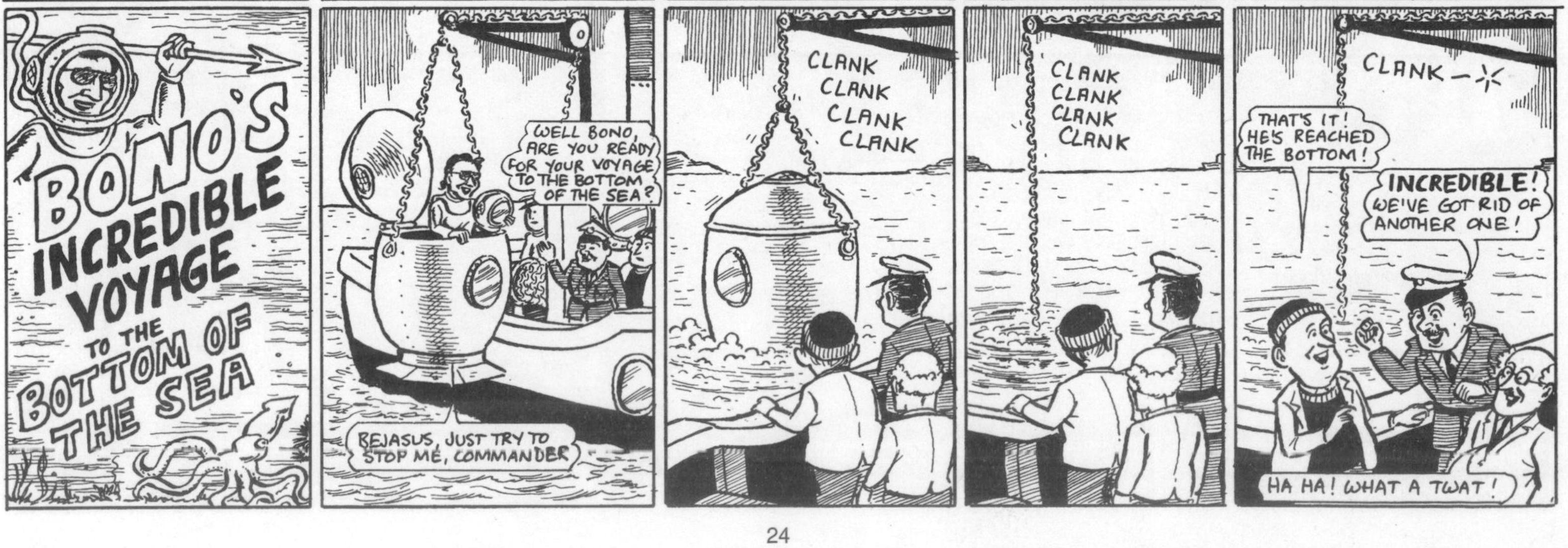

BONO'S INCREDIBLE VOYAGE TO THE BOTTOM OF THE SEA
WELL BONO, ARE YOU READY FOR YOUR VOYAGE TO THE BOTTOM OF THE SEA?
BEJASUS, JUST TRY TO STOP ME, COMMANDER
CLANK CLANK CLANK CLANK
CLANK CLANK CLANK CLANK
CLANK
THAT'S IT! HE'S REACHED THE BOTTOM!
INCREDIBLE! WE'VE GOT RID OF ANOTHER ONE!
HA HA! WHAT A TWAT!

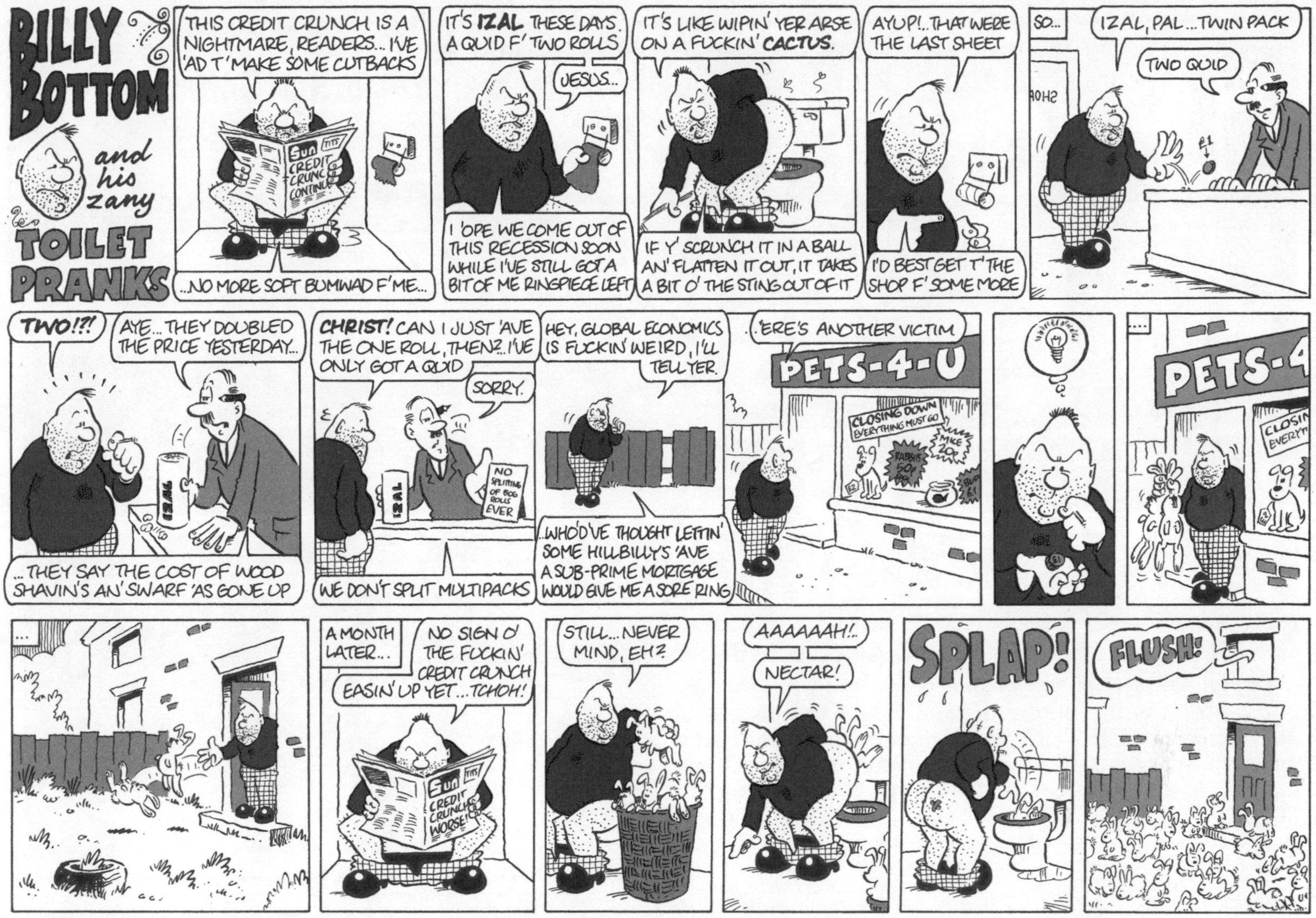
BILLY BOTTOM
and his zany
TOILET PRANKS
THIS CREDIT CRUNCH IS A NIGHTMARE, READERS... I'VE 'AD T' MAKE SOME CUTBACKS
...NO MORE SOFT BUMWAD F' ME...
IT'S IZAL THESE DAYS. A QUID F' TWO ROLLS
JESUS...
I 'OPE WE COME OUT OF THIS RECESSION SOON WHILE I'VE STILL GOT A BIT OF ME RINGPIECE LEFT
IT'S LIKE WIPIN' YER ARSE ON A FUCKIN' CACTUS.
IF Y' SCRUNCH IT IN A BALL AN' FLATTEN IT OUT, IT TAKES A BIT O' THE STING OUT OF IT
AYUP!.. THAT WERE THE LAST SHEET
I'D BEST GET T' THE SHOP F' SOME MORE
SO...
IZAL, PAL... TWIN PACK
TWO QUID
TWO!?!
AYE... THEY DOUBLED THE PRICE YESTERDAY...
...THEY SAY THE COST OF WOOD SHAVIN'S AN' SWARF 'AS GONE UP
IZAL
CHRIST! CAN I JUST 'AVE THE ONE ROLL, THEN?.. I'VE ONLY GOT A QUID
SORRY.
NO SPLITTING OF BOG ROLLS EVER
WE DON'T SPLIT MULTIPACKS
HEY, GLOBAL ECONOMICS IS FUCKIN' WEIRD, I'LL TELL YER
...WHO'D'VE THOUGHT LETTIN' SOME HILLBILLY'S 'AVE A SUB-PRIME MORTGAGE WOULD GIVE ME A SORE RING
...'ERE'S ANOTHER VICTIM
PETS-4-U
CLOSING DOWN EVERYTHING MUST GO
...
...
A MONTH LATER...
NO SIGN O' THE FUCKIN' CREDIT CRUNCH EASIN' UP YET... TCHOH!
CREDIT CRUNCH WORSE!
STILL... NEVER MIND, EH?
AAAAAAH!..
NECTAR!
SPLAP!
FLUSH!

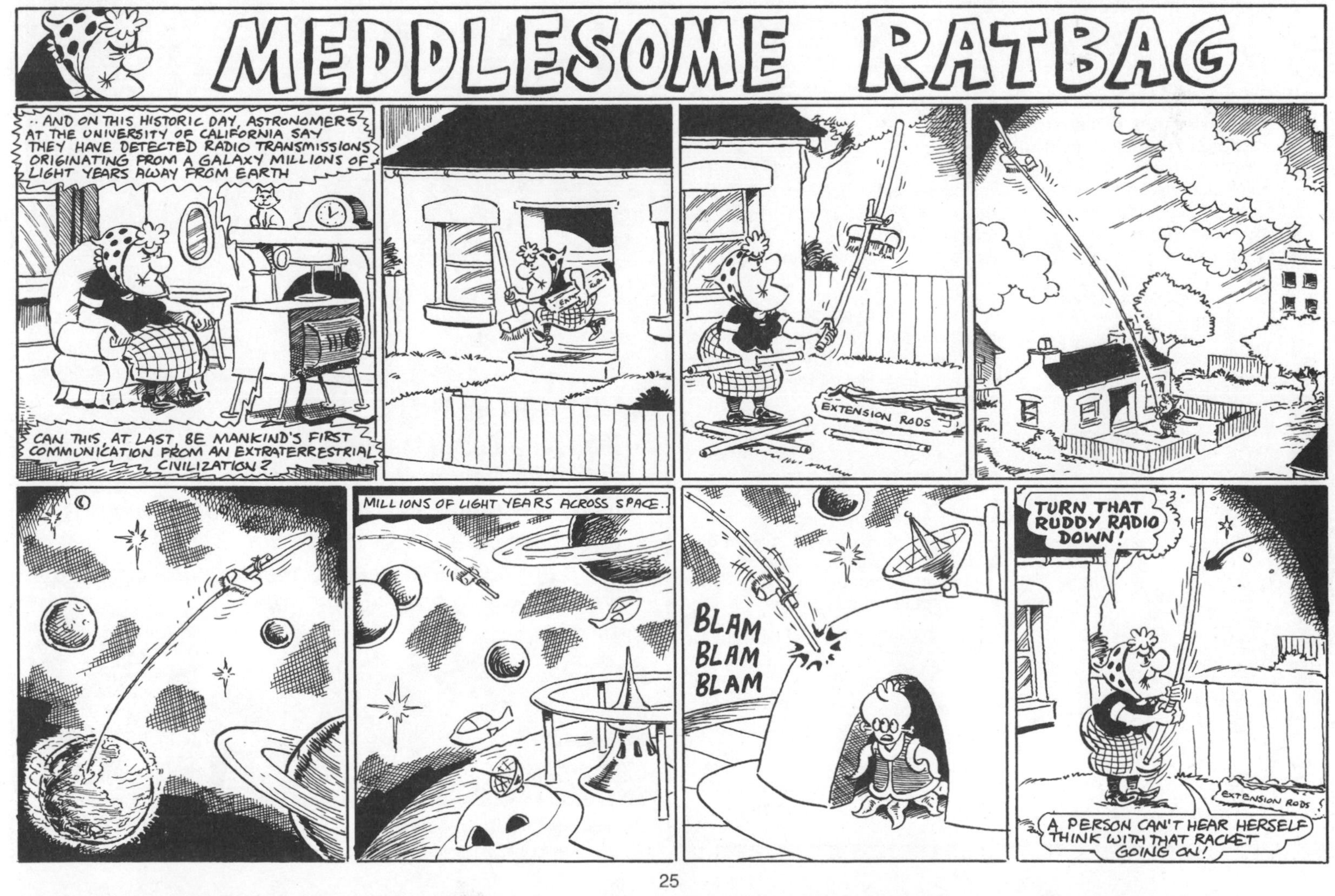
MEDDLESOME RATBAG
..AND ON THIS HISTORIC DAY, ASTRONOMERS AT THE UNIVERSITY OF CALIFORNIA SAY THEY HAVE DETECTED RADIO TRANSMISSIONS ORIGINATING FROM A GALAXY MILLIONS OF LIGHT YEARS AWAY FROM EARTH
CAN THIS, AT LAST, BE MANKIND'S FIRST COMMUNICATION FROM AN EXTRATERRESTRIAL CIVILIZATION?
EXTENSION RODS
MILLIONS OF LIGHT YEARS ACROSS SPACE..
BLAM BLAM BLAM
TURN THAT RUDDY RADIO DOWN!
EXTENSION RODS
A PERSON CAN'T HEAR HERSELF THINK WITH THAT RACKET GOING ON!

"Proud of my English Roots" ~BNP Griffin

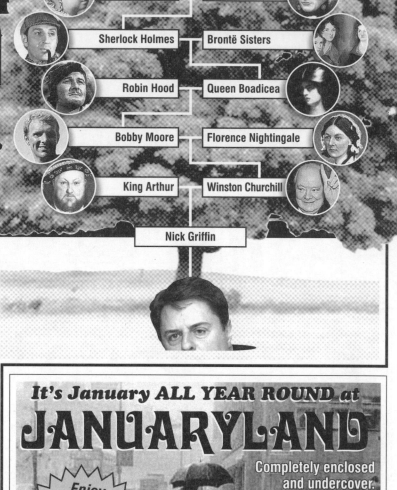

The Descent of Man: How Griffin Evolved

An English monkey
St George
Queen Victoria
Admiral Nelson
Sherlock Holmes
Brontë Sisters
Robin Hood
Queen Boadicea
Bobby Moore
Florence Nightingale
King Arthur
Winston Churchill
Nick Griffin

ACCORDING to evolutionary anthropologists, Africa is the cradle of humanity. Examination of modern DNA proves that early hominids who lived on the plains of Ethiopia thousands of years ago are the direct ancestors of the earth's 6 billion people.

Except one. For British National Party leader Nick Griffin claims to be descended from a monkey that lived not in Africa ... but right here in ***BRITAIN***.

The robustly-opinionated MEP today spoke of his relief at discovering that he is descended from a completely British genetic line.

BASTARD

"I had always felt certain that there was no way that I could of came from Africa," the Cambridge-educated ignorant bastard told German newspaper *Der Spiegl*. "I've spent the last six months tracing my ancestry, and just as I suspected, it turns out that I'm descended from a one hundred percent British monkey."

"What's more, the fossil record shows that my ancient ancestor lived up a tree in an area of the country that is now occupied by Buckingham Palace, and you can't get no more British than that," he added.

Griffin's discovery is set to be bad news for the rest of the UK population. For, as the only true indigenous Briton, Griffin is now planning to send us ALL back where we came from.

TWAT

The big racist continued: "I'm not a racialist, but I believe that Britain should be for the British. And that's me, so I would like to see the rest of the UK population repatriated back to their country of origin."

"This island is already overcrowded enough without throwing the Neolithic floodgates wide open and letting every Homo-erectus and his dog into the country," said Griffin.

ARSEHOLE

"They've come over here twenty-five thousand years ago and taken all my jobs. I mean I've got nothing against everybody else in the country, it's just that I wouldn't want one of them marrying my daughter," he continued, beginning to froth slightly at the corners of his mouth.

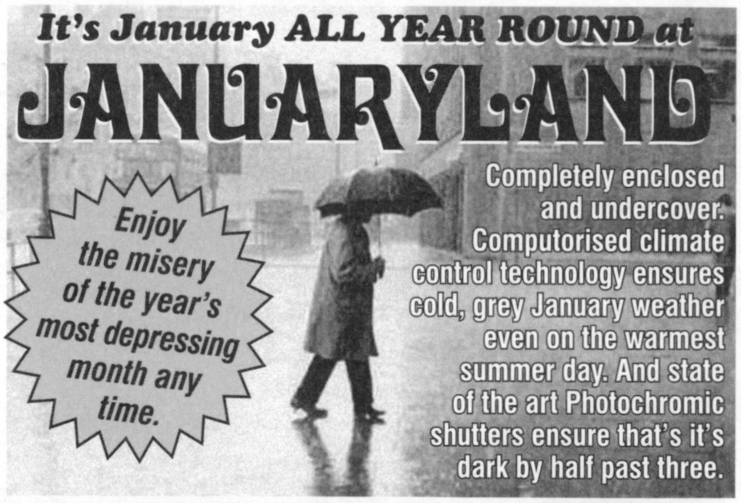

"And I'll tell you another thing, it was a WHITE monkey what I evolved off of," the fat, bozz-eyed shitter added.

NATIONAL CUNT: **BNP MEP Griffin yesterday.**

It's January ALL YEAR ROUND at

JANUARYLAND

Enjoy the misery of the year's most depressing month any time.
Completely enclosed and undercover. Computorised climate control technology ensures cold, grey January weather even on the warmest summer day. And state of the art Photochromic shutters ensure that's it's dark by half past three.

WHILE YOU'RE THERE, WHY NOT...

Closed 31st Dec - 1st Feb

- ***Wait for a bus in the sleet in our authentic Januarytown city centre...***
- ***Enjoy a warming cup of Lemsip in our famous Capricorn cafe...***
- ***Snap up 'bargains' in our JanuaryLand Gift Shop, where it's sale time all the time!***

JANUARYLAND

"I was there for two hours one day last May and I wanted to cut my fucking wrists."

Mrs B., Essex

WE ARE HERE

JanuaryLand - where a day will seem like a lifetime

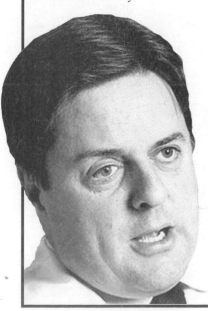

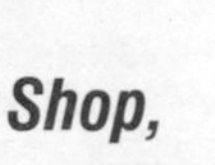

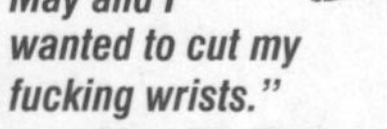

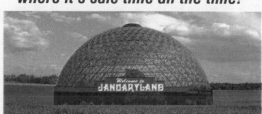

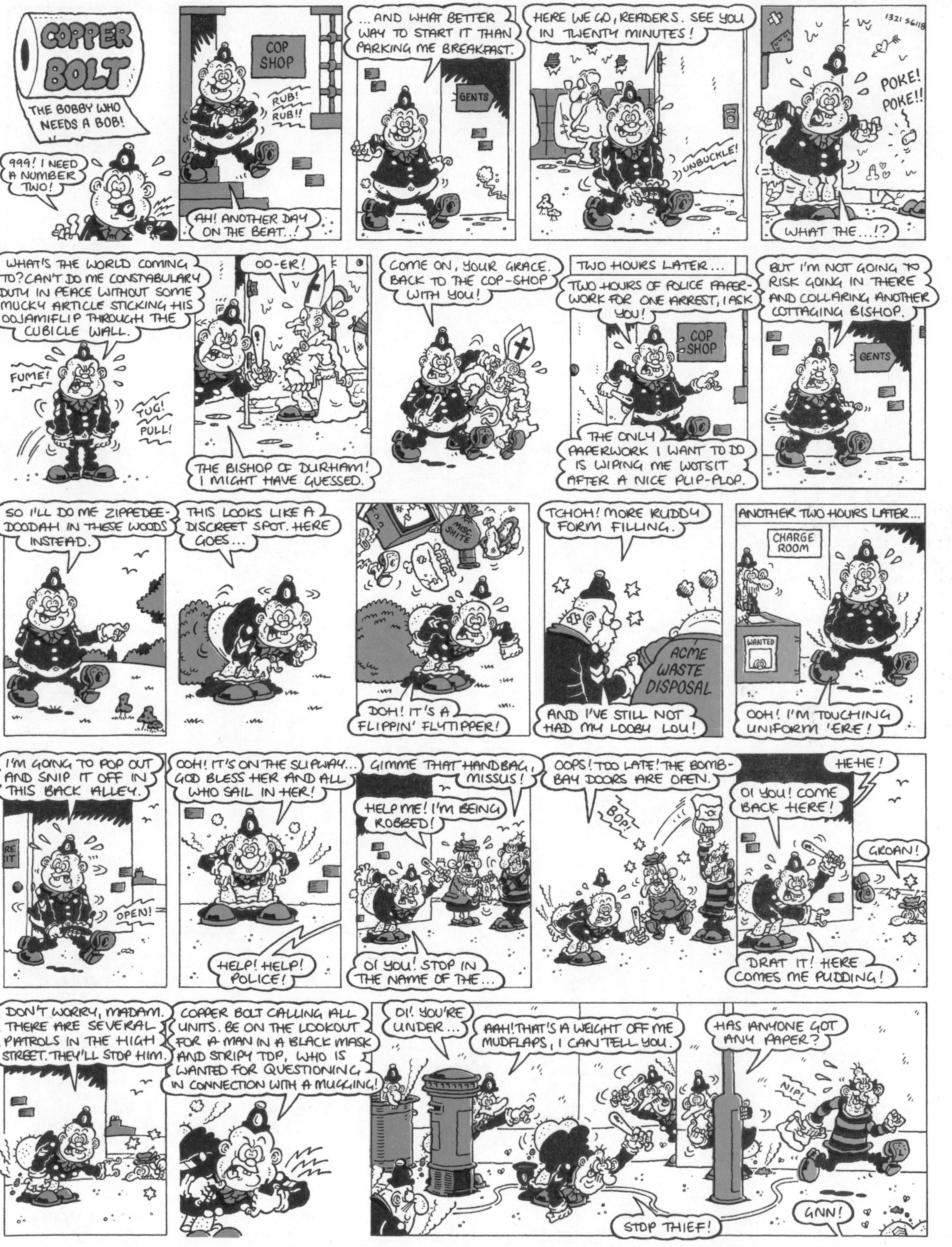
COPPER BOLT
THE BOBBY WHO NEEDS A BOB!
999! I NEED A NUMBER TWO!
COP SHOP
RUB! RUB!!
AH! ANOTHER DAY ON THE BEAT..!
... AND WHAT BETTER WAY TO START IT THAN PARKING ME BREAKFAST.
GENTS
HERE WE GO, READERS. SEE YOU IN TWENTY MINUTES!
UNBUCKLE!
POKE! POKE!!
WHAT THE ...!?
WHAT'S THE WORLD COMING TO? CAN'T DO ME CONSTABULARY DUTY IN PEACE WITHOUT SOME MUCKY ARTICLE STICKING HIS OOJAMIFLIP THROUGH THE CUBICLE WALL.
FUME!
TUG! PULL!
OO-ER!
THE BISHOP OF DURHAM! I MIGHT HAVE GUESSED.
COME ON, YOUR GRACE. BACK TO THE COP-SHOP WITH YOU!
TWO HOURS LATER ...
TWO HOURS OF POLICE PAPERWORK FOR ONE ARREST, I ASK YOU!
COP SHOP
THE ONLY PAPERWORK I WANT TO DO IS WIPING ME WOTSIT AFTER A NICE PLIP-PLOP.
BUT I'M NOT GOING TO RISK GOING IN THERE AND COLLARING ANOTHER COTTAGING BISHOP.
GENTS
SO I'LL DO ME ZIPPEDEE-DOODAH IN THESE WOODS INSTEAD.
THIS LOOKS LIKE A DISCREET SPOT. HERE GOES...
MISC. SHITE
DOH! IT'S A FLIPPIN' FLYTIPPER!
TCHOH! MORE RUDDY FORM FILLING.
ACME WASTE DISPOSAL
AND I'VE STILL NOT HAD MY LOOBY LOU!
ANOTHER TWO HOURS LATER...
CHARGE ROOM
WANTED
OOH! I'M TOUCHING UNIFORM 'ERE!
I'M GOING TO POP OUT AND SNIP IT OFF IN THIS BACK ALLEY.
OPEN!
OOH! IT'S ON THE SLIPWAY... GOD BLESS HER AND ALL WHO SAIL IN HER!
HELP! HELP! POLICE!
GIMME THAT HANDBAG, MISSUS!
HELP ME! I'M BEING ROBBED!
OI YOU! STOP IN THE NAME OF THE...
OOPS! TOO LATE! THE BOMB-BAY DOORS ARE OPEN.
BOP!
HE HE!
OI YOU! COME BACK HERE!
GROAN!
DRAT IT! HERE COMES ME PUDDING!
DON'T WORRY, MADAM. THERE ARE SEVERAL PATROLS IN THE HIGH STREET. THEY'LL STOP HIM.
COPPER BOLT CALLING ALL UNITS. BE ON THE LOOKOUT FOR A MAN IN A BLACK MASK AND STRIPY TOP, WHO IS WANTED FOR QUESTIONING IN CONNECTION WITH A MUGGING!
OI! YOU'RE UNDER...
AAH! THAT'S A WEIGHT OFF ME MUDFLAPS, I CAN TELL YOU.
HAS ANYONE GOT ANY PAPER?
NIP!
STOP THIEF!
GNN!

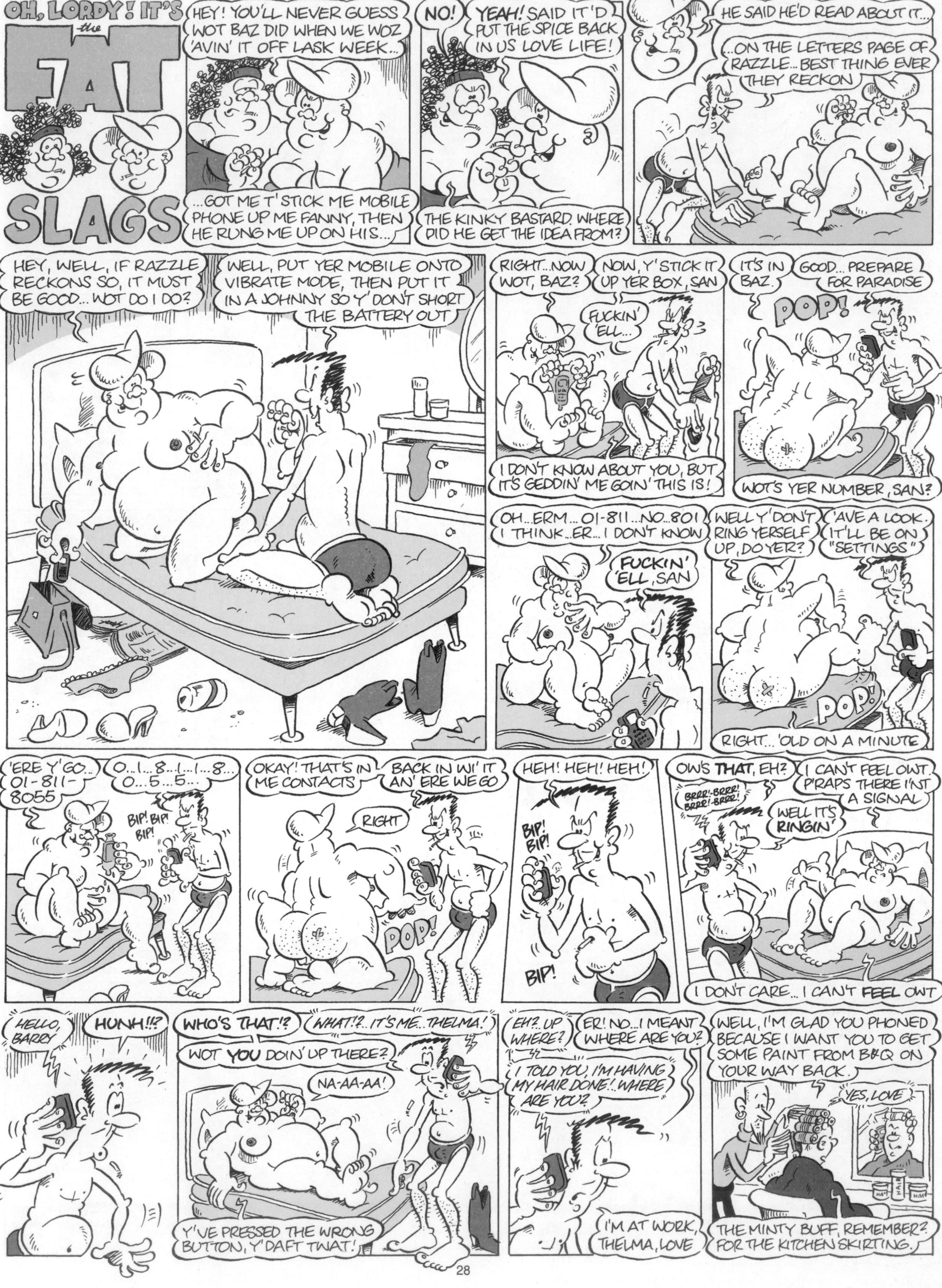
OH, LORDY! IT'S the FAT SLAGS
HEY! YOU'LL NEVER GUESS WOT BAZ DID WHEN WE WOZ 'AVIN' IT OFF LASK WEEK...
...GOT ME T' STICK ME MOBILE PHONE UP ME FANNY, THEN HE RUNG ME UP ON HIS...
NO!
YEAH! SAID IT'D PUT THE SPICE BACK IN US LOVE LIFE!
THE KINKY BASTARD. WHERE DID HE GET THE IDEA FROM?
HE SAID HE'D READ ABOUT IT...
...ON THE LETTERS PAGE OF RAZZLE... BEST THING EVER THEY RECKON
HEY, WELL, IF RAZZLE RECKONS SO, IT MUST BE GOOD... WOT DO I DO?
WELL, PUT YER MOBILE ONTO VIBRATE MODE, THEN PUT IT IN A JOHNNY SO Y' DON'T SHORT THE BATTERY OUT
RIGHT...NOW WOT, BAZ?
NOW, Y' STICK IT UP YER BOX, SAN
FUCKIN' 'ELL...
I DON'T KNOW ABOUT YOU, BUT IT'S GEDDIN' ME GOIN' THIS IS!
IT'S IN BAZ.
GOOD... PREPARE FOR PARADISE
POP!
WOT'S YER NUMBER, SAN?
OH...ERM... 01-811...NO..801 I THINK..ER... I DON'T KNOW
FUCKIN' 'ELL, SAN
WELL Y' DON'T RING YERSELF UP, DO YER?
'AVE A LOOK. IT'LL BE ON "SETTINGS"
POP!
RIGHT... 'OLD ON A MINUTE
'ERE Y' GO... 01-811-8055
0...1...8...1...1...8... 0...5...5...
BIP! BIP! BIP!
OKAY! THAT'S IN ME CONTACTS
BACK IN WI' IT AN' 'ERE WE GO
RIGHT
POP!
HEH! HEH! HEH!
BIP! BIP!
BIP!
OW'S THAT, EH?
BRRR! BRRR! BRRR! BRRR!
I CAN'T FEEL OWT. P'RAPS THERE I'N'T A SIGNAL
WELL IT'S RINGIN'
I DON'T CARE... I CAN'T FEEL OWT
HELLO, BARRY
HUNH!!?
WHO'S THAT!?
WHAT!?.. IT'S ME... THELMA!
WOT YOU DOIN' UP THERE?
NA-AA-AA!
Y'VE PRESSED THE WRONG BUTTON, Y' DAFT TWAT!
EH?.. UP WHERE?
ER! NO...I MEANT WHERE ARE YOU?
I TOLD YOU, I'M HAVING MY HAIR DONE! WHERE ARE YOU?
I'M AT WORK, THELMA, LOVE
WELL, I'M GLAD YOU PHONED BECAUSE I WANT YOU TO GET SOME PAINT FROM B&Q ON YOUR WAY BACK.
YES, LOVE
THE MINTY BUFF, REMEMBER? FOR THE KITCHEN SKIRTING.

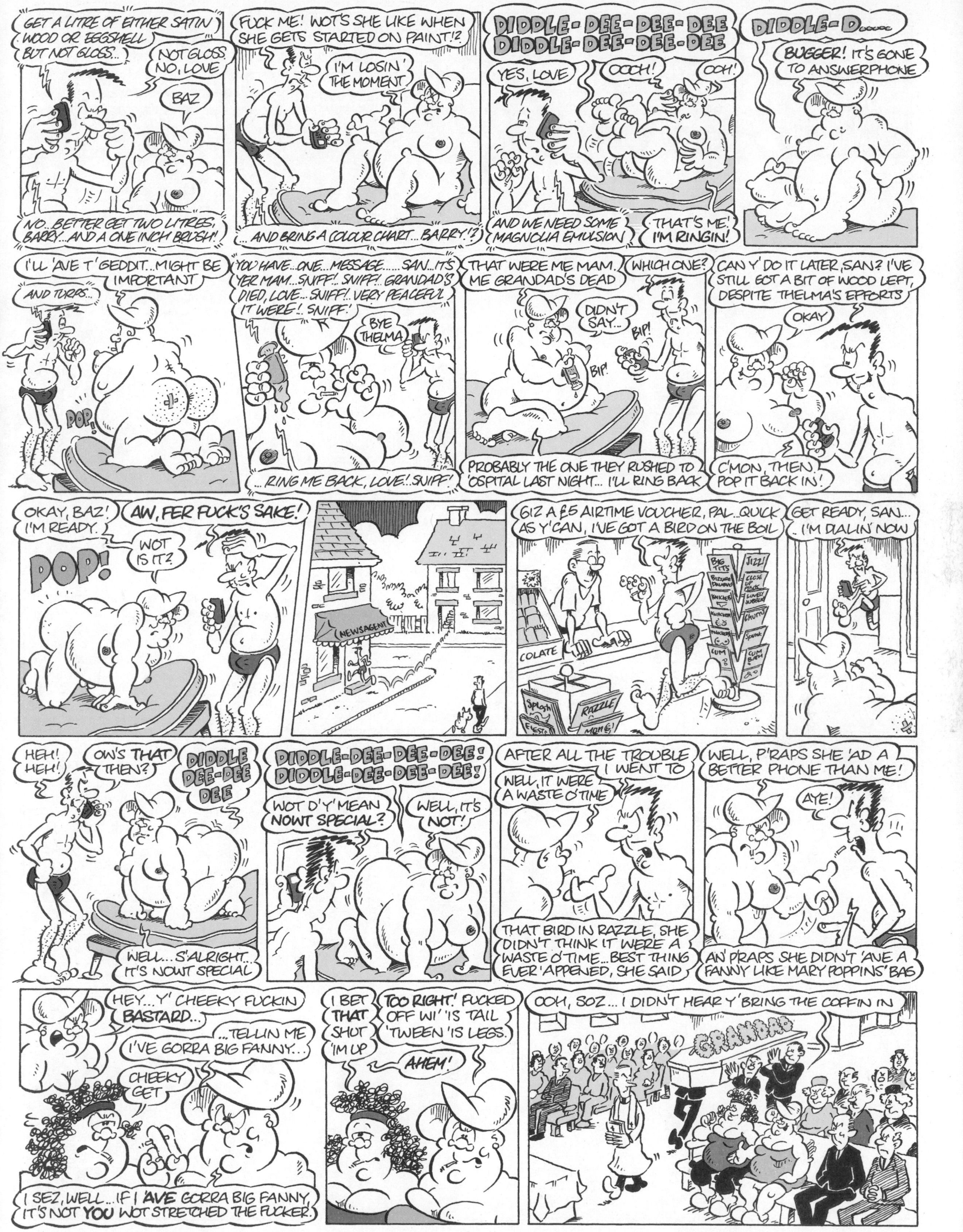
GET A LITRE OF EITHER SATIN WOOD OR EGGSHELL BUT NOT GLOSS...
NOT GLOSS, NO, LOVE
BAZ
NO... BETTER GET TWO LITRES, BARRY... AND A ONE INCH BRUSH!
FUCK ME! WOT'S SHE LIKE WHEN SHE GETS STARTED ON PAINT!?
I'M LOSIN' THE MOMENT
...AND BRING A COLOUR CHART... BARRY!?
DIDDLE-DEE-DEE-DEE DIDDLE-DEE-DEE-DEE
YES, LOVE
OOCH!
OOH!
AND WE NEED SOME MAGNOLIA EMULSION
THAT'S ME! I'M RINGIN!
DIDDLE-D.....
BUGGER! IT'S GONE TO ANSWERPHONE
I'LL 'AVE T' GEDDIT... MIGHT BE IMPORTANT
AND TURPS...
POP!
YOU HAVE... ONE... MESSAGE...... SAN... IT'S YER MAM... SNIFF! SNIFF! GRANDAD'S DIED, LOVE... SNIFF! VERY PEACEFUL IT WERE! SNIFF!
BYE THELMA
...RING ME BACK, LOVE! SNIFF!
THAT WERE ME MAM. ME GRANDAD'S DEAD
WHICH ONE?
DIDN'T SAY...
BIP!
BIP!
PROBABLY THE ONE THEY RUSHED TO 'OSPITAL LAST NIGHT... I'LL RING BACK
CAN Y' DO IT LATER, SAN? I'VE STILL GOT A BIT OF WOOD LEFT, DESPITE THELMA'S EFFORTS
OKAY
C'MON, THEN. POP IT BACK IN!
OKAY, BAZ! I'M READY.
AW, FER FUCK'S SAKE!
WOT IS IT?
POP!
NEWSAGENT
GIZ A £5 AIRTIME VOUCHER, PAL... QUICK AS Y'CAN, I'VE GOT A BIRD ON THE BOIL
BIG TITS
JIZZ!
COLATE
RAZZLE
GET READY, SAN... ...I'M DIALIN' NOW
HEH! HEH!
OW'S THAT THEN?
DIDDLE DEE-DEE DEE
WELL... S'ALRIGHT... IT'S NOWT SPECIAL
DIDDLE-DEE-DEE-DEE! DIDDLE-DEE-DEE-DEE!
WOT D'Y' MEAN NOWT SPECIAL?
WELL, IT'S NOT!
AFTER ALL THE TROUBLE I WENT TO
WELL, IT WERE A WASTE O' TIME
THAT BIRD IN RAZZLE, SHE DIDN'T THINK IT WERE A WASTE O' TIME... BEST THING EVER 'APPENED, SHE SAID
WELL, P'RAPS SHE 'AD A BETTER PHONE THAN ME!
AYE!
AN' P'RAPS SHE DIDN'T 'AVE A FANNY LIKE MARY POPPINS' BAG
HEY... Y' CHEEKY FUCKIN BASTARD...
...TELLIN ME I'VE GORRA BIG FANNY...
CHEEKY GET
I SEZ, WELL... IF I 'AVE GORRA BIG FANNY, IT'S NOT YOU WOT STRETCHED THE FUCKER!
I BET THAT SHUT 'IM UP
TOO RIGHT! FUCKED OFF WI' 'IS TAIL 'TWEEN 'IS LEGS.
AHEM!
OOH, SOZ... I DIDN'T HEAR Y' BRING THE COFFIN IN
GRANDAD

MOST DECISIONS in our lives are made democratically. Whether it's deciding which kind of takeaway we get, what we watch on TV or where we go on holiday, it's important to listen to everyone's opinion before we collectively make our choice. Having said that, we all prefer it when we get our own way, and none of us particularly likes it when a decision goes against us. Although most of us are able to simply shrug such setbacks off and put them down to experience, others insist on getting their own way whatever the cost. And whilst we all like to think that we uphold democratic values, it's a frightening thought that any one of us could be an evil despot without actually knowing it. It just needs the right set of circumstances to come together for our true tyrannical nature to reveal itself. Why not take our fun test to find out:

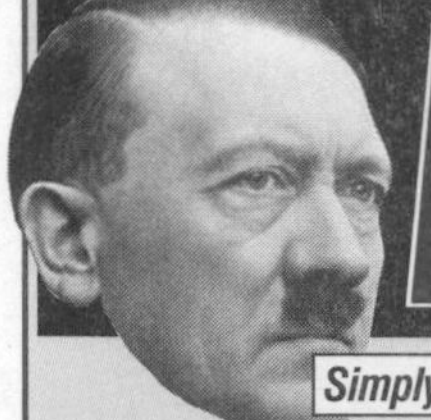

Are YOU a Closet Dictator?

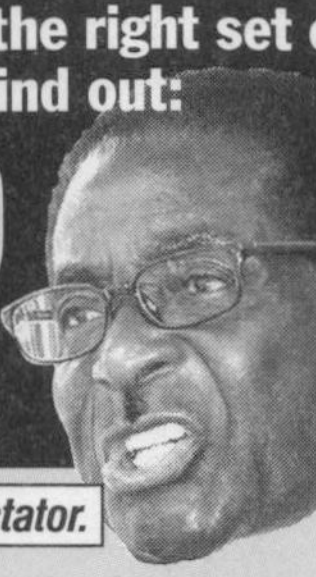

Simply answer the following questions a, b or c, then tot up your totalitarian tally to find out if you've got what it takes to become a Great Dictator.

1 You're going to the cinema with a bunch of your mates. You want to see the latest Adam Sandler flick but your pals are keen to see a movie starring Ben Affleck. How would you go about resolving the issue?

a) Take an informal straw poll in the cinema foyer, then go and see the film that received the most votes.
b) Decide that everyone can go and see the movie that they prefer, before meeting up for a drink in the bar afterwards.
c) Publicly execute the ring-leader of the Ben Affleck faction, then round up the families of your other pals, placing them in internment camps. Order your henchmen to burn all prints of Ben Affleck's films, before frogmarching your mates into the cinema to watch the Adam Sandler film at gunpoint.

2 You go into Freeman Hardy & Willis to buy yourself a new pair of shoes. What sort do you choose?

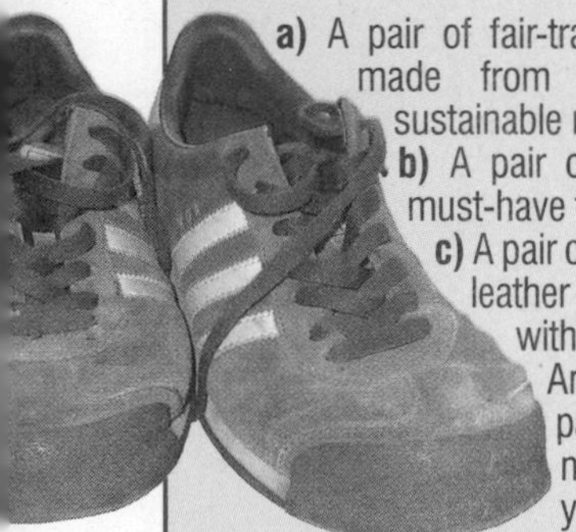

a) A pair of fair-trade sandals, made from ecologically sustainable materials.
b) A pair of the latest, must-have trainers.
c) A pair of shiny black leather riding boots with clicky heels. And 10,000 pairs of Jimmy Choos for your wife.

3 It is time to change your car. Which model do you go for?

a) An economical, battery-powered car such as a Toyota Prius or G-Whizz.
b) A sleek, sporty coupe, such as an Audi A3 or Alfa Brera.
c) An enormous, open-topped vintage Mercedes with flags on the front mudguards, to be driven down the street by a trenchcoat-wearing chauffeur whilst you stand up in the back looking resolute and occasionally saluting.

4 Your house is looking a bit shabby, so your wife asks you to decorate it. What do you do?

a) Give the woodwork a lick of paint, and brighten the rooms with some ethnic rugs, throws and scatter cushions.
b) Strip the doors, put up fashionable wallpaper in the living room and hang some stylish framed prints over the fireplace.
c) Demolish every house in the street with tanks, before erecting an enormous marble, gold and alabaster palace filled with priceless, looted art treasures in the space you have created.

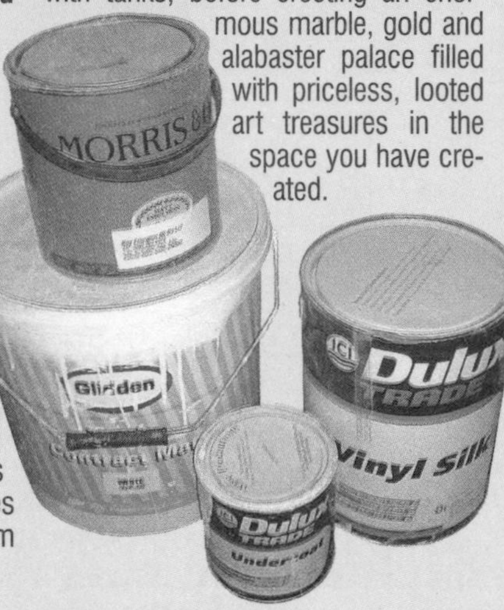

MORRIS
Glidden
Dulux
TRADE
Vinyl Silk
Dulux
TRADE

5 It is tea-time and your wife is cooking a meat pie. To go with it, she proposes to do either mashed potato or chips. She doesn't want to go to the bother of preparing both, so she asks the family which they would prefer. You want chips but everybody else wants mash. What do you do?

a) You settle for mash, because that's what everyone else wants, and you don't want to make any extra work.
b) You offer to make a few chips for yourself, so that everyone gets what they want.
c) You climb up on the table and give a wild-eyed, charismatic speech during which you declare the start of a glorious ten thousand-year epoch of chips for tea. Then go in the kitchen and destroy the potato masher.

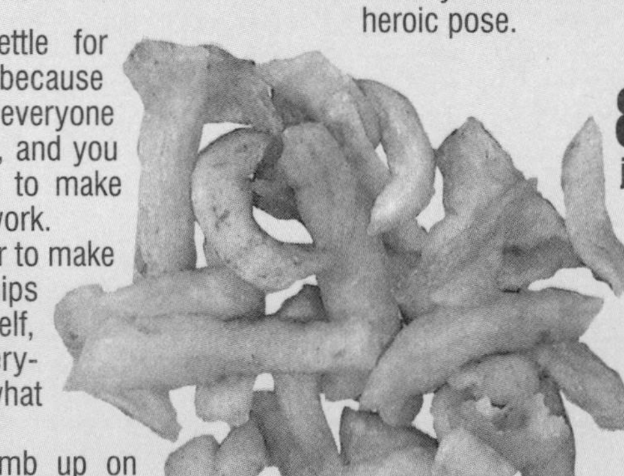

6 It's Saturday evening and *TV Burp* is on at the same time as *Strictly Come Dancing*. You want to watch Harry Hill on ITV, but other members of the family are keen to enjoy the dancing on BBC1. In the end, you agree to toss a coin to decide which channel to tune in to. You call heads, but when you peek under your hand you see that the coin has come down tails. What would you do?

a) Come clean, and settle down to watch *Strictly Come Dancing* with everyone else.
b) Go into the kitchen and grumpily watch *TV Burp* on the black & white portable set in there.
c) Keep the coin covered up with your hand, and promise to reveal the result of the toss as soon as possible. Then get an armed gang of thugs to spend the next three weeks bullying and intimidating your wife and children into watching *TV Burp.*

7 You are on a family beach holiday, and your children enlist your help in a sand sculpture competition to be judged by the local mayor. What do you decide to build?

a) A fairytale castle, complete with elaborate turrets and flags.
b) A medieval fort, complete with castellated battlements and a sea-water moat.
c) A hundred-foot high statue of yourself in sunglasses and a high-ranking military officer's uniform, striking an heroic pose.

8 What do you have on your jacket lapel?

a) An AIDS Awareness ribbon and a CND badge.
b) A Remembrance Day poppy and a small, enamel Rotary Club badge.
c) 400 medals that you have awarded to yourself.

9 You have spent the last year as chairman of your local allotment society. It is your last day in office, and you are chairing your final committee meeting at the village hall. How do you conclude your valedictory speech?

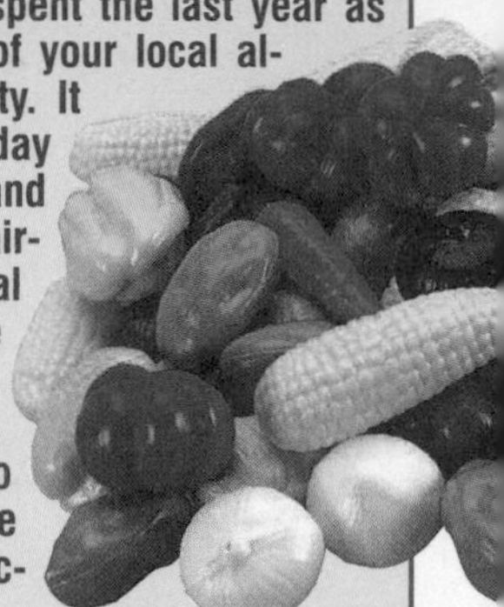

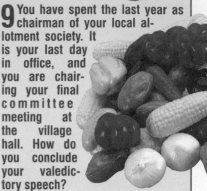

a) By thanking all your fellow members and wishing your successor good luck.
b) By making a few cheeky in-jokes about the size of other members' vegetables.
c) By refusing to leave, claiming you have been mandated by God to stay in charge of the allotment society for ever. Then declaring your 2-year-old son President for Life, before having all the other committee members dragged out of the room one by one by your goons and summarily executed behind the compost bins.

10 Your son gets his A-level results and is thrilled to find that he has got two Ds and an E and has been accepted on the Media Studies course at De Montfort University. How do you respond to his news?

a) Congratulate him warmly, and perhaps take him out for a slap-up meal to celebrate.
b) Give him a pat on the back, whilst wryly pointing out that exams must be getting easier these days.
c) Denounce him as a bourgeois intellectual capitalist running dog, and behead him with a sickle. Then go out into the street and do the same to anybody wearing spectacles, before piling up their sun-bleached skulls in your shed.

HOW DID YOU DO?

MOSTLY As
Oh dear, you really don't have what it takes to cut it as a tyrannical, autocratic dictator. You're so busy kow-towing to everyone else that you're destined to never get your own way. Quite frankly, you couldn't run a raffle, so you can forget about brutally ruling a country under an iron fist; it's just not going to happen.

MOSTLY Bs
Close, but no big Cuban cigar. Whilst you've clearly got a genuinely ruthless streak, there's no doubt that at heart you're just a softy who'd balk at committing genocide to get your own way.

MOSTLY Cs
Congratulations, you're an odious despot! A tyrannical bully boy to your core, you are gripped by insane egotism and prepared to stop at nothing in your desperate quest to wield supreme power over lesser mortals. So what are you waiting for? The world's lumpen populace is just sitting there, waiting for someone just like you to come along and use brute force take charge of them. Go for it!

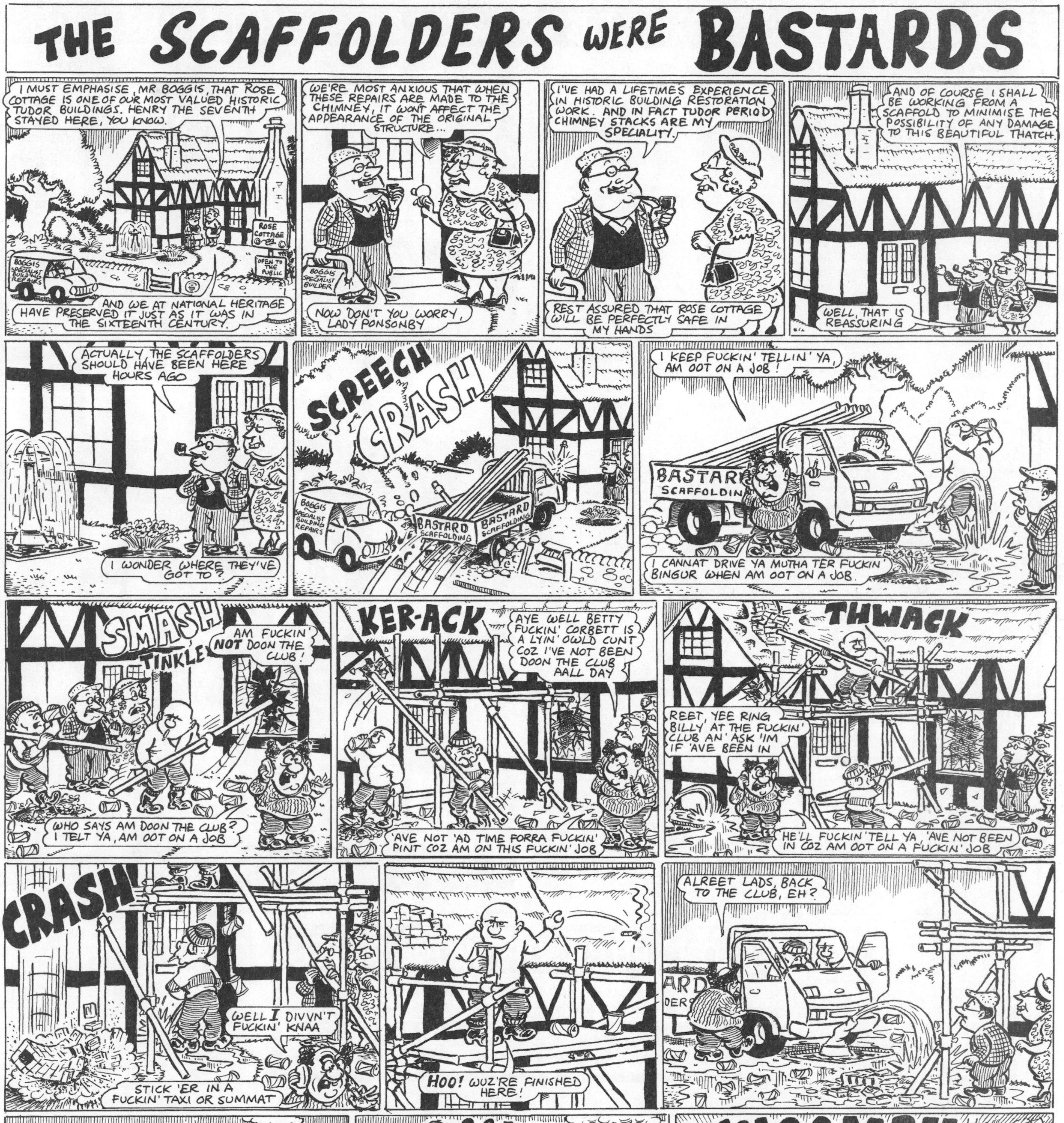
THE SCAFFOLDERS WERE BASTARDS
I MUST EMPHASISE, MR BOGGIS, THAT ROSE COTTAGE IS ONE OF OUR MOST VALUED HISTORIC TUDOR BUILDINGS. HENRY THE SEVENTH STAYED HERE, YOU KNOW.
ROSE COTTAGE
OPEN TO THE PUBLIC
BOGGIS SPECIALIST BUILDING REPAIRS
AND WE AT NATIONAL HERITAGE HAVE PRESERVED IT JUST AS IT WAS IN THE SIXTEENTH CENTURY.
WE'RE MOST ANXIOUS THAT WHEN THESE REPAIRS ARE MADE TO THE CHIMNEY, IT WON'T AFFECT THE APPEARANCE OF THE ORIGINAL STRUCTURE...
BOGGIS SPECIALIST BUILDER
NOW DON'T YOU WORRY, LADY PONSONBY
I'VE HAD A LIFETIME'S EXPERIENCE IN HISTORIC BUILDING RESTORATION WORK. AND IN FACT TUDOR PERIOD CHIMNEY STACKS ARE MY SPECIALITY.
REST ASSURED THAT ROSE COTTAGE WILL BE PERFECTLY SAFE IN MY HANDS
AND OF COURSE I SHALL BE WORKING FROM A SCAFFOLD TO MINIMISE THE POSSIBILITY OF ANY DAMAGE TO THIS BEAUTIFUL THATCH.
WELL, THAT IS REASSURING
ACTUALLY, THE SCAFFOLDERS SHOULD HAVE BEEN HERE HOURS AGO
I WONDER WHERE THEY'VE GOT TO?
SCREECH
CRASH
BOGGIS SPECIALIST BUILDING REPAIRS
BASTARD SCAFFOLDING
BASTARD SCAFFOLDING
I KEEP FUCKIN' TELLIN' YA, AM OOT ON A JOB!
BASTARD SCAFFOLDIN
I CANNAT DRIVE YA MUTHA TER FUCKIN' BINGUR WHEN AM OOT ON A JOB.
SMASH
TINKLE
AM FUCKIN' NOT DOON THE CLUB!
WHO SAYS AM DOON THE CLUB? I TELT YA, AM OOT ON A JOB
KER-ACK
AYE WELL BETTY FUCKIN' CORBETT IS A LYIN' OWLD CUNT COZ I'VE NOT BEEN DOON THE CLUB AALL DAY
'AVE NOT 'AD TIME FORRA FUCKIN' PINT COZ AM ON THIS FUCKIN' JOB
THWACK
REET, YEE RING BILLY AT THE FUCKIN' CLUB AN' ASK 'IM IF 'AVE BEEN IN
HE'LL FUCKIN' TELL YA, 'AVE NOT BEEN IN COZ AM OOT ON A FUCKIN' JOB
CRASH!
WELL I DIVVN'T FUCKIN' KNAA
STICK 'ER IN A FUCKIN' TAXI OR SUMMAT
HOO! WUZ'RE FINISHED HERE!
ALREET LADS, BACK TO THE CLUB, EH?
VROOM
CRUNCH
BASTARD SCAFFOLDING
C-R-A-C-K
WHOOMPH

++ SILVER PUBES FOR ALL BY 2015 +++ SILVER PUBES

Short & Curlies to Face Chop

PRIME Minister Gordon Brown has announced ambitious plans to phase out traditional pubic hair by 2015. Out will go old fashioned, wiry pubes that traditionally sprout around the genitals, to be replaced by space-age silvery tinsel.

Addressing a packed Downing Street press conference, Mr Brown said: "We have entered the 21st century. Britain is at the leading edge in all spheres of scientific progress. All aspects of our world are progressing at an ever faster speed yet our antiquated pubes are lagging behind."

"Today we take for granted such innovations as microwave ovens, mobile telephones and broadband internet access. We have even put a man on the moon. We have advanced so far in so many areas, yet our old-fashioned, backwards-looking pubes have remained unchanged since caveman times."

The Prime Minister said it was an unacceptable situation that he had resolved to put right, and went on to outline his plans for a nationwide switchover to space-age, spangly pubic hair within the next six years.

"A pilot scheme has been running in Milton Keynes for the past 8 months and has been largely successful," he continued. "Over fifty thousand people have undergone the tinselic pubification process without any problems whatsoever. Following on from this project, I now propose to roll the programme out across the whole country."

"It is my pledge to the country that, within the next six years, every British citizen's groin will boast modern, efficient, metallic pubic hair," Mr Brown said.

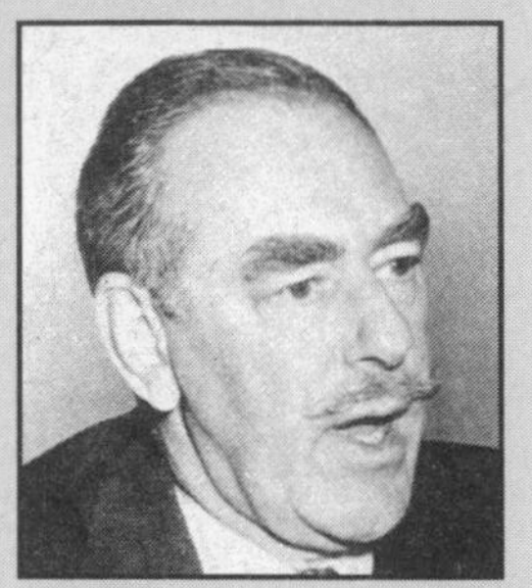

PUBIC HAIR TODAY, GONE TOMORROW: Shadow Pensions Minister Derek Wilton.

But opposition parties were quick to criticise the switchover plan. Interviewed by Evan Davies on Radio 4's *Today* programme, Shadow Pensions Minister Derek Wilton said: "As usual, the Prime Minister has simply not thought these plans through before making his announcement."

"Whilst I accept that most people under the age of thirty or so will adapt to tinsel pubic hair with no problem, the older elements of society may well find the changeover to silvery underthatching confusing, upsetting or even distressing," he continued.

"Some senior citizens may have had the same pubes for eighty years or more. Forcing them to give up what they are used to finding in their pants is simply inhumane. Nobody denies that the switchover has to take place, but it should be phased in over several years to give elderly people the chance to get used to the idea," he added.

PUBIC ENEMY NUMBER ONE: Gordon Brown sounds death knell for hair-based muffs and old-fashioned clocksprings.

PINION...PUBIC OPINION...PUBIC O

THE Prime Minister's plan to replace everybody's pubes with tinsel has aroused fierce debate on all sides. But what do the people who've already had it done think? We went to the Buckinghamshire town of Milton Keynes where, in a pilot scheme, every resident has had silvery pubic hair since last November.

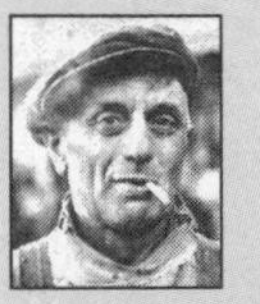

"I WASN'T so sure at first, but you have to move with the times, don't you. Now I wouldn't go back to normal hair pubes."

Fred, 42, builder

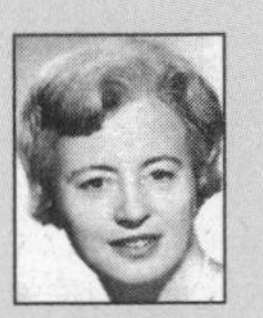

"I HATE them. They take ages to dry after a bath, and you can't use a hairdrier like you would on real pubes because there's a danger of electric shocks."

Sally, 38, nurse

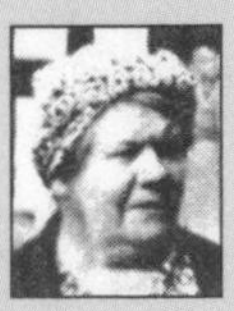

"MY OLD hairy pubes frequently got infested with pubic lice as a result of my sexual promiscuity. They were the very devil to get rid of, but now I just have to tap my new tinsel bush and they fall off into the toilet."

Audrey, 61, magistrate

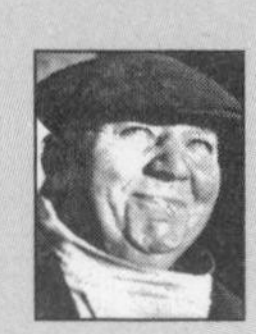

"WHAT was wrong with good old-fashioned short and curlies? I used to enjoy intimate relations with my wife, but these days when I try to flick her bean it's like fingering a robot."

Frank, 50, GP

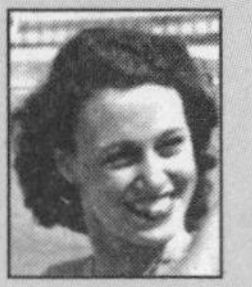

"I'M YOUNG, so I like modern things like iPods, skatebboards, training pumps and pop groups. Tinsel pubes are modern so I think they're really cool."

Mabel, 18, student

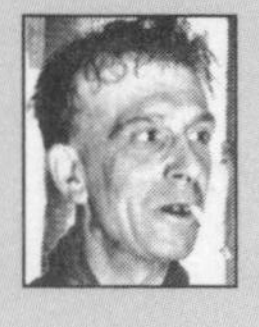

"I'M A postman. I wear nylon underpants and when I'm on my rounds a large amount of static charge builds up which regularly shorts to earth through my bell end. That never happened with my old hair pubes."

Sam, 48, postman

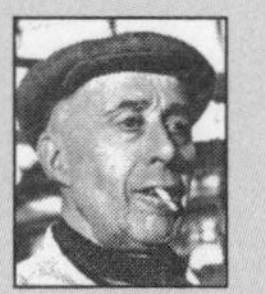

"I'M THE Lord Mayor of Milton Keynes and I love having tinsel pubes. My wife says it makes my cock look like a Christmas tree with two knackers for baubles."

Sid, 61, mayor

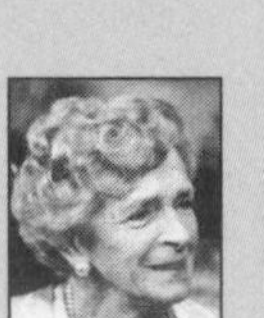

"TINSEL pubes are just another example of Gordon Brown's Big Brother society. You mark my words, they'll be wanting to put computer chips up our arses next."

Glenda, 56, cheesemonger

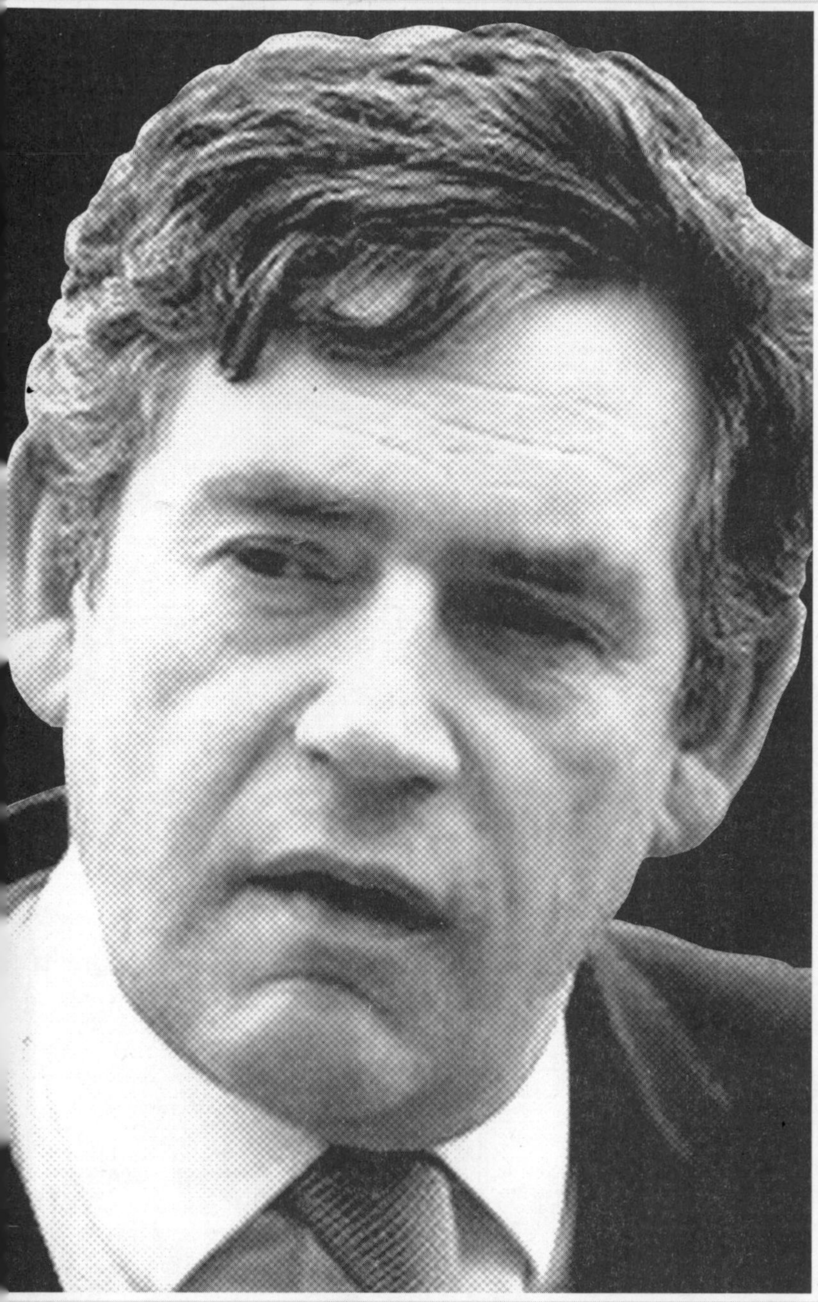

Adult stars set to strike for exemption from new law

PORN FREE

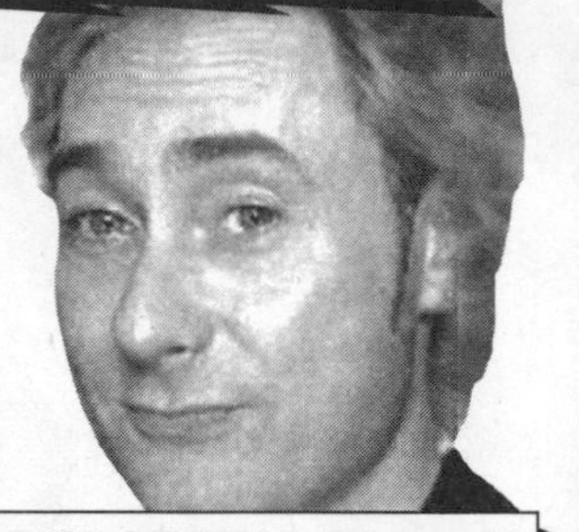

PUBE-BARB GRUMBLE: Priapismic actor Dover yesterday.

UNIONS representing pornographic film actors are demanding that their industry is exempted from draconian new tinsel pube laws.

According to Rockbert Hardon, President of NUSFADPO, the National Union of Scud Flick Actors and Double Penetration Operatives, tinselic pubification could damage the porn business, leading to widespread blowjob losses.

He told us: "The majority of adult film producers now require shaven havens. Hairless parts are now industry standard throughout the world. For Gordon Brown to now insist that my members get tinsel pubes is nothing short of scandalous."

"Porn is a global business," he continued. "British adult stars have been shaving their pubes off for years to compete in the international wank flick marketplace. Forcing them to tinsel up will leave them at a competitive disadvantage against their foreign counterparts."

And Mr Hardon warned that he couldn't rule out industrial action if an exemption from the new legislation was not made for his members' members. "They could decide to down tools," he added, entirely predictably.

But anal bongo vid veteran Ben Dover, real name Honeybunch Linseed, last night offered a cautious welcome to the proposed regulations. "Porn is a constantly evolving business, and I can foresee tinsel-pubed material filling a sizeable gap in the market," he told us.

And Dover, 74, confirmed that he is already working on several new tinsel-pubed productions, including *Jingle Bell End, Hymen Ho Silver, Shiny Flappy People* and *Fuck My Tinselly Cunt.*

TINSELIC PUBIFICATION How it will be done

Explained by: **Rt. Hon. GLENDA JACKSON MP** Minister for Pubes

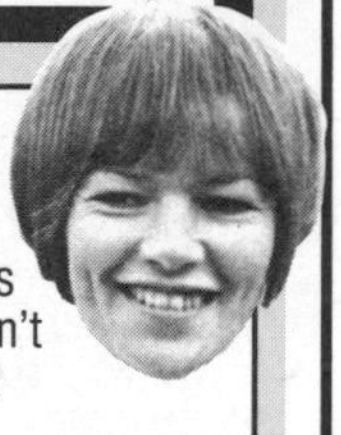

MANY OF you are understandably concerned about undergoing the tinselic pubification process. Let me put your minds at rest at once. There is nothing at all to worry about. The process is now safer than it has ever been. Here is a handy timeline which explains exactly what will happen when you are called to your local processing centre.

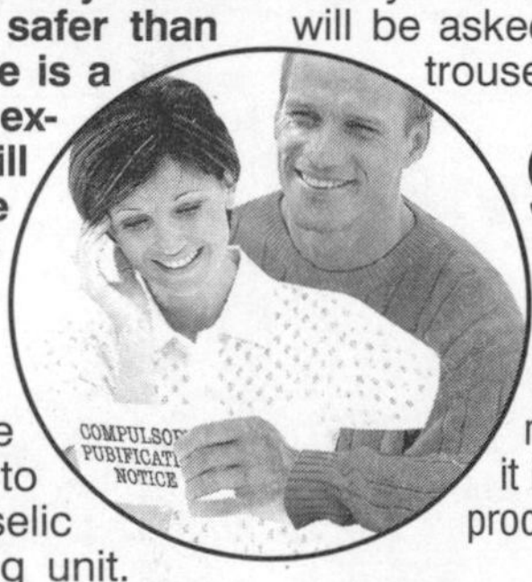

You will receive an appointment through the post, giving you a day to attend your local tinselic pubification processing unit. This could be a school, church hall or community centre although it is more likely to be a purpose built compound surrounded by chain-link fencing. You must inform the authorities if you are unable to attend on the specified day. This is important, as if you fail to turn up, a van may be sent to collect you and you may incur a charge. You will be asked to wear loose-fitting trousers.

9.00am On arrival, you will be given a unique reference number which will be clipped to your shirt. Do not lose this number as you will need it in order to leave when the process is complete.

9.05am You will be shown into a holding bay where you will be asked to remove your trousers and underpants.

9.06am Men and women will be separated into two secure compounds at this point in order to preserve their modesty.

9.10am You will be taken into the tinselic pubification room where the process will be carried out by trained operatives. It takes between twenty minutes and half an hour, depending on the amount of pubic hair you have.

9.35am *(approx)* It's all done! You will be carried into a recovery area where you will be offered a choice of a tea, orange squash or a biscuit.

9.36am Time to go home. You will be helped to your feet and given a pair of trousers. Due to the sheer numbers involved, it is unlikely that the these trousers will be your own. So don't arrive in your best pair!

9.37am On your way out you will be given a leaflet containing useful information, such as when it is safe to remove the dressings and common side effects and complications to look out for. There will be also be an emergency helpline number with a 24-hour automated response and details of a website.

9.38am And that's it! Off you go with your modern new tinsel pubes! The whole process has taken less than three quarters of an hour from start to finish.

POSTMAN PLOD

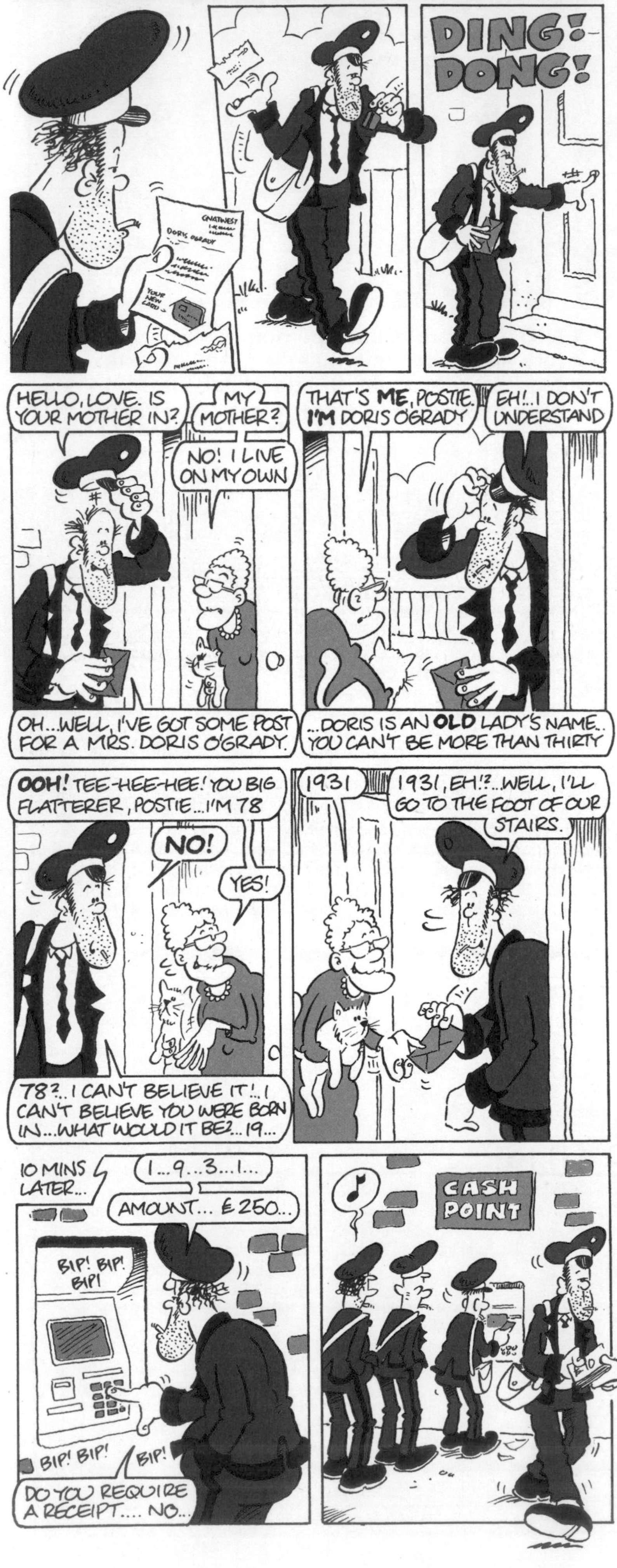
DING! DONG!
HELLO, LOVE. IS YOUR MOTHER IN?
MY MOTHER?
NO! I LIVE ON MY OWN
OH...WELL, I'VE GOT SOME POST FOR A MRS. DORIS O'GRADY.
THAT'S **ME**, POSTIE. **I'M** DORIS O'GRADY
EH!..I DON'T UNDERSTAND
...DORIS IS AN **OLD** LADY'S NAME.. YOU CAN'T BE MORE THAN THIRTY
OOH! TEE-HEE-HEE! YOU BIG FLATTERER, POSTIE...I'M 78
NO!
YES!
78?..I CAN'T BELIEVE IT!..I CAN'T BELIEVE YOU WERE BORN IN...WHAT WOULD IT BE?...19...
1931
1931, EH!?...WELL, I'LL GO TO THE FOOT OF OUR STAIRS.
10 MINS LATER...
1...9...3...1...
AMOUNT... £250...
BIP! BIP! BIP!
BIP! BIP! BIP!
DO YOU REQUIRE A RECEIPT.... NO...
CASH POINT

MAJOR MISUNDERSTANDING

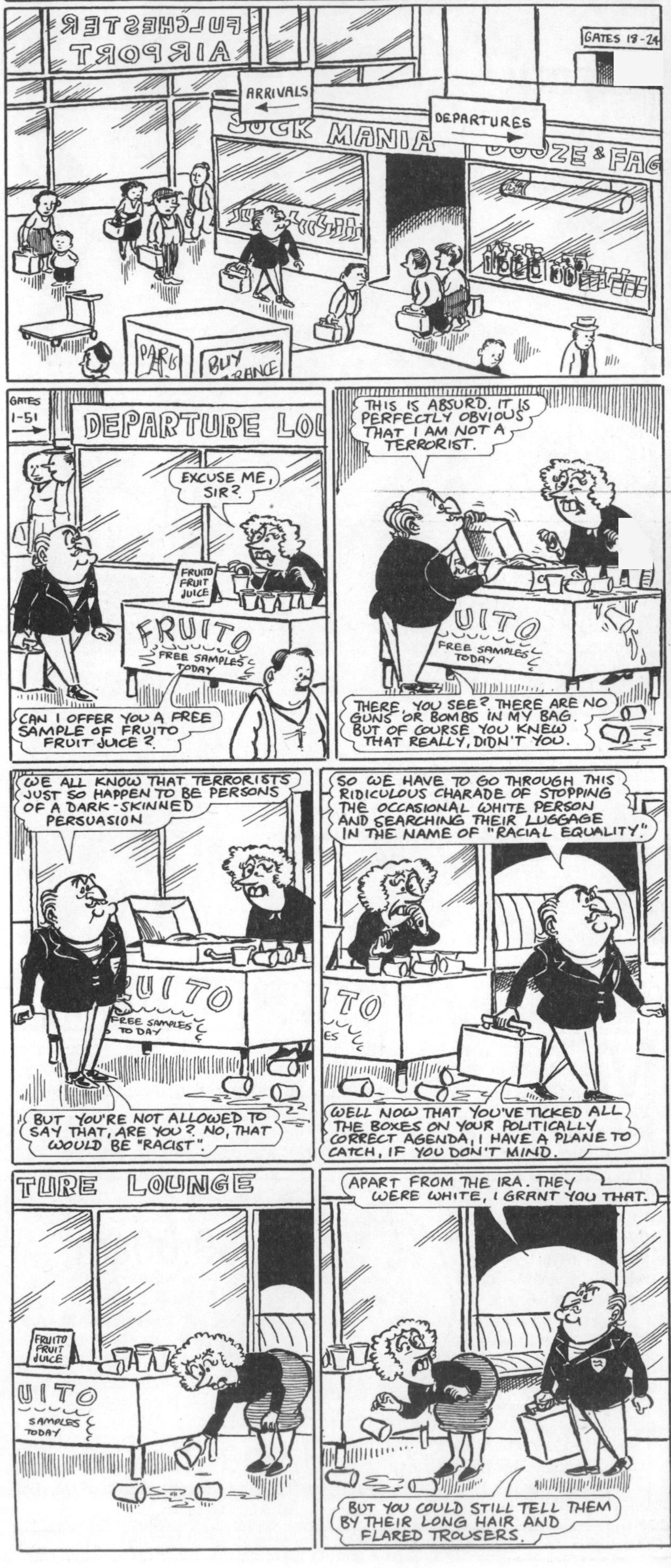
FULCHESTER AIRPORT
GATES 18-24
ARRIVALS
DEPARTURES
SOCK MANIA
GATES 1-51
DEPARTURE LOU
EXCUSE ME, SIR?
FRUITO FRUIT JUICE
FRUITO FREE SAMPLES TODAY
CAN I OFFER YOU A FREE SAMPLE OF FRUITO FRUIT JUICE?
THIS IS ABSURD. IT IS PERFECTLY OBVIOUS THAT I AM NOT A TERRORIST.
THERE, YOU SEE? THERE ARE NO GUNS OR BOMBS IN MY BAG. BUT OF COURSE YOU KNEW THAT REALLY, DIDN'T YOU.
WE ALL KNOW THAT TERRORISTS JUST SO HAPPEN TO BE PERSONS OF A DARK-SKINNED PERSUASION
BUT YOU'RE NOT ALLOWED TO SAY THAT, ARE YOU? NO, THAT WOULD BE "RACIST".
SO WE HAVE TO GO THROUGH THIS RIDICULOUS CHARADE OF STOPPING THE OCCASIONAL WHITE PERSON AND SEARCHING THEIR LUGGAGE IN THE NAME OF "RACIAL EQUALITY".
WELL NOW THAT YOU'VE TICKED ALL THE BOXES ON YOUR POLITICALLY CORRECT AGENDA, I HAVE A PLANE TO CATCH, IF YOU DON'T MIND.
TURE LOUNGE
FRUITO FRUIT JUICE
APART FROM THE IRA. THEY WERE WHITE, I GRNT YOU THAT.
BUT YOU COULD STILL TELL THEM BY THEIR LONG HAIR AND FLARED TROUSERS.

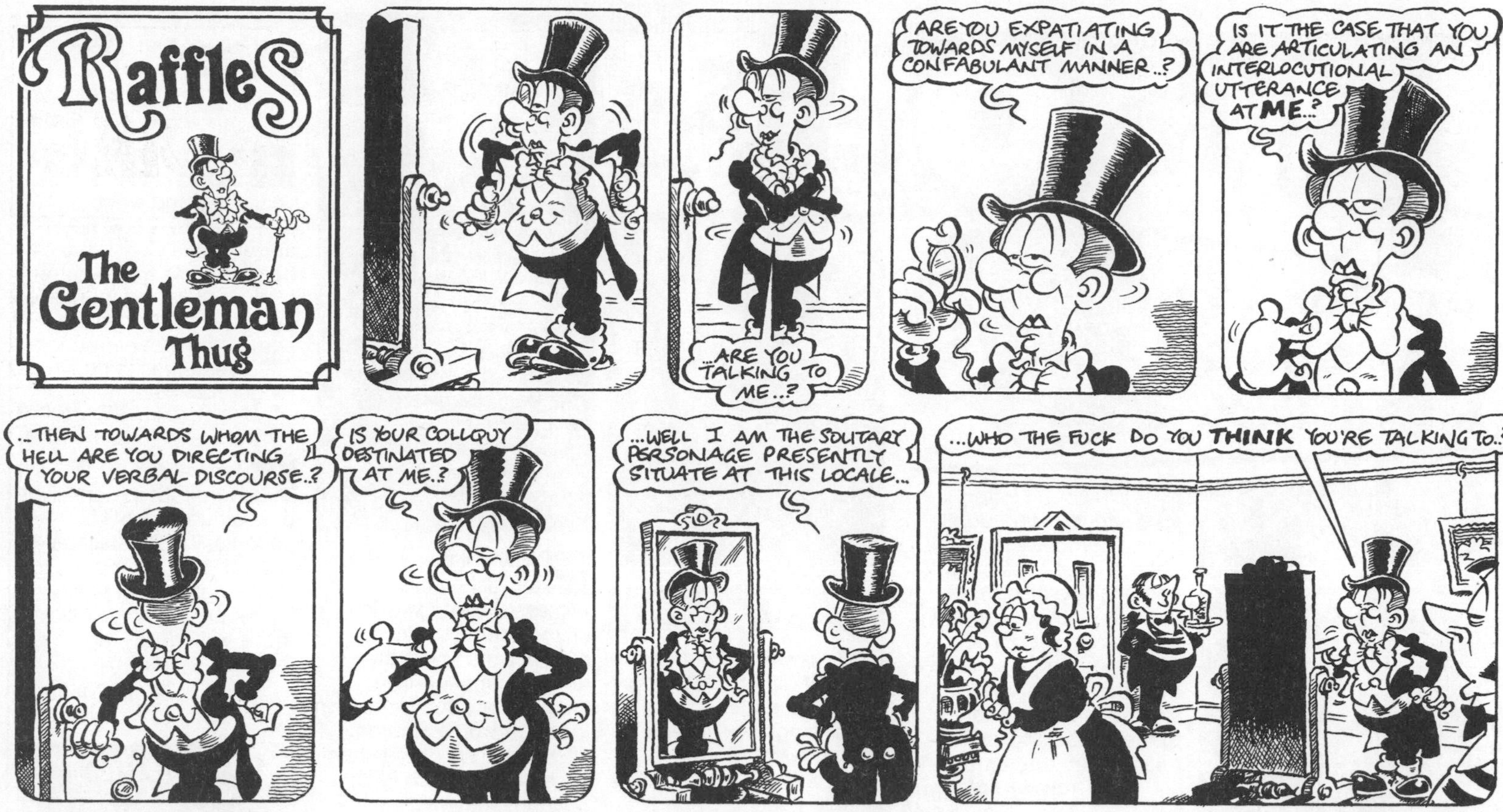
Raffles
The Gentleman Thug
...ARE YOU TALKING TO ME..?
ARE YOU EXPATIATING TOWARDS MYSELF IN A CONFABULANT MANNER..?
IS IT THE CASE THAT YOU ARE ARTICULATING AN INTERLOCUTIONAL UTTERANCE AT **ME**..?
...THEN TOWARDS WHOM THE HELL ARE YOU DIRECTING YOUR VERBAL DISCOURSE..?
IS YOUR COLLOQUY DESTINATED AT ME..?
...WELL I AM THE SOLITARY PERSONAGE PRESENTLY SITUATE AT THIS LOCALE...
...WHO THE FUCK DO YOU **THINK** YOU'RE TALKING TO..?

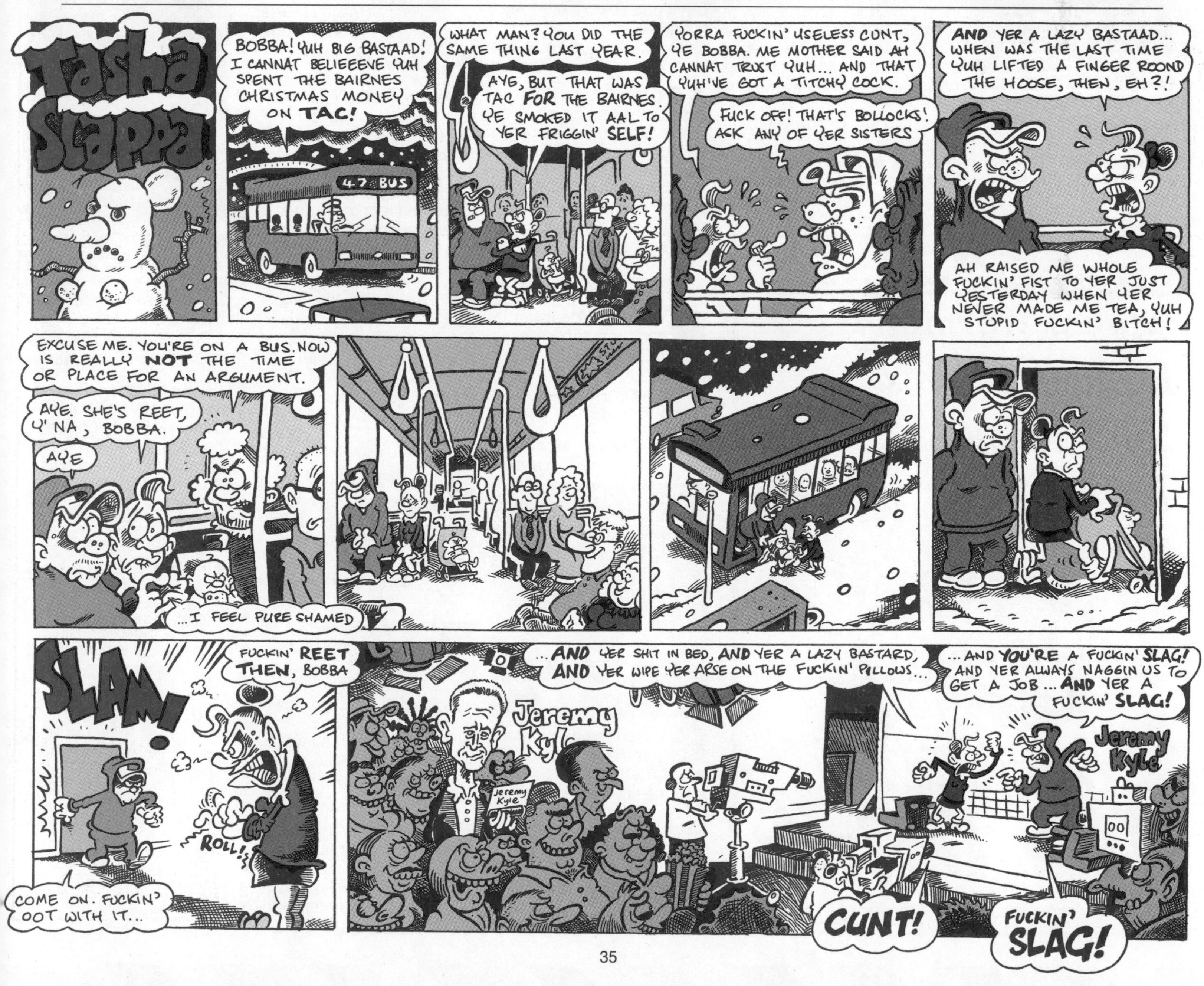
Tasha Slappa
BOBBA! YUH BIG BASTAAD! I CANNAT BELIEEEVE YUH SPENT THE BAIRNES CHRISTMAS MONEY ON **TAC**!
47 BUS
WHAT MAN? YOU DID THE SAME THING LAST YEAR.
AYE, BUT THAT WAS TAC **FOR** THE BAIRNES. YE SMOKED IT AAL TO YER FRIGGIN' **SELF**!
YORRA FUCKIN' USELESS CUNT, YE BOBBA. ME MOTHER SAID AH CANNAT TRUST YUH... AND THAT YUH'VE GOT A TITCHY COCK.
FUCK OFF! THAT'S BOLLOCKS! ACK ANY OF YER SISTERS
AND YER A LAZY BASTAAD... WHEN WAS THE LAST TIME YUH LIFTED A FINGER ROOND THE HOOSE, THEN, EH?!
AH RAISED ME WHOLE FUCKIN' FIST TO YER JUST YESTERDAY WHEN YER NEVER MADE ME TEA, YUH STUPID FUCKIN' BITCH!
EXCUSE ME. YOU'RE ON A BUS. NOW IS REALLY **NOT** THE TIME OR PLACE FOR AN ARGUMENT.
AYE. SHE'S REET, Y' NA, BOBBA.
AYE
...I FEEL PURE SHAMED
SLAM!
FUCKIN' **REET THEN**, BOBBA
ROLL!
COME ON. FUCKIN' OOT WITH IT...
...**AND** YER SHIT IN BED, **AND** YER A LAZY BASTARD, **AND** YER WIPE YER ARSE ON THE FUCKIN' PILLOWS...
...AND **YOU'RE** A FUCKIN' **SLAG**! AND YER ALWAYS NAGGIN US TO GET A JOB... **AND** YER A FUCKIN' **SLAG**!
Jeremy Kyle
CUNT!
FUCKIN' SLAG!

LeTTERbOcks

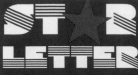

PO Box 656, North Shields, NE30 4XX

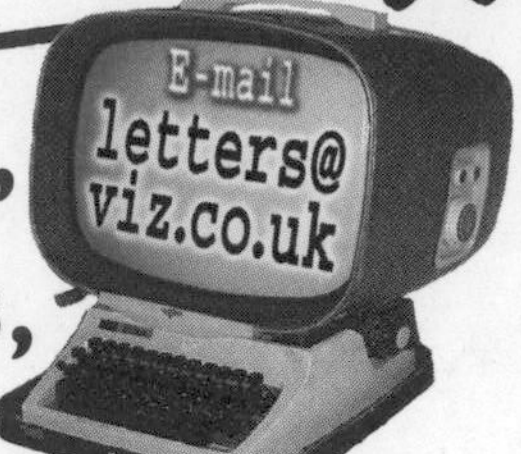

E-mail
letters@
viz.co.uk

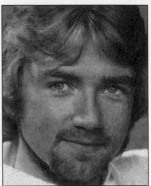

Why don't lottery winners who don't want the money to change their lives enter something a little more low-key instead, such as a raffle or tombola? Or would winning a tin of peaches still represent too much of a challenge to their shocking lack of imagination and ambition.

Crawford Maughn
e-mail

I was watching *Noel's HQ* on Sky1 the other night, and the tidy-bearded presenter blamed 'health and safety zealots' for the downfall of the country. I think that's a bit rich coming from somebody who dropped some poor sod 250 feet from a crane in the name of entertainment.

Frank Plasterboard
London

The last time I was in Marks and Spencer, I was confronted with a large sign saying 'Your M&S.' Yet when I tried to walk out with a case of booze under each arm, I was arrested for shoplifting. I don't know, it seems like the possessive second person is not what it used to be.

Vijay Gange
e-mail

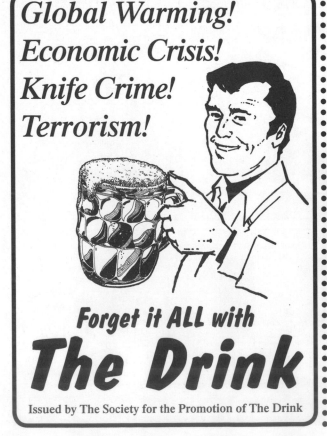

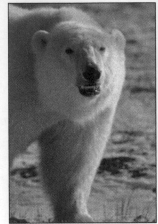

I saw an advert on the telly last night telling me that, for £3, I could adopt a polar bear. Now I can understand how you might want to adopt a fluffy kitten or a cuddly puppy, but a polar bear? Are they fucking mad?

Alan Heath
Cardiff

In their advert, Domestos point out that there are more germs on my kitchen work surfaces than in my toilet. This might be the case, but could I point out to them that the ones in my kitchen didn't come out of my arse.

Milton Kaynes
Milton Keynes

Why does Heath Ledger automatically win an Oscar just because he died? Kenneth Williams didn't get one for *Carry On Camping*. It doesn't seem fair.

Skipper McKipper
e-mail

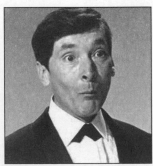

Would the gentleman in the cinema seat who talked throughout my illegally downloaded camcorder copy of *The Uninvited* please note that he's ruining it for everybody else.

Luke Newkand
e-mail

STAR LETTER

I recently attended an annual dinner for financial institutions in the City of London, where the Bank of England chairman Mervyn King gave a sobering and bleak assessment of the UK's economic prospects. Still, he was loads funnier than Jimmy Carr who was booked last year.

James Brown, Edinburgh

Why is it that Mormons and Jehovah's Witnesses come knocking on my door trying to convince me to join their religion? I mean, I love football, but I don't knock on their doors on a Saturday afternoon trying to get them to come and watch Blyth Spartans with me.

Arnold Heurta
Newcastle

I always read my horoscope in the newspaper with trepidation as it always brings bad news. Could the authors not change the name from 'horoscope' to 'nice-o-scope' and perhaps my future and that of many other readers will be better.

Geoff Price
e-mail

The new *Viz* website is so disappointing, I'm going to put my foot through my monitor and send you the bill. After I've sent this e-mail, of course. And had a quick wank.

Mark
e-mail

I don't know why judges just don't go bald gracefully, and not shell out on these expensive, hand-made wigs.

Barry Cartlidge Jnr
Jaipur

I had a cracking evening in last night. I ate a Punjab Pizza (Lloyd Grossman curry sauce on naan bread), washed down with 6 pints of Cobra, then farted so loudly that I woke up next door's baby.

Barry Cartlidge Jnr
Jaipur

My friend Anthony Philips told me that he has chicken pox all over his balls and to tell nobody. Could I assure him through your pages that his secret is safe with me?

Mina Morgan
e-mail

A born again Christian came up to me yesterday and wanted to tell me the good news about Jesus Christ. Well, I happen to be in the current affairs publishing industry and I can assure you that something that happened 2000 years ago is no longer news.

Alan Heath
e-mail

Ten years after Dr Harold Shipman killed over a hundred of his patients, the BBC asked if enough had been done to stop it happening again. I think this is very unlikely that it will happen again as the man is dead.

Edna Coaldust
Pinner

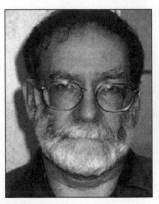

I know a young man whose father and I are brothers. Do any of you readers know what relation this makes him to me?

Frank Aubergine
Lincoln

The other day I heard fire engines in our street and I looked through the curtains to see that a car parked on my driveway was on fire. My wife and I stood on our doorstep and watched the fire crew fight the blaze for about half an

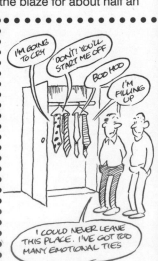

I'M GOING TO CRY
DON'T! YOU'LL START ME OFF
BOO HOO
I'M FILLING UP
I COULD NEVER LEAVE THIS PLACE. I'VE GOT TOO MANY EMOTIONAL TIES

hour before finally putting it out. After all the excitement I went to bed and forgot about it. Imagine my surprise when I got up to drive to work the next morning and realised that the car I'd watched going up in smoke was mine.

Hector Crossling
London

They say "When in Rome, Do as the Romans do." So last year, whilst visiting the Italian capital, I released a pack of lions into a church, and then forced any survivors to fight to the death.

Hector Cement
e-mail

In these days of economic uncertainty, I don't trust the banks to look after my money. I live alone in a remote farmhouse outside the village of Puxfot in Yorkshire, and I keep my life savings of £20,000 in a teapot in the kitchen where I know it will be safe.

Edna Hipjoints
Cabbage Farm, Puxfot

I have been doing the National Lottery every week now for five years and have never won a penny, yet my neighbour who has only been doing it for three years has won £10 twice! What are the chances of that? Nobody can tell me it's not fixed.

Alaric Barton
e-mail

Has anyone heard the rumour that HRH Prince Phillip is on his way out, and if so, is there any truth in it? It's just that I want to be first to the video shop when they change the telly schedules.

Rex Fry
e-mail

With reference to the above letter, I don't think Mr Fry need worry about changes in the TV schedules on the death of Prince Philip. The nature and length of TV coverage on the death of a royal reflects their popularity and influence. If the bad tempered fart is lucky, he might make the 'and finally' bit on News at Ten.

Albatross Benson
e-mail

What an utter waste of time it is recycling plastic bottles. They only go and make them into more of the ruddy things.

Claude Proudhorse
Northumberland

UP THE RSC CORNER

Sender: J Harding, East Sussex

Sender: M Jackson, Kent

top tips

ALCOHOLICS. Increase the strength of your booze by 1/8 by giving a pint of blood immediately before going on a bender.

Lionel Peppercorn, e-mail

DISCARDED heels from gentlemens' shoes make ideal front doors for mouse holes.

Kevin Fluf, e-mail

OLDER WOMEN. Don't spend a fortune on anti-ageing cosmetics as they will jeopardise your chances of being offered a seat on a bus.

Lord Wilberforce, e-mail

MOTORISTS. Stick a cardboard cut-out ear to the back of your mobile phone. That way, when using the phone whilst driving it will look like you are fiddling with your ear, which is not illegal.

Andrew Laurence, e-mail

FRUIT lovers. Wearing a top hat instantly solves the age old pineapple transportation problem.

Nisbet Crawford, e-mail

WHEN tickling a friend or relative, try saying "tickie-tickie! Tickie-tickie!" as this guarantees around 37% more laughter than standard silent tickling.

Bridie Boo, e-mail

CHOCOLATE lovers. Beat the credit crunch by buying two-fingered KitKats instead of four, snapping them in two lengthways and rejoining the two pieces side by side.

Mr Tomo, e-mail

TV EXECUTIVES. Looking for a fresh, new idea for top TV Star Danny Wallace? Simply steal one from a book without asking. The authors probably won't mind.

Hampton Framley, e-mail

toptips@viz.co.uk

Have your Say

FOR THE third year running, BBC weather girl CAROL KIRKWOOD has been named TV Weather Presenter of the Year at the prestigious Television and Radio Industries Club awards. And it's a subject that seemed to have stirred *Viz* readers' interest, because it had you writing in in your millions. In fact, such was the response that our e-mail server crashed under the weight of traffic, and the post office in North Sheilds had to take on 60 extra staff to handle all your letters. Here are 3 or 4 of the best we received...

...CAROL is certainly at the top of her game. The way she reads the weather off an autocue, moves her hand across a map of Britain and then tells us she'll be back to do it again in half an hour is something other weather presenters can only dream of.

Dewey Mobley, e-mail

...NO one deserves the award more than Carol. She is always so pleasant and cheerful, whatever the weather. Even if it was an earthquake or a tsunami or something than cost thousands of lives, she'd still present it to us with a smile and a giggle.

Maximo Hampton, e-mail

..I LOVE Carol's style. She makes all her presentations from outside in the Blue Peter garden, so not only does she tell us what the weather is, she shows us as well, just in case anyone doesn't know what rain looks like.

Roxy Bronwyn, e-mail

...IN Liam Dutton and Everton Fox, the BBC have two perfectly good black men who present the weather, yet once again, the award goes to a white woman. I think this points to a culture of institutional racism and inverted sexism at the BBC.

Sandy Fountain, e-mail

...WHEN being told what the forthcoming meteorological conditions might be, one needs to feel confident in the presenter. Only a middle aged gentleman in a suit can give the reassurance that they know what they are talking about, someone like Rob McElwee or Peter Gibbs. In the medical profession, nobody would trust a young lady doctor, and I don't see why we are expected to have confidence in a young weathergirl.

Sterling Cooper, e-mail

...LAST October, Carol Kirkwood said the weather in the south east would be overcast but dry, and guess what... it rained. I'm afraid giving Kirkwood the award is akin to given Sir Fred Goodwin a massive payoff for getting things wrong in his profession.

Chuck Salgado, e-mail

...ALTHOUGH Carol Kirkwood deserves the award, I think this year's win could be her last. 'New girl on the block' Hannah Bayman, with her unique hand-indication style has set new standards for demonstrating the probable movement of weather systems across Britain.

Neal Dumas, e-mail

SPOILT BASTARD
GO HAWKS
HAWKS
?
FOTO-PRINT
10x8 £1.50
30x40 £10

MR. T'S WORLD OF SLEAZE

With C-list A-Team B.A. Baracus actor Mr. T

Top Tory Lined Pockets at Public Expense

PARLIAMENTARY records leaked from the House of Commons Fees Office reveal that Conservative MP FRANCIS MAUDE claimed more than £8,500 to have his trouser pockets lined with mink. In a statement, the shadow minister for the cabinet office apologised for what he called an "honest mistake".

He said: "I had taken my trousers to a Jermyn Street tailor to have a small tear in the pockets repaired. I did not check the bill and so did not realise that the tailor had lined my pockets with expensive animal pelts."

"I fully intend to give the impression that I will be writing a cheque to pay every penny of that money back," he added.

Prescott "On Expenses Gravy Train"

FORMER Deputy Prime Minister JOHN PRESCOTT was last night fighting for his political life after it was revealed that he had spent a quarter of a million pounds of taxpayers' money on a gravy-powered steam railway system at his home.

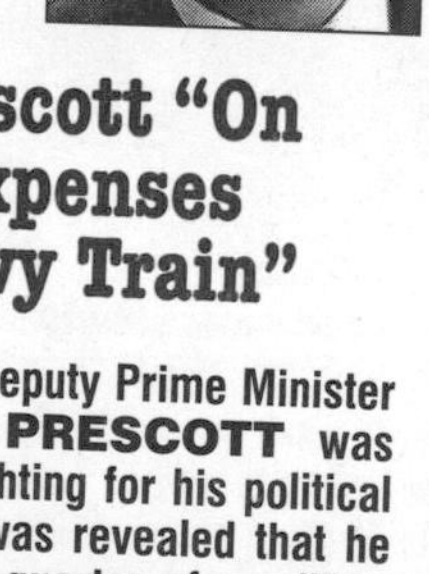

According to leaked documents, a narrow-gauge locomotive, 6 carriages and more than 2 miles of track were installed around the grounds of Mr Prescott's Hull Castle between 2004 and 2008. The MP is believed to spend up to 2 hours each day driving the train around his estate, wearing a Casey Jones hat and tooting the whistle.

He told reporters: "A system that allows me to waste money on a gravy-powered personal railway is clearly wrong. It's absolutely ludicrous, and I am angrier than anyone that I have been allowed to take advantage of the parliamentary expenses system in this way."

"We need to go back and look long and hard at the rules, to prevent people like me from doing anything like this again in the future," he added.

Liberal MP "Lived High on Hog" with Taxpayer Cash

LIB DEM Member of Parliament LEMSIP OPEK has offered to repay almost six million pounds that he claimed after he built an enormous marble pig with a house on the top in his Monmouth constituency.

"It was a complete oversight for which I apologise unreservedly," he told BBC political correspondent John Pienaar. "The six million pound bill was accidentally submitted to the fees office along with a claim for rail fares and taxi receipts."

"I only realised my mistake when I came to check my bank records. I understand the public's anger, but I would like to reassure them that I am taking steps to ensure that it should not happen again," he added.

Don't miss B.A. BARACUS' WORLD OF KNACKERS AND MARACAS next week!

3-2-1 STAR IN SEX SWAP SHOCK

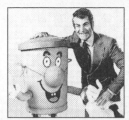

DUSTY MEMORIES: **Bin with Ted Rogers.**

SHOWBIZ legend DUSTY BIN stunned fans yesterday by announcing that he had had a sex change.

In a revealing interview with Sir Trevor McDonald, Bin, 49, revealed that he had always felt like a woman bin trapped in the body of a man bin. And following gender reassignment surgery, the anthropomorphic radio-controlled waste receptacle said that she now wishes to be known as Lauren Bin.

In the interview to be screened in the Autumn on ITV's little-watched Tonight programme, Lauren tells Sir Trevor: "As a youngster, I hated the games that the local boys played. I preferred messing about with my sister's dolls and prams."

"Like all kids, we played doctors and nurses, but I always wanted to be the nurse bin. My parents told me I would grow out of it as I got older, and I believed them," she adds.

FAME

When the 19-year-old was picked from dozens of other bins in 1978 to star in *3-2-1*, he rocketed to fame. But he kept his trademark hobnail boots with wheels in the bottom, spring legs and big red nose. "Showbusiness was good for me," he explains. "I was surrounded by people who were playing parts. On 3-2-1, I was a cheeky geezer, a man's bin. But that was just a part I was playing. It was a crazy time and I was happy to go along for the ride."

But in 1988, the inexplicably popular gameshow that made Bin a household name was axed. The famous booby prize was suddenly out of work and facing a personal crisis.

"3-2-1 had been my life and now I was left with a big void. The problems I had put on the back burner for ten years were coming to the boil. I was faced with a stark choice: turn the heat down, or take the pan off the hob altogether... I decided to have a sex change."

HORMONE

The gender realignment process began years ago when Dusty was told by doctors that he could begin hormone therapy. "They diagnosed me with gender dysphoria, and said I could start the run-up to the op," he tells McDonald. "I had the last lot of reconstructive surgery six months ago when surgeons gave me false eyelashes, red lipstick and fastened a large spotty bow onto the handle of my lid. When I looked in the mirror, I was finally how I wanted to be."

"I'm much happier now, and all my friends and family have been really supportive," says Lauren.

BUGSY MALONE

During the soul-searching interview, McDonald broaches the sensitive subject of Bin's relationship with her former *3-2-1* co-star Ted Rogers. What would he have made of it all?

"I'm sure he would have been very understanding," says Lauren, wiping away a tear produced by an adapted windscreen washer motor. "Ted and I were great friends and we went through a lot together. When he died back in 2001 I took the news very badly. I was so upset that my trademark smile was turned upside down."

But for now Lauren isn't dwelling on the past. "I'm opening a fete tomorrow with a Barron Knight," she says, stiffly waving goodbye with her vacuum cleaner hose arms.

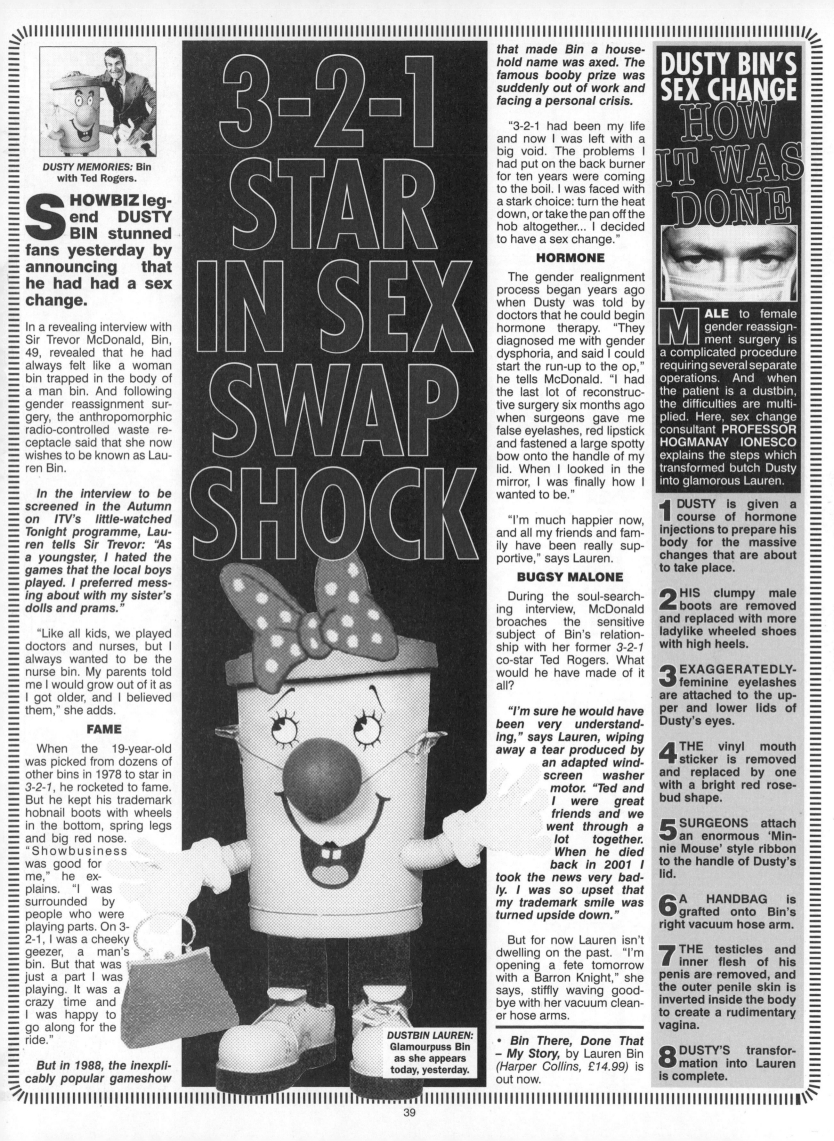

DUSTBIN LAUREN: Glamourpuss Bin as she appears today, yesterday.

• ***Bin There, Done That – My Story,*** by Lauren Bin *(Harper Collins, £14.99)* is out now.

DUSTY BIN'S SEX CHANGE HOW IT WAS DONE

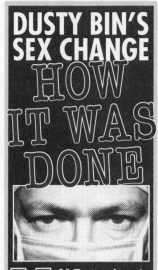

MALE to female gender reassignment surgery is a complicated procedure requiring several separate operations. And when the patient is a dustbin, the difficulties are multiplied. Here, sex change consultant **PROFESSOR HOGMANAY IONESCO** explains the steps which transformed butch Dusty into glamorous Lauren.

1 DUSTY is given a course of hormone injections to prepare his body for the massive changes that are about to take place.

2 HIS clumpy male boots are removed and replaced with more ladylike wheeled shoes with high heels.

3 EXAGGERATEDLY-feminine eyelashes are attached to the upper and lower lids of Dusty's eyes.

4 THE vinyl mouth sticker is removed and replaced by one with a bright red rosebud shape.

5 SURGEONS attach an enormous 'Minnie Mouse' style ribbon to the handle of Dusty's lid.

6 A HANDBAG is grafted onto Bin's right vacuum hose arm.

7 THE testicles and inner flesh of his penis are removed, and the outer penile skin is inverted inside the body to create a rudimentary vagina.

8 DUSTY'S transformation into Lauren is complete.

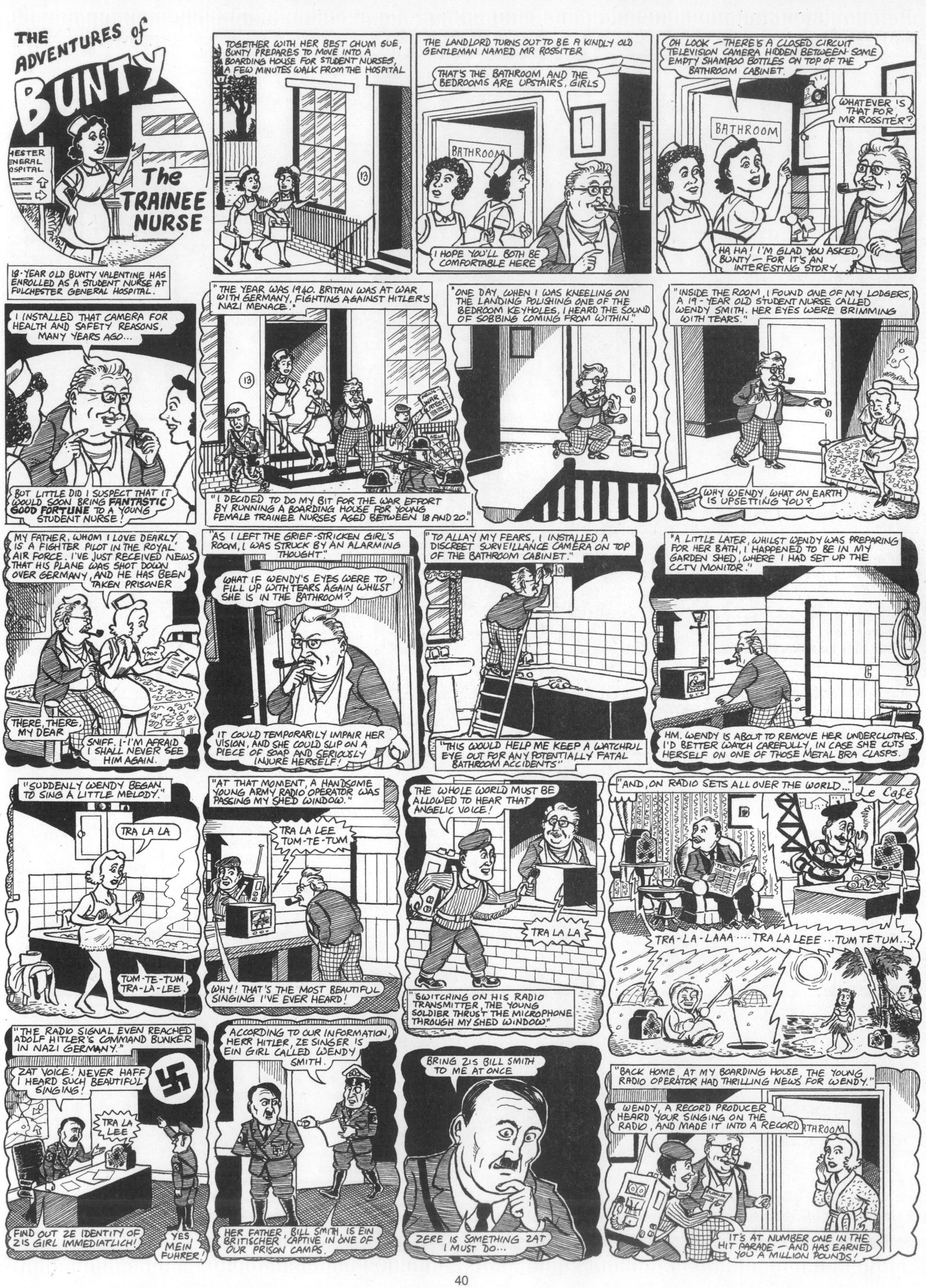
THE ADVENTURES of BUNTY
The TRAINEE NURSE
18-YEAR OLD BUNTY VALENTINE HAS ENROLLED AS A STUDENT NURSE AT FOLCHESTER GENERAL HOSPITAL.
TOGETHER WITH HER BEST CHUM SUE, BUNTY PREPARES TO MOVE INTO A BOARDING HOUSE FOR STUDENT NURSES, A FEW MINUTES WALK FROM THE HOSPITAL
THE LANDLORD TURNS OUT TO BE A KINDLY OLD GENTLEMAN NAMED MR ROSSITER
THAT'S THE BATHROOM, AND THE BEDROOMS ARE UPSTAIRS, GIRLS
BATHROOM
I HOPE YOU'LL BOTH BE COMFORTABLE HERE
OH LOOK — THERE'S A CLOSED CIRCUIT TELEVISION CAMERA HIDDEN BETWEEN SOME EMPTY SHAMPOO BOTTLES ON TOP OF THE BATHROOM CABINET.
WHATEVER IS THAT FOR, MR ROSSITER?
BATHROOM
HA HA! I'M GLAD YOU ASKED, BUNTY — FOR IT'S AN INTERESTING STORY
I INSTALLED THAT CAMERA FOR HEALTH AND SAFETY REASONS, MANY YEARS AGO...
BUT LITTLE DID I SUSPECT THAT IT WOULD SOON BRING FANTASTIC GOOD FORTUNE TO A YOUNG STUDENT NURSE!
"THE YEAR WAS 1940. BRITAIN WAS AT WAR WITH GERMANY, FIGHTING AGAINST HITLER'S NAZI MENACE."
ARP
NEWS WAR LATEST
"I DECIDED TO DO MY BIT FOR THE WAR EFFORT BY RUNNING A BOARDING HOUSE FOR YOUNG FEMALE TRAINEE NURSES AGED BETWEEN 18 AND 20."
"ONE DAY, WHEN I WAS KNEELING ON THE LANDING POLISHING ONE OF THE BEDROOM KEYHOLES, I HEARD THE SOUND OF SOBBING COMING FROM WITHIN."
"INSIDE THE ROOM, I FOUND ONE OF MY LODGERS, A 19-YEAR OLD STUDENT NURSE CALLED WENDY SMITH. HER EYES WERE BRIMMING WITH TEARS."
WHY WENDY, WHAT ON EARTH IS UPSETTING YOU?
MY FATHER, WHOM I LOVE DEARLY, IS A FIGHTER PILOT IN THE ROYAL AIR FORCE. I'VE JUST RECEIVED NEWS THAT HIS PLANE WAS SHOT DOWN OVER GERMANY, AND HE HAS BEEN TAKEN PRISONER
THERE, THERE, MY DEAR
SNIFF. I-I'M AFRAID I SHALL NEVER SEE HIM AGAIN.
"AS I LEFT THE GRIEF-STRICKEN GIRL'S ROOM, I WAS STRUCK BY AN ALARMING THOUGHT."
WHAT IF WENDY'S EYES WERE TO FILL UP WITH TEARS AGAIN WHILST SHE IS IN THE BATHROOM?
IT COULD TEMPORARILY IMPAIR HER VISION, AND SHE COULD SLIP ON A PIECE OF SOAP AND SERIOUSLY INJURE HERSELF!
"TO ALLAY MY FEARS, I INSTALLED A DISCREET SURVEILLANCE CAMERA ON TOP OF THE BATHROOM CABINET."
"THIS WOULD HELP ME KEEP A WATCHFUL EYE OUT FOR ANY POTENTIALLY FATAL BATHROOM ACCIDENTS"
"A LITTLE LATER, WHILST WENDY WAS PREPARING FOR HER BATH, I HAPPENED TO BE IN MY GARDEN SHED, WHERE I HAD SET UP THE CCTV MONITOR."
HM. WENDY IS ABOUT TO REMOVE HER UNDERCLOTHES. I'D BETTER WATCH CAREFULLY, IN CASE SHE CUTS HERSELF ON ONE OF THOSE METAL BRA CLASPS.
"SUDDENLY WENDY BEGAN TO SING A LITTLE MELODY."
TRA LA LA
TOM-TE-TUM, TRA-LA-LEE.
"AT THAT MOMENT, A HANDSOME YOUNG ARMY RADIO OPERATOR WAS PASSING MY SHED WINDOW."
TRA LA LEE TUM-TE-TUM
WHY! THAT'S THE MOST BEAUTIFUL SINGING I'VE EVER HEARD!
THE WHOLE WORLD MUST BE ALLOWED TO HEAR THAT ANGELIC VOICE!
TRA LA LA
"SWITCHING ON HIS RADIO TRANSMITTER, THE YOUNG SOLDIER THRUST THE MICROPHONE THROUGH MY SHED WINDOW"
"AND, ON RADIO SETS ALL OVER THE WORLD..."
Le Café
TIMES
TRA-LA-LAAA.... TRA LA LEEE ...TUM TETUM...
"THE RADIO SIGNAL EVEN REACHED ADOLF HITLER'S COMMAND BUNKER IN NAZI GERMANY."
ZAT VOICE! NEVER HAFF I HEARD SUCH BEAUTIFUL SINGING!
TRA LA LEE
FIND OUT ZE IDENTITY OF ZIS GIRL IMMEDIATLICH!
YES, MEIN FUHRER!
ACCORDING TO OUR INFORMATION, HERR HITLER, ZE SINGER IS EIN GIRL CALLED WENDY SMITH.
HER FATHER, BILL SMITH, IS EIN BRITISCHER CAPTIVE IN ONE OF OUR PRISON CAMPS.
BRING ZIS BILL SMITH TO ME AT ONCE
ZERE IS SOMETHING ZAT I MUST DO...
"BACK HOME AT MY BOARDING HOUSE, THE YOUNG RADIO OPERATOR HAD THRILLING NEWS FOR WENDY."
WENDY, A RECORD PRODUCER HEARD YOUR SINGING ON THE RADIO, AND MADE IT INTO A RECORD
BATHROOM
IT'S AT NUMBER ONE IN THE HIT PARADE — AND HAS EARNED YOU A MILLION POUNDS!

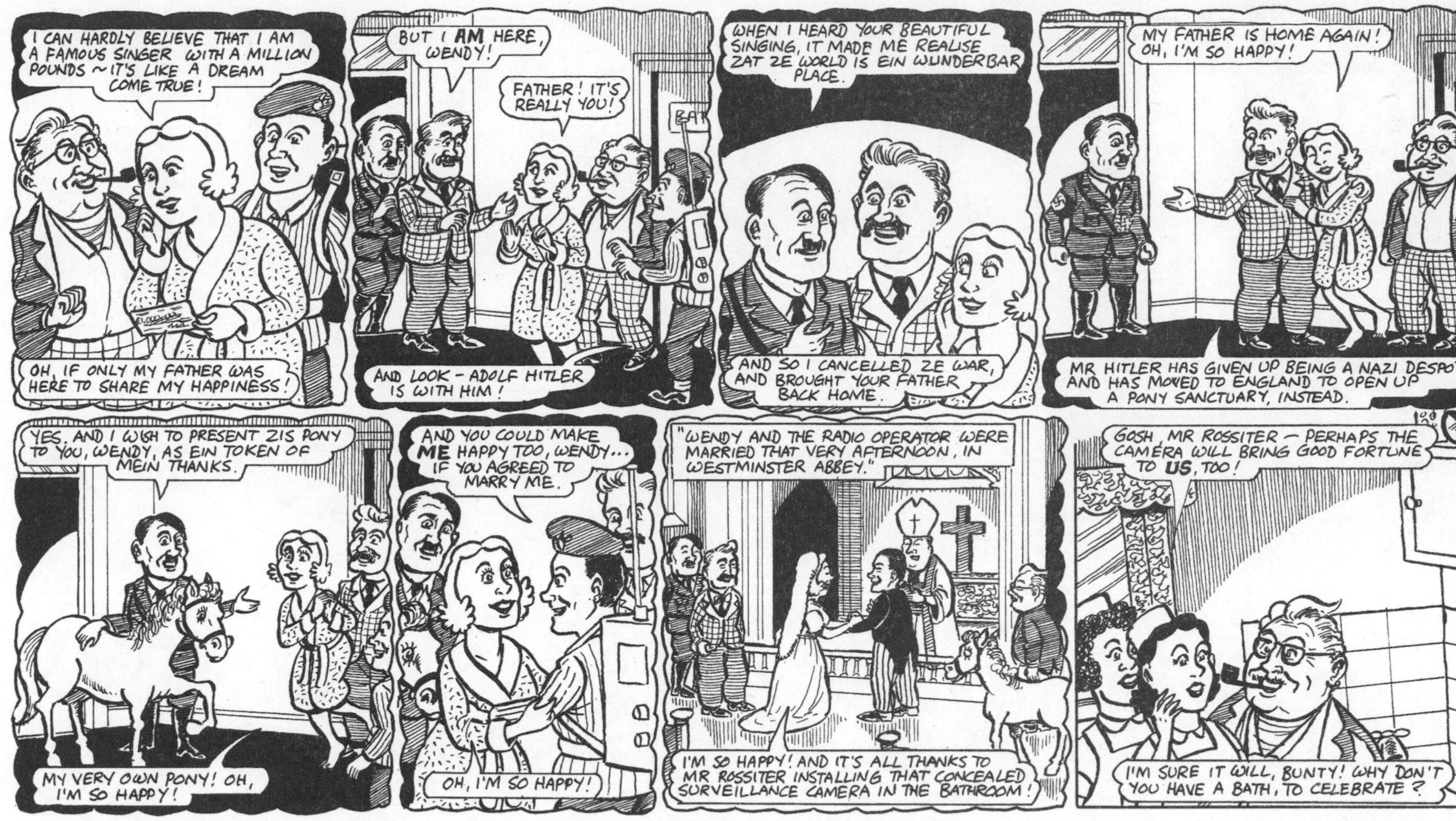
I CAN HARDLY BELIEVE THAT I AM A FAMOUS SINGER WITH A MILLION POUNDS ~ IT'S LIKE A DREAM COME TRUE!
OH, IF ONLY MY FATHER WAS HERE TO SHARE MY HAPPINESS!
BUT I AM HERE, WENDY!
FATHER! IT'S REALLY YOU!
AND LOOK - ADOLF HITLER IS WITH HIM!
WHEN I HEARD YOUR BEAUTIFUL SINGING, IT MADE ME REALISE ZAT ZE WORLD IS EIN WUNDERBAR PLACE.
AND SO I CANCELLED ZE WAR, AND BROUGHT YOUR FATHER BACK HOME.
MY FATHER IS HOME AGAIN! OH, I'M SO HAPPY!
MR HITLER HAS GIVEN UP BEING A NAZI DESPOT, AND HAS MOVED TO ENGLAND TO OPEN UP A PONY SANCTUARY, INSTEAD.
YES, AND I WISH TO PRESENT ZIS PONY TO YOU, WENDY, AS EIN TOKEN OF MEIN THANKS.
MY VERY OWN PONY! OH, I'M SO HAPPY!
AND YOU COULD MAKE ME HAPPY TOO, WENDY... IF YOU AGREED TO MARRY ME.
OH, I'M SO HAPPY!
"WENDY AND THE RADIO OPERATOR WERE MARRIED THAT VERY AFTERNOON, IN WESTMINSTER ABBEY."
I'M SO HAPPY! AND IT'S ALL THANKS TO MR ROSSITER INSTALLING THAT CONCEALED SURVEILLANCE CAMERA IN THE BATHROOM!
GOSH, MR ROSSITER — PERHAPS THE CAMERA WILL BRING GOOD FORTUNE TO US, TOO!
I'M SURE IT WILL, BUNTY! WHY DON'T YOU HAVE A BATH, TO CELEBRATE?

PUBLIC INFORMATION

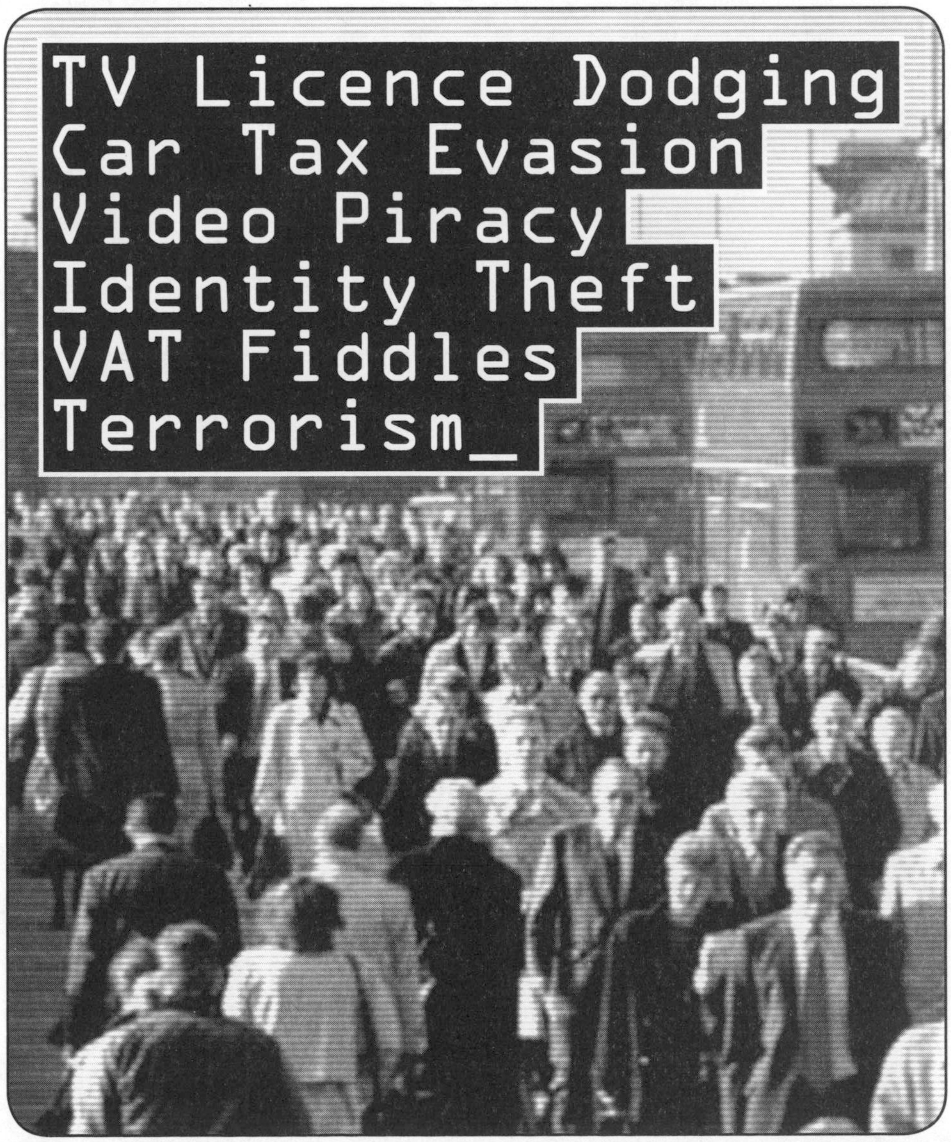
TV Licence Dodging
Car Tax Evasion
Video Piracy
Identity Theft
VAT Fiddles
Terrorism_

We know that you're *ALL* up to something.

And we won't rest until every last person in Britain is behind bars.

Issued by
H.M. Government

www.wedonttrustyouasfaraswecanfuckingthrowyou.gov

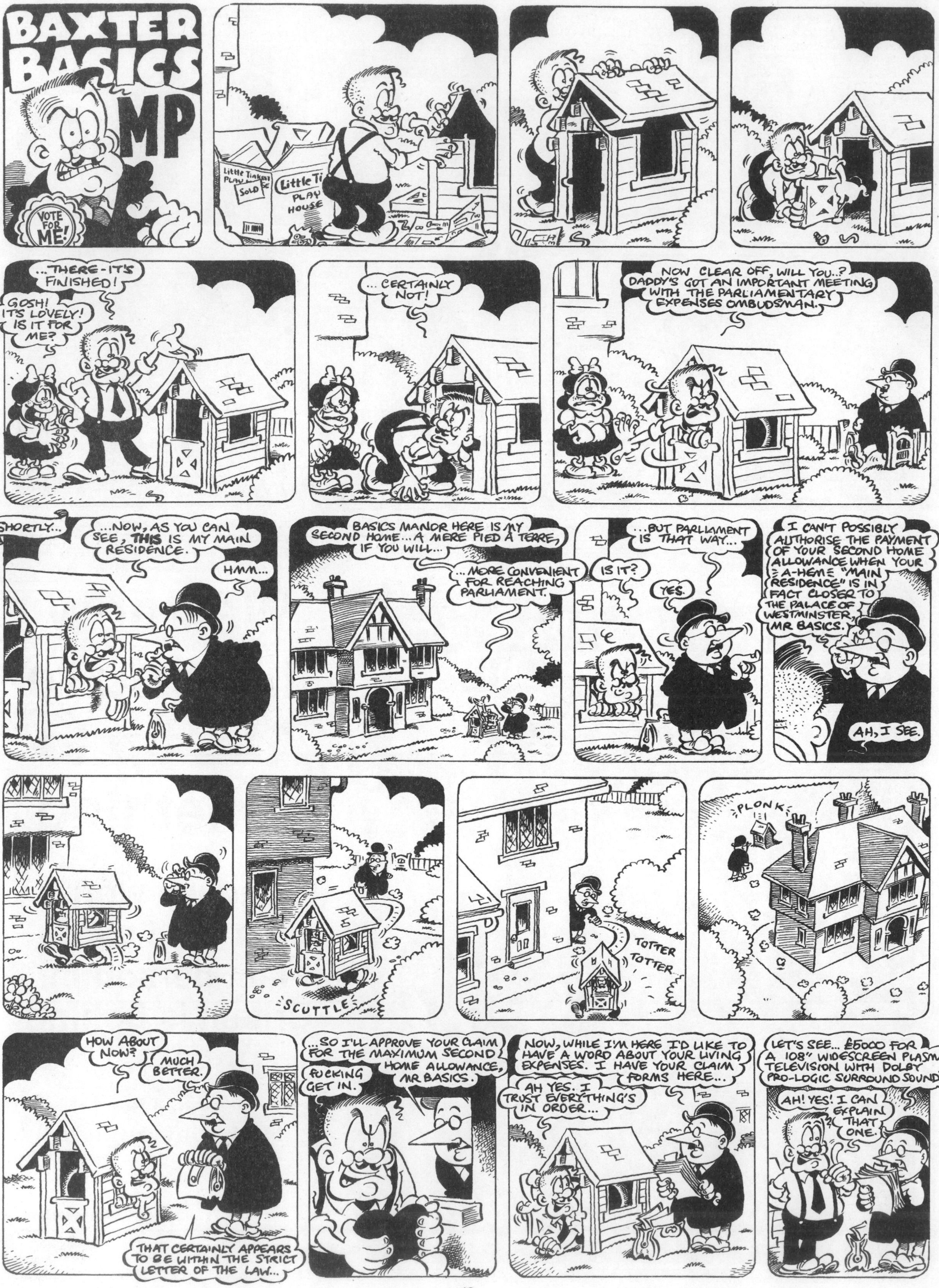
BAXTER BASICS MP
VOTE FOR ME!
SOLD
PLAY HOUSE
...THERE - IT'S FINISHED!
GOSH! IT'S LOVELY! IS IT FOR ME?
...CERTAINLY NOT!
NOW CLEAR OFF, WILL YOU..? DADDY'S GOT AN IMPORTANT MEETING WITH THE PARLIAMENTARY EXPENSES OMBUDSMAN.
SHORTLY...
...NOW, AS YOU CAN SEE, THIS IS MY MAIN RESIDENCE.
HMM...
BASICS MANOR HERE IS MY SECOND HOME... A MERE PIED A TERRE, IF YOU WILL...
...MORE CONVENIENT FOR REACHING PARLIAMENT.
...BUT PARLIAMENT IS THAT WAY...
IS IT?
YES.
I CAN'T POSSIBLY AUTHORISE THE PAYMENT OF YOUR SECOND HOME ALLOWANCE WHEN YOUR A-HEM "MAIN RESIDENCE" IS IN FACT CLOSER TO THE PALACE OF WESTMINSTER, MR BASICS.
AH, I SEE.
SCUTTLE
TOTTER TOTTER
PLONK
HOW ABOUT NOW?
MUCH BETTER.
THAT CERTAINLY APPEARS TO BE WITHIN THE STRICT LETTER OF THE LAW...
...SO I'LL APPROVE YOUR CLAIM FOR THE MAXIMUM SECOND HOME ALLOWANCE, MR BASICS.
FUCKING GET IN.
NOW, WHILE I'M HERE I'D LIKE TO HAVE A WORD ABOUT YOUR LIVING EXPENSES. I HAVE YOUR CLAIM FORMS HERE...
AH YES. I TRUST EVERYTHING'S IN ORDER...
LET'S SEE... £5000 FOR A 108" WIDESCREEN PLASMA TELEVISION WITH DOLBY PRO-LOGIC SURROUND SOUND?
AH! YES! I CAN EXPLAIN THAT ONE.

IT WAS AN ESSENTIAL PURCHASE TO ENABLE ME TO KEEP ABREAST OF CURRENT AFFAIRS... NEWSNIGHT, PANORAMA AND WHAT-HAVE-YOU...

I SEE.

WHAT ABOUT THIS? A £25,000 FITTED KITCHEN WITH IMPORTED ITALIAN GRANITE WORKTOPS THROUGHOUT..?

ERM...

AH! SIMPLE. SO I CAN MAKE MYSELF A CUP OF TEA WHEN I COME IN AFTER AN ALL-NIGHT SITTING AT THE COMMONS.

RIGHT.

I CAN ASSURE YOU THAT THESE ARE ALL LEGITIMATE EXPENSES INCURRED IN THE COURSE OF MY DUTIES AS A BUSY M.P.

£50,000 FOR A PAIR OF "HIS & HERS" ROLEX OYSTER WATCHES, MR BASICS..?

I'M GLAD YOU BROUGHT THAT UP. YOU SEE, WHAT PEOPLE DON'T REALISE IS THAT THE HOUSE OF COMMONS RUNS LIKE CLOCKWORK... LIKE CLOCKWORK.

YOU NEED TO KNOW THE TIME ACCURATELY. YOU CAN USE A CHEAP WATCH FOR A WEEK - FOR A MONTH, EVEN - BUT AT THE END OF THE DAY, YOU NEED A TIMEPIECE YOU CAN RELY ON.

MY DIAMOND-ENCRUSTED ROLEX CHRONOMETER ISN'T A LUXURY - IT'S AN ESSENTIAL TOOL THAT ENABLES ME TO DO MY JOB AS A POLITICIAN.

YOU CLAIMED FOR A PAIR...

"HIS & HERS"?

LISTEN - IF I'M ON A SELECT COMMITTEE, I'VE GOT TO BE THERE TO MOVE THOSE AMMENDMENTS AT PRECISELY 9-30... AND SO HAS MY MISTRESS.

I MEAN SECRETARY OF COURSE.

YES, WELL THAT ALL SEEMS FINE TO ME, MR BASICS...

...HOWEVER, THERE IS A CLAIM HERE THAT, I'M AFRAID, CAUSES SOME CONCERN.

OH!?

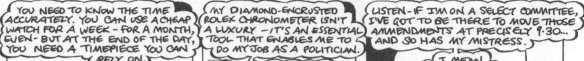

INDEED - THE RENTAL OF TWO PAY-PER-VIEW ADULT MOVIES.

AH... YES... ERM... I... ER...

EXPENSES ADDITIONAL FEATURE £5

ADDITIONAL FEATURE

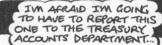

I'M AFRAID I'M GOING TO HAVE TO REPORT THIS ONE TO THE TREASURY ACCOUNTS DEPARTMENT...

B-BUT...

...TAKING ADVANTAGE OF THE SYSTEM LIKE THIS LOOKS BAD, MR BASICS.

SO YOU'D BETTER HAVE A GOOD EXPLANATION READY FOR WHEN THE PRESS GET HOLD OF THIS.

SHORTLY...

HAZY DAZE RETIREMENT REST HOME

...NOW LISTEN, GRANNY. I WOULDN'T BE ASKING YOU TO DO IT IF IT WASN'T IMPORTANT, WOULD I..?

NEXT DAY...

BBC LIVE

PRESS

PRESS

...I FULLY UNDERSTAND WHY PEOPLE HAVE BEEN ANGERED BY MY ACTIONS. I SHOULD NOT HAVE USED PUBLIC MONEY TO FUND MY VIEWING OF "BEN DOVER'S BUKKAKE JIZZ BATH" AND "BARELY LEGAL SPUNK GUZZLERS" AND I APOLOGISE FOR ANY EMBARRASSMENT I HAVE CAUSED MY GRANDSON...

PAXMAN FLATTENS KNACKERS IN VICE

BBC2 flagship current affairs programme *Newsnight* will have a temporary host for the next six weeks after regular presenter Jeremy Paxman suffered a bizarre accident at his Holland Park home.

The £1million-a-year newsreader was rushed to hospital early on Saturday morning after apparently squeezing his testicles flat in a vice. A BBC spokesman told us: "We can confirm that Jeremy suffered a mishap at the weekend. He had just had a bath and had decided to do a spot of DIY. Unfortunately he was wearing a loosely-fitting dressing gown which came open at an inopportune moment whilst he was adjusting the jaws of a metal-working vice."

Details of what exactly happened are still sketchy, but an unofficial source at St Bart's Hospital said that Paxman's injuries were coinsistent with someone tightening his private parts in a vice. "I saw his testicles when they brought him in in the ambulance. They were in a sorry state, I can tell you," he told us. "They looked like a pair of purple whoopee cushions."

A *Newsnight* spokesman explained that Paxman was still in too much pain to tell doctors exactly what had happened. "When the paramedics arrived they found Jeremy alone in the shed with the door locked from the inside," he told us. "Jeremy was in a great deal of distress with his knackers trapped in the vice."

"It had been tightened so firmly that it took two firemen with a length of scaffolding pole to open it," he continued.

He confirmed that Paxman, 59, was expected to be out of action for several weeks while he recovered from his injuries. "When newsreaders suffer this kind of mishap they are usually back at work after five or six weeks," he added.

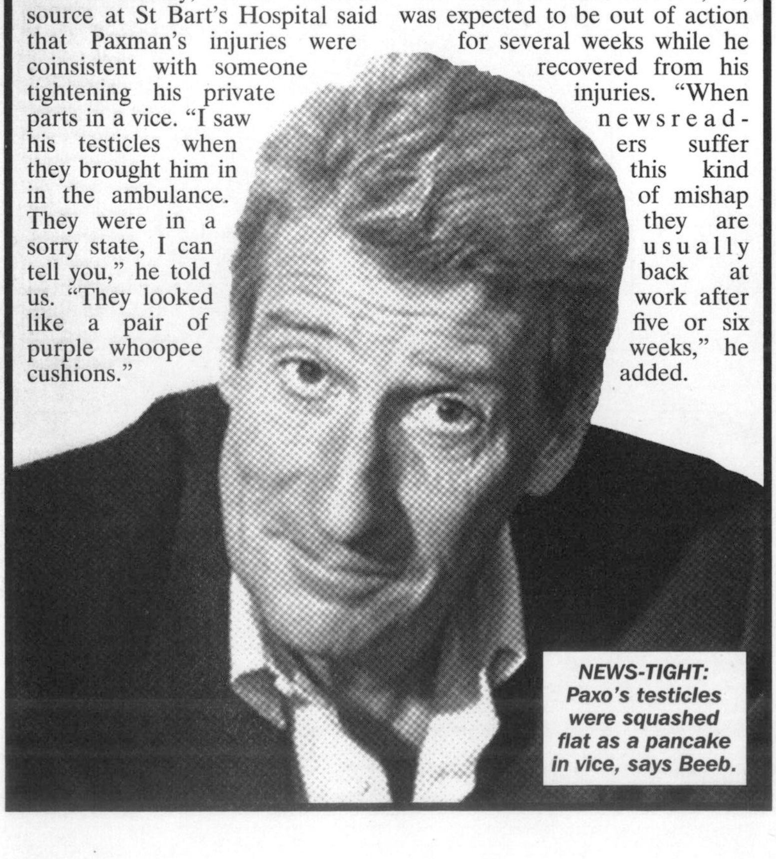

NEWS-TIGHT: Paxo's testicles were squashed flat as a pancake in vice, says Beeb.

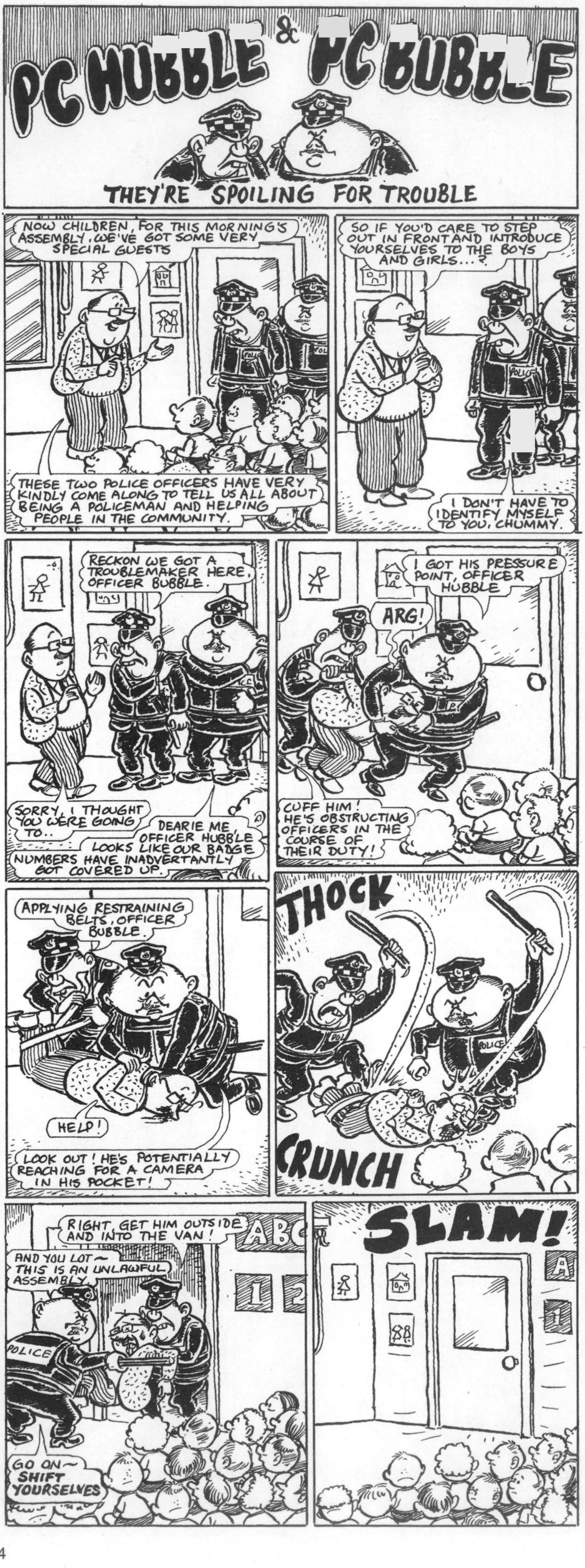
PC HUBBLE & PC BUBBLE
THEY'RE SPOILING FOR TROUBLE
NOW CHILDREN, FOR THIS MORNING'S ASSEMBLY, WE'VE GOT SOME VERY SPECIAL GUESTS
THESE TWO POLICE OFFICERS HAVE VERY KINDLY COME ALONG TO TELL US ALL ABOUT BEING A POLICEMAN AND HELPING PEOPLE IN THE COMMUNITY.
SO IF YOU'D CARE TO STEP OUT IN FRONT AND INTRODUCE YOURSELVES TO THE BOYS AND GIRLS...?
I DON'T HAVE TO IDENTIFY MYSELF TO YOU, CHUMMY.
RECKON WE GOT A TROUBLEMAKER HERE, OFFICER BUBBLE.
SORRY, I THOUGHT YOU WERE GOING TO..
DEARIE ME, OFFICER HUBBLE LOOKS LIKE OUR BADGE NUMBERS HAVE INADVERTANTLY GOT COVERED UP.
I GOT HIS PRESSURE POINT, OFFICER HUBBLE
ARG!
CUFF HIM! HE'S OBSTRUCTING OFFICERS IN THE COURSE OF THEIR DUTY!
APPLYING RESTRAINING BELTS, OFFICER BUBBLE.
HELP!
LOOK OUT! HE'S POTENTIALLY REACHING FOR A CAMERA IN HIS POCKET!
THOCK
CRUNCH
RIGHT, GET HIM OUTSIDE AND INTO THE VAN!
AND YOU LOT — THIS IS AN UNLAWFUL ASSEMBLY.
POLICE
GO ON — SHIFT YOURSELVES
SLAM!

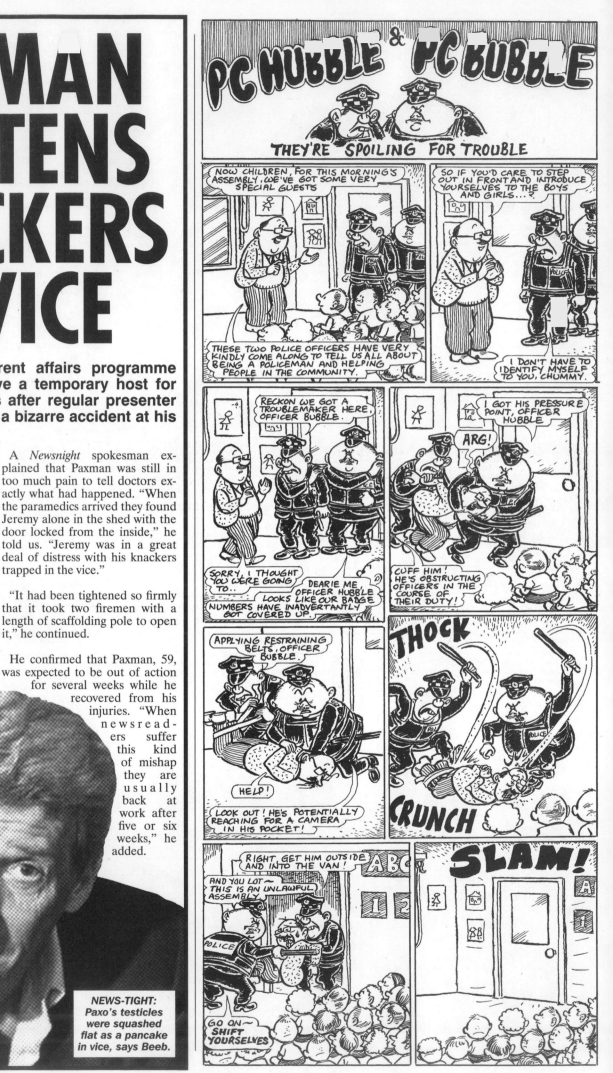

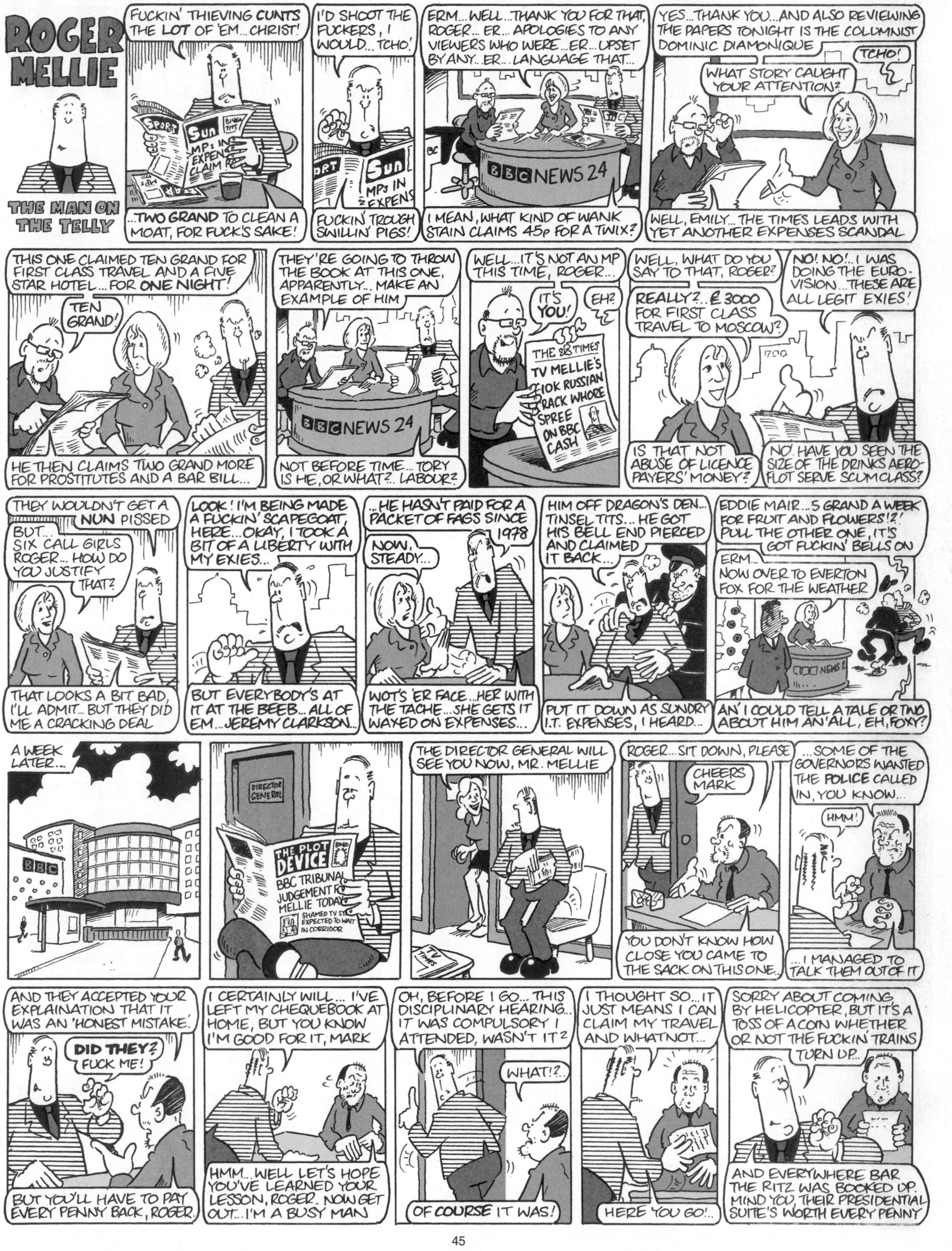
ROGER MELLIE
THE MAN ON THE TELLY
FUCKIN' THIEVING CUNTS THE LOT OF 'EM... CHRIST!
SPORT Sun BINGO TITS MPs IN EXPENSE CLAIM R
...TWO GRAND TO CLEAN A MOAT, FOR FUCK'S SAKE!
I'D SHOOT THE FUCKERS, I WOULD... TCHO!
FUCKIN' TROUGH SWILLIN' PIGS!
ERM... WELL... THANK YOU FOR THAT, ROGER... ER... APOLOGIES TO ANY VIEWERS WHO WERE... ER... UPSET BY ANY... ER... LANGUAGE THAT...
BBC NEWS 24
I MEAN, WHAT KIND OF WANK STAIN CLAIMS 45p FOR A TWIX?
YES... THANK YOU... AND ALSO REVIEWING THE PAPERS TONIGHT IS THE COLUMNIST DOMINIC DIAMONIQUE
TCHO!
WHAT STORY CAUGHT YOUR ATTENTION?
WELL, EMILY... THE TIMES LEADS WITH YET ANOTHER EXPENSES SCANDAL
THIS ONE CLAIMED TEN GRAND FOR FIRST CLASS TRAVEL AND A FIVE STAR HOTEL... FOR ONE NIGHT!
TEN GRAND!
HE THEN CLAIMS TWO GRAND MORE FOR PROSTITUTES AND A BAR BILL...
THEY'RE GOING TO THROW THE BOOK AT THIS ONE, APPARENTLY... MAKE AN EXAMPLE OF HIM
BBC NEWS 24
NOT BEFORE TIME... TORY IS HE, OR WHAT?.. LABOUR?
WELL... IT'S NOT AN MP THIS TIME, ROGER...
IT'S YOU!
EH?
THE TIMES TV MELLIE'S £10K RUSSIAN CRACK WHORE SPREE ON BBC CASH
WELL, WHAT DO YOU SAY TO THAT, ROGER?
REALLY?.. £3000 FOR FIRST CLASS TRAVEL TO MOSCOW?
IS THAT NOT ABUSE OF LICENCE PAYERS' MONEY?
NO! NO!.. I WAS DOING THE EURO-VISION... THESE ARE ALL LEGIT EXIES!
NO! HAVE YOU SEEN THE SIZE OF THE DRINKS AERO-FLOT SERVE SCUM CLASS?
THEY WOULDN'T GET A NUN PISSED
BUT... SIX CALL GIRLS ROGER... HOW DO YOU JUSTIFY THAT?
THAT LOOKS A BIT BAD, I'LL ADMIT... BUT THEY DID ME A CRACKING DEAL
LOOK! I'M BEING MADE A FUCKIN' SCAPEGOAT, HERE... OKAY, I TOOK A BIT OF A LIBERTY WITH MY EXIES...
BUT EVERYBODY'S AT IT AT THE BEEB... ALL OF 'EM... JEREMY CLARKSON...
...HE HASN'T PAID FOR A PACKET OF FAGS SINCE 1978
NOW, STEADY...
WOT'S 'ER FACE... HER WITH THE TACHE... SHE GETS IT WAXED ON EXPENSES...
HIM OFF DRAGON'S DEN... TINSEL TITS... HE GOT HIS BELL END PIERCED AND CLAIMED IT BACK...
PUT IT DOWN AS SUNDRY I.T. EXPENSES, I HEARD...
EDDIE MAIR... 5 GRAND A WEEK FOR FRUIT AND FLOWERS!?! PULL THE OTHER ONE, IT'S GOT FUCKIN' BELLS ON
ERM... NOW OVER TO EVERTON FOX FOR THE WEATHER
AN' I COULD TELL A TALE OR TWO ABOUT HIM AN' ALL, EH, FOXY?
A WEEK LATER...
BBC
DIRECTOR GENERAL
THE PLOT DEVICE BINGO
BBC TRIBUNAL JUDGEMENT FOR MELLIE TODAY
SHAMED TV STAR EXPECTED TO WAIT IN CORRIDOR
THE DIRECTOR GENERAL WILL SEE YOU NOW, MR. MELLIE
TV TIMES
ROGER... SIT DOWN, PLEASE
CHEERS MARK
YOU DON'T KNOW HOW CLOSE YOU CAME TO THE SACK ON THIS ONE...
...SOME OF THE GOVERNORS WANTED THE POLICE CALLED IN, YOU KNOW...
HMM!
...I MANAGED TO TALK THEM OUT OF IT
AND THEY ACCEPTED YOUR EXPLAINATION THAT IT WAS AN 'HONEST MISTAKE'.
DID THEY? FUCK ME!
BUT YOU'LL HAVE TO PAY EVERY PENNY BACK, ROGER.
I CERTAINLY WILL... I'VE LEFT MY CHEQUEBOOK AT HOME, BUT YOU KNOW I'M GOOD FOR IT, MARK
HMM... WELL LET'S HOPE YOU'VE LEARNED YOUR LESSON, ROGER. NOW GET OUT... I'M A BUSY MAN
OH, BEFORE I GO... THIS DISCIPLINARY HEARING... IT WAS COMPULSORY I ATTENDED, WASN'T IT?
WHAT!?..
OF COURSE IT WAS!
I THOUGHT SO... IT JUST MEANS I CAN CLAIM MY TRAVEL AND WHATNOT...
HERE YOU GO!..
SORRY ABOUT COMING BY HELICOPTER, BUT IT'S A TOSS OF A COIN WHETHER OR NOT THE FUCKIN' TRAINS TURN UP...
AND EVERYWHERE BAR THE RITZ WAS BOOKED UP. MIND YOU, THEIR PRESIDENTIAL SUITE'S WORTH EVERY PENNY

People Who Help Us... THE POLICEMAN

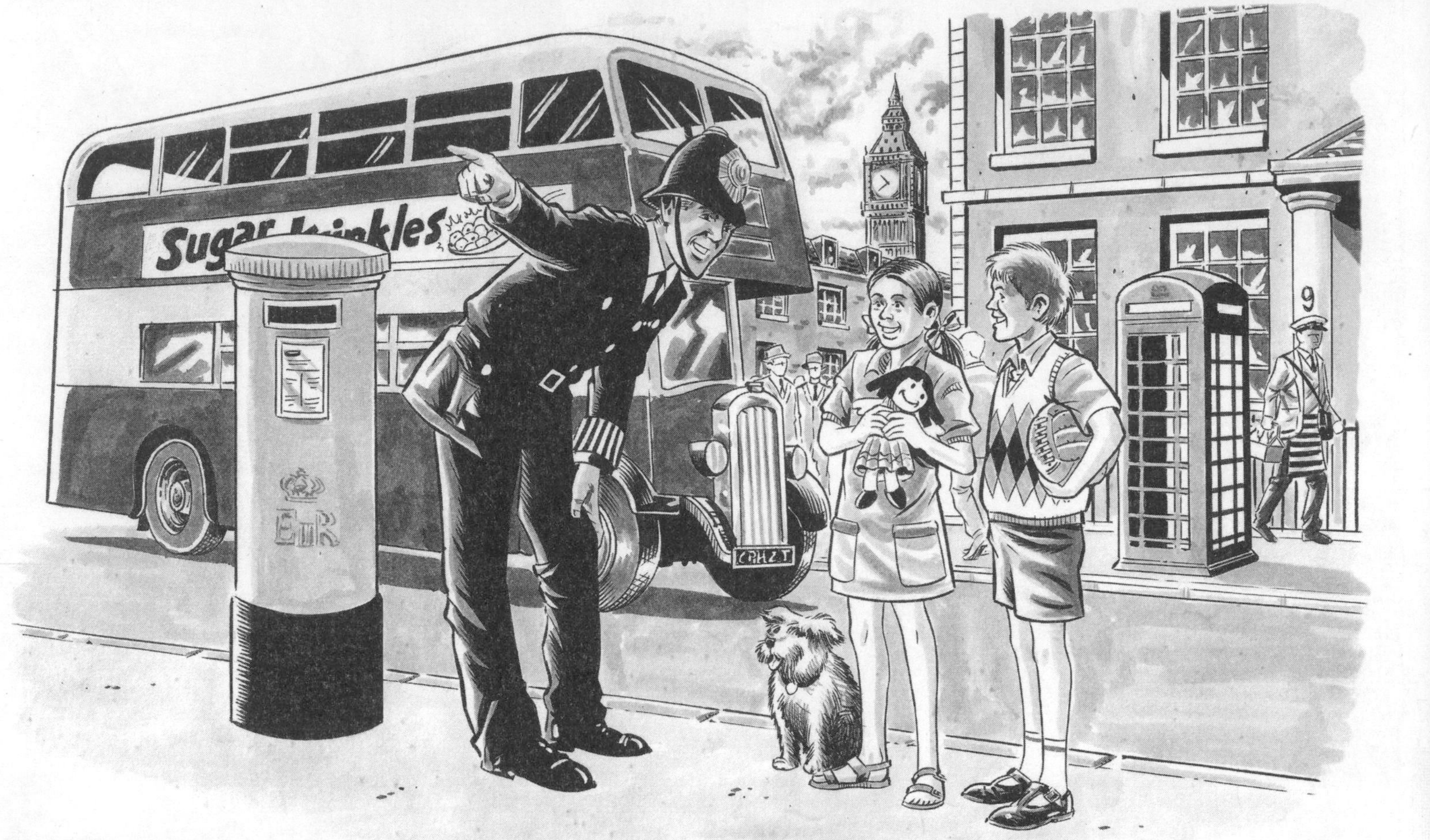
9

THE BRITISH POLICEMAN is the envy of the world. Whether he's telling someone the time, helping an old lady with her shopping or chasing a masked bank robber, we see him every day on the streets of our cities, towns and villages. He's as much a part of the traditional British scene as Westminster Abbey, the tower of Big Ben and himselves on bicycles, two by two.

Unlike his intimidating, gun-toting foreign counterpart, our approachable bobby does his job armed with nothing more than a friendly smile, his sense of fair play and a 2-foot long extendable steel baton. Not surprisingly, it's every little boy's dream to be a policeman when he grows up, and if he works hard at school and passes all his exams he'll probably go and do something else. But what's it like being a policeman? Here are just a few of the situations that an ordinary copper might meet during an ordinary day on the job...

VICTIMS of burglary are often deeply traumatised by the experience of having their homes broken into. Here, an elderly lady has dialled 999 after discovering that her house has been ransacked. The sharp-eyed Scenes of Crimes officer notices that the thieves have omitted to take a priceless antique clock, some valuable war medals and a biscuit tin of cash from the sideboard. He decides to take them home, where he can examine them carefully for clues. Realising that the homeowner would be distressed if she saw these precious pieces of evidence being removed from her house, he gets his colleague to distract her whilst he puts them in a holdall.

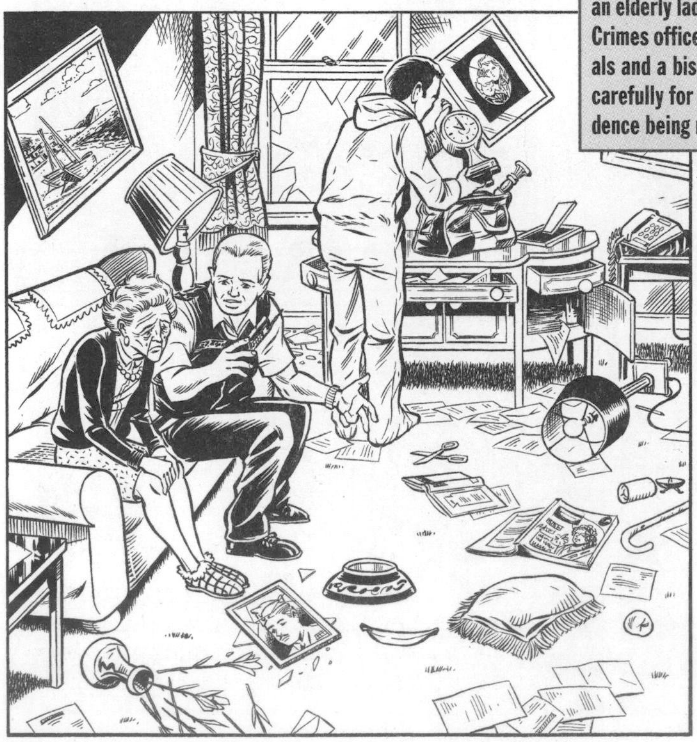

A POLICEMAN often relies on a mysterious sixth sense to tell him when a crime may have been committed. In this scene, a traffic patrolman has pulled over a passing car in order to make some routine enquiries. A young man driving a fancy motor wouldn't usually arouse suspicion, but there is something about this particular driver that makes the policeman suspect that he may be guilty of an offence. The driver is asked to produce his documents. His insurance and MOT certificates are all in order and a quick check with the police computer proves he is the legitimate owner of the vehicle. But alarm bells are still ringing in the officer's head, so just to be on the safe side, the driver is tazered, taken back to the police station, roughed up, DNA-fingerprinted and held for 48 hours before being released without charge. He may have got away with whatever it might have been this time, but he knows that he'd better watch his step. The police are onto his little game, and they won't rest until they've got him safely behind bars for something.

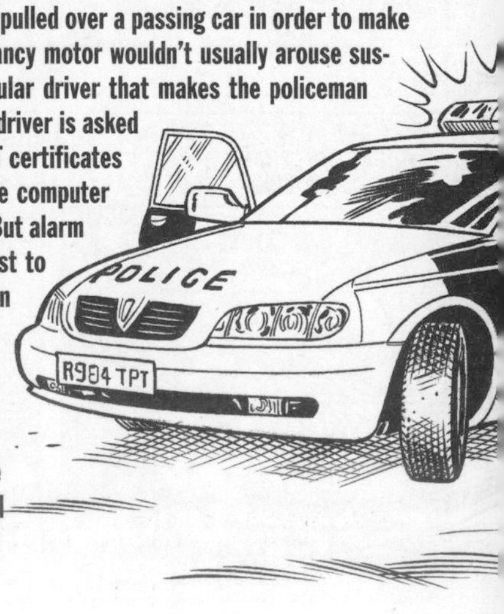
POLICE
R984 TPT

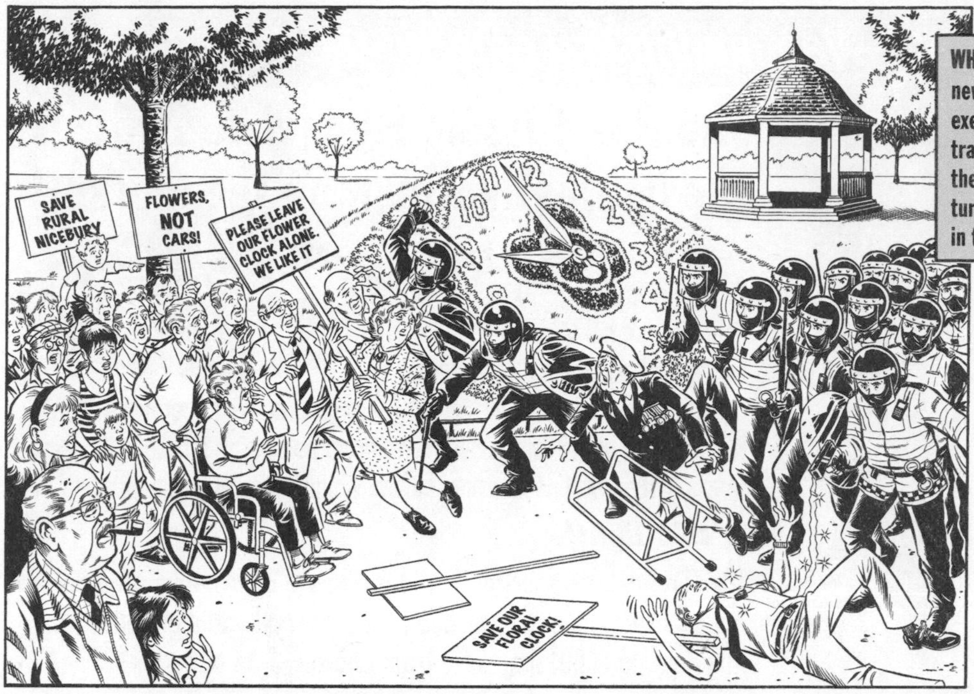
WHETHER they are demonstrating against illegal wars, globalisation, or new laws that infringe civil rights, large groups of people often gather to exercise their right to protest. It is part of our country's proud, democratic tradition. But these troublemakers have to be kept under control and it is the police's job to maintain order, using force if necessary. Here a demo has turned ugly and a group of Tactical Support Group officers has had to move in to defuse a potential riot.
SAVE RURAL NICEBURY
FLOWERS, NOT CARS!
PLEASE LEAVE OUR FLOWER CLOCK ALONE. WE LIKE IT
SAVE OUR FLORAL CLOCK!

THE FIGHT against crime entered the technological age many years ago. These days, as much detective work is done behind a computer terminal as out on the street. Thanks to the police's massive database, few offenders can hope to hide from the long arm of the law for long. Here, a copper uses a car registration number to look up the home address of a driver, as a favour for a friend who has been cut up in traffic. The miscreant will later receive a late night visit from his victim, and a lesson in road manners that will hopefully make him think twice in future about the correct use of his indicators.

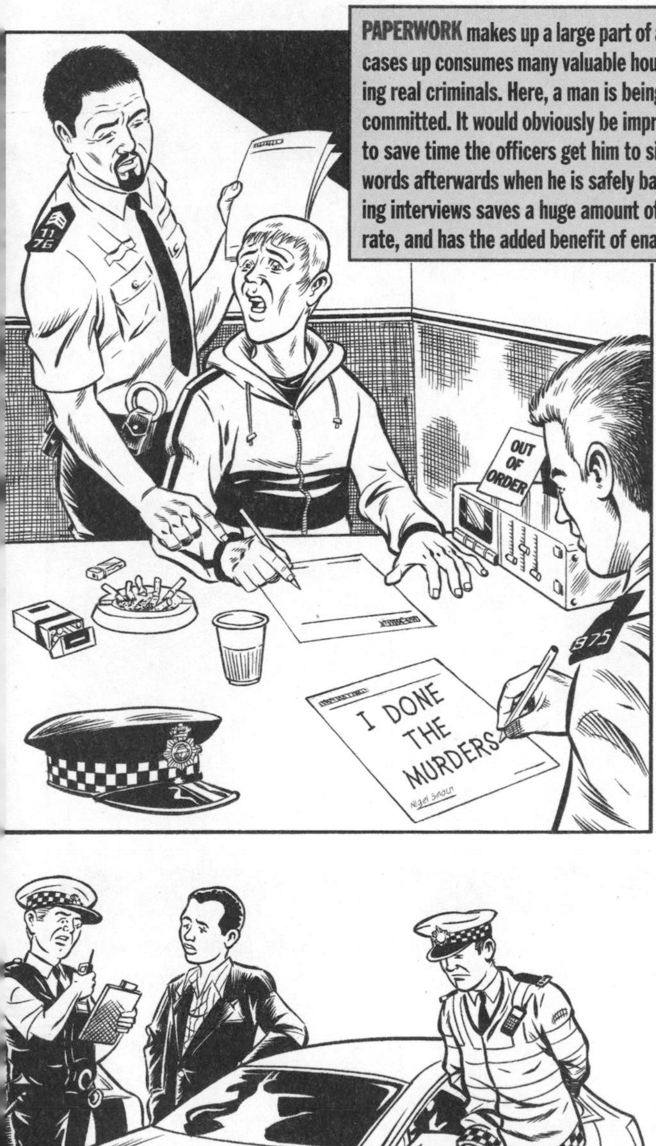
PAPERWORK makes up a large part of a modern bobby's duties. Filling in forms and writing cases up consumes many valuable hours that would be better spent out on the beat, fighting real criminals. Here, a man is being interviewed about a serious crime which has been committed. It would obviously be impractical to write down his words as he says them, so to save time the officers get him to sign several blank statement sheets first, adding his words afterwards when he is safely back in the cells. This creative approach to transcribing interviews saves a huge amount of police time, leads to a much higher crime clear-up rate, and has the added benefit of enabling trials to be completed much more quickly.
OUT OF ORDER
I DONE THE MURDERS

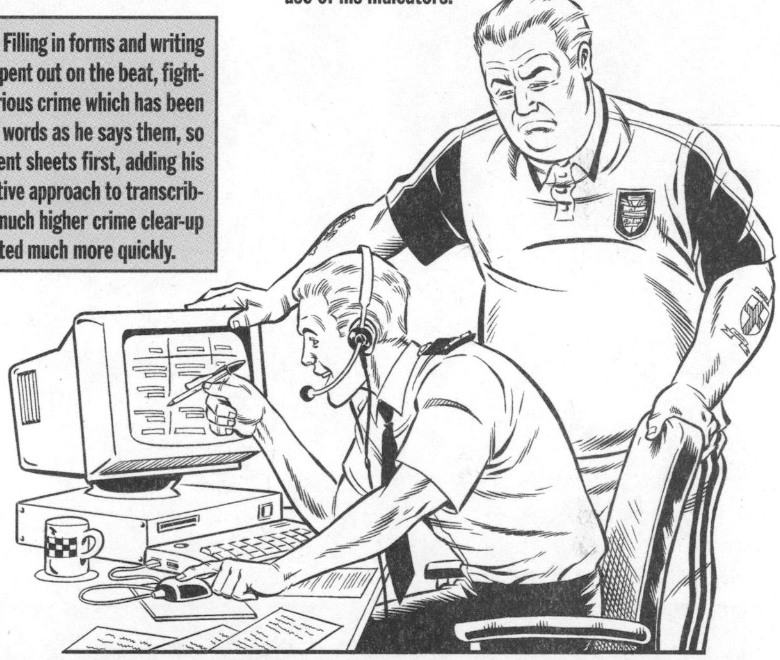

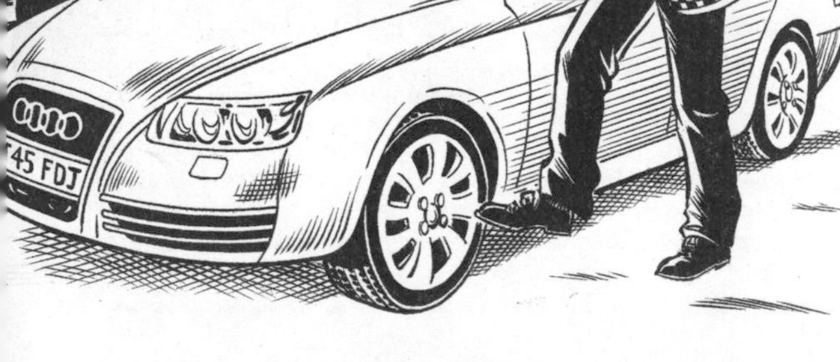
45 FDT

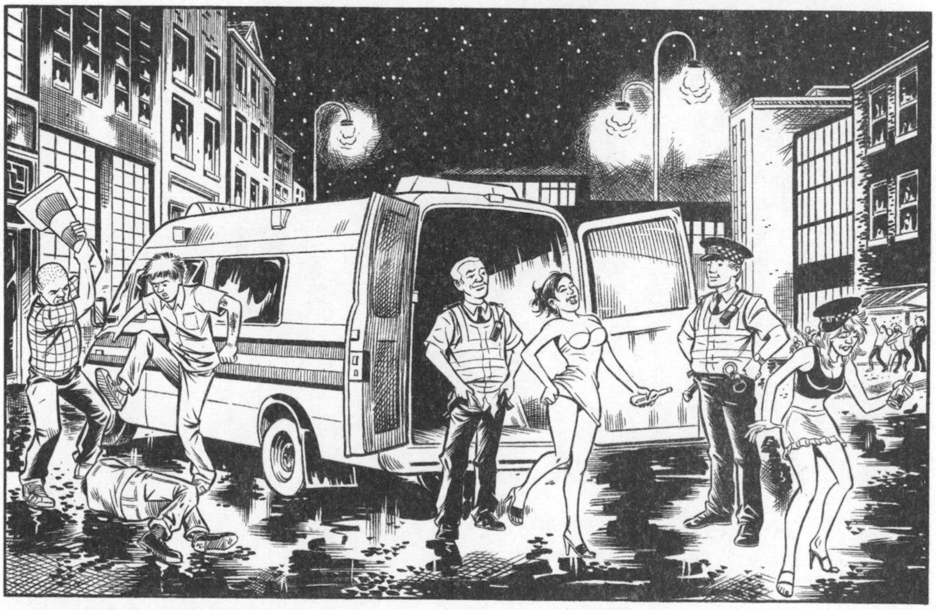

DRUNKENNESS is one of the most common criminal offences that our police have to deal with. However, arresting and prosecuting people who have had a few drinks too many on a night out is not always the best way to deal with the problem. Here, a pair of bobbies who are stationed in a busy town centre at closing time have taken a couple of tipsy young ladies into the back of their van to give them a good hard talking to about the importance of drinking sensibly.

The Rex Rissole FlimsyLite 2000™ ~ *Vacuuming just entered the 20th Century!*

Useless for stairs...
Push it backwards and forwards on your stairs if you like.
...Futile on settees...
Crevice tool leaves dirt alone in hard-to reach places.
...but SO light!
Upper handle - Ergonomic cross section fits snugly into hand
Mid handle - Joins Upper and Lower handles
Lower handle - Unadjustable for simplicity of use
Switch - Toggles between 'on' and 'off' settings up to several times before it breaks
REX RISSOLE FlimsyLite2000
Ultra-lightweight body - Injection-moulded plastic for brittleness
Superficially realistic floor nozzle tool - No discernible function whatsoever
ONLY £15.99 plus £84.01 p+p
so it's not really worth going to the trouble of sending it back for a refund

The Rex Rissole FlimsyLite 2000™ is the lightest vacuum on the market!

REX RISSOLE FlimsyLite2000

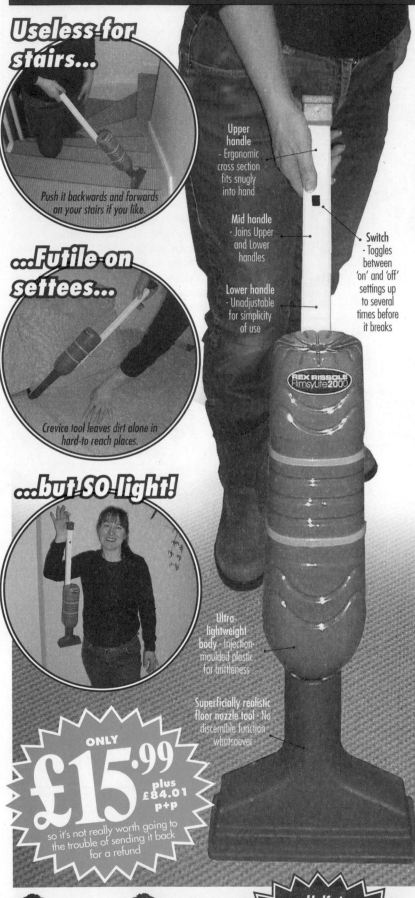

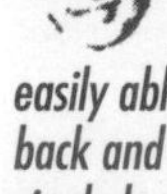

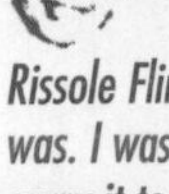

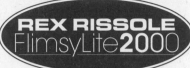

Weighing just 1½ lb, the Rex Rissole FlimsyLite 2000 makes light work of being pushed fruitlessly backwards and forwards around your home. It effortlessly makes a vacuum cleaner noise whilst leaving your house unaffected from top to bottom. And because it doesn't function, it doesn't need a bag, saving weight, time and expense.

It's SO light!

The FlimsyLite's powerful 3V motor hums at dust, crumbs and pet hairs leaving them undisturbed with ease. And you'll get up to 20 minutes vague buzzing noise from one set of AA batteries.

100% lightweight. 100% of the time!

Just look how light the Rex Rissole FlimsyLite 2000 is on these typical family spills...

Spill	Rex Rissole weight
Crisps trodden into carpet	1½ lbs.
Dropped birthday cake	1½ lbs.
Hole punch debris	1½ lbs.
Cigarette ash	1½ lbs.

Take the effort & cleaning out of cleaning day!

...in fact, whatever cleaning job you throw at it, the Rex Rissole FlimsyLite 2000 will still weigh just 1½ lb!

Utterly ineffectual!

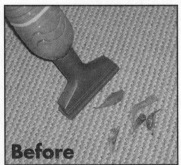

Before

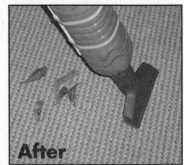

After

~ Customer Priority Order Form ~

Fill in your details on the form and send it to: ***Rex Rissole Consumer Products Ltd., Inefficacious House, Leeds.***

Please send me .... Rex Rissole FlimsyLite 2000 vacuums.

Name .... Address ....

.... Postcode ....

Telephone .... Email..

Credit/Debit card number ☐☐☐☐ ☐☐☐☐ ☐☐☐☐ ☐☐☐☐

PIN number ☐☐☐☐ Security code ☐☐☐

Mother's maiden name .... Date of birth ..../...../.....

Signature ....

We claim to despatch orders on receipt. However, more than likely we will sit on your money for the thick end of a month. We will certainly do nothing about sending off your order until you have complained at least twice and written about us to Watchdog. You may be deluged for the rest of your life with further offers from carefully selected companies selling products that do not work. If you do not wish to receive these offers, please call in person at our Customer Service Office; 10354 Prairie Street Northwest, Saskatoon, Saskatchewan, Canada any Monday between 6.30 am and 7.00 am. Your statutory rights are not respected.

"My Rex Rissole is so light I was easily able to push it back and forth over a single lentil for more than twenty minutes."
Mrs A, Wessex

"I couldn't believe how light the Rex Rissole FlimsyLite 2000 was. I was able to carry it to the tip with one finger!"
Mrs B, Essex

Half the weight of vacuums twice as heavy. It's so light you'll feel like you haven't vacuumed at all. Which you won't have.

Black BAG — THE FAITHFUL BORDER BIN LINER

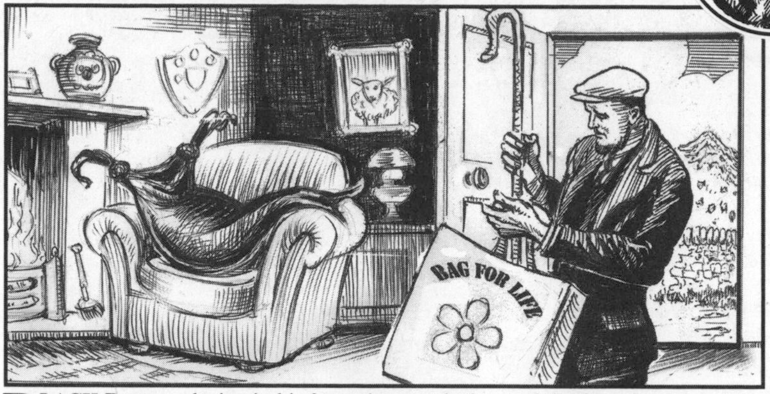
BAG FOR LIFE

BLACK Bag was dozing in his favourite spot in front of the fire when his master Andrew Selkirk the shepherd returned from a shopping trip into the local town. “Och, look whit I got from the Spar in Peebles,” he told his faithful binliner. “It’s a Bag fair Life. They’re a’ the rage, ye ken. Michty ecological and braw modern. But I’m afraid it means ye’re going fer landfill, auld pal.”

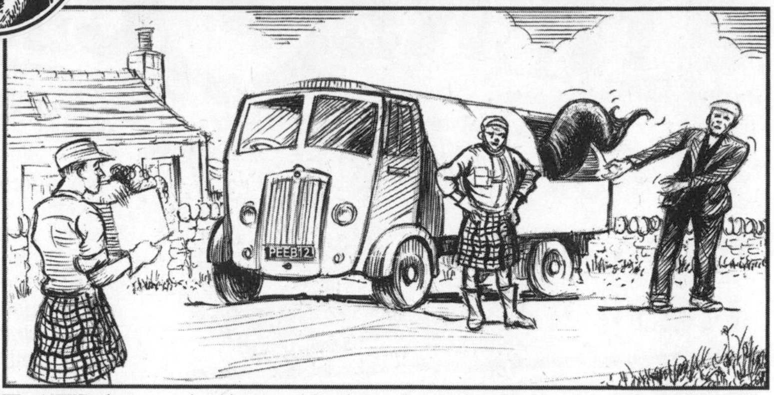
PEEB12

LATER that morning, it was with a heavy heart that the shepherd tossed his faithful polythene companion into the back of the council dustcart. “In ye go, Baggie,” he said. “We’ve had muckle adventures together, ye an’ me. But ma new Bag fair Life is greener an’ kinder tae the planet’s fragile ecosytem. He’s biodegradable, while ye’re carbon bagprint will stull be aroond in ten thoosand years frae noo.”

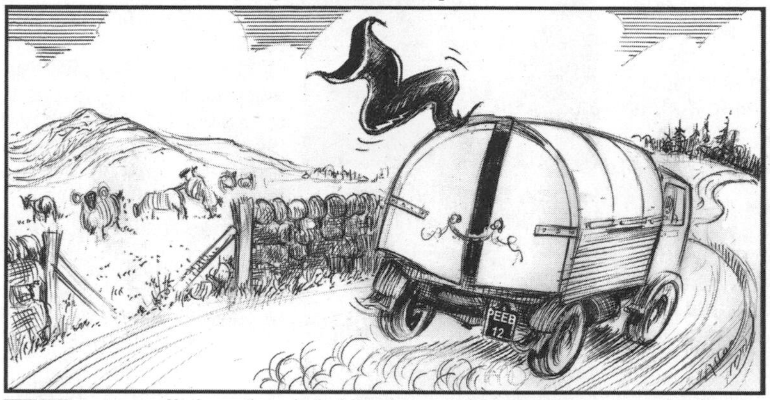
PEEB 12

THE cart set off along the windy hillside road that would take it to the Peebles County Council dump and the dreadful fate that awaited Black Bag there. But as the lorry rounded a corner, the wily binliner saw his chance. Taking advantage of a sudden gust of wind, he leapt from the wagon and made his escape over the heather-covered hills and mossy crags.

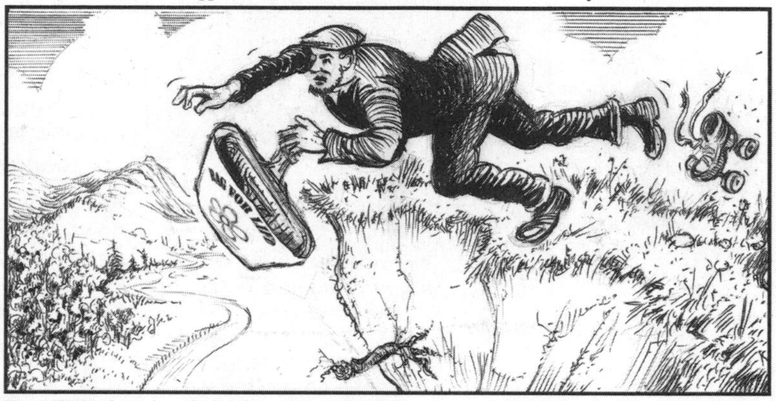
BAG FOR LIFE

LATER that day, Selkirk and Bag for Life went up onto the moors to check the shepherd’s flock of prize Herdwick sheep. “This is De’il’s Crag, the most dangerous part o’ the croft,” he explained. “Yon is a saxty foot sheer drop ontae the rocks below.” Suddenly, Selkirk let out a shout of alarm as he slipped on a carelessly-discarded roller skate. “Och! Help m’ boab! I’m fallin’!” he cried.

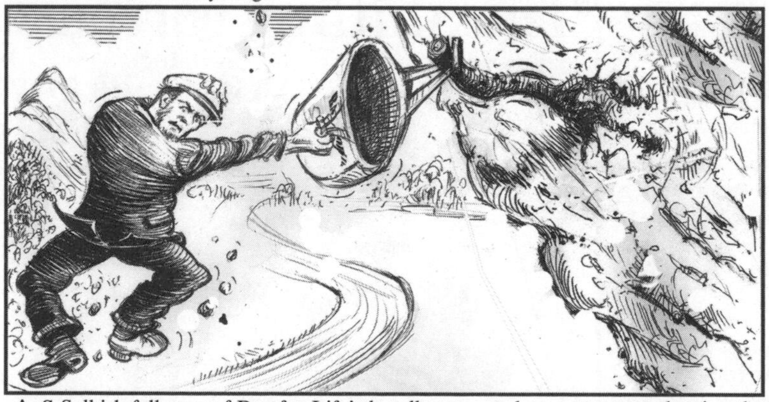

AS Selkirk fell, one of Bag for Life’s handles snagged on a tree root, leaving the shepherd dangling perilously above the rocks. “Michty me! Whit a thing tae happen, the noo!” he gasped. But when the shepherd looked up, he saw to his horror that Bag for Life’s hold on the tree root was getting weaker. “Crivvens! Yon wee handle is coming awa,” he said. “An’ a’ paid fufty pence for it an’ a’.”

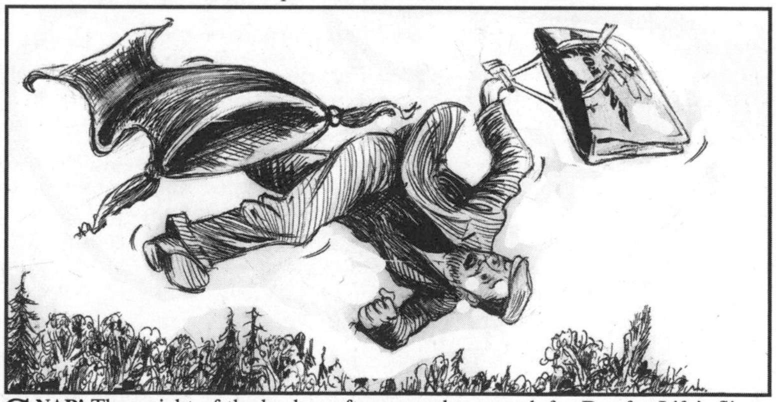

SNAP! The weight of the burly crofter proved too much for Bag for Life’s flimsy handles, and he plummeted towards the ground. But as he fell, out the corner of his eye, Selkirk glimpsed a familiar sight. The faithful border binliner that he had tossed in the dustcart that very morning was blowing towards him for all he was worth. “Here, boy! Baggie! Awa’ here!” he shouted.

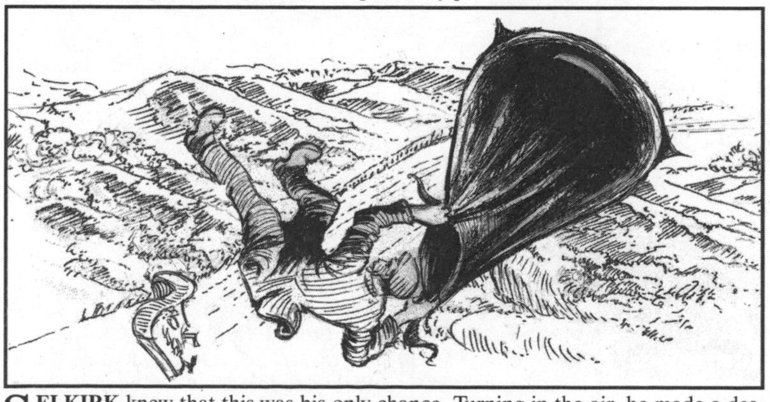

SELKIRK knew that this was his only chance. Turning in the air, he made a desperate lunge for Black Bag. “Hoots! Gotcha!” he whooped as he grabbed the binliner’s corners. The trusty bag caught the air and billowed out. And acting as a parachute, he lowered his master gently and safely to the ground below. “Och, boy. Am a’ pleased tae see ye,” he grinned.

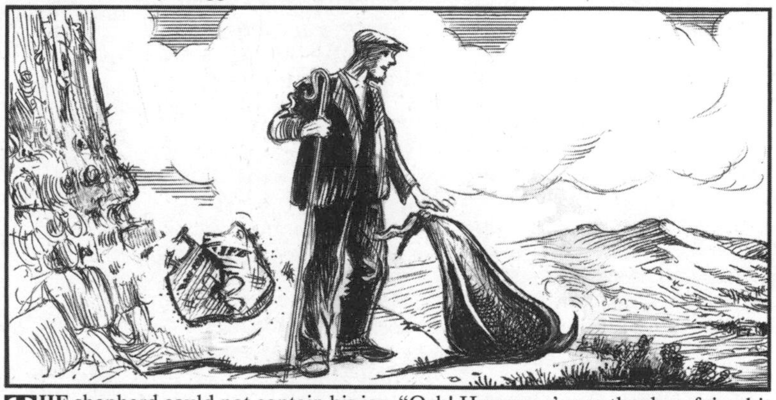

THE shepherd could not contain his joy. “Och! Hoo can a’ ever thank ye fair whit ye’ve dairn,” he cried. “I should never hae sent ye fair land fill. I was tryin’ tae save the environment. But in the end it was ye whit saved ma’ life!” The big shepherd had tears in his eyes. “Thae modern eco-bags are pure shite,” he said. “Ah’m goin’ tae fill Bag fair Life wi’ stoons an’ throw him in the River Peeb.”

THE END

LeTTERbOcks

PO Box 656,
North Shields,
NE30 4XX

E-mail
letters@
viz.co.uk

STAR LETTER

◆ COULD I use your pages to advise internet porn producers that there is no point titling a video clip 'Two Lesbians'? There is, for the purposes of light relief, no such thing as 'one lesbian.' The numbering of lesbians in video titles should begin at three, and anything more than five should be termed 'lots', because of the alliteration of the letter 'L'. The word 'licking' could also be added to emphasise this furthur. Unfortunately, I can't think of a word for fanny that begins with 'L'.

Alistair, Perth

◆ IF Febreze eliminates odours so well, why do they waste their time making the stuff with a lavender smell?

Dean Moncaster, e-mail

◆ I JUST saw Dr Hilary Jones talking about diabetes on GMTV. He said that there are currently 3 million sufferers in the UK and that figure is set to rise by 2025 to 4 million. Well, he may be a good doctor, but he's clearly rubbish at maths.

Paul Solomons, e-mail

◆ IF swimming is so good for you, why are whales so fat? Once again, the health Nazis seem to have got it wrong.

Paul Arger, e-mail

◆ I THINK I've worked out why the BBC3 sketch show *Horne and Corden* has been panned by the critics. All successful

comedy double acts have had the two syllable name first followed by the one syllable name, eg. Morecambe and Wise, Cannon and Ball, Little and Large, Mitchell and Webb... the list goes on. If they'd called the show Corden and Horne, and perhaps written something that wasn't shit, I'm sure they would have stood a better chance with the critics.

Bellman Marcela, e-mail

◆ WHEN you went into hospital in the seventies, all the nurses would be dressed like Barbara Windsor in *Carry On Doctor* with stockings and suspenders, high heels and little short aprons. Nowadays they wear mens' clothes like baggy green trousers, clogs and shapeless tops. No wonder the health service is in the state it is.

Downum Kraig, e-mail

◆ WHAT is it with these aliens always probing peoples' rectums? Surely if they've got the technology to travel halfway across the universe, they've got the imagination to think of something better to do than stick things up our arses.

Swartzell Yong, e-mail

◆ "I WON'T let the sun go down on me," sang pint-sized pop star Nik Kershaw in 1983. The only way he could have done that is to have spent the last quarter of a century circling the world in a jet at around 1000mph. Perhaps that's why he hasn't troubled the hit parade recently.

Lord Charles Gokkle of Geer

◆ HOW can historians be sure that Hitler committed suicide in his Berlin bunker in 1945? Admittedly they

found a body, but how did they know it wasn't the keyboard player out of Sparks? Or Blakey out of *On the Buses*?

Abbey Chavez, e-mail

◆ IT'S all very well Terry Pratchett campaigning for Altzheimer's awareness now that he's got it. He didn't seem to care too much about it when he didn't. Now he expects us to give two hoots about it when we haven't got it.

Funglin Zycixu, e-mail

◆ IN these economic times, I wonder if Sir Bob Geldof might ask those third world countries he got us to help a while ago if we could have a bit of our money back. they must be over their problems by now.

James Hollamby, e-mail

◆ LAST week I went to the doctor to get my haemorrhoids looked at, and she told me that a visit to the toilet for a number 2 should take no longer than 20 seconds. 20 SECONDS! Do any other

«top tips»

CATHOLIC emos. Avoid breaking with your religious doctrine by only cutting yourself with a fish knife on Friday.

Francine Conklin, e-mail

BIRO pen tops make authentic Battle of Hastings re-enactment helmets for stick insects.

Luke Gale, e-mail

WINDSCREEN covered in frost and late for work? Don't waste time scraping it off, simply drive around leaning out of your window like the woman in the Black A-Class Mercedes in rush hour traffic in Sedgley in the West Midlands.

Jonny Eye, e-mail

DRINKERS. Don't waste valuable time stopping to eat. Simply place a sausage end-up in your pint, then each time you take a sip, you can take a bite of your meaty beer-marinated treat.

Jamie Nedved, e-mail

PIGS. Avoid having your head on a dinner table by not eating whole apples.

Neil Polt, e-mail

RADIOHEAD. Make £150 million, then give away an album free saying you are against the business side of the music industry.

Colin, e-mail

INCREASE your life expectancy by expecting to live longer than you did beforehand.

Stavros Curlini, e-mail

GOTHS. Save money on expensive black nail polish by striking each fingernail sharply with a toffee hammer.

Ed Anger, e-mail

ALZHEIMER'S sufferers make perfect April Fool's Day prank victims all year round.

Adam Wigglesworth, e-mail

VERY OLD people in nursing homes. Go to bed each night in a suit and lie on your back with your arms crossed neatly over your chest. This could save a fair amount of money on undertakers' fees.

Fred Funk, e-mail

ANGLERS. Have both of your arms surgically extended by 4ft to add extreme exaggeration when describing the size of your catch.

Prof. Phil McCaverty, e-mail

The Shitting Forecast for Thursday 7th May 0700 GMT

SE Iceland
Faeroes
Bailey
Fair Isle
Viking
N Utsire
Hebrides
Cromarty
S Utsire
Rockall
Malin
Forties
Forth
Fisher
Tyne
Dogger
Irish Sea
German Bight
Shannon
Humber
Fastnet
Lundy
Thames
Dover
Sole
Plymouth
Wight
Portland
Fitzroy
Biscay

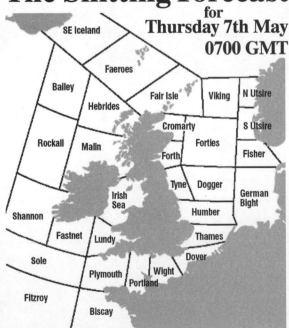

Viking, North Utsire, South Utsire: Constipation, backing up throughout the morning turning to egg-bound by late afternoon. **Forties, Cromarty, Forth, Tyne, Dogger, Fisher, German Bight:** Looseness for a time, moderate, turning rough later. **Humber, Thames, Dover, Wight, Portland, Plymouth, Biscay:** Stomach pains, severe, moving south later. Pebbledashing by early evening. **Fitzroy, Sole, Lundy, Fastnet:** Squitters, firming up later, leading to rabbit tods by afternoon. **Irish Sea, Shannon, Rockall, Malin, Hebrides:** Intermittent bubblepoo throughout the day with occasional squally showers. **Bailey, Fair Isle, Faeroes, Southeast Iceland:** Cramping and burbulence at first, turning flatulent by mid morning with rectal Krakatoas later.

readers' doctors talk a load of bollocks?

Jimmy Saxo, e-mail

◆ I HAVE a picture of a pub called the 'The Black Cock' which I feel is well suited for your *Letterbocks* page. Being ethnic myself, I do not believe it to be racist. Do you agree?

Alakh Saini, e-mail

THE BLACK COCK

** THAT'S a tricky one, Alakh. Let's throw the debate open to our readers. Whilst it is undoubtably childish to laugh at a pub called The Black Cock, is it racist as well? Write in to the usual address and let us know what YOU think. Mark your envelope 'The Big Black Cock Mass Debate.'*

◆ IN one of his books, Professor Richard Dawkins points out how lucky we are to be born, outlining the great scientists, poets and authors that could have been born in our place, but weren't. According to him, I should be full of joy that I made it here. As I sit here in my stained underwear, watching *Bargain Hunt* and eating a cream cake, I wonder if the eminent professor would like to rethink a few basic principles.

Nick, Dublin

◆ WOULD the lady on checkout 13 at ASDA in Wolverhampton please end her conversation with the colleague next to her and start scanning my goods before they go out of date.

Jonny Eye, e-mail

◆ I THINK whoever nicknamed The Titanic 'The Unsinkable Ship' was just asking for an ironic turn of events to occur when it set sail.

Ethan, e-mail

◆ HOW about a picture of Tom Jones after burns surgery standing next to a car made out of plywood and bits of leftover lean-to?

Jason Hazeley, London

HUSTLER

** A tricky one, Jason, but we finally managed to track one down.*

◆ I WAS watching the air hostesses demonstating the safety procedures on an Easyjet flight recently. When they came to the bit about evacuating during a crash in the sea they produced life jackets with Easyjet.com all over them. Now I don't know much about marketing, but I would think having your logo emblazened on the life vests of dead or injured crash victims would not be the best advert for your company.

Martin Christoff, e-mail

◆I WAS appalled to read in your last issue that Carol Kirkwood had been awarded the title Weather Presenter of the Year. The prize should have gone to BBC South East weathergirl Kaddy Lee-Preston who gives much better weather and has fantastic tits.

Sim on Cassini, e-mail

◆ WHEN I paid money into the bank, the nice lady behind the counter appeared to put it somewhere safe in a drawer behind her knee ready for when I came to collect it. Now it appears that as soon as I was out of sight one of her colleagues nipped down the bookies with it. In future I shall take all my money to the bookies myself and deposit it there for safekeeping.

Stevros, e-mail

◆ COULD I advise all your male readers that if you find yourself home alone in front of the TV watching porn and busting to crack one off, ensure that your front door is locked and your missus has not told Olive next door that she can let herself in and use your washing machine because hers is fucked.
If this should happen, remember, it's trolleys up, then the remote control, and not the other way round, as in the panic you may end up doing neither. Imagine that.

Jason Crawford, e-mail

◆ I LIKE eggs and I love sausages, but I don't like Scotch eggs. What's going on there, then?

I Dobson, e-mail

◆ 'YOU don't have to be a pilot to fly in the RAF' claims the advert. Imagine my confusion then as I was led away in handcuffs from one of their jets.

Jeremy Flynn, e-mail

UP THE ARSE

Sender:
M Armstrong, Buxton

CORNER

NAPALM DEATH AND THE MYSTERY of the HAUNTED WINDMILL
ONE DAY
WOW! CHECK OUT THE SPOOKY OLD WINDMILL, GUYS!
WOOOO!
OH MY GOSH! IT'S HAUNTED BY A G-G-GHOST!
WAIT A MINUTE! THIS ISN'T A REAL GHOST...
..IT'S JUST THE JANITOR, IN DISGUISE!
POLICE CHIEF
NICE WORK, NAPALM DEATH - YOU'VE SOLVED THE MYSTERY! NOW, HOW ABOUT PLAYING US ONE OF YOUR SONGS?
OK GUYS - LET'S GO! 1-2-3-4 -
YOU SUFFER BUT WHY?
NAPALM DEATH
THANKS FELLERS! THAT WAS GREAT!
PLEASE ACCEPT THESE WINDMILL-SHAPED SALT 'N' PEPPER SHAKERS, AS A REWARD
NO THANKS, CHIEF. I THINK WE'VE HAD QUITE ENOUGH OF WINDMILLS FOR ONE DAY!
HA HA!

Crisp ad King Lineker lifts lid on backstage cock-ups

BAGS OF FUN WITH GARY

GARY LINEKER'S hilarious crisp commercials have kept the country's sides splitting since 1994. But according to the former England captain, what happens behind the scenes is often even wackier than what finally makes it onto our television screens.

Speaking at a party to mark fifteen years as the telly face of Walkers Crisps, Gary revealed: "Honestly, if the viewers at home could see some of the stuff that happens when the cameras aren't rolling, they wouldn't believe their eyes!"

STEAL

"One of the earliest adverts I did featured me and my former England team-mate Paul Gascoigne in the crowd at a football match. The script called for me to catch him trying to steal one of my crisps and squeeze his fingers," says Lineker. "The ad ended with Gazza crying his eyes out, just like when he got booked in the 1990 World Cup."

"Everyone agreed it was one of the funniest ones yet."

"But it was nearly ME who was in floods of tears after filming ended for the day, when I looked at my pay cheque and realised that the agency had accidentally left a zero off the end of the amount!" he laughs. "It was made out for just £50,000!"

"You can be sure I went and had them fill in the correct figure straight away!"

Lineker, 49, has appeared in more than seventy TV spots for Walkers Crisps, so it's hardly surprising that it's not the only madcap mishap that has happened to him on set.

SAPPHIRE

"Another time I was starring in a commercial with the Spice Girls, when they were at the height of their fame," he recalls. "I had to flirt with each of them in turn, before finally pinching Sporty's bag of crisps and delivering the punchline: 'This is what I want, what I really, really want'."

"Everyone agreed it was one of the funniest ones yet."

"But I certainly wasn't laughing when I went into the bank later on that afternoon and the teller pointed out that my six-figure cheque for doing the ad had been incorrectly filled in. It was January, and the accountant at the agency had accidentally put the previous year in the box."

"I had them fetch the bank manager, but he wouldn't let me pay the money into my account either."

"I immediately rang up the agency and told them that what I really, really wanted was a six-figure cheque with the correct f***ing date on it," grins Gary. "Needless to say, they had one biked round pretty sharpish!"

WALKERS
Roast Chicken
CRISPS: A bag of Walkers yesterday.

GARY: **Behind the scenes goofs are laugh-a-minute.**

Over the years, Lineker's adverts have featured the popular Grandstand host in a variety of oddball costumes and disguises. "You name an outfit and chances are I've done a crisp ad in it," he laughs.

RUBY

"I'll never forget the time they had me dressed up as Cliff Richard in Summer Holiday, driving a double-decker bus. The script called for me to be so preoccupied with eating a bag of Walkers Crisps that I didn't notice a warning sign for a low bridge in the road ahead."

"The ad ended up with the bus sliced in half, and me driving off still eating my crisps!"

"Everyone agreed it was one of the funniest ones yet."

"But there was nothing funny about what happened when I opened my pay packet later that day. There had been some sort of a mix-up, and my cheque for a million pounds had been made out to someone called 'Gray Lineker'."

"Luckily, I was able to see the funny side. After a series of angry phonecalls, the agency provided me with a new cheque with the correct name on it, as well as a grovelling letter of apology."

"I still have a little chuckle to myself when I think back about that one."

WELD

After a decade and a half as their TV face, the former England legend says that the famous crisps have earned a special place in his heart. "They are a part of my life," he grins.

"Filming the Walkers ads is such a laugh that I honestly sometimes think I'd do them for nothing," he says. "But I wouldn't. It's really just the money I'm interested in."

IT'S THE BACONS...
MUTHA FATHA BIFFA
BZZZZ!!
HOO, BIFFA... KEEP STILL, SON...
SLOOP!
...THEZ A FUCKIN' WAASP ON YER NURZE... KEEP STILL...
SMACK!!
OOF!
HOO! WOT'S GANNIN' ON?
THEZ A WAASP ON BIFFA!
FUCKIN' 'ELL... KEEP STILL
SMACK! BIFF!! SOCK! SMASH!!
DINVEN'T MOVE, SON, OR IT'LL GAN FUCKIN' RADGE
BOOT! HOOF!
THERE! GORRIT... LUCKY WE WOZ 'ERE, BIFFA.
AYE! IF THAT BASTAAD 'AD OF STANG YUZ, IT'D OF HORT LIKE FUCK, MAN.

WARNING! READERS OF THIS PROBLEM PAGE MUST BE 18 OR OVER. ANYONE UNDER 18 MUST TURN TO T AGE

Your Seven Frame Freeview Starts Here!

Red Hot Miriam's Photocasebook

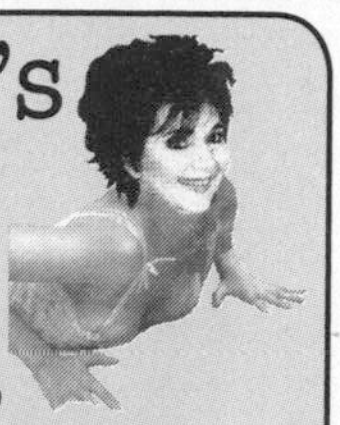

Kristel's Boiler Problem ~ Day 3

Young porn actress Kristel Gazer had paid £4000 to have a new boiler installed in her flat. But after just one week, it broke down. She invited her friend Suzi over for coffee to discuss the problem...

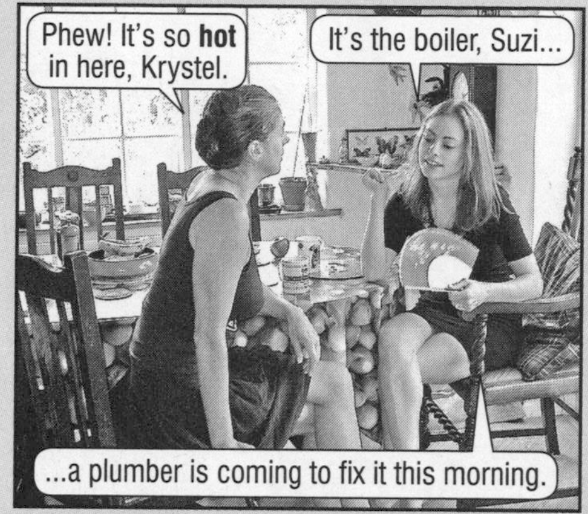
Phew! It's so **hot** in here, Krystel.
It's the boiler, Suzi...
...a plumber is coming to fix it this morning.

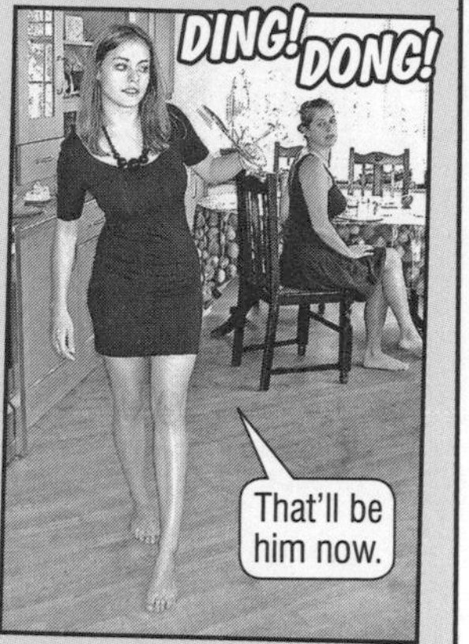
DING! DONG!
That'll be him now.

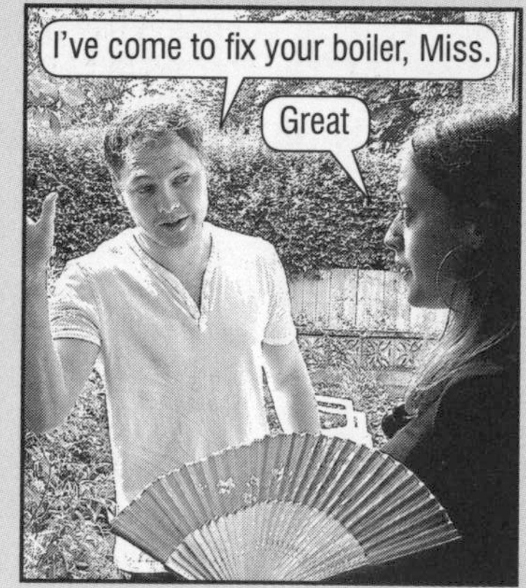
I've come to fix your boiler, Miss.
Great

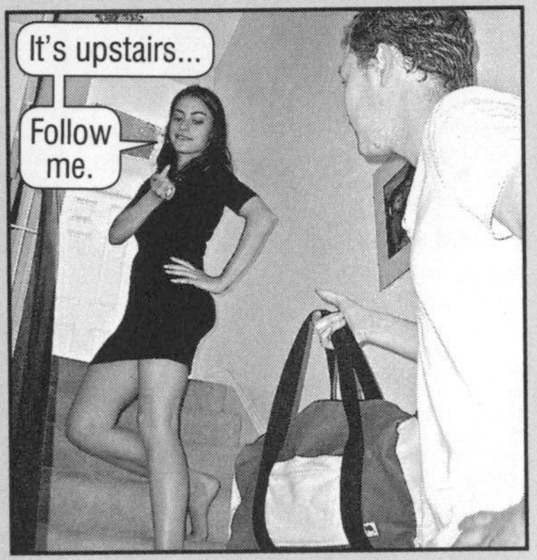
It's upstairs...
Follow me.

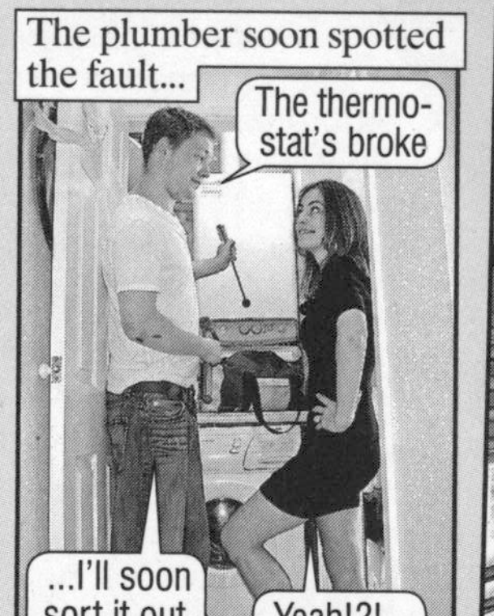
The plumber soon spotted the fault...
The thermo-stat's broke
...I'll soon sort it out.
Yeah!?!...

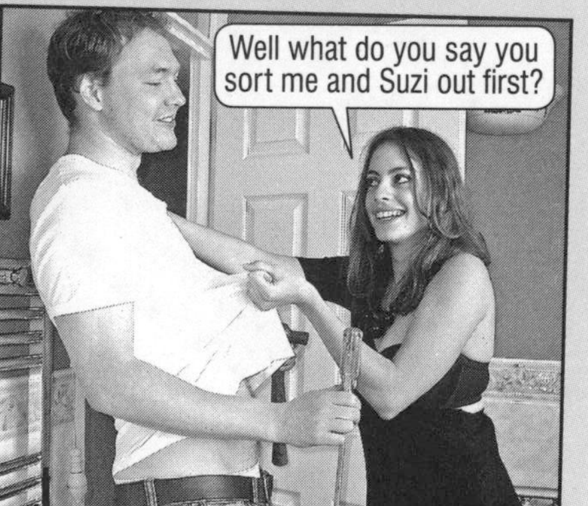
Well what do you say you sort me and Suzi out first?

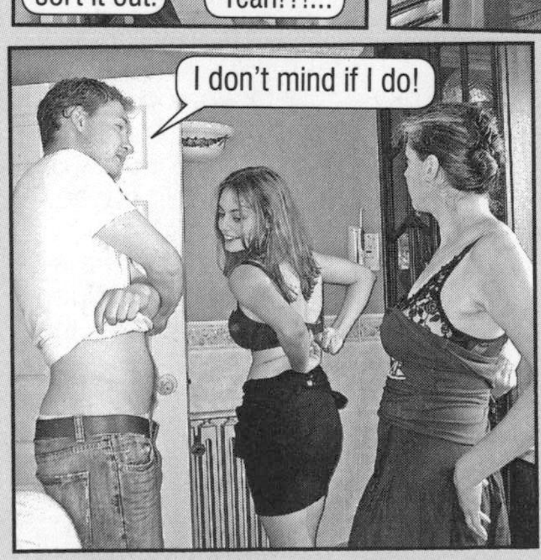
I don't mind if I do!

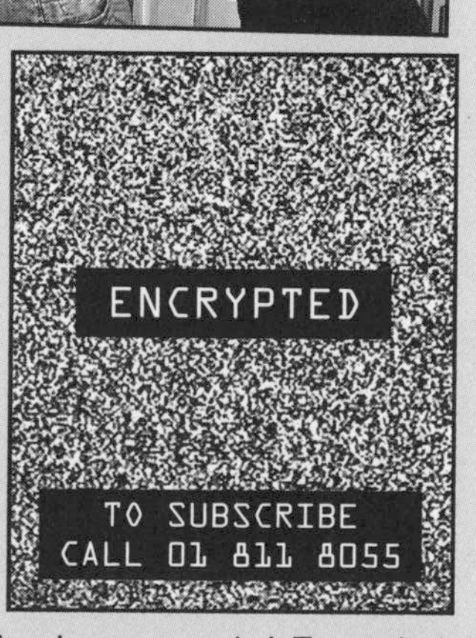
ENCRYPTED
TO SUBSCRIBE
CALL 01 811 8055

The ***Red Hot Miriam Photoproblem*** Freeview has now ended. To continue watching the action, simply call **01 811 8055** and subscribe to ***Red Hot Miriam Photoproblems*** for just £10 per issue. You can pay by credit or debit card and complete privacy is assured. The words 'Red Hot Miriam' will not appear on your bill.

Red Hot Miriam

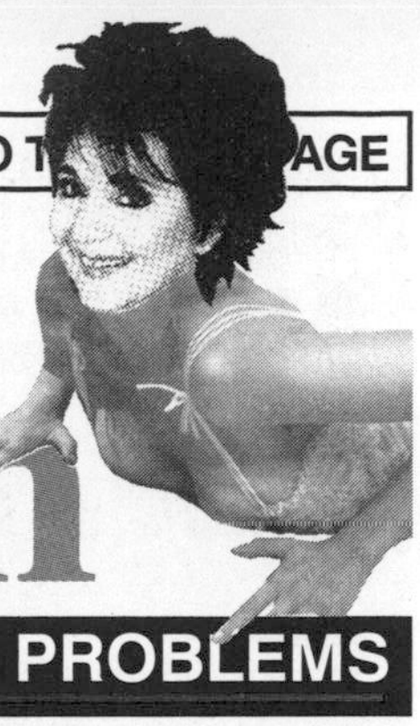

ANSWERS *YOUR* HARDCORE PROBLEMS

Cock-up in Limousine

Dear Red Hot Miriam,

THE OTHER day I was being driven through town in my stretched limousine when we stopped at a red traffic light. Suddenly, four gorgeous blonde women climbed in and sat beside me.

I am 23 and all the girls were 21. This happens to me on a regular basis so I wasn't really that surprised.

As usual, the conversation very quickly turned sexual and two of them began stroking my thigh. One thing led to another, and before long we were all completely naked, except for the stockings and suspenders that the girls were wearing. I was having sex with two of them whilst the other two performed a lesbian show on the seat opposite.

Just as I was about to do the money shot, it struck me that since it was being filmed for *Television X*, this sexual act could be classified as business. However, my insurance policy on the limo only covers me for social, domestic and pleasure. Would my insurance have been invalid if we had been involved in an accident?

Rod O'Steel, London

• *Red Hot Miriam says...*

YOUR insurance would certainly have been invalid had you been involved in an accident. However, social, domestic and pleasure cover does permit you to travel to and from your place of work. So in future, if you shoot these films on your way to the Television X studios, you will technically be covered.

Dear Red Hot Miriam,

MY GIRLFRIEND likes us to have sex in public places. She says the chance of getting caught makes her really horny.

I am 26 and she is 25 and we have been going out for a year.

Recently we went for a walk along a path which runs by our local golf course. Without warning, she pulled me down into a bunker, and we had it off in the sand while golfers strolled past just yards away, completely oblivious to the red hot action taking place right under their noses. The risk of being discovered turned her into a wild animal and we had the best sex ever.

Now she says she wants to give me oral somewhere even more public - at the Last Night of the Proms! As we live on the outskirts of Stevenage, I was wondering if you could recommend a good route to get us to the Royal Albert Hall.

Glint Thrust, Luton

• *Red Hot Miriam says...*

FROM the A602 roundabout, take the 5th exit onto the A1(M). Stay on the A1 till the Fiveways Corner roundabout, where you should take the 2nd exit. Stay on the A41past Brent Cross Interchange, go straight across the traffic lights at Swiss Cottage, before turning right onto the A501 at Baker Street junction. Then go left onto Old Marylebone Road, forward onto the A4209, take the A402, then left onto the A4204. At the lights, turn left into Kensington High Street, follow it for half a mile and you're there.

On track for lust

Dear Red Hot Miriam,

I COMMUTE into work every day on the train, whiling away the boring journey by doing a crossword in my daily paper. The other day, I was musing on a tricky clue when a busty young blonde woman entered my compartment and sat down on the opposite seat.

I am 38 and she was 22. She was wearing a really sexy short skirt and I couldn't help looking at her over my newspaper.

Imagine my excitement when she uncrossed her legs and I realised she was wearing stockings and no knickers. "Do you like what you see?" she said. "Perhaps you'd like to take a closer look." Needless to say, I didn't need asking twice!

I was soon stripped naked, having a steamy clinch with this horny nymphomaniac as the train rattled through the sleepy suburbs. The clue was 8 down; "Short Commercial break is without purpose" and I had blank D-blank-I-blank-blank. Do you have any idea what the answer might have been?

Cory Ramrod, Peterborough

• *Red Hot Miriam says...*

THE answer will have been "ADRIFT". "Ad" is the short commercial, a "rift" is a break and, according to my dictionary, one of the meanings of adrift is "without purpose".

Woooooo GARY DAVIES!

Ghost DJ's Bi in the Middle of the Night!

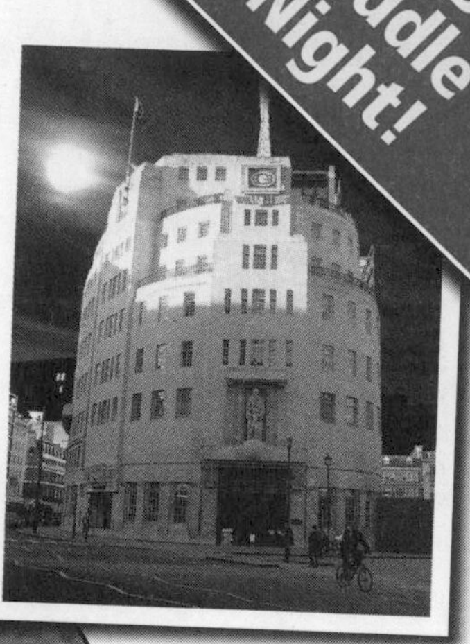

Exorcists were last night called in to rid Radio1 of a ghost that has been haunting the studios for the last three months. The spectre is believed to be that of former DJ Gary Davies who worked for the station up until 1993 and who, bizarrely, is still alive!

BBC bosses summoned ghostbusters after terrified staff reported seeing a lightweight shadowy figure drifting along the corridors late at night. Several staff also saw Davies's spook in studios, playing jingles and adjusting levels on a mixing desk.

Davies yesterday said he was gobsmacked when he heard about the hauntings. Speaking from his plush £12,000 bachelor flat in South Elmsall, he told us: "As listeners to my show on Dewsbury Hospital Radio will testify, I'm not often lost for words, but this whole episode has literally left me speechless. I don't even believe in ghosts, so to find out that a ghost of me is haunting Radio 1 has left me flabbergasted."

"Perhaps my spirit is restless. Maybe it has unfinished business at the station and is fated to endlessly roam the corridors of Broadcasting House in search of its lost career. I only hope the exorcists can finally lay my incorporeal soul to rest and put me out of my torment," he added.

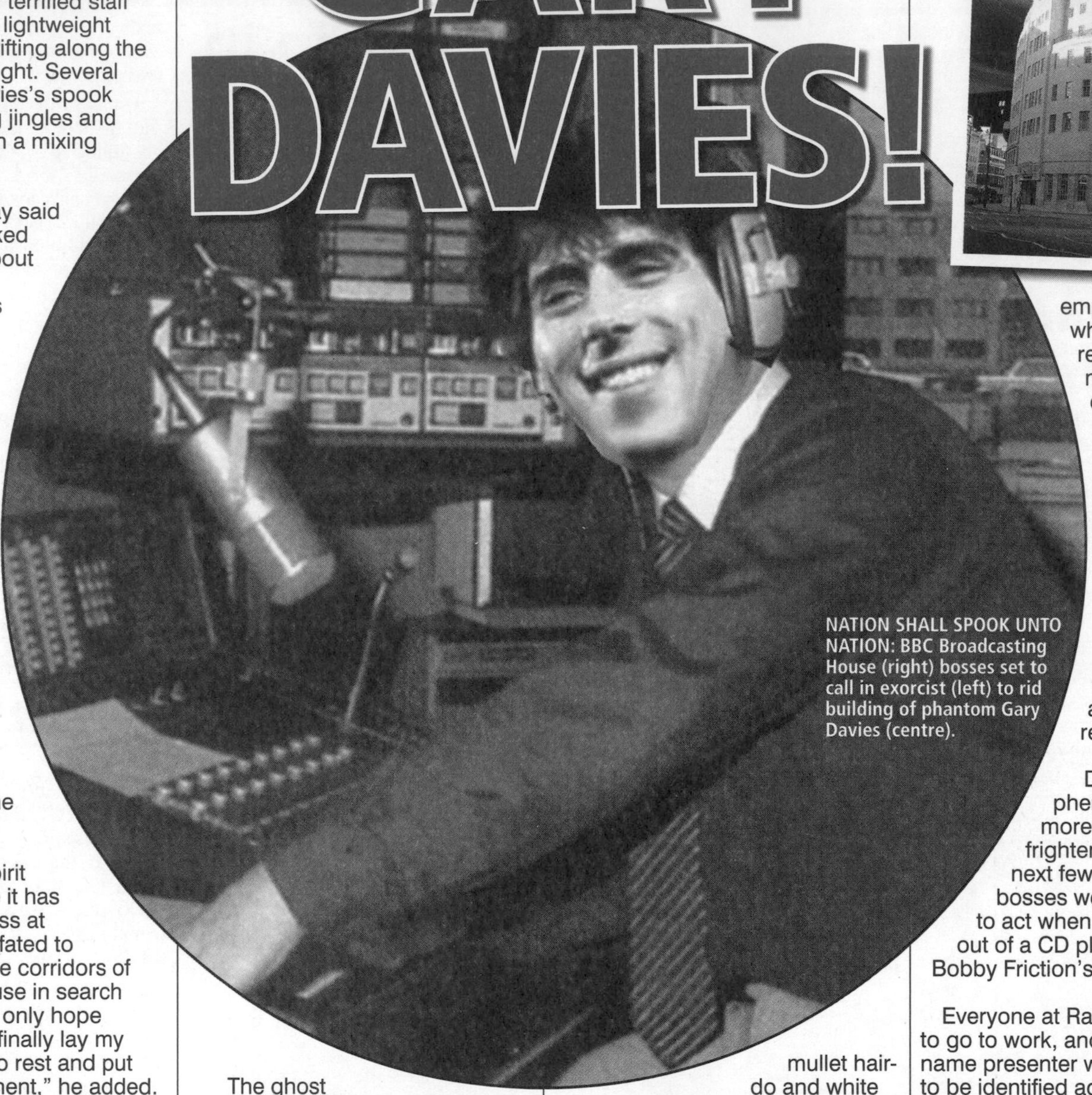

NATION SHALL SPOOK UNTO NATION: BBC Broadcasting House (right) bosses set to call in exorcist (left) to rid building of phantom Gary Davies (centre).

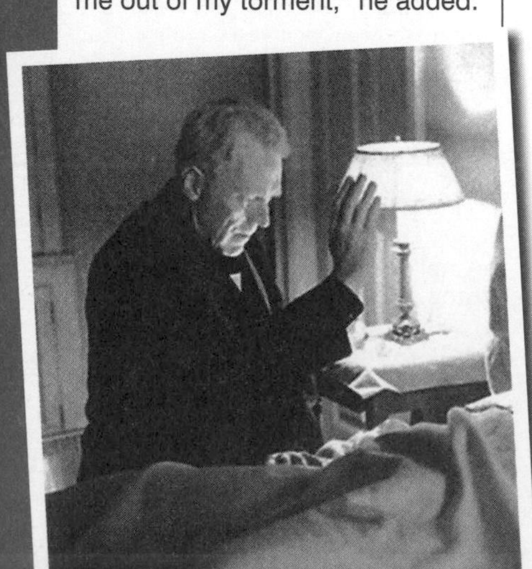

The ghost of Davies was first seen before Christmas by a BBC producer who asked us not to reveal his name. He told us: "I had stayed late one night to compile a playlist for the next day's breakfast show. I was in an editing suite when I suddenly felt that I wasn't alone. I looked up and saw a grey mist in the corner of the room which slowly began to take human form. With his big nose, mullet hair-do and white trainers, I recognised him immediately as Davies.

"The thing was, he was completely transparent. As soon as he manifested, the temperature and listening figures dropped. I couldn't get out of there fast enough, I don't mind telling you," he added.

"I don't even believe in ghosts, so to find out that a ghost of me is haunting Radio 1 has left me gobsmacked."

Other staff have also had frightening encounters with the spook. Many have heard unexplained bumps and thumps coming from empty rooms, whilst others have reported hearing mirthless laughter echoing through the station's corridors. Cups of coffee have regularly been upset in studios, and presenters have experienced unseen hands pulling CDs off shelves and flinging them around the record library.

Davies's ghostly phenomena became more extreme and frightening over the next few weeks. BBC bosses were finally forced to act when blood gushed out of a CD player during Bobby Friction's midnight show.

Everyone at Radio1 is pertrified to go to work, and one household name presenter who didn't wish to be identified admitted that he had soiled his pants during one encounter with the spook. He told us: "Chizzle my drizzle, dog. That spooky gangsta walked in through the wall mad straight, bang in my face. Word up. I dropped da bomb in my Calvin Kleins, big stylee."

Davies's phantom is not the first time that Radio 1 has been the centre of a ghost scare. In 2006, psychic researchers were called into the station when staff reported seeing a mysterious grey lady with red eyes walking slowly out of one of the studios. However, it later emerged that this was veteran broadcaster Annie Nightingale going to the toilet during her popular Saturday 5.00 am show.

Take a Viz

Woooo B40!

Spectre of Unemployment Looms for Ghosts

Millions of spooks, phantoms and spectres could be facing an uncertain eternal future as the global credit crunch begins to bite in the supernatural realm. Ghost analysts fear that the present downturn in the economy could leave millions of ghouls, poltergeists and wraiths out of work.

According to the Society for Psychical Research, demand for paranormal manifestations has dropped by 35% in the past 12 months, and the downward trend looks set set to continue for the foreseeable future. Traditional sources of employment for disembodied spirits, such as stately homes, former coaching inns and Victorian theatres, have all seen dramatic falls in visitor numbers, and so the market for restless supernatural presences to haunt them has declined accordingly.

Typical of employers who have been forced to lay off a number of ghosts is Ralph Goodchild, Chairman of the National Trust. He told us: "In 2005 we had over three thousand spooks haunting various historic properties around the UK. From headless horsemen galloping through castle grounds at midnight to sobbing children standing at the ends of beds on the anniversary of their deaths, we provided steady work for large numbers of phantasmagorical entities."

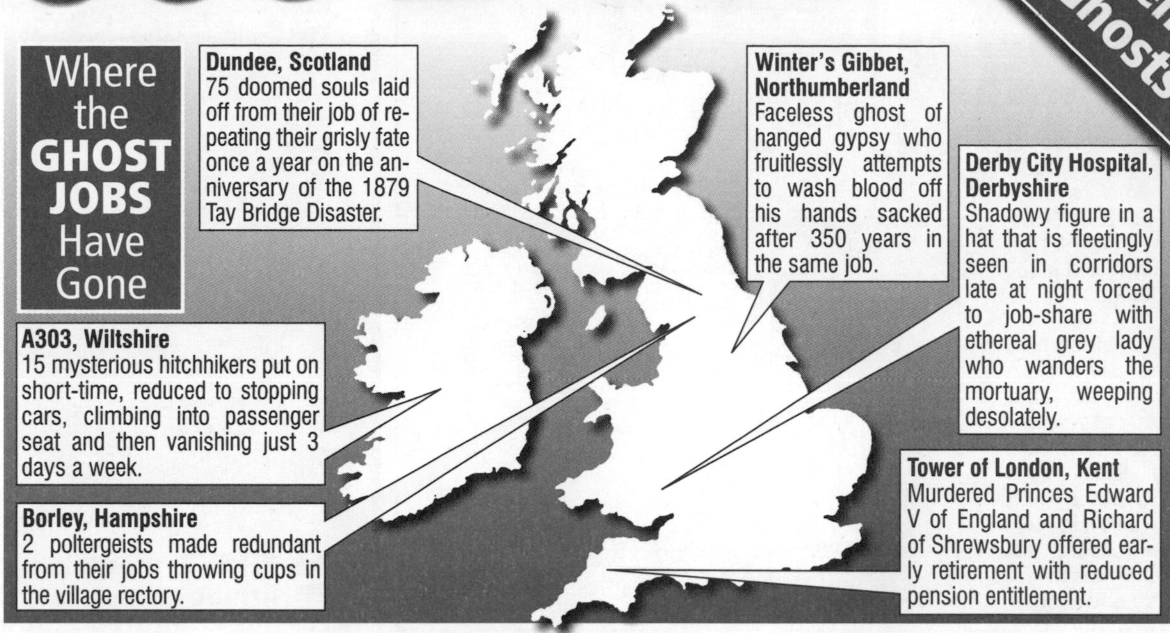

Where the GHOST JOBS Have Gone
Dundee, Scotland
75 doomed souls laid off from their job of repeating their grisly fate once a year on the anniversary of the 1879 Tay Bridge Disaster.
Winter's Gibbet, Northumberland
Faceless ghost of hanged gypsy who fruitlessly attempts to wash blood off his hands sacked after 350 years in the same job.
Derby City Hospital, Derbyshire
Shadowy figure in a hat that is fleetingly seen in corridors late at night forced to job-share with ethereal grey lady who wanders the mortuary, weeping desolately.
A303, Wiltshire
15 mysterious hitchhikers put on short-time, reduced to stopping cars, climbing into passenger seat and then vanishing just 3 days a week.
Borley, Hampshire
2 poltergeists made redundant from their jobs throwing cups in the village rectory.
Tower of London, Kent
Murdered Princes Edward V of England and Richard of Shrewsbury offered early retirement with reduced pension entitlement.

"But the financial crisis has hit our business hard," he added. "Today we've got fewer than fifty ghosts left on our books. In the last week alone I've had to lay off a cohort of Roman soldiers that it was said could often be seen at dusk, walking through the cellar of one our properties near York, a dozen lighthouse keepers who perished in fires whilst refusing to abandon their station and six headless Mary Queen of Scotses."

*Eek!*onomic Downturn Hits Things That Go Bump in the Night

And it's a story that is repeated across the country. Landlady Ann Berryman, who runs the Tudor Inn at Haddington, near Edinburgh, told us: "My pub was built on the site of an ancient graveyard where many plague victims were buried in the middle ages. We often used to joke that there were more spirits in the cellar than there were behind the bar!"

But according to Berryman, the pub trade has also fallen victim to the credit crunch. "We've had to make most of our ghosts redundant," she continued.

"We've only kept two on - a part-time grey lady who haunts the upstairs corridor at weekends and a shrieking fourteenth century priest who materialises in the toilets when there's a full moon."

Sudden unemployment can come as a shock to discarnate souls who have been used to centuries of steady haunting work. Some phantoms have been manifesting in the same place for hundreds - or even thousands - of years, and the realities of afterlife on the ghost dole can hit them hard. A DSS spokesman explained: "Claiming their entitlements is particularly hard for many spooks as many of them died before there were National Insurance numbers. The vast majority of wraiths have never paid into the Social Security system, so they usually only qualify for a one-off, discretionary hardship payment."

The spokesman continued: "To add to their difficulty, many restless presences only manifest at very specific times, such as All Hallows' Eve or midnight on the anniversary of their murder, so attending the Benefits Office at, for example, 11.15 in the morning every other Thursday can be problematic."

"And even if they do get there on time, the fact that they are made of ethereal ectoplasm makes it very hard for them to pick up a pen and sign on. Often, the best they can manage is to poltergeist it across the room," he added.

Haunted House Prices **"SET TO FALL FURTHER"**

In February, haunted house prices fell for the twelfth month in a row, according to figures released today by the Ghost of the Northern Rock Building Society. This means that an average two-poltergeist terrace in Leeds that would have cost £150,000 last year is now worth just £98,000. The slump in spectre-infested property values has left numerous haunted homeowners in negative equity. Many are now facing the very real prospect of having their possessed properties repossessed by their lenders.

Meanwhile, the present lower prices seem to be doing nothing to stimulate movement in the market. Igor Cushing of Addams Munster, a specialist haunted property agent, told us that sales of spirit-riddled dwellings are sluggish all round the country. He told us: "As an example, we have one property on our books that is an absolute snip at £200,000. It is a rickety, detatched Gothic building benefitting from a bat-infested belfry, permanently-locked attic, extensive cobwebbing throughout and perpetual exterior thunderstorm. This desirable property is set in its own generously-proportioned graveyard, and boasts fully-refurbished creaking floorboards, a charmingly sinister bricked up cellar complete with nightly scratching and muffled sobbing and all fixtures and fittings, to comprise paintings of previous tenants with moving eyes, animate suits of armour to all vestibules, landings and staircases, and self-ringing servants' bells."

"Eighteen months ago, this house would have sold for the full asking price of £350,000 as soon as we put the sign up," Cushing continued. "But since it went on the market a year ago, only one couple has been to see it, and they didn't even make an offer."

"Mind you, by the time they left the house after their viewing they had both lost their minds and their hair had turned white," he added.

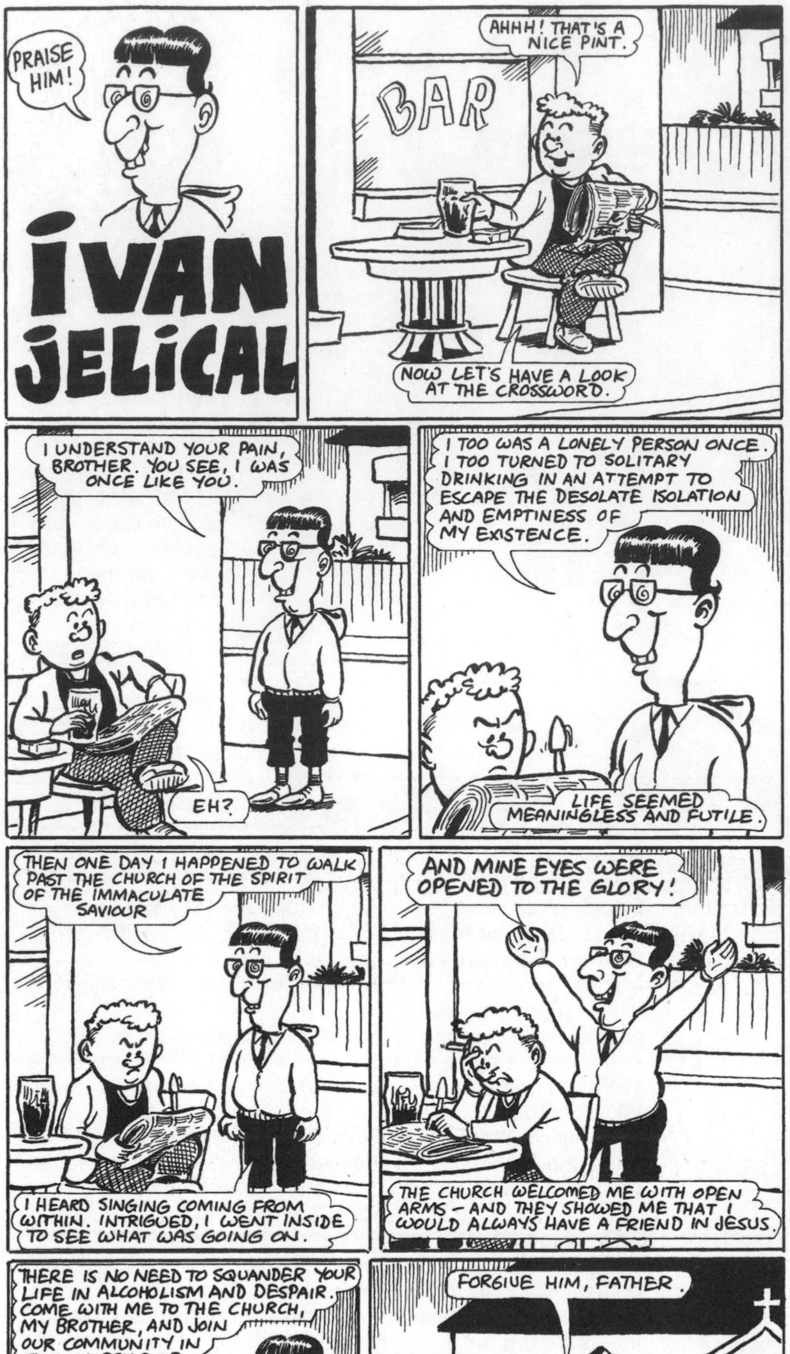
PRAISE HIM!
IVAN JELICAL
AHHH! THAT'S A NICE PINT.
BAR
NOW LET'S HAVE A LOOK AT THE CROSSWORD.
I UNDERSTAND YOUR PAIN, BROTHER. YOU SEE, I WAS ONCE LIKE YOU.
EH?
I TOO WAS A LONELY PERSON ONCE. I TOO TURNED TO SOLITARY DRINKING IN AN ATTEMPT TO ESCAPE THE DESOLATE ISOLATION AND EMPTINESS OF MY EXISTENCE.
LIFE SEEMED MEANINGLESS AND FUTILE.
THEN ONE DAY I HAPPENED TO WALK PAST THE CHURCH OF THE SPIRIT OF THE IMMACULATE SAVIOUR
I HEARD SINGING COMING FROM WITHIN. INTRIGUED, I WENT INSIDE TO SEE WHAT WAS GOING ON.
AND MINE EYES WERE OPENED TO THE GLORY!
THE CHURCH WELCOMED ME WITH OPEN ARMS - AND THEY SHOWED ME THAT I WOULD ALWAYS HAVE A FRIEND IN JESUS.
THERE IS NO NEED TO SQUANDER YOUR LIFE IN ALCOHOLISM AND DESPAIR. COME WITH ME TO THE CHURCH, MY BROTHER, AND JOIN OUR COMMUNITY IN THE WORSHIP OF CHRIST JESUS.
NO, YOU'RE ALRIGHT, TA.
FORGIVE HIM, FATHER.
CHURCH OF THE SPIRIT OF THE IMMACULATE SAVIOUR
FOR HE DOES NOT REALISE HOW HIS TRAGIC LIFE COULD BE TRANSFORMED BY JOINING THE FELLOWSHIP OF YOUR CHOSEN PEOPLE
LATER
CHRIST, WHAT A MESS. ONE OF THOSE APOCALYPTIC END-OF-THE-WORLD SECTS, WERE THEY, INSPECTOR?
CHURCH OF THE SPIRIT OF THE IMMACULATE SAVIOUR
LOOKS LIKE IT
Repent
POLICE DO NOT CROSS
THEY ALL TOPPED THEMSELVES BY DRINKING POISONED ORANGE JUICE

MAGICAL MYSTERY BORE: **Blaine plans playground stunt.**

Swinging in the Blaine

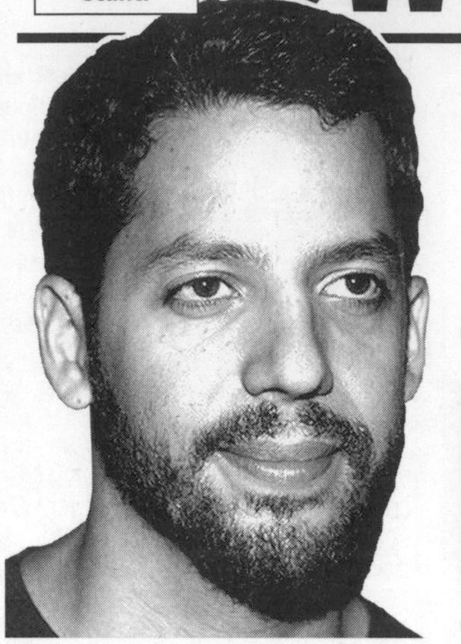

STREET magician *DAVID BLAINE* has confirmed plans to bring his latest death-defying stunt to a children's playground close to London's Royal Albert Hall.

The 36 year old New Yorker made the announcement during an appearance on ITV's *This Morning* programme. Speaking to a hungry Eamonn Holmes, Blaine said that he'd been using self-hypnosis and mind control techniques in a bid to become the first man to go all the way around on a playground swing.

FEAT

The feat was last attempted in 1921 by Harrry Houdini as part of a Royal Variety Show at the Alexandra Palace. But the renowned escapologist was killed when the trick went wrong, and many friends think Blaine is foolish to attempt to recreate what experts consider the world's most dangerous stunt.

Although he remained tight-lipped about how intends acheive the full 360 degree revolution, the spooky entertainer told *This Morning*'s unemployable viewers: "It has been a lifetime's ambition for me. Ever since kindergarten my dream has been to loop the loop on the swings. I've been working out both physically and mentally for over three years and now believe I'm ready to go."

OWL

But Oxford University Professor of Playground Propulsion Dynamics, David McGuinness told us: "To go all the way around on a swing, Blaine will have to be travelling at close to the speed of sound. In order to achieve this he will have to generate enormous momentum and thrust."

EXCLUSIVE

"He'll probably have to start stood up, give it a few good heaves and then when he's almost horizontal drop down onto the seat and lean right back. It's not impossible, but it will require superhuman strength and concentration," he added.

According to a source close to the magician, Blaine's father Albert will be on hand to give his son a few good pushes to get him going. "He's going to give David about half a dozen big pushes, and then he's on his own," he said.

ROCK ARKANSAS

But local council officials warned that the event may have to be put on hold as it contravenes strict health and safety regulations.

Park keeper Roy Jobsworth told reporters: "This playground is packed at the weekends, and there are often youths sitting on the swings drinking cider and refusing to get off."

"If Blaine turns up expecting to get a go on the swings, he could be in for a long wait," he warned.

& LARGE

Blaine, famous for spectacular stunts such as holding his breath, standing still and sitting down in a box last hit the headlines in 2006 when he successfully went down a hill on a bike doing no hands.

Riley's PLACE of PIES

WITH TV PIE EXPERT LISA RILEY

(who did *You've Been Framed* after Jeremy Beadle but before Harry Hill)

Wood you Pie-lieve it? with RONNIE WOOD

WOULD you believe the largest pie in the world was over 2 feet across...? Well over 2 feet across in fact, because it was more than 30 feet across! Much, much, more, because it was 85 feet across. And that wasn't even to the middle, because it was actually 280 feet across! Nobody knows who made it, where it was, or when, but it's a pie record breaker!

Wood you Pie-lieve it? with RONNIE WOOD

IN 1923, legendary escapologist Harry Houdini had himself baked into an enormous steak and kidney pie which was then pushed off the top of the Empire State Building. During his 1200 foot plunge, Houdini managed to eat his way through the pastry crust using a knife and fork which he had concealed up his bottom. He broke free of his pastry prison just two feet before it smashed into the pavement below.

MY SISTER once made me a pie as a birthday surprise which she said was a shepherd's pie. However, on eating it, I found that it consisted of mashed potato over a minced beef filling. I informed her that it was actually a cottage pie, as a genuine shepherd's pie is made from minced lamb. She insisted I was wrong and we had an argument that developed into a slanging match. That was over twenty years ago, and I haven't spoken a single word to her since that day, which at times has been difficult as we are Siamese twins joined at the forehead.

Mavis Dalrymple
Herts

I LOVE pies, and my favourite nursery rhyme is Simple Simon, because it contains several references to pies. Yum! Yum!

Group Captain E Barnes-Wallace
Letchworth

I AM the chairman of EMI Records, and I love pies so much that I'm releasing Pie Gold, a box-set of albums consisting of nothing but songs about pies. Unfortunately, I have only thought of one song so far - American Pie by Don McClean, and unfortunately, I am unable to include it as it is on Atlantic Records. Can any of readers think of 100 or so songs about pies that are on EMI Records? The box-set has been flagged in the press with a release date of 20th September, so I would appreciate ideas sooner rather than later.

Tony Wadsworth
EMI Records

I LOVE pies, and in 1940 I joined a monastery because I was told I could lead a very pious lifestyle. What a load of bollocks. I've spent almost seven decades with no trousers or socks, praising God and shit and pulling on a bastard rope to ring a fucking bell. If that wasn't arseache enough, they wake me up at four in the morning to chant and tend a fucking beehive. As for pies, there hasn't been a sniff of one since the day I joined. All we eat is fucking porridge.

Brother Dominic Anselm
Brinkburn Priory

AMERICANS often say something is "as good as Mom's apple pie". Well, I could not use my mother's apple pies as a standard of excellence, as they were truly dreadful. She suffered from lifelong diarrhoea and had a psychological aversion to washing her hands. Consequently, her apple pies, as well as everything else she cooked, had a distinctly unpleasant aroma of excrement about them.

Hector Fibreboard
London

WITH reference to Tony Wadsworth's letter *(above)*, how about the Jennifer Lopez song Cherry Pie? It's always been my favourite song about pie, and I would love to see it included in the box set.

Hampton Doubleday
Surrey

** I PASSED your suggestion onto Mr Wadsworth, but he pointed out that Cherry Pie was a track on the 2005 album Rebirth and was never released as a single. He added that he was really looking for chart singles about pies.*

THE OTHER day I baked a lovely pie. It was piping hot from the oven so I opened a window and placed it on the ledge to cool. Now in the olden days, the worst that would happen would be the smell attracting an ever-hungry, overweight public schoolboy, who would snaffle the pie and run away chortling. However, on this occasion, a small, hooded youth climbed in through the window, completely ignoring the pie, stole my video and did a duty on my living room carpet. What a sad indictment of British society.

Marjorie Curbishley
Leeds

I READ the chairman of EMI's letter regarding songs about pies and was immediately reminded of The Four Tops' single Sugar Pie, Honey Bunch, my all-time favourite song about pies. No box-set about pies worth its salt would be without that one.

Toby Carvery
Dundee

** WHEN I passed on your suggestion, Mr Wadsworth insisted that the song you referred to was I Can't Help Myself. Sugar Pie, Honey Bunch was actually a subtitle of the song, added in brackets after the main one. Mr Wadsworth was insistent that, to be included on the box-set, the word "Pie" must appear in the main title.*

IN 1972 my husband and I went on holiday to Cairo, as it had always been our dream to see the Pyramids and the Sphinx. On our first night in the hotel, we were served pie in the restaurant, and it was absolutely delicious. So delicious in fact, that we spent the whole fortnight in the hotel restaurant eating pies and never got to see the wonders of ancient Egypt. We have been back to the same hotel every year since, and although we have yet to see the Pyramids and the Sphinx, we have eaten a lot of lovely pies!

Eileen Monopoly
Exeter

WITH REFERENCE to Tony Wadsworth's request for songs about pies. What about Piggy Pie by Insane Clown Posse?

Hilda Eckersdyke
Halifax

** MR Wadsworth said that the box-set would be aimed at a family audience. The first verse of Piggy Pie reads "Come and get it! Wooo! We got some fresh vittles for your fat, chicken ass to snack on, bitch! So here, start wit' a slice of this fresh piggy pie, muthafukka!", and he fears that an explicit lyrics sticker could alienate a part of his target audience.*

FURTHER to Tony Wadsworth's request for pie songs. What about Pie Jesu by Charlotte Church?

Barry Island
Cardiff

** MR Wadsworth says that unfortunately, although it is spelled "pie" it is actually pronounced "pee-ay", and so could not be included in a box-set of songs about pies.*

Tell Me Pie

• **I'VE JUST** cooked a lovely apple pie in an 8 inch pie dish, that is to say, one with a radius of 4 inches. Could you tell me if there is a universal mathematical constant which governs the relationship between the radius, circumference and area of my pie?

Edna Shakuntaladevi
Troon

with Dr Magnus Pie(k)

Dr Pie(k) answers...

THERE is indeed, and you are not going to believe its name... It's called "Pie"! And it's exactly equal to 3 and a bit. The aroundness of your pie is equal to the twice the radius of your pie, timesed by Pie. So that's 8 times 3 and a bit, which means that your pie is exactly 24 and 8 bits of an inch around. As for the area of your pie, that is defined by the formula Pie timesed by the radius of your pie squared. 4 squared equals 16, times 3 and a bit gives 48 and 16 bits. Since there are a lot of bits, they'll probably add up to about two, so the answer will be almost exactly 50 inches, give or take one or two bits of an inch.

PIE JOKES

Q: What do you call a queer pie? And no, I wont use the word 'gay' as the politically correct brigade would have us do. It's sodomy, pure and simple, and no amount of dressing it up with fancy words will change that.
A: A fruit pie.

Major Hepscott-White
Woking

Q: What sort of pie has anal and/or oral sex with men in a public lavatory?
A: A cottage pie.

Major Hepscott-White
Woking

Q: What pie parades around the place with an affected feminine gait, waggling its buttocks from side to side, attempting to entice men into a public lavatory in order to engage in anal and/or oral sex with it in a filthy cubicle?
A: A mince pie

Major Hepscott-White
Woking

Wood you Pie-lieve it? with RONNIE WOOD

IN 1996, Cary Grant married Marilyn Monroe inside a giant pie! Construction of the wedding venue required 3800 chickens, 2 double decker buses full of button mushrooms, enough pastry to cover Wembley Stadium and as much gravy as the Post Office Tower. The couple later consummated the marriage in a four-poster Cornish pasty in the bridal suite of the Beverly Hills Hilton.

Wood you Pie-lieve it? with RONNIE WOOD

CRIMEAN WAR nurse Florence Nightingale invented the pie chart in 1855 in order to demonstrate graphically to the military commanders that hospital-borne infections were killing more soldiers than the enemy. Ironically the pie itself wasn't invented until 1895 by Sir Thomas Ginster, who named his circular foodstuff after the round charts invented by Nightingale forty years earlier!

Door-to-Door Salesman Nigel Lifts Lid on Life of Celebrity Nookie!

My Brushes

WE ALL dream of having sex with the stars. Whether it's enjoying a passionate kiss with Patsy Kensit, a frantic bonk with Fiona Bruce or unprotected anal with Ursula Andress, it's everyone's secret fantasy to go all the way with a famous stunner. But for one man, door-to-door brush salesman NIGEL WINKLE, that dream of celebrity romps comes true on a daily basis.

In a career spanning 20 years, the Essex-based Romeo has hawked his products to literally hundreds of stars from stage and screen. And Nigel, 62, says that his celebrity customers' appetite for rumpy-pumpy is still as insatiable as ever. In a new book out today that will send shock waves through the showbiz world, he lifts the lid on his orgy-filled lifestyle of brushes and sex.

"A brush salesman is every woman's secret fantasy lover," says Nigel. "They see him as a mysterious stranger, a bit like Clint Eastwood in High Plains Drifter. He's an enigmatic loner wandering from town to town, and that charismatic persona drives women wild."

"And believe you me, the stars are no different," he adds with a wink.

Nigel admits that he plays up to the customers' expectations of him. "I do turn on the charm with the ladies," he smiles. "And thanks to my shiny suit, smart grey slip-ons and with a suitcase of brush samples slung rakishly under my arm, I'm simply irresistible."

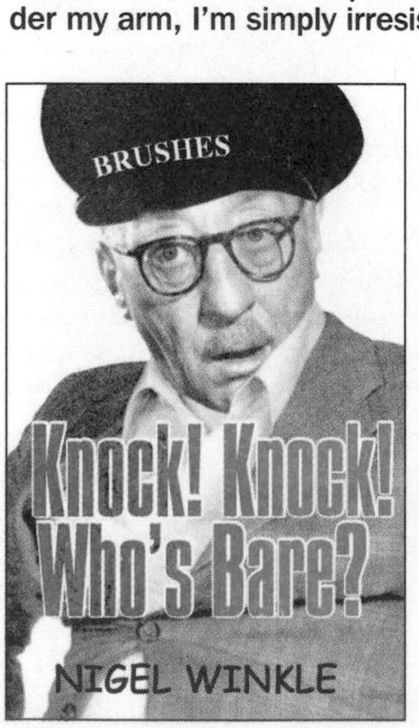
BRUSHES
Knock! Knock! Who's Bare?
NIGEL WINKLE

The roll-call of celebrity stunners who have fallen under Nigel's spell reads like a Who's Who of showbiz A-Z listers. And now, in a series of explosive extracts from his book, *Knock! Knock! Who's Bare?* (Branflakes Books, £1.99), **he spills the beans on his saucy brushes with the stars and the legions of showbiz beauties he swept off their feet.**

I got my 'Jolies' off Angelina

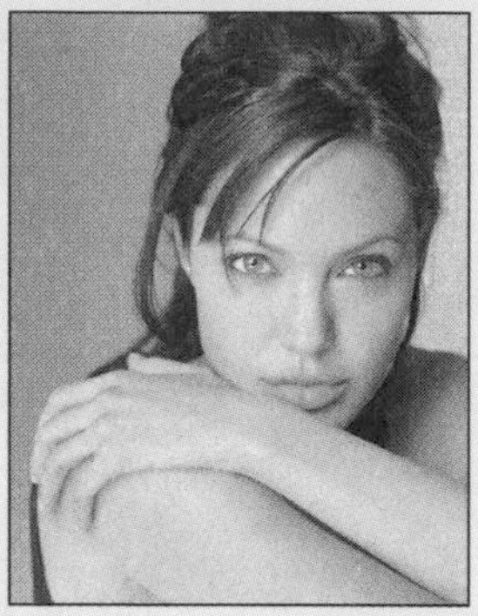

PERHAPS one of the most amazing episodes in my career happened when I was doing the doors on an upmarket estate in Buckinghamshire. I knocked on the door of one of the biggest houses on the block and was surprised when it was answered by *Tomb Raider* stunner Angelina Jolie.

I remembered reading in the paper that she was renting a house while her husband Brad Pitt made a film at nearby Pinewood Studios. I opened my case and showed her my products, and she seemed particularly interested in the *Hercules 3000*, a rather good lavatory brush that was new to my range.

It was quite a piece of kit. The head boasted 3000 polypropylene bristles, and the handle had a comfortable moulded handgrip. It also incorporated an ergonomically-designed 20° kink in the handle so it could get right into the U-bend and shift really awkward skidmarks. We were banging them out for £1.70, and that included a sleek drip stand.

Angelina asked if she could see it in action, quipping that her hubby had had a bad case of the Brad Pitts the night before. Sniffing a sale, I rolled up my sleeves and followed her upstairs to the bathroom. Imagine my surprise when I lifted the lid to find the toilet nipping clean. But I was in for an even bigger shock when I turned round. Angelina was standing there watching me and licking her trademark lips... dressed in her Lara Croft costume!

The story about the dirty toilet had been nothing more than a ruse to get me upstairs where she wanted me.

I'm too much of a gentleman to recount what happened next, suffice to say that *The Bone Collector* star added another one to her collection that afternoon. And far from being *Gone in Sixty Seconds*, I reckon I lasted nearly twice that before going off. It was a couple of minutes of erotic lust and sexual abandon that I will never forget. However, our tryst ended on a sour note.

As we lay gasping and spent on the silken sheets of her king-sized bed, I asked Angelina how she would like to pay for her toilet brush. To my dismay, she said that she would not be buying one, as she had seen something similar in the local Spar for £1.59. I pointed out the quality of the *Hercules 3000* and explained that if you buy cheaply, you buy twice, but she was having none of it. Sadly, I picked up my samples case and left the house without making a sale.

My Mixed Doubles Love Match with Tennis Ace Anna

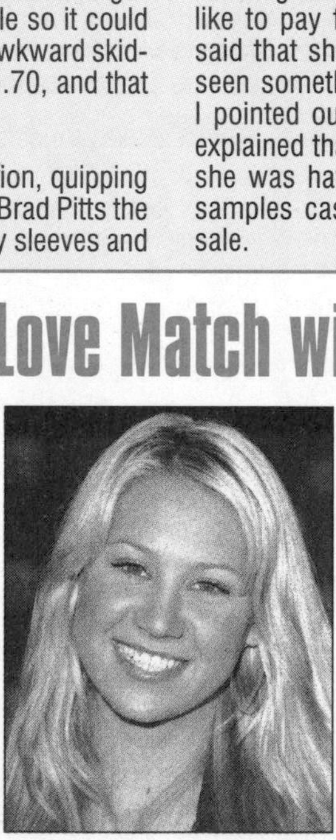

LEGGY blonde tennis star Anna Kournikova travels the world as one of the biggest attractions of the tennis circuit. So it was quite a surprise to find her pegging out the washing as I walked up the drive of a £20 million Wimbledon mansion. I knew she was sexy, because I'd seen pictures of her on the internet, but in real life she was even more attractive than I had imagined. She had long, flaxen hair, gorgeous, slender legs, skin like purest alabaster and laughing eyes that twinkled in the sun like limpid pools of the purest azure. And cracking tits.

I asked her if she would be interested in seeing some brushes and when she said she was, I opened my case to show her some of the items I had on offer that week. She pointed to a dustpan and brush, the *Crumbmaster GX Compact*, and asked if it could cope with cigarette ash. I explained that thanks to the unique ionised bristles, the *Crumbmaster* literally repels dirt and debris into the dustpan, leaving the floor AND the brush perfectly clean - *Crumbmaster* clean. I explained that in independent tests, the *Crumbmaster* had easily outperformed other leading brushes costing twice as much.

She flashed me a cheeky grin and asked me to prove it, saying that she had knocked an ashtray off her bedside table onto the polished floorboards of her bedroom.

There is something about a man demonstrating a brush that seems to act on some primitive sexual instinct in a woman. Anna was suddenly a wild animal, and I was her prey. I had only swept up half of her dog-ends when she leapt on me and dragged me onto her giant fur-covered waterbed.

What happened next was very private and between the two of us, but I will say this: if you think she makes a lot of grunting noises playing on the tennis court, you should have hear her receiving service from yours truly. It was a love game that quickly went to three sets, and when it was over we both fell back exhausted, panting and unable to speak.

When I finally got my breath back after my shattering climax, I suggested to Anna that she might want to settle up for her dustpan and brush. She went very red, and said that £2.99 was a lot of money and that she would have to think about it. I said that she could have it on approval for a week with nothing to pay, but she declined. I left her an order form in case she changed her mind and left the house.

A week later, a friend of mine told me he had read an interview with Anna Kournikova in *Take A Break* magazine where she was talking about a dustpan and brush set that she'd bought from Wilkinson's for 98p. I have never felt so used in all my life.

with Fame

BB Davina McCalled Me to Diary Room... for Sex!

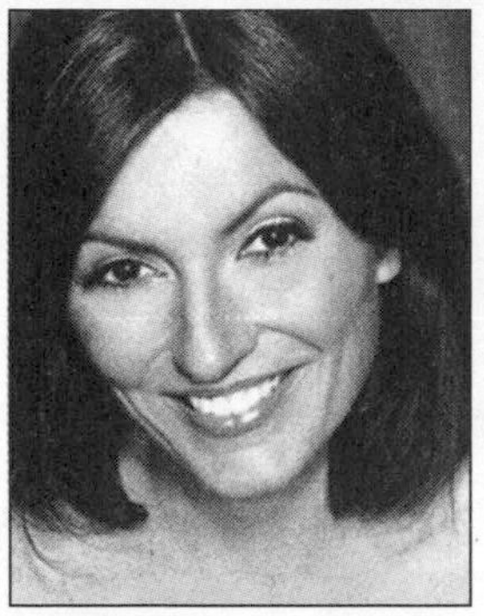

I WAS out on my rounds a couple of years ago when I saw a house that looked familiar. I couldn't place it at first, but when I rang the bell and the door was answered by a gorgeous brunette, the truth sufddenly dawned on me. It was the *Big Brother* house, and I was stood on the step talking to TV beauty Davina McCall!

I opened my case and stuck my foot in the door as usual, but there was no need. Davina invited me in, telling me that she was just tidying the house up in preparation for the new series, and she wanted an upholstery brush to get some lint off the Diary Room chair. It just so happened that I had with me a sample of a brand new product - the *Rontel FuzzBeGone* - and I offered to give her a demonstration.

She led me up a corridor to the Diary Room. I had seen it a thousand times on television, but it was much smaller in real life. We were pushed quite close together as I started my demonstration. Davina watched me with her sexy, dark brown eyes as I explained the secret of the *FuzzBeGone*'s effectiveness - its revolutionary patented directional bristle system. I couldn't believe my eyes at what happened next. She started undoing her dress while I showed her how, brushed one way across upholstery it lifts lint out of the pile like a magnet and then, unlike other products on the market, when you brush it the other way onto a cloth, how it deposits the fluff.

By the time I got to the bit about how the *FuzzBeGone* always maintains its full 100% capacity to pick up stray threads, pet hairs and fluff, Davina was completely naked. She made a grab for the front of my trousers and pushed me back roughly onto the Diary Room chair. I can only think that my brush patter had worked its magic even more effectively than usual. She was like a wild cat, desperate to sink her claws into my flesh.

I'm too much of a gentleman to go into detail about what happened next. But as every single moment was captured by hidden *Big Brother* cameras, I'm sure the entire two minutes of unbridled sex action will make its way onto the internet sooner or later.

Panting for breath, I pulled up my trousers and fastened my flies. Davina, still flushed from her multiple orgasms, picked up her underpants from the floor and got dressed. I popped the *FuzzBeGone* back into its packaging and handed it to her, explaining that the price of £3.50 included a free, washable lint-removal cloth. To my astonishment, she told me she wasn't going to buy it. The budget money, she said, would instead have to be spent on a new Diary Room chair.

When I turned round, I saw what she meant. The *Big Brother* chair was just a smouldering pile of splintered wood, torn cloth and bent springs. In the throes of our passion, we had quite literally bonked it to bits!

Cheeky Girls Touched my Bum... and my Cock!

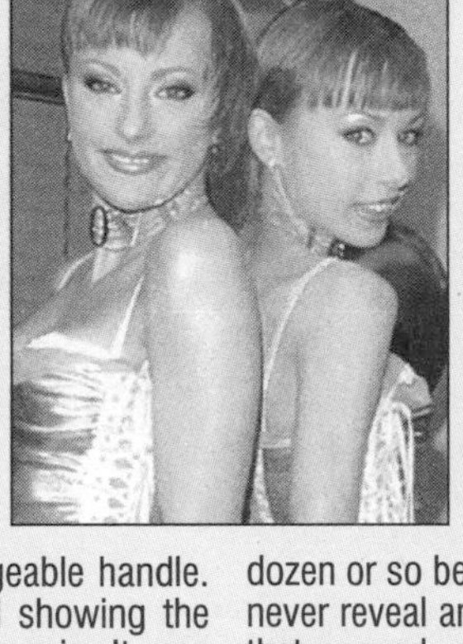

WHEN I knocked on the door of a flat near to the Houses of Parliament, I didn't expect a pair of successful singing stars to answer the door ... and they didn't. Instead it was the Cheeky Girls, who invited me inside. They explained in broken English that their husband, Liberal MP Lemsip Opek, was out taking part in an important debate about the Iraq War, whilst they had stayed at home doing their hair.

As luck would have it, I'd just taken delivery of a new range of ergonomically-designed hairbrushes with an interchangeable handle. I opened my case and had just started showing the girls my wares when the doorbell rang again. It was the Pussycat Dolls, Girls Aloud and Atomic Kitten. The room was soon full of gorgeous women and Kerry Katona.

The girls crowded round me as I launched into a pitch for the new brushes. I was explaining how the nylon bristles generate a static charge that prevents split ends and tangles, but they weren't listening. Every single one of them was undressing me with her eyes, imagining what lay underneath my stylish polyester suit and aertex underwear.

Like a true professional, I continued with my demonstration, showing how the various versatile heads could be used for brushing, teasing and backcombing. But I soon became aware that they weren't undressing me with their eyes any more, they were undressing me with their fingers!

Pretty soon I was standing naked in front of them. There were gasps when the girls caught sight of my salesmanhood. What happened in the next couple of minutes is between me and those dozen or so beautiful pop stars and Kerry Katona. I will never reveal any details of the frantic, sweaty sex orgy that ensued, save to say that every woman present reached a height of passion that she could previously only have imagined in her wildest dreams.

Afterwards, I got a thick wad of order forms out of my case, expecting that each of the girls I had just bonked would be buying a set of brushes at the introductory price of just £4.99 a set. And it really was a bargain - they should have been £6.99. But sadly, I didn't make a single sale that afternoon. My love-making had exhausted them all so much that each and every one of them was fast asleep.

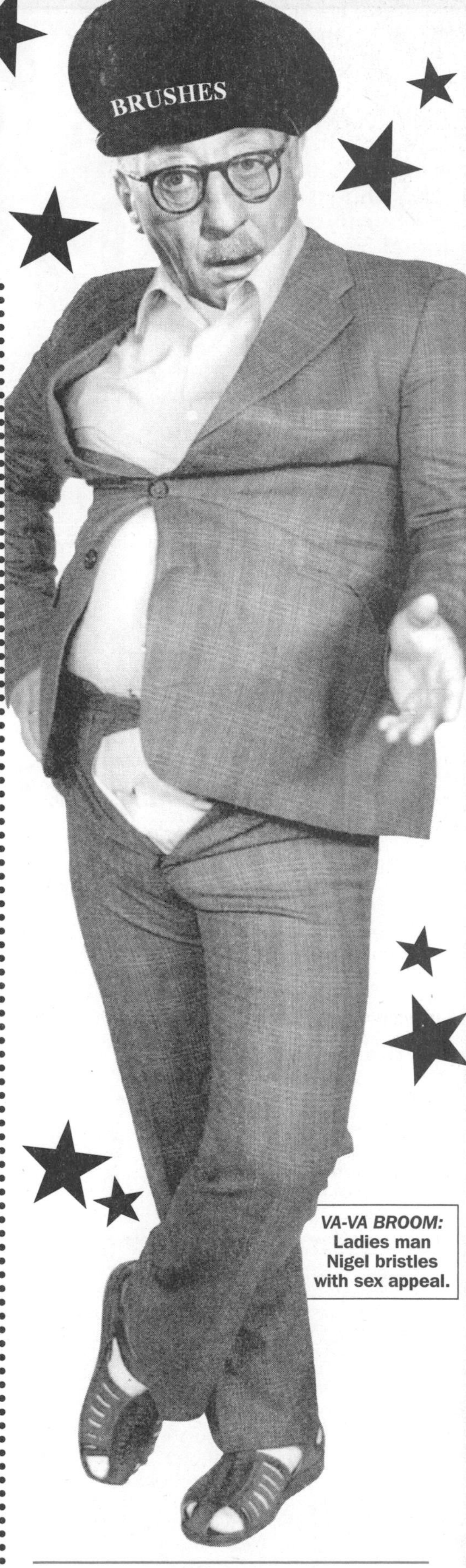
BRUSHES

VA-VA BROOM: **Ladies man Nigel bristles with sex appeal.**

NEXT WEEK ***The time Nigel knocked on the door of Buckingham Palace and Zara Philips answered. "She rode me like a stallion all round the throne room, and then didn't buy a squeegee mop for £1.86."***

Nigel Twinkle's book ***Knock! Knock! Who's Bare?*** *(Branflakes Books, £1.99)* is available from the reception desk of the Salvation Army Men's Hostel, Braintree and all good bookshops.

Now Google Photographs our *Bottoms!*

Scandal of Internet Arse-View Technology

WEBSEARCH engineers GOOGLE have revealed that they have taken pictures of the buttocks of every single person in the UK. And in a move that will horrify every law-abiding citizen in the country, they have posted them ONLINE!

Google 'Arse-View' pinhole cameras, normally used in keyhole surgery, were placed through drain covers outside people's houses. The tiny fibre-optic devices were then pushed up people's drainpipes into the bottoms of their toilet bowls, where heat-seeking technology identified whether the seats were occupied. It is believed that unmarked 'Arse-View' vans patrolled Britain's streets for over a year to collect the 60million images which are now on the database. Internet users can swivel and zoom in or out with a 3-D 'rectal-viewer' tool.

outrage

Civil liberties and privacy groups are said to be outraged that Google has taken high quality digital 360-degree photographs of the anii of everyone in Britain without their knowledge. A spokesman for the sinister web giants defended the controversial project. He told us: "Google has put in place adequate safeguards to protect the privacy and safety of individuals."

security issues

However, an examination of the 'Arse-View' site quickly found problems that may raise security issues. It took our reporter just a few clicks to obtain images of the Prime Minister wiping feeshus from his rectal sphincter in his private toilet at 10 Downing Street. It took slightly longer to find Home Secretary Jacqui Smith's bottom because she claims money for several addresses in and around London and the West Midlands, but her posterior was still found in a matter of minutes.

With images of cabinet minister's bottoms being so easily accessed, many security experts are anxious about the consequences of Al-Qaida or the Real IRA making use of the information. "If Osama Bin laden wanted to plant a bomb up the Prime Minister's back passage, he knows what it looks like and where to find it," one IT expert warned yesterday. "Frankly, it's only a matter of time before something like this happens," he added.

Images Arses News Video Mail more ▾
Google
Arse UK
london
Search Arses
Show search options
Get Directions My Maps
Print Send
London
UK
Explore this arse »
Photos
102 Elgin Crescent, Kensington, England, United Kingdom
Address is approximate

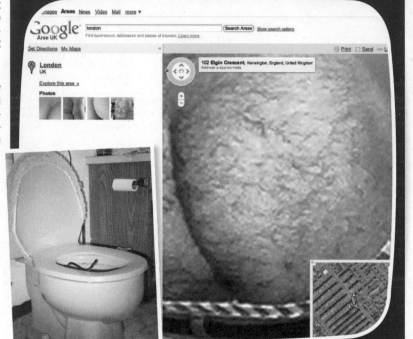

BROWN EYE: **Web surfers can access pics of PM's anus.**

SHITE HONOURABLE: **Photos of Home Secretary defecating freely available to snoopers.**

PERHAPS the most worrying aspect of Google Arse-View is that it allows perverts, stalkers and snoopers unfetted access to top celebrities' most private moments. It's a shameful and disgusting invasion of their privacy.

Here are some Google Arse-View images of celebrity bottoms which took us just minutes to access. The celebrities names have been ommitted to protect their privacy.

DISGRACE!

■ Eeuurgh! Eeuurgh! Eeuurgh! Goodness gracious, how's about that then? This must be the least glittering "ring" that this jewellery-bedecked ex-DJ owns.

INVASION!

■ Nice to see poo, to see poo, nice! This veteran all round entertainer is half way through dropping a copper bolt. Good game, good game!

OUTRAGE!

■ What a Liberty. It's a "Shami" that this Human Rights and Civil Liberties champion should find her pert Chakra*botty* plastered over the internet.

APPALLING!

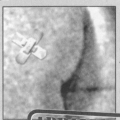

■ Surprise! Surprise! There's a lorra lorra ginger anal "hurr" sprouting from between the bum cheeks of this shrill scouse songstress.

DISGUSTING!

■ Judging by the winnets clustered round this Irish rocker's clackervalve, he still hasn't found what he's looking for... the lavatory paper!

SCANDAL!

■ Only fools and arses. This actor has has a touch of the *trotters* and has left the pan far from "perfik". G...G...G... Granville! Fetch a bog brush! It's David Jason's ringpiece.

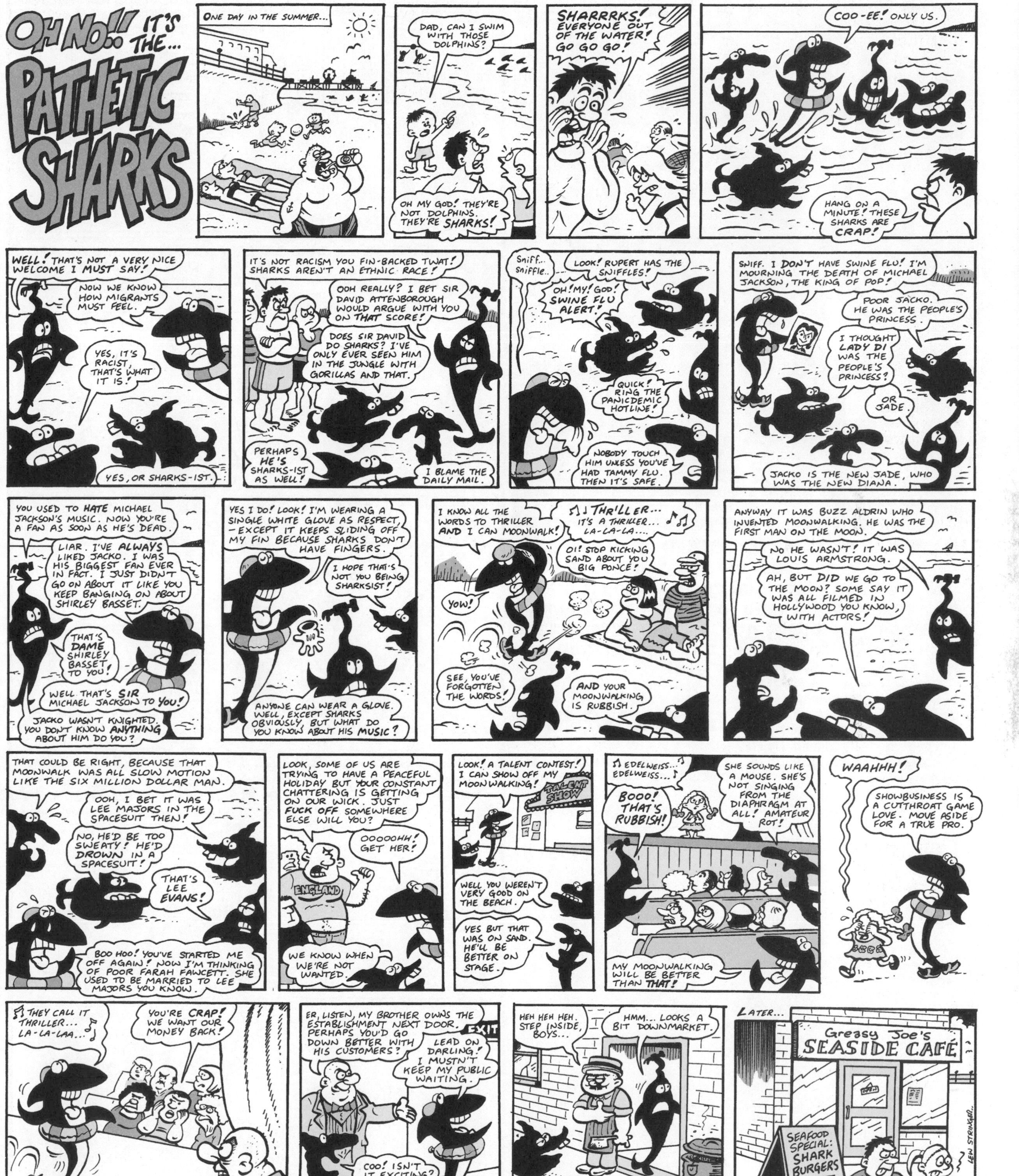
OH NO!! IT'S THE... PATHETIC SHARKS
ONE DAY IN THE SUMMER...
DAD, CAN I SWIM WITH THOSE DOLPHINS?
OH MY GOD! THEY'RE NOT DOLPHINS. THEY'RE SHARKS!
SHARRRKS! EVERYONE OUT OF THE WATER! GO GO GO!
COO-EE! ONLY US.
HANG ON A MINUTE! THESE SHARKS ARE CRAP!
WELL! THAT'S NOT A VERY NICE WELCOME I MUST SAY!
NOW WE KNOW HOW MIGRANTS MUST FEEL.
YES, IT'S RACIST, THAT'S WHAT IT IS!
YES, OR SHARKS-IST.
IT'S NOT RACISM YOU FIN-BACKED TWAT! SHARKS AREN'T AN ETHNIC RACE!
OOH REALLY? I BET SIR DAVID ATTENBOROUGH WOULD ARGUE WITH YOU ON THAT SCORE!
DOES SIR DAVID DO SHARKS? I'VE ONLY EVER SEEN HIM IN THE JUNGLE WITH GORILLAS AND THAT.
PERHAPS HE'S SHARKS-IST AS WELL!
I BLAME THE DAILY MAIL.
Sniff... sniffle..
LOOK! RUPERT HAS THE SNIFFLES!
OH! MY! GOD! SWINE FLU ALERT!
QUICK! RING THE PANICDEMIC HOTLINE!
NOBODY TOUCH HIM UNLESS YOU'VE HAD TAMMY FLU. THEN IT'S SAFE.
SNIFF. I DON'T HAVE SWINE FLU! I'M MOURNING THE DEATH OF MICHAEL JACKSON, THE KING OF POP!
POOR JACKO. HE WAS THE PEOPLE'S PRINCESS.
I THOUGHT LADY DI WAS THE PEOPLE'S PRINCESS?
OR JADE.
JACKO IS THE NEW JADE, WHO WAS THE NEW DIANA.
YOU USED TO HATE MICHAEL JACKSON'S MUSIC. NOW YOU'RE A FAN AS SOON AS HE'S DEAD.
LIAR. I'VE ALWAYS LIKED JACKO. I WAS HIS BIGGEST FAN EVER IN FACT. I JUST DIDN'T GO ON ABOUT IT LIKE YOU KEEP BANGING ON ABOUT SHIRLEY BASSET.
THAT'S DAME SHIRLEY BASSET TO YOU!
WELL THAT'S SIR MICHAEL JACKSON TO YOU!
JACKO WASN'T KNIGHTED. YOU DON'T KNOW ANYTHING ABOUT HIM DO YOU?
YES I DO! LOOK! I'M WEARING A SINGLE WHITE GLOVE AS RESPECT, — EXCEPT IT KEEPS SLIDING OFF MY FIN BECAUSE SHARKS DON'T HAVE FINGERS.
I HOPE THAT'S NOT YOU BEING SHARKSIST!
ANYONE CAN WEAR A GLOVE. WELL, EXCEPT SHARKS OBVIOUSLY, BUT WHAT DO YOU KNOW ABOUT HIS MUSIC?
I KNOW ALL THE WORDS TO THRILLER AND I CAN MOONWALK!
THRILLER... IT'S A THRILLER... LA-LA-LA....
OI! STOP KICKING SAND ABOUT YOU BIG PONCE!
YOW!
SEE, YOU'VE FORGOTTEN THE WORDS!
AND YOUR MOONWALKING IS RUBBISH.
ANYWAY IT WAS BUZZ ALDRIN WHO INVENTED MOONWALKING. HE WAS THE FIRST MAN ON THE MOON.
NO HE WASN'T! IT WAS LOUIS ARMSTRONG.
AH, BUT DID WE GO TO THE MOON? SOME SAY IT WAS ALL FILMED IN HOLLYWOOD YOU KNOW, WITH ACTORS!
THAT COULD BE RIGHT, BECAUSE THAT MOONWALK WAS ALL SLOW MOTION LIKE THE SIX MILLION DOLLAR MAN.
OOH, I BET IT WAS LEE MAJORS IN THE SPACESUIT THEN!
NO, HE'D BE TOO SWEATY! HE'D DROWN IN A SPACESUIT!
THAT'S LEE EVANS!
BOO HOO! YOU'VE STARTED ME OFF AGAIN! NOW I'M THINKING OF POOR FARAH FAWCETT. SHE USED TO BE MARRIED TO LEE MAJORS YOU KNOW.
LOOK, SOME OF US ARE TRYING TO HAVE A PEACEFUL HOLIDAY BUT YOUR CONSTANT CHATTERING IS GETTING ON OUR WICK. JUST FUCK OFF SOMEWHERE ELSE WILL YOU?
OOOOOHH! GET HER!
ENGLAND
WE KNOW WHEN WE'RE NOT WANTED.
LOOK! A TALENT CONTEST! I CAN SHOW OFF MY MOONWALKING!
TALENT SHOW
WELL YOU WEREN'T VERY GOOD ON THE BEACH.
YES BUT THAT WAS ON SAND. HE'LL BE BETTER ON STAGE.
EDELWEISS... EDELWEISS...
BOOO! THAT'S RUBBISH!
SHE SOUNDS LIKE A MOUSE. SHE'S NOT SINGING FROM THE DIAPHRAGM AT ALL! AMATEUR ROT!
MY MOONWALKING WILL BE BETTER THAN THAT!
WAAHHH!
SHOWBUSINESS IS A CUTTHROAT GAME LOVE. MOVE ASIDE FOR A TRUE PRO.
THEY CALL IT THRILLER... LA-LA-LAA...
YOU'RE CRAP! WE WANT OUR MONEY BACK!
GET OFF STAGE YOU TWAT! YOU'RE RUINING MY SHOW!
ER, LISTEN, MY BROTHER OWNS THE ESTABLISHMENT NEXT DOOR. PERHAPS YOU'D GO DOWN BETTER WITH HIS CUSTOMERS?
EXIT
LEAD ON DARLING! I MUSTN'T KEEP MY PUBLIC WAITING.
COO! ISN'T IT EXCITING?
WE COULD BE THE NEXT GARETH GATES!
HEH HEH HEH. STEP INSIDE, BOYS...
HMM... LOOKS A BIT DOWNMARKET.
ALL THE GREATS HAVE TO START SOMEWHERE. THIS COULD BE OUR BIG BREAK.
LATER...
Greasy Joe's SEASIDE CAFÉ
SEAFOOD SPECIAL: SHARK BURGERS
URRRGH. THEY EVEN TASTE CRAP.
LEW STRINGER
VIZ 188

Bono Launches Campaign to Save Staples

"USE 2" SAYS U2 BELL END

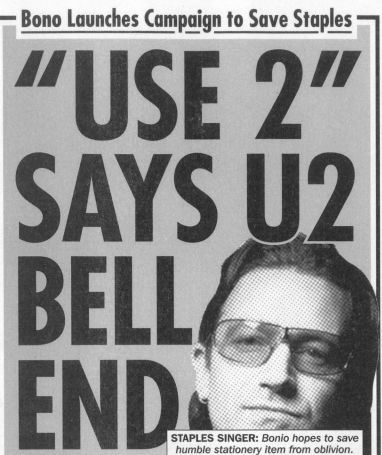

STAPLES SINGER: *Bonio hopes to save humble stationery item from oblivion.*

TWATTISH rocker BONO has backed a campaign to put the ailing staple industry back on a firm footing. According to official figures, the world used to spend twice as much on staples as it does now. But the advent of the paperless office has seen this amount drop by a half to 50% of its previous level.

But the U2 frontman believes there is still a place for the bent wire paper fasteners in our lives, and he is confident that his ***'Use 2'*** campaign will be just the boost the industry needs.

"I'm asking that every time anyone staples some paper together, they use two staples instead of one," he told the United Nations. "It's a small thing that each of us can do, but it will double turnover for staple manufacturers in one fell swoop," he continued.

QUAVERING

His voice quavering with emotion, the Dublin-born shortarse outlined how his fears for the future had led him to come up with his Use 2 crusade. "E-mails, digital storage of documents and treasury tags are all pushing the staple to the brink of extinction," he said. "And once the staple makers close down, they will never open up again."

"I fear that my children will grow up in a world where staples are just dusty objects on the shelves of a museum."

SPACE RAIDERING

"The earth is standing on a precipice, staring into the abyss,"

EXCLUSIVE

he added, overdramatically. "It's a nightmarish, staple-less, dystopian vision of the future and we have to act now if we want to prevent it becoming reality."

Bono continued: "The world's staples unite paper for people, and now the world's people must unite for staples." And he unveiled a poster of himself holding up some papers which had been stapled twice, featuring the slogan *"Clunk-clunk! U2 says Use 2".*

MONSTER MUNCHING

However, a former band employee last night claimed that the singer was failing to practise what he preached. Retired pilot Patrick Sparkes told reporters: "I know for a fact that Bono only ever uses one staple at a time."

"When I got my instructions every morning for where I had to fly his hat in an empty jumbo jet, the separate pages were always held together with a single staple," said Sparkes. "And the pilots of his trousers and shoe planes would tell you the same thing."

OH, LORDY! IT'S... THE FAT SLAGS
XMAS DAY...
'ERE, SAN... WOT'S ALL THESE BITS OF RUBBER ON THE FLOOR?
EH?
OH, THEY'RE ME SHAG BANDS. BAZ GOT 'EM ME FOR CHRISTMAS
SHAG BANDS? WOT'S THEM?
THEY'RE LIKE COLOURED RUBBER BRACELETS...
... EACH COLOUR STANDS FORRA DIFFERENT SEX ACT...
WHITE'S A KISS... YELLOW'S TOPS... BLUE'S FINGERS... BLACK'S A NOSH... PURPLE'S A SHAG AN' BROWN'S A BOSTON PANCAKE
OOH, I SAY!... 'OW DO THEY WORK?
WELL, IF SOMEBODY SNAPS ONE, YOU 'AVE T' GIVE THAT PERSON THAT SEX ACT...
I DON'T THINK BY LAW. THEY SELL 'EM IN THE POUND SHOP
BAZ BOUGHT ME SIX PURPLES, WHICH MEANT HE COULD GIVE ME SIX FUCKS.
HE WAS GOIN' T' SNAP ONE EVERY DAY TILL NEW YEAR...
BUT THEY WERE A BIT SMALL FOR ME WRISTS, AN' THEY ALL SNAPPED AS HE WAS TRYIN' T' GET 'EM ON THIS MORNIN.
FANCY!... SO WOT 'APPENED?
WELL, HE ONLY MANAGED T' GERRIT UP FOUR TIMES BEFORE HIS NUTS WENT FLAT, THEN HE NODDED OFF. I'LL GET THE OTHER TWO OFF 'IM WHEN HE WAKES UP

Jack the Ripper 'was Blakey'

THE AUTHOR of a new book on Jack the Ripper claims to have uncovered shocking new evidence that proves the world's most notorious serial killer was none other than BLAKEY from 70s sitcom *On the Buses*.

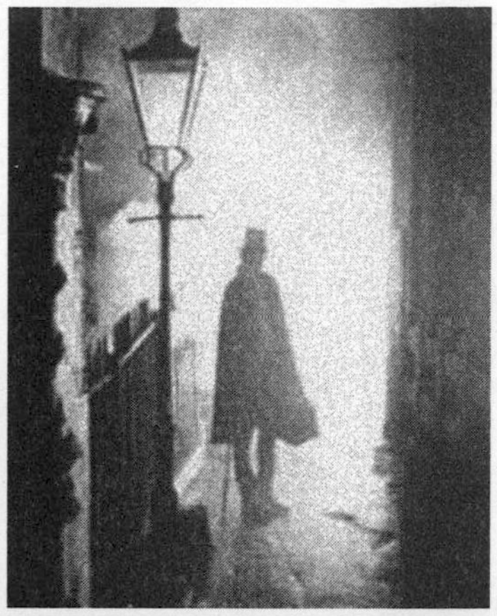

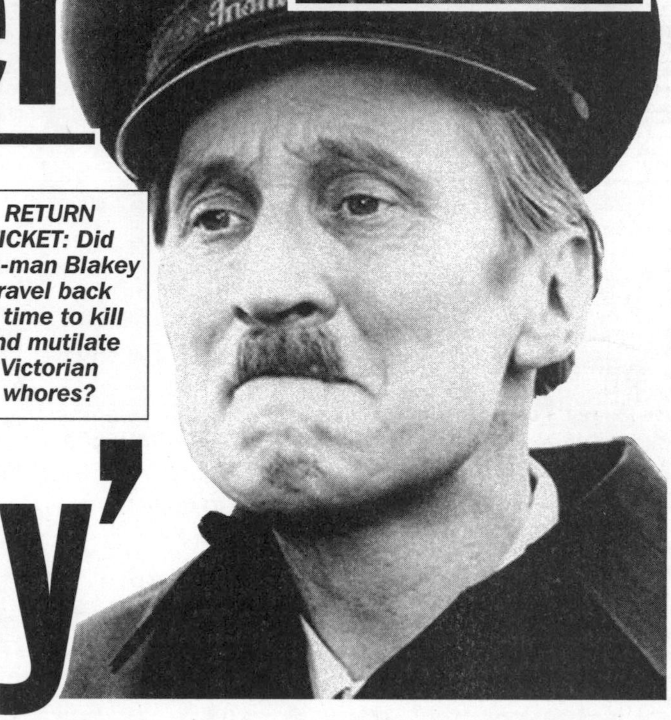
TOWN

RETURN TICKET: ***Did bus-man Blakey travel back in time to kill and mutilate Victorian whores?***

The book, *I'll Get You, Prostitutes* details how the thin-lipped fictional bus inspector was so consumed by hatred for Stan Butler and his lazy conductor friend Jack Harper that it caused a tear in the fabric of the space-time continuum through which Blakey was able to travel back to the 1880s and brutally murder prostitutes.

"Everything clicked into place," said author Aaron Denkie Jr. "I was sat at home one morning watching the episode of On the Buses where Blakey and Butler had a falling out because Butler had been warming himself on the bus engine, despite it being against regulations."

"Blakey had a single-minded obsession with rules and punctuality, whereas Reg and Jack were more interested in chatting up dolly birds than running an effective transport service. It was an incendiary combination that could only end in time-travelling murder."

Denkie continued: "Blakey's loathing for Butler was no secret, and I believe he was ultimately driven insane by the workshy driver's inability to get a bus out on time. This seething hatred must of somehow opened up a time wormhole like in Primeval."

"This allowed Blakey to go back in time to the foggy back streets of the Victorian East End, possibly in a commandeered yellow and green bus, where he killed and sexually mutilated a series of Victorian hookers."

"His background in public transport would have given him an excellent knowledge of London streets, making it easy for him to evade police," Denkie added.

Fascinated by his theory, the author re-examined famous Ripper evidence to find a series of chilling clues. Blakey was a stickler for doing things by the book. He hated his buses to deviate from their official routes or their set timetables. Similarly, Jack the Ripper was a deeply methodical man, with an obsession for the ritual of killing.

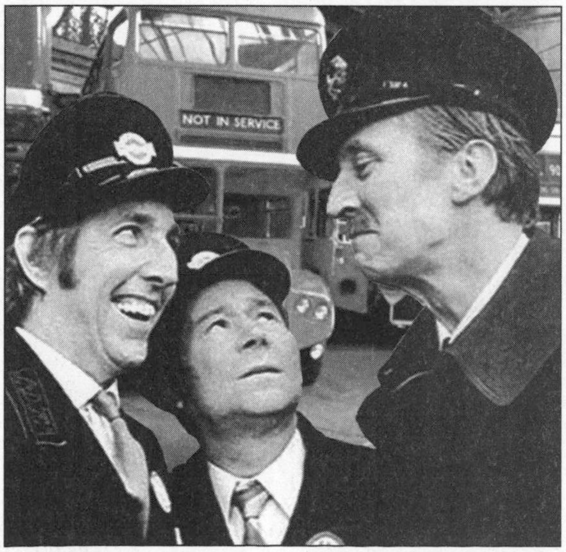
NOT IN SERVICE

"Blakey was driven to murder by his workshy driver's inability to get a bus out on time."

But perhaps the most damning piece of evidence that points the finger of blame at the deranged bus inspector is the so-called 'Goulston Street Grafitti'. This was a hastily-scrawled line of writing chalked on a wall near to one of the victims that was believed to be a message from the killer.

"Police at the time transcribed it as 'The Juwes are the men who will not be blamed for nothing'," said Denkie Jr. "But if you re-arrange the letters, take some of them away and add some other ones, a new phrase appears: 'Get that bus out or I'll 'ave you, Butler'." For Denkie, this was the final piece of the jigsaw.

The question remains: Why didn't Blakey simply kill Butler? Why did he choose to vent his anger on five unknown nineteenth century prostitutes? Jenkie believes he has the answer.

"Inspector Blake was in a state of psychological conflict," he explained. "Despite his hatred for him, he nevertheless liked Butler's mum and harboured repressed romantic feelings for his ugly sister Olive."

"Indeed, Blakey had even been to the Butlers' house for tea on a couple of occasions, most notably in the episode Bye Bye, Blakey, where he was given kippers."

"He knew that if he killed his bus-driving nemesis it would upset Mrs Butler and Olive, so he was forced to find another outlet for his loathing. He decided to enact his evil plan in a different era where he would be less likely to get caught."

Denkie's book also makes the astonishing accusation that Blakey may have been protected by an Establishment cover-up.

"As a famous bus inspector, Blakey would have known Queen Victoria and the Prime Minister the Marquess of Salisbury," he continued. "They would have used their influence to shield Blakey from Scotland Yard's investigation, possibly even getting him a new identity as a diplomat or lamp lighter until he was able to re-open the time vortex and travel back to the 70s to make the increasingly unfunny On The Buses feature films," he added.

Denkie Jr is currently working on a new book based on his theory that 70s Confessions film actor Robin Askwith was responsible for the kidnap and murder of the Lindbergh baby.

LeTTERbOcks

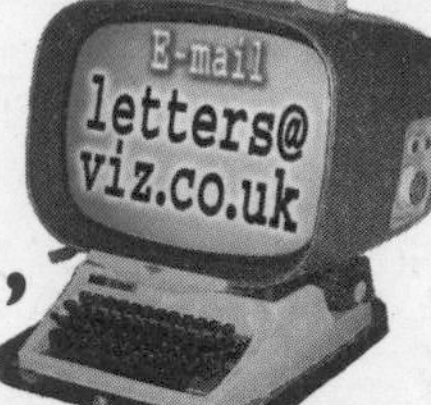
E-mail
letters@
viz.co.uk

PO Box 656,
North Shields,
NE30 4XX

STAR LETTER

◆ IF I WERE to invent a time machine, the first thing I'd do is go back to the time of Noah and his Ark and make sure the crocodiles weren't let on. Then I'd whizz forward a few thousand years and laugh in delight as Jimmy Nail's pop career flops after his first single *Shoes* fails to break into the top 40. That'll learn the prick.

Paul Greasley, e-mail

◆ **AFTER** popping into my local pub the other night, I was shocked at how many Australians there were working behind the bar. It was only the next day when I sobered up that I remembered that I live in Sydney.

Glenn McGrath
Sydney

◆ **PROFESSOR** Stephen Hawking was taken into hospital and was reported to be undergoing tests. Just how clever do they want him to prove that he is? He wrote *A Brief History of Time*, for God's sake.

Billy Bookcase
e-mail

◆ **I CAN'T** understand why some people are so worried about a decline in the bee population. They've clearly never been stang off of one. Or a wasp.

Clinton Clunge
e-mail

◆ **MY DAD** supplied Renato out of Renée and Renato with a blue and grey velour sweater for his video *Save Your Love* in 1982. And I can prove

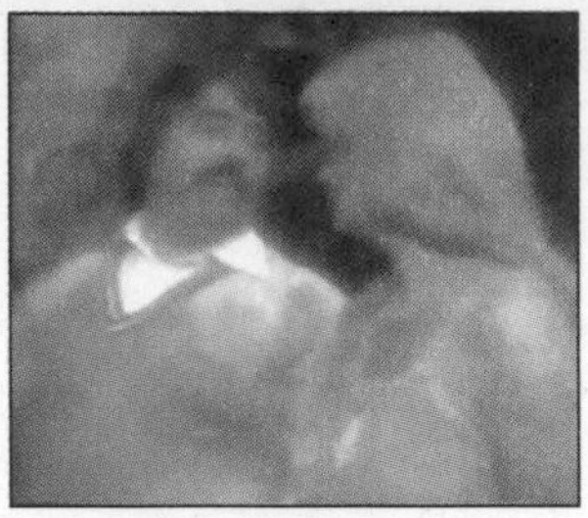

it. Fucking top that you crowd of cunts.

Kevin Smallman
Birmingham

** WELL, Kevin, it's very easy to go around boasting that your dad supplied Renato out of Renée and Renato's jumper, but to be honest, we don't believe you. We think you've made it up in order to impress some girls. So we're calling your bluff, and we want to see the proof.*

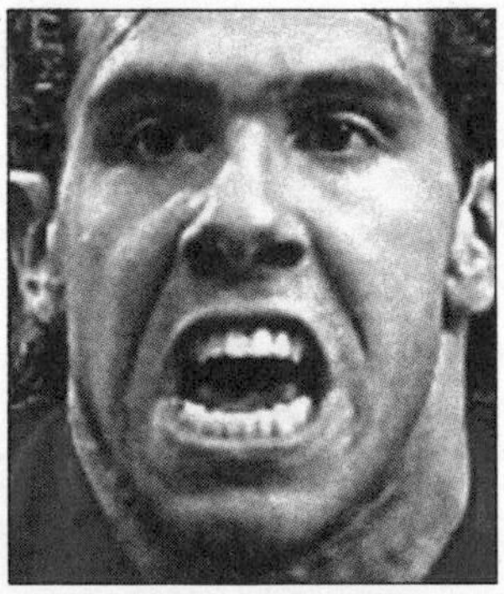

◆ **IF IT'S** true that dogs resemble their owners, then Manchester City striker Carlos Tevez probably has a bulldog with an arse where its face should be.

Karen Matthews
e-mail

◆ **I WAS** disgusted to learn that a certain popular clothing retailers use child labour to make their clothes. That would explain the awful state of stitching on my jeans. Couldn't they stretch their budget a bit and at least employ some teenagers?

Donald Troosers
e-mail

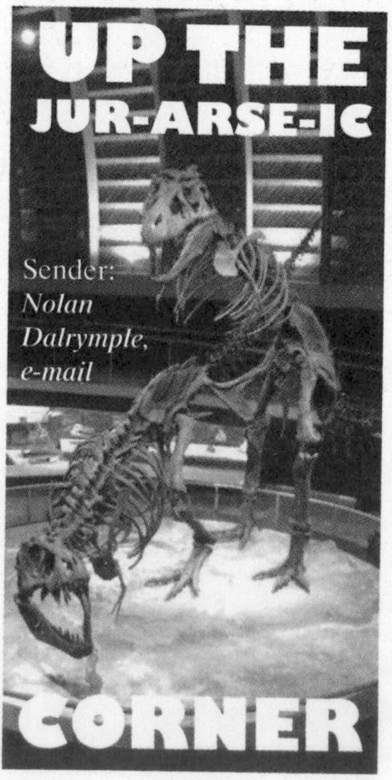
UP THE
JUR-ARSE-IC
Sender:
Nolan
Dalrymple,
e-mail
CORNER

◆ **MY WIFE** says I fart all the time, yet at around 100 farts per day, each lasting roughly 3 seconds, this means I actually fart for 300 seconds in every 24 hours. This is about five minutes, which equates to one twelfth of an hour spread over 24, and there my maths skills fail me. Perhaps any boffins reading this could let me know precisely what percentage of each day I spend farting.

Bifford Norton
e-mail

◆ **I'LL TELL** you something those Sheila's Wheels women leave out of their advert - the £25 administration fee for phoning up to change address. Mind you, I suppose it would be a little difficult to incorporate that information into the song.

Christina Martin
e-mail

◆ **WITH** all the sleaze about politicians and their expenses making the news, Sir Fred Goodwin seems to have dropped out of the public eye. So I am just writing in to remind everybody what a greedy bastard he is.

RBS Thompson
e-mail

◆ **DOES** anyone want an empty biscuit tin?

Richard Stainton
e-mail

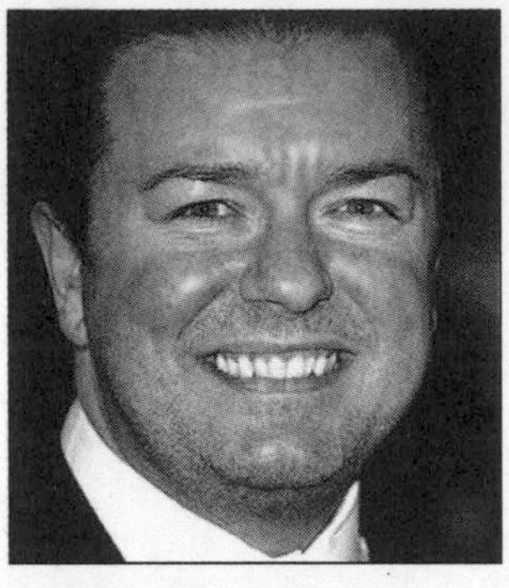

◆ **THAT** Ricky Gervais is funny. I love it when he pretends to be a cunt and tells us how many Golden Globes he's won. I never tire of hearing that, fortunately.

Stuart Powers
e-mail

◆ **ARE** sports stars all stupid? I have yet to see a bottle of Champagne with 'Shake Before Opening' written on it, yet they all do it. Surely they must know what's going to happen.

Dean Moncaster
e-mail

◆ **I WOULD** like to ask T-Mobile why it is that I can't get a reception from my house in Cheshire on my mobile, but Osama Bin Laden can send death threats by videophone around the world from a cave in Afganistan. Is there a special tarrif for terrorist calls?

H O'Hooligan
e-mail

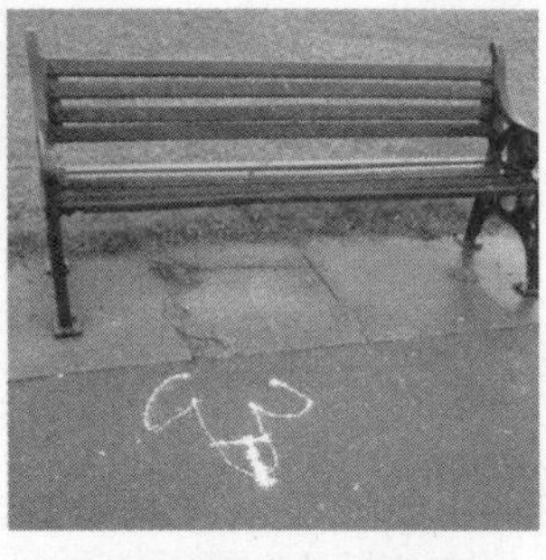

◆ **WHILST** visiting Seaton Carew the other day, I sat on a bench to take in the breathtaking views across Hartlepool Bay when I saw this grafitti cock on the ground. It added a little light heartedness to an otherwise dreary day.

Perigrine Measor,
Hartlepool

THE NAME OF THE PET

WE never asked you to write in and tell us how your pets got their names, but you did anyway, in your droves. Here's a selection of the best that we never wanted to receive.

WE'VE got a pet mouse called Boutros, because we bought him from the pet shop on the 14th November, the birthday of Boutros Boutros-Ghali, the sixth secretary general of the United Nations.

Edith Cholera, Sheffield

OUR Persian cat is called Mr Blofeld after the James Bond villain. And like him, I sometimes think our Mr Blofeld would like to take over the world - he's certainly taken over our house!

Ada Lumbago, Tooting

I WON a goldfish at a fair in 1972, and I called her Hoop-La, after the stall on which I won her. If she were alive today she would have been 37, but unfortunately she died of a fungal rot the day after I got her home.

Dolly Osteoporosis, Gwent

I'VE got a Jack Russell called Holly. We gave her that name because me and my late husband got her for Christmas. We could have called her Mistletoe, but we didn't like that name as much.

Edna Arthritis, Goole

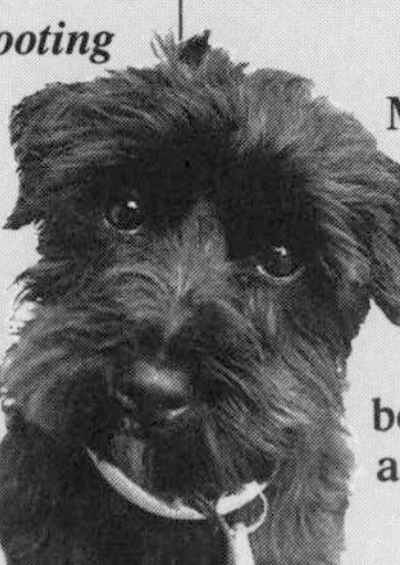

ME and my husband have got a bulldog who we named Winston Chuchill, because he looks like the fertility expert Professor Robert Winston, and the pet shop where we bought him from was next door to a church on top of a hill.

Mavis Plague, Taunton

WE called our budgie Noel, because he hatched out of his egg a few days before Christmas, just like TV presenter Noel Edmonds. Although he probably didn't hatch out of an egg.

Doris Ricketts, Dundee

**** HAVE you got a funny or cute story about how your pet got its name? Don't write in to the usual address and tell us, because nobody gives a shit. Don't mark your envelope 'My Pet's Name.'***

Shame of Street

TV HORROR BAG *Janet Street Porter* admitted yesterday that she was 'shocked' and 'embarrassed' when she recently saw herself on the television for the first time.

Speaking to the *Radio Times*, Street-Porter, at least 60, revealed that despite somehow earning a living from broadcasting for over 30 years, she had never watched a single programme she'd been involved with. "I always thought the idea of watching yourself on the telly was very self obsessive" she told reporter Matthew Bolleaux.

INTERVIEW

In the interview, the veteran arts harridan explained how she accidentally caught her appearance on a recent edition of the BBC's *Question Time*. "I was sat in a bar and there was a television on behind me," she said. "All I could hear was the

EXCLUSIVE!

annoying, ear-splitting cacophony of some woman screeching over the top of everyone else on the panel."

"I couldn't believe it when I turned around and saw that the awful racket was coming from me!"

ALBION

She continued: "In my head I always thought I came across as well spoken, polite and thoughtful with a lovely speaking voice, like Hannah Gordon or Joanna Lumley. To actually hear myself as a crass, loudmouth boor was quite a revelation. Honestly, I sounded like a murder of crows."

"Everyone likes to think they sound like a newsreader. I now realise that I actually sound like an hysterical witch playing a giant kazoo in a dustbin."

LEEDS COVERED

Janet Street Porter admitted that if she had known she was so annoying she wouldn't have taken a job in broadcasting. "My father owned a bakery," she said. "I should have gone into that instead."

◆ **I ONCE** got bitten off of an otter. Can any of your readers top that?

Edith Shotgun e-mail

∗ WELL readers, CAN you top that? Perhaps you've got bitten off of TWO otters, maybe THREE. Write and let us know how many otters you've been bitten off of. Mark your envelope 'I've been bitten off of a number of otters.'

◆ **WITH** all these gloomy headlines, the government should give each household a cheeky chimpanzee to lift the nation's mood. Their comical antics and japes would certainly keep everyone smiling through these difficult times. Obviously, as they are also quite dangerous they would have to be killed and stuffed. And vegetarians needn't worry - they could choose a stuffed dolphin instead.

Andy Mansh e-mail

◆ **I JUST** wondered if anyone misses licking stamps.

Stanley Gibbons Twickenham

◆ **WITH** reference to the letter on your previous Letterbocks page, BBC weather girl Kaddy-Lee Preston may be a step up from Carol Kirkwood, but BBC London's Wendy Hurrell is even tastier. No wonder ITV is going down the khazi.

A Royffe i-Phone

◆ **CHURCH** leaders were complaining about a football match scheduled on Easter Sunday, saying it was disrespectful. What hypocrites! Whenever I walk past a church on a Sunday they're always open. They should practise what they preach.

Morten Christmas e-mail

◆ **FOLLOWING** on from the above letter, if God said Sunday is the day of rest, why do Christians and that lot choose Sunday to go bothering him with prayers. Let the man have a lie in.

Rik Lothian e-mail

Political Interviewer Joke No. 6521a

THERE'S A ROBIN ON THE WATERING CAN

«TOP TIPS»

RABBIS. Get with the times by dressing up like chart teen sensations The Jonas Brothers instead of 80s rockers ZZ Top.

Jofus O'Hooligan, e-mail

NEED a day off work? Convince your boss you have a cold over the phone by slipping your tongue into a boiling hot Pop Tart before you call.

Andy Mapps, e-mail

A MIXTURE of human hair, carrot peelings and some congealed fat makes an excellent makeshift plug for any kitchen sink

Simon T Bosun, e-mail

OFFICE workers. Before shredding paper, write the numbers 1 to 30 across the top. That way you will easily be able to put the paper back together if you accidentally shred something you meant to keep.

T Ketchup, e-mail

BEAT the credit crunch. When you hear your neighbour running a bath, get a friend to go round and distract them until the water comes over their overflow pipe. Then stand under it for a free hot shower.

Anton Seventies, e-mail

LADIES. Leaving your curtains open when undressing will ensure that, in the event of any unfortunate accident, anyone watching you through binoculars can quickly summon help.

Rab Saughton, e-mail

FEMALE newsreaders. Tell viewers at the start of each bulletin wheather or not you are wearing a bra, then we won't waste half an hour trying to figure it out for ourselves.

Chris, e-mail

SMOKERS. A sliver of chicken in the end of your cigarette turns an anti-social smell into an irrisistable barbecue aroma, ensuring your popularity in public places.

Trevor Topsoil, e-mail

BLUE PETER presenters. Bring the old home-made toy telephone up to date by not using anything to join two paper cups together.

Twitchy John, e-mail

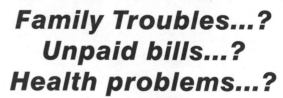

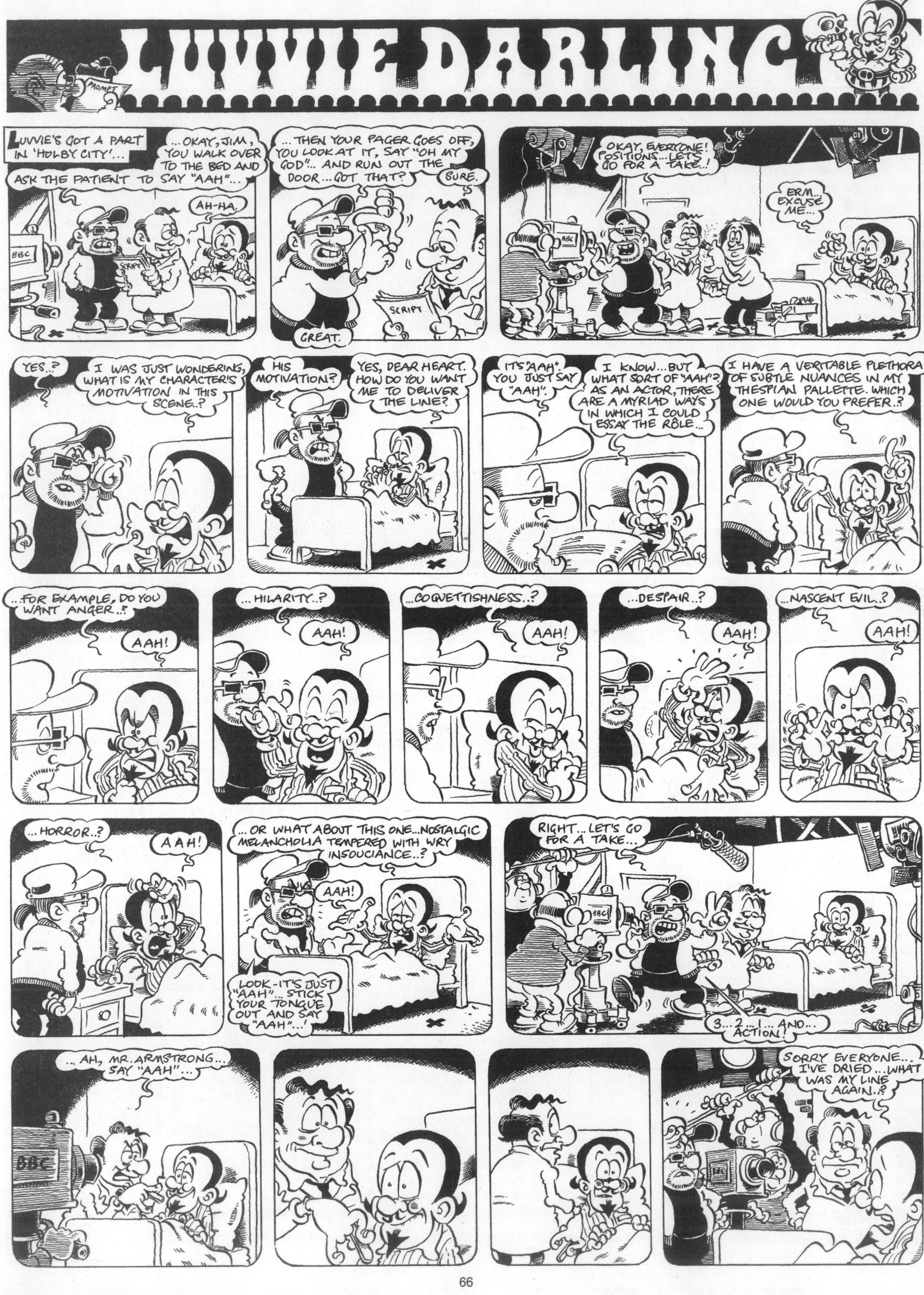
LUVVIE DARLING
PROMPT
LUVVIE'S GOT A PART IN 'HOLBY CITY'...
...OKAY, JIM, YOU WALK OVER TO THE BED AND ASK THE PATIENT TO SAY "AAH"...
AH-HA.
BBC
SCRIPT
...THEN YOUR PAGER GOES OFF, YOU LOOK AT IT, SAY "OH MY GOD"... AND RUN OUT THE DOOR... GOT THAT?
SURE.
SCRIPT
GREAT.
OKAY, EVERYONE! POSITIONS... LET'S GO FOR A TAKE..!
ERM... EXCUSE ME...
BBC
YES..?
I WAS JUST WONDERING, WHAT IS MY CHARACTER'S MOTIVATION IN THIS SCENE..?
HIS MOTIVATION?
YES, DEAR HEART. HOW DO YOU WANT ME TO DELIVER THE LINE?
IT'S "AAH". YOU JUST SAY "AAH".
I KNOW... BUT WHAT SORT OF "AAH"? AS AN ACTOR, THERE ARE A MYRIAD WAYS IN WHICH I COULD ESSAY THE RÔLE...
I HAVE A VERITABLE PLETHORA OF SUBTLE NUANCES IN MY THESPIAN PALLETTE. WHICH ONE WOULD YOU PREFER..?
...FOR EXAMPLE, DO YOU WANT ANGER..?
AAH!
...HILARITY..?
AAH!
...COQUETTISHNESS..?
AAH!
...DESPAIR..?
AAH!
...NASCENT EVIL..?
AAH!
...HORROR..?
AAH!
...OR WHAT ABOUT THIS ONE... NOSTALGIC MELANCHOLIA TEMPERED WITH WRY INSOUCIANCE..?
AAH!
LOOK - IT'S JUST "AAH"... STICK YOUR TONGUE OUT AND SAY "AAH"...!
RIGHT... LET'S GO FOR A TAKE...
BBC
3... 2... 1... AND... ACTION!
...AH, MR. ARMSTRONG... SAY "AAH"...
BBC
SORRY EVERYONE... I'VE DRIED... WHAT WAS MY LINE AGAIN..?

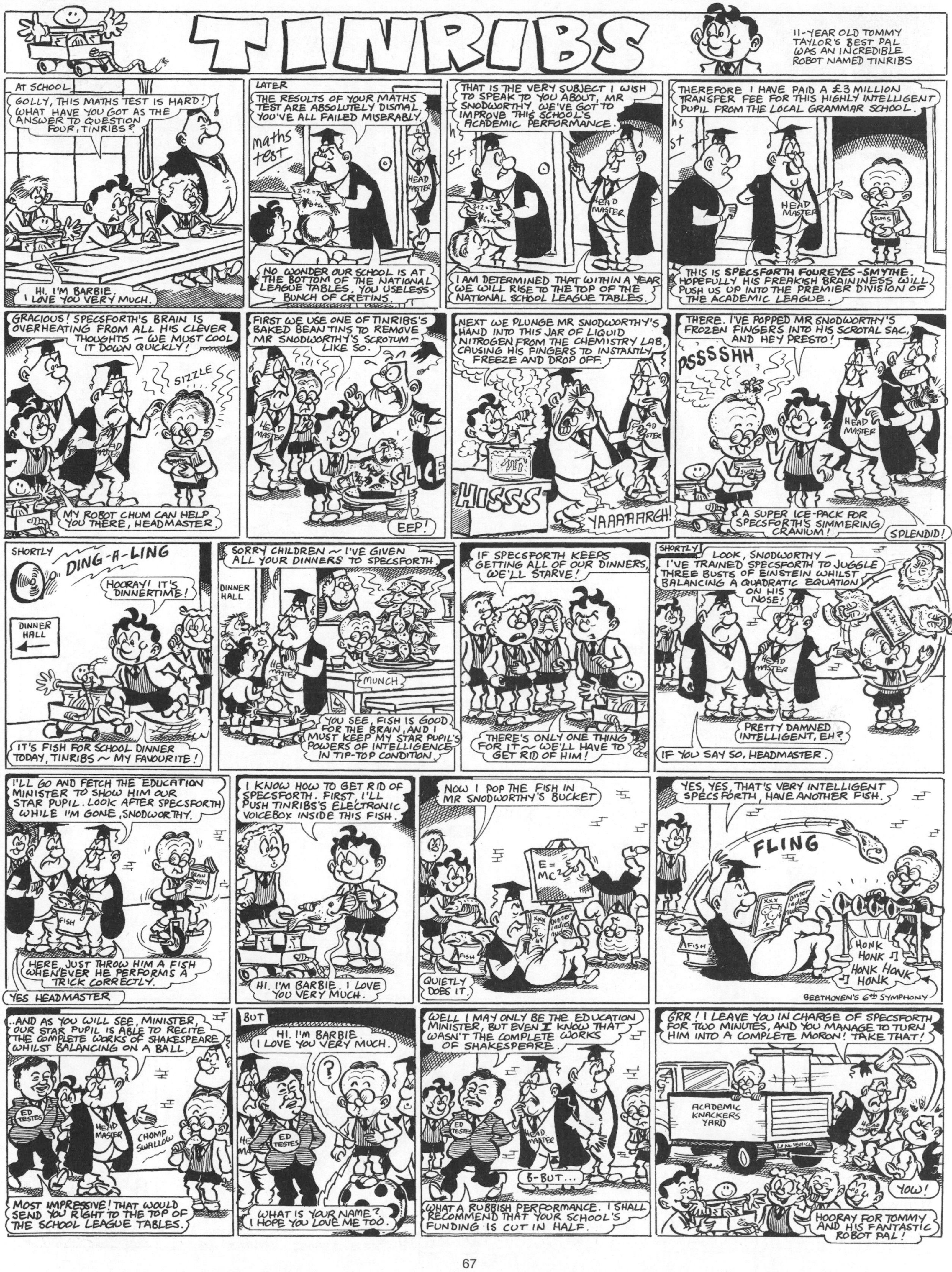
TINRIBS
11-YEAR OLD TOMMY TAYLOR'S BEST PAL WAS AN INCREDIBLE ROBOT NAMED TINRIBS
AT SCHOOL
GOLLY, THIS MATHS TEST IS HARD! WHAT HAVE YOU GOT AS THE ANSWER TO QUESTION FOUR, TINRIBS?
HI, I'M BARBIE. I LOVE YOU VERY MUCH.
LATER
THE RESULTS OF YOUR MATHS TEST ARE ABSOLUTELY DISMAL. YOU'VE ALL FAILED MISERABLY.
maths test
HEAD MASTER
NO WONDER OUR SCHOOL IS AT THE BOTTOM OF THE NATIONAL LEAGUE TABLES, YOU USELESS BUNCH OF CRETINS.
THAT IS THE VERY SUBJECT I WISH TO SPEAK TO YOU ABOUT, MR SNODWORTHY. WE'VE GOT TO IMPROVE THIS SCHOOL'S ACADEMIC PERFORMANCE.
HEAD MASTER
I AM DETERMINED THAT WITHIN A YEAR WE WILL RISE TO THE TOP OF THE NATIONAL SCHOOL LEAGUE TABLES.
THEREFORE I HAVE PAID A £3 MILLION TRANSFER FEE FOR THIS HIGHLY INTELLIGENT PUPIL FROM THE LOCAL GRAMMAR SCHOOL.
HEAD MASTER
SUMS
THIS IS SPECSFORTH FOUREYES-SMYTHE. HOPEFULLY HIS FREAKISH BRAININESS WILL PUSH US UP INTO THE PREMIER DIVISION OF THE ACADEMIC LEAGUE.
GRACIOUS! SPECSFORTH'S BRAIN IS OVERHEATING FROM ALL HIS CLEVER THOUGHTS — WE MUST COOL IT DOWN QUICKLY!
SIZZLE
MY ROBOT CHUM CAN HELP YOU THERE, HEADMASTER.
FIRST WE USE ONE OF TINRIBS'S BAKED BEAN TINS TO REMOVE MR SNODWORTHY'S SCROTUM — LIKE SO.
HEAD MASTER
SLICE
EEP!
NEXT WE PLUNGE MR SNODWORTHY'S HAND INTO THIS JAR OF LIQUID NITROGEN FROM THE CHEMISTRY LAB, CAUSING HIS FINGERS TO INSTANTLY FREEZE AND DROP OFF.
HISSS
YAAAAARRGH!
THERE. I'VE POPPED MR SNODWORTHY'S FROZEN FINGERS INTO HIS SCROTAL SAC, AND HEY PRESTO!
PSSSSHH
HEAD MASTER
SUMS
A SUPER ICE-PACK FOR SPECSFORTH'S SIMMERING CRANIUM!
SPLENDID!
SHORTLY
DING-A-LING
HOORAY! IT'S DINNERTIME!
DINNER HALL
IT'S FISH FOR SCHOOL DINNER TODAY, TINRIBS ~ MY FAVOURITE!
SORRY CHILDREN ~ I'VE GIVEN ALL YOUR DINNERS TO SPECSFORTH.
DINNER HALL
HEAD MASTER
MUNCH
YOU SEE, FISH IS GOOD FOR THE BRAIN, AND I MUST KEEP MY STAR PUPIL'S POWERS OF INTELLIGENCE IN TIP-TOP CONDITION.
IF SPECSFORTH KEEPS GETTING ALL OF OUR DINNERS, WE'LL STARVE!
THERE'S ONLY ONE THING FOR IT ~ WE'LL HAVE TO GET RID OF HIM!
SHORTLY
LOOK, SNODWORTHY — I'VE TRAINED SPECSFORTH TO JUGGLE THREE BUSTS OF EINSTEIN WHILST BALANCING A QUADRATIC EQUATION ON HIS NOSE!
HEAD MASTER
PRETTY DAMNED INTELLIGENT, EH?
IF YOU SAY SO, HEADMASTER.
I'LL GO AND FETCH THE EDUCATION MINISTER TO SHOW HIM OUR STAR PUPIL. LOOK AFTER SPECSFORTH WHILE I'M GONE, SNODWORTHY.
FISH
HERE, JUST THROW HIM A FISH WHENEVER HE PERFORMS A TRICK CORRECTLY.
YES HEADMASTER
I KNOW HOW TO GET RID OF SPECSFORTH. FIRST, I'LL PUSH TINRIBS'S ELECTRONIC VOICEBOX INSIDE THIS FISH.
HI. I'M BARBIE. I LOVE YOU VERY MUCH.
NOW I POP THE FISH IN MR SNODWORTHY'S BUCKET
E = MC²
FISH
QUIETLY DOES IT.
YES, YES, THAT'S VERY INTELLIGENT SPECSFORTH, HAVE ANOTHER FISH.
FLING
FISH
HONK HONK
HONK HONK HONK
BEETHOVEN'S 6th SYMPHONY
..AND AS YOU WILL SEE, MINISTER, OUR STAR PUPIL IS ABLE TO RECITE THE COMPLETE WORKS OF SHAKESPEARE WHILST BALANCING ON A BALL.
ED TESTES
HEAD MASTER
CHOMP SWALLOW
MOST IMPRESSIVE! THAT WOULD SEND YOU RIGHT TO THE TOP OF THE SCHOOL LEAGUE TABLES.
BUT
HI. I'M BARBIE. I LOVE YOU VERY MUCH.
?
ED TESTES
WHAT IS YOUR NAME? I HOPE YOU LOVE ME TOO.
WELL I MAY ONLY BE THE EDUCATION MINISTER, BUT EVEN I KNOW THAT WASN'T THE COMPLETE WORKS OF SHAKESPEARE.
ED TESTES
HEAD MASTER
B-BUT...
WHAT A RUBBISH PERFORMANCE. I SHALL RECOMMEND THAT YOUR SCHOOL'S FUNDING IS CUT IN HALF.
GRR! I LEAVE YOU IN CHARGE OF SPECSFORTH FOR TWO MINUTES, AND YOU MANAGE TO TURN HIM INTO A COMPLETE MORON! TAKE THAT!
ACADEMIC KNACKERS YARD
YOW!
HOORAY FOR TOMMY AND HIS FANTASTIC ROBOT PAL!

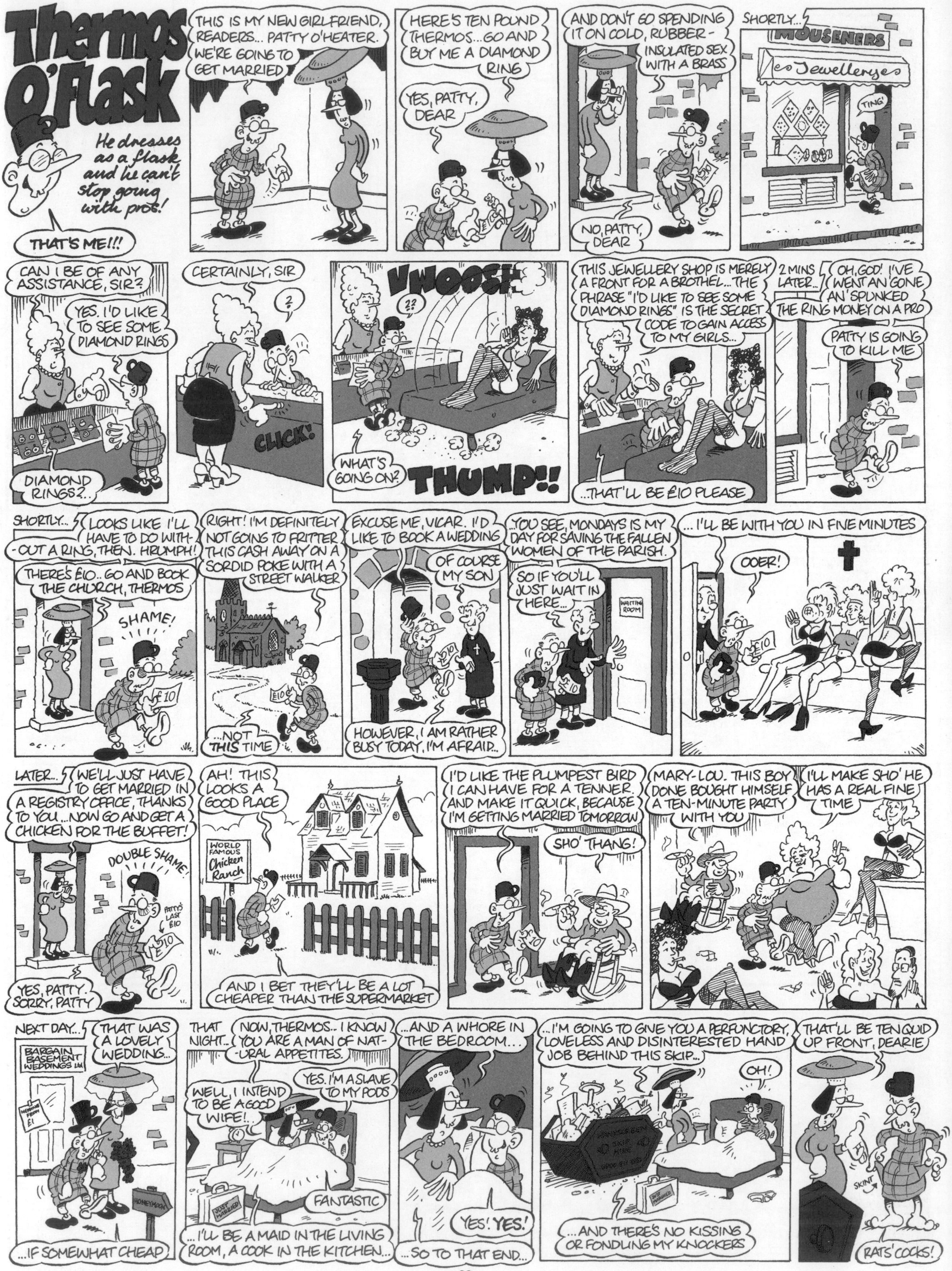
Thermos O'Flask
He dresses as a flask and he can't stop going with pros!
THAT'S ME!!!
THIS IS MY NEW GIRLFRIEND, READERS... PATTY O'HEATER. WE'RE GOING TO GET MARRIED
HERE'S TEN POUND THERMOS... GO AND BUY ME A DIAMOND RING
YES, PATTY, DEAR
AND DON'T GO SPENDING IT ON COLD, RUBBER-INSULATED SEX WITH A BRASS
NO, PATTY, DEAR
SHORTLY...
MOUSENERS
es Jewelleryes
TING!
CAN I BE OF ANY ASSISTANCE, SIR?
YES. I'D LIKE TO SEE SOME DIAMOND RINGS
DIAMOND RINGS?..
CERTAINLY, SIR
?
CLICK!
VWOOSH!
??
WHAT'S GOING ON?
THUMP!!
THIS JEWELLERY SHOP IS MERELY A FRONT FOR A BROTHEL... THE PHRASE "I'D LIKE TO SEE SOME DIAMOND RINGS" IS THE SECRET CODE TO GAIN ACCESS TO MY GIRLS...
...THAT'LL BE £10 PLEASE
2 MINS LATER...
OH, GOD! I'VE WENT AN' GONE AN' SPUNKED THE RING MONEY ON A PRO
PATTY IS GOING TO KILL ME
SHORTLY...
LOOKS LIKE I'LL HAVE TO DO WITH-OUT A RING, THEN. HRUMPH!
THERE'S £10.. GO AND BOOK THE CHURCH, THERMOS
SHAME!
£10
RIGHT! I'M DEFINITELY NOT GOING TO FRITTER THIS CASH AWAY ON A SORDID POKE WITH A STREET WALKER
...NOT THIS TIME
EXCUSE ME, VICAR. I'D LIKE TO BOOK A WEDDING
OF COURSE MY SON
HOWEVER, I AM RATHER BUSY TODAY, I'M AFRAID...
...YOU SEE, MONDAYS IS MY DAY FOR SAVING THE FALLEN WOMEN OF THE PARISH.
SO IF YOU'LL JUST WAIT IN HERE...
WAITING ROOM
... I'LL BE WITH YOU IN FIVE MINUTES
OOER!
LATER...
WE'LL JUST HAVE TO GET MARRIED IN A REGISTRY OFFICE, THANKS TO YOU... NOW GO AND GET A CHICKEN FOR THE BUFFET!
DOUBLE SHAME!
PATTY'S LAST £10
YES, PATTY. SORRY, PATTY
AH! THIS LOOKS A GOOD PLACE
WORLD FAMOUS Chicken Ranch
AND I BET THEY'LL BE A LOT CHEAPER THAN THE SUPERMARKET
I'D LIKE THE PLUMPEST BIRD I CAN HAVE FOR A TENNER. AND MAKE IT QUICK, BECAUSE I'M GETTING MARRIED TOMORROW
SHO' THANG!
MARY-LOU. THIS BOY DONE BOUGHT HIMSELF A TEN-MINUTE PARTY WITH YOU
I'LL MAKE SHO' HE HAS A REAL FINE TIME
NEXT DAY...
THAT WAS A LOVELY WEDDING...
BARGAIN BASEMENT WEDDINGS Ltd
...IF SOMEWHAT CHEAP
HONEYMOON
THAT NIGHT...
NOW, THERMOS.. I KNOW YOU ARE A MAN OF NAT-URAL APPETITES.
YES. I'M A SLAVE TO MY PODS
WELL, I INTEND TO BE A GOOD WIFE!..
FANTASTIC
JUST MARRIED
...I'LL BE A MAID IN THE LIVING ROOM, A COOK IN THE KITCHEN...
...AND A WHORE IN THE BEDROOM...
YES! YES!
...SO TO THAT END...
...I'M GOING TO GIVE YOU A PERFUNCTORY, LOVELESS AND DISINTERESTED HAND JOB BEHIND THIS SKIP...
OH!
SKIP HIRE
...AND THERE'S NO KISSING OR FONDLING MY KNOCKERS
THAT'LL BE TEN QUID UP FRONT, DEARIE
SKINT
RATS' COCKS!

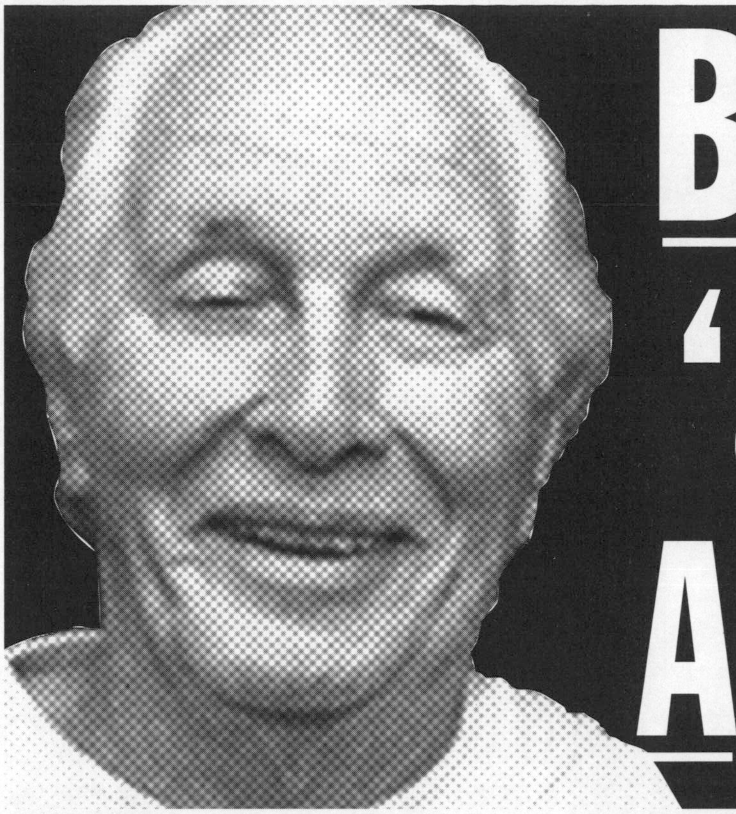

Biggs 'at it Again'

HOME SECRETARY Jack Straw has been left red-faced after agreeing to the release of Great Train Robber RONNIE BIGGS from prison on compassionate grounds. For, it has been revealed, after less than 24 hours of freedom, the veteran cockney robber was already planning a *NEW HEIST* on a mail train.

EXCLUSIVE!

According to an insider at the nursing home where Biggs was moved after leaving Wandsworth prison's hospital wing, the 80-year-old villain wasted no time in getting up to his old tricks.

"As soon as he arrived here, a load of his underworld pals turned up," said the source, who works as a cleaner at the Sunset Grange Nursing Home, "We thought they were here to say their final farewells to their old mate so we left them together in private."

BEDPAN

"However, when I went back into the room a few minutes later to empty Biggs's bedpan, I saw that they had balanced a model railway siding on a board on top of his life support machine. Ronnie was pushing a little model train and removals van around it, whilst the others took notes. There was also a blackboard on an easel with all arrows drawn on it. I thought it was a bit odd, but didn't take much notice."

But later, whilst emptying Biggs's catheter bag after his visitors had left, the source came across evidence which showed that the octogenarian thief was planning a final hurrah.

"Scrumpled up in the bin, there were bits of paper covered with scrawled notes, train timetables, an equipment list and details of flights to Brazil. And there was also a newspaper clipping about a trainload of used banknotes that was due to be moved along a small Essex branch line in the next few weeks."

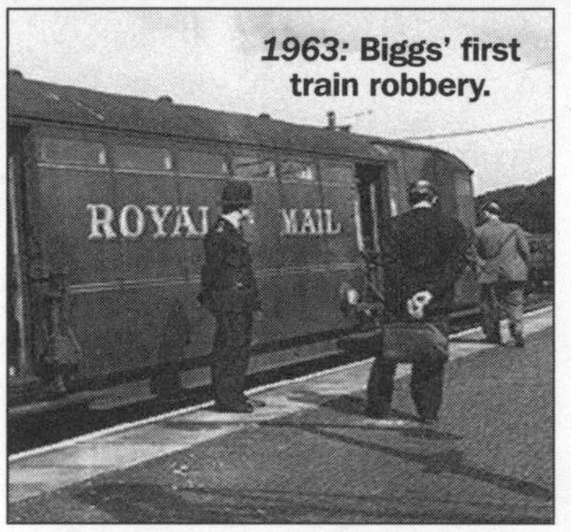
ROYAL MAIL
1963: **Biggs' first train robbery.**

SAUCEPAN

Piecing together the evidence, it appears that Biggs and his gang were planning a second Great Train Robbery that would have made its 1963 predecessor's haul of £2.6m look like chicken feed.

Jack Straw said he was pleased that the plans had failed to come to fruition, but Conservative backbencher Anthony Regents-Gobshite demanded that the Home Secretary resign for what he called "Yet another case of political correctness gone mad."

SAUCE BOTTLE

Speaking on Radio 4's *Today* programme, Mr Regents-Gobshite said: "I am literally incandescent with rage. Releasing criminals from prison so they can offend again and again is yet another case of political correctness gone mad."

"A leopard doesn't change his spots and life should mean life. It's yet another case of political correctness gone mad," he added.

Political Interviewer Joke No. 6519

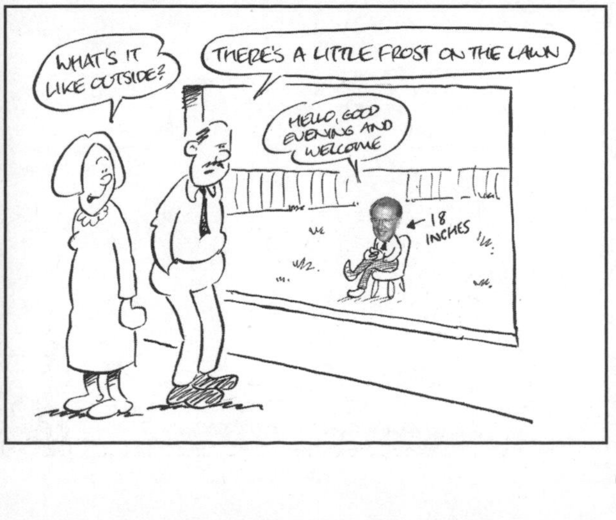
WHAT'S IT LIKE OUTSIDE?
THERE'S A LITTLE FROST ON THE LAWN
HELLO, GOOD EVENING AND WELCOME
← 18 INCHES

How it was to be done

AS THIS time line shows, the second Great Train Robbery was set to be every bit as spectacular as the first.

23.40 Biggs's hospital bed is loaded into a stolen ambulance and driven at high speed to a remote railway siding in Essex

23.45 Other gang members make their way to the siding in a removals lorry

23.58 Biggs's bed is placed at the trackside with a red light attached to it

00.02 The train driver, confusing the red light for a stop signal, brings his train to a halt

00.03 Wire cutters hidden in Biggs's bedpan are used to snip through telephone wires to prevent the alarm being raised

00.04 Gang members use a block & tackle to hoists Biggs's bed into the guard's van of the train

00.25 Bigg's bed is pushed the length of the train to the driver's compartment

00.45 Biggs's bed arrives at the driver's compartment where the driver is forced, at gunpoint, to lower his head to Biggs's bedside

00.46 Biggs is woken up and handed a specially-made 'easy-grip' cosh

00.47 Two other gang members raise Biggs to a sitting position and adjust and secure the ratchet mechanism on his bed

00.58 Biggs is woken again and given his medication, whilst another gang member patiently explains to him who he is and what he is doing

01.02 A gang member helps Biggs to raise the cosh above the back of the driver's head

01.03 Biggs's hand is released and the cosh drops, dealing the driver a feeble blow. The process is repeated until the driver is unconscious

08.45 With the driver unconscious, gang members quickly begin removing hundreds of sacks of money from the train into the removals van

08.46 Biggs's bed is loaded back into the ambulance and driven back to the nursing home

FRU T. BUNN
THE MASTER BAKER & HIS GINGERBREAD SEX DOLLS

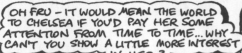

COOEE! FRU! WE'RE BACK FROM THE PET SHOP, DEAR!

≋HRUMPH≋

CHELSEA BOUGHT HERSELF A RABBIT, LOOK.

≋TSK≋

SHE SAYS SHE LOVES HIM SO MUCH SHE'S GOING TO CALL HIM AFTER YOU...

DADDY! DADDY! ≋GIGGLE≋

...ISN'T THAT LOVELY..?

≋TCHOH≋

OH FRU - IT WOULD MEAN THE WORLD TO CHELSEA IF YOU'D PAY HER SOME ATTENTION FROM TIME TO TIME... WHY CAN'T YOU SHOW A LITTLE MORE INTEREST IN HER..?

WHY!?.. WHY!??...I'LL TELL YOU WHY, SHALL I, NOREEN..?

...WHILE YOU WERE OUT, I GOT A PHONE CALL...

.. FROM THE HOSPITAL!

OH MY.

IT WAS...≋GULP≋... IT WAS ABOUT MY GRANDMOTHER.

...WAS IT BAD NEWS, FRU..?

I'LL SAY IT'S BAD NEWS...SHE'S HAD A STROKE IF YOU MUST KNOW...THERE!

OH NO!

SHE'S ON LIFE SUPPORT.

EVEN IF SHE DOES PULL THROUGH, SHE'LL PROBABLY END UP AS A VEGETABLE, THE DOCTOR SAID.

OH FRU! I DIDN'T THINK... I FEEL TERRIBLE.

I'M NOT SURPRISED. YOU SHOULD DO.

I'VE BEEN SO SELFISH, THINKING ABOUT MY OWN ENJOYMENT WHILE YOUR POOR GRANNY WAS IN INTENSIVE CARE...

YES, YES YOU HAVE.

IT'S ALL SELF, SELF, SELF WITH YOU, ISN'T IT..? NEVER A THOUGHT FOR THE SUFFERING OF OTHERS.

WHERE ARE YOU GOING?

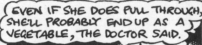

WHERE DO YOU THINK!? TO THE HOSPITAL - TO BE AT THE SIDE OF MY POOR SICK GRANDMOTHER...SHE'S BEEN CALLING OUT FOR ME...

I WANT TO BE THERE IF...IF...

≋SQUEAK≋

SLAM!

≋CHOKE≋

VROOOOM!

≋BOO-HOO!≋

≋SNIFF≋

BUNN THE BAKER

HEH-HEH! OH FRU, YOU CRAFTY OLD DEVIL, YOU. YOU'VE ONLY BEEN AND DONE IT AGAIN! NOREEN FELL FOR YOUR LITTLE FIB HOOK, LINE AND SINKER!

JUST IMAGINE HER FACE IF SHE KNEW THE TRUTH - THAT YOU WERE ON YOUR WAY TO A PARTY HEAVING WITH UNATTACHED BISCUIT FANNY!

≋SLURP!≋

BUNN THE BAKER

GOING TO VISIT MY GRAND-MOTHER ON HER DEATHBED, MY BAKER'S ARSE!

POULSON COURT

...≋GROAN≋ IS THAT YOU, FRUBERT LOVE..?

THERE, THERE, MRS BUNN...

... I SPOKE TO YOUR GRANDSON ON THE PHONE MORE THAN AN HOUR AGO... I'M SURE HE'LL BE HERE VERY SOON.

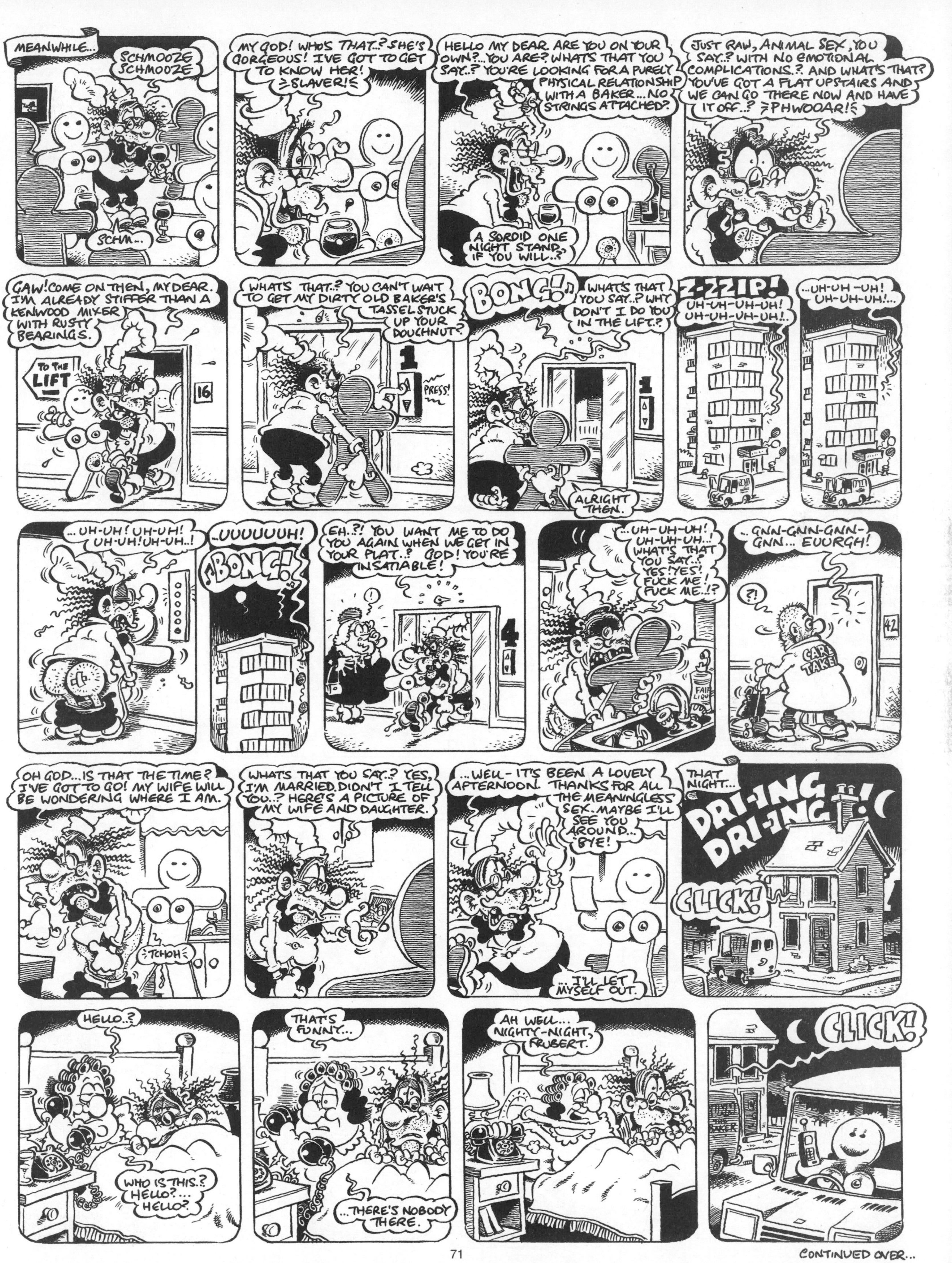
MEANWHILE...
SCHMOOZE SCHMOOZE
SCHM...
MY GOD! WHO'S THAT..? SHE'S GORGEOUS! I'VE GOT TO GET TO KNOW HER!
≥SLAVER!≤
HELLO MY DEAR. ARE YOU ON YOUR OWN?...YOU ARE? WHAT'S THAT YOU SAY..? YOU'RE LOOKING FOR A PURELY PHYSICAL RELATIONSHIP WITH A BAKER...NO STRINGS ATTACHED?
A SORDID ONE NIGHT STAND, IF YOU WILL..?
JUST RAW, ANIMAL SEX, YOU SAY..? WITH NO EMOTIONAL COMPLICATIONS..?. AND WHAT'S THAT? YOU'VE GOT A FLAT UPSTAIRS AND WE CAN GO THERE NOW AND HAVE IT OFF..? ≥PHWOOAR!≤
GAW! COME ON THEN, MY DEAR. I'M ALREADY STIFFER THAN A KENWOOD MIXER WITH RUSTY BEARINGS.
TO THE LIFT
16
WHAT'S THAT..? YOU CAN'T WAIT TO GET MY DIRTY OLD BAKER'S TASSEL STUCK UP YOUR DOUGHNUT?
1
PRESS!
BONG!
WHAT'S THAT YOU SAY..? WHY DON'T I DO YOU IN THE LIFT..?
1
ALRIGHT THEN.
Z-ZZIP!
UH-UH-UH-UH! UH-UH-UH-UH!..
...UH-UH-UH! UH-UH-UH!...
...UH-UH! UH-UH! UH-UH! UH-UH..!
..UUUUUUH!
BONG!
EH..?! YOU WANT ME TO DO YOU AGAIN WHEN WE GET IN YOUR FLAT..? GOD! YOU'RE INSATIABLE!
4
...UH-UH-UH! UH-UH-UH... WHAT'S THAT YOU SAY..? YES! YES! FUCK ME! FUCK ME..!?
...GNN-GNN-GNN-GNN... EUURGH!
42
CARE TAKE
OH GOD... IS THAT THE TIME? I'VE GOT TO GO! MY WIFE WILL BE WONDERING WHERE I AM.
TCHOH
WHAT'S THAT YOU SAY..? YES, I'M MARRIED. DIDN'T I TELL YOU..? HERE'S A PICTURE OF MY WIFE AND DAUGHTER.
...WELL- IT'S BEEN A LOVELY AFTERNOON. THANKS FOR ALL THE MEANINGLESS SEX. MAYBE I'LL SEE YOU AROUND... 'BYE!
...I'LL LET MYSELF OUT.
THAT NIGHT...
DRI-ING DRI-ING
CLICK!
HELLO..?
WHO IS THIS..? HELLO?... HELLO?
THAT'S FUNNY...
...THERE'S NOBODY THERE.
AH WELL... NIGHTY-NIGHT, FRUBERT.
CLICK!
THE BAKER

CONTINUED OVER...

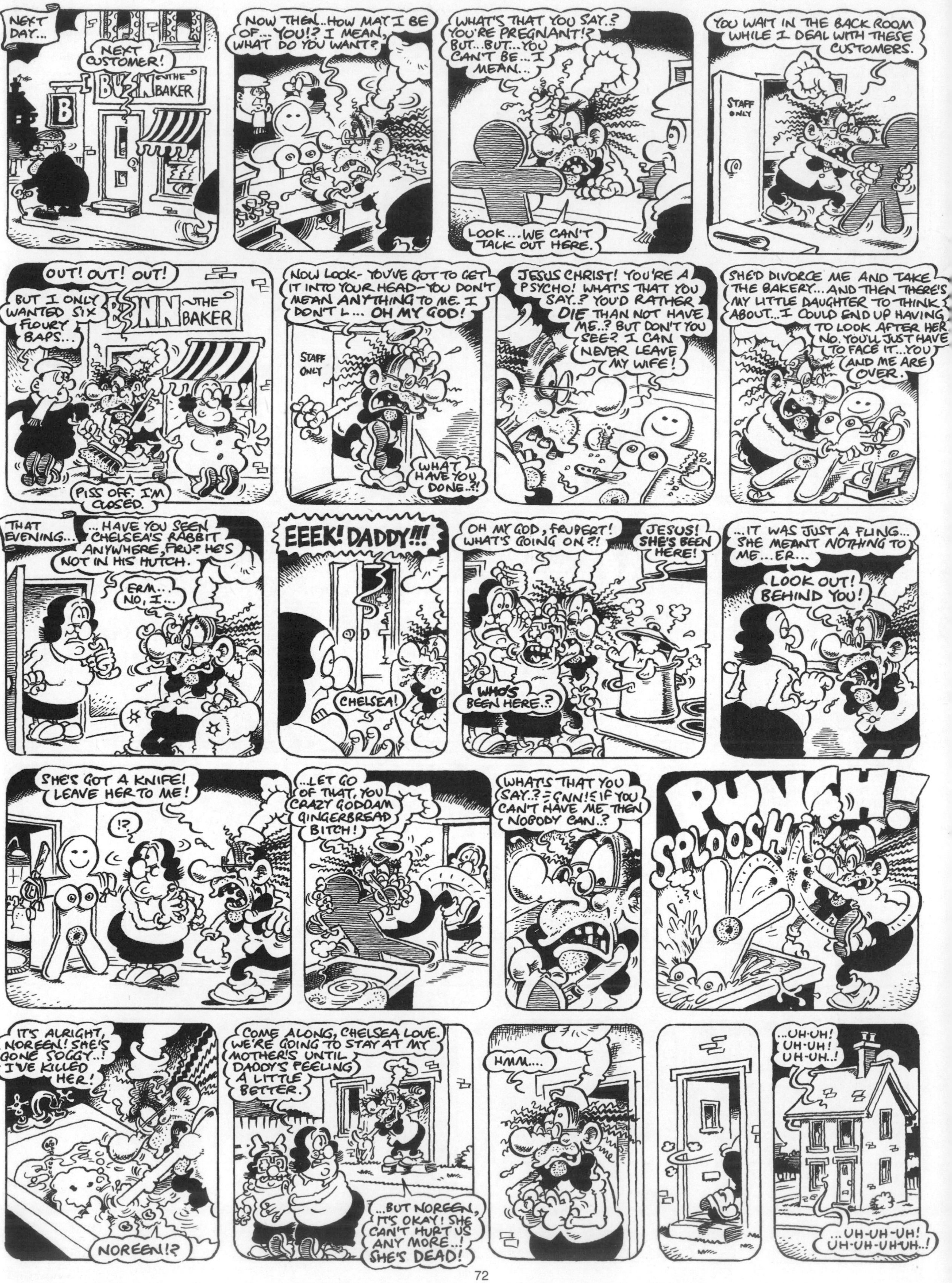
NEXT DAY...
NEXT CUSTOMER!
BUN THE BAKER
NOW THEN... HOW MAY I BE OF... YOU!? I MEAN, WHAT DO YOU WANT?
WHAT'S THAT YOU SAY..? YOU'RE PREGNANT!? BUT... BUT... YOU CAN'T BE... I MEAN...
LOOK... WE CAN'T TALK OUT HERE.
YOU WAIT IN THE BACK ROOM WHILE I DEAL WITH THESE CUSTOMERS.
STAFF ONLY
OUT! OUT! OUT!
BUT I ONLY WANTED SIX FLOURY BAPS...
BUNN THE BAKER
PISS OFF. I'M CLOSED.
NOW LOOK- YOU'VE GOT TO GET IT INTO YOUR HEAD- YOU DON'T MEAN ANYTHING TO ME. I DON'T L... OH MY GOD!
STAFF ONLY
WHAT HAVE YOU DONE..?!
JESUS CHRIST! YOU'RE A PSYCHO! WHAT'S THAT YOU SAY..? YOU'D RATHER DIE THAN NOT HAVE ME..? BUT DON'T YOU SEE? I CAN NEVER LEAVE MY WIFE!
SHE'D DIVORCE ME AND TAKE THE BAKERY... AND THEN THERE'S MY LITTLE DAUGHTER TO THINK ABOUT... I COULD END UP HAVING TO LOOK AFTER HER.
NO. YOU'LL JUST HAVE TO FACE IT... YOU AND ME ARE OVER.
THAT EVENING...
...HAVE YOU SEEN CHELSEA'S RABBIT ANYWHERE, FRU? HE'S NOT IN HIS HUTCH.
ERM... NO, I...
EEEK! DADDY!!!
CHELSEA!
OH MY GOD, FRUBERT! WHAT'S GOING ON?!
JESUS! SHE'S BEEN HERE!
WHO'S BEEN HERE..?
...IT WAS JUST A FLING... SHE MEANT NOTHING TO ME... ER...
LOOK OUT! BEHIND YOU!
SHE'S GOT A KNIFE! LEAVE HER TO ME!
!?
...LET GO OF THAT, YOU CRAZY GODDAM GINGERBREAD BITCH!
WHAT'S THAT YOU SAY..? =GNN!= IF YOU CAN'T HAVE ME THEN NOBODY CAN..?
PUNCH!
SPLOOSH!
IT'S ALRIGHT, NOREEN! SHE'S GONE SOGGY..! I'VE KILLED HER!
NOREEN!?
COME ALONG, CHELSEA LOVE. WE'RE GOING TO STAY AT MY MOTHER'S UNTIL DADDY'S FEELING A LITTLE BETTER.
...BUT NOREEN, IT'S OKAY! SHE CAN'T HURT US ANY MORE..! SHE'S DEAD!
HMM....
...UH-UH! UH-UH! UH-UH..!
...UH-UH-UH! UH-UH-UH'UH..!

Love kept them together, but a secret threatened to tear them apart!

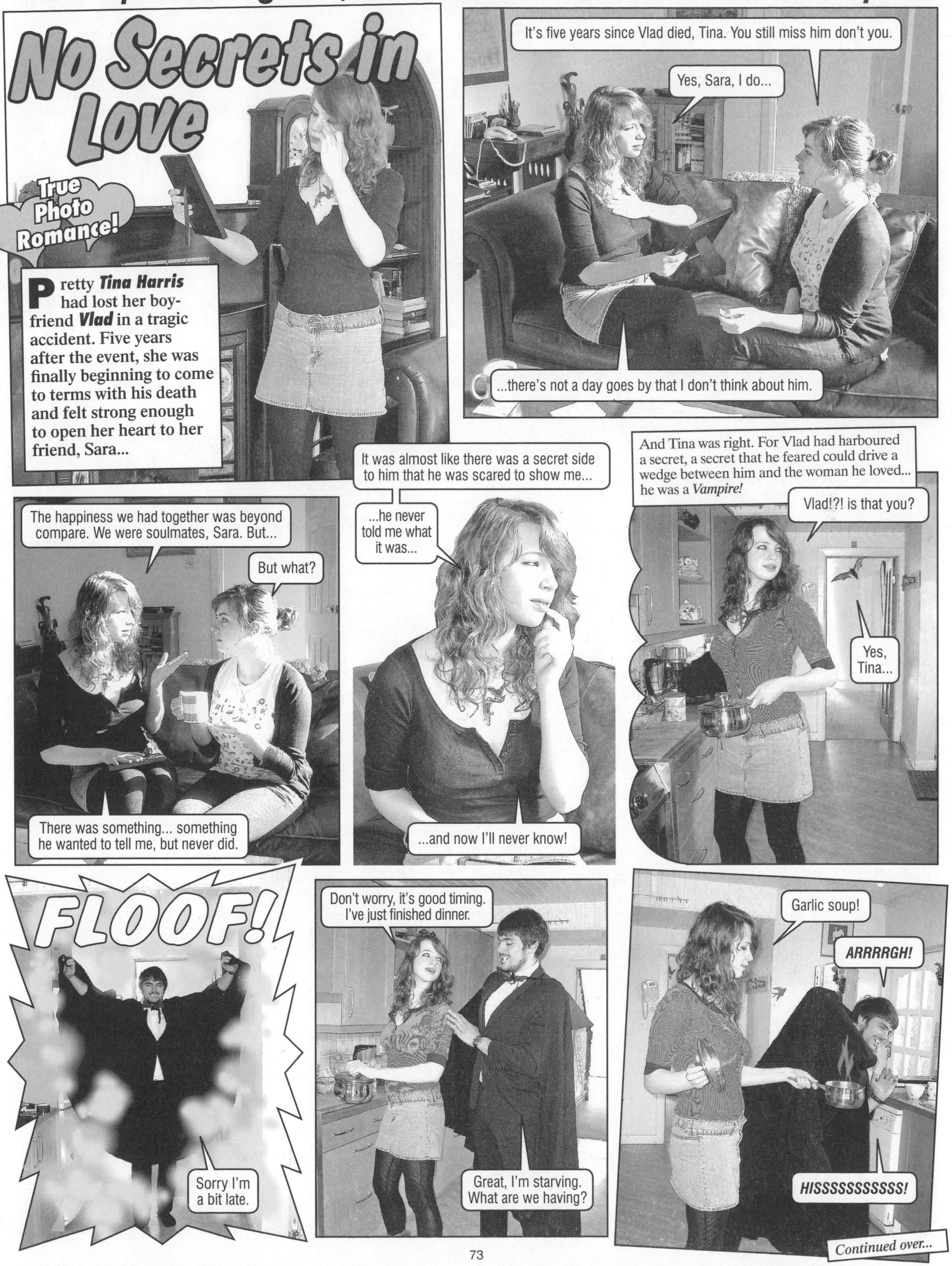
No Secrets in Love
True Photo Romance!
Pretty Tina Harris had lost her boy-friend Vlad in a tragic accident. Five years after the event, she was finally beginning to come to terms with his death and felt strong enough to open her heart to her friend, Sara...
It's five years since Vlad died, Tina. You still miss him don't you.
Yes, Sara, I do...
...there's not a day goes by that I don't think about him.
The happiness we had together was beyond compare. We were soulmates, Sara. But...
But what?
There was something... something he wanted to tell me, but never did.
It was almost like there was a secret side to him that he was scared to show me...
...he never told me what it was...
...and now I'll never know!
And Tina was right. For Vlad had harboured a secret, a secret that he feared could drive a wedge between him and the woman he loved... he was a Vampire!
Vlad!?! is that you?
Yes, Tina...
FLOOF!
Sorry I'm a bit late.
Don't worry, it's good timing. I've just finished dinner.
Great, I'm starving. What are we having?
Garlic soup!
ARRRRGH!
HISSSSSSSSSSS!

Continued over...

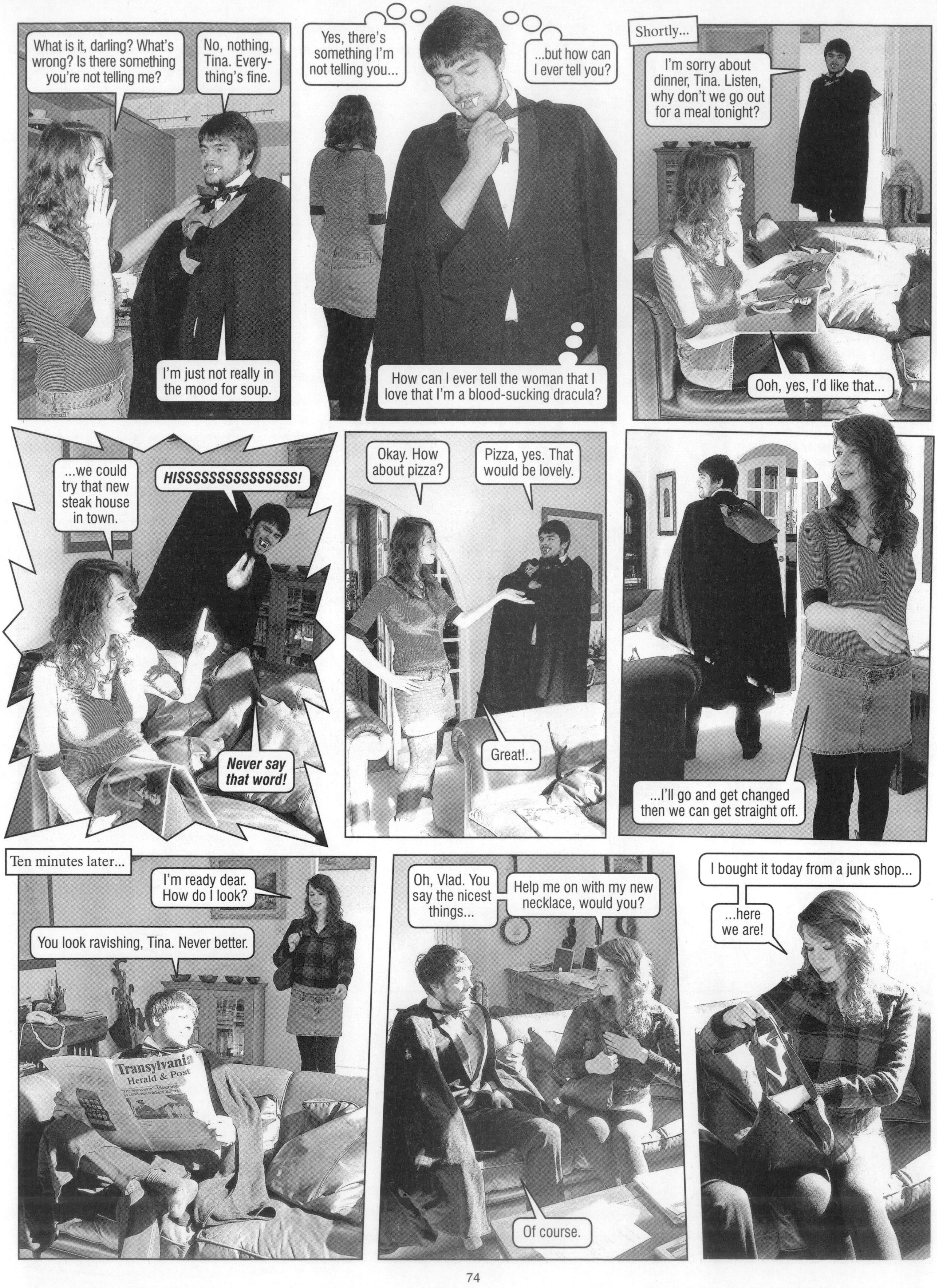
What is it, darling? What's wrong? Is there something you're not telling me?
No, nothing, Tina. Every-thing's fine.
I'm just not really in the mood for soup.
Yes, there's something I'm not telling you...
...but how can I ever tell you?
How can I ever tell the woman that I love that I'm a blood-sucking dracula?
Shortly...
I'm sorry about dinner, Tina. Listen, why don't we go out for a meal tonight?
Ooh, yes, I'd like that...
...we could try that new steak house in town.
HISSSSSSSSSSSSSSS!
Never say that word!
Okay. How about pizza?
Pizza, yes. That would be lovely.
Great!..
...I'll go and get changed then we can get straight off.
Ten minutes later...
I'm ready dear. How do I look?
You look ravishing, Tina. Never better.
Transylvania Herald & Post
Oh, Vlad. You say the nicest things...
Help me on with my new necklace, would you?
Of course.
I bought it today from a junk shop...
...here we are!

HISSSSSSSSSSSSSSSSSSSSSSSSSSSSSSSSSSSS!

Take it away! It burns! IT BURNS!

COUGH! COUGH! COUGH! COUGH!

Alright, alright! If you don't like it I won't wear it.

Thank you!

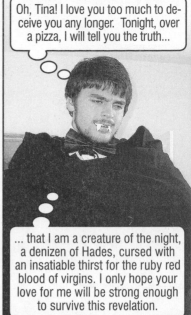

Oh, Tina! I love you too much to deceive you any longer. Tonight, over a pizza, I will tell you the truth...

... that I am a creature of the night, a denizen of Hades, cursed with an insatiable thirst for the ruby red blood of virgins. I only hope your love for me will be strong enough to survive this revelation.

Tina. There is something I need to get off my chest, something I can't keep to myself any longer...

I knew there was Vlad. What is it? You can tell me. Whatever it is I'll understand.

I only hope that's true, Tina...

...however...

...I fear what you hear may change the way you think about me for ever!

Come on, I'll tell you over dinner.

Okay, Vlad, darling. I'll get the car.

Vlad had tried many times to tell Tina he was a Nosferatu. Tonight he was determined she would know the truth...

I'll just back it out, Vlad.

Okay!

Hello!?! Looks like we've got a couple of scratches on the boot...

UNA 250K

...I wonder how they got there.

...I'll have to T-Cut those out at the weekend.

I'll just check the mirror to see if it's all clear...

Continued over...

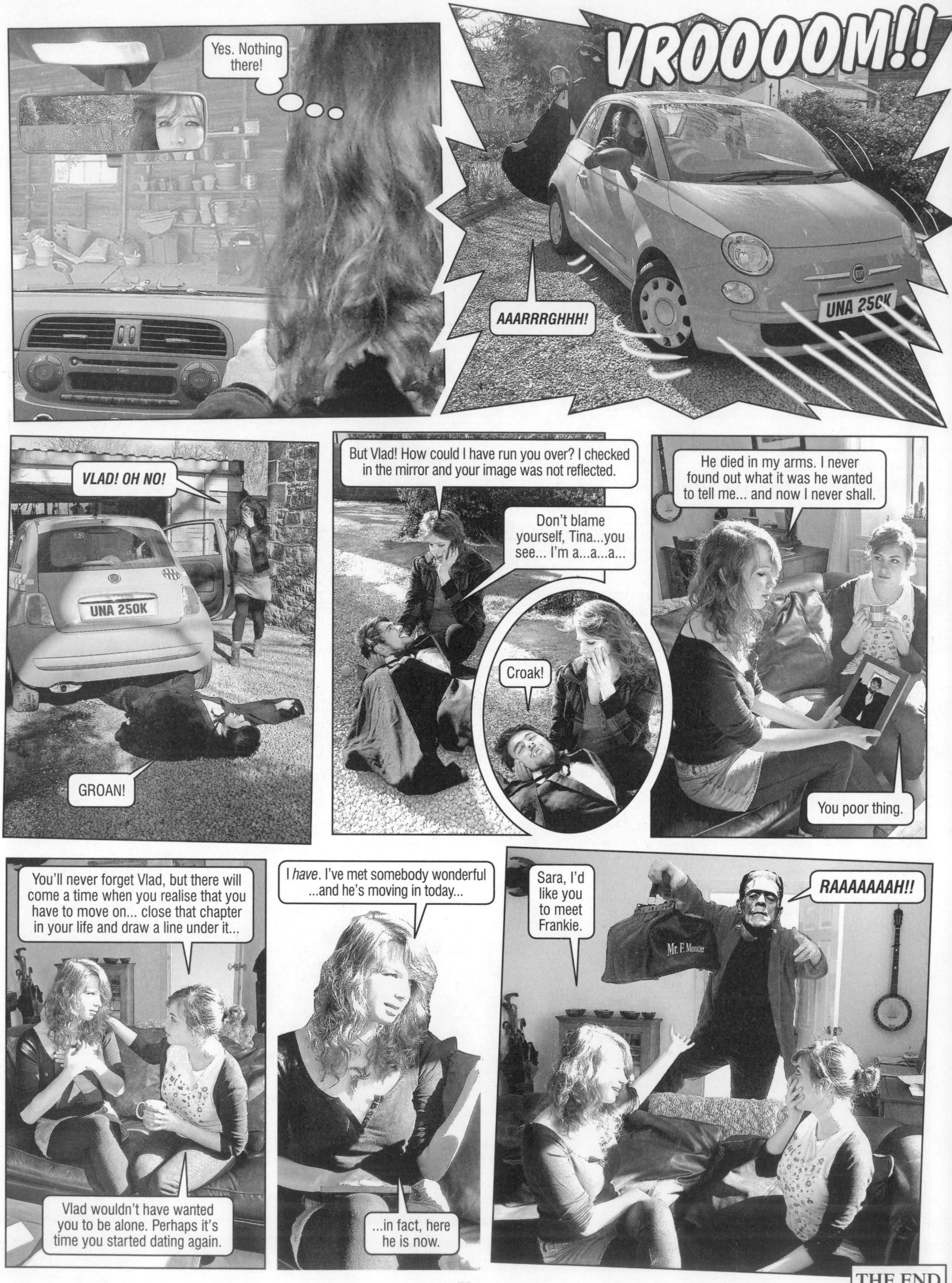
Yes. Nothing there!
VROOOOM!!
UNA 250K
AAARRRGHHH!
VLAD! OH NO!
UNA 250K
GROAN!
But Vlad! How could I have run you over? I checked in the mirror and your image was not reflected.
Don't blame yourself, Tina...you see... I'm a...a...a...
Croak!
He died in my arms. I never found out what it was he wanted to tell me... and now I never shall.
You poor thing.
You'll never forget Vlad, but there will come a time when you realise that you have to move on... close that chapter in your life and draw a line under it...
Vlad wouldn't have wanted you to be alone. Perhaps it's time you started dating again.
I *have*. I've met somebody wonderful ...and he's moving in today...
...in fact, here he is now.
Sara, I'd like you to meet Frankie.
RAAAAAAAH!!
Mr. F. Monster
THE END

THE VIZ

...MICHAEL JACKSON SPECIAL...!

"1000 words by lunchtime? No problem."

READ TONY PARSEHOLE'S TRIBUTE TO JACKO INSIDE

THE MICHAEL JACKSON I KNEW

TO THE WORLD, Michael Jackson was a pop idol, a true musical genius in every sense of the word. His string of hits defined an era, and the legacy of his tragically early death is a collection of chart-topping music that is recognised across the globe.

But behind his public mask, Jackson was a deeply troubled soul. During his infamous child abuse trial, Jackson's defence counsel painted a picture of a troubled man who was haunted by his past - a lonely Peter Pan, afraid of growing up and trapped in an eternal adolescence where he could only be himself amid the company of children.

No longer the fresh-faced Prince of Pop who had won the public's heart in the Jackson 5, to the media he was now Wacko Jacko - an extremely eccentric, even disturbed individual. Whether he was dangling a baby from a hotel balcony, sharing his home with a chimpanzee or sleeping in an oxygen tent, stories of his weird behaviour filled the newspapers.

Continued on Next Page

EXCLUSIVE
DEATH
BED PIC
INSIDE!

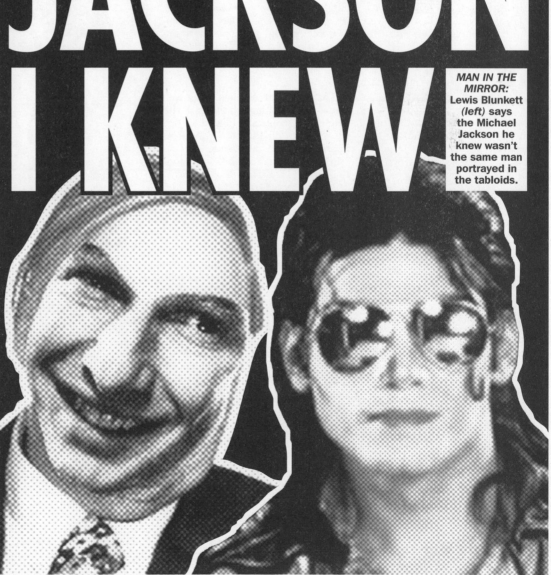

MAN IN THE MIRROR: **Lewis Blunkett *(left)* says the Michael Jackson he knew wasn't the same man portrayed in the tabloids.**

"Everyone knew him Prince of Pop. But t knew could not have

From Front Page

But in Cheshire, Stalybridge carpet fitter Lewis Blunket always took these reports with a pinch of salt. Because the Michael Jackson he knew was very different to the one that grabbed the tabloid headlines. And now, following the singer's death, he says it is finally time to set the record straight.

"I often wondered if the press made these stories up because they describe a very different Michael Jackson to the one I knew," Blunket says, shaking his head sadly. "Because the Michael Jackson I knew was a 23 year-old carpet fitter from Glossop."

These two Michael Jacksons were born in different decades, on different continents and were fated never to meet. They were destined to follow very contrasting careers, one the greatest superstar the world has ever seen and the other in the domestic/light commercial contract flooring business. They were in every way as different as chalk and cheese. But in his personal biography, *The Michael Jackson I Knew* (Kedgeree Books), Blunket tells of the bizarre way in which the lives of these two very different people often mirrored each other closely.

"I remember I first met Mike when I started work at Kwik-Lay Carpets in Mottram. He'd been there about two years when I joined and knew the ropes. The gaffer put him in charge of me and over the next six months he taught me everything there was to know about fitting carpets. As I got to know him, it became clear that he was absolutely nothing like his famous namesake. He was white for a start, and he couldn't sing or dance to save his life. Pop star Michael was a teetotal Jehovah's Witness, whereas my mate Mike loved a drink. And forget about kiddies, it was the birds what flicked Mike's switch, let me tell you.

"But there were strange parallels in the two Michaels' lives, odd coincidences that on their own were unremarkable, but together made me wonder if some strange forces were at work.

BLUNKET COVERAGE: Carpet fitter Lewis yesterday.

The pop star Michael was well know for rubbing shoulders with celebrities, counting Elizabeth Taylor, Brooke Shields and Diana Ross amongst his closest friends. And according to Blunket, this start-studded aspect of Jacko's life was eerily mirrored by his friend Michael who would also hob-nob with the stars. "He has put carpets in for all the big names in his time - the cousin of Big Brother reject Bubble, the man who worked Zippy's mouth on Rainbow, Jet off of Gladiators, you name them. His list of clients reads like a Who's Who of showbiz A-listers.

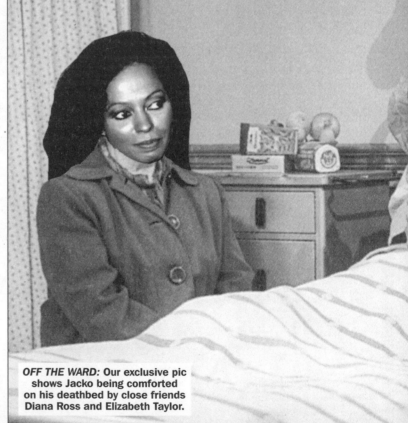

OFF THE WARD: Our exclusive pic shows Jacko being comforted on his deathbed by close friends Diana Ross and Elizabeth Taylor.

"I remember one time going round to an old lady's house to do a job, and she quickly let it be known that she was the auntie of the drummer from Black Lace. She picked the carpet she wanted and then asked for the cheapest underlay. But being the true professional, Michael advised her that it would be false economy to put cheap underlay down. He explained that a thin underlay would cause the carpet to wear more quickly, especially in the heavy traffic areas like at the top of the stairs and outside the bathroom. Although it was £4.99 per square metre as opposed to £1.99, he told her it would save money in the long run, so she eventually agreed. He got the money off her up front and then put the cheap stuff down like he always did.

"Because her nephew had a hit with Agadoo in the 70s she probably expected some kind of preferential treatment. But just like his Motown legend namesake, Mike was never star struck and so she got the same treatment as everybody else."

Towards the end of his musical career, pop star Michael hit the headlines for all the wrong reasons. Allegations of child abuse dogged him to the end of his life, even after he was acquitted of all charges. And in another bizarre echo, his carpet-fitting namesake on this side of the pond also found himself having to answer embarrassing questions about sexual indiscretions.

"It was about a year after the Jackson abuse trial in America, and we were fitting some Axminster in the hallway of a house in Gamesley. The woman who owned it was a cracking bit of stuff and Michael was giving her some pretty fruity banter. Anyway, halfway

as Wacko Jacko, the e Michael Jackson I been more different."

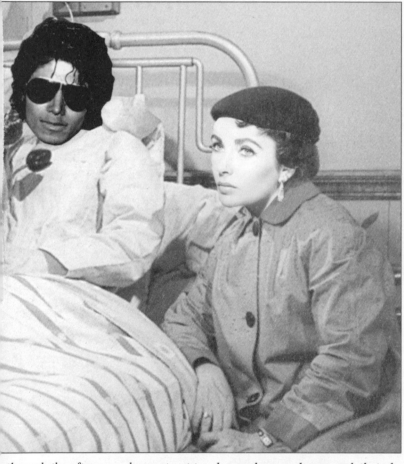

through the afternoon she went out to the shops and as usual Michael nipped upstairs to have a sniff around the bedroom. He'd been gone about five minutes when he called me up. I found him standing by a chest of drawers, grinning from ear to ear, holding up a really sexy black lace basque. I left him up there going through the rest of her stuff like a kid in a sweet shop while I went back downstairs to finish off putting the gripper rods round the skirting.

"Anyway, the next morning the gaffer called us both into his office. Apparently, the woman had phoned up in hysterics claiming that someone had wanked into her underwear drawer and that she was going to call the police.

"Well, Michael just smiled and said that it wasn't him. He pointed out it could easily have been the man who had called to read the gas meter while we were there, but he wasn't fooling anybody. We all knew it was Michael, as he did it at most of the houses we went to and he had had several warnings in the past. Needless to say, the homeowner was furious, but she knew she couldn't prove anything. Eventually she let it drop after our gaffer offered to knock the cost of dry cleaning her undies off the bill. And Michael got another warning."

Lewis once again put the similarity of the situations down to nothing more than a coincidence. But then something amazing happened which convinced him that the two Michael Jacksons' lives really might be following parallel paths.

"We were fitting a deep pile carpet in somebody's front room in Hadfield. It was a cushy number - the owners were out all day, and Mike was calling chatlines on their phone - and we were trying to stretch the job out. We'd got in at half past eight, but by lunchtime we were still sat down with the paper. I remember reading the story of how Michael Jackson's hair had caught fire whilst he was filming a Pepsi advert. Me and Mike were joking about it, trying to think up songs that he could cover that had references to fire or hair in the title.

"I was laughing, but deep down I was uneasy. I felt that it was an omen, and that at any time Mike too could suffer a terrible accident at work. And it wasn't long before I was proved right.

"Just after dinner, we decided to do five minutes work in case he owners came back early. As Mike went over to the skirting board to pick up his hammer, he let out an agonising yell. My blood ran cold. He had knelt on a tack. Fortunately, it was on its side so it hadn't pierced the skin, but it had left a nasty indentation on his knee. The following day, he phoned the gaffer to say that he wouldn't be in to work. Pop star Jackson was out of the burns unit and back in the studio within two weeks of his accident, but Mike wasn't so lucky. His injury laid him up for nearly six weeks, and he only finally felt fit enough to come back to work the day after his statutory sic pay ran out.

Blunket was now watching the career of Michael Jackson very carefully, convinced that his friend and the stateside Pop Prince were set on the same course of destiny. And if he did have any lingering doubts that he could be wrong, they were put to bed when he went to work one day last October.

"We had been sent lay a Wilton in a house not far from Tintwhistle. It was a simple job, one that we would usually rush so that we could spend the afternoon in the pub. But Mike seemed very quiet and introverted that day and said he didn't really fancy a drink. He usually liked to draw a big cock and balls or some other obscene image in felt pen on the floorboards before he put the underlay down, but on this morning he couldn't even be bothered with that.

"It was clear that his heart really wasn't in his work. I asked him what was wrong, and he told me. He had got a girl pregnant and was going to have to get married.

"I tried to cheer him up, asking him who the lucky girl was. When he told me, I was not in the least surprised. In America, Michael Jackson's first bride had been Lisa-Marie Presley, daughter of rock star Elvis. Over in England, Mike's bride was to be Kirsty Small, daughter of the local butcher Les Small.

"And whilst Elvis is known to the world as the King of Rock 'n' Roll, Les Small is affectionately known in Glossop as The King of the Sausage Roll."

Although he was now convinced of the link between the two Michael Jacksons, Lewis still thought the men's parallel lives were nothing more than an interesting aberration - a series of million-to-one coincidences. But with the recent death of the US pop idol, the association has taken a sinister twist.

"We used to laugh and joke about the similarity of events in the two Michael Jacksons' lives," Blunket says in the final chapter of his book. "But now, following Jacko's death, it doesn't seem so funny any more. I have this awful fear that one day, I don't know when, Mike will follow the same path as Jacko and die. I hope to God I am wrong." **99**

Lewis Blunket
THE MICHAEL JACKSON I KNEW

• *The Michael Jackson I Knew* (Kedgeree Books) is currently being printed in Bristol before being delivered directly to a pulping mill in Totnes.

TONY PARSEHOLE

Why I grieve for Jacko

THERE is only one word which comes close to describing the phenomenom that was Michael Jackson.

That word is genius.

But the word genius doesn't even come close to describing the phenomenom that was Michael Jackson. It's too small a word. Too inadequate a word. It's too meagre a word.

Too small, because Jackson's talent was infinite. It was bigger than the solar system. It was bigger than the galaxy. It was bigger, yes, than the universe itself.

Too inadequate, because compared to the phenomenom that was Michael Jackson, all other so called geniuses of history pale into insignificance.

Could Einstein moonwalk? No.

Could Isaac Newton of written Thriller? No.

Could Leonardo da Vinci moonwalk either? No. He could not. A thousand times no.

I'll just do a quick word count. 124. Bloody hell. I thought I'd nearly finished.

What was after inadequate? Oh, yes, meagre.

Too meagre, because the phenomenom that was Michael Joseph Jackson towered above the six insubstantial letters that make up the word genius. He towered over them like Mount Everest.

But not a Mount Everest made out of stone and snow. No. Michael Jackson was a Mount Everest made out of talent.

Musical talent. Singing talent. Dancing talent. Moonwalking talent.

More than that, Michael Jackson was a Mount Everest of talent that wore a single iconic glove. A single iconic glove that touched hearts. He touched my heart. He touched your heart. Yes, he touched all our hearts.

He also touched children. But not their hearts. Their bottoms.

He was not perfect. Not by any means. And I for one will never say he was. In fact, perfection was the one quality which was not possessed by the phenomenom that was Michael Jackson. Amidst all the hype, we must never forget that.

297. That's more like it. Nearly a third of the way through. I'll have this finished in time for Cash in the Attic.

Perfection. No other word comes close to describing the phenomenom that was Michael Joseph Jackson, born in Gary, Indiana, USA. Actually, I should call it the United States of America, not USA, because that takes up five words instead of one.

The United States of America was transformed by Michael Joseph Jackson of Gary, Indiana. Because before Michael Joseph Jackson of Gary, Indiana, the United States of America was a dark place. It was a gloomy place. And, yes, it was a place bereft of light.

But then came Michael Joseph Jackson of Gary, Indiana, blazing a trail of blinding brilliance like a comet. But not a comet made out of loose collections of ice, dust and small rocky particles, ranging from a few kilometres to tens of kilometres across.

No. Michael Joseph Jackson of Gary, Indiana, was a comet made out of star quality.

Like a comet, he flew through the heavens. The light of his brilliance illuminated the sinister shadows of the American psyche. Yes, I like that bit. I'll use that again in the Farrah Fawcett one next week.

Born into a society which was riven by racial tensions, war and inequality, Michael's music healed the rifts between black and white. He bestrode the colour barrier like the Colossus of Rhodes.

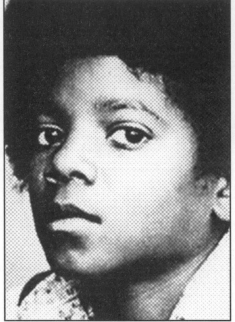

He was the black Elvis. He was the white James Brown.

He did more to bring about today's equal, racism-free America than a thousand Rosa Parkes's could of done in a million years of catching buses. She is not fit to shine his shoes. 578. Getting there.

He was an angel in every sense of the word. He came down from heaven, and to heaven he hath returned. But like all angels, he was beset by demons. Sinister demons. Wicked demons. And yes, bad demons. Very bad demons. Very bad demons indeed.

And it was these very very bad demons that were to destroy him in the end.

As a child, Michael Joseph Jackson of Gary, Indiana spent his childhood not being a child. As an adult, having been denied a childhood as a child, he spent his adulthood in a fruitless search for the childhood that he had been denied as a child.

He tried to get in touch with the child inside him by touching the children outside him. 705. Just 295 words to go.

Michael Jackson tried to recreate the innocence, the wonderment and the innocent wonderment of his lost childhood by building his own personal theme park. Neverland Ranch was a fairytale playground where he could retreat from the pressures, strains and stresses of the showbiz merry-go-round - his very own Disneyland.

And in many ways, Michael came to resemble the characters from the Disney films which served as a magical window into the childhood hopes and dreams which had been denied to him so cruelly.

Like Peter Pan, he could never grow up and would often appear unexpectedly in children's bedrooms late at night.

Like Mickey Mouse, his face changed over the years and he spoke in a high-pitched voice.

Like Mowgli in the Jungle Book, he befriended a monkey, only to have that friendship turn to ashes when the secret of man's red fire was let loose on his hair during the filming of a Pepsi commercial.

Like Pinocchio, he longed to be a real boy rather than a wooden marionette controlled by the puppet-masters of the international music industry. And he did manage to cut those strings, only to find himself swallowed up by the monstrous whale of corporate greed and avarice.

Like Snow White, he was graceful and his skin was the colour of the purest alabaster. Jacko was pure of heart, but fell victim to the cruel, poisoned apple of success.

Like Happy, he experienced great moments of joy when performing in front of his adoring fans.

Like Bashful, he shunned publicity away from the stage.

Like Dopey, his senses were often dulled by the prescription drugs to which he was tragically addicted.

Like Sneezy, his nose was often sore, especially after plastic surgery.

Like Grumpy, he wasThere that's 1000. Invoice enc.

NEXT WEEK: "She flew through the heavens. The light of her brilliance illuminated the sinister shadows of the American psyche." **PARSEHOLE ON FARRAH FAWCETT**

ONE SMALL STEP FOR JACKSON

BLAME IT ON THE TRICK PHOTOGRAPHY: Faker Jackson performs his famous moonwalk in the Billy Jean video.

IN 1934, London gynaecologist Robert Kenneth Wilson was on holiday in the Highlands when he took a photograph of what he claimed was an aquatic monster living in Loch Ness. The legend of Nessie was born, and people from all over the world spent the next 60 years flocking to the Scottish loch in search of the mysterious long-necked creature. It was not until 1994 that it was revealed that the picture had been faked.

This was not the first time, nor the last, that the world would fall victim to a skillful hoax. The Cottingley Fairies, the Roswell alien autopsy film and the notorious Hitler diaries are all examples of the gullible public being duped by mischievous pranksters.

And now one Yorkshire teenager is ready to blow the lid on another seemingly impossible event. For he says he can prove that the late Michael Jackson's famous moonwalk was **FAKED!**

On the 25th March 1983, anyone watching the TV show *Motown 25* would have witnessed the unforgettable moment of the first moonwalk. For it was during a performance of his song Billy Jean that the late Michael Jackson moved his legs as though walking forwards whilst actually travelling backwards. But Gritley Mews, an unemployed school-leaver from Wakefield, believes Jacko's famous 'backwards walk' never took place, and that a massive cover-up has been organised to prevent the truth coming out.

Jacko repeated his stunt hundreds of times over the following decades, and Mews believes that this overperformance is the undoing of the hoax. And with the death of the star earlier this year, he believes that the shell of lies surrounding the truth of what really happened will quickly crumble.

"You can fool people easily once, but the more times you try to do it, the more chances there are that you will make a mistake," he told reporters at a press conference held in his bedroom. "I've spent the last 4 years watching videos of Jackson moonwalking on the internet, and I've collected enough evidence to prove that the whole thing was faked," he added.

"Like all hoaxes, it's really quite simple when you know how it was done. In his videos, Jackson was filmed walking forwards, then the director would simply run the film backwards on the final cut. It's a very convincing effect, but there are one or two things that give it away," he explained.

"If you look in the background during the Billy Jean moonwalk sequence, you can just make out that the second hand on the drummer's wristwatch appears to be going **BACKWARDS**. In addition to this, there is what appears to be a bead of sweat on the lead guitarist's cheek that mysteriously rolls **UPWARDS** towards his forehead. And in the brass section, the trumpeter's cheeks are clearly seen being sucked **IN**."

According to Mews, the king of pop was so worried about the truth being revealed, that everyone involved with the making of the Billy Jean video was killed in order to prevent them from talking.

"Once shooting was over, Jackson invited the cast and crew back to his Neverland Ranch as a thank-you for their help," he said. "There, he handed out free tickets for the rollercoaster, and everyone piled on hoping for the ride of their life."

"What they got was the ride of their DEATH!"

"The rollercoaster made its way up the track, but when it got to the top the wheels all fell off," said Mews.

According to the teenager, twenty-five carriages, along with their 250 passengers plummeted to the ground. There were no survivors. Their silence had been assured and Jacko's secret was safe.

The death of 250 people may have been considered a small price to prevent the truth coming out. But what about when Jackson performed the stunt live on stage in front of thousands of fans? Mews thinks he has the answer.

"Jackson regularly did his moonwalk before massive stadium audiences of 100,000 or more. I doubt that even he, with his vast wealth and influence, could have had that many people killed without attracting unwanted attention. And on a practical level, the queuing time to get on the rollercoaster would have run into many hours, and lots of his fans would have got bored and gone home before they could be killed.

*"So onstage, Jackson needed another way of moving backwards whilst appearing to walk for-*wards, and after studying hundreds of hours of live footage, I think I know how he did it," he told reporters.

"With his right foot about ten inches behind his left and with his toe on the ground, he slid his left foot backwards with the sole on the ground until it was ten inches behind his right. At this point, he snapped his right foot flat to the ground whilst simultaneously lifting his left onto the toe. He then repeated this process which gave the impression that he was walking forwards whilst actually moving back. The hoax was complete."

Mews' article, *How Michael Jackson Faked his Moonwalk* is available to download from www.mjmoonwalk-hoax.co.uk and all crackpot conspiracy theory websites.

MICHAEL JACKSON'S moonwalk is just one of a catalogue of spectacular hoaxes that the music industry has pulled off over the years. Here are some of the most famous deceptions in the history of pop.

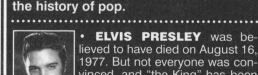

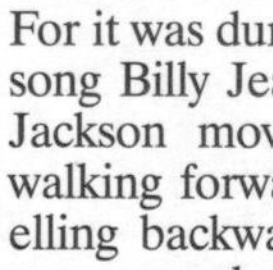

• **ELVIS PRESLEY** was believed to have died on August 16, 1977. But not everyone was convinced, and "the King" has been spotted by so many people in the last three decades that it is now widely accepted that he faked his own death in an attempt to revive his flagging career.

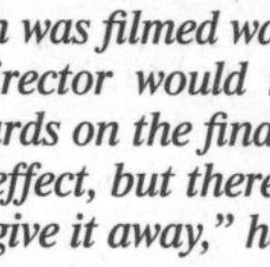

MUSIC FAKERS

• Art rockers **KLF** famously burnt £1million in cash on a Scottish island as a publicity stunt. But in 2007 it was revealed by band front man Bill Drummond that the wads of notes were Monopoly money with only the top ones being real tenners. In actuality, a mere £250 went up in flames.

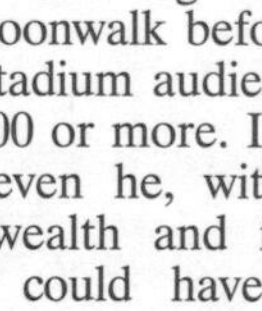

• In 1982, Manchester-born Stephen **MORRISSEY** began his career with The Smiths. For the next three decades he convinced the public that he was a deep, tortured lyricist, but in 2008 it was revealed by a music business insider that he was just a big twat.

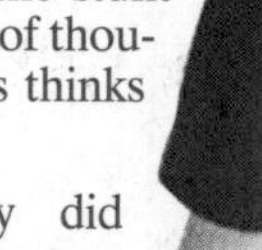

• For many years, fans of U2 believed that lead singer **BONO** was a normal 5 feet 10 inches tall. However, two years ago, a Dublin cobbler divulged that the Irish star had bought a pair of shoes in for repair, the heels of which were a full 4 inches thick, revealing the star to be just 5 feet 6. Shortly afterwards, the cobbler was killed when a Ferris wheel in the grounds of Bono's Dublin mansion mysteriously came off its axle and rolled off a cliff.

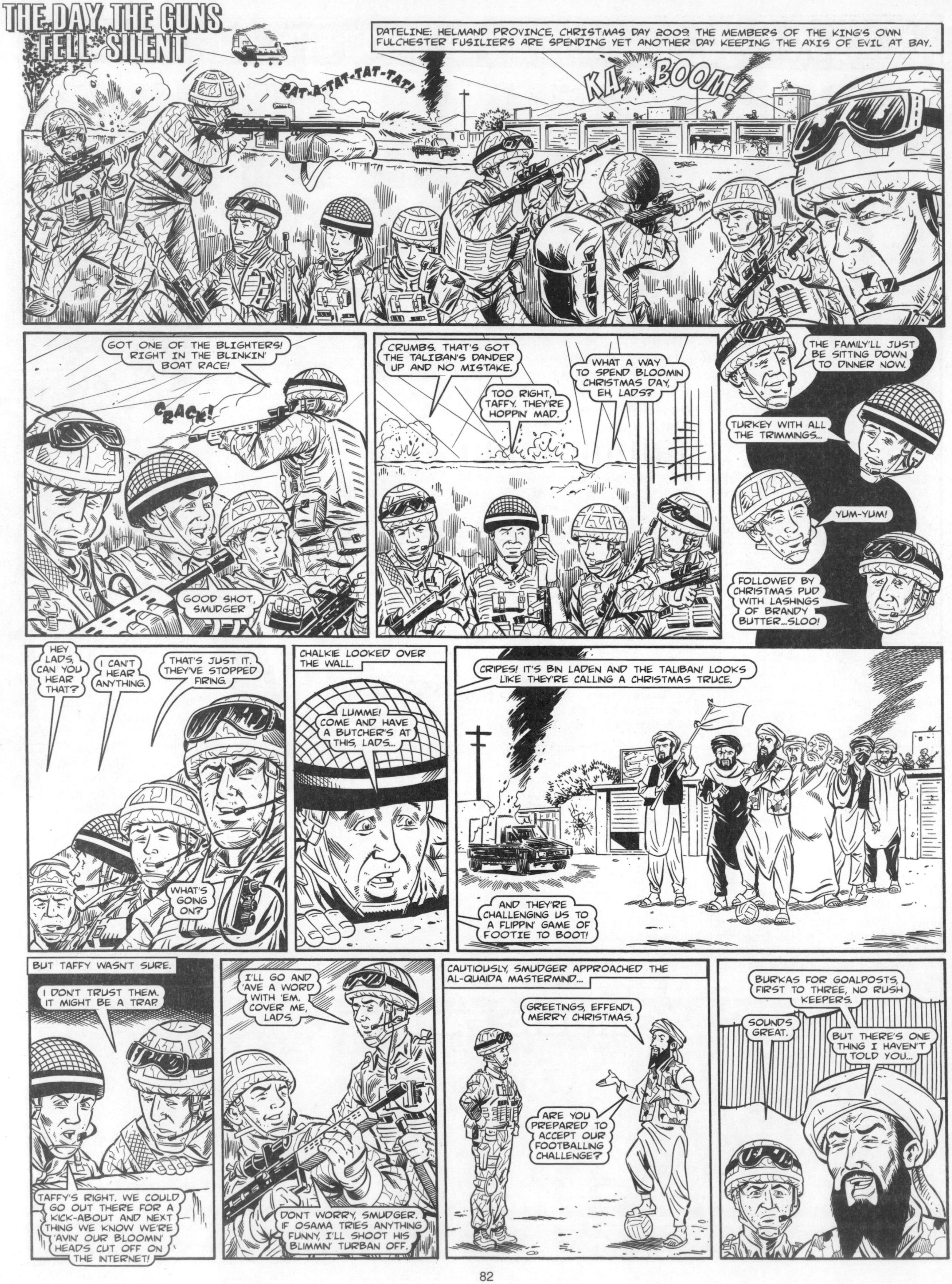
THE DAY THE GUNS FELL SILENT
DATELINE: HELMAND PROVINCE, CHRISTMAS DAY 2009. THE MEMBERS OF THE KING'S OWN FULCHESTER FUSILIERS ARE SPENDING YET ANOTHER DAY KEEPING THE AXIS OF EVIL AT BAY.
RAT-A-TAT-TAT-TAT!
KA BOOM!
GOT ONE OF THE BLIGHTERS! RIGHT IN THE BLINKIN' BOAT RACE!
CRACK!
GOOD SHOT, SMUDGER
CRUMBS. THAT'S GOT THE TALIBAN'S DANDER UP AND NO MISTAKE.
TOO RIGHT, TAFFY. THEY'RE HOPPIN' MAD.
WHAT A WAY TO SPEND BLOOMIN CHRISTMAS DAY, EH, LADS?
THE FAMILY'LL JUST BE SITTING DOWN TO DINNER NOW.
TURKEY WITH ALL THE TRIMMINGS...
YUM-YUM!
FOLLOWED BY CHRISTMAS PUD WITH LASHINGS OF BRANDY BUTTER...SLOO!
HEY LADS, CAN YOU HEAR THAT?
I CAN'T HEAR ANYTHING.
THAT'S JUST IT. THEY'VE STOPPED FIRING.
WHAT'S GOING ON?
CHALKIE LOOKED OVER THE WALL.
LUMME! COME AND HAVE A BUTCHER'S AT THIS, LADS...
CRIPES! IT'S BIN LADEN AND THE TALIBAN! LOOKS LIKE THEY'RE CALLING A CHRISTMAS TRUCE.
AND THEY'RE CHALLENGING US TO A FLIPPIN' GAME OF FOOTIE TO BOOT!
BUT TAFFY WASN'T SURE.
I DON'T TRUST THEM. IT MIGHT BE A TRAP.
TAFFY'S RIGHT. WE COULD GO OUT THERE FOR A KICK-ABOUT AND NEXT THING WE KNOW WE'RE 'AVIN' OUR BLOOMIN' HEADS CUT OFF ON THE INTERNET!
I'LL GO AND 'AVE A WORD WITH 'EM. COVER ME, LADS.
DON'T WORRY, SMUDGER. IF OSAMA TRIES ANYTHING FUNNY, I'LL SHOOT HIS BLIMMIN' TURBAN OFF.
CAUTIOUSLY, SMUDGER APPROACHED THE AL-QUAIDA MASTERMIND...
GREETINGS, EFFENDI. MERRY CHRISTMAS.
ARE YOU PREPARED TO ACCEPT OUR FOOTBALLING CHALLENGE?
BURKAS FOR GOALPOSTS, FIRST TO THREE, NO RUSH KEEPERS.
SOUNDS GREAT.
BUT THERE'S ONE THING I HAVEN'T TOLD YOU...

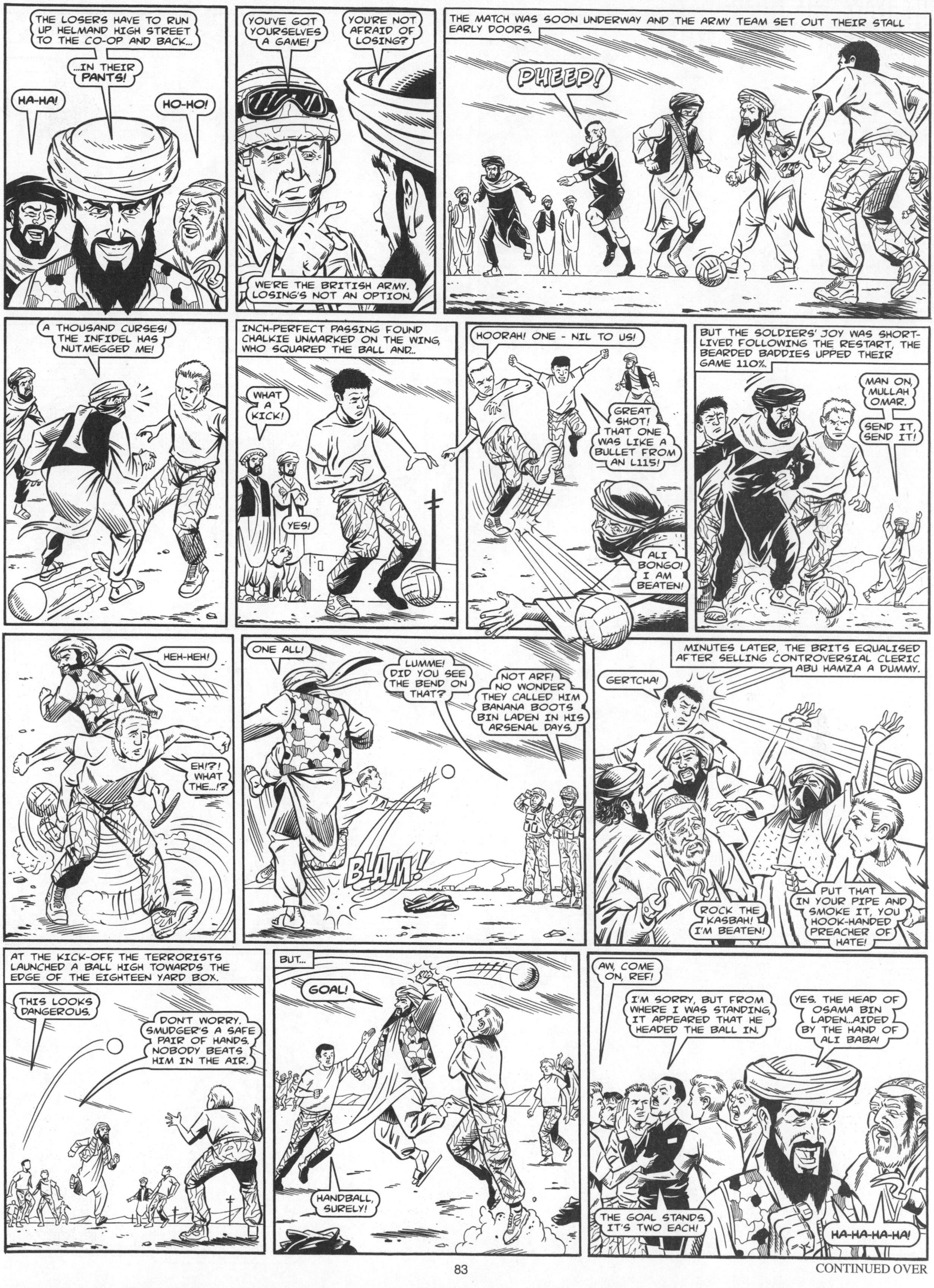
THE LOSERS HAVE TO RUN UP HELMAND HIGH STREET TO THE CO-OP AND BACK...
...IN THEIR PANTS!
HA-HA!
HO-HO!
YOU'VE GOT YOURSELVES A GAME!
YOU'RE NOT AFRAID OF LOSING?
WE'RE THE BRITISH ARMY. LOSING'S NOT AN OPTION.
THE MATCH WAS SOON UNDERWAY AND THE ARMY TEAM SET OUT THEIR STALL EARLY DOORS.
PHEEP!
A THOUSAND CURSES! THE INFIDEL HAS NUTMEGGED ME!
INCH-PERFECT PASSING FOUND CHALKIE UNMARKED ON THE WING, WHO SQUARED THE BALL AND...
WHAT A KICK!
YES!
HOORAH! ONE - NIL TO US!
GREAT SHOT! THAT ONE WAS LIKE A BULLET FROM AN L115!
ALI BONGO! I AM BEATEN!
BUT THE SOLDIERS' JOY WAS SHORT-LIVED. FOLLOWING THE RESTART, THE BEARDED BADDIES UPPED THEIR GAME 110%.
MAN ON, MULLAH OMAR.
SEND IT, SEND IT!
HEH-HEH!
EH!?! WHAT THE...!?
ONE ALL!
LUMME! DID YOU SEE THE BEND ON THAT?
NOT ARF! NO WONDER THEY CALLED HIM BANANA BOOTS BIN LADEN IN HIS ARSENAL DAYS.
BLAM!
MINUTES LATER, THE BRITS EQUALISED AFTER SELLING CONTROVERSIAL CLERIC ABU HAMZA A DUMMY.
GERTCHA!
ROCK THE KASBAH! I'M BEATEN!
PUT THAT IN YOUR PIPE AND SMOKE IT, YOU HOOK-HANDED PREACHER OF HATE!
AT THE KICK-OFF, THE TERRORISTS LAUNCHED A BALL HIGH TOWARDS THE EDGE OF THE EIGHTEEN YARD BOX.
THIS LOOKS DANGEROUS.
DON'T WORRY. SMUDGER'S A SAFE PAIR OF HANDS. NOBODY BEATS HIM IN THE AIR.
BUT...
GOAL!
HANDBALL, SURELY!
AW, COME ON, REF!
I'M SORRY, BUT FROM WHERE I WAS STANDING, IT APPEARED THAT HE HEADED THE BALL IN.
YES. THE HEAD OF OSAMA BIN LADEN...AIDED BY THE HAND OF ALI BABA!
THE GOAL STANDS. IT'S TWO EACH!
HA-HA-HA-HA!

CONTINUED OVER

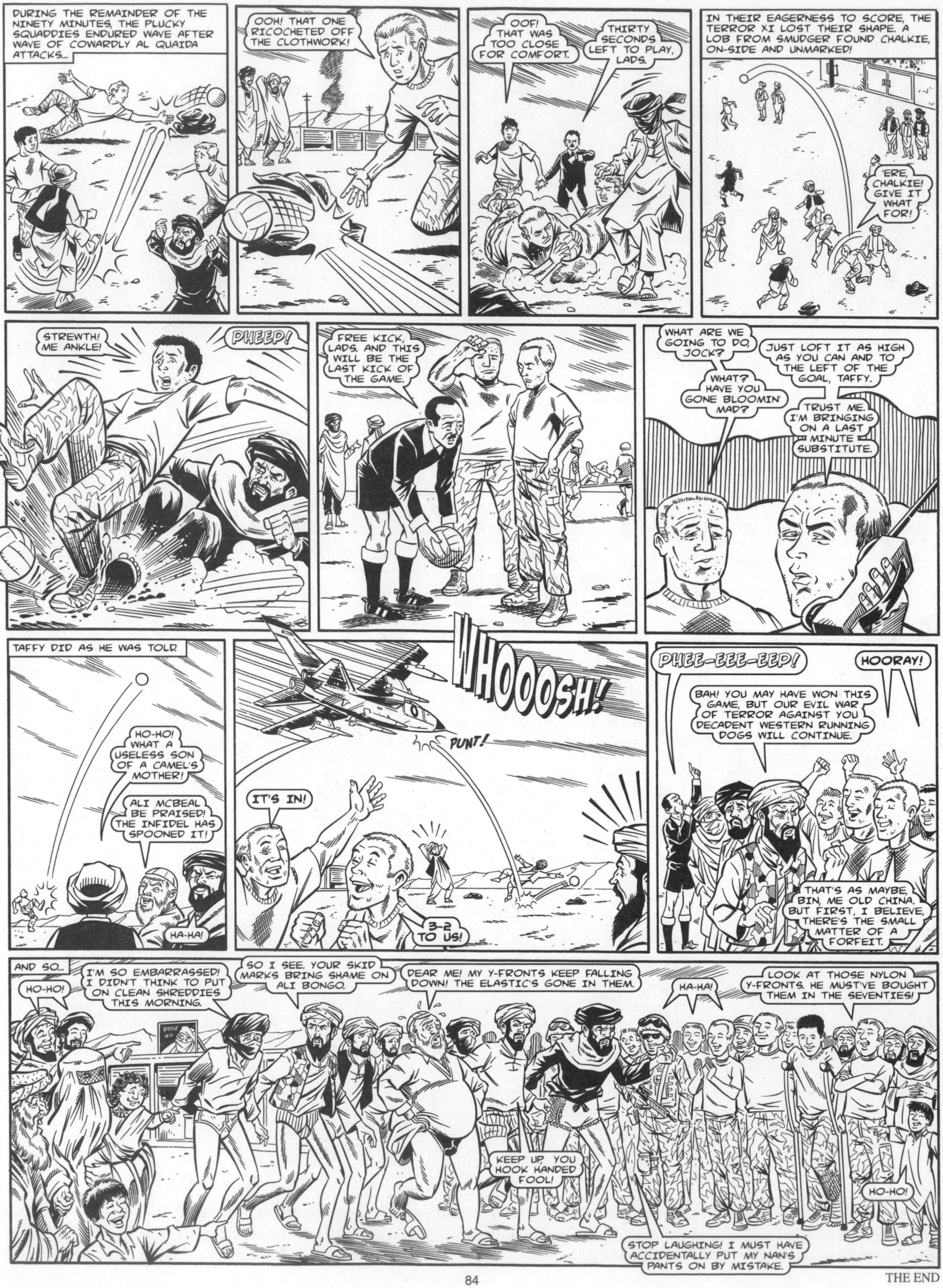
DURING THE REMAINDER OF THE NINETY MINUTES, THE PLUCKY SQUADDIES ENDURED WAVE AFTER WAVE OF COWARDLY AL QUAIDA ATTACKS...
OOH! THAT ONE RICOCHETED OFF THE CLOTHWORK!
OOF! THAT WAS TOO CLOSE FOR COMFORT.
THIRTY SECONDS LEFT TO PLAY, LADS.
IN THEIR EAGERNESS TO SCORE, THE TERROR XI LOST THEIR SHAPE. A LOB FROM SMUDGER FOUND CHALKIE, ON-SIDE AND UNMARKED!
'ERE, CHALKIE! GIVE IT WHAT FOR!
STREWTH! ME ANKLE!
PHEEP!
FREE KICK, LADS, AND THIS WILL BE THE LAST KICK OF THE GAME.
WHAT ARE WE GOING TO DO, JOCK?
JUST LOFT IT AS HIGH AS YOU CAN AND TO THE LEFT OF THE GOAL, TAFFY.
WHAT? HAVE YOU GONE BLOOMIN' MAD?
TRUST ME. I'M BRINGING ON A LAST MINUTE SUBSTITUTE.
TAFFY DID AS HE WAS TOLD.
HO-HO! WHAT A USELESS SON OF A CAMEL'S MOTHER!
ALI MCBEAL BE PRAISED! THE INFIDEL HAS SPOONED IT!
HA-HA!
WHOOOSH!
PUNT!
IT'S IN!
3-2 TO US!
PHEE-EEE-EEP!
HOORAY!
BAH! YOU MAY HAVE WON THIS GAME, BUT OUR EVIL WAR OF TERROR AGAINST YOU DECADENT WESTERN RUNNING DOGS WILL CONTINUE.
THAT'S AS MAYBE, BIN, ME OLD CHINA. BUT FIRST, I BELIEVE, THERE'S THE SMALL MATTER OF A FORFEIT.
AND SO...
HO-HO!
I'M SO EMBARRASSED! I DIDN'T THINK TO PUT ON CLEAN SHREDDIES THIS MORNING.
SO I SEE. YOUR SKID MARKS BRING SHAME ON ALI BONGO.
DEAR ME! MY Y-FRONTS KEEP FALLING DOWN! THE ELASTIC'S GONE IN THEM.
HA-HA!
LOOK AT THOSE NYLON Y-FRONTS. HE MUST'VE BOUGHT THEM IN THE SEVENTIES!
KEEP UP, YOU HOOK HANDED FOOL!
HO-HO!
STOP LAUGHING! I MUST HAVE ACCIDENTALLY PUT MY NAN'S PANTS ON BY MISTAKE.

THE END

Rantzen to Have Sex with Gorilla

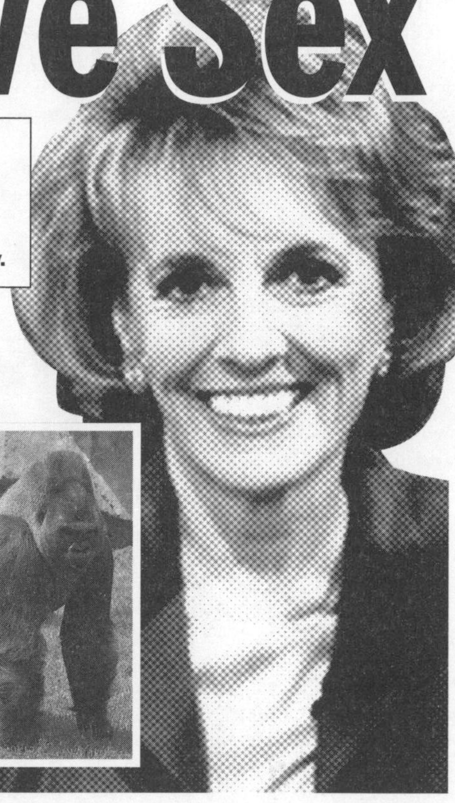

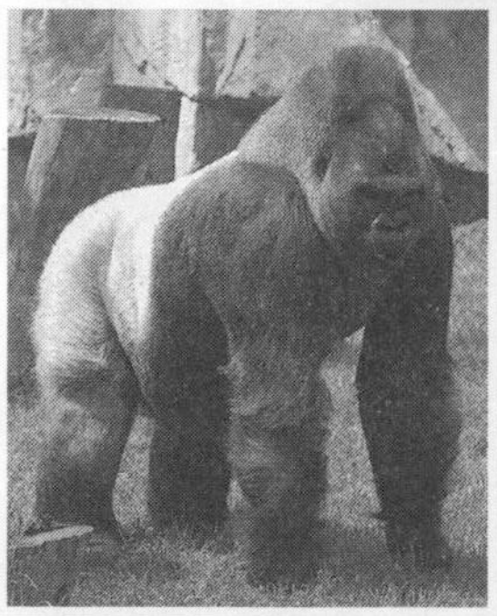

MONKEY BUSINESS: **Rantzen (right) and (inset) her 40-stone lover-to-be, yesterday.**

FORMER *That's Life* presenter ESTHER RANTZEN has revealed her New Year's Resolution for 2009. And it's not to give up smoking, lose weight or join a gym... it's to have SEX with GORILLA!

EXCLUSIVE!

Speaking on Radio 4's *Desert Island Discs,* the veteran broadcaster told Kirsty Young that there were many experiences she wanted to try before she got too old, and this was one of them.

"There is something magical and exciting about a male gorilla. That immense power combined with such great gentleness is something I find deeply erotic," said Rantzen. "Ever since I was in my twenties I've wondered what it would be like to bed one of these wonderful creatures."

"As one get's older one realises time is running out. I'm all too aware that I'm not getting any younger and I kept thinking to myself, 'if not now, when?' That's when I resolved to do it this year," the 68-year-old presenter added.

Rantzen has already made plans to visit Longleat in the spring to meet Blimbo, the safari park's 23-year-old mountain gorilla. She intends to strip naked and climb into Blimbo's enclosure, luring him down from his tyre and allowing the 40-stone primate to run his huge, leathery hands over every inch of her still girlish body. Esther expects her nipples to harden expectantly as wave after electric wave of desire courses through her, as the beast's teasing fingers make their way inexorably down towards the womanly treasure that has waited so long for their tender simian touch.

Now fully aroused, it is thought that Blimbo will then take the Hearts of Gold star in his arms and consummate the relationship. As his massive throbbing apehood enters her, Rantzen anticipates that she will be elevated to heights of orgasmic rapture that she could previously not have imagined in her wildest dreams. Again and again, the gorilla's powerful thrusts - ten times stronger than those of a man - will cause the toothy Accident Advice Helpline spokeswoman to cry out, 'Oh Blimbo, oh Blimbo, oh Blimbo!'

Finally, just when she feels that she may faint with ecstasy, Rantzen and her primate lover are will simultaneously reach a shattering climax before both collapsing, utterly spent, onto the straw of his pen.

"If I don't have sex with a gorilla this year, I never will," said Esther. "And that would be a tragedy."

But monkey expert Hazelnut Monkbottle last night sounded a note of caution about the plan. "Gorillas are notoriously difficult to arouse," he told us. "Esther might find that she has to slap a bit of blue paint on her arse before Blimbo gets a bone-on."

Star Brushes Off Rumours of Death

JACKO STILL ALIVE!

EXCLUSIVE

THE NEWS that Jacko had suffered a massive heart attack and died stunned the world. But no one was more shocked than Jacko himself, who heard the report whilst listening to the radio in the bath.

"I thought there must have been some mistake when I heard that I had been rushed to hospital in Los Angeles," Jacko out of Brush Strokes told a reporter at a hastily-arranged press conference. "Then an hour later, the news came through that I had died and I knew for certain there'd been a mix up."

RELIEF

"It was such a relief when my wife explained that they were talking about the other Jacko, the American one who wasn't in Brush Strokes," he added.

But Jacko confessed that after the initial relief, he was concerned that the confusion may have an adverse effect on his career. And he urged news agencies across the world to make it clear in their reports that the Jacko who died was not the one out of Brush Strokes.

PRODUCER

"If the BBC was thinking of bringing back the series after an 18-year rest, they might decide not to bother if they hear that the show's star is dead," continued jacko. "Or what if a Hollywood director like Stephen Spielberg or George Lucas was planning to make a big budget movie version of Brush Strokes? He would cast another major star in my role as the randy painter and decorator if he thought I'd passed on. Similarly, if the people I walk dogs for see in the paper that I've popped my clogs, they're going to get somebody else to do it. And that would leave me out of pocket to the tune of £65 per week."

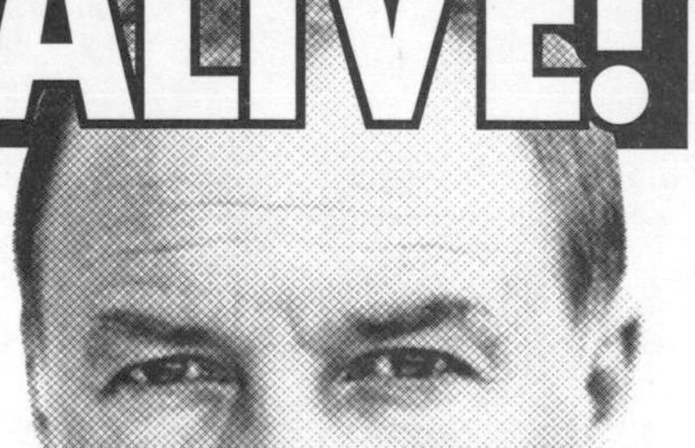

Jacko freely admits that the confusion could have been avoided if he was more widely known by his real name, rather than as a character he played in a lame sitcom nearly twenty years ago. "The problem is, I can't remember what my real name is," he told the reporter. "And neither can any of my friends or family."

COACH TRAVEL

"During the 90s, I was convinced that I was Terry the chef from Fawlty Towers, but then somebody told me he was called Brian Hall, and that didn't ring any bells with my wife," he continued.

"I even went down the library to try and look myself up on a computer, but I couldn't understand how to work the internet," he added.

Do YOU know the real name of Jacko out of Brush Strokes? Perhaps you went to school with him, or maybe you used to be his postman. Or do you have a video of the sitcom that you accidentally recorded 20 years ago with his name in the credits? Write in and tell us at the usual address, and we'll pass all the suggested names onto him. Mark your envelope: "I think I might know what Jacko out of Brush Strokes's real name is."

Internet 'to Reach Wales by 2020'

TWO THIRDS of the Welsh population will have internet access by the year 2020, according to a progress report issued today.

The world wide web currently stops at Chester, but Welsh internet bosses are hopeful that the information superhighway will make its way across the border in the next decade, allowing the principality's population to join the electronic communications revolution.

"We've got a lot of exciting plans for the 'Wales Wide Web' when we finally get it up and running," said Dyffwyn Gryffydd, head of the Welsh Council for Technological Development.

"We're hoping to install a computer in Cardiff, one in Swansea and another in Llanfairfechan. They will be joined together by a network of three long wires. People will be allowed to pre-book time on them to 'surf the web', and there will be a technician on hand to operate the keyboard for them," he added.

Users of the Welsh internet will be able to access dozens of useful websites, such as ones showing tide times in Harlech, Aberystwyth and Prestatyn, what's on at the Mold Arts Centre, the height of Snowdon and up-to-the-minute news about slate.

"We're even planning to have a website for the kids, called Clwb Sboncyn," continued Gryffydd. "It's going to feature a cartoon about Eisteddfods, a fun male-voice choir-based video game and a searchable version of the Mabinogion. It should be great fun."

And the Welsh internet will also incorporate an e-mail service, similar to the one already in use on the world wide web. Gryffydd explained: "To send an e-mail, the user would simply write their message on paper and post it to the operator of his nearest computer, where it would be typed in and 'e-mailed' to the computer which was closest to its recipient."

"Here the message would be printed out, placed in an envelope and mailed to the addressee's local post office. To check their e-mail in-box, the recipient would simply pop along to their local post office and ask the old lady behind the counter if they had received any e-mails that day," he continued.

"We haven't finalised the costings yet, but we anticipate that the price of sending an e-mail across the Wales Wide Web should be no more than fifty to sixty pence," added Gryffydd.

Meanwhile, Wales's glitterati are said to be queuing up to launch their own websites. Gravel-voiced crooner Bonnie Tyler told us: "I'm really excited about the Welsh internet. I'm planning to set up my own web page, www.bonnietyler.co.gogoch, where my fans can look at a picture of me and see a list of shops where they can buy my latest cassette, which has been top of the Welsh Album Charts - Ppop y Topydd Cymraeg - since 1988."

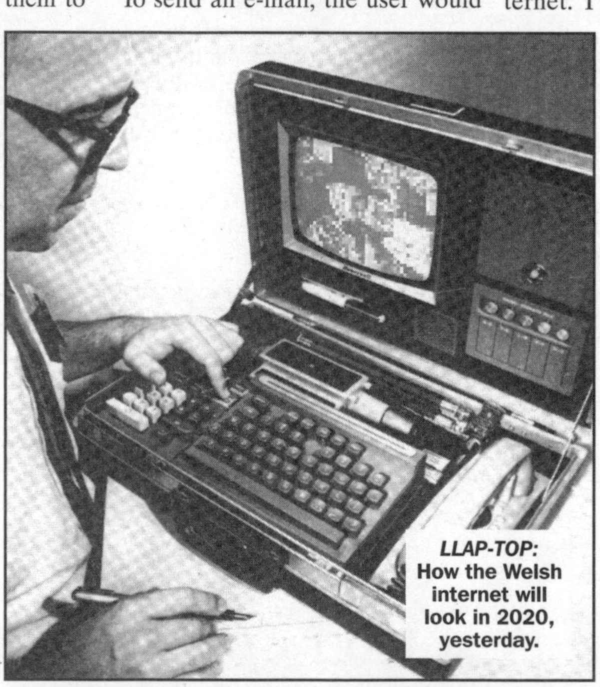

LLAP-TOP: How the Welsh internet will look in 2020, yesterday.

Other Welsh A-listers who are also said to be interested in setting up their own sites include Max Boyce, Ruth Madoc and Pricey out of *Please Sir.*

The Welsh internet will run from 9.30am to 4.00pm weekdays and 9.30am - 12.00pm on Saturdays. It will be closed on Sundays and Bank Holidays.

Dr. Finlay's Facebook

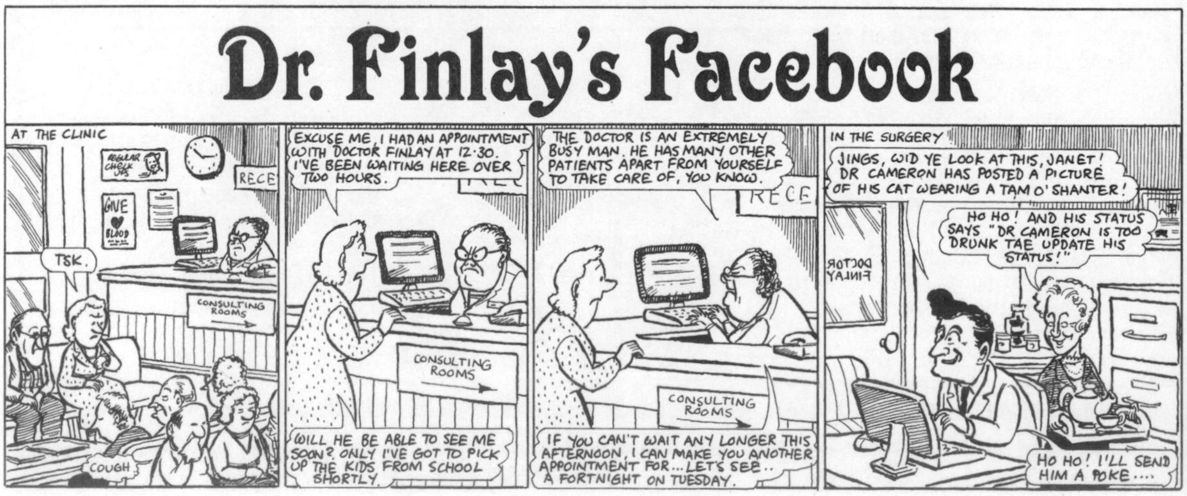
AT THE CLINIC
REGULAR CHECK UPS
RECE
GIVE BLOOD
TSK.
CONSULTING ROOMS
COUGH
EXCUSE ME, I HAD AN APPOINTMENT WITH DOCTOR FINLAY AT 12·30. I'VE BEEN WAITING HERE OVER TWO HOURS.
CONSULTING ROOMS
WILL HE BE ABLE TO SEE ME SOON? ONLY I'VE GOT TO PICK UP THE KIDS FROM SCHOOL SHORTLY.
THE DOCTOR IS AN EXTREMELY BUSY MAN. HE HAS MANY OTHER PATIENTS APART FROM YOURSELF TO TAKE CARE OF, YOU KNOW.
RECE
CONSULTING ROOMS
IF YOU CAN'T WAIT ANY LONGER THIS AFTERNOON, I CAN MAKE YOU ANOTHER APPOINTMENT FOR... LET'S SEE.. A FORTNIGHT ON TUESDAY.
IN THE SURGERY
JINGS, WID YE LOOK AT THIS, JANET! DR CAMERON HAS POSTED A PICTURE OF HIS CAT WEARING A TAM O' SHANTER!
HO HO! AND HIS STATUS SAYS "DR CAMERON IS TOO DRUNK TAE UPDATE HIS STATUS!"
HO HO! I'LL SEND HIM A POKE....

Miria

ANSWERS YOUR BLACK FILM COMEDIAN PRO

Angered by neighbour's behaviour

Dear Miriam

I have lived in my house for 12 years and I have always got on well with my neighbour. We have never been great friends, but have always passed the time of day and been very pleasant to each other.

However, that all changed last Sunday when he was outside watering his lawn. I was cleaning out my gutters, and as I was moving my ladder I lost hold of it. It slipped and went straight through his front room window.

I went to apologise and offer to pay for the damage, but he was pretty angry, and before I could say anything, he'd gone over to my car and torn the windscreen wipers off. I felt quite aggrieved at this, so I went over to his house and pulled some bits of wood off his porch. This angered him even more and he ripped the bonnet off my car and threw it under a steam roller.

I don't want this episode to escalate out of control, but I didn't start it. What should I do next?

SL , Hollywood

Miriam says...

You should rip his flower boxes off and push them through his remaining windows, stamp all over his flowerbeds and pull his front door off. If you can't manage this yourself, get an overweight friend to help you. Your neighbour will inevitably strip your car down to the chassis as a result, but this is the only thing you can do in this situation.

Dr Miriam's Siler

The slapstick comedy adv

Fallen into a shallow tray of whitewa

018 118 055

Hit round the head with a scaffold pla

0 181 18055

Sink plunger stuck on forehead

01811 80 55

Legs tied round neck in bow

0 1811805 5

m

HITE
S

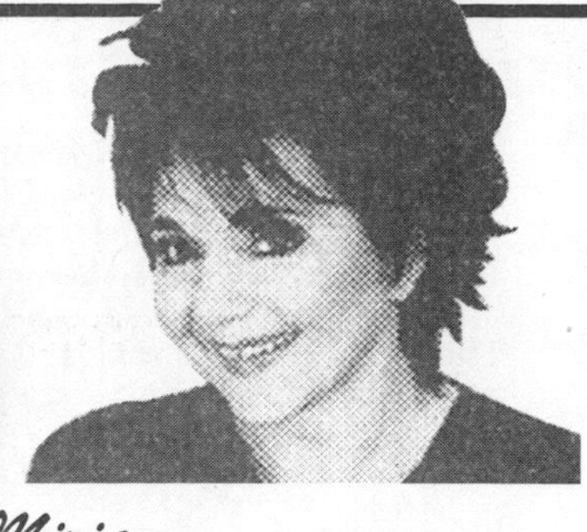

Hubby's brush with law

Dear Miriam

Me and my husband had the most terrifying experience the other morning. We had just got up and were having breakfast when the police broke down our front door.

I am 32 and my husband is 35. We have been married for ten years and neither of us have ever been in trouble with the law.

Twelve police officers ran in whilst somebody played a piano very quickly. They didn't say anything, but the one at the front hit my husband over the head with a large truncheon. Then they ran out as quickly as they came in, dragging my husband with them and bundled him into the back of an open-top police car before climbing in themselves.

Then, the car pulled away so quickly that they all fell out backwards in a heap. The car carried on, and they all got up and ran after it, holding their hats on.

That was two days ago and I haven't seen my husband since. Please help me, as I don't know what to do.

Margerie Sennet, Hollywood

Miriam says...

Anyone arrested must be charged or released within 48 hours. In any case, the next of kin must be informed as to their whereabouts within 12 hours. I suggest that you put on a long coat and a hat with fruit on it and march into the police station. Make a fuss with the desk sergeant until all the officers come out of a back room. When they are standing in a line, shove the front one hard in the chest so as they fall like dominoes while somebody plays a swanee whistle.

Dear Miriam

The other night, my husband came home from work, and he was slightly drunk. I have never seen him drunk before and t took me by surprise.

I am 28 and he is 31 and we have been married for seven years.

When I asked him why he had been drinking he became very defensive. An argument broke out which became very heated. Suddenly, he lost his temper. He grabbed hold of my hat, filled it with molasses and jammed it back on my head really tight, giving it a tap on top with a wooden spoon for good measure. I just stood there for a few seconds while the molasses ran down my face.

I have never seen him do anything like that before and I didn't know how to react. I am worried that he might do it again. What should I do?

Edna Hardy, Hollywood

Miriam says...

It's always very difficult when arguments become physical. Retaliating might provoke him into further action, but you cannot let him get away with it in case it becomes the norm. If it happens again, I would advise you do something to let him know you are upset, like cut his braces and empty a tin of beans into his trousers. Or perhaps cut a bit of his fringe off with a bread knife and stick it on his chin with treacle.

Worried my boyfriend may end up getting hurt

Dear Miriam

My boyfriend tried to impress me by climbing up the side of a building, and now I fear it's all going to end in tears.

I am 22 and my boyfriend is 26. We have been going out for nearly three years.

I work in an office and my boyfriend decided to pay me a surprise visit during my lunch hour to bring me a bunch of flowers. He arrived just as I was explaining to another girl how much I loved him and wanted to marry him. My boyfriend overheard the conversation but misunderstood, thinking I was talking about another, much richer man who's been pestering me to go out with him.

To cut a long story short, my boyfriend decided the only way to win my love was to climb up the outside of the building. Now he's hanging by his fingertips off the hand of a clock outside my eighteenth floor office, holding his straw hat on with his other hand. The clock face has come away from the works on a big spring and I'm terrified he might fall to his death. Please help me, Miriam

Bebe Daniels, Hollywood

Miriam says...

You must let your boyfriend know how you feel about him. As long as he imagines that the only way to win your affection is to perform dangerous stunts, it will be impossible to put your relationship on the solid footing that you so desperately crave. Why not look out of the window with a shocked expression on your face, alternately covering your mouth with the back of your slightly curved fist and clasping both your hands together over the left side of your chest.

Miriam's Photo Problem Casebook

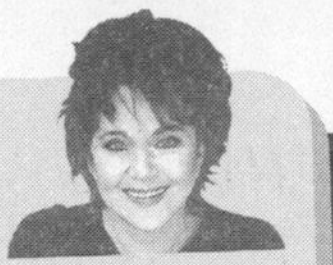

Kirsty's Harpo Dilemma ~ Day 4

Office worker *Kirsty Sweetman* had been dating *Harpo Marx* for 18 months, and she desperately wanted to start a family. But discussing things with her boyfriend was not easy...

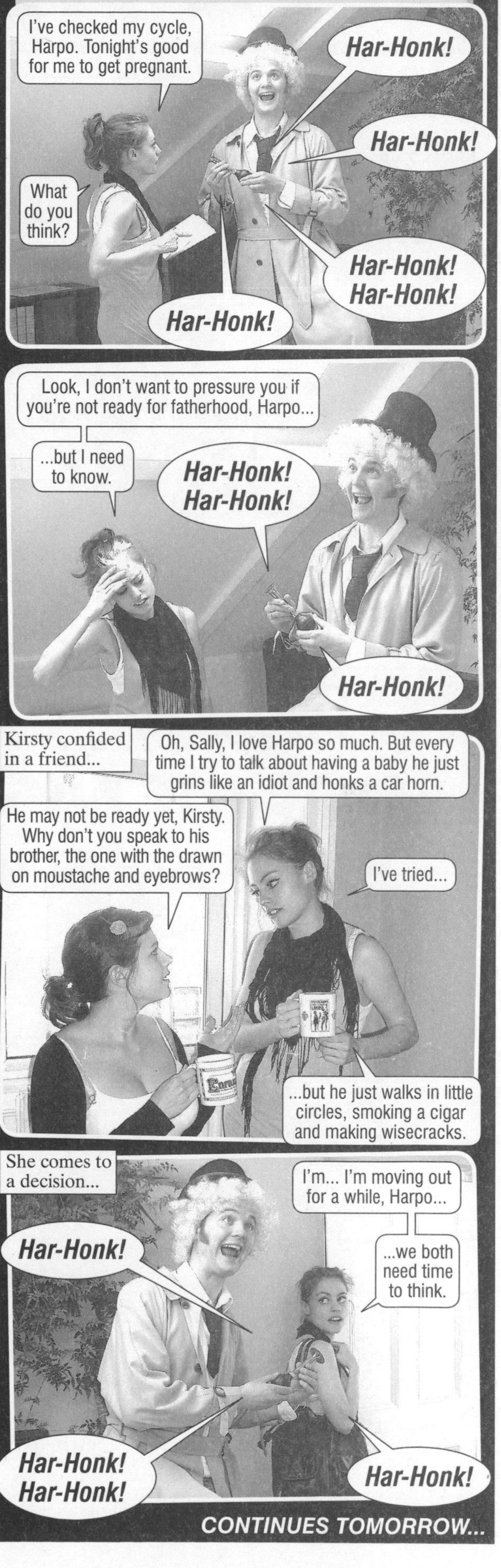

I've checked my cycle, Harpo. Tonight's good for me to get pregnant.
Har-Honk!
Har-Honk!
What do you think?
Har-Honk! Har-Honk!
Har-Honk!
Look, I don't want to pressure you if you're not ready for fatherhood, Harpo...
...but I need to know.
Har-Honk! Har-Honk!
Har-Honk!
Kirsty confided in a friend...
Oh, Sally, I love Harpo so much. But every time I try to talk about having a baby he just grins like an idiot and honks a car horn.
He may not be ready yet, Kirsty. Why don't you speak to his brother, the one with the drawn on moustache and eyebrows?
I've tried...
...but he just walks in little circles, smoking a cigar and making wisecracks.
She comes to a decision...
I'm... I'm moving out for a while, Harpo...
...we both need time to think.
Har-Honk!
Har-Honk! Har-Honk!
Har-Honk!

CONTINUES TOMORROW...

Zombie Attack Livens up Humberside Council Meeting

Lord Mayor of GHOUL!

NIGHTMARE: **An artist's impression of how the Mayor of Goole may have looked after the zombie attack.**

COUNTY COUNCILLORS at Goole Town Hall yesterday attended a meeting they will never forget. For twenty minutes into proceedings, their deliberations were interrupted ... by a *ZOMBIE!*

Members of the Planning Committee were discussing an application for the erection of a mobile telephone mast in Snaith when the doors to the debating chamber burst open and the uninvited flesh-eating visitor shambled in.

"At first we thought it was a tramp who'd come in for a bit of a warm," Councillor Margaret Pratt told local paper, *The Humber Sceptre*. "Then we noticed that his skin was decomposed and green, and peeling off his bones in big lumps. Also one of his eyes was hanging out of its socket. He was a zombie. The foetid stench of rotting human flesh was overpowering."

"The smell was so bad, several councillors ended up holding their noses!" added Mrs Pratt.

As the whiffsome interloper lurched towards the front of the hall, committee chairman Alderman Eric Thonks raised a point of order. He told us: "I informed the creature that this particular session was not open to the public, unlike the regular Thursday evening council meetings, when the first floor spectators' gallery is available to visitors who have an interest in the workings of the municipal authority."

BLOOD

But the soul-less corpse wasn't listening and seemed more interested in feasting on the Mayor's blood. Councillors watched in amazement as it made its way onto the dais and hungrily sank its teeth into council leader Jack Proudfoot's neck, ripping out huge chunks of his flesh and severing his jugular vein and windpipe.

***SCENE OF ATTACK:* Goole Town Hall yesterday.**

At this point, the Lady Mayoress began using the town's ceremonial mace in a fruitless attempt to beat the cadaverous cannibal off her husband. "Mrs Proudfoot was trying to bonk the zombie on the head, but she kept missing and hitting the Mayor instead," said Mrs Pratt. "I know it's wrong to laugh, but it was such a comical spectacle that everybody was in stitches."

HOOK

Eventually the uninvited guest was shooed out of the council chamber by several committee members. The planning meeting, which had been temporarily adjourned, was then re-convened. Alderman Thonks moved a motion that the Mayor, who was now lying dead on the platform, should be destroyed before he became zombified himself and bit any other members of the council.

At this point Herbert Sparks, independent councillor for the East Cowick ward, raised a point of order, reminding the committee members that Mr Thonks's proposition was not on the official agenda. "He argued that any vote on a proposal would only be binding if it had been tabled as an extraordinary motion, " said Mrs Pratt.

As Mr Sparks began explaining how, according to the standing orders of the council, any ruling passed through the chair would still be open to appeal even if it had been sustained in an open ballot, the Mayor suddenly sat up, lumbered to his feet and lurched towards him, hissing through his teeth.

SENSIBLE

A motion was quickly moved that the meeting be suspended to allow Town Hall caretaker Fred Varney to be summoned. Following a vote, the proposal was passed by a majority of six to four, with two abstentions. The caretaker was called and dispatched the re-animated Mayor's corpse by swinging a heavy fire-axe into the back of its skull.

"Mr Proudfoot's head exploded like a watermelon, showering the chamber with rotting brains and blood," said Mrs Pratt, who admitted that she can't remember a more eventful council session in over 40 years as a member.

"Who would have thought that the presence of a member of the undead could liven up a meeting so much?" she quipped.

When the committee re-convened, following a break to allow the caretaker to clean up the chamber, the proposal for the erection of the mobile telephone mast in Snaith was passed by a majority of six to four, with two abstentions.

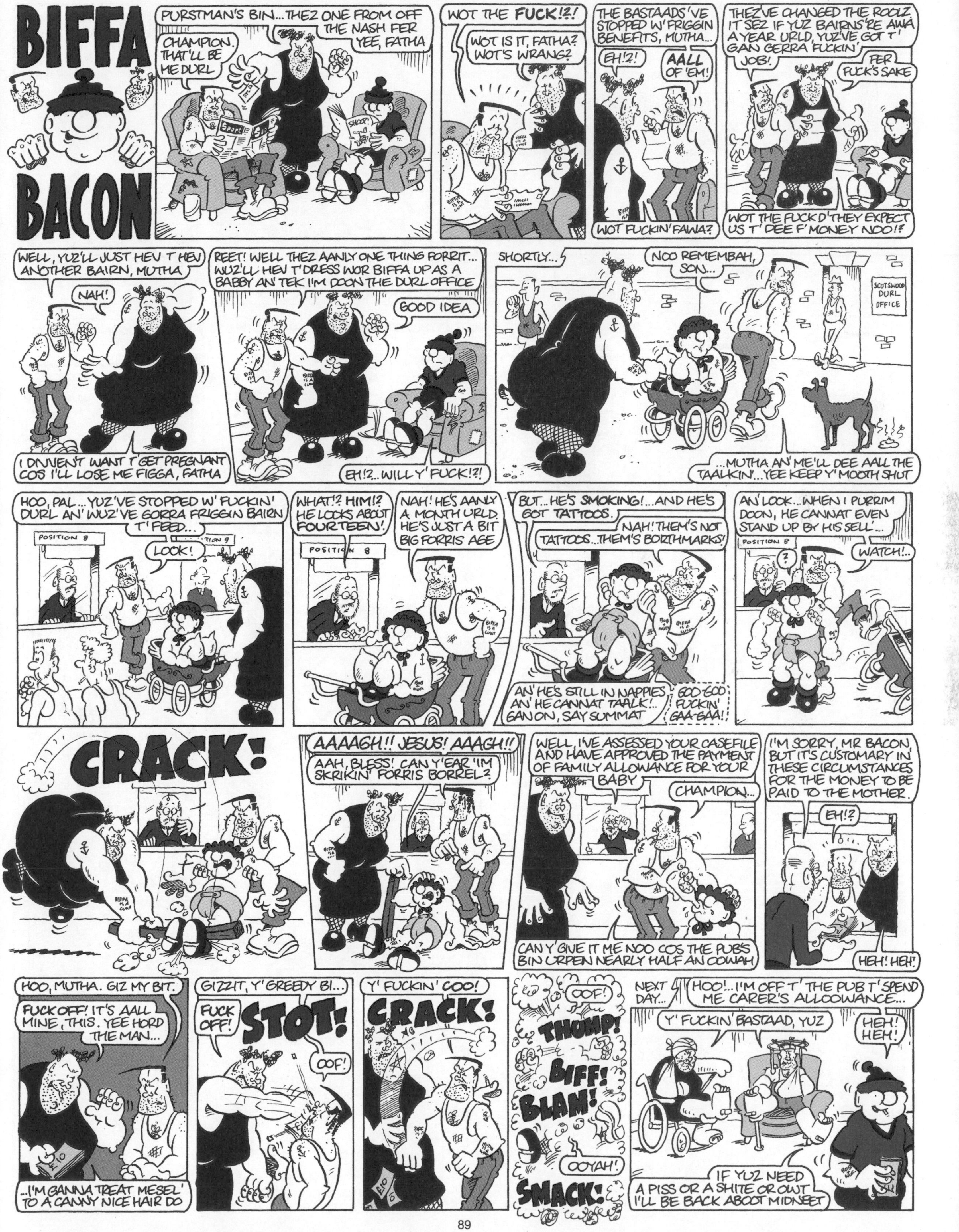
BIFFA BACON
PURSTMAN'S BIN... THEZ ONE FROM OFF THE NASH FER YEE, FATHA
CHAMPION. THAT'LL BE ME DURL
WOT THE FUCK!?!
WOT IS IT, FATHA? WOT'S WRANG?
THE BASTAADS 'VE STOPPED W' FRIGGIN BENEFITS, MUTHA...
EH!?!
AALL OF 'EM!
WOT FUCKIN' FAWA?
THEZ'VE CHANGED THE ROOLZ. IT SEZ IF YUZ BAIRNS 'RE AWA A YEAR URLD, YUZ'VE GOT T' GAN GERRA FUCKIN' JOB!
FER FUCK'S SAKE
WOT THE FUCK D'THEY EXPECT US T' DEE F' MONEY NOO!?
WELL, YUZ'LL JUST HEV T' HEV ANOTHER BAIRN, MUTHA
NAH!
I DIVVEN'T WANT T' GET PREGNANT COS I'LL LOSE ME FIGGA, FATHA
REET! WELL THEZ AANLY ONE THING FORRIT... WUZ'LL HEV T' DRESS WOR BIFFA UP AS A BABBY AN' TEK I'M DOON THE DURL OFFICE
GOOD IDEA
EH!?.. WILL Y' FUCK!?!
SHORTLY...
NOO REMEMBAH, SON...
SCOTSWOOD DURL OFFICE
...MUTHA AN' ME'LL DEE AALL THE TAALKIN'... YEE KEEP Y' MOOTH SHUT
HOO, PAL... YUZ'VE STOPPED W' FUCKIN' DURL AN' WUZ'VE GORRA FRIGGIN BAIRN T' FEED...
POSITION 8
POSITION 9
LOOK!
WHAT!? HIM!? HE LOOKS ABOUT FOURTEEN!
NAH! HE'S AANLY A MONTH URLD. HE'S JUST A BIT BIG FORRIS AGE
POSITION 8
BUT... HE'S SMOKING!... AND HE'S GOT TATTOOS.
NAH! THEM'S NOT TATTOOS... THEM'S BORTHMARKS!
AN' HE'S STILL IN NAPPIES AN' HE CANNAT TAALK!.. GAN ON, SAY SUMMAT
GOO-GOO FUCKIN' GAA-GAA!
AN' LOOK... WHEN I PURRIM DOON, HE CANNAT EVEN STAND UP BY HIS SELL'...
POSITION 8
?
WATCH!..
CRACK!
AAAAGH!! JESUS! AAAGH!!
AAH, BLESS! CAN Y'EAR 'IM SKRIKIN' FORRIS BORREL?
WELL, I'VE ASSESSED YOUR CASEFILE AND HAVE APPROVED THE PAYMENT OF FAMILY ALLOWANCE FOR YOUR BABY
CHAMPION...
CAN Y' GIVE IT ME NOO COS THE PUB'S BIN URPEN NEARLY HALF AN OWAH
I'M SORRY, MR BACON, BUT IT'S CUSTOMARY IN THESE CIRCUMSTANCES FOR THE MONEY TO BE PAID TO THE MOTHER.
EH!?
HEH! HEH!
HOO, MUTHA. GIZ MY BIT.
FUCK OFF! IT'S AALL MINE, THIS. YEE HORD THE MAN...
...I'M GANNA TREAT MESEL' TO A CANNY NICE HAIR DO
GIZZIT, Y' GREEDY BI...
FUCK OFF!
STOT!
OOF!
Y' FUCKIN' COO!
CRACK!
OOF!
THUMP!
BIFF!
BLAM!
OOYAH!
SMACK!
NEXT DAY...
HOO!... I'M OFF T' THE PUB T' SPEND ME CARER'S ALLOOWANCE...
Y' FUCKIN' BASTAAD, YUZ
HEH! HEH!
IF YUZ NEED A PISS OR A SHITE OR OWT I'LL BE BACK ABOOT MIDNEET

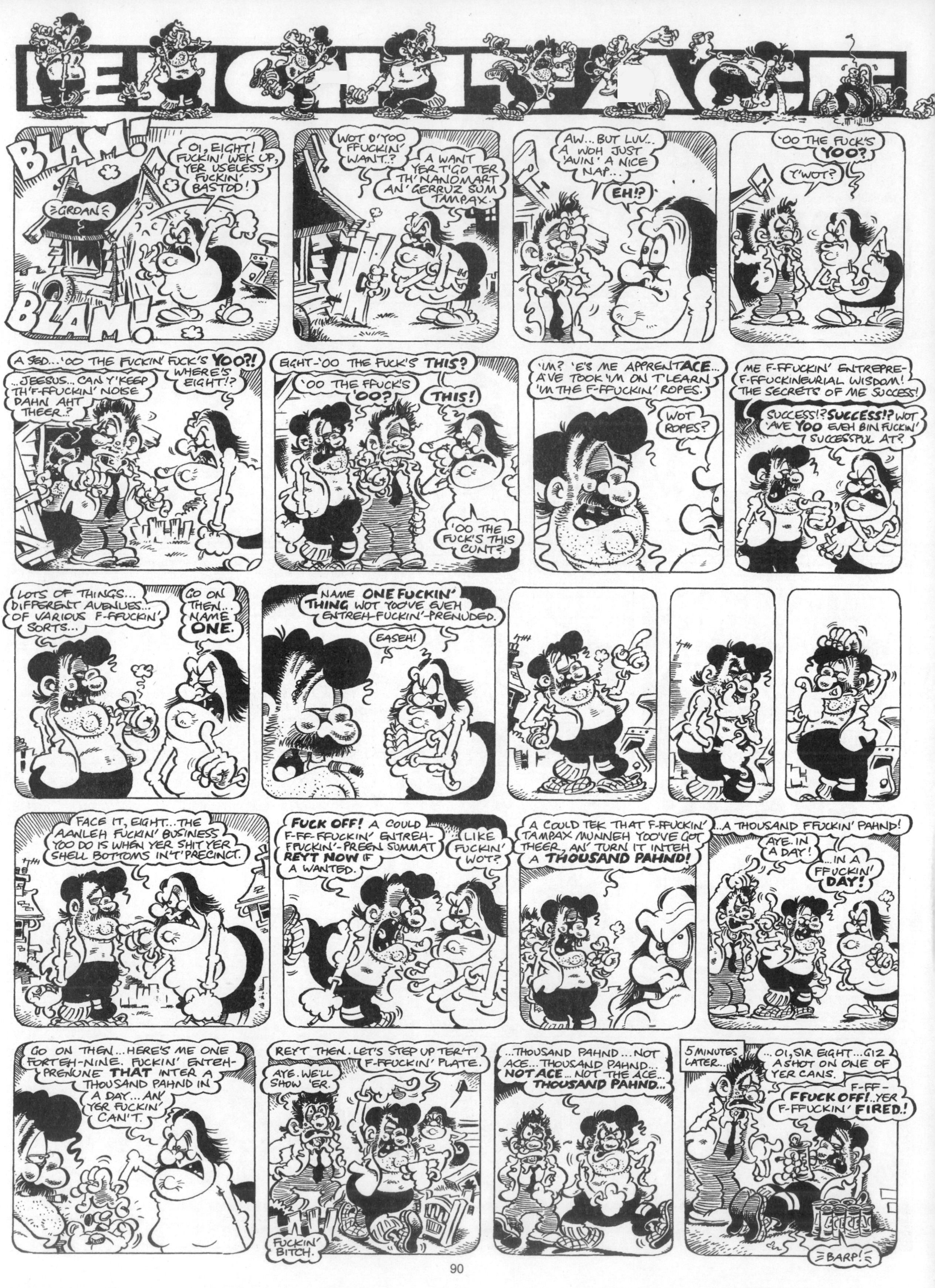
BLAM!
OI, EIGHT! FUCKIN' WEK UP, YER USELESS FUCKIN' BASTOD!
GROAN
BLAM!
WOT D'YOO FFUCKIN' WANT..?
A WANT YER T'GO TER TH' NANOMART AN' GERRUZ SUM TAMPAX.
AW... BUT LUV.. A WOH JUST 'AVIN' A NICE NAP...
EH!?
'OO THE FUCK'S YOO?
Y'WOT?
A SED... 'OO THE FUCKIN' FUCK'S YOO?!
WHERE'S EIGHT!?
...JEESUS... CAN Y'KEEP TH'F-FFUCKIN' NOISE DAHN AHT THEER..?
EIGHT-'OO THE FUCK'S THIS?
'OO THE FFUCK'S 'OO?
THIS!
'OO THE FUCK'S THIS CUNT?
'IM? 'E'S ME APPRENTACE... A'VE TOOK 'IM ON T'LEARN 'IM THE F-FFUCKIN' ROPES.
WOT ROPES?
ME F-FFUCKIN' ENTREPRE-F-FFUCKINEURIAL WISDOM! THE SECRETS OF ME SUCCESS!
SUCCESS!? SUCCESS!? WOT 'AVE YOO EVEH BIN FUCKIN' SUCCESSFUL AT?
LOTS OF THINGS... DIFFERENT AVENUES... OF VARIOUS F-FFUCKIN' SORTS...
GO ON THEN... NAME ONE.
NAME ONE FUCKIN' THING WOT YOO'VE EVEH ENTREH-FUCKIN'-PRENUDED.
EASEH!
FACE IT, EIGHT... THE AANLEH FUCKIN' BUSINESS YOO DO IS WHEN YER SHIT YER SHELL BOTTOMS IN'T' PRECINCT.
FUCK OFF! A COULD F-FF-FFUCKIN' ENTREH-FFUCKIN'-PREEN SUMMAT REYT NOW IF A WANTED.
LIKE FUCKIN' WOT?
A COULD TEK THAT F-FFUCKIN' TAMPAX MUNNEH YOO'VE GOT THEER, AN' TURN IT INTEH A THOUSAND PAHND!
...A THOUSAND FFUCKIN' PAHND!
AYE. IN A DAY!
...IN A FFUCKIN' DAY!
GO ON THEN... HERE'S ME ONE FORTEH-NINE. FUCKIN' ENTEH-PRENUNE THAT INTER A THOUSAND PAHND IN A DAY... AN' YER FUCKIN' CAN'T.
REYT THEN. LET'S STEP UP TER'T' F-FFUCKIN' PLATE.
AYE. WE'LL SHOW 'ER.
FUCKIN' BITCH.
...THOUSAND PAHND... NOT ACE... THOUSAND PAHND... NOT ACE... NOT THE ACE... THOUSAND PAHND...
5 MINUTES LATER...
...OI, SIR EIGHT... GIZ A SHOT ON ONE OF YER CANS.
F-FF-FFUCK OFF!..YER F-FFUCKIN' FIRED.!
BARP!

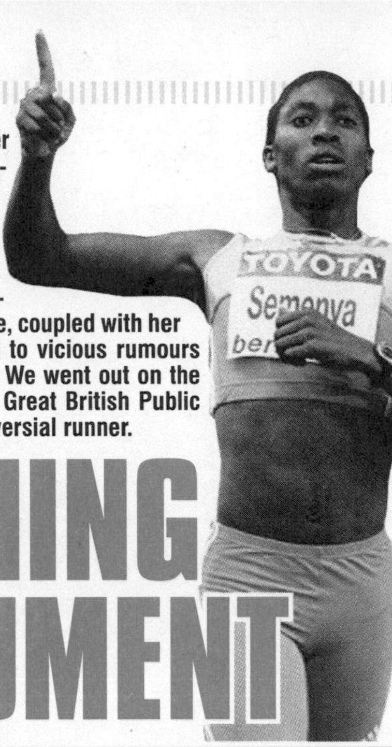

SOUTH AFRICAN Caster Semenya took the Athletics World Championships by storm, winning the Women's 800m in the year's best time of 1 minute 55.45 seconds. But Semenya's impressive performance, coupled with her muscular physique, has led to vicious rumours that SHE is a actually a HE. We went out on the streets to find out what the Great British Public had to say about the controversial runner.

RUNNING ARGUMENT

"...**MY** *husband is a great fan of female sports, particularly the beach volleyball and mud wrestling. However, when Caster Semenya lined up for the start of her race in Berlin, he went to the kitchen to make himself a cup of tea, which set alarm bells ringing in my mind at least."*

Mrs C Saalvesen, Deal

"...***ATHLETICS*** authorities should put a saucy French maid bending over to dust something on the final bend of every woman's race. Any runners who stop to slap the backs of their necks or pull their collar to one side to allow steam to escape are clearly men and should be disqualified."

Crane Fruehauf, Canterbury

"...**EVERYONE'S** *far too hung up on gender issues these days, in my opinion. We're all human beings, so why can't we just put our differences to one side and start getting on with each other for a change?"*

Reg Laurie, Yellowlaurie

"...**THE** *present controversy is nothing more than sexism gone mad. Men seem to think that unless female athletes have got enormous breasts and are running in high-heeled shoes, they are not women. Mind you, if they were like that, they might get a few more punters in to watch than that flat-chested South African bird."*

Boalloy Tautliner, Wye

"...***HAVING*** separate races for men and women is a form of sexual apartheid. They wouldn't have different competitions for black runners and white runners, so why have them for male and female athletes? It's political correctness gone mad."

Dennis Binlorry, Dover

"...***I FEEL*** very sorry for Caster Semenya, but she has brought a lot of this on herself. If she'd worn a nice pair of flowery shorts or a pretty brooch on her running vest, people wouldn't have been as quick to point the finger at her."

Leyland Routemaster, Sandwich

"...**IT HARDLY** *seems fair to use Semanya's lack of a bust as evidence of her masculinity. It doesn't prove anything. There wasn't a woman athlete at the games who had anything more than fried eggs for tits. Meanwhile, the male shot-putters had knockers like Dolly Parton."*

Scammell Flatbed, Maidstone

"...***I GREW*** up in the seventies, when Mary Peters won the Pentathlon at the Munich Olympics. She looked like Desperate Dan in a wig, yet nobody asked to put their hand down her knickers."

Diesel Artic, Margate

"...**GENDER** *confusion is nothing new. My mother had a full set of male genitals, a thick, bushy beard and smoked a pipe, yet she was no less a woman for all that. Actually, it might have been my father, now I come to think of it."*

E Stobart, Faversham

"...***I WAS*** a swimming judge in the 1970s, and I used to regularly hide behind the lockers in the women's changing rooms during competitions. And let me tell you, they were all women in those days. If the IOC want me to hide in the athletics changing rooms during any forthcoming events, I would be more than happy to verify the athletes' gender status."

Ifor Williamstrailers, Sittingbourne

"...**I HOLIDAY** *regularly in Bangkok, and often encounter difficulty telling men from women. They should do what I do and look in her pants and see if she's got a cock. Then, if she has, he should be stripped of her medal."*

Norbert Dentressangle, Tunbridge Wells

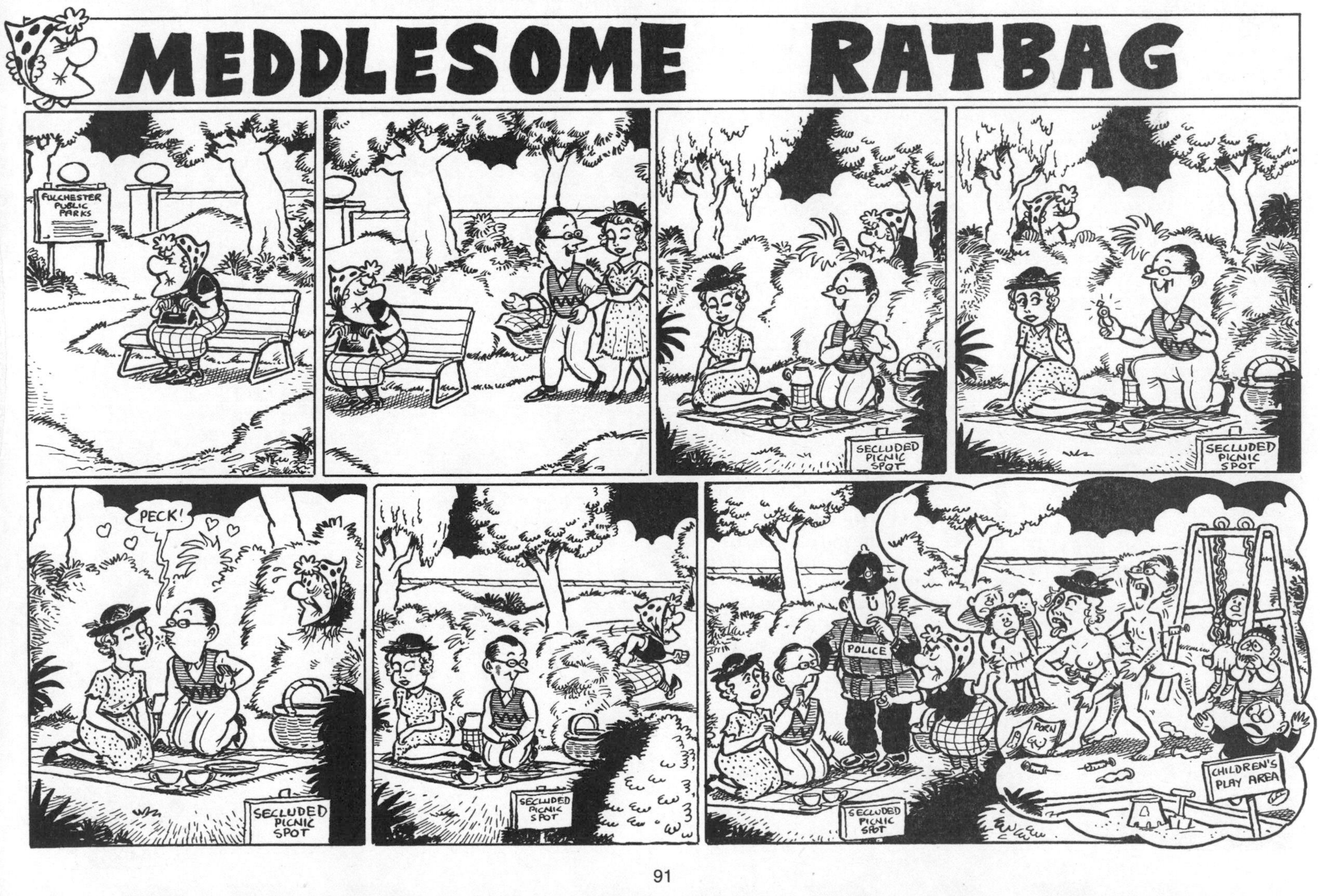
MEDDLESOME RATBAG
FULCHESTER PUBLIC PARKS
SECLUDED PICNIC SPOT
SECLUDED PICNIC SPOT
PECK!
SECLUDED PICNIC SPOT
SECLUDED PICNIC SPOT
POLICE
PORN
CHILDREN'S PLAY AREA
SECLUDED PICNIC SPOT

LUNARBOCKS

Britain's Moon Landing 40th Anniversariest Letters Page

PO Box 656,
North Shields,
NE30 4XX

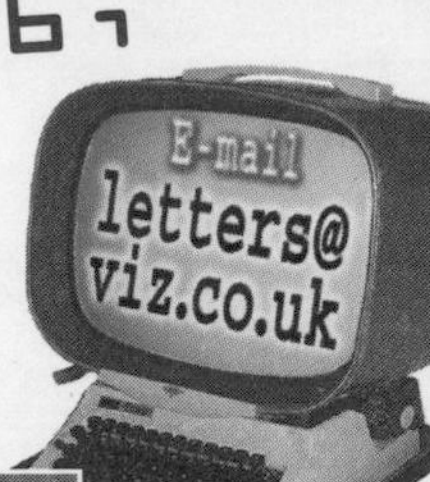
E-mail
letters@
viz.co.uk

STAR LETTER

HAVE any of your readers spotted my mother lately? She was supposed to come home last night at about 11.30pm with a Marks and Spencer ready meal for me. She's in her late 80s and slightly hunchbacked.

Sebastian Groves-Chortleson, e-mail

** SEBASTIAN wins a fantastic weekend trip to the Moon in the Viz rocket plus £200 spending money.*

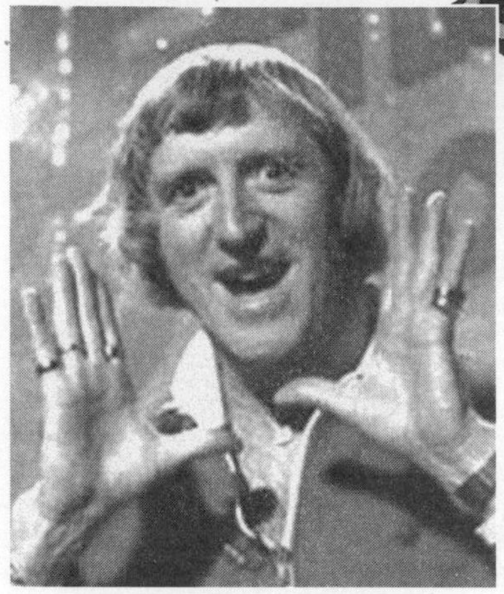

How's About that, Then?

IN THE 70s, Jimmy Savile was never off our screens telling us to "Clunk! Click! Every trip!" What a hypocrite. I drove past him in Leeds recently and did he have his seat belt on? Did he heck as like. Admittedly he was walking into a café in Kippax, but nevertheless, the sheer hypocrisy of the man stinks.

Bernie Inn
Garforth

IT'S FUNNY how different people have different reaction times. For instance, the parents of a newborn baby and a young toddler who turned up at the York Dungeon last weekend. Everyone in the queue noticed immediately their wildly inappropriate choice of day out. However, it took then 35 minutes of their children crying and showing obvious distress before this revelation finally permeated their pea brains.

Christina Martin
e-mail

DOWNUM Kraig *(Letterbocks page 50)* says that the NHS was better in the 70s as you got nurses dressed like Barbara Windsor with suspenders, high heels and little aprons. But what he forgets is that there was a good chance you'd be treated by Bernard Bresslaw in the same uniform. Frankly, if the price of ensuring I won't get a cross-dressing behemoth of a nurse in hospital is baggy green uniforms, it's one I'm willing to pay.

Jonathan Richardson
e-mail

The Weakest Link

HAS ANYONE ever noticed the word 'turd' in Saturday? It doesn't seem fair, as I think it's the nicest day of the week.

Tom Aspel
Dorking

I'VE renamed my cat Halle Berry. Now if I want to fantasise about having deranged sex with a Hollywood movie star, I just tap a tin of Whiskers with a fork and get cracking.

A Tuzzlebut
e-mail

PULL THE other one, David Blunkett. You claim to be blind, yet you can obviously see well enough to do your tie up. And whenever you are on the telly, you always know where the camera is. If you were really blind, statistics would say that you would do half your interviews facing the wrong way.

Edna Spermbanks
Tooting

MY DVD rental service recently recommended Most Haunted series 3, based on the fact that I once rented Monty Python series 3. I think they're focussing on the wrong aspect. I'm not going to automatically like the third series of any given show.

Arthur Rumsfeld
Manchester

Mind Your Language

WHY DO foreign film makers always add English sub-titles to their films? You'd think foreigners would be able to understand films in their own languages.

Adam Gatward
e-mail

AFTER watching Crimewatch last night, the presenter said 'Please, don't have nightmares.' I wish he'd said it a bit sooner, as I had just eaten some cheese.

Greg Bown
e-mail

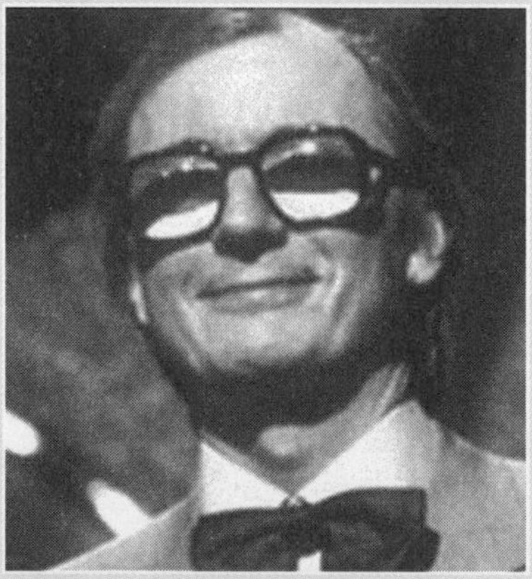

THEY SAY every little helps. Well not my neighbour, washed-up comedian Syd Little. I was recently coming up my path struggling under the weight of half a dozen bags of shopping, and he just sat in a deck chair in his garden and watched.

Angus Steakhouse
Fleetwood

YOU NEVER see those pirate DVD warnings on pirate DVDs, do you? They're targeting the wrong people if you ask me.

Christmas Martinez
e-mail

Eye Wonder

I AM I the only person who thinks that Stevie Wonder is just pretending that he can't see? If he was really blind, he wouldn't be able to see the keys on his piano and he would play all the wrong notes. He'd probably even try to play it with the lid down.

Edna Spermbanks
Tooting

BBC announcers are forever saying to us viewers "press your red buttons now". Well I'm married to the actor Red Buttons (who was in *The Poseidon Adventure*) and he's getting sick of me pressing him.

Ada Buttons
Peterborough

Red or Dead?

I SUSPECT that the letter *(above)* has been sent in by an impostor, as I know for a fact that Red Buttons died of vascular disease in 2006. And anyway, he lived in Hollywood where the BBC interactive digital service isn't available.

Tarquin Brutus
Manchester

Summit Stinks

I HAVE just bought some Harpic Odour Stop Mountain Air. Now my toilet smells like mountain air... if you were to smell the air up a mountain just after someone had done a big shit at the summit.

Matt
e-mail

A LITTLE goes a long way, or so they say. Well I disagree. My next door neighbour is washed-up comedian Syd Little, and I saw him going down to the shop yesterday for a bottle of milk and a paper. It couldn't have been more than a 200 yards round trip.

Angus
Steakhouse
Fleetwood

Last Meals

Each week we ask someone called Last to choose what they would eat for their final meal if they were about to be executed. This week, German bandleader JAMES LAST.

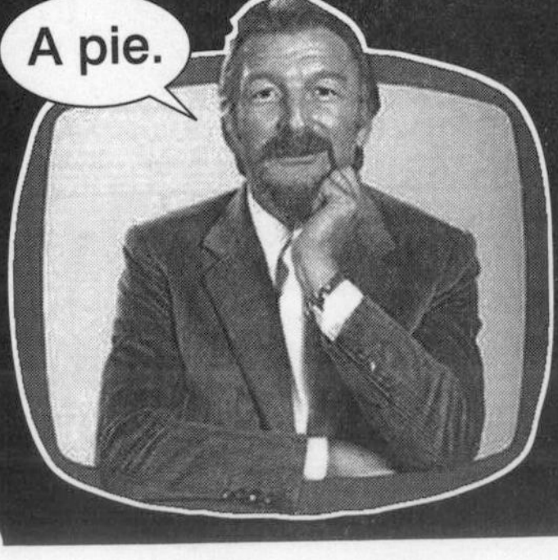
A pie.

◆ **THAT EPIC** poet John Milton (1608~1674) was no more blind than I am. The ten books of *Paradise Lost* were a classic work of literature. If he was blind, he

would have been banging away at the typewriter producing reams of utter gibberish. And even if he wrote it with a pen, chances are the last few books would have been blank because he wouldn't of known when his biro had ran out.

Edna Spermbanks
Tooting

What a Card

◆ **I ONCE** received a birthday card from my aunt and uncle after my uncle had died. My aunt, instead of not sending it, had chosen to scrawl over my deceased uncle's signature in red pen, which incidentally made it look like she had perhaps killed him. Anyway, has anyone received a more sinister birthday greeting?

Chris Lou
e-mail

◆ **FOR 50** years, I kept an old biscuit tin full of buttons in the sideboard. Hundreds of them, all shapes and sizes. I held onto them just in case they came in useful. But last week, I was having a clear out and I decided that, as I had never used a single one of them, I would chuck the lot away. Would you believe it, the very next day my husband came in and asked me if I had hundreds of spare buttons as he had decided to become a Pearly King!

Mrs TFI Friday
Gateshead

Top...Tips...Top...Tips...

CELERY with a bit of jam on makes an excellent rhubarb substitute.

Tova Dolin
e-mail

PROLONG the life of your carpets by rolling them up each night before bed and storing them in the shed.

R Babbington
e-mail

WASPS make ideal doormen for beehives.

Bill Broonzy
e-mail

HOLLYWOOD film makers. Stuck for an idea for a new movie? Simply select the name of an animal or occupation at random and stick the words 'Beverly Hills' in front of it.

Peter Britton
e-mail

MEN. Save energy drying recently washed pots and pans by blasting each of them for 30 seconds in the microwave.

Peter Smith
e-mail

RHUBARB steeped in bleach makes a fantastic substitute for celery.

Tova Dolin
e-mail

IAN HISLOP. Win *Have I Got News for You* by being funnier than Paul Merton and looking less like Penfold from *Dangermouse*.

Dave Downes
Nottingham

CREATE that 'just been to the swimming pool' feeling by spraying yourself with bleach, rubbing chilli sauce in your eyes and stuffing your ears with Blu-Tac.

Rob Cottam
e-mail

DAILY Express editors. Test your readers' memory by constantly filling your paper with inflammatory articles about asylum seekers and immigrants and then feigning disgust when the BNP get elected.

Mark
e-mail

CORONATION Street cast. Don't eat cereal for breakfast as you'll only stab at it moodily with a spoon before pushing it away uneaten. Eat toast and you can wave it about happily while chatting with people.

Arigato Ian Hughes
e-mail

SAVE money on batteries by only putting them into your clock when you wish to know the time.

Matthew Wilson
e-mail

ZOOKEEPERS. Get round politically correct rules against holding chimps' tea parties by dressing bears up as chimps. This can be done using a grass skirt, a wig made of leaves and two coconut shell halves attached to their jaws. To make things go with a swing, put honey on the currant buns.

Johnny Pring, e-mail

THAT'S TEETH
with Esther Rantzen

I've been inundated with letters from old people informing me of their age and the fact that they still have their own teeth. Here's a few of the best I've received.

Dear Esther,
I'M 82 and I've still got all my own teeth.

Edna Bucket
Tring

Dear Esther,
I'M 86 and I've still got all my own teeth.

Dolly Scrotum
Troon

Dear Esther,
I'VE still got all my own teeth. I'm 88, you know.

Cissy Spaceship
Truro

Dear Esther,
I'M 92, but unfortunately, I haven't got my own teeth. However, my husband has still got all his, and they're beautiful and pearly white. Mind you, he's only 23.

Sylvia Teapot
Troste

Dear Esther,
MY grandaughter works for a dentist and she says that Edna Bucket (*That's Teeth, this issue*) was in there last week and she had a new top plate fitted. She's a ruddy liar is Edna Bucket, Esther, and that's swearing. And I'll tell you another thing, her net curtains haven't seen the inside of a washer since last Christmas.

Winnie Clitworth
Tring

Dear Esther,
I SUFFER from the tragic accelerated ageing illness progeria. I'm four years old, and I've still got all my own milk teeth, you know.

Mabel Shufflebottom
Trump

Dear Esther,
THAT Winnie Clitworth (*That's Teeth, this issue*) has got a ruddy cheek accusing me of having dirty nets. I've been in her house and you wouldn't believe the dirt. Eeeh! I didn't want to sit down. And she turns round and comes on your page calling me. What a ruddy sauce. And that's swearing.

Edna Bucket
Tring

Dear Esther,
HOW dare that Edna Bucket (*That's Teeth, this issue*) talk about me like that. Who does she think she is? If anybody's got a filthy house it's her. I went to her toilet once to do a duty and, eeeh! the state of the pan. I couldn't go. I had to hold it in. Course I couldn't go when I got home because me bowel had spasmed. The nurse at the practice had to manipulate me back body to get me motions going.

Winnie Clitworth
Tring

Dear Esther,
YOU know me, I'm not one to start slinging mud, but if you want to see a dirty toilet you want to get round to Winnie Clitworth's house. Eeeeh! I've never seen anything like it. You'd think she'd never heard of bleach. And when her husband was in North Africa during the war, she never went without nylons, if you know what I mean. Talk of the street she was, the way she carried on.

Edna Bucket
Tring

Dear Esther,
I'M 95 and I've still got all my own teeth. But I'll tell you what, that woman next door, well her niece had a black baby.

Elsie Fourpence
Totnes

WELL, it looks like Elsie Fourpence from Totnes is the oldest person in Britain with her own teeth. That is, of course, unless YOU know different... *Esther*

Mothball Plan for Queen

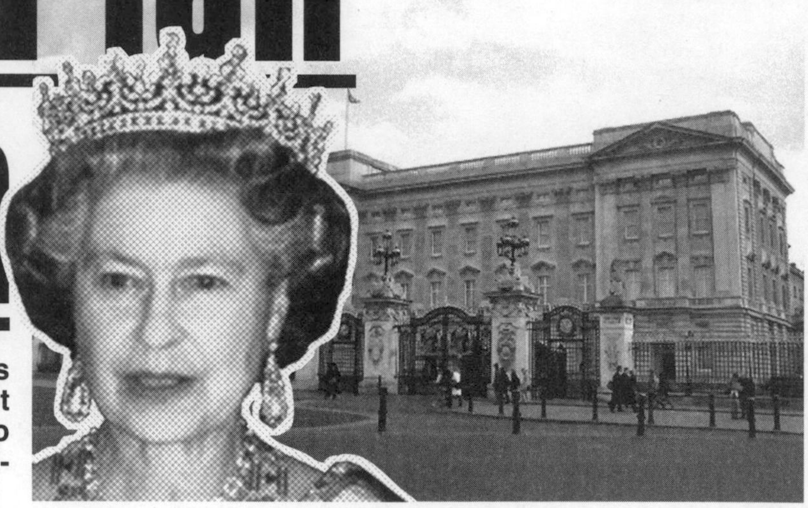

QUEEN MUMMY?: Palace chiefs aim to mothball monarch till present crisis is over.

HER Majesty the Queen is set to be mothballed as part of a series of cost-cutting measures brought in by the government. Plans have been made to store the sovereign in the basement of Buckingham Palace until the present economic recession is over.

EXCLUSIVE!

With an estimated annual upkeep cost of £500 million, the Queen is the world's most expensive ceremonial head of state. Treasury analysts have decided that it is simply too costly to maintain her in the current financial climate. "UK plc is virtually bankrupt and Her Majesty is a luxury the country just cannot afford at the moment," a Bank of England source told us. But he stressed that simply scrapping the ageing monarch is not an option. "When exchange rates recover, she'll be needed once again to fulfill her traditional role of making Britain an attractive holiday destination for foreign tourists," he added. "At that point she will be brought out of storage and put back to work."

PLANS

But the controversial plans have already come under fire. Clive Shacklady, who runs the website www.queenelizabeth2fanclub.co.uk, fumed: "It's ridiculous to think that the Queen could be brought out of storage and simply start reigning again straight away. There would have to be a lengthy period of adjustment during which Her Majesty could be re-familiarised with her various regal duties such as looking down at people, waving and pulling open little curtains at sports centres."

SQUIRREL

"The enormous expense of this process could easily outweigh any savings made by mothballing her," he added.

The Queen is not the first celebrity to face being mothballed due to a change in circumstances. In 1986, sinister TV star Noel Edmonds was placed into a barrel in the cellar of Television Centre after he killed someone on his *Late Late Breakfast Show.* Nearly 20 years later he was brought back out of storage and once again took his place on our screens when his unique skills were needed to host a series of shows such as *Deal or No Deal, Are You Smarter than a 10-Year-Old?* and *Noel's HQ.*

Why not... **Be a Plumber**

AND MEET UP TO 40,000 WOMEN p.a

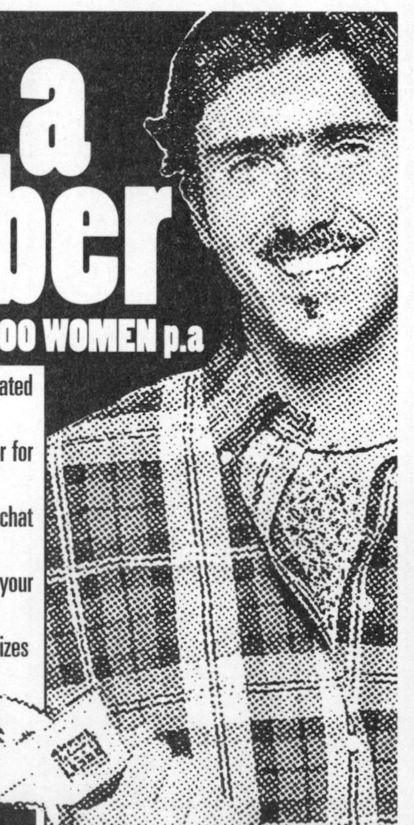

- 400 new bored housewives are created every month
- BY 2020, there could be one plumber for 100 housewives
- NO previous experience in cheeky chat leading to a quickie upstairs needed
- BIG belts featuring pockets for all your massive tools
- LUMBERJACK shirts in all shaoes & sizes
- HOT lesbian sex

Are you HANDY at showing the sexually frustrated young things of Great Britain & Wales the ins and outs of male & female coupling parts that screw together like so?

Become fully trained in spouting complex EU regulations in order to drastically increase your quote AND impress the lady.

Call NOW to arrange to pop round mid-morning after yer fellas gone - for an informal chat with someone wearing a see-thru nightie or dressing gown fresh from the shower:

☎ 0898 000 000 000

How will it be Done?

With some analysts estimating that the credit crunch could last for ten years or more, we asked several high profile celebrities how they would go about preserving the Queen for an indefinite period.

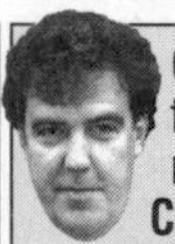

OUTSPOKEN motorhead petrol-mouth **JEREMY CLARKSON** explained how he would treat the monarch like a valuable classic car. "I would lift her off the floor on bricks, cover her with a dust cloth and leave her in a well-ventilated garage," he told us. "Every two weeks or so I would couple her tits up to some jump leads and turn her heart over a couple of times and leave her waving for five minutes or so. That way, she would always be ready to be re-commissioned at a moment's notice, a bit like a Green Goddess."

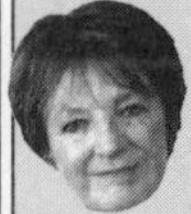

DRUNKEN soccer outburst TV pan-basher ***DELIA SMITH*** *suggested sealing the Queen in a giant can. "Tinned foods last for ever," she slurred. "So I would pop Her Majesty into an oil-drum and weld the lid tightly shut. Providing her can doesn't get dinted, the Queen should stay fresh indefinitely."*

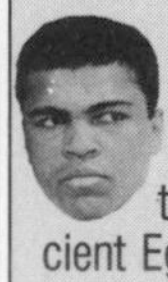

HARRODS boss **MOHAMMED AL FAYED** reckoned the authorities should take a leaf out of his ancestors' book. "The Pharaohs of ancient Egypt wrapped themselves in bandages to protect them against the ravages of time," the nut-job shopkeeper explained. "Sealed in solid gold sarcophaguses deep within their massive granite pyramids, they have remained in perfect condition for many thousands of years. However, if the Queen were to do the same, there is a risk that whoever dug her out in the future would fall foul of her curse and die a horrible death."

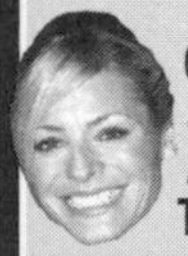

COMMON-voiced *Strictly Come Dancing* beauty **TESS DALY** recommended popping Her Majesty in the freezer. "It may sound old fashioned," she said, "but freezing is still the best way of keeping something fresh until it is needed. And I bet there's plenty of Queen-sized fridges in the kitchens at Buckingham Palace!" However, Tess sounded a note of caution. "They would have to allow the chilled Royal a good 48 hours to thaw about before expecting her to undertake any ceremonial duties. It wouldn't do if she went to change the guard and she was still frozen solid in the middle."

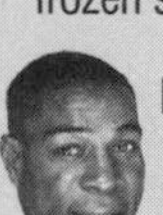

LOVABLE ex-thump-monger **FRANK BRUNO** thought that pickling the Queen in vinegar like an onion would be a good idea. "But I'm not talking about the sort of cheap vinegar you get at the chip shop, know what I mean, Harry? They would have to use really expensive Balsamic stuff from Fortnum and Mason. Or Waitrose at least," he told us. "A-hur-hur-hur. A-hur-hur-hur," he added.

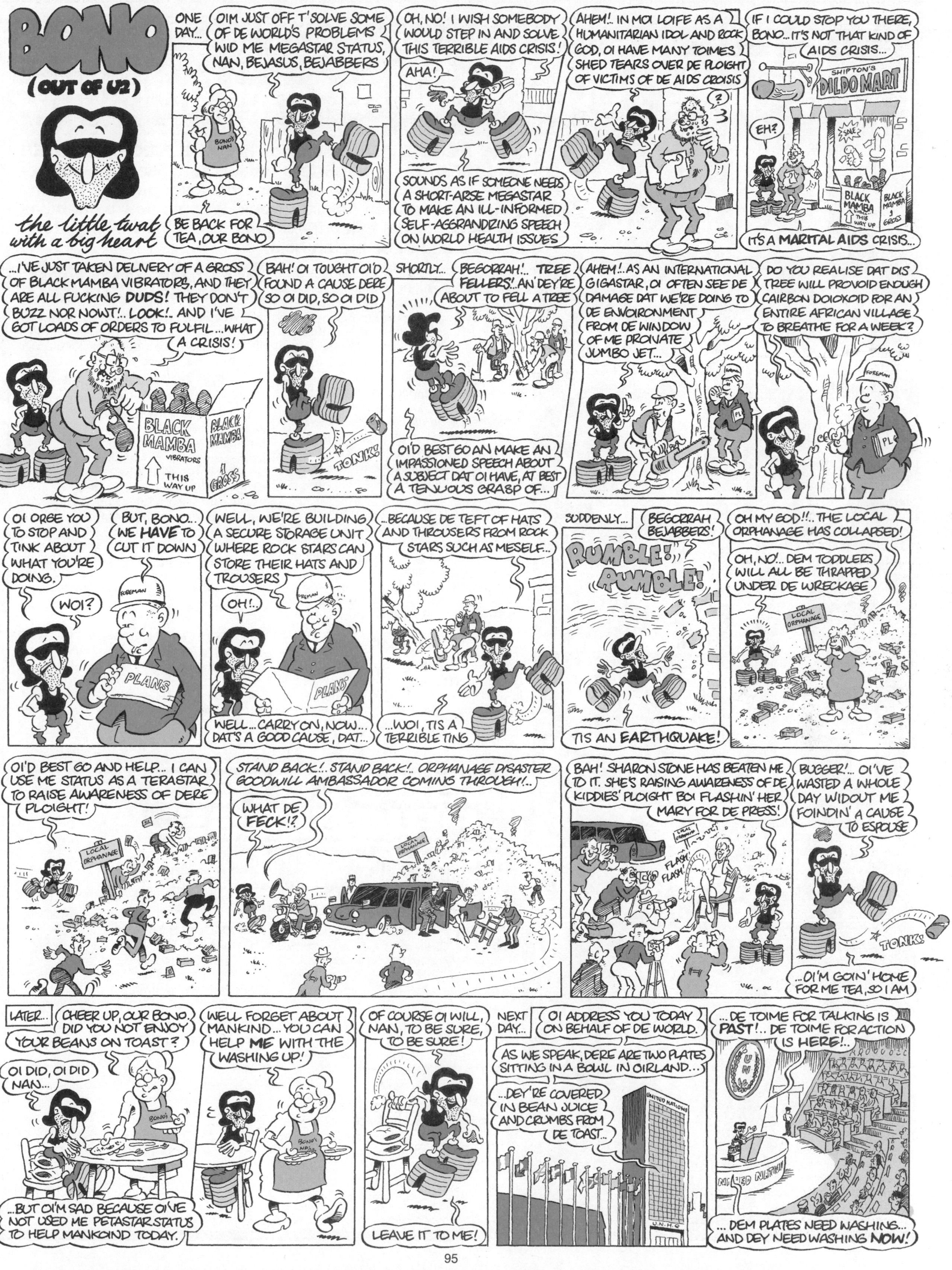
BONO
(OUT OF U2)
the little twat with a big heart
ONE DAY...
OIM JUST OFF T'SOLVE SOME OF DE WORLD'S PROBLEMS WID ME MEGASTAR STATUS, NAN, BEJASUS, BEJABBERS
BONO'S NAN
BE BACK FOR TEA, OUR BONO
OH, NO! I WISH SOMEBODY WOULD STEP IN AND SOLVE THIS TERRIBLE AIDS CRISIS!
AHA!
SOUNDS AS IF SOMEONE NEEDS A SHORT-ARSE MEGASTAR TO MAKE AN ILL-INFORMED SELF-AGGRANDIZING SPEECH ON WORLD HEALTH ISSUES
AHEM!.. IN MOI LOIFE AS A HUMANITARIAN IDOL AND ROCK GOD, OI HAVE MANY TOIMES SHED TEARS OVER DE PLOIGHT OF VICTIMS OF DE AIDS CROISIS
?
IF I COULD STOP YOU THERE, BONO... IT'S NOT THAT KIND OF AIDS CRISIS...
SHIPTON'S DILDO MART
EH?
SALE
BLACK MAMBA THIS WAY UP
BLACK MAMBA 1 GROSS
IT'S A MARITAL AIDS CRISIS...
...I'VE JUST TAKEN DELIVERY OF A GROSS OF BLACK MAMBA VIBRATORS, AND THEY ARE ALL FUCKING DUDS! THEY DON'T BUZZ NOR NOWT!.. LOOK!.. AND I'VE GOT LOADS OF ORDERS TO FULFIL... WHAT A CRISIS!
BLACK MAMBA VIBRATORS THIS WAY UP
BLACK MAMBA 1 GROSS
BAH! OI TOUGHT OI'D FOUND A CAUSE DERE SO OI DID, SO OI DID
TONK!
SHORTLY...
BEGORRAH!.. TREE FELLERS!.. AN' DEY'RE ABOUT TO FELL A TREE
OI'D BEST GO AN MAKE AN IMPASSIONED SPEECH ABOUT A SUBJECT DAT OI HAVE, AT BEST A TENUOUS GRASP OF...
AHEM!.. AS AN INTERNATIONAL GIGASTAR, OI OFTEN SEE DE DAMAGE DAT WE'RE DOING TO DE ENVOIRONMENT FROM DE WINDOW OF ME PROIVATE JUMBO JET...
PL
DO YOU REALISE DAT DIS TREE WILL PROVOID ENOUGH CAIRBON DOIOXOID FOR AN ENTIRE AFRICAN VILLAGE TO BREATHE FOR A WEEK?
FOREMAN
PL
OI ORGE YOU TO STOP AND TINK ABOUT WHAT YOU'RE DOING.
BUT, BONO... WE HAVE TO CUT IT DOWN
WOI?
FOREMAN
PLANS
WELL, WE'RE BUILDING A SECURE STORAGE UNIT WHERE ROCK STARS CAN STORE THEIR HATS AND TROUSERS
OH!..
FOREMAN
PLANS
WELL... CARRY ON, NOW... DAT'S A GOOD CAUSE, DAT...
...BECAUSE DE TEFT OF HATS AND THROUSERS FROM ROCK STARS SUCH AS MESELF...
...WOI, TIS A TERRIBLE TING
SUDDENLY...
BEGORRAH BEJABBERS!
RUMBLE! RUMBLE!
TIS AN EARTHQUAKE!
OH MY GOD!!.. THE LOCAL ORPHANAGE HAS COLLAPSED!
OH, NO!.. DEM TODDLERS WILL ALL BE THRAPPED UNDER DE WRECKAGE
LOCAL ORPHANAGE
OI'D BEST GO AND HELP... I CAN USE ME STATUS AS A TERASTAR TO RAISE AWARENESS OF DERE PLOIGHT!
LOCAL ORPHANAGE
STAND BACK!.. STAND BACK!.. ORPHANAGE DISASTER GOODWILL AMBASSADOR COMING THROUGH!..
WHAT DE FECK!?
LOCAL ORPHANAGE
BAH! SHARON STONE HAS BEATEN ME TO IT. SHE'S RAISING AWARENESS OF DE KIDDIES' PLOIGHT BOI FLASHIN' HER MARY FOR DE PRESS!
LOCAL ORPHANAGE
FLASH! FLASH!
BUGGER!.. OI'VE WASTED A WHOLE DAY WIDOUT ME FOINDIN' A CAUSE TO ESPOUSE
TONK!
...OI'M GOIN' HOME FOR ME TEA, SO I AM
LATER...
CHEER UP, OUR BONO. DID YOU NOT ENJOY YOUR BEANS ON TOAST?
OI DID, OI DID NAN...
BONO'S
...BUT OI'M SAD BECAUSE OI'VE NOT USED ME PETASTAR STATUS TO HELP MANKOIND TODAY.
WELL FORGET ABOUT MANKIND... YOU CAN HELP ME WITH THE WASHING UP!
BONO'S NAN
OF COURSE OI WILL, NAN, TO BE SURE, TO BE SURE!
LEAVE IT TO ME!
NEXT DAY...
OI ADDRESS YOU TODAY ON BEHALF OF DE WORLD.
AS WE SPEAK, DERE ARE TWO PLATES SITTING IN A BOWL IN OIRLAND...
...DEY'RE COVERED IN BEAN JUICE AND CRUMBS FROM DE TOAST...
UNITED NATIONS
U.N.H.Q
...DE TOIME FOR TALKING IS PAST!.. DE TOIME FOR ACTION IS HERE!..
UN
...DEM PLATES NEED WASHING... AND DEY NEED WASHING NOW!

Media Couple's Lives on Hold as Script Strike Bites

PETE & KATIE LOSE THE PLOT!

ONGOING industrial action by KATIE PRICE and PETER ANDRE's scriptwriters looked no closer to being resolved yesterday as their strike over pay and working conditions entered its sixth week. With no new plots being produced for the celebrity couple, their long-running storyline has had to be put on hold.

A source close to Price and Andre confided that the pair are in limbo. "Pete and Katie always got their new scripts first thing on Monday morning, telling them what twists and turns their relationship was going to take that week," the friend said. "Without fresh plots to live out in the public eye, they really haven't got a clue what's going to happen to them next."

"Peter has no idea from one day to another whether he's going to be photographed snogging a mystery blonde outside a nightclub or tearfully taking his kids to the zoo," he added. "He simply hasn't got a clue."

The last episode to be completed before the strike began saw the pair split up when singer Andre became jealous of his model wife's relationship with a handsome dressage coach. A rumoured Christmas episode in which the couple were to renew their marriage vows on the beach in Tahiti now looks almost certain to be shelved.

STRIKE

OK! magazine editor Marjorie Shitbucket says that the strike action is having knock-on effects throughout the celebrity industry. "Six weeks without any fresh Katie and Peter storylines has left us with hundreds of extra pages to fill," she told

EXCLUSIVE!

us. "We're really feeling the pinch. There's only so many times we can run features about Kerry Katona being back on drugs before the public will start to turn off."

FIVE GO MAD IN DORSET

Meanwhile Len Turdbridge, chairman of NUKPS, the National Union of Katie and Peter Scriptwriters, said that his members were anxious to get back to work. However, he was adamant that they would stay out on the picket lines as long as it took for their demands to be met. "We've got loads of great ideas for plots," he told Radio 4's *Today* programme. "A boob job that goes wrong leaving Katie in a coma, a mystery caller at their house who claims to be Princess Tiiaami's father and a fantastic double episode when Katie's stables burn down and Pete is arrested and charged with arson."

"These are all great ideas, but unless we get better pay and conditions, they're never going to see the light of day," he added.

Price and Andre were yesterday unable to comment. "Without their scripts, they simply have no idea what they think or what to say," said a spokesman.

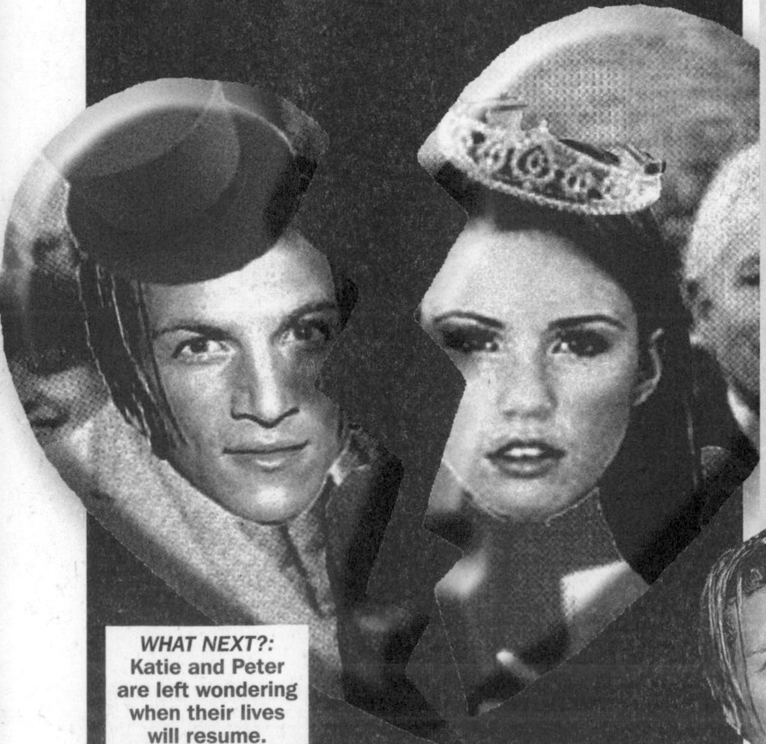

WHAT NEXT?: Katie and Peter are left wondering when their lives will resume.

ABSOLUTELY PRICELESS

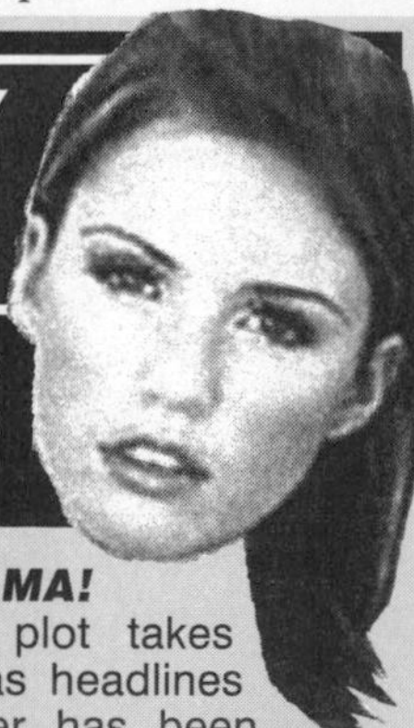

THANKS to some great plotlines, Katie and Pete's rollercoaster life together has always been popular with the public.

2004 ***ROMANCE!*** The couple meet for the first time in the Australian jungle whilst filming *I'm a Celebrity Get Me Out of Here!* Their love affair with publicity has begun.

2005 ***LOVE!*** Millions line the pockets of *OK!* magazine to see exclusive coverage of their ostentatiously tacky wedding at a fairytale castle.

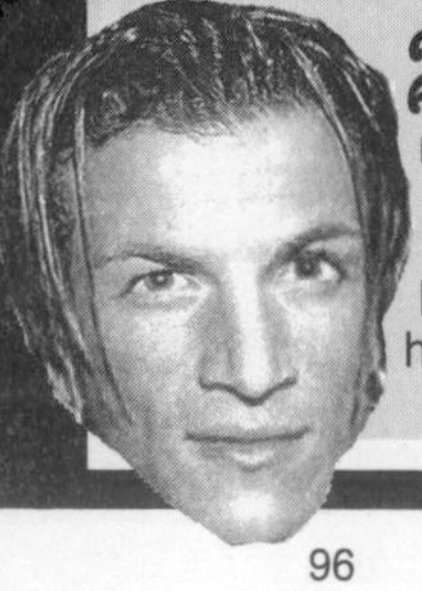

2006 ***JOY!*** The couple cement their love as photographic rights to pictures of their beautiful babies are flogged to the highest bidder.

2007 ***DRAMA!*** The plot takes a sinister turn as headlines report that Peter has been rushed to hospital with fatal meningitis. Fortunately he gets better.

2008 ***EMOTION!*** In a lavish, wallet-rending ceremony in an exclusive South African resort, the couple renew their wedding vows in front of close *OK!* magazine photographers.

2006 ***TRAGEDY!*** Scriptwriters announce the couple's most dramatic plot yet - their separation. Will they ever get back together? Watch this space!

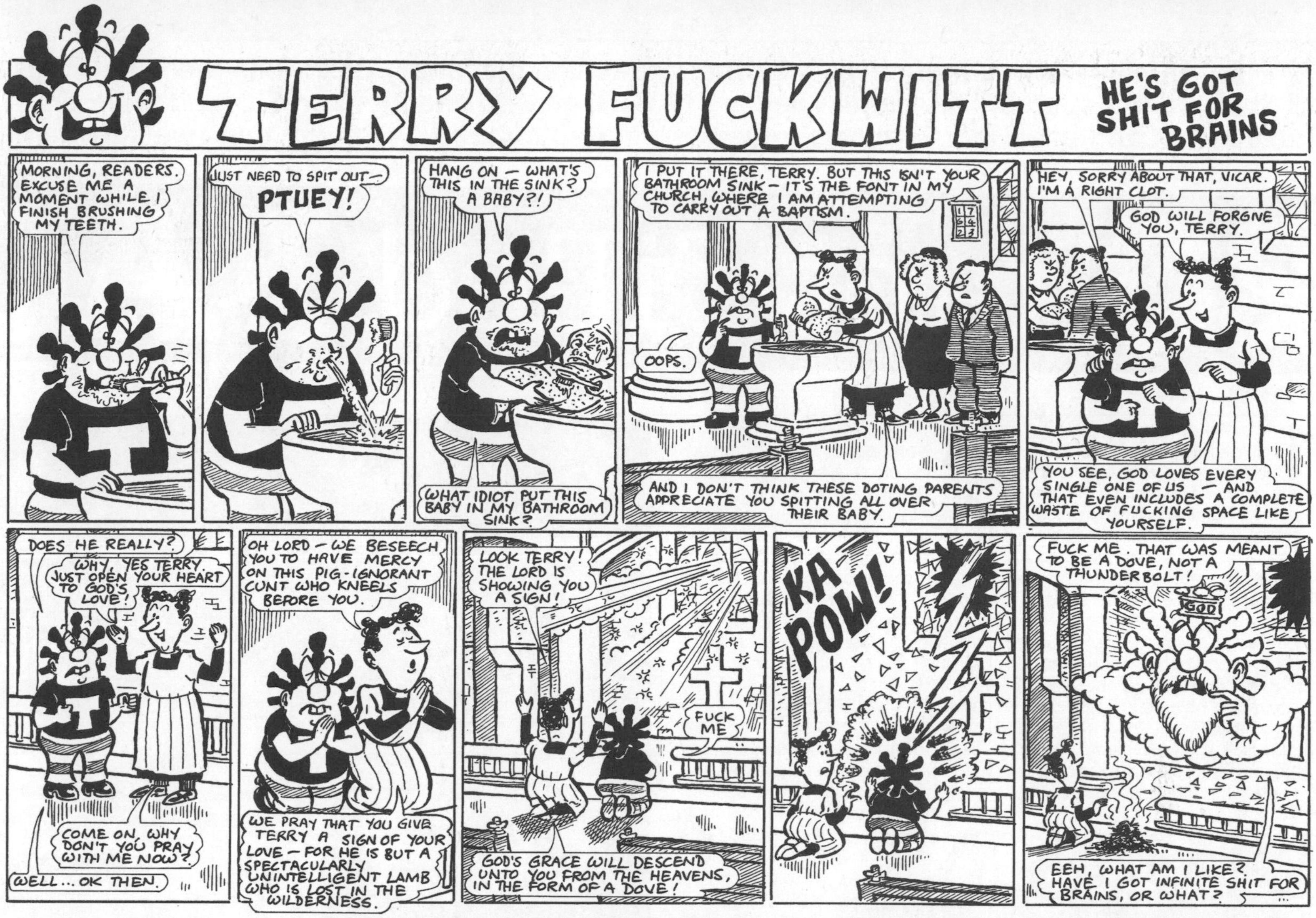
TERRY FUCKWITT
HE'S GOT SHIT FOR BRAINS
MORNING, READERS. EXCUSE ME A MOMENT WHILE I FINISH BRUSHING MY TEETH.
JUST NEED TO SPIT OUT—
PTUEY!
HANG ON — WHAT'S THIS IN THE SINK? A BABY?!
WHAT IDIOT PUT THIS BABY IN MY BATHROOM SINK?
I PUT IT THERE, TERRY. BUT THIS ISN'T YOUR BATHROOM SINK – IT'S THE FONT IN MY CHURCH, WHERE I AM ATTEMPTING TO CARRY OUT A BAPTISM.
OOPS.
AND I DON'T THINK THESE DOTING PARENTS APPRECIATE YOU SPITTING ALL OVER THEIR BABY.
HEY, SORRY ABOUT THAT, VICAR. I'M A RIGHT CLOT.
GOD WILL FORGIVE YOU, TERRY.
YOU SEE, GOD LOVES EVERY SINGLE ONE OF US — AND THAT EVEN INCLUDES A COMPLETE WASTE OF FUCKING SPACE LIKE YOURSELF.
DOES HE REALLY?
WHY, YES TERRY. JUST OPEN YOUR HEART TO GOD'S LOVE!
COME ON, WHY DON'T YOU PRAY WITH ME NOW?
WELL... OK THEN.
OH LORD — WE BESEECH YOU TO HAVE MERCY ON THIS PIG-IGNORANT CUNT WHO KNEELS BEFORE YOU.
WE PRAY THAT YOU GIVE TERRY A SIGN OF YOUR LOVE — FOR HE IS BUT A SPECTACULARLY UNINTELLIGENT LAMB WHO IS LOST IN THE WILDERNESS.
LOOK TERRY! THE LORD IS SHOWING YOU A SIGN!
FUCK ME
GOD'S GRACE WILL DESCEND UNTO YOU FROM THE HEAVENS, IN THE FORM OF A DOVE!
KA POW!
FUCK ME. THAT WAS MEANT TO BE A DOVE, NOT A THUNDERBOLT!
GOD
EEH, WHAT AM I LIKE? HAVE I GOT INFINITE SHIT FOR BRAINS, OR WHAT?

Mind Our Language!

Foreigners warned to BUCK UP or SHUT UP

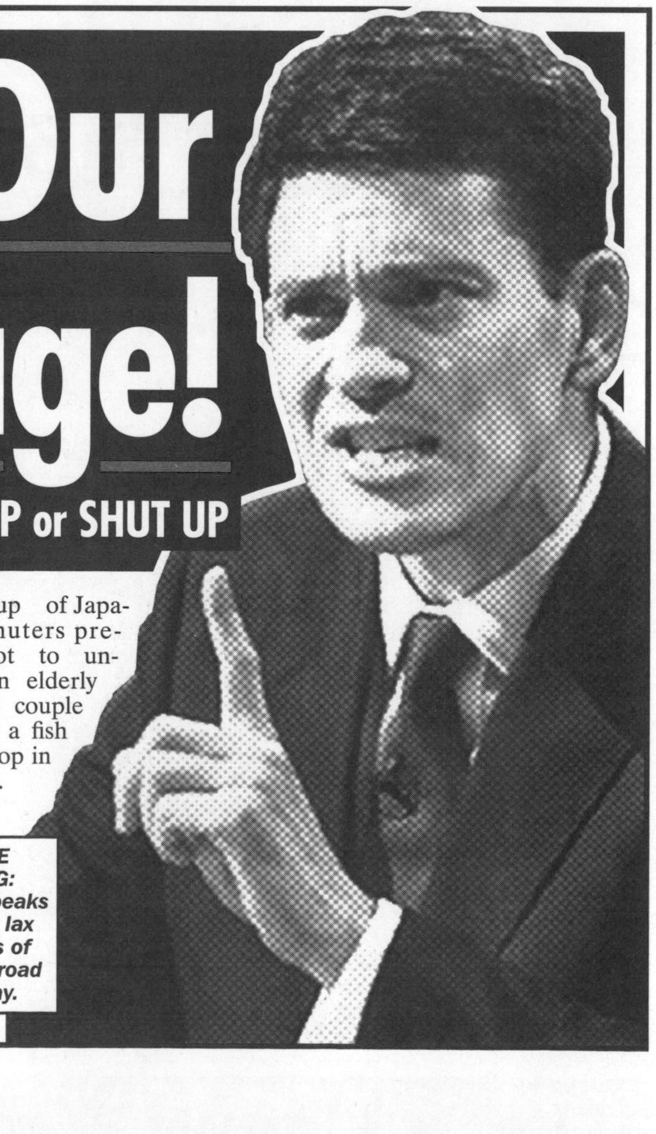

TONGUE LASHING: Miliband speaks out abour lax standards of English abroad yesterday.

BRITISH holidaymakers are to be warned against travelling to other countries after a government report revealed that standards of spoken English abroad have fallen to an all time low.

The Foreign Office report found that many sunseekers have their holidays completely ruined by locals who are unable or unwilling to converse using the Queen's English. Foreign Secretary David Miliband slammed abroad, and told a general meeting of the UN that British Citizens would no longer tolerate foreigners pointing at things, pulling faces or shrugging as substitutes for conversation.

LANGUAGE

Speaking slowly and loudly to UN Secretary General Banky Moon, Mr Milliband said: "The British people are tolerant and fair, but you lot have had long enough to pick the language up. It's sheer laziness."

Ps & Qs

Tangerine-hued *Wish You Were Here* presenter Judith Chalmers backed the plan. "I've travelled all over the world and it never ceases to amaze me how many foreigners simply can't be bothered to speak to me in my native tongue," she told reporters. "And it's even worse when they start jibber-jabbering on in their own ridiculous languages."

100s & 1000s

To ram the message home, a £12m advertising campaign entitled 'English: Local Language of the World' will be launched in newspapers, TV, radio and the internet this summer. The adverts will show scenes of Germans confusing V's and W's, French speakers unable to pronouce "th" and a group of Japanese commuters pretending not to understand an elderly Glaswegian couple looking for a fish and chip shop in Matsuyama.

THEY are always true and never incorrect. In fact the dictionary describes them as things that are indisputably the case. They are FACTS, and we see them on TV, read them on the internet and use them to answer questions in pub quizzes. We might think we know all

20 fact-filled FAC

1 We all know facts about something, but the person in the world who knows the most facts is *University Challenge* egg-head Gail Trimble. She learnt her first fact at the tender age of three when her father informed her that newts were impervious to fire. Her mother gave her her second fact the next day, telling her that every golf ball had a bag of deadly poison in the middle. Gail was bitten by the fact bug and vowed to learn ten new facts every day. Now at the age of 26, she knows a staggering 83,950 facts. 83,951 after we phoned her up and told her that Burt Reynolds has an 11 inch cock.

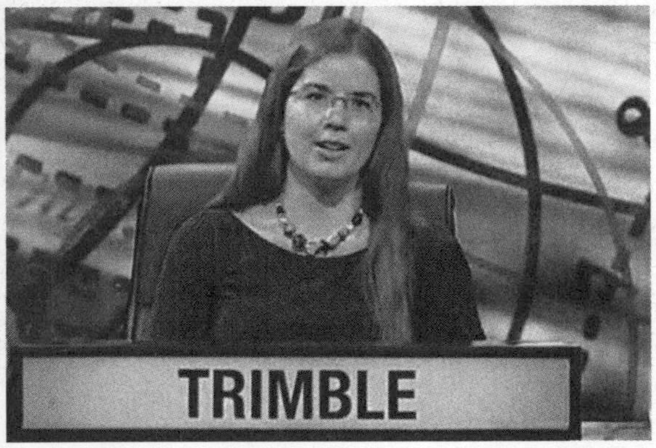
TRIMBLE

2 Facts have their own unique units of measurement. Tall things are not measured in feet and inches or even metres, but in double decker buses, Nelson's Columns and Eiffel Towers. Weights are measured in elephants, jumps by insects are measured in men jumping over St Paul's Cathedrals and loud noises are measured in Concordes taking off. Multiple things that could be laid end to end are expressed in terms of how many times they would circle the globe or reach the moon and back.

3 It is sometimes difficult to establish whether or not a fact is true. For example, it is a well known fact that 80s singer Marc Almond once had to have his stomach pumped after swallowing $1^{1}/_{2}$ pints of semen. However, there is no reason to suppose this fact is anything more than a rumour. The actual quantity of semen Almond imbibed could have been a pint or even two pints. The true facts are impossible to establish.

4 The smallest facts in the world are those concerning the world's smallest man, Calvin Phillips, who stood just 8 inches tall in his stockinged feet. Indeed, it has been estimated that if all the indisputable items of knowledge about him were written down, they would fill a fact file no bigger than a postage stamp, and you would need a microscope to read it.

5 The world's biggest collection of facts can be found in the British Library. It's shelves groan under the weight of 14 million books, each one containing over 60,000 facts. If all those facts were laid end to end, they would stretch to the moon and back over 80 times. And that's a fact!

6 You might think that you would find facts in a book. But think again. Just because something is written down or printed doesn't make it a fact. Indeed, even this fact may not be true... and if it isn't, then it *is* a fact after all.

7 Most of us rely on newspapers to give us the facts about what is going on in the world. But that is a mistake, as no newspapers print any facts at all. All the elements of newspaper stories are a mixture of unsubstantiated tittle-tattle, deliberately misleading PR press releases, exaggerated repeats of other journalists' made up rumours and unreliable information cut and pasted from a cursory Google search.

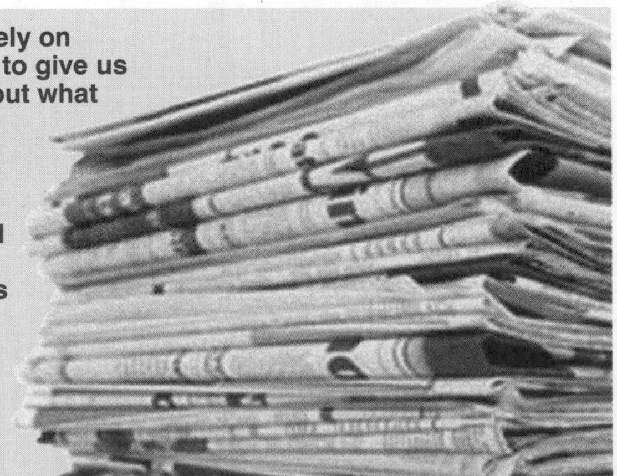

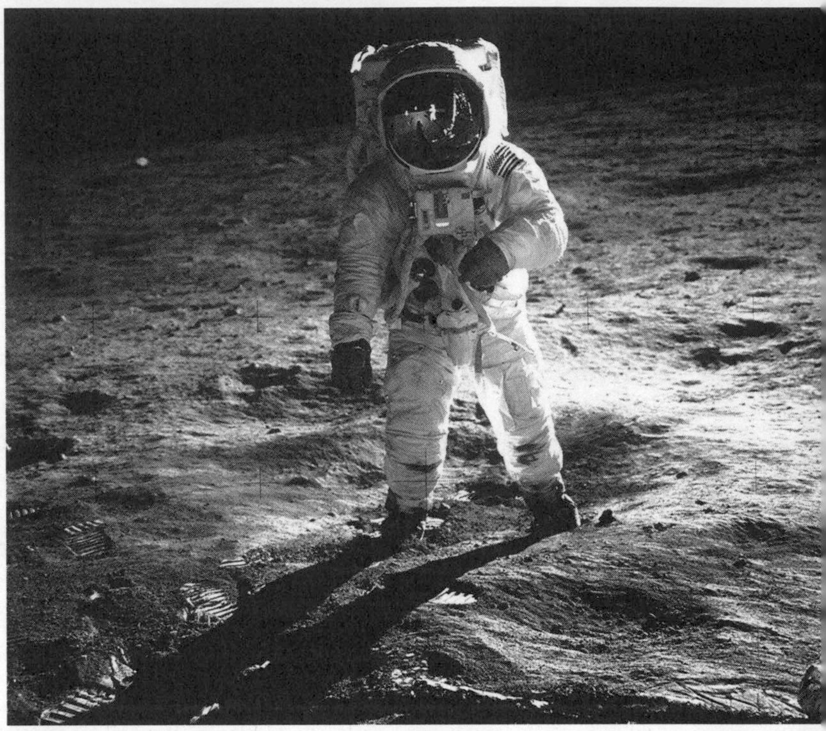

8 Politicians often go on "fact-finding" missions. However, they usually return having gleaned few undisputable certitudes or incontestable actualities. That's because a fact-finding mission is actually a chance for an elected representatives to fly first class to an exclusive golfing resort in the Seychelles with his mistress.

9 Facts are changing all the time. Advances in science and technology mean that yesterday's facts are today's fiction. You might find it difficult to believe that people once accepted as fact the ridiculous notions that the earth was flat, that people would die if they travelled at more than 15mph, and that Jimmy Carr was a comedian.

10 Immediately after their inauguration, every president of the United States is taken into a secret room at the White House and told a series of facts that only he is allowed to know. These facts include: American astronauts never went to the moon and all the photographs are fakes; they've invented a car that runs on water but the oil companies won't let them market it; it was a French mafia hitman dressed as a cop who shot Kennedy from the grassy knoll and Lee Harvey Oswald was a patsy; they've got a working flying saucer and two living aliens in a tank at Area 51 in Roswell; Desmond Lynam has got 'Fuck Off' tattooed on his top lip and that's why he's got a moustache.

about them, but do we really? How many are there? Where do they come from? What do they mean? Let's face it, there is a lot of nonsense talked about facts, so it's time to set sail on a voyage of discovery to separate the fact from the fiction.

TS about FACTS

11 If you need to know a fact about any subject in the world - from ants to xylophones - chances are you'll find it in the pages of the Encyclopaedia Britannica. This is a 26-volume dictionary of facts which was invented in 1871 by a door-to-door salesman who had run out of brushes.

12 Like most things, facts can be catagorised. These catagories of facts include sport, history, geography, famous people, TV and film, books, pop music and nature. Any fact that doesn't fit under one of these headings is given its own special group, called general knowledge.

13 If you want to win a pub quiz, you might think you would need to know thousands of facts on hundreds of subjects. But you'd be wrong. That's because most pub quiz masters are notoriously unimaginative and base all their questions on James Bond films. Simply being able to remember the actor who played 007 in each movie and who sang the theme tune is usually enough to get you 60 to 70%. And in the picture round, the blonde woman is usually Paris Hilton, and the black man will be Wesley Snipes.

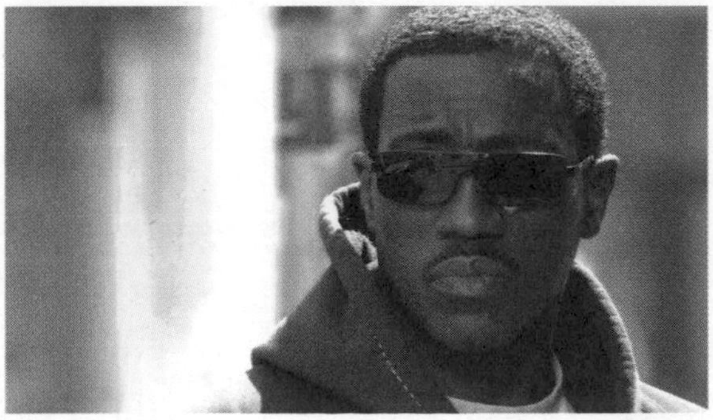

14 The oldest known fact in the world is that dinosaurs had a brain had a brain the size of a walnut, which was scrawled on the wall of a cave by a stone age man over 1,000,000 years ago. The ancient fact was only discovered last week which means, ironically, that the fact that it is the oldest known fact in the world is actually the *newest* fact in the world!

15 People who work in the media know a lot of fascinating facts that are kept from the general public. Some of these are kept secret in the interests of national security, whilst others remain undisclosed for different reasons, such as the ones about Paul Daniels and Debbie McGee, Cliff Richard, Jimmy Savile and Gary Lineker. And a really, really good one about Una Stubbs.

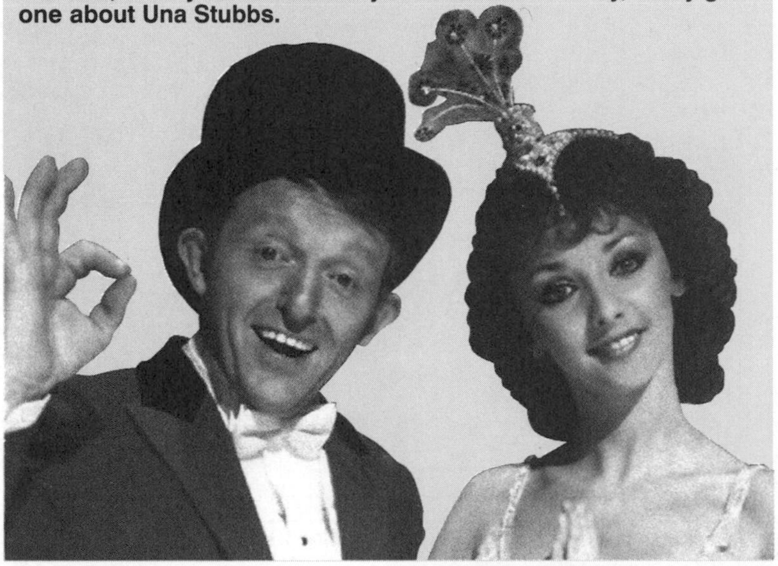

16 A 'factoid' is a small packet of unreliable information copyrighted by the Radio 2 DJ Steve Wright. 'Penguins don't have ears', 'there are no stones in Holland', and 'importing kiwi fruit uses more than it's own weight in aviation fuel', are some of the pointless statements read out by Wright and his arse-licking posses of loud-mouthed twats in an effort to fill up space between bouts of false applause on his long-running afternoon show.

17 You may find it hard to believe, but scientists have discovered that female brains are better at storing information than male brains. Amazingly, a woman can hold up to 20% more facts in her memory than a man. However, the facts they store tend to be trivial, concerning such things as dress sizes, the price of shoes and what they overheard somebody telling somebody else in a shop. Men's brains, on the other hand, are filled with facts about important football statistics, useful routes they have driven along and vital information about the names of the characters from Captain Pugwash.

18 There are many little known facts in the world, such as that Chinese women's fannies go from side to side instead of up and down like normal. That this is a little known fact is a surprising fact in itself, since China has a population of one and a half billion and you would have thought that at least half of them would be aware of it, and the rest might find out eventually too.

19 The animal that has the least number of facts about it is the swan. Despite being one of the world's most attractive birds, there are only five facts about these creatures. 1. That they all belong to the Queen. 2. That they mate for life. 3. That they only make a sound when they are dying. 4. That they can break your arm with their wing. 5. That there are only five facts about them.

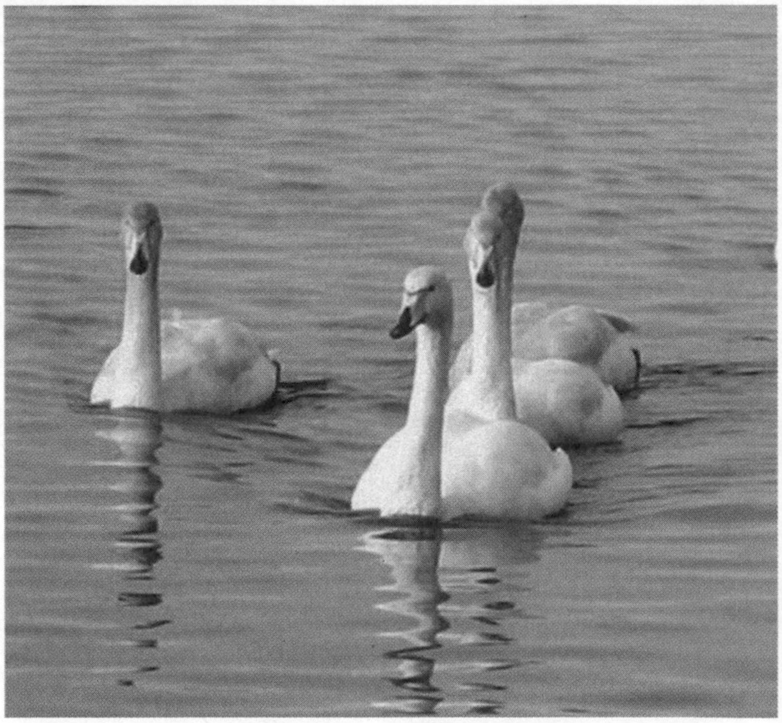

20 Despite the fact that there are millions of facts in the world, the 19 facts on this page are the only known facts about facts themselves. And this fact brings that total up to 20.

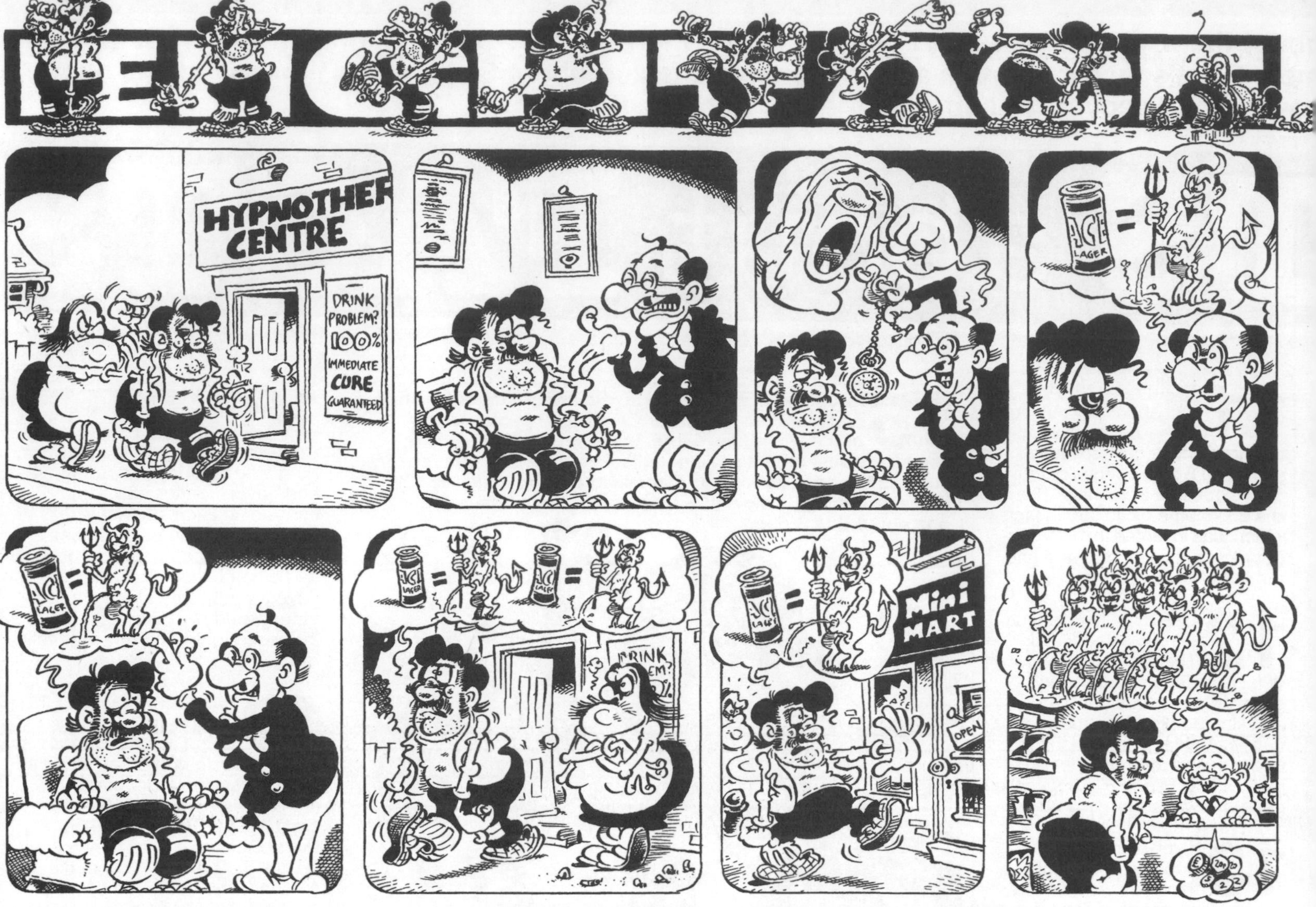
HYPNOTHER
CENTRE
DRINK PROBLEM? 100% IMMEDIATE CURE GUARANTEED
ACE LAGER
ACE LAGER
ACE LAGER
ACE LAGER
ACE LAGER
Mini MART
OPEN

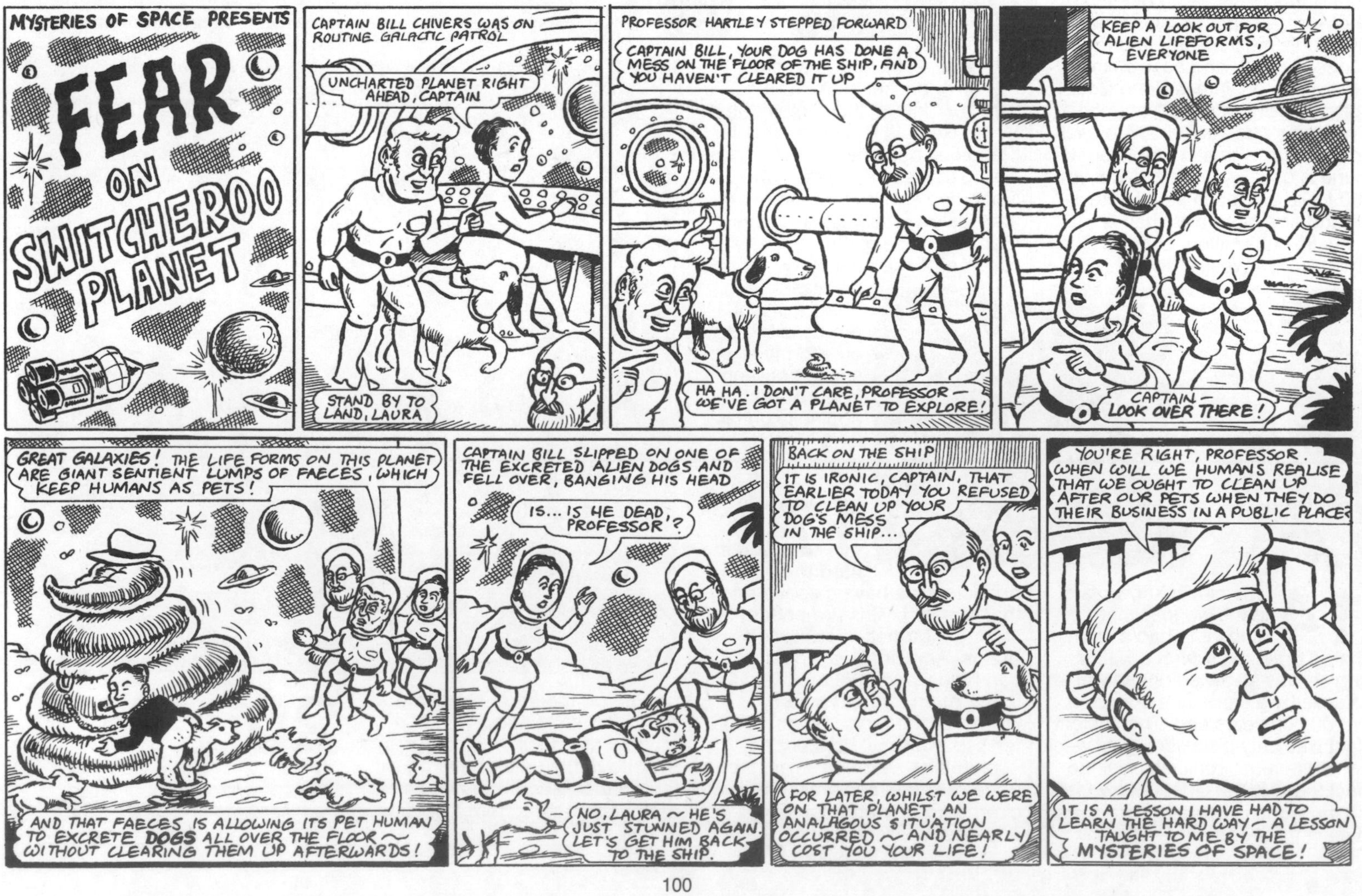
MYSTERIES OF SPACE PRESENTS
FEAR ON SWITCHEROO PLANET
CAPTAIN BILL CHIVERS WAS ON ROUTINE GALACTIC PATROL
UNCHARTED PLANET RIGHT AHEAD, CAPTAIN
STAND BY TO LAND, LAURA
PROFESSOR HARTLEY STEPPED FORWARD
CAPTAIN BILL, YOUR DOG HAS DONE A MESS ON THE FLOOR OF THE SHIP, AND YOU HAVEN'T CLEARED IT UP
HA HA. I DON'T CARE, PROFESSOR ~ WE'VE GOT A PLANET TO EXPLORE!
KEEP A LOOK OUT FOR ALIEN LIFEFORMS, EVERYONE
CAPTAIN ~ LOOK OVER THERE!
GREAT GALAXIES! THE LIFE FORMS ON THIS PLANET ARE GIANT SENTIENT LUMPS OF FAECES, WHICH KEEP HUMANS AS PETS!
AND THAT FAECES IS ALLOWING ITS PET HUMAN TO EXCRETE DOGS ALL OVER THE FLOOR ~ WITHOUT CLEARING THEM UP AFTERWARDS!
CAPTAIN BILL SLIPPED ON ONE OF THE EXCRETED ALIEN DOGS AND FELL OVER, BANGING HIS HEAD
IS... IS HE DEAD, PROFESSOR?
NO, LAURA ~ HE'S JUST STUNNED AGAIN. LET'S GET HIM BACK TO THE SHIP.
BACK ON THE SHIP
IT IS IRONIC, CAPTAIN, THAT EARLIER TODAY YOU REFUSED TO CLEAN UP YOUR DOG'S MESS IN THE SHIP...
FOR LATER, WHILST WE WERE ON THAT PLANET, AN ANALAGOUS SITUATION OCCURRED ~ AND NEARLY COST YOU YOUR LIFE!
YOU'RE RIGHT, PROFESSOR. WHEN WILL WE HUMANS REALISE THAT WE OUGHT TO CLEAN UP AFTER OUR PETS WHEN THEY DO THEIR BUSINESS IN A PUBLIC PLACE?
IT IS A LESSON I HAVE HAD TO LEARN THE HARD WAY ~ A LESSON TAUGHT TO ME BY THE MYSTERIES OF SPACE!

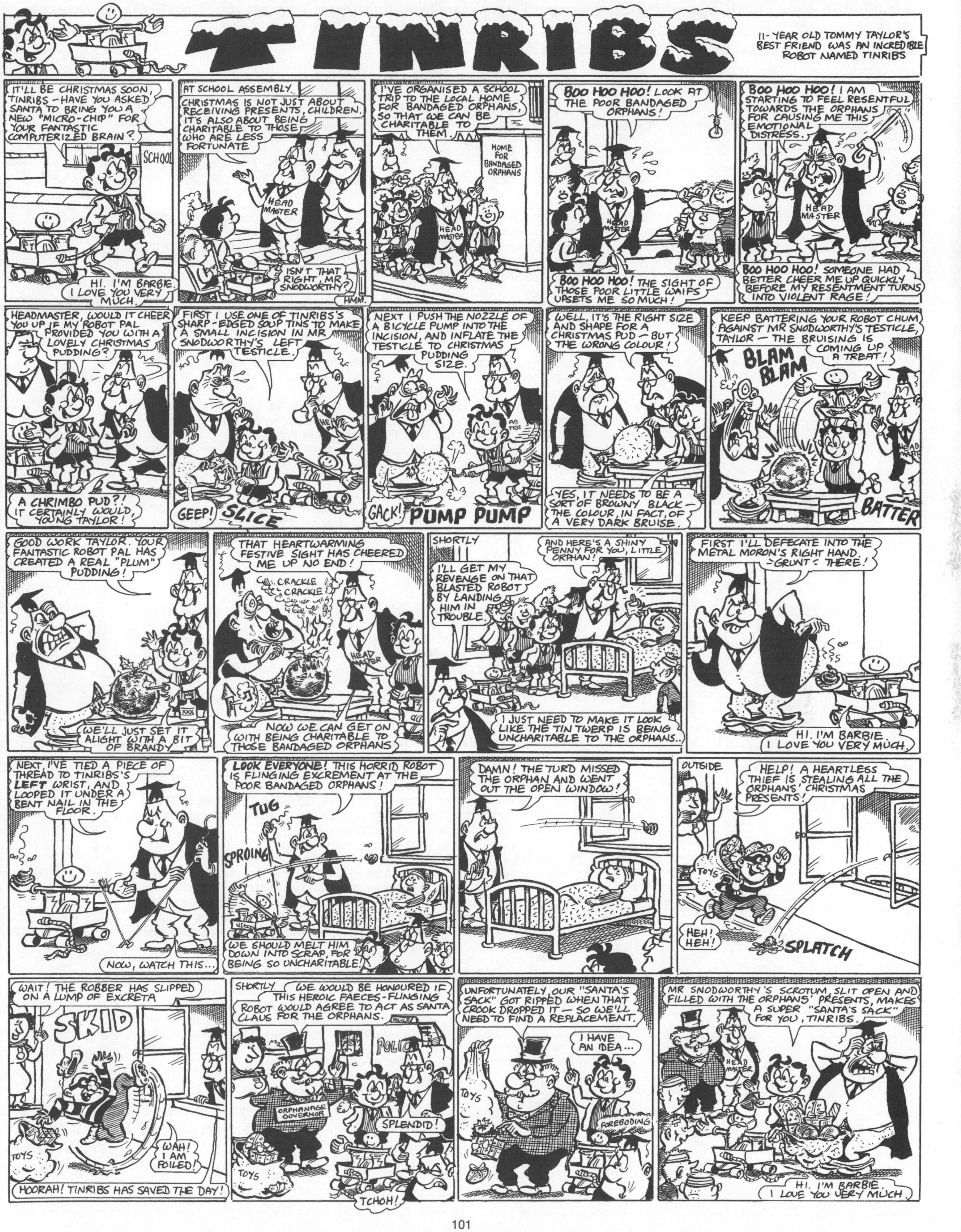
TINRIBS
11-YEAR OLD TOMMY TAYLOR'S BEST FRIEND WAS AN INCREDIBLE ROBOT NAMED TINRIBS
IT'LL BE CHRISTMAS SOON, TINRIBS - HAVE YOU ASKED SANTA TO BRING YOU A NEW "MICRO-CHIP" FOR YOUR FANTASTIC COMPUTERIZED BRAIN?
SCHOOL
HI. I'M BARBIE. I LOVE YOU VERY MUCH.
AT SCHOOL ASSEMBLY.
CHRISTMAS IS NOT JUST ABOUT RECEIVING PRESENTS, CHILDREN. IT'S ALSO ABOUT BEING CHARITABLE TO THOSE WHO ARE LESS FORTUNATE
HEAD MASTER
ISN'T THAT RIGHT, MR SNODWORTHY?
HMM.
I'VE ORGANISED A SCHOOL TRIP TO THE LOCAL HOME FOR BANDAGED ORPHANS, SO THAT WE CAN BE CHARITABLE TO THEM.
HOME FOR BANDAGED ORPHANS
HEAD MASTER
BOO HOO HOO! LOOK AT THE POOR BANDAGED ORPHANS!
HEAD MASTER
BOO HOO HOO! THE SIGHT OF THOSE POOR LITTLE WAIFS UPSETS ME SO MUCH!
BOO HOO HOO! I AM STARTING TO FEEL RESENTFUL TOWARDS THE ORPHANS FOR CAUSING ME THIS EMOTIONAL DISTRESS.
HEAD MASTER
BOO HOO HOO! SOMEONE HAD BETTER CHEER ME UP QUICKLY BEFORE MY RESENTMENT TURNS INTO VIOLENT RAGE!
HEADMASTER, WOULD IT CHEER YOU UP IF MY ROBOT PAL PROVIDED YOU WITH A LOVELY CHRISTMAS PUDDING?
A CHRIMBO PUD?! IT CERTAINLY WOULD, YOUNG TAYLOR!
FIRST I USE ONE OF TINRIBS'S SHARP-EDGED SOUP TINS TO MAKE A SMALL INCISION IN MR SNODWORTHY'S LEFT TESTICLE.
GEEP!
SLICE
NEXT I PUSH THE NOZZLE OF A BICYCLE PUMP INTO THE INCISION, AND INFLATE THE TESTICLE TO CHRISTMAS PUDDING SIZE.
GACK!
PUMP PUMP
WELL, IT'S THE RIGHT SIZE AND SHAPE FOR A CHRISTMAS PUD — BUT THE WRONG COLOUR!
YES, IT NEEDS TO BE A SORT OF BROWNY BLACK — THE COLOUR, IN FACT, OF A VERY DARK BRUISE.
KEEP BATTERING YOUR ROBOT CHUM AGAINST MR SNODWORTHY'S TESTICLE, TAYLOR — THE BRUISING IS COMING UP A TREAT!
BLAM BLAM
HEAD MASTER
BATTER
GOOD WORK TAYLOR. YOUR FANTASTIC ROBOT PAL HAS CREATED A REAL "PLUM" PUDDING!
XXX
WE'LL JUST SET IT ALIGHT WITH A BIT OF BRANDY
THAT HEARTWARMING FESTIVE SIGHT HAS CHEERED ME UP NO END!
CRACKLE CRACKLE
HEAD MASTER
NOW WE CAN GET ON WITH BEING CHARITABLE TO THOSE BANDAGED ORPHANS
SHORTLY
AND HERE'S A SHINY PENNY FOR YOU, LITTLE ORPHAN!
I'LL GET MY REVENGE ON THAT BLASTED ROBOT BY LANDING HIM IN TROUBLE.
I JUST NEED TO MAKE IT LOOK LIKE THE TIN TWERP IS BEING UNCHARITABLE TO THE ORPHANS...
FIRST I'LL DEFECATE INTO THE METAL MORON'S RIGHT HAND. -GRUNT- THERE!
HI. I'M BARBIE. I LOVE YOU VERY MUCH.
NEXT, I'VE TIED A PIECE OF THREAD TO TINRIBS'S LEFT WRIST, AND LOOPED IT UNDER A BENT NAIL IN THE FLOOR.
NOW, WATCH THIS...
LOOK EVERYONE! THIS HORRID ROBOT IS FLINGING EXCREMENT AT THE POOR BANDAGED ORPHANS!
TUG
SPROING
WE SHOULD MELT HIM DOWN INTO SCRAP, FOR BEING SO UNCHARITABLE!
DAMN! THE TURD MISSED THE ORPHAN AND WENT OUT THE OPEN WINDOW!
OUTSIDE
HELP! A HEARTLESS THIEF IS STEALING ALL THE ORPHANS' CHRISTMAS PRESENTS!
TOYS
HEH! HEH!
SPLATCH
WAIT! THE ROBBER HAS SLIPPED ON A LUMP OF EXCRETA
SKID
WAH! I AM FOILED!
TOYS
HOORAH! TINRIBS HAS SAVED THE DAY!
SHORTLY
WE WOULD BE HONOURED IF THIS HEROIC FAECES-FLINGING ROBOT WOULD AGREE TO ACT AS SANTA CLAUS FOR THE ORPHANS.
ORPHANAGE GOVERNOR
SPLENDID!
TOYS
TCHOH!
UNFORTUNATELY, OUR "SANTA'S SACK" GOT RIPPED WHEN THAT CROOK DROPPED IT — SO WE'LL NEED TO FIND A REPLACEMENT.
I HAVE AN IDEA...
TOYS
FOREBODING
MR SNODWORTHY'S SCROTUM, SLIT OPEN AND FILLED WITH THE ORPHANS' PRESENTS, MAKES A SUPER "SANTA'S SACK" FOR YOU, TINRIBS.
HEAD MASTER
HI. I'M BARBIE. I LOVE YOU VERY MUCH.

WHO'S THE MOST W

BARBARA

Born in Shoreditch with the sound of the Bow Bells ringing in her ears, Babs is as Cockney as they come and could play the spoons before she could walk or talk. Like all true Londoners, Babs eats nothing but pie & mash, whelks and boiled beef & carrots. A season ticket holder at West Ham, she only misses out on full points in this round because her *EastEnders* filming commitments prevent her from spending as much time as she would like going down The Strand. Having a banana.

No Christmas day would be complete without every family in Britain gathering round the TV to watch traditional *EastEnders* Christmas Special. Always action-packed, the show is a seasonal treat for millions of viewers, featuring extra-entertaining storylines. Whether it's a suicide under the Christmas tree, a murder over the turkey or a rape taking place to a soundtrack of carol singers wassailing in Albert Square, there's no telling what will happen. But one thing is for certain. Peggy Mitchell will be there watching over proceedings from behind the bar of the Rover's Return.

Although she was born plain Barbara Deeks, bubbly *Carry On*-star Babs is well known to her millions of fans by her ultra-English stage name of Windsor. However, the surname on her birth certificate is just as British as her adopted stage monicker. Even though Deeks rhymes with leeks and there is therefore a slim chance it may be a Welsh surname, it's nevertheless another high-scoring round for the nation's favourite cockney sparrow.

Dubbed "the British Diana Dors" back in her 60s heyday, Barbara Windsor was a blonde bombshell who turned heads wherever she went. Whether she was being examined by priapic doctor Jim Dale, having her nurse's uniform accidentally torn off by Bernard Breslaw or bending over to pick something up in front of Sid James, she never failed to raise the audience's blood pressure. And with curves in all the right places (arse and tits) and her trademark saucy wiggle, Babs's on-screen sex appeal has "carried on" bringing her own brand of *Va-Va-Voom* to the silver screen right up until the present day.

If Barbara Windsor opened a fruit shop and you innocently decided to compliment her on her magnificent melons, you would almost certainly be treated to her popular catchphrase: "Hehehehe! Saucy!" Likewise, if she set up a stall selling door furniture in your local market and you asked if you could have a look at her knockers, you may well receive the same response. And if Babs had an appointment at your mobile mammogram clinic and you asked if she would like you to examine her breasts, the answer would no doubt be the same. Indeed, it is hard to imagine a situation when Windsor's much-loved innuendo-laden catchphrase could not be employed.

The bubbly starlet has had her fair share of relationships with a succession of lovable rogues such as no-nonsense businessman Ronnie Knight; thirsty footballer George Best, scrotum-faced Casanova Sid James and cockney murderer Reggie Kray. Although she is now happily married to her middle-aged toyboy lover Scott, Babs's past boyfriends' colourful antics ensured they were never far from the headlines. Whether they were running away to the Costa del Crime, scoring goals for Manchester United, dropping dead on the stage of the Sunderland Empire or stabbing somebody's neck to the floor of an East End pub, their roguish hijinks were always guaranteed to keep the nation enthralled and entertained.

Bubbly Babs's family tree is as full of illustrious forebears as her bikini top is full of tits. For the cockney Sparrow's ancestry reads like a *Who's Who* of famous names from history. Her fourth cousin, six times removed was Haywain painter John Constable, and her maternal grandmother was the famous Music Hall star Fat Nan, who made her name at the Britannia Theatre, Hoxton. And as if this were not enough fame in one family, her mother's daughter - Barbara Deeks - grew up to be none other than Barbara Windsor, star of over 8, but fewer than 10 *Carry On* films in the 70s and 80s!

Everyone in Britain is familiar with the famous scene in *Carry On Camping* where buxom Babs pings her brassierre into Kenneth Williams's horrified face whilst doing her morning PT. Nevertheless, this is a low scoring round, since the sequence was actually a product of special effects trickery. Babs's bikini top didn't shoot off her chest, but was pulled off using a length of fishing line by a props man hiding behind a bush . Film director Gerald Thomas then threw an identical bra into Williams's face to complete the effect. The noise of the bra shooting off was recorded using the spring off a pogo stick, a megaphone and a Swanee whistle, then dubbed on afterwards.

9	COCKNEYOS
8	CHRISTMAS BROADCAS
7	ENGLISHNE OF SURNA
8	SEX FACTO
7	CATCHPHRA VERSATILI
8	BOYFRIEN
9	ANCESTRY
0	FIRING BR OFF INTO MA FACE DURI STRETCHIN EXERCISE

56

AND THE WINDSOR IS...
Our Grand National race was close ru but once the scores have been totte up it is clear that the country's favourite Windsor is Her Majesty the Quee Babs held the lead throughout but fell at the final fence. She can "carry o

Ve love them both equally, but which one do we love the most? Is it actress Babs with her saucy sense of umour, her pneumatic figure and her infectious giggle? Or is it Monarch Elizabeth with her majestic air, her orgis and her castles full of gold? We put them to the ultimate test to discover...

NDERFUL WINDSOR?

ELIZABETH

OCKNEYOSITY 6

Like Barbara, Her Majesty the Queen was also born in London. However, there the similarities end. For, although she is fluent in French and her native German, Her Majesty the Queen speaks almost no Rhyming Slang, the native tongue of the true Cockney. In addition, at state banquets and ceremonial dinners, she eschews jellied eels in their own liquor and flatly refuses to touch cockney staples like cockles, mussels and winkles in case they give her the shits.

RISTMAS DAY ROADCASTS 7

Her Majesty made her first Christmas Day broadcast back in 1952, and she's been playing the same character - the stuck-up, starchy Queen Elizabeth II - ever since. Her Christmas shows may have been running for more than half a century, but they are completely lacking in excitement and drama. Repetitive storylines about people in the Commonwealth enjoying the festive season, summings-up of her state visits to distant lands and praise for the work of her armed forces both abroad and at home leave viewers yawning every Christmas. It's a poor scoring round for Her Majesty.

NGLISHNESS F SURNAME 6

Oh dear. Despite being the Queen of England, Her Majesty was actually christened with the distinctly teutonic-sounding name of Elizabeth Saxe Coburg Battenburg de Gotha. At the height of anti-German feeling during the war, this was changed by deed poll to the more publically-acceptable surname of Windsor. However, as a married lady, the Queen's correct title is actually the equally foreign-sounding Mrs Elizabeth Pappadopolopolopoulos!

SEX FACTOR 7

Unlike her film star namesake, the Queen has always projected a dowdy public image. Although she was undoubtedly a good-looking woman in her youth, she always kept her crown jewels well wrapped up away from the lustful eyes of her male subjects. Had she opened Parliament wearing nothing but a skimpy, spangled bikini, trooped the colour in a diaphanous babydoll nightie or attended the Queen Mum's funeral in a push-up basque, split-crotch panties, stockings and suspenders, she might have fared better in this round. As it is, our frumpy turn-off monarch makes yet another poor showing.

ATCHPHRASE ERSATILITY 6

By comparison, the Queen's famous catchphrase is far less versatile. If Her Majesty had been booked to open a new carpet warehouse and the manager cheekily offered to slip her a length, or if a chicken farmer on her Balmoral estate asked her if she fancied a look at his prize cock, the reponse "My husband and I" would make no sense at all. In fact, it could only be used in very specific circumstances, such as if a waiter in a posh restaurant were to enquire: "Who ordered the swans?". As a result, it's yet another runaway win for Barbara Windsor and a right royal disappointment for her regal namesake in this round.

OYFRIENDS 7

Before her marriage, the Queen's name was also romantically linked to a series of suitors. Clive Dunn, Patrick Moore, Professor Magnus Pyke and Terry-Thomas were all at one time or another rumoured to be courting the pretty young heir to the British throne. However, the world was shocked when, in 1947, the palace announced her engagement to Philip Pappadopolopolopoulos, a waiter she met whilst on holiday in Greece. Since the day they married, the gaffe-prone Duke of Edinburgh has seldom been out of the headlines ... but for all the wrong reasons. With his penchant for walking along with his hands behind his back, making racist comments and being wrongly suspected of having affairs with actresses, he has kept the our toes curling for more than six decades.

ANCESTRY 8

Very little is known about the ancestry of Her Majesty, although she is believed to be descended from a German family who came over to rule Britain sometime before WW1. Whilst the identity of the Queen's father remains a mystery, genealogists have established that her mother was Queen Elizabeth the Queen Mother, who died in 2002, taking the secret of her husband's identity to the grave. It is believed that she had a sister who wore sunglasses, drank gin and sucked off Peter Sellers. Although, in a bid for fame, one of her sons attempted to break into television, he was completely shit at it. Just like everything else he ever did or ever will do.

IRING BRA F INTO MAN'S ACE DURING STRETCHING EXERCISE 10

During her coronation on June 2nd 1953, the Princess Elizabeth and her Ladies in Waiting were limbering up with a few bending and stretching exercises prior to that day's grueling investiture ceremony at Westminster Abbey. As tradition demanded, the Princess was wearing the Bra of India, an ermine-trimmed item of ceremonial lingerie which had been worn by all female monarchs at their coronations since Elizabeth I. Without warning, the bra's antique clasp gave way under the strain of a particularly vigorous star jump, and the garment was catapulted into the face of the Archbishop of Canterbury, Dr Geoffrey Fisher, who spluttered "Take them away, Matron".

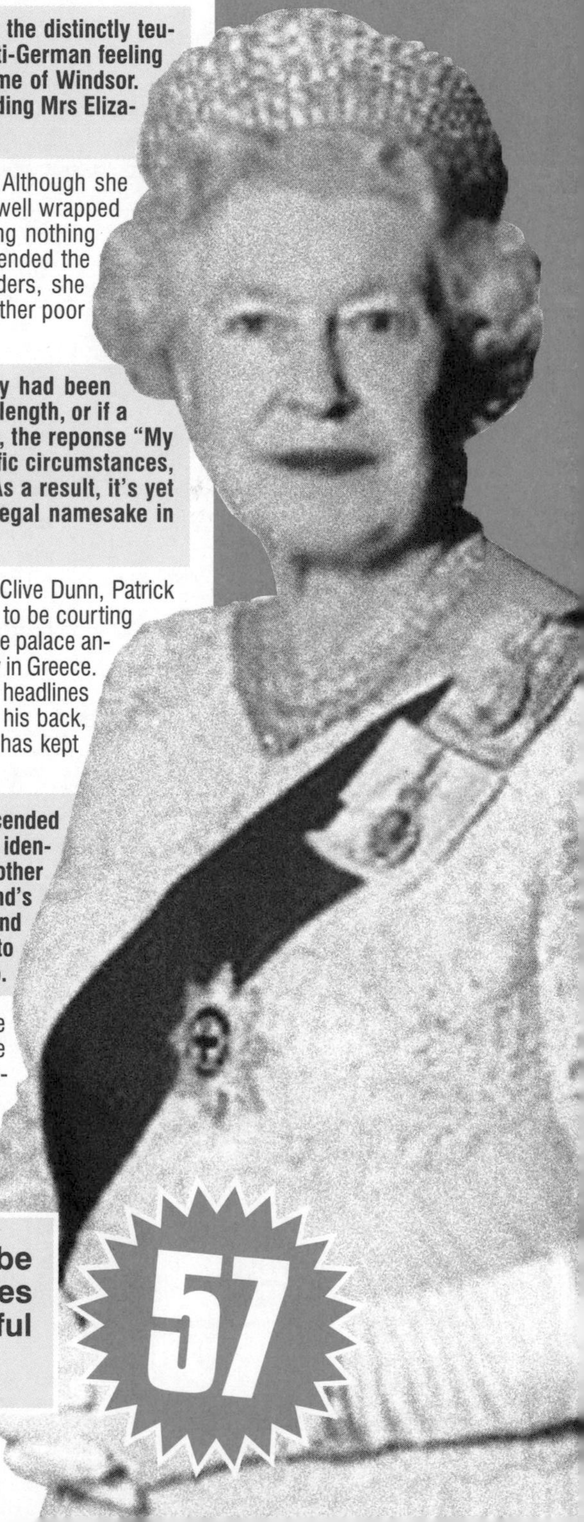

omplaining all she likes, but surely it's time for this moth-eaten old nag to be arted off to the knacker's yard. Meanwhile, our right royal favourite makes er Majestic way to the winners' enclosure to receive the plaudits of a grateful ation. God Save the Queen!

57

EXCLUSIVE!

Tragic Jade Set for Telly Comeback

■ *By* Our Showbiz Correspondent
ANNIE AULDGUFF

JADE GOODY is to make a triumphant return to TV screens this month, when the late reality TV star's GHOST makes an appearance as the star of an hour-long special edition of *Most Haunted.*

Sources say Jade signed the £1m deal with Living TV last week via an ouija board, continuing the successful relationship she had with the channel when she was alive.

TAPERS

Publicist Max Clifford told anyone who would listen: "Jade's ghost is just as feisty and unique as Jade was. The only noticeable difference is you can pass your hand through her now, and instead of legs, she just sort of tapers off towards the ground.

"Jade was always determined that her career wouldn't pass away just because she did, so it's fitting that her ghost should take up the reins.'

TIGIRS

Yitney *Most Haunted* presenter and pretend blonde Yvette Fielding says she can't wait to be scared of the tragic star's wraith. "I never met Jade when she was alive, so this is the next best thing," she gushed.

Jade's ghost is expected to be quite loud.

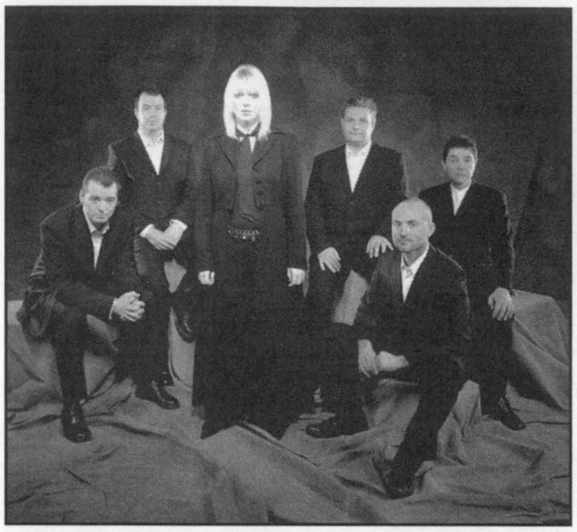

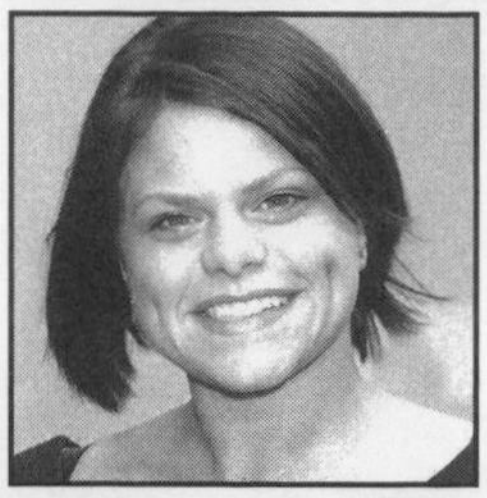

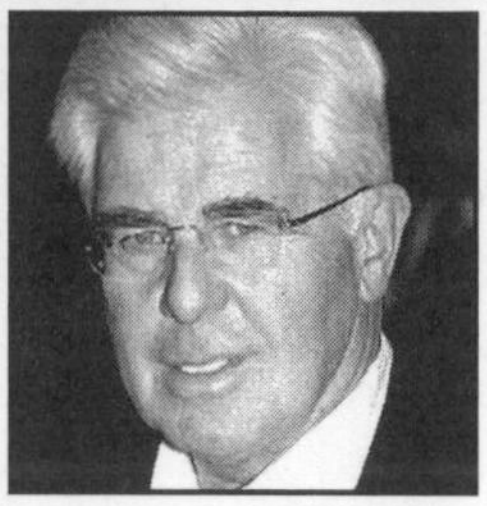

THE PEOPLE'S PEOPLE'S PRINCESS: Goody *(top)* will be back in spirit form on Most Haunted *(left)* says Max Clifford *(above)*.

• *Most Haunted Special is on Living TV at 9pm, 10pm and 11pm every night for the rest of time.*

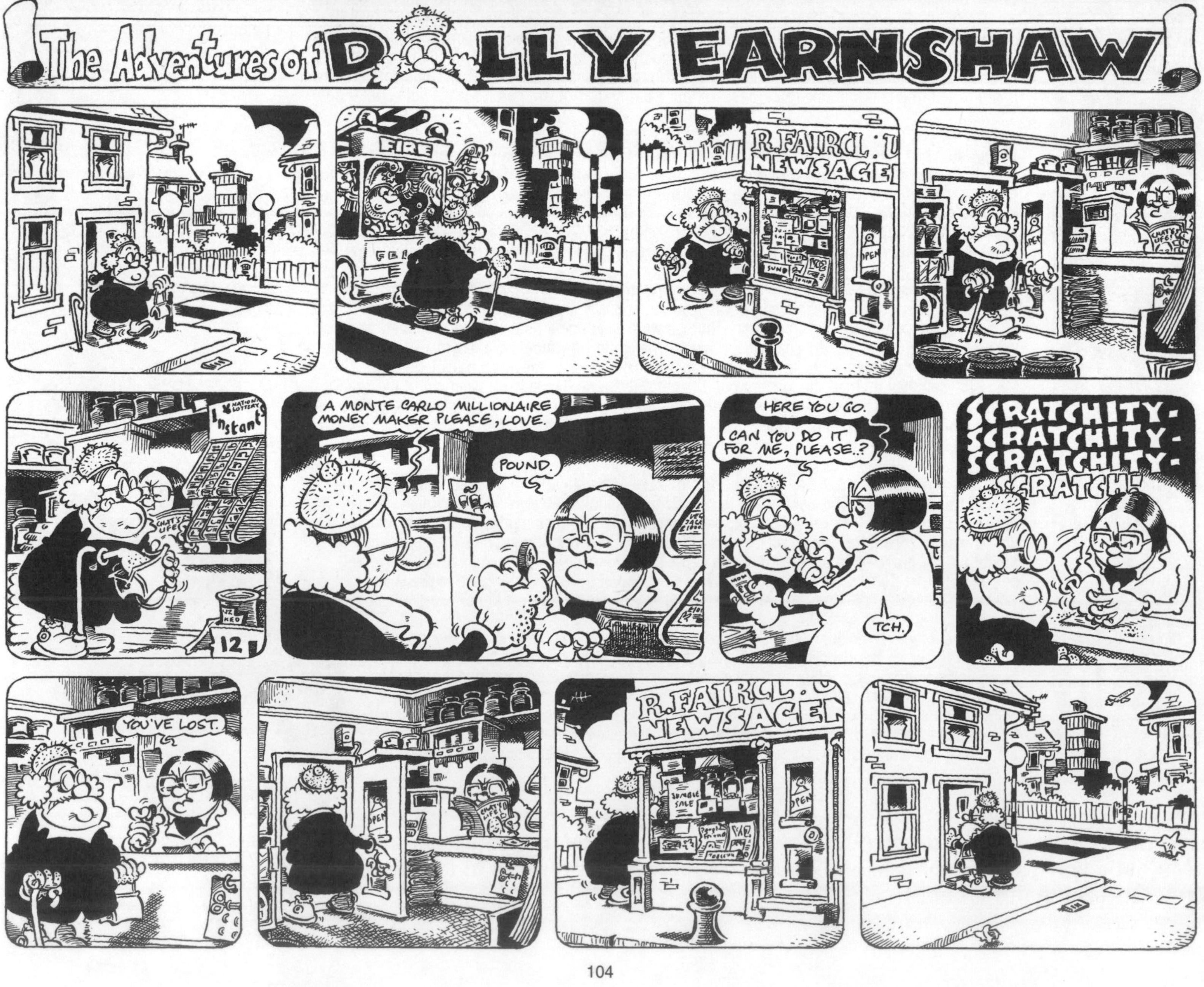
The Adventures of DOLLY EARNSHAW
FIRE
R.FAIRCL.U NEWSAGE
A MONTE CARLO MILLIONAIRE MONEY MAKER PLEASE, LOVE.
POUND.
HERE YOU GO.
CAN YOU DO IT FOR ME, PLEASE..?
TCH.
SCRATCHITY-SCRATCHITY-SCRATCHITY-SCRATCH!
YOU'VE LOST.
R.FAIRCL.U NEWSAGEN

MAJOR MISUNDERSTANDING

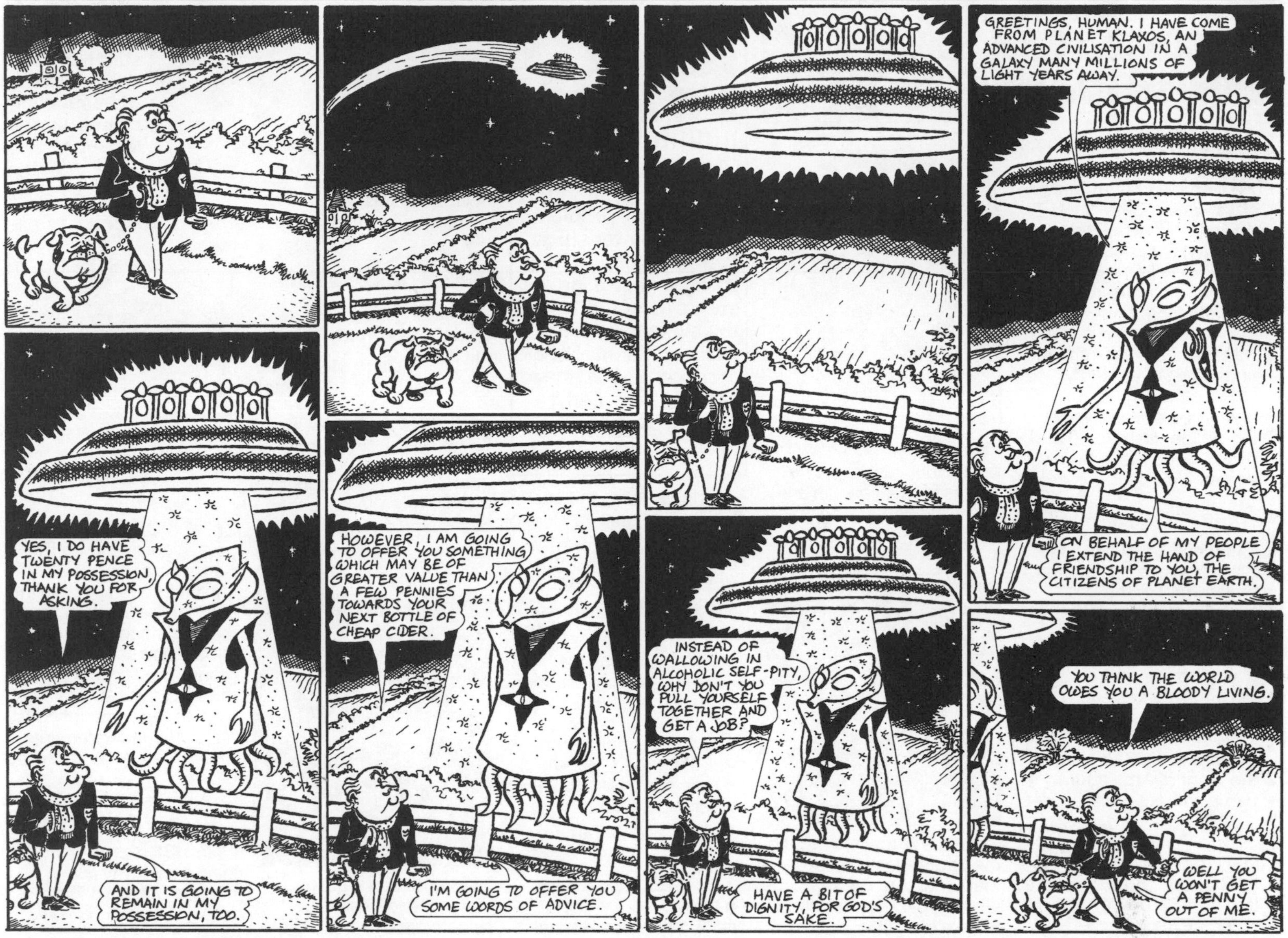
GREETINGS, HUMAN. I HAVE COME FROM PLANET KLAXOS, AN ADVANCED CIVILISATION IN A GALAXY MANY MILLIONS OF LIGHT YEARS AWAY.
ON BEHALF OF MY PEOPLE I EXTEND THE HAND OF FRIENDSHIP TO YOU, THE CITIZENS OF PLANET EARTH.
YES, I DO HAVE TWENTY PENCE IN MY POSSESSION, THANK YOU FOR ASKING.
AND IT IS GOING TO REMAIN IN MY POSSESSION, TOO.
HOWEVER, I AM GOING TO OFFER YOU SOMETHING WHICH MAY BE OF GREATER VALUE THAN A FEW PENNIES TOWARDS YOUR NEXT BOTTLE OF CHEAP CIDER.
I'M GOING TO OFFER YOU SOME WORDS OF ADVICE.
INSTEAD OF WALLOWING IN ALCOHOLIC SELF-PITY, WHY DON'T YOU PULL YOURSELF TOGETHER AND GET A JOB?
HAVE A BIT OF DIGNITY, FOR GOD'S SAKE.
YOU THINK THE WORLD OWES YOU A BLOODY LIVING.
WELL YOU WON'T GET A PENNY OUT OF ME.

Kyle Honoured with Cunt Status

EXCLUSIVE!

CONTROVERSIAL TV host JEREMY KYLE has been adopted by the International Science Community as the new System of Units (SI) standard cunt for scientific purposes.

❑ By our science correspondent **INGLEDEW BOTTERILL**

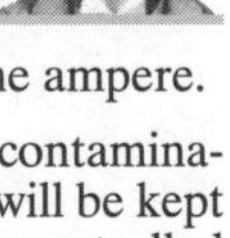

The Cunt, which is the measure of absolute intolerability, was recalibrated by the French Academe de Sciences after the previous standard cunt, Jim Davidson, degraded over time to 0.9942 of a cunt.

cunt

Kyle will take up his position as the new international standard cunt on 1 November, when he will be deposited in the National Archives in Paris for reference, alongside such global standards as the metre, the gramme and the ampere.

To avoid distortion or contamination, the oily trash-baiter will be kept in an atmospherically controlled glass cabinet bearing a brass plaque reading LE CON, which is French for CUNT.

cunt

"Kyle was found quite by accident," said Professor Jean-Michel Jahwobble. "But once we had taken a look at his programme, my colleagues and I agreed we had never seen such an unalloyed cunt."

"Of course, sealing Kyle in a glass box will mean the cunt is unable to present his TV show, so that is an unexpected bonus," added the professor.

Cunt Kyle was not available for comment last night, but a source close to the cunt told us: "I can't think of a better choice for a yardstick cunt. The man is a 100% cunt, a cunt through and through. An utter cunt."

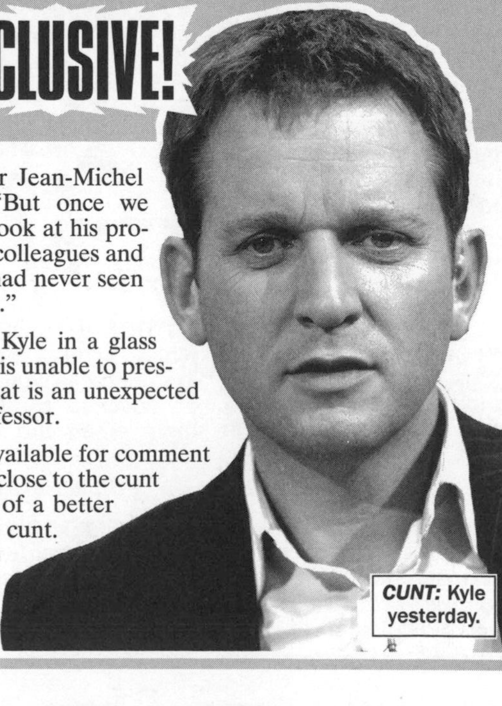

CUNT: Kyle yesterday.

LETTERBOCKS

VIZ COMIC, PO Box 656, North Shields, NE30 4XX

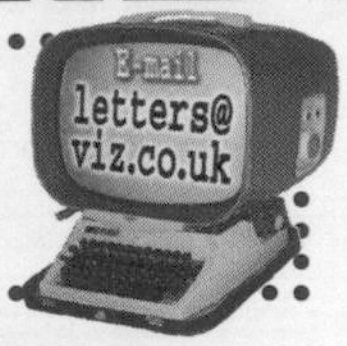
E-mail
letters@
viz.co.uk

STAR LETTER

MY train was late this morning owing to 'signalling problems due to a power surge.' You would have thought that a power surge would make the signals work extra well, so in my book the train should have actually been early.

Edna Battering-Ram Longfields

I'M fed up with the nonsensical motoring laws we all have to endure these days. Last month whilst driving on the M5, there were road markings and signs up telling motorists to 'keep two chevrons from the vehicle in front.' Well the Porsche in front of me was four chevrons ahead and doing over ninety. I tried catching him up, only to be pulled over by the police, fined £200 and given six points. It hardly seems fair.

A Heath Cardiff

WHILST watching the BBC's recent Wimbledon coverage, I found it a breath of fresh air to hear Sue Barker say that she was looking forward to watching the men's semis. Most former women tennis professionals are raging lezzers and wouldn't show the slightest interest in the sight of Andy Murray's partially erect cock.

Ian Squibs London

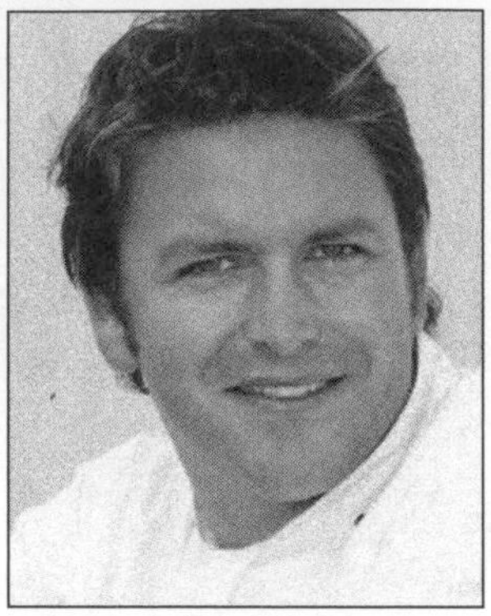

DO ANY of your readers know which county *Saturday Kitchen* chef James Martin is from? I think it might be Yorkshire, but I'm not sure as he never seems to mention it in any of his shows.

Percy Twelvepencils e-mail

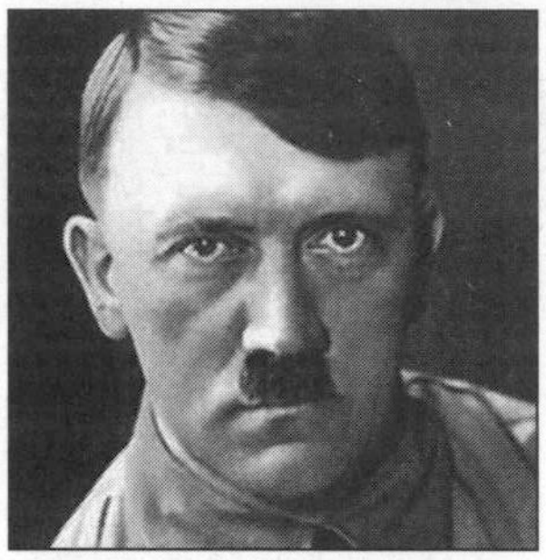

I KNOW this may make me unpopular, but I think that Hitler had the right idea. Apparently, he used to take his butter out of the fridge about an hour before he intended to use it, thus ensuring it spreaded easily. Call me a right-wing lunatic if you like, but this seems like good old-fashioned common sense to me.

Andy Hepworth e-mail

DOCTORS say that swimming is good for you because it uses every muscle in your body. Well, doctors don't know everything, because when I go swimming I like to keep my left leg straight.

Bryan Jones e-mail

I PASSED a road sign on the M6 last week that said 'Road works - delays until September.' I think the department of transport are scaremongering a bit, as I got through in about ten minutes.

Dean Moncaster e-mail

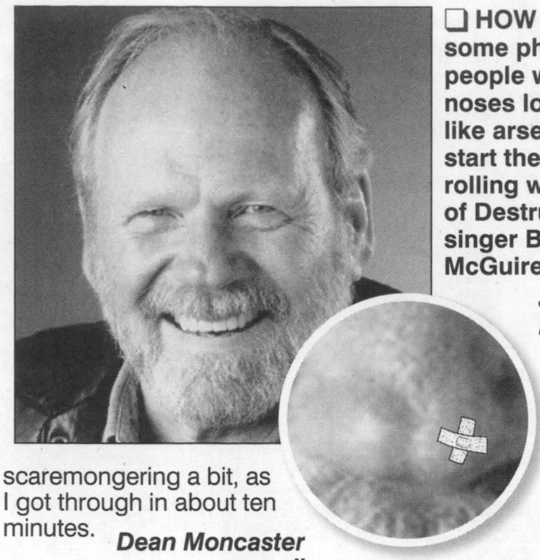

HOW about some photos of people whose noses look like arses? I'll start the ball rolling with Eve of Destruction singer Barry McGuire.

J Thorn, Hexham

I SAW a sign recently that read 'Church may Just Surprise You.' They were right. I went along and it was far more tedious than I had imagined.

Morgan Crumbs e-mail

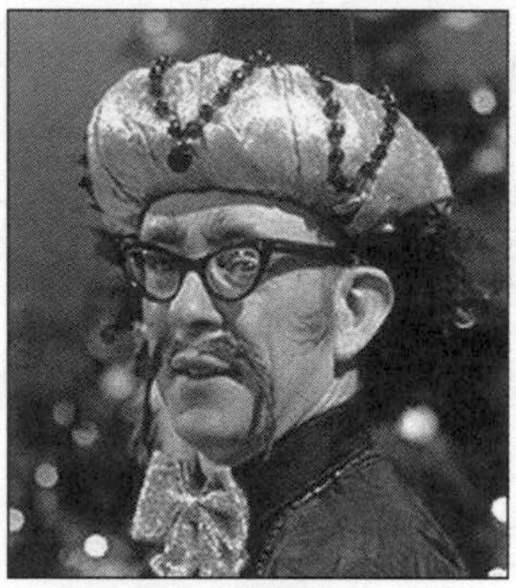

MAY I use your magazine to offer my sincere condolences to the Bongo family, first on the death of magician Ali and then tragically his brother Omar, President of Gabon. Whether it was pulling a long line of brightly-coloured knotted hankies out of a sleeve or skimming off millions of dollars of aid into Swiss bank accounts while your countrymen starve, the antics of the Bongo brothers will be missed by us all.

Norman e-mail

WHEN I open a packet of digestive biscuits, I save the top disc of celeophane and insert it back into the tube to ensure the top biscuit always remains fresh. Do any of your other readers feel that their life has no meaning?

Mr Marbles London

WHY is it that when I have a wank onto a bird's knockers, it dribbles out like the tears of a weeping widow? But when I have a wank on my own it goes all over the shirt I was about to wear for work?

JC de la Cruz e-mail

I'M SICK and tired of people collecting for Dr. Barnardo's children. If he can't afford to bring them up, then he shouldn't have them. In my opinion they should use some of the money they collect getting the amorous old sod the snip. In the words of your Major Misunderstanding, "they won't get a penny out of me."

Ryan McDonald Hamilton

IF HSBC are the world's local bank, why is my nearest branch 8 fucking miles away?

Tony e-mail

I WAS watching God TV recently and they were having an 'understanding male homosexuality conference.' I must admit, 'understanding' in this context seemed to mean 'judging harshly.'

Crawfort Martins e-mail

UP THE *Arts* CORNER

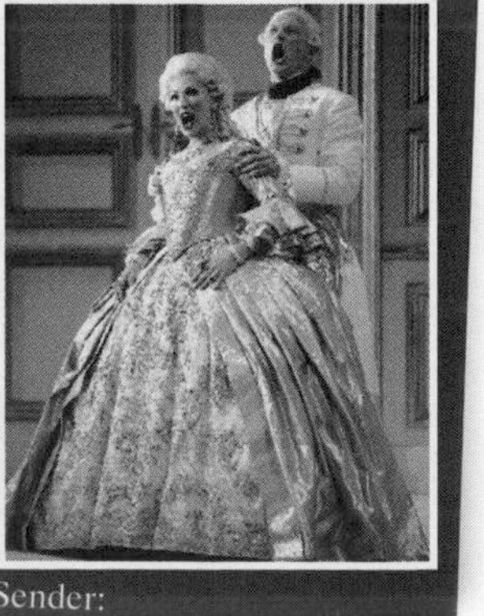

Sender:
Max Tomwell, Edinburgh

TOP TIPS

PUB landords. Save money on posters and printing by having one huge sign that reads 'Big Screen Sports Here, No Smoking, Car Wash, Lease This Pub, For Sale.'

John Smith, Nottingham

HARDCORE Hispanic gangsters from south central L.A. Save money on expensive hairnets by using the satsuma bags from Aldi in Redcar.

Chat Mon Yat, e-mail

VIEWERS of *Mock the Week*. Get the funniest gags from the new series about a month early by simply reading them in the pages of *Viz*.

Mike Tatham, e-mail

DRIVERS. Save money on tinted windows by setting a small fire in the glove compartment and allowing the plastic to burn long enough to deposit a thin layer of soot on the glass. Remember not to wind your windows down or it will come off.

Bazalini, e-mail

ASTRONAUTS. If contemplating another moon landing, increase your chance of success by travelling there when the moon is full.

Chris Higson, e-mail

GENTLEMEN. I find a copy of *Razzle Readers' Wives Special* makes obeying that tricky 10th commandment about not coveting thy neighbour's wife that bit easier.

Brendan Stitch, e-mail

MECHANICS. A pencil makes an absolutely perfect, if somewhat fragile, replacement for a 8mm allen key.

Thomas Thomas, e-mail

HOUSEWIVES. The handy, resealable bags that Cathedral cheese comes in can be re-used to keep some nice cheese in.

Scotty, e-mail

CINEMA goers. Ensure you get more for your money by only going to see longer films.

John Shoved, London

PAINTBALLERS. Attach a paintbrush onto the end of your gun to use as a 'bayonet' in case you run out of ammo.

H Broom, e-mail

❑ **I SEE** that woman who openly criticised Vladimir Putin was kidnapped and executed in Chechnya yesterday. Let that be a lesson to interfering old ratbags who think they can change the world by slagging off despotic and barbarian world leaders.

Rhys Evans
e-mail

❑ **I RECKON** that we can't find the missing link because at some time in the future, someone will invent time travel, go back in time and fuck a monkey. I bet these so-called scientists haven't thought of that one.

Malcolm
e-mail

❑ **WHEN** I was a kid, the height of excitement was finding a soggy jazz mag in the bushes and taking it home to restore it - it was always more thrilling than buying one. The other day I found a bongo DVD by the road, but even after I carefully cleaned it up, it wouldn't play. Call me old fashioned, but I don't think that's progress.

Rooster
e-mail

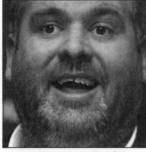

❑ **ON** the cover of the current *Radio Times*, Chris Moyles says he feels that his great-grandfather's story is his own. I was unaware that his great-grandfather was a twat whose name was a byword for broadcasting mediocrity, but I'll take his word for it.

Mike Morris
e-mail

❑ **I BLAME** all this terrorism on hot weather. You only have to look at where the trouble is - the Middle East, the Far Fast, South America. Even the southern states of the USA and northern Australia. I'm sure it affects the brain, as people in temperate countries don't seem to have half the problems. And the situation is only going to get worse with global warming.

Terry Dutson
e-mail

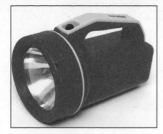

❑ **NOW** that the nights are starting to get darker again, how about running a competition to win a big, powerful torch?

Hugh Letpackard
Glasgow

* *Good idea, Mr Letpackard. Here's the competition question:* ***Who invented the torch and why?*** *Send your answers to 'Big Powerful Torch Competition, Viz Comic, PO Box 656, North Shields, NE30 4EZ. The first correct answer out of the hat will win a big, powerful torch. Ten runners up will each win a smaller, much more feeble torch.*

❑ **I WENT** to the zoo last week and spent the whole time trying to steal glimpses of gorillas through the thick greenery on their island. Now I'm all for animal welfare, but I preferred it when they were in concrete enclosures with nothing to amuse them but a half-eaten carrot. They may have spent the whole time rocking back and forth, fingering their shit about and eating their own hands, but at least you could see the fuckers.

Andy Mansh
e-mail

❑ **FOR** the past 3 months I have shoplifted my copy of *Viz* from WHSmith. Now I feel bad and want to pay you back, so I'm planning to win £10 with the Star Letter so you can deduct the last three issues from my winnings and send me the remainder. So I just need something to write in with. Any ideas?

Richard Tea-Bag Hawkins
e-mail

❑ **HAS** anyone seen La Toya Jackson lately? Only I've got a £50 bet that needs settled.

Mike Tatham
e-mail

❑ **COULD** I ask the fit birds on *Big Brother* to get their tits and basils out in the first minute of the show so I don't have to sit through the whole hour long episode? I do have a life, you know.

Biff
e-mail

❑ I heard Welsh sportsman Joe Calzaghe on the radio recently, launching an anti-bullying campaign. Imagine my horror when I saw him later on TV repeatedly punching a man about the head and body.

Darren Conway
e-mail

❑ **SO** Iran's supreme leader calls Britain the most evil foreign power. Well that shows what that plonker knows, because Britain isn't foreign for a start.

B Guy
e-mail

❑ IT'S A long way to Tipperary, or so the song says. Well not for me - I live in Ballynamrossagh, about mile and a half away.

Aldrick Baldwin
e-mail

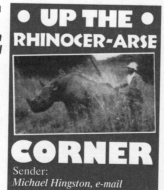

• UP THE •
RHINOCER-ARSE

CORNER

Sender:
Michael Hingston, e-mail

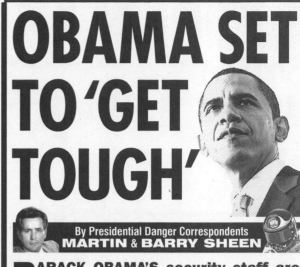

OBAMA SET TO 'GET TOUGH'

By Presidential Danger Correspondents
MARTIN & BARRY SHEEN

BARACK OBAMA'S security staff are to take drastic action to protect the US president from assassination attempts – by soaking him overnight in VINEGAR and then BAKING him to make him really hard.

President Obama was surrounded by a shield of bulletproof plexiglass at his inauguration in January, but experts say such protection is simply not practical for his day to day duties. A plan for the president to roll around public meetings in a reinforced giant hamster ball was rejected after a 7-year-old girl with a bunch of flowers was crushed to death during initial tests last month in Vermont.

SITTING DUCK

The soaking and baking of the world's most powerful man is expected to take place behind closed doors next week. It is hoped the procedure will render the Commander In Chief as hard as knockers and invulnerable to attack from terrorists or domestic extremists.

Experts insist they are not overreacting. 'The president is classfied as a high risk target, and when he's performing his official duties, such as attending state dinners, opening supermarkets or judging sandcastle competitions, he's a sitting duck,' said the White House's Chief Security Advisor, Hymen Prepuce III.

TOILET BULL

Prepuce explained: "If we can get Mr President rock hard, like a mahogany table, bullets will just bounce off his stony head and ricochet from his broad, impenetrable chest like grains of rice tossed vainly at a granite obelisk."

This is not the first time a leader of the US has been treated to protect him against attacks. Following John Hinckley's 1981 assassination attempt, President Ronald Reagan said his survival was down to having been painted with clear nail varnish by secret service agents immediately following his inauguration.

Obama's hair is expected to smell of chipshops until 2011.

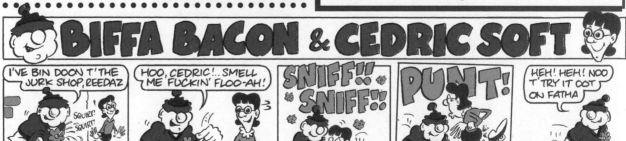

BIFFA BACON & CEDRIC SOFT
I'VE BIN DOON T'THE JURK SHOP, REEDAZ
SQUIRT! SQUIRT!
WATCH THIS
HOO, CEDRIC!.. SMELL ME FUCKIN' FLOO-AH!
OH! HOW BEAUTIFUL!
SNIFF!! SNIFF!!
PUNT!
HEH! HEH! NOO T'TRY IT OOT ON FATHA

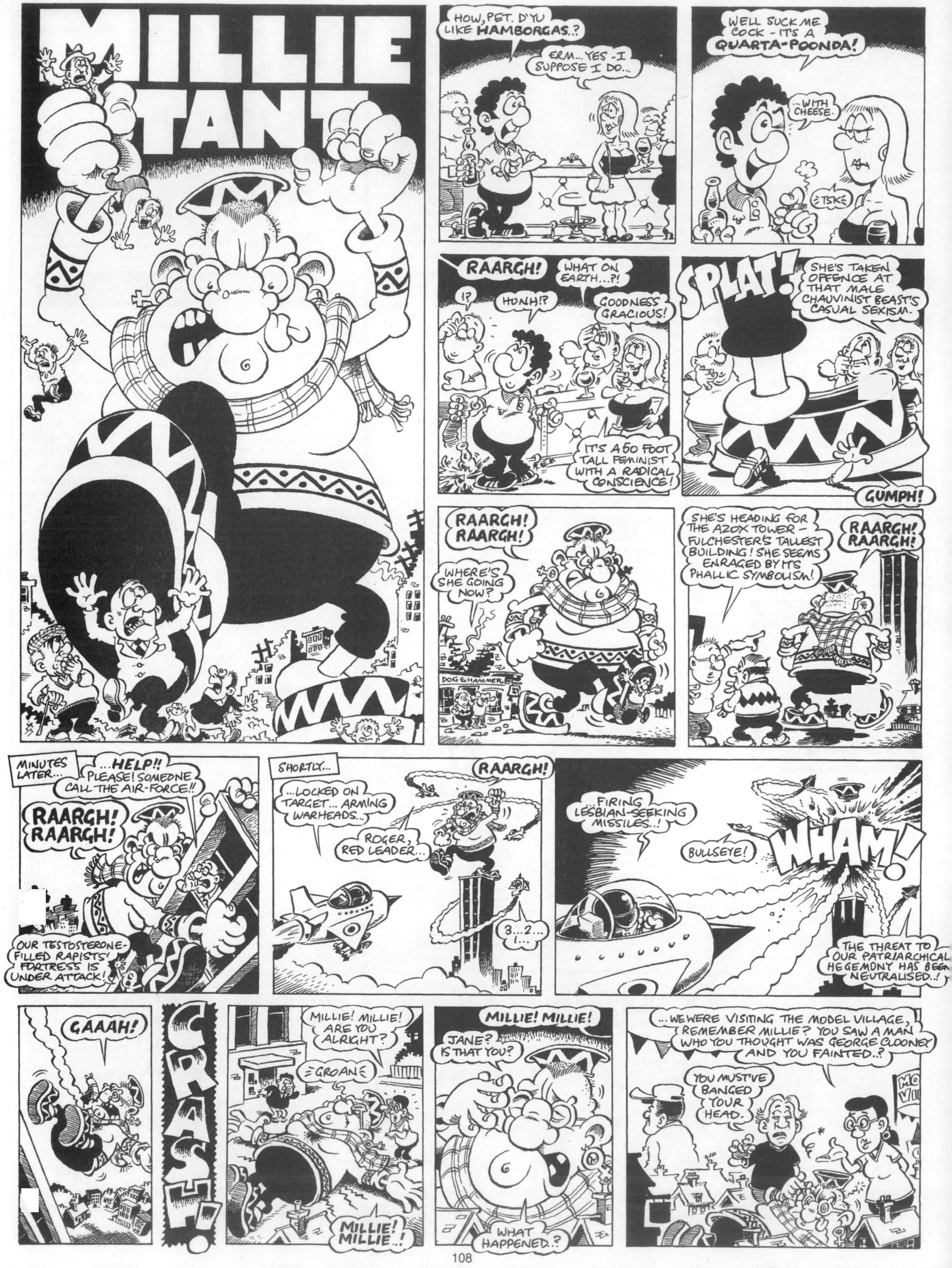
MILLIE TANT
HOW, PET. D'YU LIKE HAMBORGAS..?
ERM... YES - I SUPPOSE I DO...
WELL SUCK ME COCK - IT'S A QUARTA-POONDA!
...WITH CHEESE.
TSK
RAARGH!
WHAT ON EARTH...?!
!?
HUNH!?
GOODNESS GRACIOUS!
IT'S A 50 FOOT TALL FEMINIST WITH A RADICAL CONSCIENCE!
SPLAT!
SHE'S TAKEN OFFENCE AT THAT MALE CHAUVINIST BEAST'S CASUAL SEXISM.
GUMPH!
RAARGH! RAARGH!
WHERE'S SHE GOING NOW?
DOG & HAMMER
SHE'S HEADING FOR THE AZOX TOWER - FULCHESTER'S TALLEST BUILDING! SHE SEEMS ENRAGED BY ITS PHALLIC SYMBOLISM!
RAARGH! RAARGH!
MINUTES LATER...
...HELP!! PLEASE! SOMEONE CALL THE AIR-FORCE!!
RAARGH! RAARGH!
OUR TESTOSTERONE-FILLED RAPISTS' FORTRESS IS UNDER ATTACK!
SHORTLY...
RAARGH!
...LOCKED ON TARGET... ARMING WARHEADS...
ROGER, RED LEADER...
3...2...1...
...FIRING LESBIAN-SEEKING MISSILES...!
BULLSEYE!
WHAM!
THE THREAT TO OUR PATRIARCHICAL HEGEMONY HAS BEEN NEUTRALISED..!
GAAAH!
CRASH!
MILLIE! MILLIE! ARE YOU ALRIGHT?
GROAN
MILLIE! MILLIE..!
MILLIE! MILLIE!
JANE? IS THAT YOU?
WHAT HAPPENED..?
...WE WERE VISITING THE MODEL VILLAGE, REMEMBER MILLIE? YOU SAW A MAN WHO YOU THOUGHT WAS GEORGE CLOONEY AND YOU FAINTED..?
YOU MUST'VE BANGED YOUR HEAD.

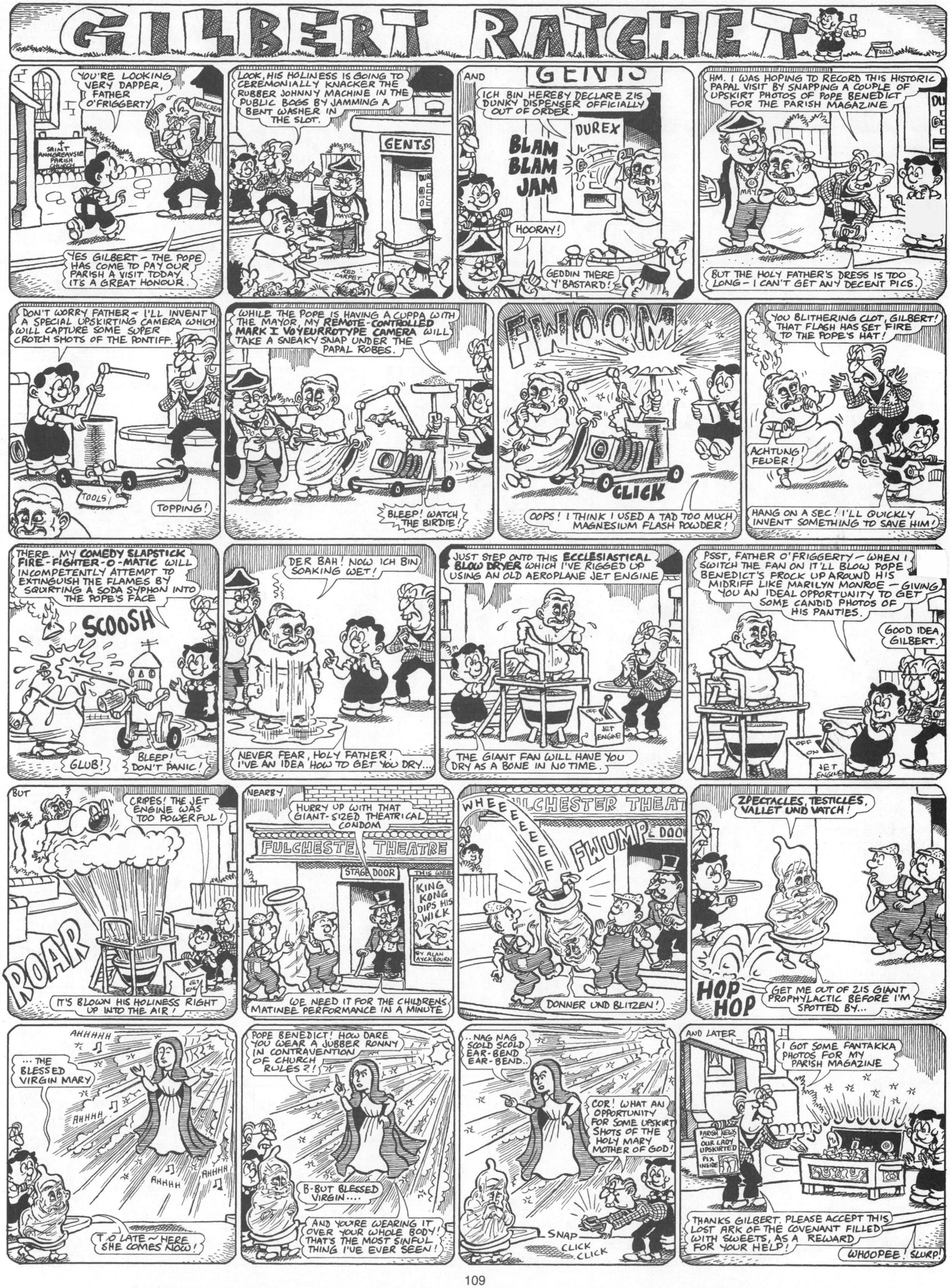
GILBERT RATCHET
TOOLS
YOU'RE LOOKING VERY DAPPER, FATHER O'FRIGGERTY
BRYLCREAM
SAINT ANNGREAVSIE PARISH CHURCH
YES GILBERT – THE POPE HAS COME TO PAY OUR PARISH A VISIT TODAY. IT'S A GREAT HONOUR.
LOOK, HIS HOLINESS IS GOING TO CEREMONIALLY KNACKER THE RUBBER JOHNNY MACHINE IN THE PUBLIC BOGS BY JAMMING A BENT WASHER IN THE SLOT.
GENTS
MAYOR
RED CARPET
AND
GENTS
ICH BIN HEREBY DECLARE ZIS DUNKY DISPENSER OFFICIALLY OUT OF ORDER.
DUREX
BLAM BLAM JAM
HOORAY!
GEDDIN THERE Y'BASTARD!
HM. I WAS HOPING TO RECORD THIS HISTORIC PAPAL VISIT BY SNAPPING A COUPLE OF UPSKIRT PHOTOS OF POPE BENEDICT FOR THE PARISH MAGAZINE
BUT THE HOLY FATHER'S DRESS IS TOO LONG – I CAN'T GET ANY DECENT PICS.
DON'T WORRY FATHER – I'LL INVENT A SPECIAL UPSKIRTING CAMERA WHICH WILL CAPTURE SOME SUPER CROTCH SHOTS OF THE PONTIFF.
TOOLS
TOPPING!
WHILE THE POPE IS HAVING A CUPPA WITH THE MAYOR, MY REMOTE-CONTROLLED MARK I VOYEURROTYPE CAMERA WILL TAKE A SNEAKY SNAP UNDER THE PAPAL ROBES.
BLEEP! WATCH THE BIRDIE!
FWOOM
CLICK
OOPS! I THINK I USED A TAD TOO MUCH MAGNESIUM FLASH POWDER!
YOU BLITHERING CLOT, GILBERT! THAT FLASH HAS SET FIRE TO THE POPE'S HAT!
ACHTUNG! FEUER!
HANG ON A SEC! I'LL QUICKLY INVENT SOMETHING TO SAVE HIM!
THERE. MY COMEDY SLAPSTICK FIRE-FIGHTER-O-MATIC WILL INCOMPETENTLY ATTEMPT TO EXTINGUISH THE FLAMES BY SQUIRTING A SODA SYPHON INTO THE POPE'S FACE
SCOOSH
GLUB!
BLEEP! DON'T PANIC!
DER BAH! NOW ICH BIN SOAKING WET!
NEVER FEAR, HOLY FATHER! I'VE AN IDEA HOW TO GET YOU DRY...
JUST STEP ONTO THIS ECCLESIASTICAL BLOW DRYER WHICH I'VE RIGGED UP USING AN OLD AEROPLANE JET ENGINE
OFF ON
JET ENGINE
THE GIANT FAN WILL HAVE YOU DRY AS A BONE IN NO TIME.
PSST, FATHER O'FRIGGERTY – WHEN I SWITCH THE FAN ON IT'LL BLOW POPE BENEDICT'S FROCK UP AROUND HIS MIDRIFF LIKE MARILYN MONROE – GIVING YOU AN IDEAL OPPORTUNITY TO GET SOME CANDID PHOTOS OF HIS PANTIES.
GOOD IDEA, GILBERT.
OFF ON
JET ENGINE
BUT
CRIPES! THE JET ENGINE WAS TOO POWERFUL!
ROAR
IT'S BLOWN HIS HOLINESS RIGHT UP INTO THE AIR!
NEARBY
HURRY UP WITH THAT GIANT-SIZED THEATRICAL CONDOM
FULCHESTER THEATRE
STAGE DOOR
THIS WEEK
KING KONG DIPS HIS WICK
BY ALAN AYCKBOURN
WE NEED IT FOR THE CHILDRENS MATINEE PERFORMANCE IN A MINUTE
WHEEEEEEEE
FULCHESTER THEAT
FWUMP
DONNER UND BLITZEN!
ZPECTACLES, TESTICLES, VALLET UND VATCH!
HOP HOP
GET ME OUT OF ZIS GIANT PROPHYLACTIC BEFORE I'M SPOTTED BY...
AHHHHH
... THE BLESSED VIRGIN MARY
AHHHH
AHHHH
AHHHH
TOO LATE – HERE SHE COMES NOW!
POPE BENEDICT! HOW DARE YOU WEAR A JUBBER RONNY IN CONTRAVENTION OF CHURCH RULES?!
B-BUT BLESSED VIRGIN....
AND YOU'RE WEARING IT OVER YOUR WHOLE BODY! THAT'S THE MOST SINFUL THING I'VE EVER SEEN!
...NAG NAG SCOLD SCOLD EAR-BEND EAR-BEND..
COR! WHAT AN OPPORTUNITY FOR SOME UPSKIRT SHOTS OF THE HOLY MARY MOTHER OF GOD!
SNAP CLICK CLICK
AND LATER
I GOT SOME FANTAKKA PHOTOS FOR MY PARISH MAGAZINE
PARISH NEWS
OUR LADY UPSKIRTED
PIX INSIDE
THANKS GILBERT. PLEASE ACCEPT THIS LOST ARK OF THE COVENANT FILLED WITH SWEETS, AS A REWARD FOR YOUR HELP!
WHOOPEE! SLURP!

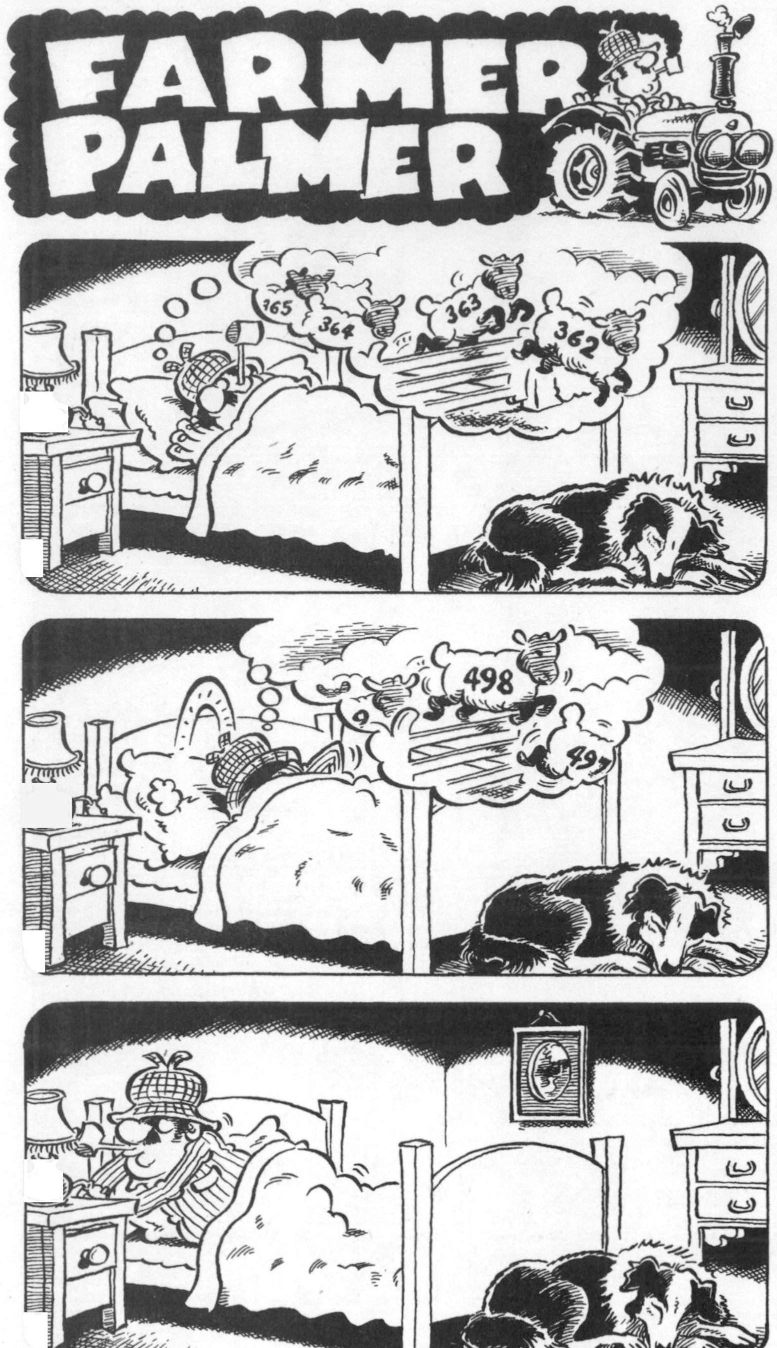
FARMER PALMER
365
364
363
362
498
497
BLAM!

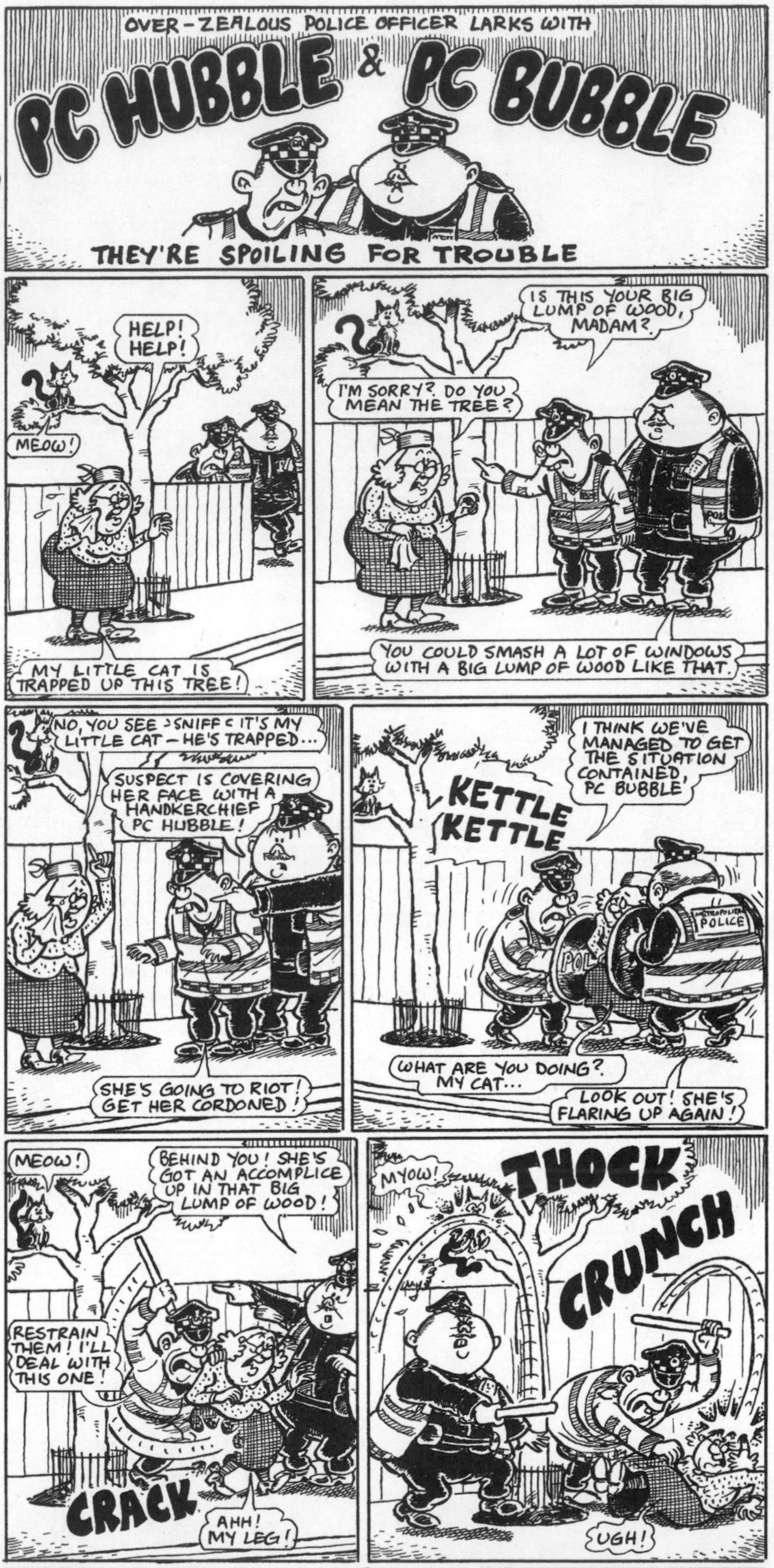
OVER-ZEALOUS POLICE OFFICER LARKS WITH
PC HUBBLE & PC BUBBLE
THEY'RE SPOILING FOR TROUBLE
HELP! HELP!
MEOW!
MY LITTLE CAT IS TRAPPED UP THIS TREE!
IS THIS YOUR BIG LUMP OF WOOD, MADAM?
I'M SORRY? DO YOU MEAN THE TREE?
YOU COULD SMASH A LOT OF WINDOWS WITH A BIG LUMP OF WOOD LIKE THAT.
NO, YOU SEE *SNIFF* IT'S MY LITTLE CAT – HE'S TRAPPED...
SUSPECT IS COVERING HER FACE WITH A HANDKERCHIEF PC HUBBLE!
SHE'S GOING TO RIOT! GET HER CORDONED!
I THINK WE'VE MANAGED TO GET THE SITUATION CONTAINED, PC BUBBLE
KETTLE KETTLE
WHAT ARE YOU DOING? MY CAT...
LOOK OUT! SHE'S FLARING UP AGAIN!
MEOW!
BEHIND YOU! SHE'S GOT AN ACCOMPLICE UP IN THAT BIG LUMP OF WOOD!
RESTRAIN THEM! I'LL DEAL WITH THIS ONE!
CRACK
AHH! MY LEG!
MYOW!
THOCK
CRUNCH
UGH!
HMM.
THUD
NEXT DAY
Daily Blah
BOMB-PLOT TERROR DUO COMMIT SUICIDE IN STREET SIEGE
POLICE OFFICERS ESCAPE INJURY

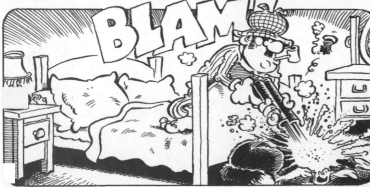

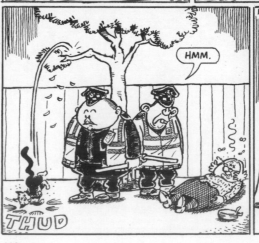

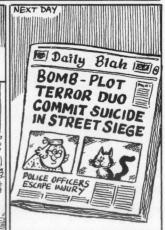

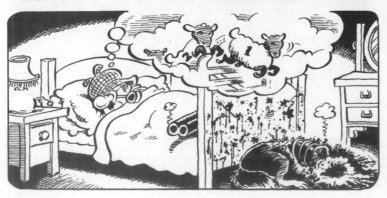

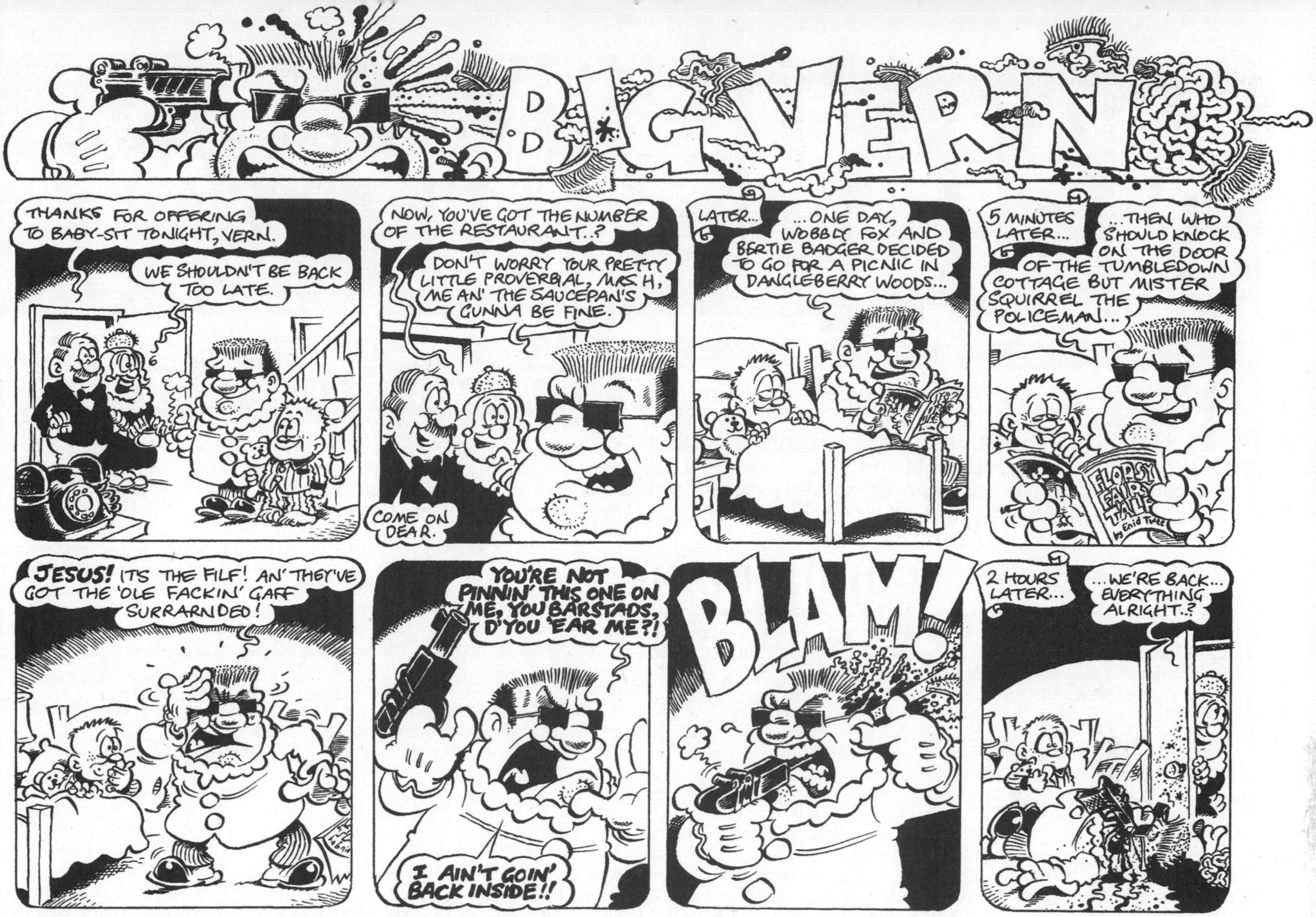
BIG VERN
THANKS FOR OFFERING TO BABY-SIT TONIGHT, VERN.
WE SHOULDN'T BE BACK TOO LATE.
NOW, YOU'VE GOT THE NUMBER OF THE RESTAURANT..?
DON'T WORRY YOUR PRETTY LITTLE PROVERBIAL, MRS. H, ME AN' THE SAUCEPAN'S GUNNA BE FINE.
COME ON DEAR.
LATER...
...ONE DAY, WOBBLY FOX AND BERTIE BADGER DECIDED TO GO FOR A PICNIC IN DANGLEBERRY WOODS...
5 MINUTES LATER...
...THEN WHO SHOULD KNOCK ON THE DOOR OF THE TUMBLEDOWN COTTAGE BUT MISTER SQUIRREL THE POLICEMAN...
FLOPSY FAIRY TALES
JESUS! IT'S THE FILF! AN' THEY'VE GOT THE 'OLE FACKIN' GAFF SURRARNDED!
YOU'RE NOT PINNIN' THIS ONE ON ME, YOU BARSTADS. D'YOU 'EAR ME?!
I AIN'T GOIN' BACK INSIDE!!
BLAM!
2 HOURS LATER...
...WE'RE BACK... EVERYTHING ALRIGHT..?

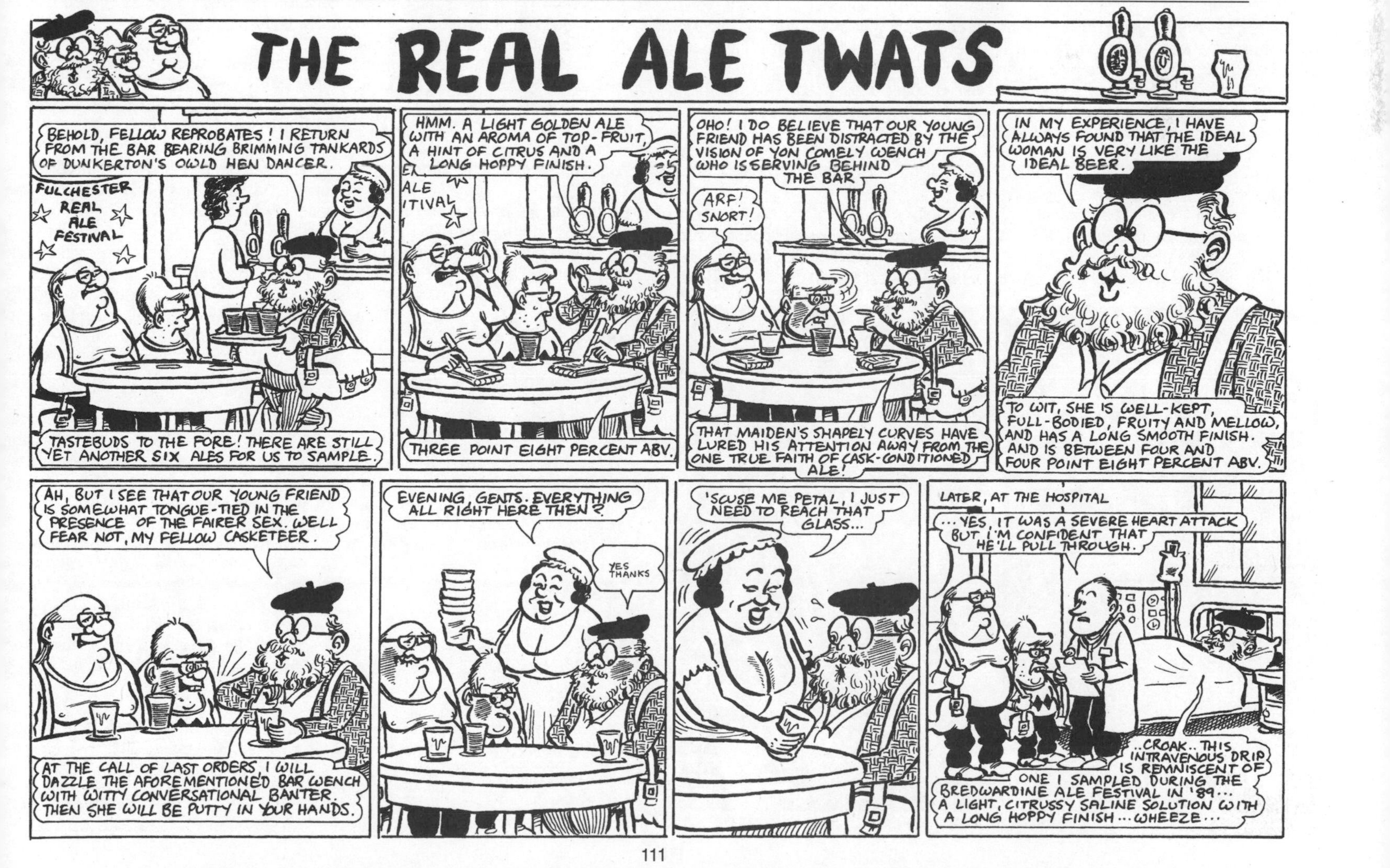
THE REAL ALE TWATS
BEHOLD, FELLOW REPROBATES! I RETURN FROM THE BAR BEARING BRIMMING TANKARDS OF DUNKERTON'S OWLD HEN DANCER.
FULCHESTER REAL ALE FESTIVAL
TASTEBUDS TO THE FORE! THERE ARE STILL YET ANOTHER SIX ALES FOR US TO SAMPLE.
HMM. A LIGHT GOLDEN ALE WITH AN AROMA OF TOP-FRUIT, A HINT OF CITRUS AND A LONG HOPPY FINISH.
THREE POINT EIGHT PERCENT ABV.
OHO! I DO BELIEVE THAT OUR YOUNG FRIEND HAS BEEN DISTRACTED BY THE VISION OF YON COMELY WENCH WHO IS SERVING BEHIND THE BAR
ARF! SNORT!
THAT MAIDEN'S SHAPELY CURVES HAVE LURED HIS ATTENTION AWAY FROM THE ONE TRUE FAITH OF CASK-CONDITIONED ALE!
IN MY EXPERIENCE, I HAVE ALWAYS FOUND THAT THE IDEAL WOMAN IS VERY LIKE THE IDEAL BEER.
TO WIT, SHE IS WELL-KEPT, FULL-BODIED, FRUITY AND MELLOW, AND HAS A LONG SMOOTH FINISH. AND IS BETWEEN FOUR AND FOUR POINT EIGHT PERCENT ABV.
AH, BUT I SEE THAT OUR YOUNG FRIEND IS SOMEWHAT TONGUE-TIED IN THE PRESENCE OF THE FAIRER SEX. WELL FEAR NOT, MY FELLOW CASKETEER.
AT THE CALL OF LAST ORDERS, I WILL DAZZLE THE AFOREMENTIONED BAR WENCH WITH WITTY CONVERSATIONAL BANTER. THEN SHE WILL BE PUTTY IN YOUR HANDS.
EVENING, GENTS. EVERYTHING ALL RIGHT HERE THEN?
YES THANKS
'SCUSE ME PETAL, I JUST NEED TO REACH THAT GLASS...
LATER, AT THE HOSPITAL
...YES, IT WAS A SEVERE HEART ATTACK BUT I'M CONFIDENT THAT HE'LL PULL THROUGH.
..CROAK.. THIS INTRAVENOUS DRIP IS REMINISCENT OF ONE I SAMPLED DURING THE BREDWARDINE ALE FESTIVAL IN '89... A LIGHT, CITRUSSY SALINE SOLUTION WITH A LONG HOPPY FINISH... WHEEZE...

Neighbours fro

TWO YEARS ago, retired car park attendant Ted Soil moved into his dream house. It had everything he'd ever wanted in a home, including double glazing, hot and cold water on tap, and even a fully-insulated roof. He spent hours lovingly cleaning it, decorating it and showing it off to friends in the quiet Leicestershire town of Ashby de la Zouch.

" I can't tell you how happy I was in my little house," recalls Ted, 66. "I had a lovely back garden for my pigeons and an indoor lavatory for the first time in my life. There was even a carpet on the living room floor."

"They say an Englishman's home is his castle. Well, I wouldn't have swapped that house for Buckingham Palace," he smiles.

But after living there for only a short while, Ted's sweet dreams of home ownership began to turn sour.

"I had only been there about a month when I noticed that the house next door had been put up for sale," says Soil. "It's not too rough an area but the prices are quite reasonable, so it wasn't on the market long before it got snapped up. One morning, a big removal van pulled up outside. I spent a good hour or two, peering out through my net curtains, waiting to catch a first glimpse of the new owner."

But Ted was in for a big surprise

|||||||||||||||||||||||||||

when his new next door neighbour turned out to be none other than washed-up eighties funnyman **EDDIE LARGE**.

"Imagine my amazement when I saw him wheezing up the path. I used to love watching him when he used to come on the telly with his partner, Tommy Ball or whatever his name was," says Ted. "I couldn't imagine what it would be like to have one of my comedy heroes living on the other side of my garden fence."

Before long Ted got chatting to Large whilst out in his back yard feeding his pigeons.. "Large told me the comedy work had dried up and times had become tough. He seemed like a really nice chap, and we soon became firm friends."

However, the friendship quickly took a dramatic turn for the worse.

"Eddie had invited me round to his place one evening for some peanuts and a game of Superbikes Top Trumps," he remembers. "It was the first time I had

been next door since he had moved in, he seemed unusually secretive when it came to letting visitors into his home. I expected it to be full of memorabilia from his showbiz career, but nothing could have been further from the truth."

"There were no signed photographs of his star pals like Brucie, Tarby and Joe Pasquale, no framed posters from pantomimes where he and Tommy had topped the bill in happier times, no BAFTA awards on the mantelpiece. Instead, there was a scruffy black cat with evil black eyes, which hissed at me as I walked in the room."

"I hadn't even realised he had a cat," says Ted. "And I made a mental note to lock the door of my pigeon loft in future."

"As well as the cat, there was a large broomstick propped up in the corner of his living room. I noticed that the shelves were filled with books about magic and spells. In the kitchen, there was a huge, black cauldron in the middle of the floor, full of green liquid that was boiling away, giving off luminous fumes that seemed to beckon me like menacing fingers."

"Eddie told me it was some garden vegetable cup-a-soups he was heating up and asked me if I would like to try some. I said yes, as I hadn't had any lunch." Ted heartily tucked into the soup, but was a little suspicious when he noticed that his host wasn't having any himself. Then he realised he had made a grave mistake.

"After a couple of sips, my throat was on fire," he says. "Smoke billowed from my mouth. I looked at my hands and they were starting to turn to stone. I looked at Eddie who had turned bright green with diabolical red eyes. He threw his head back and gave an evil cackle as he rubbed his hands together over the bubbling cauldron."

"I realised to my horror that Eddie Large was a witch and I had drunk a horrible potion."

"I dropped my mug and staggered out of the house. With every step I took I could feel myself turning to more stone. It was only a matter of time before I became a statue. Fortu-

nately, a friend of mine at the end of the road is in the St John's Ambulance, and he was able to put me right. But it was a close shave."

Mr Soil called the police and Large was arrested in a dawn raid the next day. He was found guilty of witchcraft and burned at the steak. Ted Soil thought his neighbour troubles were over. Little did he realise they had only just begun.

Jimmy's Plan was Simply not Cricket

"A few months later, I noticed a Sold sign go up next door," he recalls. "I was looking forward to the arrival of my new neighbour as I felt it would give me closure after the Eddie Large affair. I was expecting a normal member of public this time, perhaps a young couple with children or an older, retired chap like myself with an interest in pigeons."

"I certainly wasn't expecting to see washed-up eighties comic **JIMMY CRICKET** pull up one morning in a rented Luton van."

Ted had been a huge fan of the Irish funnyman in his heyday, so the pair soon became close pals.

Soil remembers: "Jimmy seemed a really friendly chap. He told me the work had dried up a bit in the last couple of decades but he had put enough by during the good times to see him by. He was happy to just stand and chat with me, cracking jokes about my pigeons and how thick he was."

A few weeks after he moved in, Cricket told Ted he was putting on a charity stand up performance at the local community centre and invited him to join the audience. Ted was delighted to attend.

"Cricket told me he was going to donate all the proceeds from the show to a local orphanage or hospice or donkey sanctuary or something, so I was only to pleased to go along and lend my support. He was really excited about it. Jimmy told me it was ages since he had performed, so he couldn't wait to get up there on stage again."

On the night of the show Soil went to the community centre but was surprised to find the place deserted. He remembers: "I checked my ticket and I'd got the right day and the right time. The seats were all

HOME MOANER: Next door neighbours were nothing to laugh about, says Soil.

DDV666Y

112

m HELL

Nightmare

aid out so I sat down and waited. Nobody lse turned up, and I started to feel sorry or Cricket. I remembered the days when e could fill the Blackpool Hippodrome, nd now it appeared he couldn't even sell ne ticket for a show at the Ashby de la Zouch Community Centre."

After half an hour, no-one else had hown up and Ted was about to give up nd go home. Then, suddenly, Jimmy appeared on the stage in puff of smoke."

"He was wearing a black cloak and ointed hat, not the usual fingerless mitens and silly wellies that I remembered rom his appearances on television. He vas holding a magic wand, waving it bout the room and chanting some kind f incantation. I looked on in horror as I aw that all the empty chairs had come to fe! Not only that, they were coming for ne! They knocked me to the ground and tarted kicking me with their wooden legs. immy then pointed his stick at a broom upboard and a load of mops and buckts danced out and joined in the attack. Now he started started conjuring fireballs rom out of thin air and hurling them at ne with his clawed, warty hands. One hit ne and set fire to my head, so I ran for he exit."

"I don't know how I managed to escape, ut somehow I got out of there with my life. I vent to my friend down the road is in the St ohn's Ambulance, so he was able to put my ead out and treat my injuries."

Soil called the police and, like Eddie Large before him, Jimmy Cricket was oon arrested. He confessed to witchcraft fter being tied to a stool and ducked in a ocal pond. Like Large, he was burned at he steak. But if Ted thought his life was bout to return to some sort of normality, e was about to get a very rude awakenng.

Ostrich Man Clifton Gave Ted the Bird

"Next door stood empty again for a ew more months," he explains. "I was relly anxious about who my new neighbour vould be this time. I had a sick feeling in ny stomach in case it turned out to be yet nother washed-up eighties comedian. o imagine my horror when the Sold sign vent up again and washed-up eighties coedian **BERNIE CLIFTON** moved into he place!"

"I couldn't believe my bad luck. Of course I knew that lightning never strikes in the same place three times, and the odds of him turning out to be a witch too were practically nil, but I wasn't taking any chances. I made no effort to befriend Clifton or speak to him in any way. If I saw him walking up the road on his comedy ostrich, I would cross over quickly to the other side. If I saw him sat in his back yard drinking beer, I would stay inside. Sometimes he would try to strike up a conversation with me over the fence when I was feeding my pigeons, but I would just ignore him and pretend I couldn't hear him. After dark, I kept my doors and windows firmly locked."

Two weeks passed during which Ted managed to avoid all contact with his new next door neighbour. But this was not enough to guarantee him his safety, as he found out to his terror one night.

"I had gone to bed and drifted off to sleep. Suddenly, on the stroke of midnight, I found myself being lifted out of bed by an unseen force. I floated out of the window, which opened by magic, and drifted into Bernie Clifton's house through his front door, which also opened by magic. Once inside, I was invisibly carried down the steps into the cellar."

"There was Clifton in his Ostrich suit hovering above the floor on a broomstick. He was wearing an evil grin the Devil himself would have been proud of. He pointed at me and began reciting a magic spell, repeating the magic words over and over again."

"Suddenly there was a bright flash and a puff of green smoke. I found I had been turned into a hamster! But worse was to come, for at that very moment a door opened and in walked washed-up eighties comedian **FREDDIE STARR**. And we all know what he does to hamsters."

Judging by the knife and fork in his grasp, Ted could see that he was on the menu that night. He recalls: "Luckily for me, I saw a small hole in the wall, through which I managed to escape. I ran down the road as fast as my little hamster legs would carry me to the house of my friend, who is in the St John's Ambulance and he turned me back into a human again. Back in my real body, I shuddered as I remembered how close I had been to being scoffed by Freddie Starr. It had been a close call. Too close for comfort."

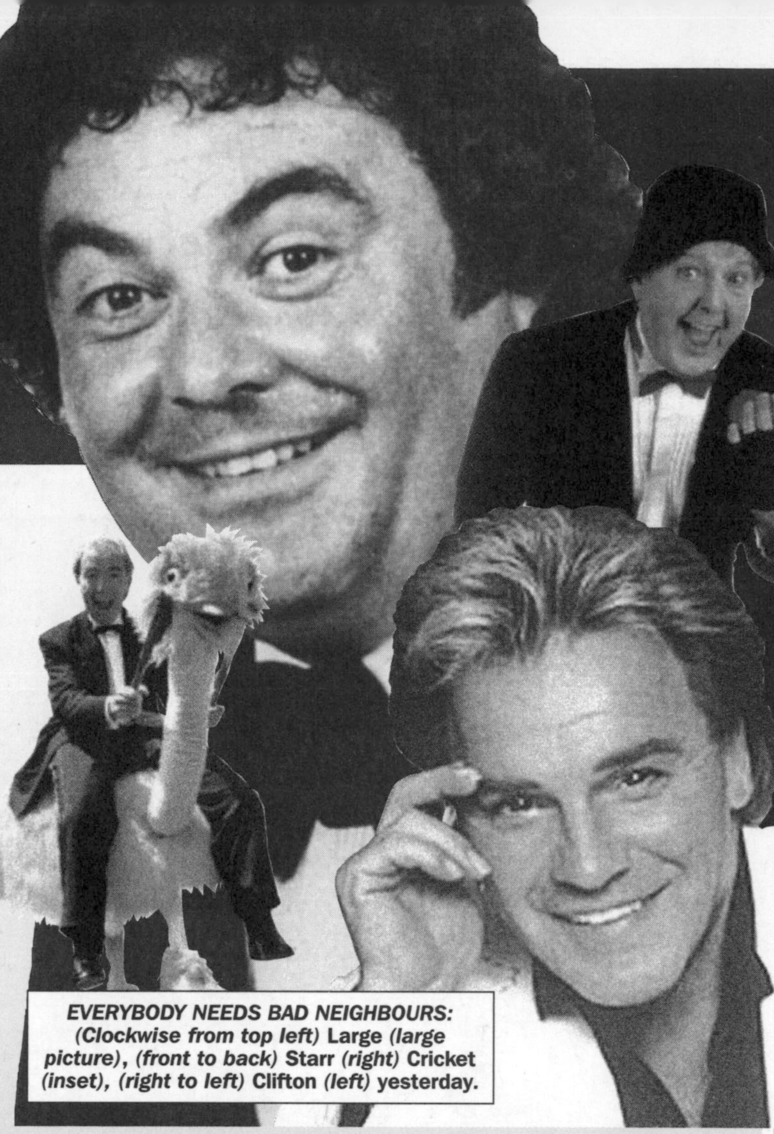

EVERYBODY NEEDS BAD NEIGHBOURS: (Clockwise from top left) Large (large picture), (front to back) Starr (right) Cricket (inset), (right to left) Clifton (left) yesterday.

The police were summoned again and Clifton was arrested. He was forced to grip a white hot crucifix and the tell-tale burn marks on the palm of his hand confirmed that he was guilty of witchcraft. He was later burnt at the steak on a bleak fen overlooking Ashby de la Zouch.

The house has now been empty for more than a year and Ted is safe for the moment. But he keeps asking himself the same questions over and over: What are the chances of three washed-up eighties comedians moving in next door, one after the other, and them all turning out to be witches? Furthermore, what is the chance that the next person to move into the house will be bring that sinister total up to four?

Ted has the answer, and it's one that doesn't bring him any comfort. "It's no coincidence," he says. "I'm being targeted and I think I know why."

"You see, shortly before I moved into my house, I went to see washed-up eighties comedian Tom O'Connor at the Hinkley Leisure Centre. I didn't reckon much to his act. It was a load of old jokes about his wife and her mother. Frankly, I'd heard it all before so, from my front row seat, I shouted out "Boo! You're rubbish Tom." He didn't say anything, being the old pro that he is, and so I thought nothing more about it."

"But thinking back, I'm sure he heard me. I could tell by the angry look on his face. I'm now convinced that, after the show, Tom told his mates about it and they decided to get together and wreak their terrible revenge on me by learning the black arts. ”

Soil says that the worry of his ordeal at the hands of washed-up eighties comedians has wrecked his health. He has now checked himself into a local clinic, where he has been busy writing his memoirs. These are set to be published in the Autumn under the provisional title *Hubble Bubble Soil in Trouble*, and will be available for 45p from the reception desk at Ashby de la Zouch Secure Mental Unit.

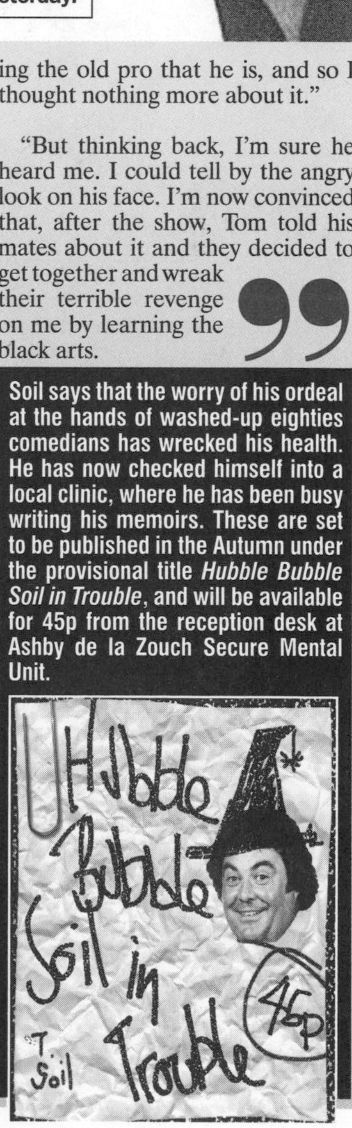
Hubble
Bubble
Soil in
Trouble
45p
T Soil

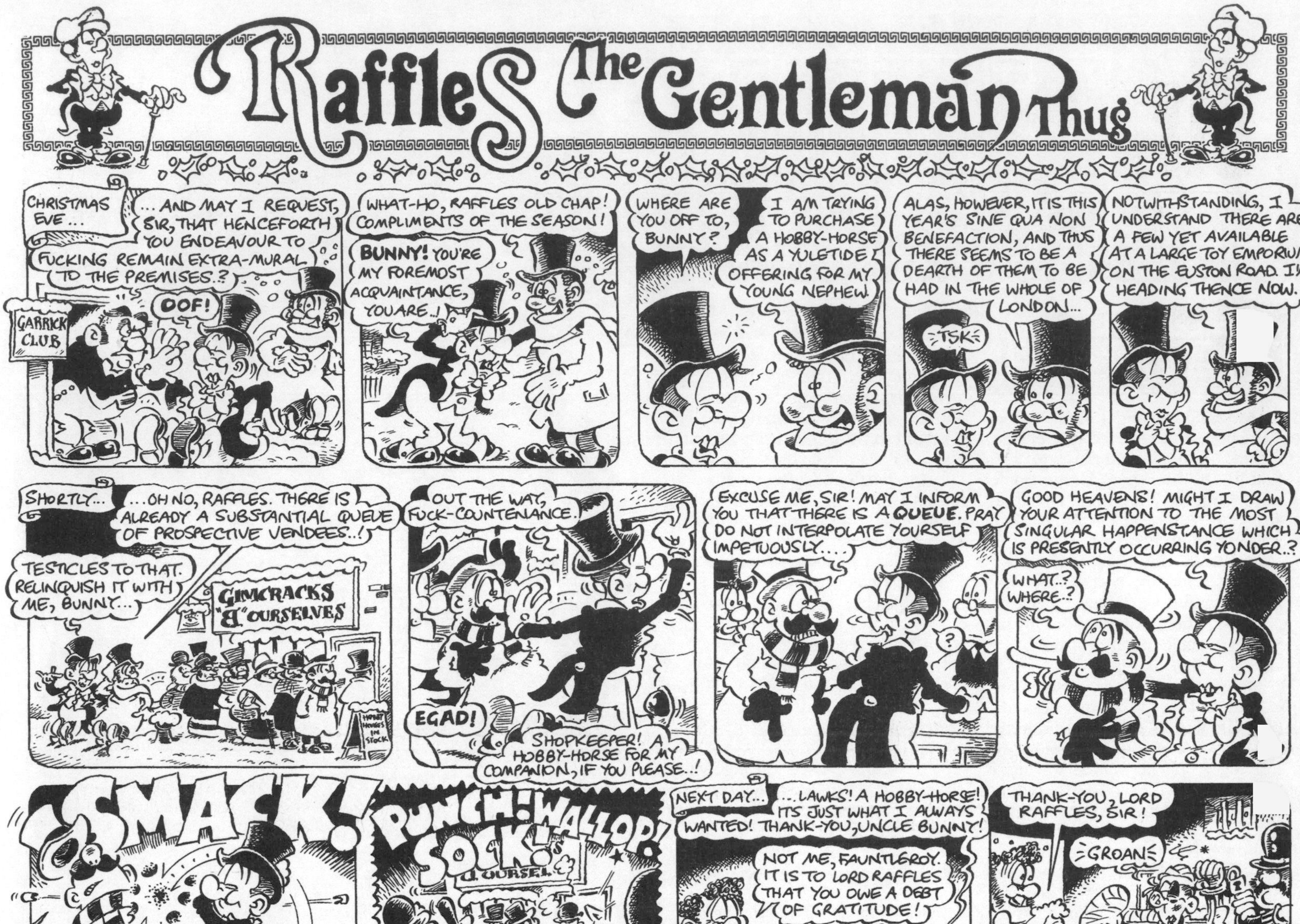
Raffles The Gentleman Thug
CHRISTMAS EVE...
...AND MAY I REQUEST, SIR, THAT HENCEFORTH YOU ENDEAVOUR TO FUCKING REMAIN EXTRA-MURAL TO THE PREMISES..?
GARRICK CLUB
OOF!
WHAT-HO, RAFFLES OLD CHAP! COMPLIMENTS OF THE SEASON!
BUNNY! YOU'RE MY FOREMOST ACQUAINTANCE, YOU ARE..!
WHERE ARE YOU OFF TO, BUNNY?
I AM TRYING TO PURCHASE A HOBBY-HORSE AS A YULETIDE OFFERING FOR MY YOUNG NEPHEW.
ALAS, HOWEVER, IT IS THIS YEAR'S SINE QUA NON BENEFACTION, AND THUS THERE SEEMS TO BE A DEARTH OF THEM TO BE HAD IN THE WHOLE OF LONDON...
TSK
NOTWITHSTANDING, I UNDERSTAND THERE ARE A FEW YET AVAILABLE AT A LARGE TOY EMPORIUM ON THE EUSTON ROAD. I'M HEADING THENCE NOW.
SHORTLY...
...OH NO, RAFFLES. THERE IS ALREADY A SUBSTANTIAL QUEUE OF PROSPECTIVE VENDEES..!
TESTICLES TO THAT. RELINQUISH IT WITH ME, BUNNY...
GIMCRACKS "R" OURSELVES
OUT THE WAY, FUCK-COUNTENANCE.
EGAD!
SHOPKEEPER! A HOBBY-HORSE FOR MY COMPANION, IF YOU PLEASE..!
EXCUSE ME, SIR! MAY I INFORM YOU THAT THERE IS A QUEUE. PRAY DO NOT INTERPOLATE YOURSELF IMPETUOUSLY....
?
GOOD HEAVENS! MIGHT I DRAW YOUR ATTENTION TO THE MOST SINGULAR HAPPENSTANCE WHICH IS PRESENTLY OCCURRING YONDER..?
WHAT..? WHERE..?
SMACK!
OOYAH!
EXTRACT THE OSSICLES FROM THAT, CUNT-BUBBLE..!
PUNCH! WALLOP! SOCK!
PHEEP!
NEXT DAY...
...LAWKS! A HOBBY-HORSE! IT'S JUST WHAT I ALWAYS WANTED! THANK-YOU, UNCLE BUNNY!
NOT ME, FAUNTLEROY. IT IS TO LORD RAFFLES THAT YOU OWE A DEBT OF GRATITUDE!
THANK-YOU, LORD RAFFLES, SIR!
GROAN
...WHAT THE FUCK EVENTUATED?

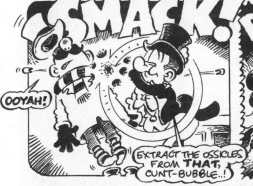

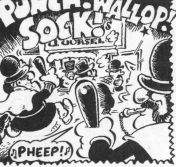

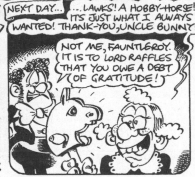

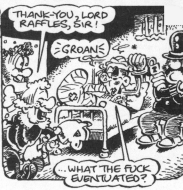

UP THE ARSE CORNER

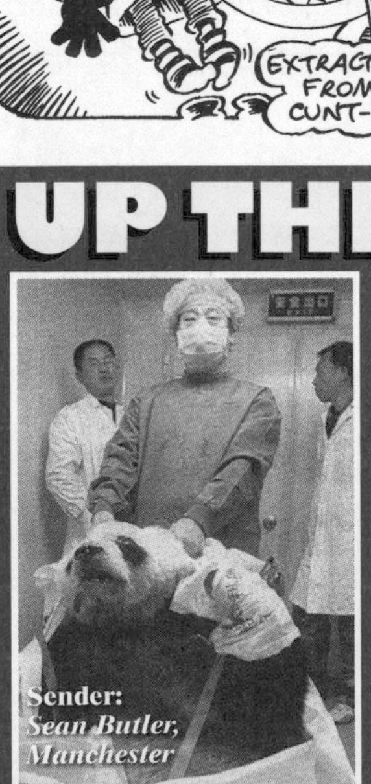
Sender: Sean Butler, Manchester

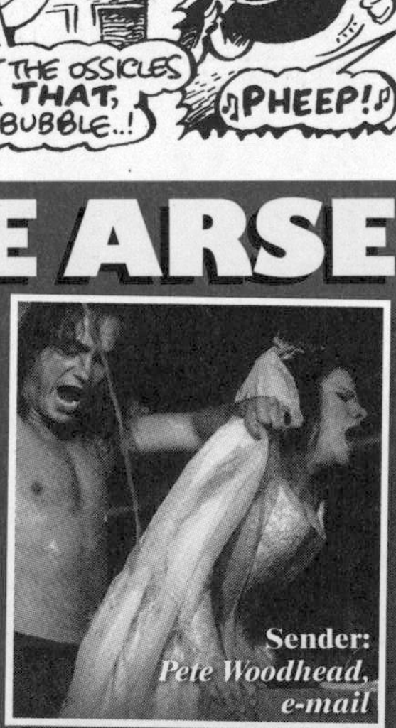
Sender: Pete Woodhead, e-mail

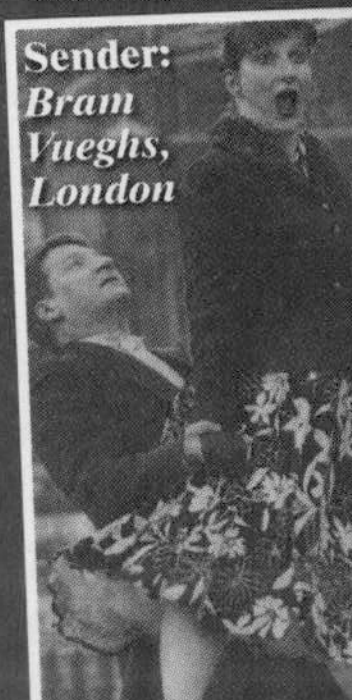
Sender: Bram Vueghs, London

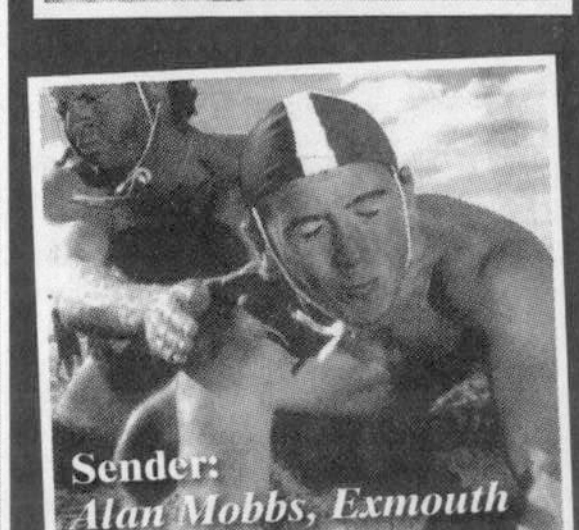
Sender: Alan Mobbs, Exmouth

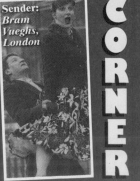

Have Your Say

RADIO 4 PRESENTER and voice of the Shipping Forecast Peter Jefferson has been given the push by the BBC after 45 years of service. The news comes coincidentally just a month after the veteran announcer let slip a 4-letter word during a live broadcast. And whilst the BBC received no complaints from listeners, many believe that it was Jefferson's on-air blooper that led to his sacking. But in this day and age, is the F-word really that offensive? Or is there never any need to say fuck on national radio. We went on the streets to find out what YOU think...

...I WAS disgusted when I heard Peter Jefferson say the F-word. I worked for forty years in the Wallsend dockyards where people regularly dropped buckets of hot rivvets on their toes. But in all that time, I never once heard any of them swear.

Cecil Gaybody, Maple Avenue

...I'VE been a nun for forty years and I listen to the shipping forecast every night before vespers. When I heard the announcer say that word, I wasn't in the least shocked, as I hear far worse in the convent every day. When some of the sisters get a prayer wrong, hit a bum note during All Things Bright and Beautiful or get a puncture on their tandems, they really come out with some choice language.

Sister Consumptia, Trinity Road

...I ALWAYS listen to the shipping forecast with my 3-year old son. On that night, he turned to me with tears in his eyes and said "Daddy, what does the F-word mean?" What could I say?

Hector Warburton, Birch Road

...MY mother was 86 and had never heard the F-word in all her life. She didn't know what it meant or even that it existed. When she heard it for the first time on the Radio 4 shipping forecast, she was so shocked that she slipped into a coma and died.

Shirley Crabtreehouse, Triangle Lane

...WHEN I heard potty-mouthed Jefferson utter his filthy expletive on air, I was so incensed that I put my foot through my radio and sent the BBC the bill. And that'll come out of the licence payer's pocket.

Pinchbeck Foreskin, Churchbalk Lane

...I'M a round-the-world yachtsman, and I was listening to the shipping forecast whilst rounding Cape Horn in my 12 foot catameringue when Jefferson turned the airwaves blue. I was so incensed that I put my foot through the radio. Unfortunately, it went not only through the radio, but also through the hull of my boat which sank.

Sir Francis Worcester, Marine Road

Street and Square in Half-Arsed Battle for Xmas Ratings

By our Soap Correspondent
BUBBLES SOAP

TV SOAP FANS look set for a roller coaster Christmas after writers announced their most intelligence-insulting storylines ever! And it could mean an epic clash of the titans as ITV's *Coronation Street* and the BBC's *EastEnders* go head-to-head with plots so ludicrous that even the most uncritical viewers will struggle to believe what they are watching.

The festive period has traditionally been the most important time of year for soaps. Double-length Christmas Day episodes and memorable storylines regularly attract millions of extra viewers. However this year telly bosses are planning to slap loyal fans in the face and have asked writers to ditch the usual mix of comedy, action and tragedy, replacing it with any old shit that pops into their heads.

IDIOTS

Granada spokesman Gary Adverts told us: "Corrie has over ten million regular viewers who tune in week-in, week-out. It doesn't seem to matter how poor the stories are. These bovine idiots will watch anything, so from now on we're not going to bother trying.

"For this year's Christmas Day episodes we just went to the pub and wrote down a few half-arsed ideas on the back of a beer mat," he said. "We've got Jack Duckworth giving birth to an eight-legged spider baby on the roof the Rovers Return, Rita and Norris being abducted by aliens, and Sally Webster getting struck by lightning and waking up back in time in Victorian Weatherfield. It's utter bollocks from start to finish."

DOGVILLE

"It's our way of demonstrating the contempt in which we hold the fuckwits who watch the show," he added.

Meanwhile scriptwriters working on rival BBC soap *EastEnders* have been told to completely disregard everything that's happened on the show in the last twenty-five years. Christmas Day episodes are set to confuse viewers by re-introducing characters who have been written out in the past, some of whom were even thought to be dead.

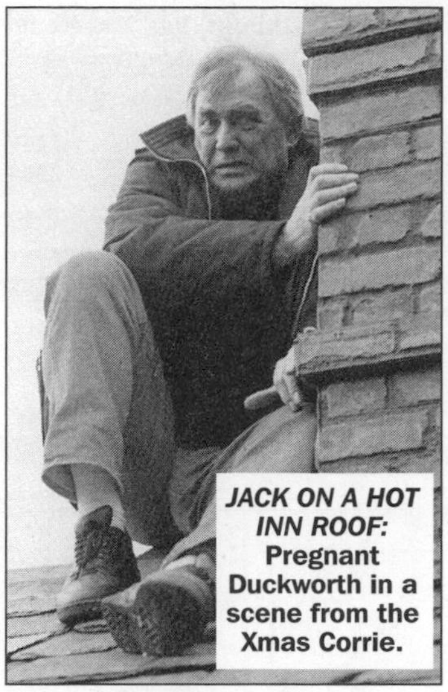

JACK ON A HOT INN ROOF: Pregnant Duckworth in a scene from the Xmas Corrie.

BBC Director General Mark Thompson told us: "Don't expect to be able to follow this one, it's going to be a real fucking shambles. It doesn't make any sense, but quite frankly nobody here gives a tuppeny wank any more.

"Any viewers who want to complain can suck my cock," he added.

ANTICHRIST

Other soaps now look set to follow suit. It is believed that Emmerdale actors have been encouraged to make their festive episode up as they go along. Meanwhile a special Christmas Eve Holby City, set on the Moon in the year 3020 is already in production.

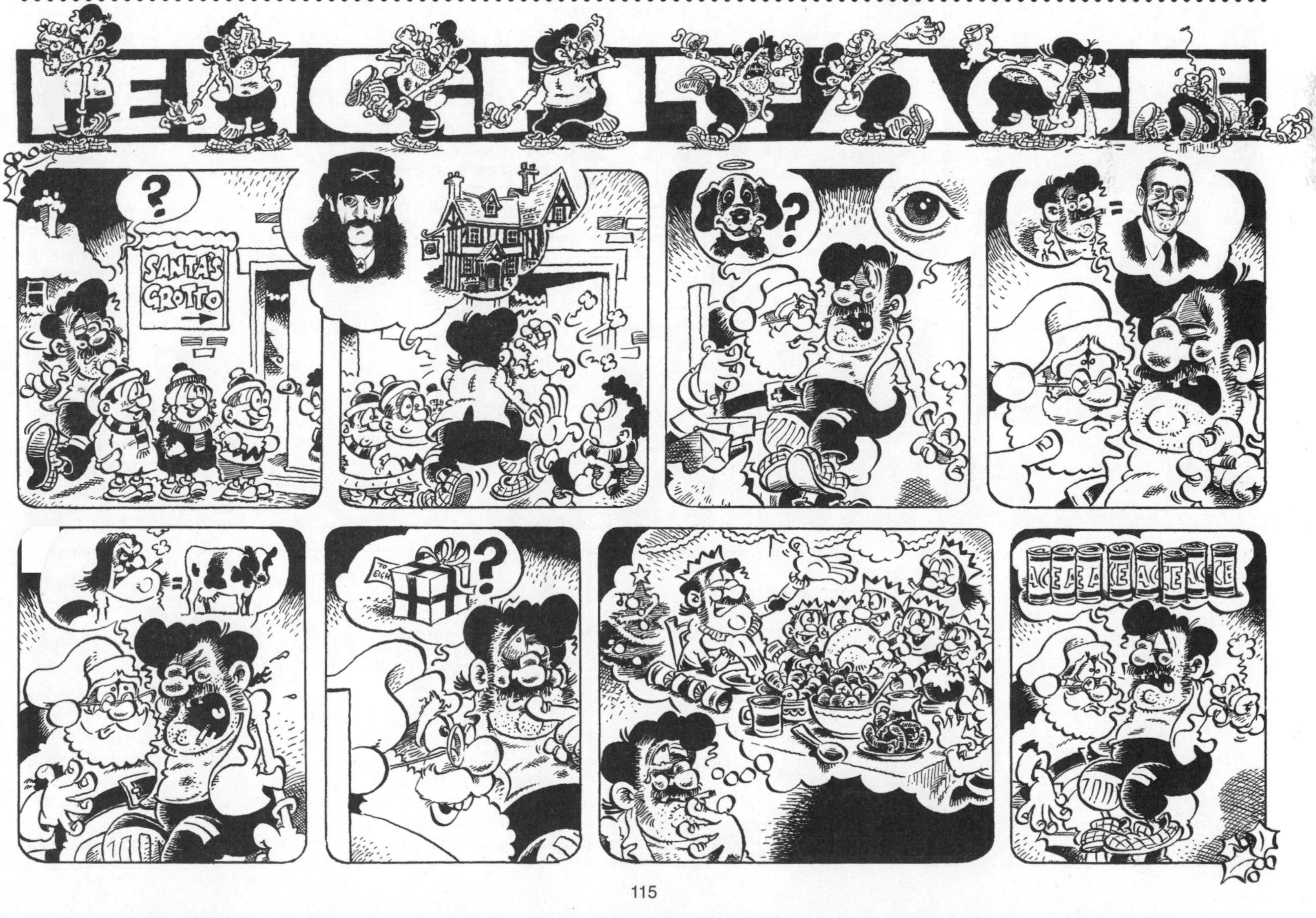
?
SANTA'S GROTTO
?
=
?
=
?

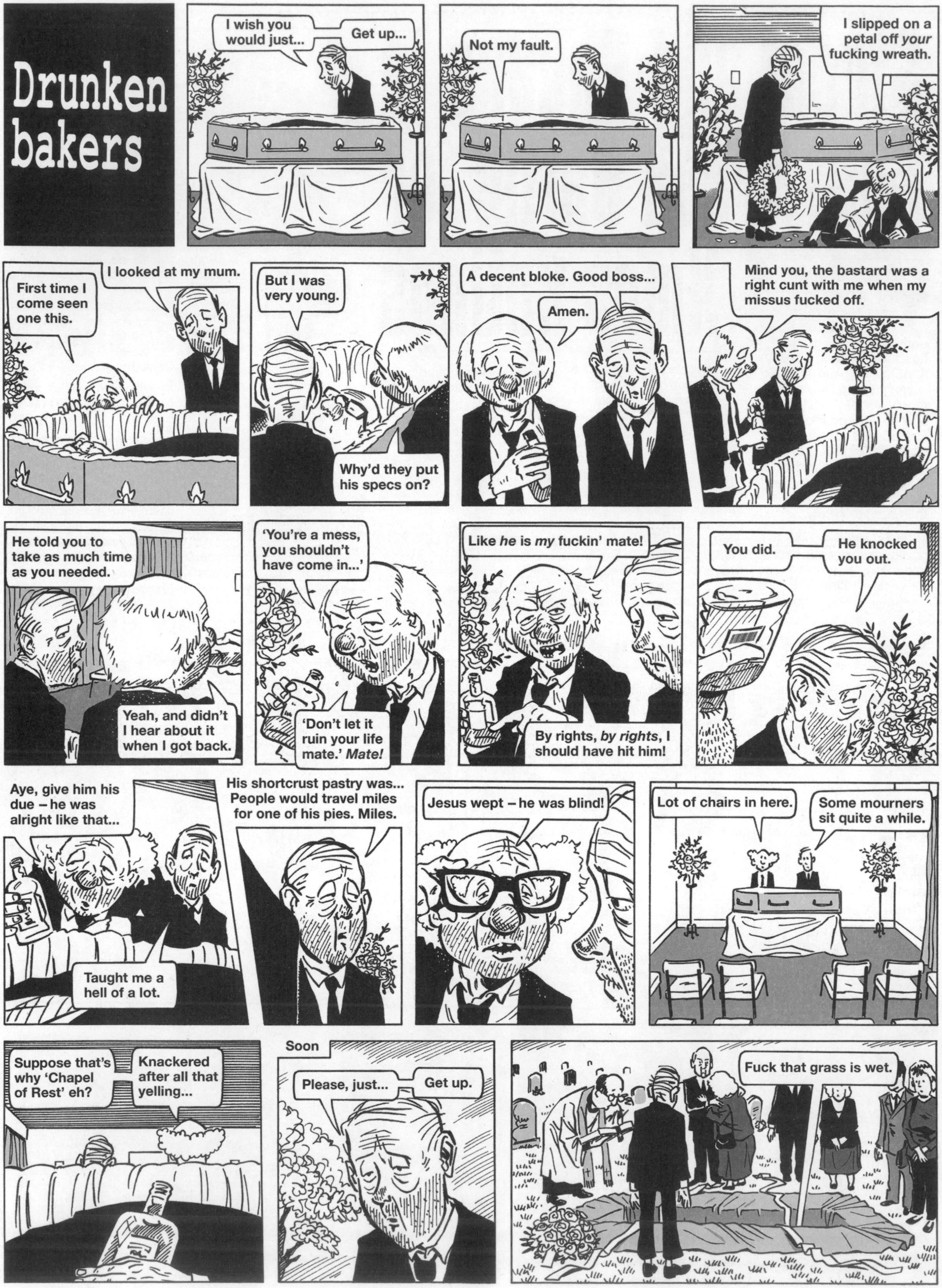
Drunken bakers
I wish you would just...
Get up...
Not my fault.
I slipped on a petal off your fucking wreath.
First time I come seen one this.
I looked at my mum.
But I was very young.
Why'd they put his specs on?
A decent bloke. Good boss...
Amen.
Mind you, the bastard was a right cunt with me when my missus fucked off.
He told you to take as much time as you needed.
Yeah, and didn't I hear about it when I got back.
'You're a mess, you shouldn't have come in...'
'Don't let it ruin your life mate.' Mate!
Like he is my fuckin' mate!
By rights, by rights, I should have hit him!
You did.
He knocked you out.
Aye, give him his due – he was alright like that...
Taught me a hell of a lot.
His shortcrust pastry was... People would travel miles for one of his pies. Miles.
Jesus wept – he was blind!
Lot of chairs in here.
Some mourners sit quite a while.
Suppose that's why 'Chapel of Rest' eh?
Knackered after all that yelling...
Soon
Please, just...
Get up.
Fuck that grass is wet.

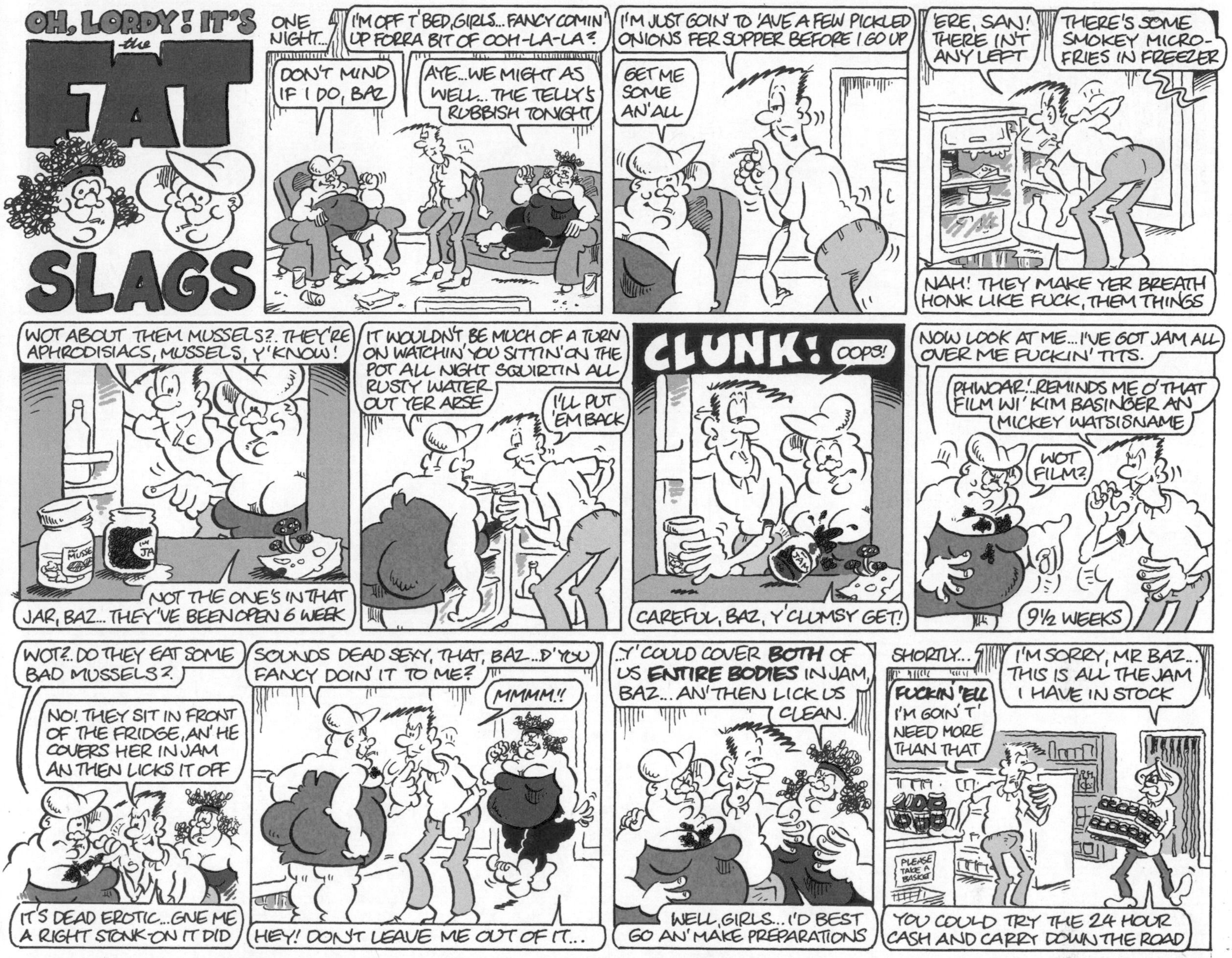
OH, LORDY! IT'S the FAT SLAGS
ONE NIGHT...
I'M OFF T'BED, GIRLS... FANCY COMIN' UP FORRA BIT OF OOH-LA-LA?
DON'T MIND IF I DO, BAZ
AYE... WE MIGHT AS WELL... THE TELLY'S RUBBISH TONIGHT
I'M JUST GOIN' TO 'AVE A FEW PICKLED ONIONS FER SUPPER BEFORE I GO UP
GET ME SOME AN'ALL
'ERE, SAN! THERE IN'T ANY LEFT
THERE'S SOME SMOKEY MICRO-FRIES IN FREEZER
NAH! THEY MAKE YER BREATH HONK LIKE FUCK, THEM THINGS
WOT ABOUT THEM MUSSELS?. THEY'RE APHRODISIACS, MUSSELS, Y'KNOW!
NOT THE ONE'S IN THAT JAR, BAZ... THEY'VE BEEN OPEN 6 WEEK
IT WOULDN'T BE MUCH OF A TURN ON WATCHIN' YOU SITTIN' ON THE POT ALL NIGHT SQUIRTIN ALL RUSTY WATER OUT YER ARSE
I'LL PUT 'EM BACK
CLUNK!
OOPS!
CAREFUL, BAZ, Y'CLUMSY GET!
NOW LOOK AT ME... I'VE GOT JAM ALL OVER ME FUCKIN' TITS.
PHWOAR!.. REMINDS ME O'THAT FILM WI' KIM BASINGER AN MICKEY WATSISNAME
WOT FILM?
9½ WEEKS
WOT?.. DO THEY EAT SOME BAD MUSSELS?.
NO! THEY SIT IN FRONT OF THE FRIDGE, AN' HE COVERS HER IN JAM AN THEN LICKS IT OFF
IT'S DEAD EROTIC... GIVE ME A RIGHT STONK-ON IT DID
SOUNDS DEAD SEXY, THAT, BAZ... D'YOU FANCY DOIN' IT TO ME?
MMMM.!!
HEY! DON'T LEAVE ME OUT OF IT...
...Y' COULD COVER **BOTH** OF US **ENTIRE BODIES** IN JAM, BAZ... AN' THEN LICK US CLEAN.
WELL, GIRLS... I'D BEST GO AN' MAKE PREPARATIONS
SHORTLY...
FUCKIN' 'ELL I'M GOIN' T' NEED MORE THAN THAT
I'M SORRY, MR BAZ.. THIS IS ALL THE JAM I HAVE IN STOCK
PLEASE TAKE A BASKET
YOU COULD TRY THE 24 HOUR CASH AND CARRY DOWN THE ROAD

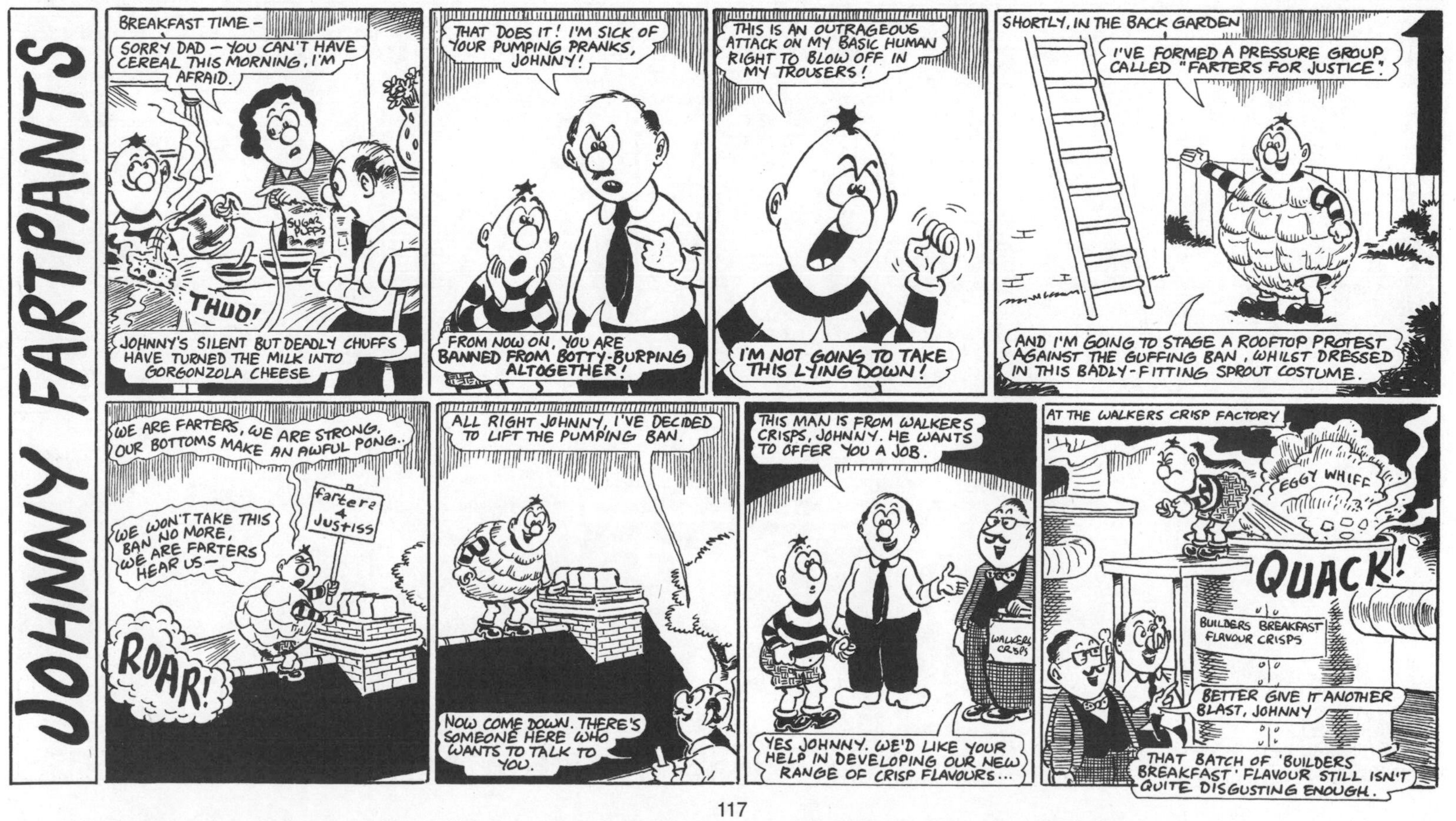
JOHNNY FARTPANTS
BREAKFAST TIME –
SORRY DAD – YOU CAN'T HAVE CEREAL THIS MORNING, I'M AFRAID.
SUGAR PUFFS
THUD!
JOHNNY'S SILENT BUT DEADLY CHUFFS HAVE TURNED THE MILK INTO GORGONZOLA CHEESE
THAT DOES IT! I'M SICK OF YOUR PUMPING PRANKS, JOHNNY!
FROM NOW ON, YOU ARE BANNED FROM BOTTY-BURPING ALTOGETHER!
THIS IS AN OUTRAGEOUS ATTACK ON MY BASIC HUMAN RIGHT TO BLOW OFF IN MY TROUSERS!
I'M NOT GOING TO TAKE THIS LYING DOWN!
SHORTLY, IN THE BACK GARDEN
I'VE FORMED A PRESSURE GROUP CALLED "FARTERS FOR JUSTICE".
AND I'M GOING TO STAGE A ROOFTOP PROTEST AGAINST THE GUFFING BAN, WHILST DRESSED IN THIS BADLY-FITTING SPROUT COSTUME.
WE ARE FARTERS, WE ARE STRONG. OUR BOTTOMS MAKE AN AWFUL PONG..
WE WON'T TAKE THIS BAN NO MORE, WE ARE FARTERS HEAR US–
farterz 4 Justiss
ROAR!
ALL RIGHT JOHNNY, I'VE DECIDED TO LIFT THE PUMPING BAN.
NOW COME DOWN. THERE'S SOMEONE HERE WHO WANTS TO TALK TO YOU.
THIS MAN IS FROM WALKERS CRISPS, JOHNNY. HE WANTS TO OFFER YOU A JOB.
WALKERS CRISPS
YES JOHNNY. WE'D LIKE YOUR HELP IN DEVELOPING OUR NEW RANGE OF CRISP FLAVOURS...
AT THE WALKERS CRISP FACTORY
EGGY WHIFF
QUACK!
BUILDERS BREAKFAST FLAVOUR CRISPS
BETTER GIVE IT ANOTHER BLAST, JOHNNY
THAT BATCH OF 'BUILDERS BREAKFAST' FLAVOUR STILL ISN'T QUITE DISGUSTING ENOUGH.

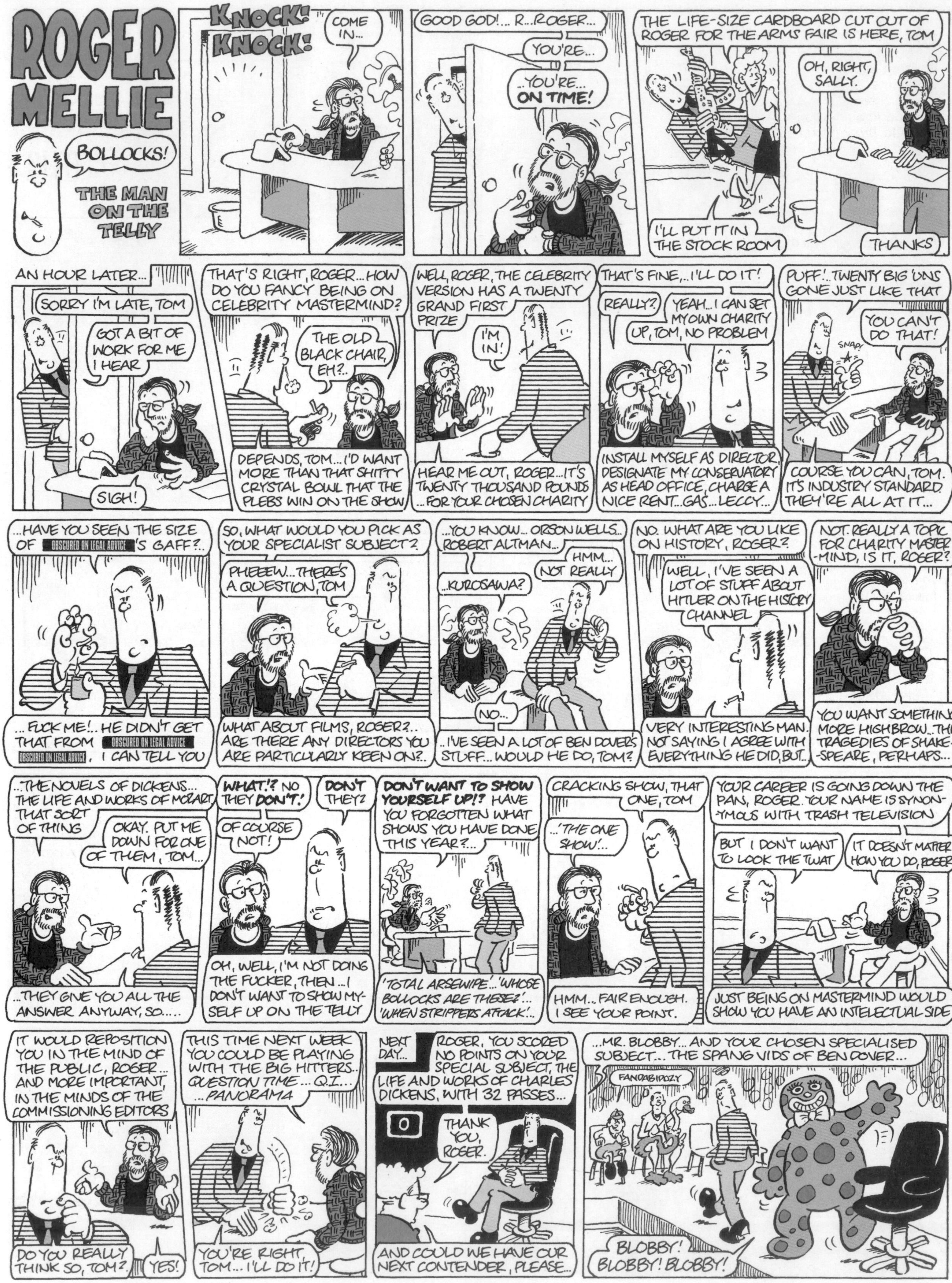
ROGER MELLIE
BOLLOCKS!
THE MAN ON THE TELLY
KNOCK! KNOCK!
COME IN...
GOOD GOD!... R...ROGER...
YOU'RE...
...YOU'RE... ON TIME!
THE LIFE-SIZE CARDBOARD CUT OUT OF ROGER FOR THE ARMS FAIR IS HERE, TOM
OH, RIGHT, SALLY.
I'LL PUT IT IN THE STOCK ROOM
THANKS
AN HOUR LATER...
SORRY I'M LATE, TOM
GOT A BIT OF WORK FOR ME I HEAR
SIGH!
THAT'S RIGHT, ROGER... HOW DO YOU FANCY BEING ON CELEBRITY MASTERMIND?
THE OLD BLACK CHAIR, EH?..
DEPENDS, TOM... I'D WANT MORE THAN THAT SHITTY CRYSTAL BOWL THAT THE PLEBS WIN ON THE SHOW
WELL, ROGER, THE CELEBRITY VERSION HAS A TWENTY GRAND FIRST PRIZE
I'M IN!
HEAR ME OUT, ROGER... IT'S TWENTY THOUSAND POUNDS ...FOR YOUR CHOSEN CHARITY
THAT'S FINE,.. I'LL DO IT!
REALLY?
YEAH... I CAN SET MY OWN CHARITY UP, TOM, NO PROBLEM
INSTALL MYSELF AS DIRECTOR, DESIGNATE MY CONSERVATORY AS HEAD OFFICE, CHARGE A NICE RENT... GAS... LECCY...
PUFF!... TWENTY BIG 'UNS GONE JUST LIKE THAT
YOU CAN'T DO THAT!
SNAP!
COURSE YOU CAN, TOM. IT'S INDUSTRY STANDARD. THEY'RE ALL AT IT...
...HAVE YOU SEEN THE SIZE OF OBSCURED ON LEGAL ADVICE 'S GAFF?..
...FUCK ME!... HE DIDN'T GET THAT FROM OBSCURED ON LEGAL ADVICE OBSCURED ON LEGAL ADVICE, I CAN TELL YOU
SO, WHAT WOULD YOU PICK AS YOUR SPECIALIST SUBJECT?
PHEEEW... THERE'S A QUESTION, TOM
WHAT ABOUT FILMS, ROGER?... ARE THERE ANY DIRECTORS YOU ARE PARTICULARLY KEEN ON?..
...YOU KNOW... ORSON WELLS... ROBERT ALTMAN...
HMM... NOT REALLY
...KUROSAWA?
NO...
...I'VE SEEN A LOT OF BEN DOVER'S STUFF... WOULD HE DO, TOM?
NO. WHAT ARE YOU LIKE ON HISTORY, ROGER?
WELL, I'VE SEEN A LOT OF STUFF ABOUT HITLER ON THE HISTORY CHANNEL
VERY INTERESTING MAN. NOT SAYING I AGREE WITH EVERYTHING HE DID, BUT...
NOT REALLY A TOPIC FOR CHARITY MASTER-MIND, IS IT, ROGER?
YOU WANT SOMETHING MORE HIGHBROW... THE TRAGEDIES OF SHAKE-SPEARE, PERHAPS...
...THE NOVELS OF DICKENS... THE LIFE AND WORKS OF MOZART THAT SORT OF THING
OKAY. PUT ME DOWN FOR ONE OF THEM, TOM...
...THEY GIVE YOU ALL THE ANSWER ANYWAY, SO.....
WHAT!? NO THEY DON'T!
DON'T THEY?
OF COURSE NOT!
OH, WELL, I'M NOT DOING THE FUCKER, THEN ...I DON'T WANT TO SHOW MY-SELF UP ON THE TELLY
DON'T WANT TO SHOW YOURSELF UP!? HAVE YOU FORGOTTEN WHAT SHOWS YOU HAVE DONE THIS YEAR?...
'TOTAL ARSEWIPE'... 'WHOSE BOLLOCKS ARE THESE?'... 'WHEN STRIPPERS ATTACK'...
CRACKING SHOW, THAT ONE, TOM
...'THE ONE SHOW'...
HMM... FAIR ENOUGH. I SEE YOUR POINT.
YOUR CAREER IS GOING DOWN THE PAN, ROGER. YOUR NAME IS SYNON-YMOUS WITH TRASH TELEVISION
BUT I DON'T WANT TO LOOK THE TWAT
IT DOESN'T MATTER HOW YOU DO, ROGER
JUST BEING ON MASTERMIND WOULD SHOW YOU HAVE AN INTELECTUAL SIDE
IT WOULD REPOSITION YOU IN THE MIND OF THE PUBLIC, ROGER... AND MORE IMPORTANT, IN THE MINDS OF THE COMMISSIONING EDITORS
DO YOU REALLY THINK SO, TOM?
YES!
THIS TIME NEXT WEEK YOU COULD BE PLAYING WITH THE BIG HITTERS.. QUESTION TIME... Q.I... ...PANORAMA
YOU'RE RIGHT, TOM... I'LL DO IT!
NEXT DAY...
ROGER, YOU SCORED NO POINTS ON YOUR SPECIAL SUBJECT, THE LIFE AND WORKS OF CHARLES DICKENS, WITH 32 PASSES...
0
THANK YOU, ROGER.
AND COULD WE HAVE OUR NEXT CONTENDER, PLEASE...
...MR. BLOBBY... AND YOUR CHOSEN SPECIALISED SUBJECT... THE SPANG VIDS OF BEN DOVER...
FANDABIDOZY
BLOBBY! BLOBBY! BLOBBY!

Fears Grow for BBC Man Trapped in Wardrobe

FRIENDS of Mihir Bose were yesterday mounting an anxious vigil outside his home as the BBC sports editor entered a second night trapped in a wardrobe. The 61-year-old broadcaster has been locked in the wardbrobe in his bedroom since Friday night, and so far all attempts to free him have failed. Emergency services now fear that unless he is released quickly, Bose could suffocate on his own farts.

TUESDAY

It is thought that Bose may entered the wardrobe on Tuesday evening looking for a magic faraway land, after being inspired by the CS Lewis Narnia Books. His mother, Edna Bose, told reporters: "I began reading The Lion, The Witch and the Wardrobe to Mihir as his bedtime story and he became very excited at the part where Lucy enters the wardrobe and the fur coats turn into trees.

TIG

"He kept asking me if there was a Narnia behind the suits in his wardrobe," she added.

Mrs Bose discovered her son's predicament when he failed to come down for breakfast the following morning.

MIG

"I went into his room to get him up, but he wasn't in his bed. Then I heard muffled cries coming from his wardrobe. I tried to open it up but found the door was stuck fast and the handle came off in my hand. I was worried because Mihir had had meatballs in Chicken Tonight for his tea the night before, and that always makes him a bit windy."

SHIELDED METAL ARC

Unable to free her award-winng sports pundit son, Mrs Bose called the fire brigade, but when they arrived they too were unable to get the wardrobe open. Two officers tried to force the door using a butter knife from the kitchen, but it bent. Two other firemen removed the mirror in the hope of finding another way in, but they discovered it was solid wood behind.

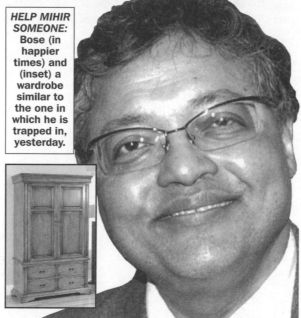

HELP MIHIR SOMEONE: Bose (in happier times) and (inset) a wardrobe similar to the one in which he is trapped in, yesterday.

Following the unsuccessful rescue attempts, Chief Fire Officer Cuthbert Flack read a statement to the press gathered outside Bose's West London home. Looking tired and drawn, he told reporters: "I can confirm that a 61-year-old man is trapped inside a wardrobe at this address. He is not in any imminent danger of injury, but he has been eating Chicken Tonight and there is a risk that his flatulence could build up to a level that might endanger life in such a confined space."

Firefighters were last night still attempting to remove Bose from his wardrobe, although hopes of a successful outcome were said to be fading fast. "We are doing everything we can, but it is only a matter of time before Mihir succumbs to his own toxic flatus," Flack added.

Meanwhile, BBC bosses were believed to be discussing the possibility of adapting Bose's plight into a Saturday evening gameshow format. *I'm a Celebrity, Get Mihir Out of There!* will feature a variety of stars coming up with harebrained schemes to free the bespectacled sports editor from his wardrobe prison before he suffocates on his own farts. Viewers will get the chance to vote for their favourite in a very expensive, rigged telephone poll.

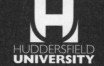

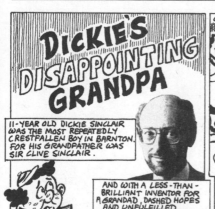

DICKIE'S DISAPPOINTING GRANDPA
11-YEAR OLD DICKIE SINCLAIR WAS THE MOST REPEATEDLY CRESTFALLEN BOY IN BARNTON, FOR HIS GRANDFATHER WAS SIR CLIVE SINCLAIR.
AND WITH A LESS-THAN-BRILLIANT INVENTOR FOR A GRANDAD, DASHED HOPES AND UNFULFILLED EXPECTATIONS WERE ALWAYS JUST AROUND THE CORNER.
ONE DAY
DICKIE! YOUR GRANDPA'S GOT SOMETHING TO SHOW YOU.
HE'S IN HIS SHED.
GOSH DICKIE! PERHAPS YOUR GRANDPA HAS INVENTED A ROCKET JET-PACK THAT WILL ENABLE YOU TO FLY!
GRANDPA SIR CLIVE'S SHED
OR MAYBE HE'S BUILT AN ARMY OF REMOTE-CONTROLLED MINIATURE ROBOT SOLDIERS!
BUT
NO. THERE'S A NOT-VERY-GOOD COMPUTER, A KIND OF BATTERY-POWERED CAR THING THAT EVERYONE LAUGHS AT.... AND A "FOLD-UP BICYCLE" WITH SILLY LITTLE WHEELS.
GRANDPA SIR CLIVE'S SHED
OH.

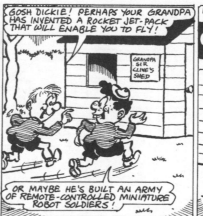

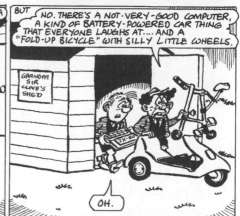

LETTERBOCKS

VIZ COMIC, PO Box 656, North Shields, NE30 4XX

E-mail letters@viz.co.uk

STATE OF NORTH BORNEO
ONE CENT
DORCH
DORSE

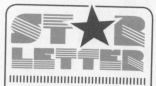

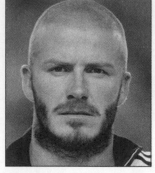

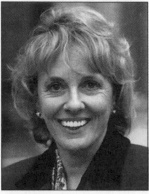

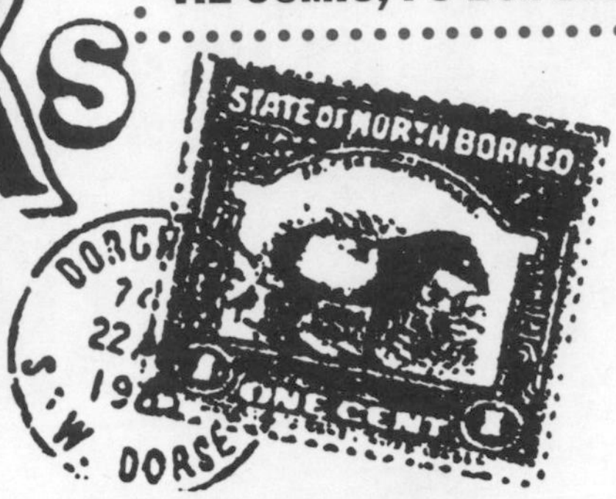

I AM a solicitor, and the other day I saw a man out of my office window standing holding a large sign that read 'GOLF SALE'. Whilst I was working hard on some case files, he was getting paid for just standing there all day, holding a sign and listening to music on his iPod. Honestly, it made me wonder why I bothered going to university to study law.

Hector Lovething
London

ESTHER Rantzen is a wonderful lady, and I will certainly vote for her at the next election. If only she could be cloned so that were 650 of her, one to stand for Parliament in every constituency in Britain. What a fantastic country Britain would be with 650 lovely Esthers at the helm.

Ada Elk
Luton

I AM that old lady who used to appear on *That's Life* each week eating worm pies on the street. Esther Rantzen was always lovely to me and I'd certainly vote for her. Unfortunately, I am no longer on the electoral roll as I died in the 1980s. Of worms.

Annie Oldcrone
Hell

I'VE just written 'David Beckham is a wanker'... with a Sharpie pen!

Ben Dixon
e-mail

THE OTHER day, my son was eating a red lolly when he was run over by a yellow lorry. I have a Jonathan Ross-style speech impediment and the coroner was Chinese. What a carry-on that was!

Rory Laurel
e-mail

THE Australians have their didgeridoos, the Scotch have got bagpipes, the Austrians have Alpine horns... It seems every country is allowed to have a national musical instrument except the English. I dare say we're not allowed one in case it "causes offence" to other nationalities. I wish there was some sort of phrase I could use to end this letter, but I can't think of one.

Charlton Mackrell
Hull

I KNOW zoos have moved on since the old days, and in general this is a trend to be welcomed. But isn't it about time they started putting chimpanzees in little trousers again? I was at the North Wales Mountain Zoo in Colwyn Bay last month, and the arse on one of their chimps turned my stomach.

Farrington Gurney
Leeds

CAN anyone remember whether Sikhs got exempted from having to wear motorcycle helmets in the end? I'm writing a letter to the *Daily Mail* on the subject, and I don't know whether to start it with 'it's a rare victory for common sense' or 'yet another case of political correctness gone mad'.

Nempnett Thrubwell
Chichester

WITH reference to the above query, Section 2A of the 1976 Motor-Cycle Crash Helmets (Religious Exemption) Act allows Sikhs to ride a motorbike or scooter wearing a turban instead of a crash helmet. So the tone of Mr Thrubwell's letter to the *Daily Mail* should be one of outrage about yet another case of political correctness gone mad.

Fifehead Neville
Bristol

WITH reference to the above two letters. I've never seen a Sikh on a motorbike in a turban or a skid-lid. I'm beginning to wonder if it's against the Sikhish religion to ride motorbikes at all.

Langford Budville
Llanfairfechan

IT'S A good job Evel Knievel wasn't a Sikh. I doubt he'd have survived his jump across the Snake River Canyon on a rocket-powered motorbike with just a bit of old cloth wrapped a couple of times round his noggin. It's certainly food for thought.

Thorne St Margaret
Uttoxeter

IT'S political correctness gone mad. What if one of these Sikhs wanted to be a Formula One driver? The safety implications of wearing a turban whilst driving a 250mph+ racing car don't bear thinking about. What if a bit of the turban came undone and got caught in the back wheel? It seems to me that it's one rule for Sikh F1 drivers and another for the rest of us.

Emerson Fittipaldi
Rio

WELL I've never seen a Sikh driving a Formula One car in a turban or a skid-lid. I'm beginning to wonder if it's against the Sikhish religion to drive Formula One cars at all.

Langford Budville
Llanfairfechan

IT SEEMS to me that the authorities have bent over backwards to accommodate the Sikhs and their religion, whilst losing sight of the bigger picture. What if one of them decided he wanted to be an astronaut? I dare say he'd be exempt from having to wear a space helmet too. He wouldn't last five minutes in the oxygen-free vacuum of space. It's political correctness gone mad.

Holcombe Rogus
Tewkesbury

STAR LETTER

IN 2007, when I bought a sofa in the DFS sale, I was told that I would have nothing to pay for the first two years. However, after two years of parties, spilled drinks and food, and the dogs sleeping on it, the sofa is completely wrecked and I've put it in the garden. Yesterday I received a letter from DFS asking for the first installment. Can you believe the cheek of them, demanding payment for a sofa that is only fit for the binmen to take away? They must think I was born yesterday.

Vermintrude Stool
Letchworth

IF SIKHS are allowed not to wear helmets when they're on motorbikes, it's only fair that they should be forced to wear helmets when they're not on motorbikes.

Huish Champflower
Durham

I'M A Hell's Angel and I hate being forced to wear a helmet. Does anyone know how I would go about joining the Sikhs and how much it costs?

Dirtyarse
Hereford Chapter

WHAT about other religions? Would a Jew be allowed to ride a motorbike just wearing one of them big wide-brimmed hats, for example? In my opinion, this would be very dangerous, as it could easily blow off and land on a car windscreen.

Chewton Mendip
Sunderland

PIG in SHIT

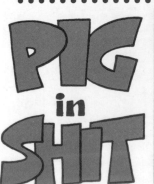

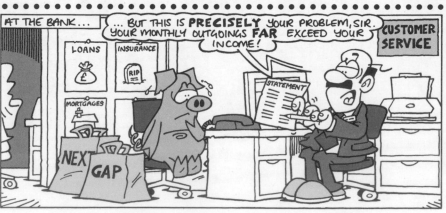

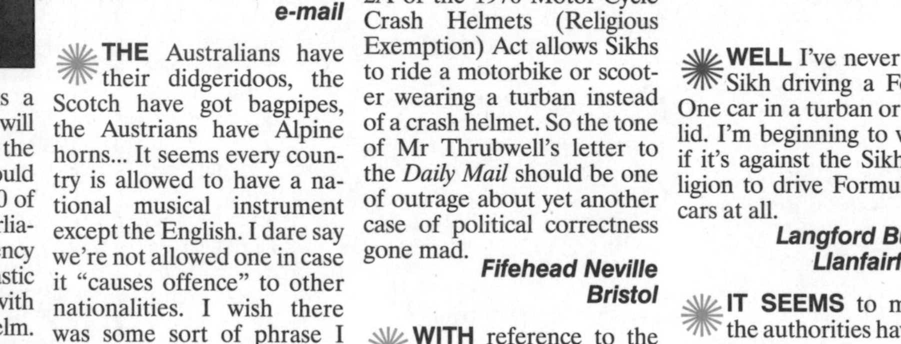

AT THE BANK...
... BUT THIS IS PRECISELY YOUR PROBLEM, SIR. YOUR MONTHLY OUTGOINGS FAR EXCEED YOUR INCOME!
CUSTOMER SERVICE
LOANS
INSURANCE
RIP
MORTGAGES
STATEMENT
NEXT
GAP

Palmer VIZ 09

TOP TIPS

RECREATE the feeling of being a five-year-old on your first day at school by going to your doctor's surgery and having a conversation with the receptionist.

Glen Stone, e-mail

LADIES. Save a fortune on expensive fashion magazines by flicking through the frock sec-

I'M the Archbishop of Canterbury and I must confess that even I am completely confused about religious exemptions from the law that requires all motorcyclists to wear helmets. And that's a shame because I've just bought a Yamaha V-Max and I fancy going for the double ton up the M2 at the weekend whilst wearing my bishop's mitre.

Dr Rowan Williams Canterbury

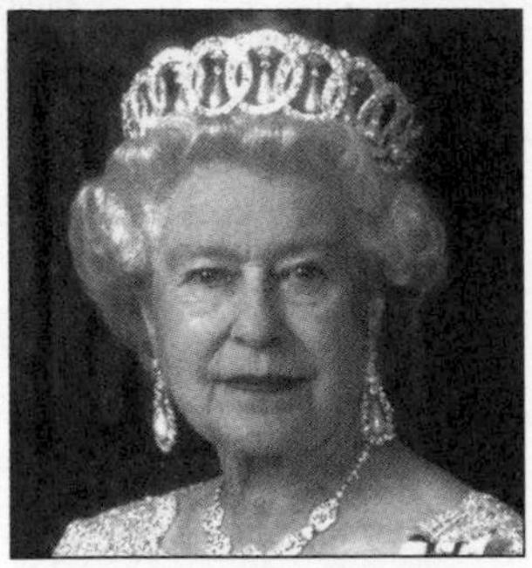

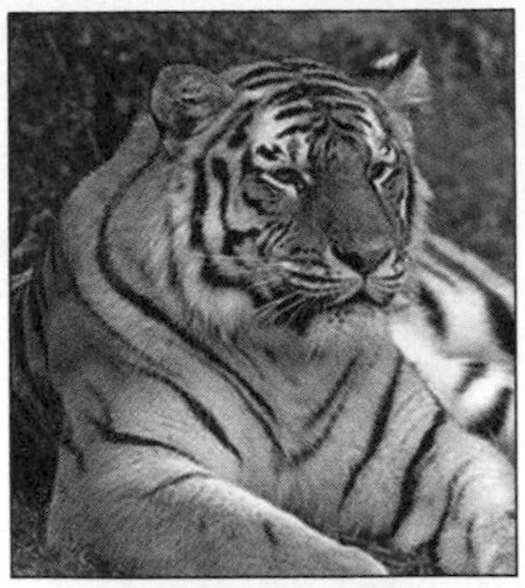

I'VE been a vegetarian for more than 40 years, and I've been an active campaigner for animal rights for longer than I care to remember. However, I woke up the other morning with the unaccountable urge to shoot a tiger. The thought of stalking one of these magnificent beasts through the jungle, lining it up in the cross-hairs of my rifle's telescopic sight, then pulling the trigger and watching it fall to its knees and die right in front of me thrills me like nothing I've ever imagined before.

Rodney Stoke Garforth

THE OTHER day, my husband said he was popping down to the shop to get a newspaper. That was six months ago and he still hasn't returned. You can imagine how hard I'm going to laugh at him when he gets home and I point out that his paper is completely out of date.

Mrs P Latio e-mail

WHILST reading a cheap magazine, I was outraged to read that the Queen keeps 12 corgis. Surely in this recession when everyone is cutting back and tightening their belts, she should set an example, and have all but three of them put down.

Acomb Boy e-mail

I DON'T know why old people keep moaning about having to buy their fruit and veg in metric. A kilogram is more than twice as heavy as a pound, so you get twice as much fruit and veg.

Shepton Beauchamp Dundee

IF YOU type "Hitler was a fucking cunt" into Google using the speech-marks, you get 2 results over the entire internet. If you type "Jeremy Kyle is a fucking cunt" you get 612. I can't do the maths, but that sounds about right.

Captain Henry e-mail

SOME people have speculated that Michael Jackson may be planning to pester children from the other side, but I for one am not worried by this prospect. For if his ghost attempts to touch a minor inappropriately, his hand will merely pass through their underpants, leaving them unmolested. His victims may experience sudden icy coldness around their genitals for a few moments, but that would be the full extent of the experience.

Bertram Millipede Epsom

THE other day I was thinking that I probably wouldn't have sex with the ginger one out of Girls Aloud, but then later on, I completely changed my mind and thought that I probably would. I like busy days like that.

Andrew Turner e-mail

THEY say a picture paints a thousand words. What nonsense! I was looking at a picture of Simon Cowell the other day, and the only words that came to mind were arsehole and cocksucker.

Steven Ranger e-mail

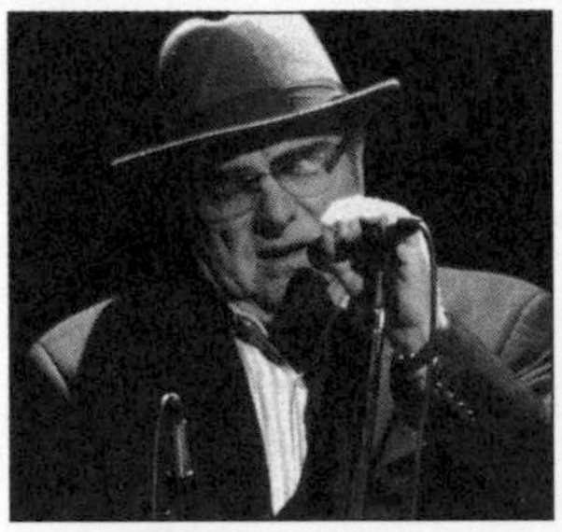

WHILST driving along the other day, I thought I saw Irish pop legend Van Morrison in my rear view mirror. What a fool I felt when I remembered that things appear reversed in mirrors. It was actually a Morrison's van.

Stephen Fuller e-mail

Rude Bishop

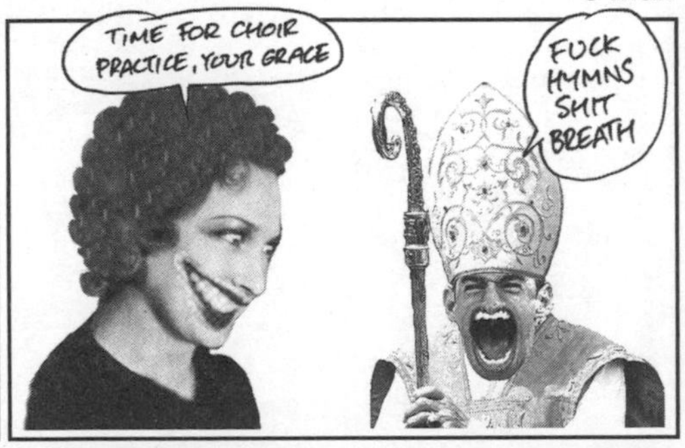
TIME FOR CHOIR PRACTICE, YOUR GRACE
FUCK HYMNS SHIT BREATH

THE NAME OF THE PET

• **WE WENT** to the local dog rescue centre to pick a puppy. The first one we saw was a pathetic little bundle of fur that had been abandoned in a skip on a winter's night. He only had three legs, his coat was all matted and he looked at us with such pleading eyes. However, we picked another dog to take home. We called him Lucky, because we could easily have picked the first one, and then he would have probably got put down.

Mrs L Budville Greenwich

• **OUR** parrot is called Janet Street-Porter because it's pulled all the feathers out of its neck so it looks really scrawny, it's always making this horrible screeching noise and it writes arsehole articles in the Independent on Sunday.

Buckhorn Weston Urmston

• **I'VE GOT** a pet bear that I call Rocky. Not because he's tough like the boxer, it's because I keep him in a cage that is so cramped he can't stand up so he spends all day just sitting on his haunches amongst his own filth, rocking backwards and forwards. He's completely mad.

Kemal Fezborough Turkey

• **MY** neighbour called her cat Mrs Havisham after a character in her favourite book, *Great Expectations* by Charles Dickens. So when I bought a kitten, I called it Madame Ranevskaya after the character in Chekov's *Uncle Vanya*, to let my neighbour know I'm much better read than she is.

Mrs Staple Fitzpaine Winchcombe

• **I'VE GOT** two elephants. One of them is called Jumbo, but the second one doesn't have a name because I can't think of another name for an elephant. I could call it Dumbo, but it hasn't got particularly big ears and anyway, it sounds too much like Jumbo and it might get confusing for the other elephant if I was shouting one of them in for its tea.

Ogwynn Golightly Retford

• **MY** husband keeps bees. As he has ten hives, each of which contains over 50,000 of the insects, it would be ridiculous to attempt to give each of them a name. But he has! I can't remember what all the bees are called, but I do know that one of them is called Buzzby.

Mrs Dewlap Farsley

• **I LEFT** the lid off a jar of jam and a wasp got stuck in it. I decided to keep it as a pet. I call him Paul Weller, not because he was "in the jam", but because he has a stupid fucking haircut with long bits hanging down the side and a ridiculous coconut bit on the top.

Huish Champflower, Dresden

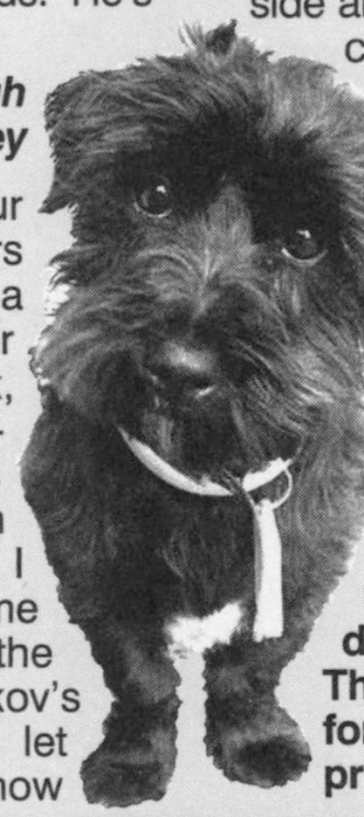

*** HAVE you got a funny or cute story about how your pet got its name? Write in to the usual address and tell us. There's a free dog for every one we print.**

tion of the Littlewoods catalogue and imagining your own facile, pointless editorial.

Martin Christmas, e-mail

INSECT PORNOGRAPHERS. Wasps make excellent shaven-haven actors when making hardcore films for bees.

F Quimby, Merseyside

RESTLESS SOULS. Speed up lengthy ouija board sittings by using text-speak abbreviations.

Mrs D Stokes, Limbo

A SPIDER painted green makes an excellent leafy bit for the top of a tomato.

B Wright, Castleford

A BLOCK of cheese makes an excellent rubber when writing on bread.

Rev J Foucault, Truro

A SOMBRERO in a bin liner makes a trendy 'hands-free' umbrella.

Bernard Eccles, e-mail

HARVEY Nichols customers. When entering the shop, always have a large wad of money in your hand so that the doorman and other staff will see that you can afford their stuff and won't look at you as if you're something that's just dropped off a tramp's arse.

Ted Bartlett, e-mail

CAR drivers. Get away with not wearing a seat belt by painting a diagonal black stripe on all your shirts.

Andy Wright, e-mail

WHEN buying a new bin, always buy two in case one isn't very good and has to be thrown away. That way you will always have something to put it in.

Paul Smeenis, e-mail

ANT & Dec. Have some fun by switching names and seeing if anybody notices or cares.

Dick & Dom, London

FELLAS. Don't waste money on expensive pornographic magazines. Simply ask female friends to pose naked whilst you masturbate.

Neil Keenan, e-mail

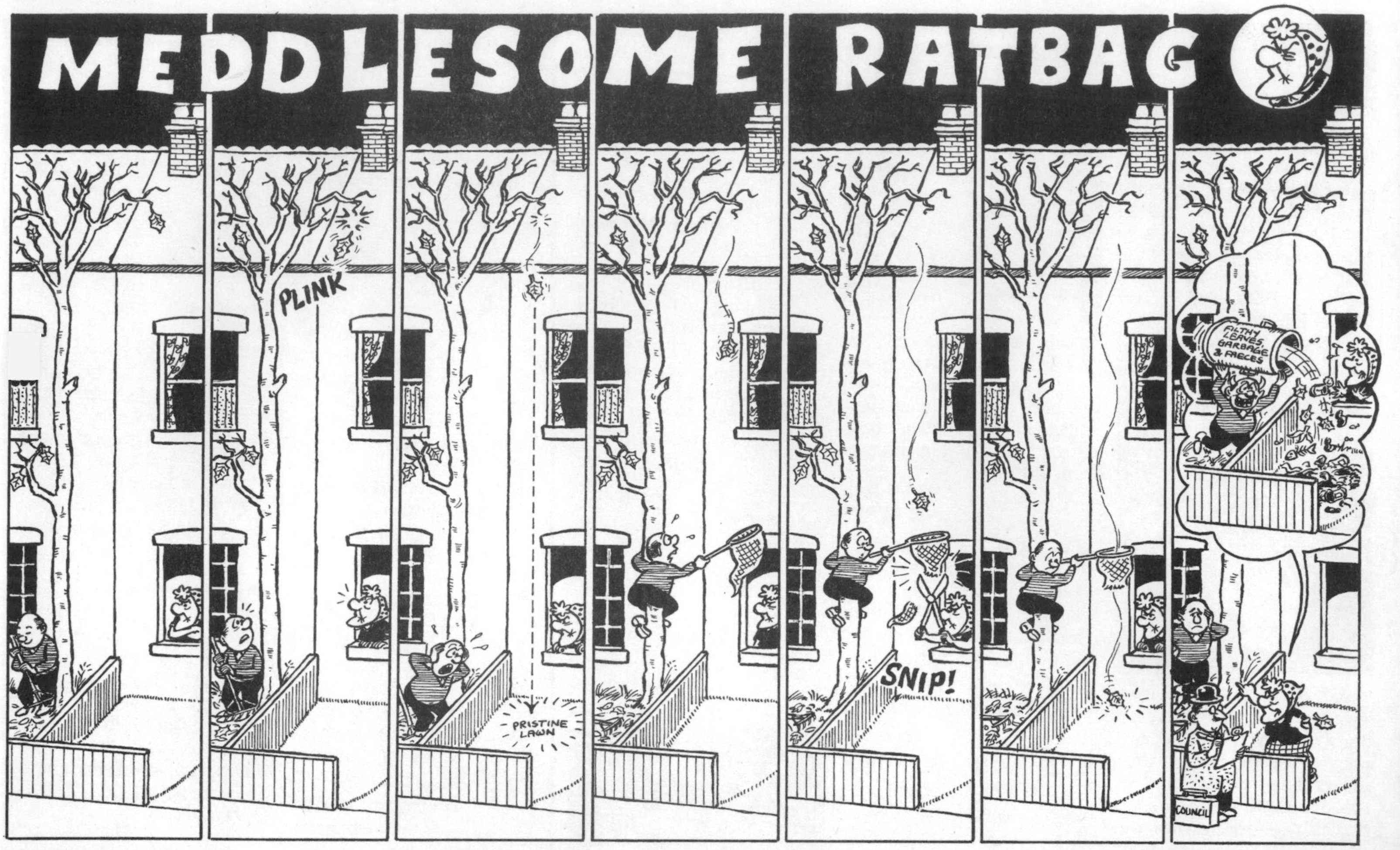
MEDDLESOME RATBAG
PLINK
PRISTINE LAWN
SNIP!
FILTHY LEAVES, GARBAGE & FAECES
COUNCIL

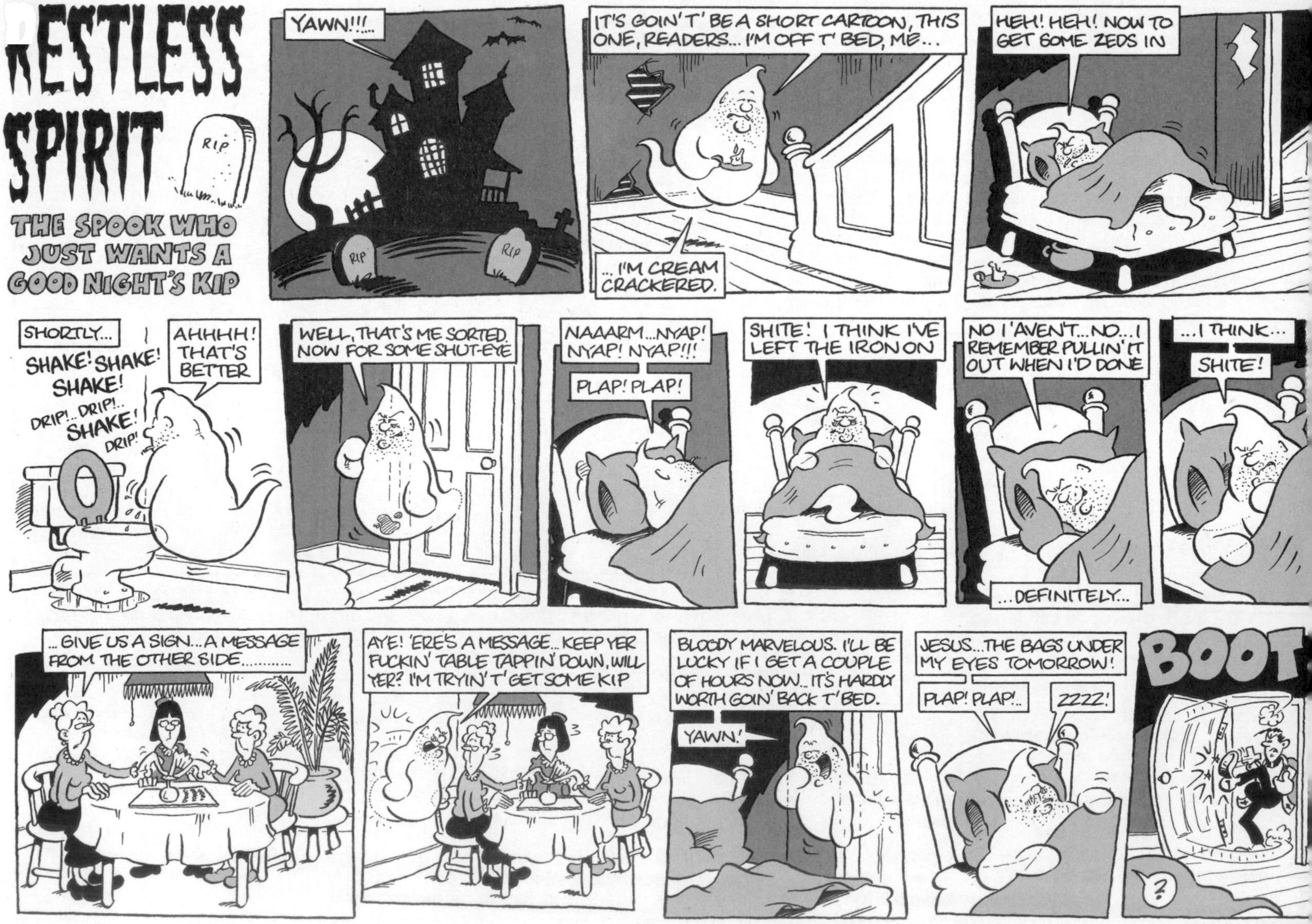
RESTLESS SPIRIT
RIP
THE SPOOK WHO JUST WANTS A GOOD NIGHT'S KIP
YAWN!!!...
RIP
RIP
IT'S GOIN' T' BE A SHORT CARTOON, THIS ONE, READERS... I'M OFF T' BED, ME...
...I'M CREAM CRACKERED.
HEH! HEH! NOW TO GET SOME ZEDS IN
SHORTLY...
SHAKE! SHAKE! SHAKE!
DRIP!.. DRIP!.. SHAKE! DRIP!
AHHHH! THAT'S BETTER
WELL, THAT'S ME SORTED. NOW FOR SOME SHUT-EYE
NAAARM...NYAP! NYAP! NYAP!!!
PLAP! PLAP!
SHITE! I THINK I'VE LEFT THE IRON ON
NO I 'AVEN'T...NO...I REMEMBER PULLIN' IT OUT WHEN I'D DONE
...DEFINITELY...
...I THINK...
SHITE!
...GIVE US A SIGN...A MESSAGE FROM THE OTHER SIDE..........
AYE! 'ERE'S A MESSAGE... KEEP YER FUCKIN' TABLE TAPPIN' DOWN, WILL YER? I'M TRYIN' T' GET SOME KIP
BLOODY MARVELOUS. I'LL BE LUCKY IF I GET A COUPLE OF HOURS NOW... IT'S HARDLY WORTH GOIN' BACK T' BED.
YAWN!
JESUS...THE BAGS UNDER MY EYES TOMORROW!
PLAP! PLAP!..
ZZZZ!
BOOT
?

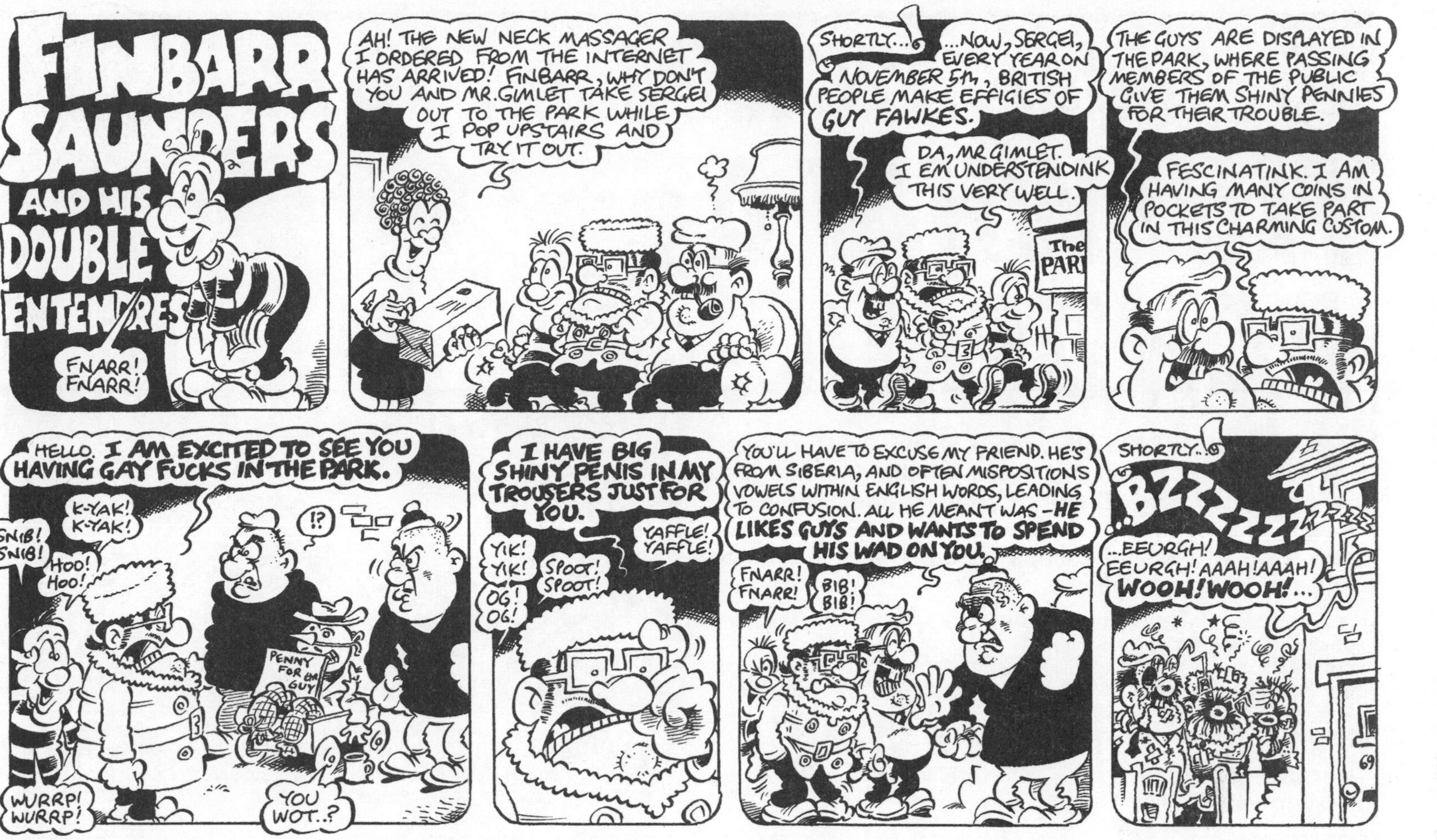
FINBARR SAUNDERS AND HIS DOUBLE ENTENDRES
FNARR! FNARR!
AH! THE NEW NECK MASSAGER I ORDERED FROM THE INTERNET HAS ARRIVED! FINBARR, WHY DON'T YOU AND MR. GIMLET TAKE SERGEI OUT TO THE PARK WHILE I POP UPSTAIRS AND TRY IT OUT.
SHORTLY...
...NOW, SERGEI, EVERY YEAR ON NOVEMBER 5th, BRITISH PEOPLE MAKE EFFIGIES OF GUY FAWKES.
DA, MR GIMLET. I EM UNDERSTENDINK THIS VERY WELL.
The PARK
THE GUYS ARE DISPLAYED IN THE PARK, WHERE PASSING MEMBERS OF THE PUBLIC GIVE THEM SHINY PENNIES FOR THEIR TROUBLE.
FESCINATINK. I AM HAVING MANY COINS IN POCKETS TO TAKE PART IN THIS CHARMING CUSTOM.
HELLO. I AM EXCITED TO SEE YOU HAVING GAY FUCKS IN THE PARK.
K-YAK! K-YAK!
SNIB! SNIB!
HOO! HOO!
!?
PENNY FOR THE GUY
WURRP! WURRP!
YOU WOT..?
I HAVE BIG SHINY PENIS IN MY TROUSERS JUST FOR YOU.
YIK! YIK!
SPOOT! SPOOT!
YAFFLE! YAFFLE!
OG! OG!
YOU'LL HAVE TO EXCUSE MY FRIEND. HE'S FROM SIBERIA, AND OFTEN MISPOSITIONS VOWELS WITHIN ENGLISH WORDS, LEADING TO CONFUSION. ALL HE MEANT WAS - HE LIKES GUYS AND WANTS TO SPEND HIS WAD ON YOU.
FNARR! FNARR!
BIB! BIB!
SHORTLY...
BZZZZZZZ
...EEURGH! EEURGH! AAAH! AAAH! WOOH! WOOH!...
69

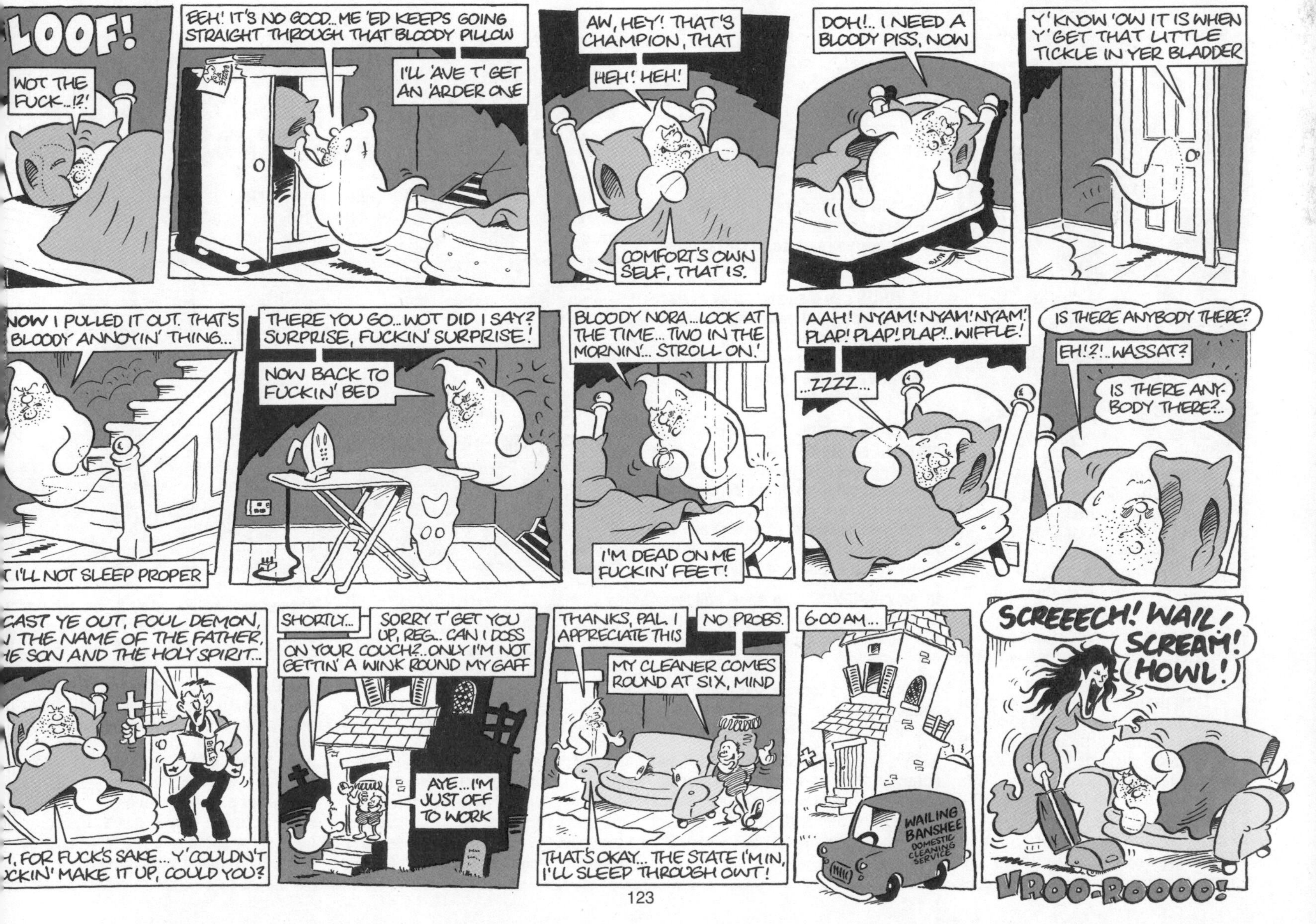
LOOF!
WOT THE FUCK..!?
EEH! IT'S NO GOOD...ME 'ED KEEPS GOING STRAIGHT THROUGH THAT BLOODY PILLOW
I'LL 'AVE T' GET AN 'ARDER ONE
AW, HEY! THAT'S CHAMPION, THAT
HEH! HEH!
COMFORT'S OWN SELF, THAT IS.
DOH!.. I NEED A BLOODY PISS, NOW
Y'KNOW 'OW IT IS WHEN Y'GET THAT LITTLE TICKLE IN YER BLADDER
NOW I PULLED IT OUT. THAT'S BLOODY ANNOYIN' THING...
I'LL NOT SLEEP PROPER
THERE YOU GO... WOT DID I SAY? SURPRISE, FUCKIN' SURPRISE!
NOW BACK TO FUCKIN' BED
BLOODY NORA... LOOK AT THE TIME... TWO IN THE MORNIN'... STROLL ON.
I'M DEAD ON ME FUCKIN' FEET!
AAH! NYAM! NYAM! NYAM! PLAP! PLAP! PLAP!.. WIFFLE!
...ZZZZ...
IS THERE ANYBODY THERE?
EH!?!.. WASSAT?
IS THERE ANY-BODY THERE?..
CAST YE OUT, FOUL DEMON,
N THE NAME OF THE FATHER,
HE SON AND THE HOLY SPIRIT...
H, FOR FUCK'S SAKE... Y'COULDN'T
CKIN' MAKE IT UP, COULD YOU?
SHORTLY...
SORRY T' GET YOU UP, REG... CAN I DOSS ON YOUR COUCH?.. ONLY I'M NOT GETTIN' A WINK ROUND MY GAFF
AYE... I'M JUST OFF TO WORK
THANKS, PAL. I APPRECIATE THIS
NO PROBS.
MY CLEANER COMES ROUND AT SIX, MIND
THAT'S OKAY... THE STATE I'M IN, I'LL SLEEP THROUGH OWT!
6:00 AM...
WAILING BANSHEE DOMESTIC CLEANING SERVICE
SCREEECH! WAIL! SCREAM! HOWL!
VROO-ROOOO!

1U Million...2U Million...3U Million...
FLU! WHAT A PANDEMIC!

THROUGHOUT HISTORY, many plagues have ravaged our shores, each one more deadly than the last. From the Black Death of 1066, to the 1666 Great Plague of London and the Spanish Flu of 1919, as each new wave of deadly infection hit our island, the death tolls ran into the millions.

But these terrible pandemics of the past are set to pale into insignificance in the face of the terrifying mutant virus that is now scything through the British population like an unstoppable combine harvester of death - **MEXICAN SWINE FLU**. The lethal new H1N1 mutant strain leaves the country facing the biggest threat to its survival since the meteorite in Jurassic times that wiped out Britain's dinosaurs.

The danger from this killer virus outbreak is so severe that the average British citizen has as much chance of surviving to see this Christmas as he has of winning the National Lottery and being struck by lightning 20 times on the same day.

There is of course an infinitely small chance that we can survive, but it's a bleak prospect.

But thanks to *Viz*, we can all improve our chances of survival. Because, in collaboration with the Department of Health, we're issuing these handy hints to ward of swine flu. Simply by following these few top tips, you can increase your chances of survival from virtually nil, to

Viz TOP TIPS SPECIAL!

everso slightly more than virtually nil:

THE VIRUS is spread by airborne droplets in sneezes. So avoid anything that makes you sneeze, such as pepper, or burst pillows.

THE VIRUS can also spread by surface contact, so avoid touching anything. If you accidentally touch something, wash your hands immediately afterwards, remembering of course not to touch the taps.

THE RISK of infection is greatest in crowds, so avoid gatherings where large numbers of people are present such as football matches or cinemas. Instead, go for walks on open moorland or isolated beaches, or go and see The Paul Daniels Summer Season Magic Show at the Llandudno Playhouse.

IF ANY FRIENDS who have holidayed in Mexico bring you a sombrero as a gift, boil it thoroughly before putting it on.

IF YOU HAVE a wetsuit and scuba gear, wear them at all times to guarantee you breathe clean, pathogen-free air.

APPLY for a job where you will not come into contact with other people, such as a lighthouse keeper, round the world canoeist or Summer Season box office attendant at the Llandudno Playhouse.

OF COURSE, even following these Top Tips to the letter, the chances are you will still come into contact with the virus and contract swine flu. And with this in mind, the government has set up special dedicated Swine Flu Call Centres staffed not by doctors, but by unemployed people who have been hurriedly trained to tick a series of boxes on a checklist.

However, in the panic there is a danger that so many people will call the helpline with illnesses that turn out not to be Swine Flu, such as piles, that the system will become overloaded. So before YOU call, here is a simple checklist that you can use to decide whether you're suffering from swine flu or piles.

SWINE FLU or HAEMORRHOIDS
What have YOU got?

1. You wake up one morning feeling under the weather. What exactly are your symptoms?

  a. *Headache, high temperature, feverishness, aching joints and muscles, sore throat.*

  b. *Pain like a red hot poker stuck up your bottom and blood on your toilet tissue.*

2. You are wiping your nipsy after a sit down visit. Can you feel any extremely tender grape-like structures hanging out of your anus?

  a. *No.*

  b. *Yes.*

3. What do you find is the best way of relieving your current symptoms?

  a. *Lemsip.*

  b. *Sitting on a large, inflatable doughnut with an ice-cube up your arse.*

How did FLU do? •••••••••••••••••••••••••••••••

Mostly a's: Oh, dear! The bad news is you've got Mexican Swine Flu and you're about to die a horrible death, drowning in your own blood-streaked sputum. The good news is, you've not got piles. *Mostly b's:* The good news is, you haven't got Mexican Swine Flu, so are safe for the moment. The bad news is, you've got piles. *A mixture of a's and b's:* You've got Mexican Swine Flu AND piles.

So you've done the test *(above)* and you've definitely got fatal Mexican Swine Flu. Now what? Well, the simple answer to that question is, that you're going to die. But there are still things you can do to make life a bit easier for the survivors:

AT BEDTIME, tie a luggage label around you big toe with your name and postcode on it, and go to bed in your best suit with your arms folded across your chest. Try to compose your face into a peaceful expression before you nod off. Sleeping downstairs will make it easier for surviving family members to drag your corpse into the street in the morning.

THE ONLY way to stop yourself sneezing and passing the bacteria onto other members of your family is to press your finger up under your nose. When you need both hands - for example when holding binoculars, fondling your wife's breasts or playing a banjo - use a finger-sized carrot or Ikea pencil in the same position, secured with two elastic bands round the back of your ears.

FREE!

Protect yourself with Health Secretary and Swine Flu expert ANDY BURNHAM MP's

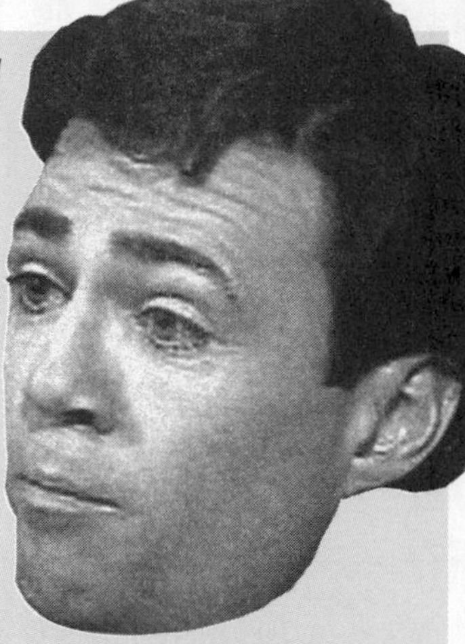

Snack 'n' Sip 'n' Smoke 'n' Survive

Anti~Swine Flu Protection Mask

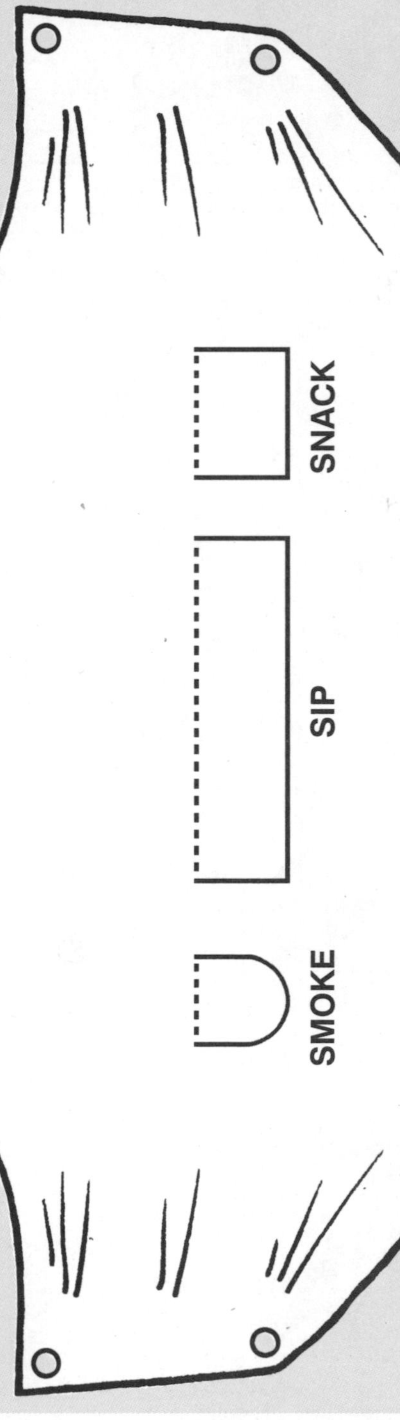

SNACK
SIP
SMOKE

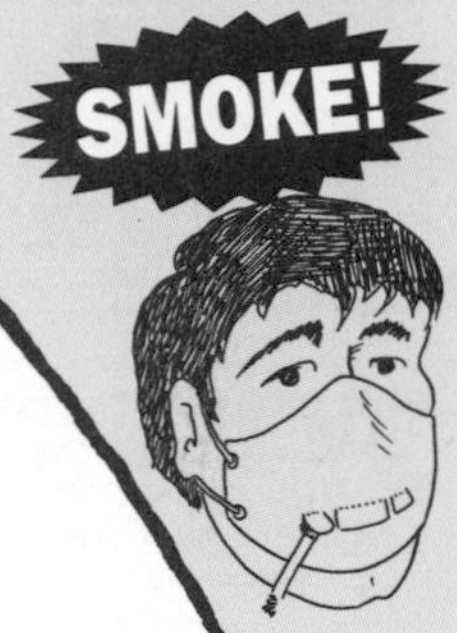

SMOKE!

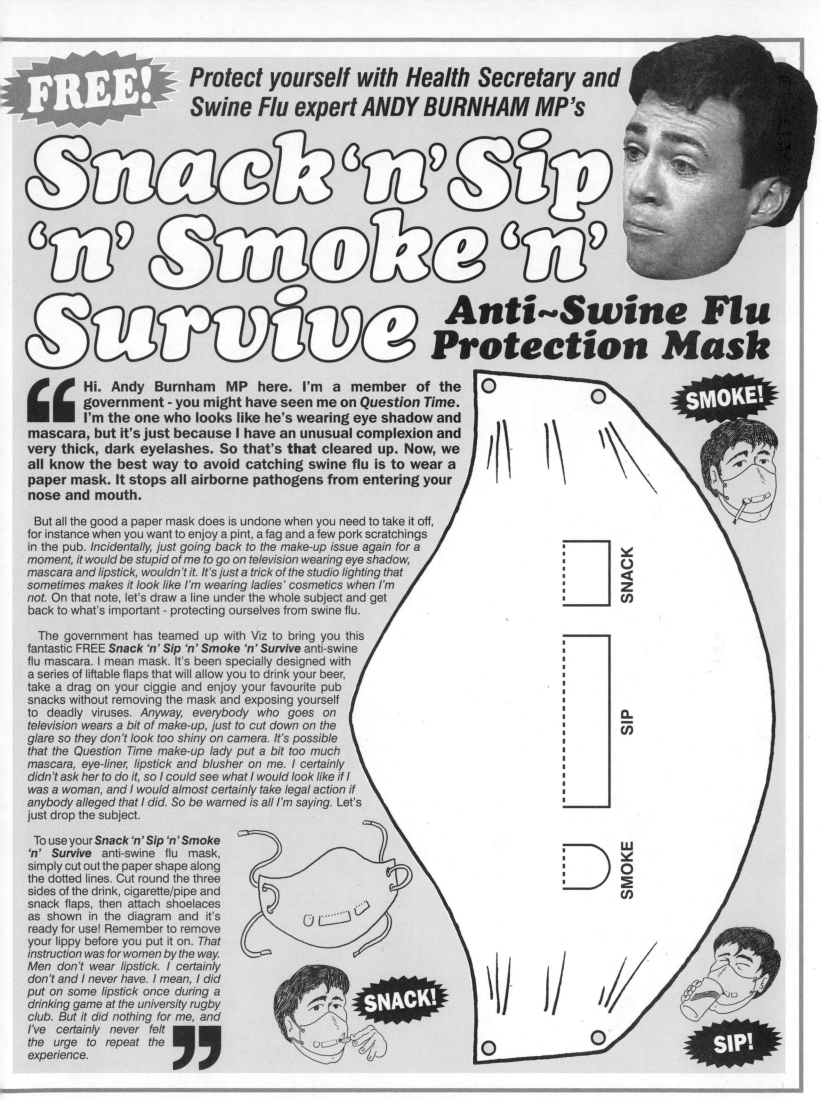

"Hi. Andy Burnham MP here. I'm a member of the government - you might have seen me on *Question Time*. I'm the one who looks like he's wearing eye shadow and mascara, but it's just because I have an unusual complexion and very thick, dark eyelashes. So that's that cleared up. Now, we all know the best way to avoid catching swine flu is to wear a paper mask. It stops all airborne pathogens from entering your nose and mouth.

But all the good a paper mask does is undone when you need to take it off, for instance when you want to enjoy a pint, a fag and a few pork scratchings in the pub. *Incidentally, just going back to the make-up issue again for a moment, it would be stupid of me to go on television wearing eye shadow, mascara and lipstick, wouldn't it. It's just a trick of the studio lighting that sometimes makes it look like I'm wearing ladies' cosmetics when I'm not.* On that note, let's draw a line under the whole subject and get back to what's important - protecting ourselves from swine flu.

The government has teamed up with Viz to bring you this fantastic FREE ***Snack 'n' Sip 'n' Smoke 'n' Survive*** anti-swine flu mascara. I mean mask. It's been specially designed with a series of liftable flaps that will allow you to drink your beer, take a drag on your ciggie and enjoy your favourite pub snacks without removing the mask and exposing yourself to deadly viruses. *Anyway, everybody who goes on television wears a bit of make-up, just to cut down on the glare so they don't look too shiny on camera. It's possible that the Question Time make-up lady put a bit too much mascara, eye-liner, lipstick and blusher on me. I certainly didn't ask her to do it, so I could see what I would look like if I was a woman, and I would almost certainly take legal action if anybody alleged that I did. So be warned is all I'm saying.* Let's just drop the subject.

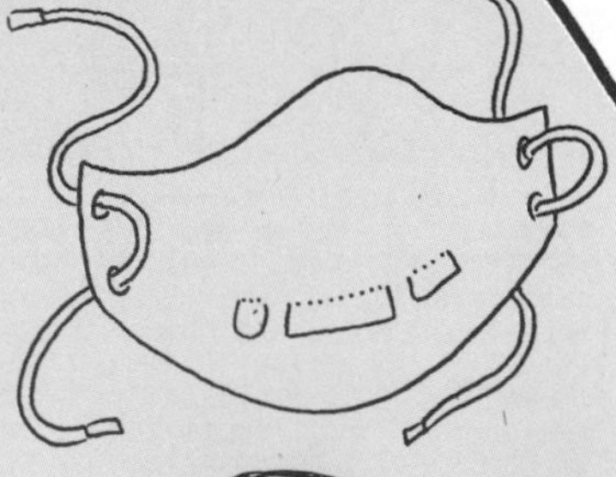

To use your ***Snack 'n' Sip 'n' Smoke 'n' Survive*** anti-swine flu mask, simply cut out the paper shape along the dotted lines. Cut round the three sides of the drink, cigarette/pipe and snack flaps, then attach shoelaces as shown in the diagram and it's ready for use! Remember to remove your lippy before you put it on. *That instruction was for women by the way. Men don't wear lipstick. I certainly don't and I never have. I mean, I did put on some lipstick once during a drinking game at the university rugby club. But it did nothing for me, and I've certainly never felt the urge to repeat the experience.*"

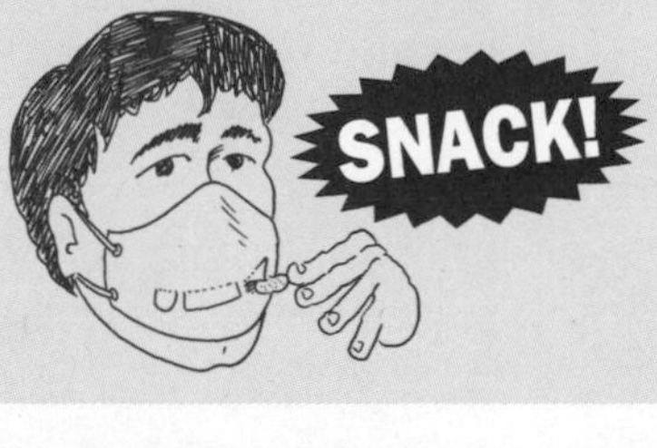

SNACK!

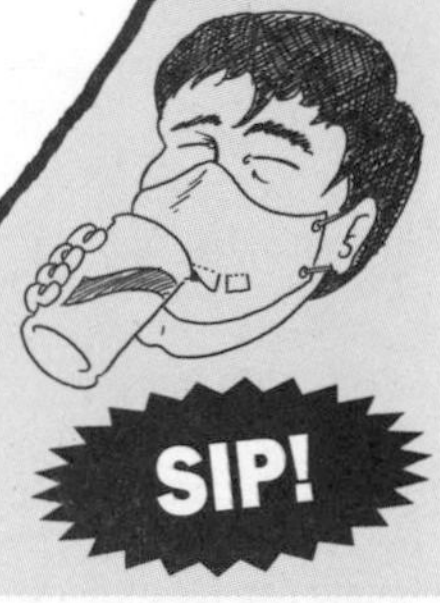

SIP!

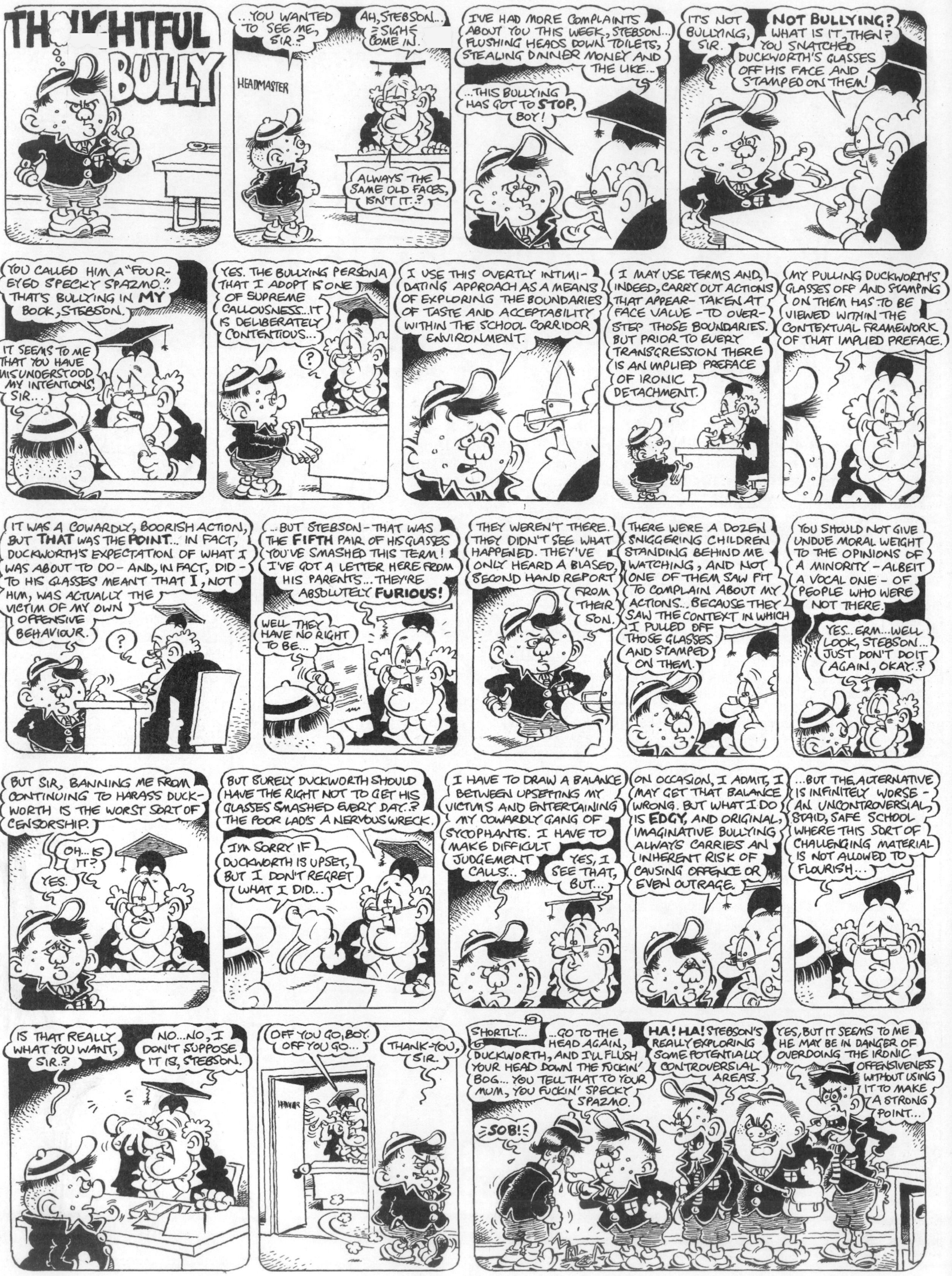
THOUGHTFUL BULLY
...YOU WANTED TO SEE ME, SIR..?
AH, STEBSON... ≡SIGH≡ COME IN.
HEADMASTER
ALWAYS THE SAME OLD FACES, ISN'T IT..?
I'VE HAD MORE COMPLAINTS ABOUT YOU THIS WEEK, STEBSON... FLUSHING HEADS DOWN TOILETS, STEALING DINNER MONEY AND THE LIKE...
...THIS BULLYING HAS GOT TO STOP, BOY!
IT'S NOT BULLYING, SIR.
NOT BULLYING? WHAT IS IT, THEN? YOU SNATCHED DUCKWORTH'S GLASSES OFF HIS FACE AND STAMPED ON THEM!
YOU CALLED HIM A "FOUR-EYED SPECKY SPAZMO..!" THAT'S BULLYING IN MY BOOK, STEBSON.
IT SEEMS TO ME THAT YOU HAVE MISUNDERSTOOD MY INTENTIONS, SIR...
YES. THE BULLYING PERSONA THAT I ADOPT IS ONE OF SUPREME CALLOUSNESS... IT IS DELIBERATELY CONTENTIOUS...
?
I USE THIS OVERTLY INTIMIDATING APPROACH AS A MEANS OF EXPLORING THE BOUNDARIES OF TASTE AND ACCEPTABILITY WITHIN THE SCHOOL CORRIDOR ENVIRONMENT.
I MAY USE TERMS AND, INDEED, CARRY OUT ACTIONS THAT APPEAR - TAKEN AT FACE VALUE - TO OVERSTEP THOSE BOUNDARIES. BUT PRIOR TO EVERY TRANSGRESSION THERE IS AN IMPLIED PREFACE OF IRONIC DETACHMENT.
MY PULLING DUCKWORTH'S GLASSES OFF AND STAMPING ON THEM HAS TO BE VIEWED WITHIN THE CONTEXTUAL FRAMEWORK OF THAT IMPLIED PREFACE.
IT WAS A COWARDLY, BOORISH ACTION, BUT THAT WAS THE POINT... IN FACT, DUCKWORTH'S EXPECTATION OF WHAT I WAS ABOUT TO DO - AND, IN FACT, DID - TO HIS GLASSES MEANT THAT I, NOT HIM, WAS ACTUALLY THE VICTIM OF MY OWN OFFENSIVE BEHAVIOUR.
?
...BUT STEBSON - THAT WAS THE FIFTH PAIR OF HIS GLASSES YOU'VE SMASHED THIS TERM! I'VE GOT A LETTER HERE FROM HIS PARENTS... THEY'RE ABSOLUTELY FURIOUS!
WELL THEY HAVE NO RIGHT TO BE...
THEY WEREN'T THERE. THEY DIDN'T SEE WHAT HAPPENED. THEY'VE ONLY HEARD A BIASED, SECOND HAND REPORT FROM THEIR SON.
THERE WERE A DOZEN SNIGGERING CHILDREN STANDING BEHIND ME WATCHING, AND NOT ONE OF THEM SAW FIT TO COMPLAIN ABOUT MY ACTIONS... BECAUSE THEY SAW THE CONTEXT IN WHICH I PULLED OFF THOSE GLASSES AND STAMPED ON THEM.
YOU SHOULD NOT GIVE UNDUE MORAL WEIGHT TO THE OPINIONS OF A MINORITY - ALBEIT A VOCAL ONE - OF PEOPLE WHO WERE NOT THERE.
YES... ERM... WELL LOOK, STEBSON... JUST DON'T DO IT AGAIN, OKAY..?
BUT SIR, BANNING ME FROM CONTINUING TO HARASS DUCKWORTH IS THE WORST SORT OF CENSORSHIP.
OH... IS IT?
YES.
BUT SURELY DUCKWORTH SHOULD HAVE THE RIGHT NOT TO GET HIS GLASSES SMASHED EVERY DAY..? THE POOR LAD'S A NERVOUS WRECK.
I'M SORRY IF DUCKWORTH IS UPSET, BUT I DON'T REGRET WHAT I DID...
I HAVE TO DRAW A BALANCE BETWEEN UPSETTING MY VICTIMS AND ENTERTAINING MY COWARDLY GANG OF SYCOPHANTS. I HAVE TO MAKE DIFFICULT JUDGEMENT CALLS...
YES, I SEE THAT, BUT...
ON OCCASION, I ADMIT, I MAY GET THAT BALANCE WRONG. BUT WHAT I DO IS EDGY, AND ORIGINAL. IMAGINATIVE BULLYING ALWAYS CARRIES AN INHERENT RISK OF CAUSING OFFENCE OR EVEN OUTRAGE.
...BUT THE ALTERNATIVE IS INFINITELY WORSE - AN UNCONTROVERSIAL, STAID, SAFE SCHOOL WHERE THIS SORT OF CHALLENGING MATERIAL IS NOT ALLOWED TO FLOURISH...
IS THAT REALLY WHAT YOU WANT, SIR..?
NO... NO, I DON'T SUPPOSE IT IS, STEBSON.
OFF YOU GO, BOY. OFF YOU GO...
THANK-YOU, SIR.
SHORTLY...
...GO TO THE HEAD AGAIN, DUCKWORTH, AND I'LL FLUSH YOUR HEAD DOWN THE FUCKIN' BOG... YOU TELL THAT TO YOUR MUM, YOU FUCKIN' SPECKY SPAZMO.
SOB!
HA! HA! STEBSON'S REALLY EXPLORING SOME POTENTIALLY CONTROVERSIAL AREAS.
YES, BUT IT SEEMS TO ME HE MAY BE IN DANGER OF OVERDOING THE IRONIC OFFENSIVENESS WITHOUT USING IT TO MAKE A STRONG POINT...

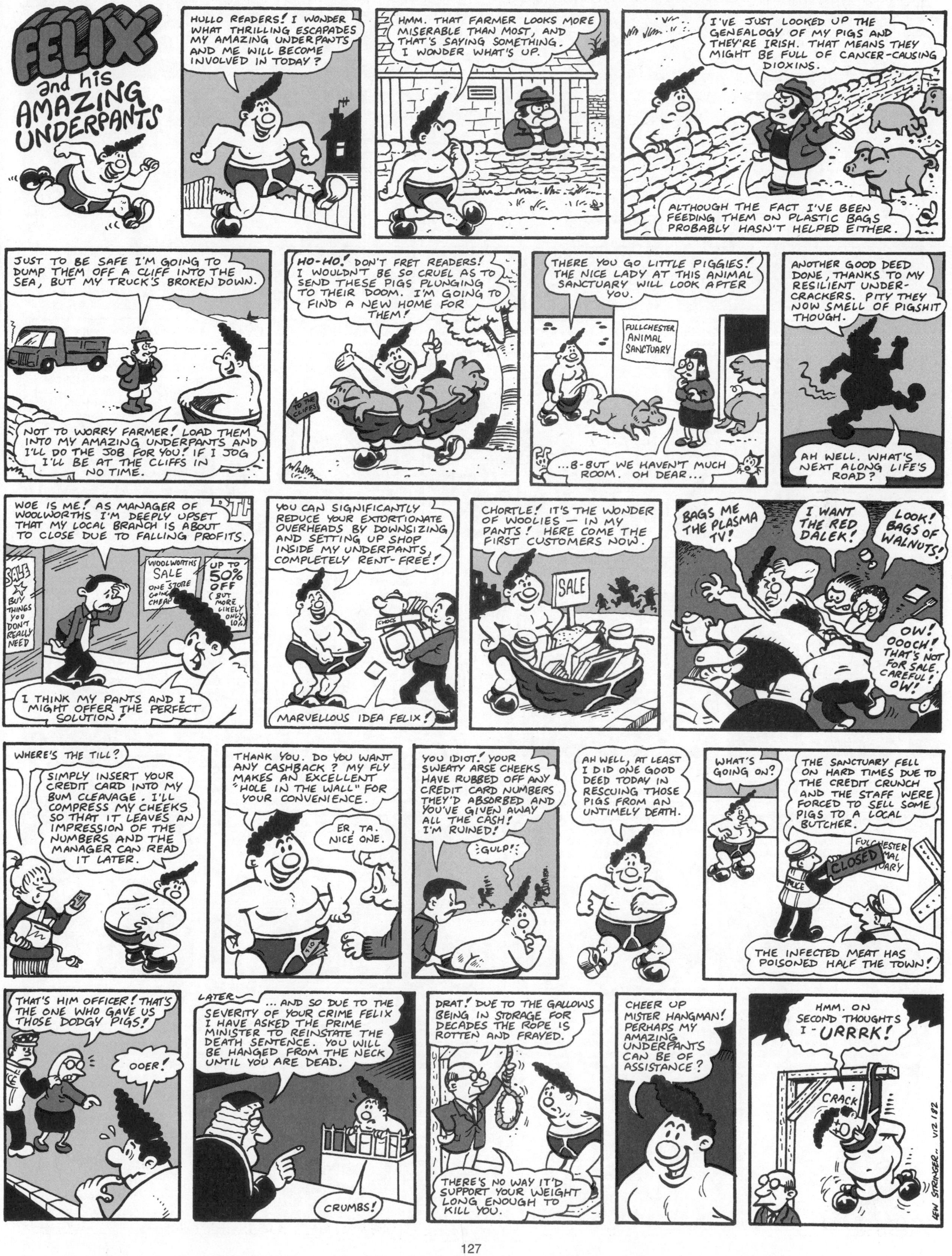
FELIX and his AMAZING UNDERPANTS
HULLO READERS! I WONDER WHAT THRILLING ESCAPADES MY AMAZING UNDERPANTS AND ME WILL BECOME INVOLVED IN TODAY?
HMM. THAT FARMER LOOKS MORE MISERABLE THAN MOST, AND THAT'S SAYING SOMETHING. I WONDER WHAT'S UP.
I'VE JUST LOOKED UP THE GENEALOGY OF MY PIGS AND THEY'RE IRISH. THAT MEANS THEY MIGHT BE FULL OF CANCER-CAUSING DIOXINS.
ALTHOUGH THE FACT I'VE BEEN FEEDING THEM ON PLASTIC BAGS PROBABLY HASN'T HELPED EITHER.
JUST TO BE SAFE I'M GOING TO DUMP THEM OFF A CLIFF INTO THE SEA, BUT MY TRUCK'S BROKEN DOWN.
NOT TO WORRY FARMER! LOAD THEM INTO MY AMAZING UNDERPANTS AND I'LL DO THE JOB FOR YOU! IF I JOG I'LL BE AT THE CLIFFS IN NO TIME.
HO-HO! DON'T FRET READERS! I WOULDN'T BE SO CRUEL AS TO SEND THESE PIGS PLUNGING TO THEIR DOOM. I'M GOING TO FIND A NEW HOME FOR THEM!
TO THE CLIFFS
THERE YOU GO LITTLE PIGGIES! THE NICE LADY AT THIS ANIMAL SANCTUARY WILL LOOK AFTER YOU.
FULLCHESTER ANIMAL SANCTUARY
...B-BUT WE HAVEN'T MUCH ROOM. OH DEAR...
ANOTHER GOOD DEED DONE, THANKS TO MY RESILIENT UNDER-CRACKERS. PITY THEY NOW SMELL OF PIGSHIT THOUGH.
AH WELL. WHAT'S NEXT ALONG LIFE'S ROAD?
WOE IS ME! AS MANAGER OF WOOLWORTHS I'M DEEPLY UPSET THAT MY LOCAL BRANCH IS ABOUT TO CLOSE DUE TO FALLING PROFITS.
SALE BUY THINGS YOU DON'T REALLY NEED
WOOLWORTHS SALE ONE STORE GOING CHEAP
UP TO 50% OFF (BUT MORE LIKELY ONLY 10%)
I THINK MY PANTS AND I MIGHT OFFER THE PERFECT SOLUTION.
YOU CAN SIGNIFICANTLY REDUCE YOUR EXTORTIONATE OVERHEADS BY DOWNSIZING AND SETTING UP SHOP INSIDE MY UNDERPANTS, COMPLETELY RENT-FREE!
CHOCS
MARVELLOUS IDEA FELIX!
CHORTLE! IT'S THE WONDER OF WOOLIES — IN MY PANTS! HERE COME THE FIRST CUSTOMERS NOW.
SALE
BAGS ME THE PLASMA TV!
I WANT THE RED DALEK!
LOOK! BAGS OF WALNUTS!
OW! OOOCH! THAT'S NOT FOR SALE. CAREFUL! OW!
WHERE'S THE TILL?
SIMPLY INSERT YOUR CREDIT CARD INTO MY BUM CLEAVAGE. I'LL COMPRESS MY CHEEKS SO THAT IT LEAVES AN IMPRESSION OF THE NUMBERS AND THE MANAGER CAN READ IT LATER.
THANK YOU. DO YOU WANT ANY CASHBACK? MY FLY MAKES AN EXCELLENT "HOLE IN THE WALL" FOR YOUR CONVENIENCE.
ER, TA. NICE ONE.
YOU IDIOT! YOUR SWEATY ARSE CHEEKS HAVE RUBBED OFF ANY CREDIT CARD NUMBERS THEY'D ABSORBED AND YOU'VE GIVEN AWAY ALL THE CASH! I'M RUINED!
GULP!
AH WELL, AT LEAST I DID ONE GOOD DEED TODAY IN RESCUING THOSE PIGS FROM AN UNTIMELY DEATH.
WHAT'S GOING ON?
THE SANCTUARY FELL ON HARD TIMES DUE TO THE CREDIT CRUNCH AND THE STAFF WERE FORCED TO SELL SOME PIGS TO A LOCAL BUTCHER.
CLOSED
POLICE
THE INFECTED MEAT HAS POISONED HALF THE TOWN!
THAT'S HIM OFFICER! THAT'S THE ONE WHO GAVE US THOSE DODGY PIGS!
OOER!
LATER—
...AND SO DUE TO THE SEVERITY OF YOUR CRIME FELIX I HAVE ASKED THE PRIME MINISTER TO REINSTATE THE DEATH SENTENCE. YOU WILL BE HANGED FROM THE NECK UNTIL YOU ARE DEAD.
CRUMBS!
DRAT! DUE TO THE GALLOWS BEING IN STORAGE FOR DECADES THE ROPE IS ROTTEN AND FRAYED.
THERE'S NO WAY IT'D SUPPORT YOUR WEIGHT LONG ENOUGH TO KILL YOU.
CHEER UP MISTER HANGMAN! PERHAPS MY AMAZING UNDERPANTS CAN BE OF ASSISTANCE?
HMM. ON SECOND THOUGHTS I- URRRK!
CRACK
LEW STRINGER.. VIZ 182

Mrs Brady Old Lady

...SO THAT'S AN OVERALL LOSS FOR THE BLUES OF £198... LET'S SEE IF THE REDS CAN DO ANY BETTER...

...MUNCH! MUNCH! MUNCH!

...NOW YOU PAID £75 FOR THIS 19th CENTURY ENAMELLED SNUFFBOX. I WONDER WHAT IT WILL MAKE AT AUCTION...

EEEEEH! MUNCH! MUNCH! THE PRICE OF 19th CENTURY ENAMELLED SNUFFBOXES THESE DAYS...

CLINK! RATTLE!

TEA'S UP, ADA.

YOU TOOK YOUR RUDDY TIME ABOUT IT, DOLLY. WHERE DID YOU GO FOR IT... RUDDY CHINA..?

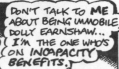

I'M SORRY, ADA, I'M NOT AS FLEET OF FOOT AS I WAS BEFORE ME STROKE.

DON'T TALK TO ME ABOUT BEING IMMOBILE, DOLLY EARNSHAW... I'M THE ONE WHO'S ON INCAPACITY BENEFITS.

AND YOU DON'T GET THEM BY BEING ABLE TO TROT IN AND OUT THE RUDDY KITCHEN MAKING CUPS OF TEA WILLY-NILLY.

..WILLY-NILLY, YES.

SPLOOT!
RUDDY 'ECK, DOLLY! THAT'S STRONG!

=SLOOP!=

AYE, SORRY ADA. ONLY I HAD ANOTHER LITTLE STROKE WHILE IT WERE MASHING... THE POT WERE WELL STEWED BY THE TIME I COME ROUND ON THE LINO.

LINO!? THAT'S MARMOLEUM IS THAT, I'LL HAVE YOU KNOW, YOU CHEEKY TROLLOP.

EEH, SORRY ADA. IT'S NICE. LOVELY MARBLING.

..'SPECIALLY FROM CLOSE UP.

YES. IT'S PROPER LINO, YOU KNOW. NONE OF THIS MARMOLEUM RUBBISH. FORTY-NINE POUND A METRE, THAT WERE, DOLLY.

EEH! FANCY.

MIND, I TOLD 'EM THEY COULD TICKLE WITH THEIR RUDDY FOREIGN MEASUREMENTS. METRES INDEED..! I HAD THEM CUT IT IN PROPER YARDS.

THE MAN FROM WALTER WALLS SAYS "MRS BRADY," HE SAYS, HE SAYS "MRS BRADY," HE SAYS, "IF YOU WANT IT IN YARDS, YOU SHALL HAVE IT IN YARDS."

SHORTBREAD, ADA?

EEURGH! YOU'VE GIVE ME A FINGER, DOLLY, AND I WANTED PETTICOAT TAILS.

SHORTBREAD'S NOT SHORTBREAD LESS IT'S IN A PETTICOAT TAIL.

SORRY ADA. IT'S ALL THEY HAD AT THE SPAR, AND THAT'S AS FAR AS I CAN MANAGE ON ME FRAME.

EEH, YOU'RE LUCKY TO GET THAT FAR. IF YOU WAS HOUSE-BOUND LIKE ME, YOU'D HAVE SOMETHING TO COMPLAIN ABOUT. I'VE NOT BEEN BEYOND THESE FOUR WALLS THESE FIVE WEEK GONE, DOLLY.

PRISONER I AM, DOLLY. PRISONER IN ME OWN HOME...

I'M DONE ON ME PAN, BY THE WAY, DOLLY. SO IF YOU'D JUST...

I'LL GET IT FOR YOU, ADA.

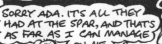

OOH! THAT'S A BEAUTY, THAT ONE. THERE'S NOWT WRONG WITH YOUR MOTIONS.

WHAT DO YOU MEAN, NOWT WRONG!? I'VE BEEN SAT ON THAT PAN ALL MORNING, TRYING.

IS IT YOUR SPASTIC BOWEL THAT'S INCAPACITATED YOU, ADA..?

NO. THAT'S JUST A SYMPTOM. DR. CHAKRABORTY SAYS HE DOESN'T KNOW WHAT IT IS. MEDICAL ENIGMA, I AM.

THEY'RE GOING TO HAVE TO RE-WRITE THE TEXT-BOOKS.

WHO'S THAT, ADA?

KNOCK-KNOCK!

THAT'LL BE THE MAN OFF THE BENEFITS COME TO DO ME ROUTINE CASE ASSESSMENT.

OOH, THAT'S NICE.

SHIFT YOURSELF, DOLLY. HE'S A BUSY MAN.

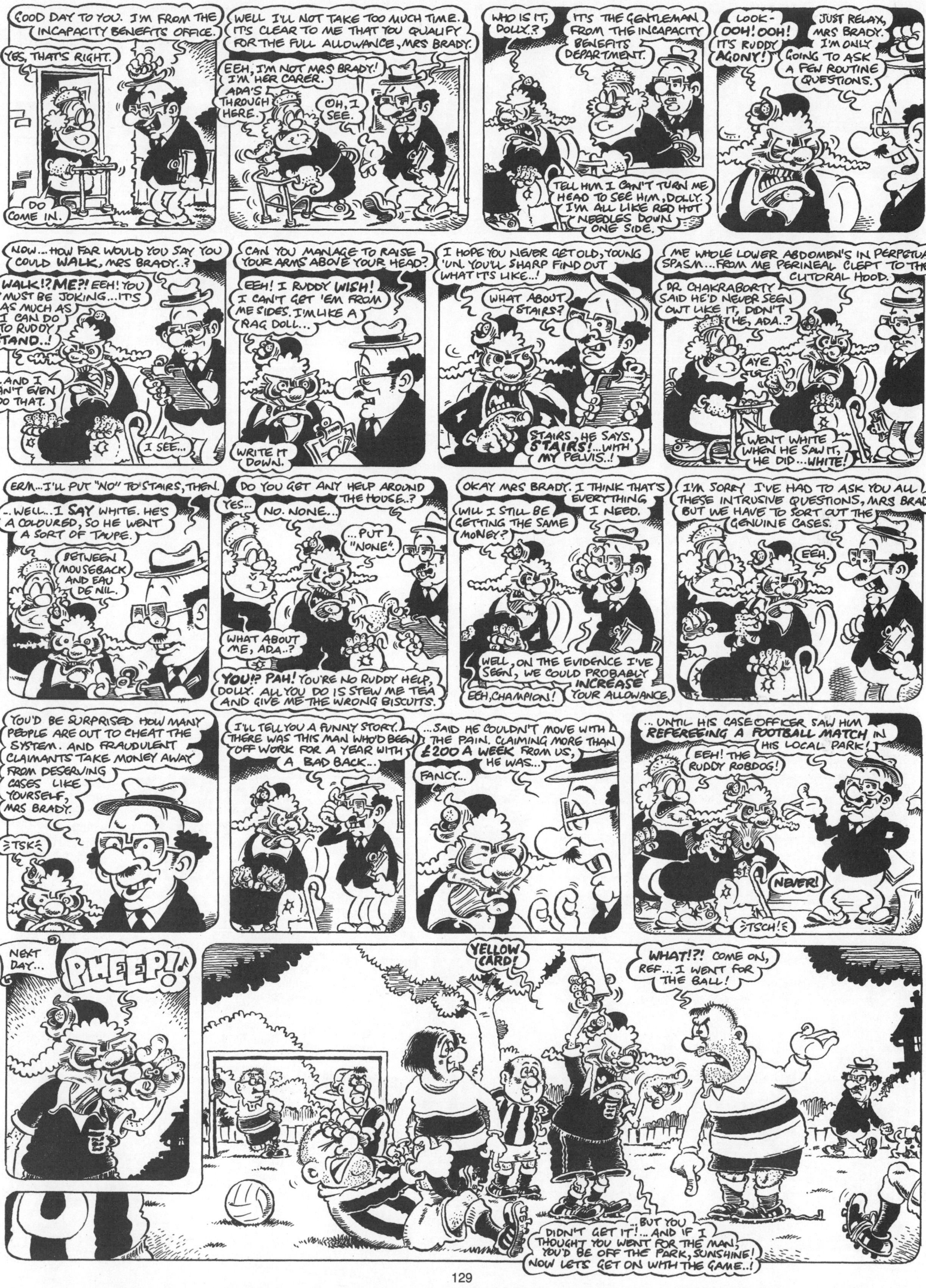
GOOD DAY TO YOU. I'M FROM THE INCAPACITY BENEFITS OFFICE.
YES, THAT'S RIGHT.
DO COME IN.
WELL I'LL NOT TAKE TOO MUCH TIME. IT'S CLEAR TO ME THAT YOU QUALIFY FOR THE FULL ALLOWANCE, MRS BRADY.
EEH, I'M NOT MRS BRADY! I'M HER CARER.
ADA'S THROUGH HERE.
OH, I SEE.
WHO IS IT, DOLLY..?
IT'S THE GENTLEMAN FROM THE INCAPACITY BENEFITS DEPARTMENT.
TELL HIM I CAN'T TURN ME HEAD TO SEE HIM, DOLLY. I'M ALL LIKE RED HOT NEEDLES DOWN ONE SIDE.
LOOK - OOH! OOH! IT'S RUDDY AGONY!
JUST RELAX, MRS BRADY. I'M ONLY GOING TO ASK A FEW ROUTINE QUESTIONS.
NOW... HOW FAR WOULD YOU SAY YOU COULD WALK, MRS BRADY..?
WALK!? ME?! EEH! YOU MUST BE JOKING... IT'S AS MUCH AS I CAN DO TO RUDDY STAND..!
...AND I CAN'T EVEN DO THAT.
I SEE...
CAN YOU MANAGE TO RAISE YOUR ARMS ABOVE YOUR HEAD?
EEH! I RUDDY WISH! I CAN'T GET 'EM FROM ME SIDES. I'M LIKE A RAG DOLL...
WRITE IT DOWN.
I HOPE YOU NEVER GET OLD, YOUNG 'UN. YOU'LL SHARP FIND OUT WHAT IT'S LIKE...!
WHAT ABOUT STAIRS?
STAIRS, HE SAYS, STAIRS!... WITH MY PELVIS..!
ME WHOLE LOWER ABDOMEN'S IN PERPETUAL SPASM... FROM ME PERINEAL CLEFT TO THE CLITORAL HOOD.
DR CHAKRABORTY SAID HE'D NEVER SEEN OWT LIKE IT, DIDN'T HE, ADA..?
AYE.
WENT WHITE WHEN HE SAW IT, HE DID... WHITE!
ERM... I'LL PUT "NO" TO STAIRS, THEN.
...WELL... I SAY WHITE. HE'S A COLOURED, SO HE WENT A SORT OF TAUPE.
BETWEEN MOUSEBACK AND EAU DE NIL.
DO YOU GET ANY HELP AROUND THE HOUSE..?
YES...
NO. NONE...
...PUT "NONE".
WHAT ABOUT ME, ADA..?
YOU!? PAH! YOU'RE NO RUDDY HELP, DOLLY. ALL YOU DO IS STEW ME TEA AND GIVE ME THE WRONG BISCUITS.
OKAY MRS BRADY. I THINK THAT'S EVERYTHING I NEED.
WILL I STILL BE GETTING THE SAME MONEY?
WELL, ON THE EVIDENCE I'VE SEEN, WE COULD PROBABLY INCREASE YOUR ALLOWANCE.
EEH, CHAMPION!
I'M SORRY I'VE HAD TO ASK YOU ALL THESE INTRUSIVE QUESTIONS, MRS BRADY. BUT WE HAVE TO SORT OUT THE GENUINE CASES.
EEH.
YOU'D BE SURPRISED HOW MANY PEOPLE ARE OUT TO CHEAT THE SYSTEM. AND FRAUDULENT CLAIMANTS TAKE MONEY AWAY FROM DESERVING CASES LIKE YOURSELF, MRS BRADY.
TSK
I'LL TELL YOU A FUNNY STORY. THERE WAS THIS MAN WHO'D BEEN OFF WORK FOR A YEAR WITH A BAD BACK...
...SAID HE COULDN'T MOVE WITH THE PAIN. CLAIMING MORE THAN £200 A WEEK FROM US, HE WAS...
FANCY...
... UNTIL HIS CASE OFFICER SAW HIM REFEREEING A FOOTBALL MATCH IN HIS LOCAL PARK!
EEH! THE RUDDY ROBDOG!
NEVER!
TSCH!
NEXT DAY...
PHEEP!
YELLOW CARD!
WHAT!?! COME ON, REF... I WENT FOR THE BALL!
...BUT YOU DIDN'T GET IT!... AND IF I THOUGHT YOU WENT FOR THE MAN, YOU'D BE OFF THE PARK, SUNSHINE! NOW LETS GET ON WITH THE GAME..!

STARS BE

PETE Doherty, Diana Ross, Leslie Grantham, Stephen Fry, Robert Downey Jr... the list seems endless. Name any star, and chances are that they have done time in prison. Whether it's for drink driving, fighting in a nightclub or stealing a diamond-encrusted cigarette holder, our favourite celebrities are forever finding themselves on the wrong side of the law and paying the price with a spell in stir. Indeed, these days the morning slop-out in a typical jail reads like a who's who of showbiz A-listers.

And prison is far worse for a celeb than for a normal man in the street. Whilst the average Joe would take a spell at Her Majesty's Pleasure in his stride, a star who is used to living a jet-set life of 5-star hotels, stretch limousines and champagne on tap feels the contrast a hundred times more keenly. For a famous person, a day in a cell - with no PA to arrange fresh flowers and without his guitar-shaped swimming pool to relax by - seems like a life sentence with no chance of parole.

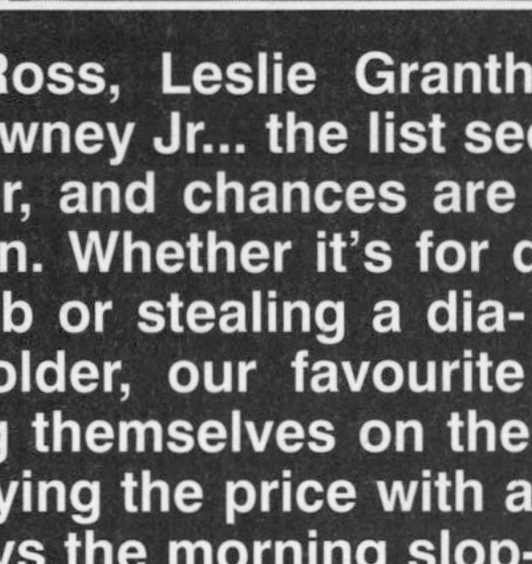

A prison yesterday.

The shocking fact is that for the stars it's not a matter of if, but when they will get locked up. And as this week's batch of celeb cons - including OJ Simpson, Boy George and Coronation Street's Betty Driver - check into the Big House, we speculate how other famous faces will cope behind bars when it's their turn to get banged up.

MOORE-SHANK REDEMPTION PLAN FOR PATRICK

SIR Patrick Moore is the boggle-eyed presenter of The Sky at Night, so we're used to seeing him peering through his telescope at heavenly bodies. But if he were to give in to temptation and train his 6-inch refractor on the heavenly bodies of his neighbours, Moore would quickly find himself looking down the wrong end of a 6-month sentence in a high security prison.

Moore would find incarceration difficult to cope with. The prison library's poor selection of books, the restricted opportunity to listen to classical music and having to shit in a bucket in front of three other cons would hit the 85-year-old stargazer hard. As a result, it is likely that his thoughts would quickly turn to methods of escape.

Inspired by the film The Shawshank Redemption, Moore would begin to tunnel through the wall of his cell using his trademark monocle as an improvised digging tool. At night he would play his xylophone to cover up the sounds made by his excavations, hiding the opening to his escape tunnel behind a glamourous pin-up poster of former British Astronomical Association President Heather Couper. After many nights of tunneling, Moore would eventually break through into a prison service shaft. Then he would use his knowledge of astronomy to wait for a solar eclipse and a meteor storm to provide cover for his audacious escape bid.

Like Tim Robbins's character Andy Dufresne in the movie, 30-stone Moore would use a rock to smash his way into a cast iron sewer pipe before squeezing inside and hauling himself half a mile along it, finally emerging into a ditch on the other side of the perimeter fence. He would then make his way back to his home in Selsey, Sussex, where he would hide in his back garden observatory, anxiously keeping watch for the prison search party with their pack of baying bloodhounds.

BK4454813 06 27 95
LOS ANGELES POLICE
HWD

PRISON LIFE IS SWEET FOR SUGAR

ALAN Sugar is famous for firing the contestants on his popular TV show The Apprentice. But were he to fire a sawn-off shotgun at terrified guards during a botched bullion raid on a security van, he would very soon find himself doing a ten-stretch in Wormwood Scrubs. Back in civvy street Sugar is in charge of the massive Amstrad group. The bearded tycoon has built up the company from scratch, so he is used to calling the shots. It is certain that his attitude would be no different behind bars.

Sugar would quickly identify the most profitable business opportunities in the clink; within a few days of starting his sentence he would be running mobile phone, cigarette and pornography rackets, making huge profits at the expense of his fellow inmates. After just a month, he would be a snout millionaire at the helm of a business empire employing dozens of other prisoners and trading in every wing of the jail.

As an entrepreneur, Sugar knows the importance of protecting his market share. In the outside world, he would deal with competitors by squeezing his suppliers, cutting prices and boosting his visibility in the retail arena. Behind bars, however, any business rivals would simply be stabbed in the face with a sharpened toothbrush.

BK4454813 06 27 95
LOS ANGELES POLICE
HWD

IIND BARS

MEET THE MAN IN THE CELLS - PAUL DANI-ELS

'HE courts would like it not a lot if under-ver RSPCA inspectors ere to present them ith blurred video foot-ge of illegal dogfights rganised by former TV nagician Paul Daniels. ndeed, if this happened t's practically certain that the Judge would have no hesitation in sentencing the Middlesbrough-born wand-waggler to 3 years in prison for animal cruelty.

On the stage, audiences have seen Daniels free himself from handcuffs, underwater milk-churns, strait-jackets and peculiarly-decorated boxes, so you might suppose he would have no difficulty in escaping from prison. However, his illusions rely on specially-made props and carefully-chosen camera angles for their mystifying effects, and so once his cell door was locked Daniels would be stuck there for the duration.

But Daniels has pure showbusiness running through his veins, and it is almost certain that his desire to entertain would remain as strong as ever. He would try to live his life on the inside as much like his life on the outside as possible, regularly holding poorly-attended magic shows in the quarter-full prison theatre. But denied access to his huge stock of props, Daniels would be forced to improvise, performing tricks using only items readily available in his cell. Pulling a rabbit out of a slop bucket, producing a bunch of pornography from up his sleeve and sawing a rapist in half would be just some of the tricks that the diminutive magic man would perform to the delight of his captive audience.

BK 4454813 06 27 95

JAILBIRD DOVER'S EYE FOR THE BIRDS

'ERYBODY in the vorld has seen por-raphic actor Ben Do-'s genitals, so it would extremely ironic if he re to be arrested for lecent exposure in his cal park and handed a year prison sentence. ıt if this did happen, how would the ınny-crazed video stickman cope with 'e on the inside?

Dover is well known for his habit of having sex at the drop of a hat, and once in prison his sex life would be no less active, although instead of a hat, it would be at the drop of some soap. In the showers, he would soon come to curse his parents for giving him a name - Ben Dover - that could be twisted into a sinister instruction rather than a friendly greeting.

At this point, he might find an injured baby sparrow on the windowledge of his cell. Nursing it back to health would take Dover many weeks, but eventually the bird would be fit enough to be released back into the wild. Many prisoners take up hobbies to block out the reality of their predicament, and following his experience with the baby bird, Dover might become as obsessed with birds as he is in his obscene videos ... though this time of the feathered variety. Their names, such as tits, choughs, big cocks and shags would all serve to remind him of happier times.

As his sentence progressed, Dover would begin to eagerly devour all the bird books he could find in the prison library, educating himself about ornithological matters and even writing articles and scientific papers about bird health. As his reputation grew, other prisoners and warders would bring sick and injured fledglings they had found to Dover's cell to be nursed back to health. Eventually even the governor himself would trust Dover enough to allow him to treat his sick budgerigar.

Over the course of his 2-year sentence, Dover would earn himself an international reputation as a renowned bird expert. On his release, however, he would forget all about it and go back to filming himself banging slappers in the back of a transit van.

BK 4454813 06 27 95
LOS ANGELES POLICE: HWD

CHOKEY NO SUMMER HOLIDAY FOR CLIFF

CLEANCUT Cliff Richards is the last person you'd expect to see getting locked up in prison. But if he refused to buy a television licence and found himself the subject of several written warnings and a County Court Judgement, he would soon be starting a mandatory 30-day stretch in his local slammer.

Initially, his strong Christian faith would help him to cope with the unfamiliar and unfriendly surroundings of prison. Richards would undoubtedly vow to keep his nose clean, stay out of trouble and do his time with the minimum of fuss. He would be only too aware that, with good behaviour, he could be back playing tennis in the grounds of his plush Surrey mansion in a fortnight. However, it's likely that after spending less than a week in the brutal prison regime, something would snap in the Peter Pan of Pop's brain, causing him to attack a fellow inmate with a pool cue.

For this, Cliff would lose all chance of parole and have an extra 6 months added to his sentence for good measure. With the possibility of an early release gone the veteran singer, whose hits include Congratulations, Living Doll and Wired for Sound, would go stir crazy and beat up a warder with a chair leg. A spell in solitary confinement would only serve to incense Cliff even more, fermenting a manic sense of injustice and a brooding hatred of authority in his unbalanced mind.

A visit in his cell from the Prison chaplain would quickly turn into a hostage situation, with Richards holding a shard of broken shaving mirror at his terrified victim's throat for several hours whilst screaming threats through his barricaded cell door. Moved to a maximum security wing, Sir Cliff would break out onto the roof where he would unfurl a sheet on which he had scrawled the words "FUK THE POLIS" in his own excrement. He would spend three days on the roof, hurling slates at the people below, before being driven back inside by cold and hunger.

His prison record could now see Richards trapped in a vicious circle of punishment and deteriorating behaviour. As a result, the authorities may decide to simply throw away the key. If that happens, it's a sad fact that this bachelor boy would well end up behind bars until his dying day.

BK 4454813 06 27 95
LOS ANGELES POLICE: HWD

Have *YOU* shared a cell with a celeb? Perhaps you've done stir with a soapstar, time with a tapdancer or porridge with a pop group? How did you get on? What were they like? Did you bum them? Ring our confidential Star Newsline on 01811 8055 and let us know. Your calls will be treated in the strictest confidence until your face is splashed all over the front of the paper next Sunday.

TOURHETT BUTLER JOKE

FRANKLY, MY DEAR, I DON'T FUCKING GIVE A CUNTING BASTARD DAMN.

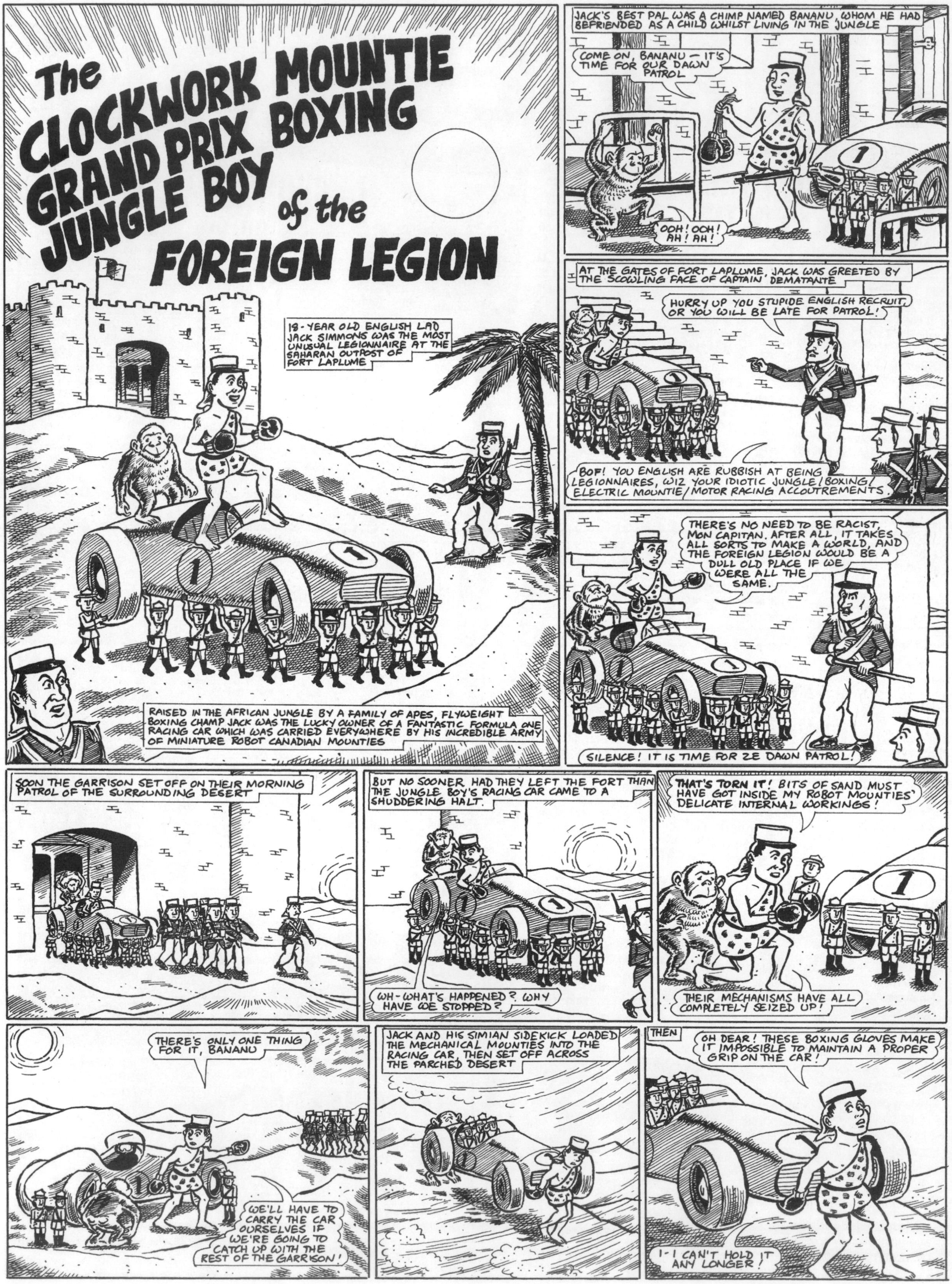
The CLOCKWORK MOUNTIE GRAND PRIX BOXING JUNGLE BOY of the FOREIGN LEGION
18-YEAR OLD ENGLISH LAD JACK SIMMONS WAS THE MOST UNUSUAL LEGIONNAIRE AT THE SAHARAN OUTPOST OF FORT LAPLUME
RAISED IN THE AFRICAN JUNGLE BY A FAMILY OF APES, FLYWEIGHT BOXING CHAMP JACK WAS THE LUCKY OWNER OF A FANTASTIC FORMULA ONE RACING CAR WHICH WAS CARRIED EVERYWHERE BY HIS INCREDIBLE ARMY OF MINIATURE ROBOT CANADIAN MOUNTIES
JACK'S BEST PAL WAS A CHIMP NAMED BANANU, WHOM HE HAD BEFRIENDED AS A CHILD WHILST LIVING IN THE JUNGLE
COME ON, BANANU – IT'S TIME FOR OUR DAWN PATROL
OOH! OOH! AH! AH!
AT THE GATES OF FORT LAPLUME, JACK WAS GREETED BY THE SCOWLING FACE OF CAPTAIN DEMATANTE
HURRY UP YOU STUPIDE ENGLISH RECRUIT, OR YOU WILL BE LATE FOR PATROL!
BOF! YOU ENGLISH ARE RUBBISH AT BEING LEGIONNAIRES, WIZ YOUR IDIOTIC JUNGLE/BOXING/ELECTRIC MOUNTIE/MOTOR RACING ACCOUTREMENTS
THERE'S NO NEED TO BE RACIST, MON CAPITAN. AFTER ALL, IT TAKES ALL SORTS TO MAKE A WORLD, AND THE FOREIGN LEGION WOULD BE A DULL OLD PLACE IF WE WERE ALL THE SAME.
SILENCE! IT IS TIME FOR ZE DAWN PATROL!
SOON THE GARRISON SET OFF ON THEIR MORNING PATROL OF THE SURROUNDING DESERT
BUT NO SOONER HAD THEY LEFT THE FORT THAN THE JUNGLE BOY'S RACING CAR CAME TO A SHUDDERING HALT.
WH-WHAT'S HAPPENED? WHY HAVE WE STOPPED?
THAT'S TORN IT! BITS OF SAND MUST HAVE GOT INSIDE MY ROBOT MOUNTIES' DELICATE INTERNAL WORKINGS!
THEIR MECHANISMS HAVE ALL COMPLETELY SEIZED UP!
THERE'S ONLY ONE THING FOR IT, BANANU
WE'LL HAVE TO CARRY THE CAR OURSELVES IF WE'RE GOING TO CATCH UP WITH THE REST OF THE GARRISON!
JACK AND HIS SIMIAN SIDEKICK LOADED THE MECHANICAL MOUNTIES INTO THE RACING CAR, THEN SET OFF ACROSS THE PARCHED DESERT
THEN
OH DEAR! THESE BOXING GLOVES MAKE IT IMPOSSIBLE TO MAINTAIN A PROPER GRIP ON THE CAR!
I-I CAN'T HOLD IT ANY LONGER!

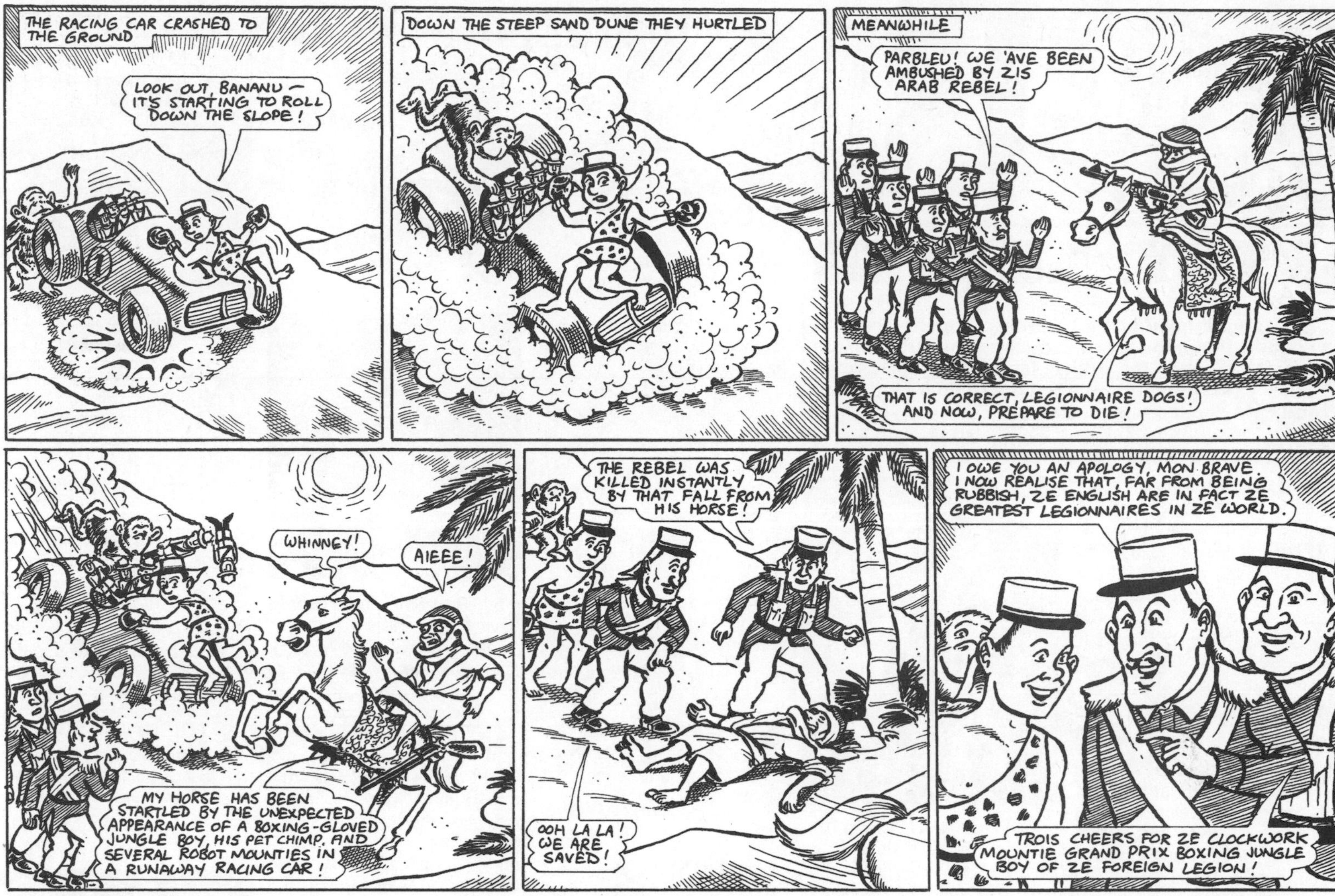
THE RACING CAR CRASHED TO THE GROUND
LOOK OUT, BANANU – IT'S STARTING TO ROLL DOWN THE SLOPE!
DOWN THE STEEP SAND DUNE THEY HURTLED
MEANWHILE
PARBLEU! WE 'AVE BEEN AMBUSHED BY ZIS ARAB REBEL!
THAT IS CORRECT, LEGIONNAIRE DOGS! AND NOW, PREPARE TO DIE!
WHINNEY!
AIEEE!
MY HORSE HAS BEEN STARTLED BY THE UNEXPECTED APPEARANCE OF A BOXING-GLOVED JUNGLE BOY, HIS PET CHIMP, AND SEVERAL ROBOT MOUNTIES IN A RUNAWAY RACING CAR!
THE REBEL WAS KILLED INSTANTLY BY THAT FALL FROM HIS HORSE!
OOH LA LA! WE ARE SAVED!
I OWE YOU AN APOLOGY, MON BRAVE. I NOW REALISE THAT, FAR FROM BEING RUBBISH, ZE ENGLISH ARE IN FACT ZE GREATEST LEGIONNAIRES IN ZE WORLD.
TROIS CHEERS FOR ZE CLOCKWORK MOUNTIE GRAND PRIX BOXING JUNGLE BOY OF ZE FOREIGN LEGION!

There's a Moth on Mi Landing, What Am I Gonna Do?

FORMER UB40 front man ALI CAMPBELL has described how he feared for his life after he became trapped in his bathroom for three days... *BY A MOTH!*

EXCLUSIVE!

The Brummie-born singer, 50, confessed to reporters that he had always had a phobia for flying insects in general, but harboured a secret terror of moths. Campbell locked himself in his bathroom when he spotted one of the furry nocturnal butterflies fluttering around his landing last Tuesday evening.

BROWN

"I was absolutely terrified," he told the *NME*. "It was one of those big brown ones and it was making a horrible flapping noise as it flew abound the lightbulb.

"I didn't know what to do, and when it flew towards my white t-shirt I panicked. I dashed back inside my bathroom and locked the door."

Sleeping fully-clothed in the bath and using the shower curtain as a makeshift duvet, the cod-reggae frontman, whose hits include *Red, Red Wine*, *Cherry Oh Baby* and *I Got You Babe* (with Chrissie Hynde), survived for two nights by drinking shampoo and eating toothpaste. He cautiously poked his head around the bathroom door late on Thursday morning.

Speaking from his Wednesbury home, Campbell told reporters: "I was hoping it had either flown away or died while I was hiding, but I couldn't believe my eyes when I saw it was still there. It was resting close to the coving at the top of the stairs. I thought about rushing past it but didn't want to wake it up, so I dived back into the bathroom where I spent a another night."

BANKS

Campbell eventually fled to his bedroom 24 hours later where he used a mobile phone to post messages on the social networking site, Twitter. "I sent a tweet explaining my plight and the response was brilliant," he said.

"I had good luck messages and advice from fans all over the world, and that kept me calm until eventually someone called the fire brigade and they rescued me. It was a bit embarrassing really as they sent a woman fire fighter round and she just hit it with her glove."

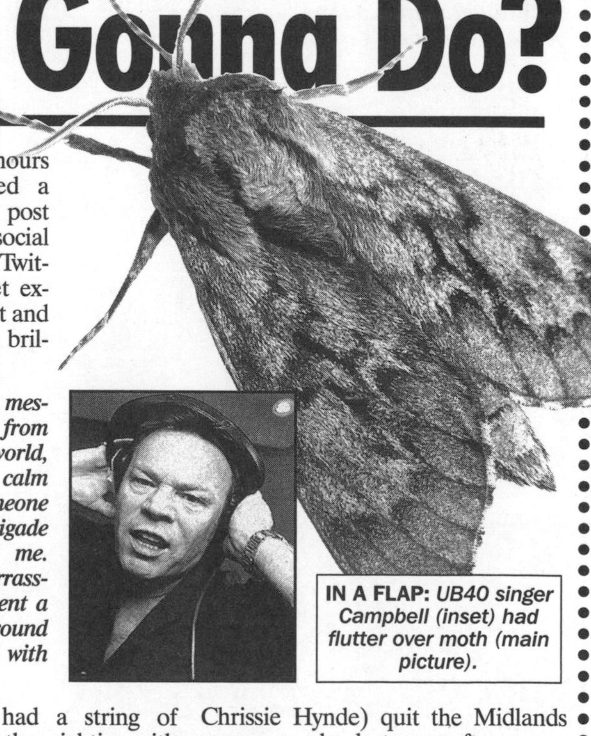

IN A FLAP: UB40 singer Campbell (inset) had flutter over moth (main picture).

Campbell, who had a string of worldwide hits in the eighties with songs such as *One in Ten*, *Rat in Mi Kitchen* and *Breakfast in Bed* (with Chrissie Hynde) quit the Midlands reggae combo last year after a row over windows being left open with the lights on.

LETTERBOCKS

VIZ COMIC, PO Box 656, North Shields, NE30 4XX

letters@viz.co.uk

STAR LETTER

❑ **SO Audi have come up with a fuel efficient car costing thousands and thousands where the engine stops when the vehicle is stationary. Whoopee do. My N-reg Escort cuts out every time I stop at a red light and it costs me sod all.**

Andy, Nottinghamshire

IT'S ALL very well environmentalists telling us we should be going everywhere by bike instead of by car to save the planet. But surely they should be encouraging us to save even more energy by going by unicycle, as these use only half as much energy as a bike.

Dennis Basso
Luton

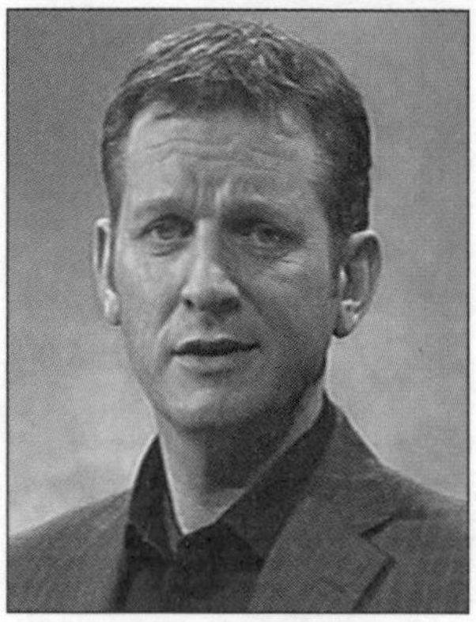

I AM a football referee and last Sunday morning I was called 'a wanker' by a player in an under 15's match. Rather than getting annoyed, I allowed myself a smile. The irony of being called a wanker by a fourteen-year old boy was not lost on me.

Marcel Drucker
Totnes

AT £1350, the Indian-built Tata Nano was billed as the world's cheapest car. What a load of nonsense. My brother bought a Mini Metro off his mate's mum for £100.

Magnus Mbanu
e-mail

THIS morning on the Jeremy Kyle show, after giving one of the guests the bad news that their boyfriend had cheated on them, he said "This is the worst part of this job." And he kept a straight face! Fair play to the man.

Kirk Folly
Manchester

LAST time I went to the dentist, he kept me waiting 45 minutes past my appointment time. Whilst in the waiting room, I noticed a sign on the wall telling me how many people had missed their appointments in the last month. I couldn't help wondering if those people had turned up, God knows what time he would have seen me.

B Makowsky
Croydon

DO ANY of your readers know where Ian Rankin resides? I've tried to do some detective work on the best-selling Scottish crime writer, but after researching several newspaper articles and listening to interviews, I'm still not too sure which city he hails from.

Craig Smith
e-mail

HAVE any of your readers ever put a slinky on an escalator, and if so, did it work?

Edward Pallet
e-mail

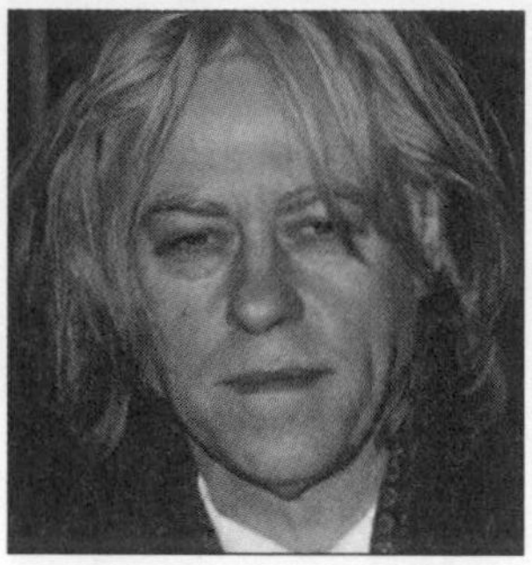

I THINK it's time that Bob Geldof got onto the giant vegetable growers of Great Britain and encouraged them to stop being selfish and reveal their secret techniques for growing whopping marrows and huge cabbages. The starving of Africa can only grow shrivelled-up measly veg, whilst these people can produce turnips weighing 14 stone. I know, because I saw one at the East of England vegetable show in Peterborough last year and it could have fed a whole family for a year, if they'd liked turnips.

Phillip O'Carroll
e-mail

THIS morning, BBC weather forecaster Carol Kirkwood told viewers not to leave home without a cardigan and umbrella. Well, my husband works on a building site, and his workmates haven't stopped taking the mickey out of him since.

Elaine Taiger
Kent

"A MILLION people want to learn to drive, and YOU could be teaching them," says the RED driving instructor school ad. Frankly, I wouldn't want to teach that many people. I'd never get a weekend off.

Rick O'Shea
e-mail

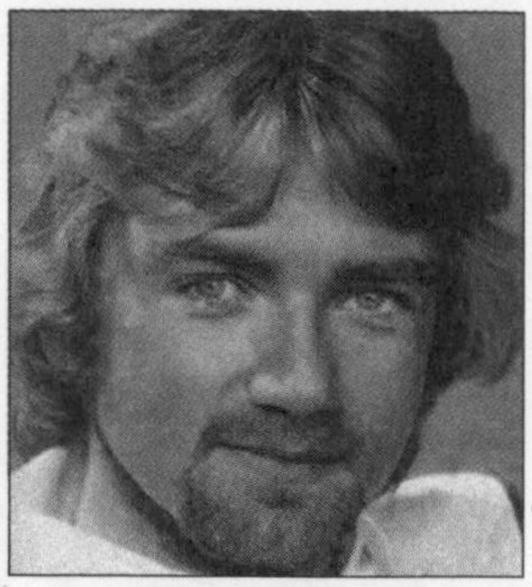

THEY say the best things in life are free. But I would happily pay £50 to see Noel Edmonds being mauled by a tiger.

Tam Dale
e-mail

**Would YOU pay £50 to see Noel Edmonds mauled by a tiger? Or for that money would you expect a pride of lions? Write in and let us know what animals you would like to see Edmonds mauled by, and how much you'd be prepared to pay.*

THERE'S no place like home, they say. Nonsense. All the houses on my estate look exactly the same.

B Butterell
e-mail

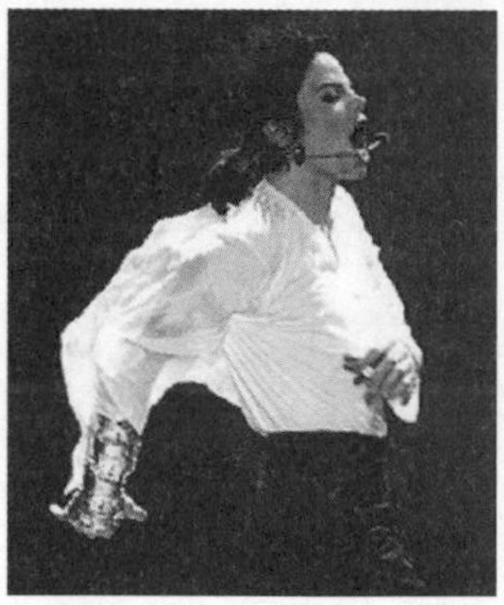

DO ANY of your readers have any idea what would have happened if Michael jackson had performed his famous moonwalk at the famous Scottish optical illusion spot The Electric Brae? Would he have appeared to be walking uphill, or maybe the two effects would cancel each other out and he would just appear to be walking on the spot?

Pedro Juan
e-mail

COULD I make an appeal to local councils? When putting down speed bumps, could you put another one 10 feet further along so we have something to land on, please?

Boy Racer
e-mail

THESE know-alls keep banging on about the polar ice-caps melting. Now

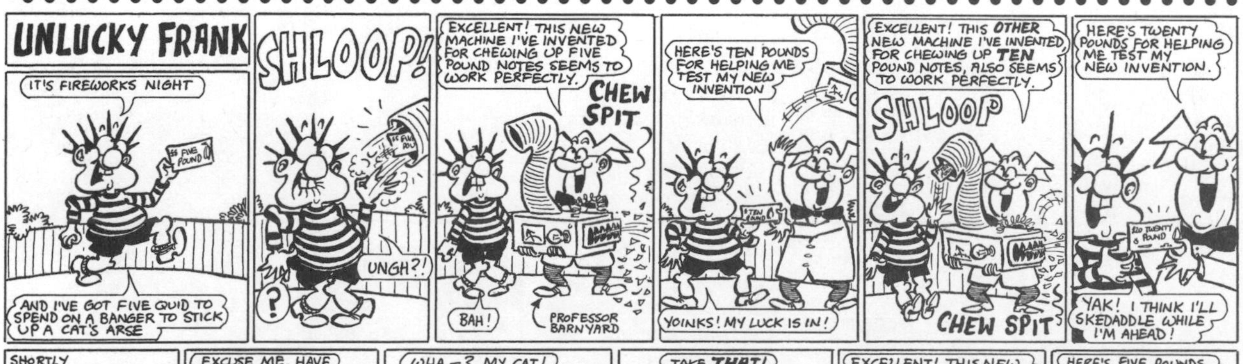
UNLUCKY FRANK
IT'S FIREWORKS NIGHT
AND I'VE GOT FIVE QUID TO SPEND ON A BANGER TO STICK UP A CAT'S ARSE
SHLOOP!
UNGH?!
?
EXCELLENT! THIS NEW MACHINE I'VE INVENTED FOR CHEWING UP FIVE POUND NOTES SEEMS TO WORK PERFECTLY.
CHEW SPIT
BAH!
PROFESSOR BARNYARD
HERE'S TEN POUNDS FOR HELPING ME TEST MY NEW INVENTION
YOINKS! MY LUCK IS IN!
EXCELLENT! THIS OTHER NEW MACHINE I'VE INVENTED FOR CHEWING UP TEN POUND NOTES, ALSO SEEMS TO WORK PERFECTLY.
SHLOOP
CHEW SPIT
HERE'S TWENTY POUNDS FOR HELPING ME TEST MY NEW INVENTION.
YAK! I THINK I'LL SKEDADDLE WHILE I'M AHEAD!
SHORTLY
THAT TWENTY QUID BOUGHT A GREAT BIG BANGER TO STICK UP A CAT'S ARSE
FIZZZ
MEOW
EXCUSE ME. HAVE YOU SEEN MY CAT, OF WHOM I AM INORDINATELY FOND?
BOOM!
WHA-? MY CAT! THAT DOES IT!
?
EH?
I'M GOING TO CAUSE YOU A HUGE AMOUNT OF PAIN!
TAKE THAT! AND THAT! AND THAT!
EXCELLENT! THIS NEW SPRAY I'VE INVENTED, WHICH MAKES PEOPLE CONFUSE "CAUSING PAIN" WITH "GIVING AWAY MONEY," SEEMS TO WORK PERFECTLY.
HERE'S FIVE POUNDS FOR HELPING ME TEST MY NEW INVENTION
CRACK
YOWK! HOW UNLUCKY!

TOP TIPS

SODA-SYPHON owners. The little green gas bottles are ideal for re-enacting the final scene from Jaws with your cat.

Charlie Farnsbarns, e-mail

FOOTBALLERS. Pass the ball slowly amongst your defenders and goalkeeper during extra time and then moan about the 'insane lottery' of a penalty shootout.

Ryan Pooh, e-mail

LATE for work? Simply sneak in the side door and hide your coat in a drawer, then grab some paper from the photocopy room and casually walk to your desk pretending to read the blank sheets of paper.

Simon, e-mail

WHEEL manufacturers. Take a tip from the marketing techniques of makers of mens' razors and release a new model every year claiming to be 'the roundest wheel yet.'

Ash Bracey, e-mail

JAMIE Oliver. When you bring out a new book, why not price it at £12 rather than £25? This would save the shops having to put 'Half price' stickers on them before they go on the shelves.

Roland Butter, e-mail

TOUPEE wearers. A duck placed on your head makes a warm and waterproof alternative to your usual syrup on those rainy days. For gentlemen with larger heads, try a small goose.

T Dude, e-mail

COMMUTERS. When reading a hardback book on the train to work, turn the dust jacket upside down to convince fellow passengers that you have inverted vision.

John Callaghan, Reading

SAINSBURYS. Make a mockery of your 'We have removed carrier bags from our tills' scheme by instructing your cahiers to offer every customer some of the bags hidden under their seats.

Andrew Stevens, Manchester

SAVE money on tap shoes by simply pushing drawing pins into the toes and heels of your feet.

Bruno Tonioli, e-mail

HAIRDRESSERS. Break even during the recession by not cutting your customers' hair so short. They'll be back for another chop in no time and you can charge them again.

Richard, Ross-on-Wye

SPAGHETTI Bolognese makes great intestines for a badly wounded Action Man.

Dean Hale, e-mail

BREAST MEN. When shopping in the supermarket, miss out the first aisle so that you are going against the flow. Arse men should follow the usual route.

Spike, e-mail

PEOPLE of normal height and build. Lose about 6 stone before taking a Virgin transatlantic flight. Not only will you now fit into the seat, you might even find it comfortable.

Tina McCormick, e-mail

AMAZON.CO.UK. If someone purchases an exercise bike from your website, don't bother sending them endless e-mails recommending further exercise bikes. They tend not to be things you buy on a regular basis.

Christina Martin, e-mail

THE Moral MAZE THIS WEEK

You Are Danny La Rue on the Titanic

SCENARIO: You are Danny La Rue performing a show on the RMS Titanic. Suddenly, it strikes an iceberg and begins to take on water. The lifeboats are launched and the cry goes out... *"WOMEN AND CHILDREN FIRST!"* As a female impersonator, do you elbow your way into a lifeboat with the real women? Or do you come clean about being a man and wait in line until all the women and children are safely off the ship?

Get on the boat with the women	Stay behind with the men
01 811 8055	**01 811 8056**

Calls charged at £1.50/minute at all times. Average call lasts 4 hrs 23 mins.

LAST WEEK ON THE MORAL MAZE: *We asked whether Rolf Harris's Jake the Peg character should be entitled to a Disabled Parking badge for his car.* **96%** *said he should.*
NEXT WEEK: *If Spit the Dog bit a child, should Bob Carolgees be put down?*

I'm no scientist, but how the fuck can it be melting when the mean summer temperature is between -15°c and -35°c? Come on, eggheads, explain that.

Darren Morse e-mail

HAVING visited Wales for the first time last week, I was extremely concerned by the amount of illegible graffiti on all the road signs. Although I do have to admit, it was very professionally done.

D Meister Shrops

I WANTED to travel to from Surbiton to Winchester by rail the other day. When I went to buy a ticket, the clown in the booth told me that as a pensioner I could get a third off my rail journey. Well, if I ask for a ticket to Winchester, I don't want to get off at Basingstoke, thank you very much.

Soloman Catheter e-mail

I HOPE all the politicians who were depressed and stressed because they got caught fiddling expenses are feeling better after their three months off. My army mate out in Helmand was worried sick about them.

Willy McWilliams e-mail

RECENTLY, a hair salon with the name Bespoke Hairdressing opened up near me. I've tried and tried, but I cannot think of a more redundant use of the word bespoke.

P Crumple e-mail

I WAS thinking about milk the other day when I burped unexpectedly. To my surprise, it tasted like milk, despite me not having drunk any. It occurred to me that I had tricked my own brain using mind power. However, when I let a tommy squeaker go in bed this morning that smelt of cat food. No matter how much I told the missus it smelt of peaches, she wouldn't have it. Her mind is strong.

S Selwood e-mail

CELEBRITY SWEARS

No. 617 ~ Terry Wogan

Shitty arse biscuits

PETER KAY-VEMAN

HEY, WHAT WAS IT LIKE BEFORE THE WHEEL, EH? DO YOU 'MEMBER? WHAT WUR WE THINKING BACK THEN, EH?
HUH HUH! HIM RIGHT!
PRIMORDIAL SOUP?! PRIMORDIAL SOUP?!
... PRIMORDIAL?
...SOUP?
HUH
HUH HUH
SUDDENLY...
...PRIMORDIAL SOUP?!
BOOM!
HEY! WHO 'MEMBERS T' DINOSAURS, EH? THEY WERE WEIRD, WEREN'T THEY! DO YOU 'MEMBER?
HUH!
HUH HUH! THAT FUNNY!

Rude Kid.
AREN'T YOU GOING TO BLOW OUT THE CANDLES ON YOUR 30TH BIRTHDAY CAKE, DEAR?
SUCK MY BIG BLACK SHITTY COCK!
HAPPY 30TH

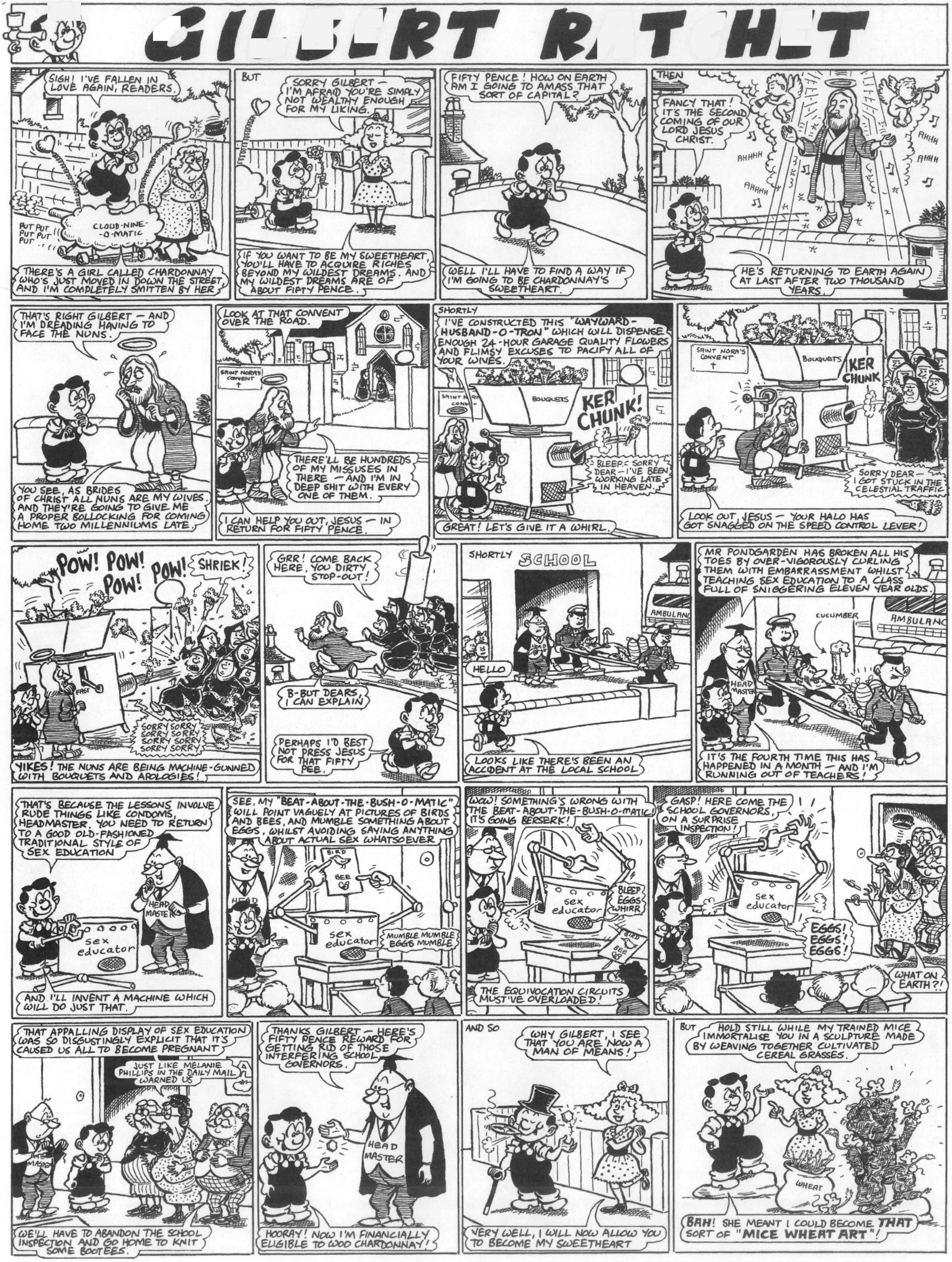
GILBERT RATCHET
SIGH! I'VE FALLEN IN LOVE AGAIN, READERS.
PUT PUT PUT PUT PUT
CLOUD-NINE-O-MATIC
THERE'S A GIRL CALLED CHARDONNAY WHO'S JUST MOVED IN DOWN THE STREET, AND I'M COMPLETELY SMITTEN BY HER
BUT
SORRY GILBERT - I'M AFRAID YOU'RE SIMPLY NOT WEALTHY ENOUGH FOR MY LIKING.
IF YOU WANT TO BE MY SWEETHEART, YOU'LL HAVE TO ACQUIRE RICHES BEYOND MY WILDEST DREAMS. AND MY WILDEST DREAMS ARE OF ABOUT FIFTY PENCE.
FIFTY PENCE! HOW ON EARTH AM I GOING TO AMASS THAT SORT OF CAPITAL?
WELL I'LL HAVE TO FIND A WAY IF I'M GOING TO BE CHARDONNAY'S SWEETHEART.
THEN
FANCY THAT! IT'S THE SECOND COMING OF OUR LORD JESUS CHRIST.
AHHH AHHHH AHHHH AHHH AHHH
HE'S RETURNING TO EARTH AGAIN AT LAST AFTER TWO THOUSAND YEARS.
THAT'S RIGHT GILBERT - AND I'M DREADING HAVING TO FACE THE NUNS.
YOU SEE, AS BRIDES OF CHRIST ALL NUNS ARE MY WIVES. AND THEY'RE GOING TO GIVE ME A PROPER BOLLOCKING FOR COMING HOME TWO MILLENNIUMS LATE.
LOOK AT THAT CONVENT OVER THE ROAD.
SAINT NORA'S CONVENT
THERE'LL BE HUNDREDS OF MY MISSUSES IN THERE - AND I'M IN DEEP SHIT WITH EVERY ONE OF THEM.
I CAN HELP YOU OUT, JESUS - IN RETURN FOR FIFTY PENCE.
SHORTLY
I'VE CONSTRUCTED THIS "WAYWARD-HUSBAND-O-TRON" WHICH WILL DISPENSE ENOUGH 24-HOUR GARAGE QUALITY FLOWERS AND FLIMSY EXCUSES TO PACIFY ALL OF YOUR WIVES.
BOUQUETS
KER CHUNK!
BLEEP.. SORRY DEAR - I'VE BEEN WORKING LATE IN HEAVEN.
GREAT! LET'S GIVE IT A WHIRL.
SAINT NORA'S CONVENT
BOUQUETS
KER CHUNK
FAST
SORRY DEAR - I GOT STUCK IN THE CELESTIAL TRAFFIC
LOOK OUT, JESUS - YOUR HALO HAS GOT SNAGGED ON THE SPEED CONTROL LEVER!
POW! POW! POW! POW!
SHRIEK!
FAST
SORRY SORRY SORRY SORRY SORRY SORRY SORRY SORRY
YIKES! THE NUNS ARE BEING MACHINE-GUNNED WITH BOUQUETS AND APOLOGIES!
GRR! COME BACK HERE, YOU DIRTY STOP-OUT!
B-BUT DEARS, I CAN EXPLAIN
PERHAPS I'D BEST NOT PRESS JESUS FOR THAT FIFTY PEE.
SHORTLY
SCHOOL
AMBULANC
HELLO
LOOKS LIKE THERE'S BEEN AN ACCIDENT AT THE LOCAL SCHOOL
MR PONDGARDEN HAS BROKEN ALL HIS TOES BY OVER-VIGOROUSLY CURLING THEM WITH EMBARRASSMENT WHILST TEACHING SEX EDUCATION TO A CLASS FULL OF SNIGGERING ELEVEN YEAR OLDS.
CUCUMBER
AMBULANC
HEAD MASTER
IT'S THE FOURTH TIME THIS HAS HAPPENED IN A MONTH - AND I'M RUNNING OUT OF TEACHERS!
THAT'S BECAUSE THE LESSONS INVOLVE RUDE THINGS LIKE CONDOMS, HEADMASTER. YOU NEED TO RETURN TO A GOOD OLD-FASHIONED TRADITIONAL STYLE OF SEX EDUCATION
HEAD MASTER
sex educator
AND I'LL INVENT A MACHINE WHICH WILL DO JUST THAT.
SEE, MY "BEAT-ABOUT-THE-BUSH-O-MATIC" WILL POINT VAGUELY AT PICTURES OF BIRDS AND BEES, AND MUMBLE SOMETHING ABOUT EGGS, WHILST AVOIDING SAYING ANYTHING ABOUT ACTUAL SEX WHATSOEVER
BIRD
BEE
sex educator
MUMBLE MUMBLE EGGS MUMBLE
WOW! SOMETHING'S WRONG WITH THE BEAT-ABOUT-THE-BUSH-O-MATIC! IT'S GOING BERSERK!
sex educator
BLEEP EGGS WHIRR
BIRD BEE
THE EQUIVOCATION CIRCUITS MUST'VE OVERLOADED!
GASP! HERE COME THE SCHOOL GOVERNORS, ON A SURPRISE INSPECTION!
sex educator
EGGS! EGGS! EGGS!
WHAT ON EARTH?!
THAT APPALLING DISPLAY OF SEX EDUCATION WAS SO DISGUSTINGLY EXPLICIT THAT IT'S CAUSED US ALL TO BECOME PREGNANT
JUST LIKE MELANIE PHILLIPS IN THE DAILY MAIL WARNED US
WE'LL HAVE TO ABANDON THE SCHOOL INSPECTION AND GO HOME TO KNIT SOME BOOTEES.
THANKS GILBERT - HERE'S FIFTY PENCE REWARD FOR GETTING RID OF THOSE INTERFERING SCHOOL GOVERNORS.
HEAD MASTER
HOORAY! NOW I'M FINANCIALLY ELIGIBLE TO WOO CHARDONNAY!
AND SO
WHY GILBERT, I SEE THAT YOU ARE NOW A MAN OF MEANS!
VERY WELL, I WILL NOW ALLOW YOU TO BECOME MY SWEETHEART
BUT
HOLD STILL WHILE MY TRAINED MICE IMMORTALISE YOU IN A SCULPTURE MADE BY WEAVING TOGETHER CULTIVATED CEREAL GRASSES.
WHEAT
BAH! SHE MEANT I COULD BECOME THAT SORT OF "MICE WHEAT ART"!

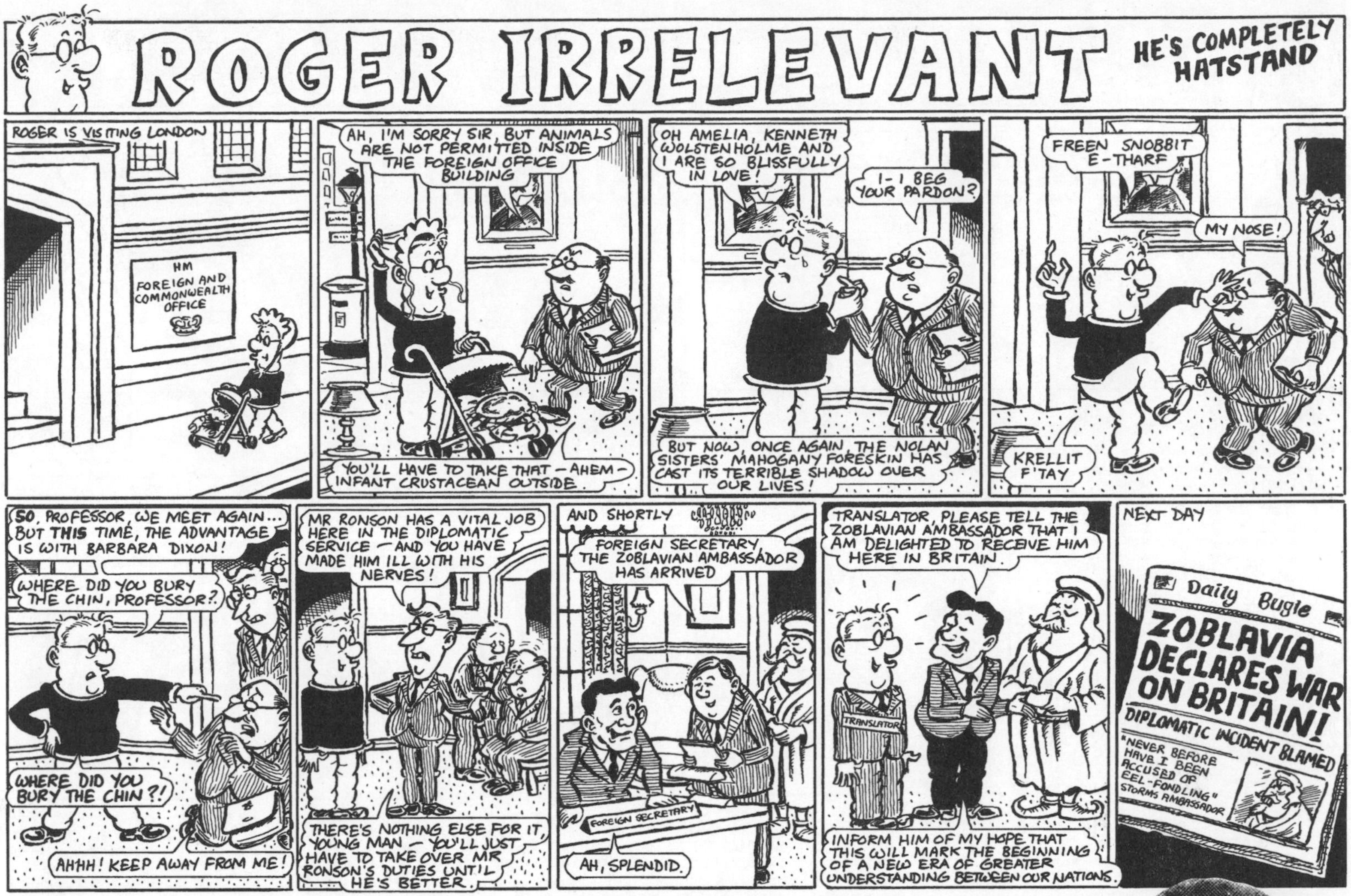
ROGER IRRELEVANT
HE'S COMPLETELY HATSTAND
ROGER IS VISITING LONDON
HM FOREIGN AND COMMONWEALTH OFFICE
AH, I'M SORRY SIR, BUT ANIMALS ARE NOT PERMITTED INSIDE THE FOREIGN OFFICE BUILDING
YOU'LL HAVE TO TAKE THAT – AHEM – INFANT CRUSTACEAN OUTSIDE.
OH AMELIA, KENNETH WOLSTENHOLME AND I ARE SO BLISSFULLY IN LOVE!
I-I BEG YOUR PARDON?
BUT NOW, ONCE AGAIN, THE NOLAN SISTERS' MAHOGANY FORESKIN HAS CAST ITS TERRIBLE SHADOW OVER OUR LIVES!
FREEN SNOBBIT E-THARF
MY NOSE!
KRELLIT F'TAY
SO, PROFESSOR, WE MEET AGAIN... BUT THIS TIME, THE ADVANTAGE IS WITH BARBARA DIXON!
WHERE DID YOU BURY THE CHIN, PROFESSOR?!
WHERE DID YOU BURY THE CHIN?!
AHHH! KEEP AWAY FROM ME!
MR RONSON HAS A VITAL JOB HERE IN THE DIPLOMATIC SERVICE – AND YOU HAVE MADE HIM ILL WITH HIS NERVES!
THERE'S NOTHING ELSE FOR IT, YOUNG MAN – YOU'LL JUST HAVE TO TAKE OVER MR RONSON'S DUTIES UNTIL HE'S BETTER.
AND SHORTLY
FOREIGN SECRETARY, THE ZOBLAVIAN AMBASSADOR HAS ARRIVED
FOREIGN SECRETARY
AH, SPLENDID.
TRANSLATOR, PLEASE TELL THE ZOBLAVIAN AMBASSADOR THAT I AM DELIGHTED TO RECEIVE HIM HERE IN BRITAIN.
TRANSLATOR
INFORM HIM OF MY HOPE THAT THIS WILL MARK THE BEGINNING OF A NEW ERA OF GREATER UNDERSTANDING BETWEEN OUR NATIONS.
NEXT DAY
Daily Bugle
ZOBLAVIA DECLARES WAR ON BRITAIN!
DIPLOMATIC INCIDENT BLAMED
"NEVER BEFORE HAVE I BEEN ACCUSED OF EEL-FONDLING" STORMS AMBASSADOR

DOGGIE PADDLE

ALMOST a century after the Titanic sank, a dog thought to be among the 1,500 fatalities of the liner's disastrous maiden voyage has turned up alive and well. And after swimming non-stop for ninety seven years, the plucky pooch has finally reunited with his now elderly master.

Pooch Reunited with Owner After Titanic Swim

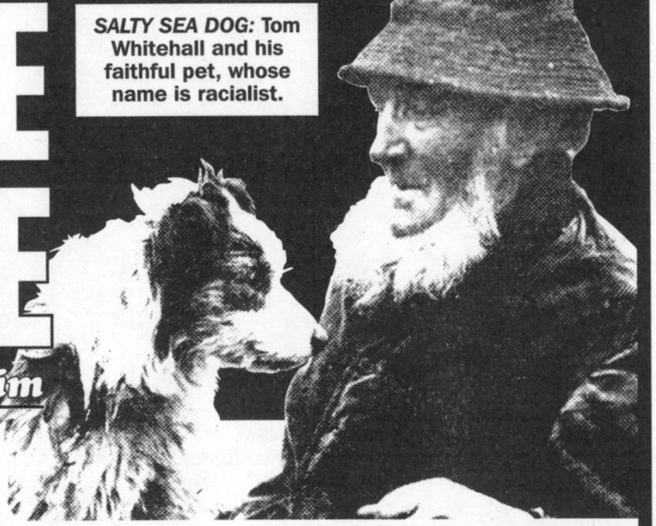

SALTY SEA DOG: **Tom Whitehall and his faithful pet, whose name is racialist.**

The dog, whose name cannot be printed due to it being racist, leaped from the arms of his young owner at the ship's launch in 1912 and ran up the gangplank of the doomed liner. Five days later, the ship struck an iceberg off Newfoundland and sank. And while the nation mourned the massive loss of life, seven year old Tom Whitehall cried for his young puppy, who he feared had perished in the icy waters of the North Atlantic.

WORKERS

However harbour workers at Southampton dock were amazed last week when a dog rescued from the Solent led them from the Quayside back to its home in the Chartwell Green area of the city.

Harbour employee Peter Strand told the Southampton Euphonium: "I spotted a bedraggled dog swimming down by the docks and fished it out of the water. The first thing I noticed was that it had a really offensive word on its name tag." Strand tried to remove the dog's collar to avoid causing any offence, but the animal escaped and ran away.

ANTE

Strand said: "I followed it through the city's streets and it soon became clear that the little fellow knew exactly where he was going."

Before long, the dog had arrived back at the house he last saw almost a century ago. And the fantastic journey was complete when the long distance pooch leapt into the arms of his delighted owner. Whitehall, 104, was overjoyed, and admitted that he had never given up hope of seeing his dog again. "I always knew we'd be reunited," he said. "But as the years went on I thought the chances of it being in this life were less and less."

The racially sensitive named dog received a thorough check up from local vets who pronounced him tired, but fit as a fiddle. They believe the hound survived thanks to his thick fur which would have protected him from the freezing temperatures of the Atlantic. "He probably kept himself going by eating fish and drinking seawater during his marathon century-long doggie paddle," said TV animal expert Terry Nutkins. "I know dogs love swimming and it's often hard to get them out of the water, but this is one of the most amazing cases I have ever come across," he added.

A still sprightly Mr Whitehall vowed to make up for lost time with his dog, but feared that he will have to give his canine companion a new name. "Lots of people called their dogs that word in the olden days. There was nothing wrong with it. Now I suppose if I shout him in at night I'll be called a racist," he told reporters.

ARSE CORNER

"It's political correctness gone mad," he added.

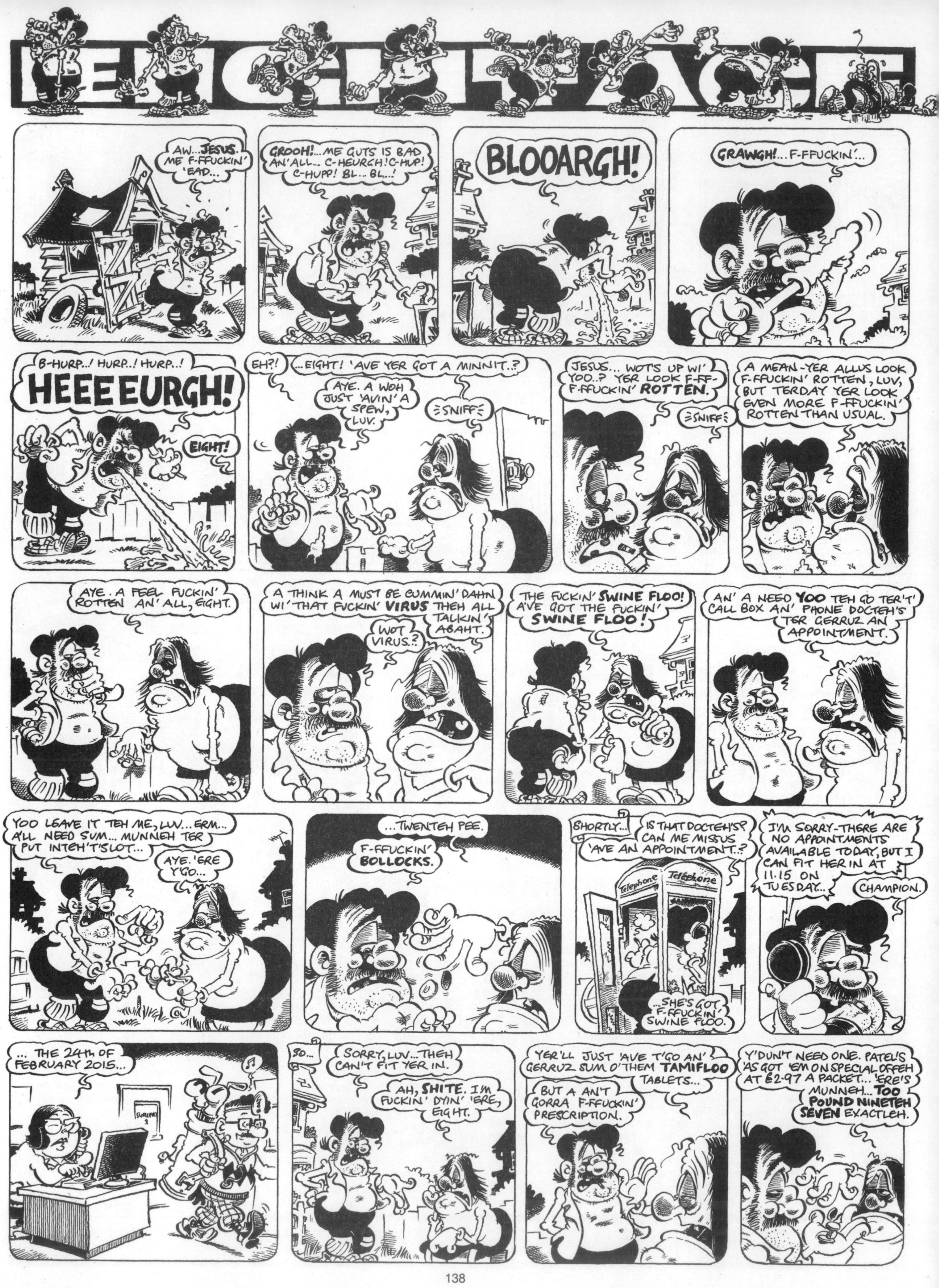

AW... JESUS. ME F-FFUCKIN' 'EAD...
GROOH!... ME GUTS IS BAD AN' ALL... C-HEURCH! C-HUP! C-HUPP! BL... BL...!
BLOOARGH!
GRAWGH!... F-FFUCKIN'...
B-HURP..! HURP..! HURP..!
HEEEEURGH!
EIGHT!
EH?!
...EIGHT! 'AVE YER GOT A MINNIT..?
AYE. A WOH JUST 'AVIN' A SPEW, LUV.
SNIFF
JESUS... WOT'S UP WI' YOO..? YER LOOK F-FF-F-FFUCKIN' ROTTEN.
SNIFF
A MEAN-YER ALLUS LOOK F-FFUCKIN' ROTTEN, LUV, BUT TERDAY YER LOOK EVEN MORE F-FFUCKIN' ROTTEN THAN USUAL.
AYE. A FEEL FUCKIN' ROTTEN AN' ALL, EIGHT.
A THINK A MUST BE CUMMIN' DAHN WI' THAT FUCKIN' VIRUS THEH ALL TALKIN' ABAHT.
WOT VIRUS..?
THE FUCKIN' SWINE FLOO! A'VE GOT THE FUCKIN' SWINE FLOO!
AN' A NEED YOO TEH GO TER'T' CALL BOX AN' PHONE DOCTEH'S TER GERRUZ AN APPOINTMENT.
YOO LEAVE IT TEH ME, LUV... ERM... A'LL NEED SUM... MUNNEH TER PUT INTEH'T'SLOT...
AYE. 'ERE Y'GO...
...TWENTEH PEE.
F-FFUCKIN' BOLLOCKS.
SHORTLY...
IS THAT DOCTEH'S? CAN ME MISSUS 'AVE AN APPOINTMENT..?
Telephone
Telephone
...SHE'S GOT F-FFUCKIN' SWINE FLOO.
I'M SORRY-THERE ARE NO APPOINTMENTS AVAILABLE TODAY, BUT I CAN FIT HER IN AT 11.15 ON TUESDAY...
CHAMPION.
... THE 24th OF FEBRUARY 2015...
SO...
SORRY, LUV... THEH CAN'T FIT YER IN.
AH, SHITE. I'M FUCKIN' DYIN' 'ERE, EIGHT.
YER'LL JUST 'AVE T'GO AN' GERRUZ SUM O'THEM TAMIFLOO TABLETS...
BUT A AN'T GORRA F-FFUCKIN' PRESCRIPTION.
Y'DUN'T NEED ONE. PATEL'S 'AS GOT 'EM ON SPECIAL OFFEH AT £2.97 A PACKET... 'ERE'S MUNNEH... TOO POUND NINETEH SEVEN EXACTLEH.

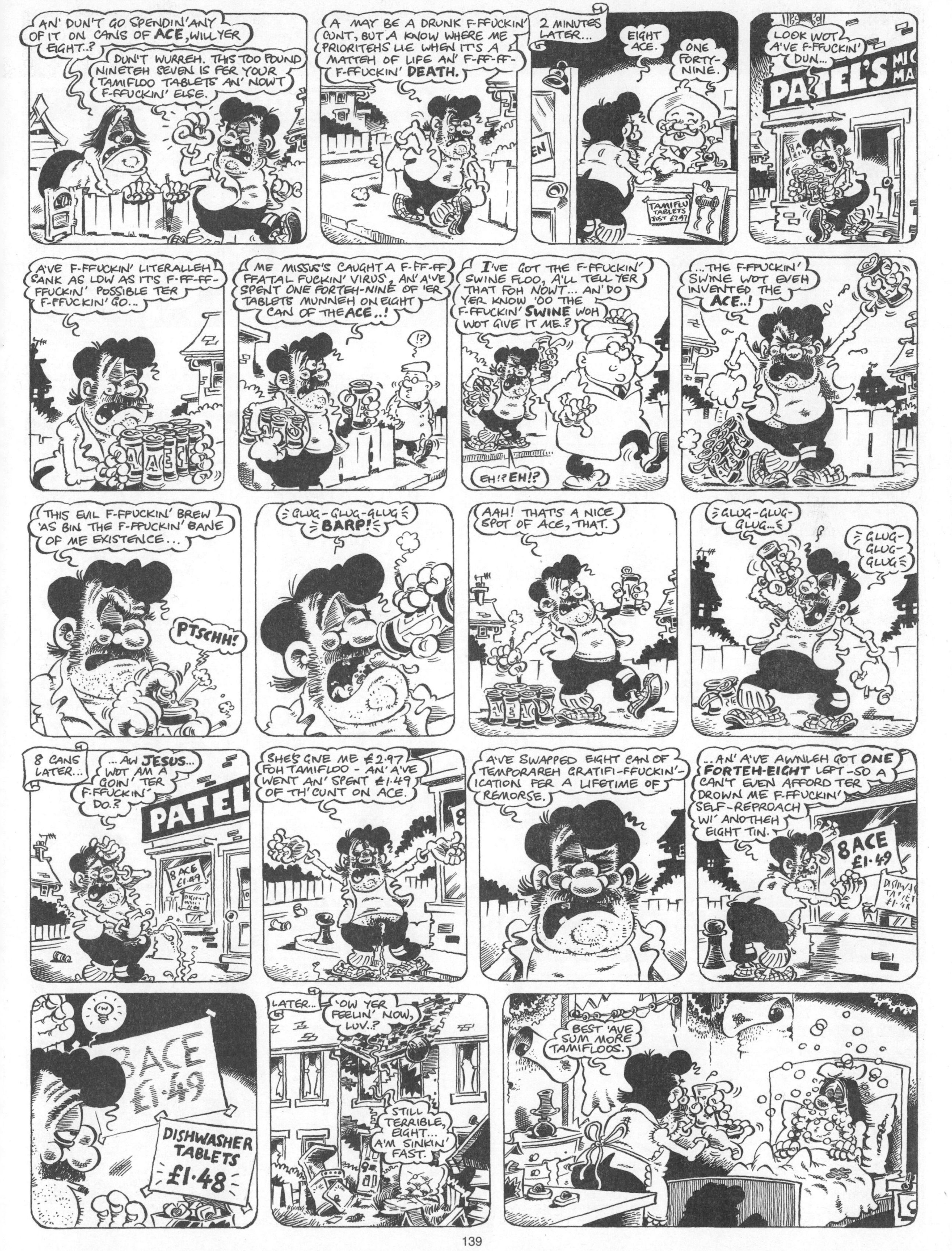
AN' DUN'T GO SPENDIN' ANY OF IT ON CANS OF ACE, WILL YER EIGHT..?
DUN'T WURREH. THIS TOO POUND NINETEH SEVEN IS FER YOUR TAMIFLOO TABLETS AN' NOWT F-FFUCKIN' ELSE.
A MAY BE A DRUNK F-FFUCKIN' CUNT, BUT A KNOW WHERE ME PRIORITEHS LIE WHEN IT'S A MATTEH OF LIFE AN' F-FF-FF-F-FFUCKIN' DEATH.
2 MINUTES LATER...
EIGHT ACE.
ONE FORTY-NINE.
TAMIFLU TABLETS JUST £2.97
LOOK WOT A'VE F-FFUCKIN' DUN...
PATEL'S
A'VE F-FFUCKIN' LITERALLEH SANK AS LOW AS IT'S F-FF-FF-FFUCKIN' POSSIBLE TER F-FFUCKIN' GO...
ME MISSUS'S CAUGHT A F-FF-FF FFATAL FUCKIN' VIRUS, AN' A'VE SPENT ONE FORTEH-NINE OF 'ER TABLETS MUNNEH ON EIGHT CAN OF THE ACE..!
!?
I'VE GOT THE F-FFUCKIN' SWINE FLOO, A'LL TELL YER THAT FOH NOWT... AN' DO YER KNOW 'OO THE F-FFUCKIN' SWINE WOH WOT GIVE IT ME..?
EH!? EH!?
...THE F-FFUCKIN' SWINE WOT EVEH INVENTED THE ACE..!
THIS EVIL F-FFUCKIN' BREW 'AS BIN THE F-FFUCKIN' BANE OF ME EXISTENCE...
PTSCHH!
GLUG-GLUG-GLUG BARP!
AAH! THAT'S A NICE SPOT OF ACE, THAT.
GLUG-GLUG-GLUG...
GLUG-GLUG-GLUG
8 CANS LATER...
...AW JESUS... WOT AM A GOIN' TER F-FFUCKIN' DO..?
PATEL
8 ACE £1·49
SHE'S GIVE ME £2·97 FOH TAMIFLOO - AN' A'VE WENT AN' SPENT £1·49 OF TH' CUNT ON ACE.
A'VE SWAPPED EIGHT CAN OF TEMPORAREH GRATIFI-FFUCKIN'-ICATION FER A LIFETIME OF REMORSE.
...AN' A'VE AWNLEH GOT ONE FORTEH-EIGHT LEFT - SO A CAN'T EVEN AFFORD TER DROWN ME F-FFUCKIN' SELF-REPROACH WI' ANOTHEH EIGHT TIN.
8 ACE £1·49
8ACE £1·49
DISHWASHER TABLETS £1·48
LATER...
'OW YER FEELIN' NOW, LUV..?
STILL TERRIBLE, EIGHT... A'M SINKIN' FAST.
BEST 'AVE SUM MORE TAMIFLOOS.

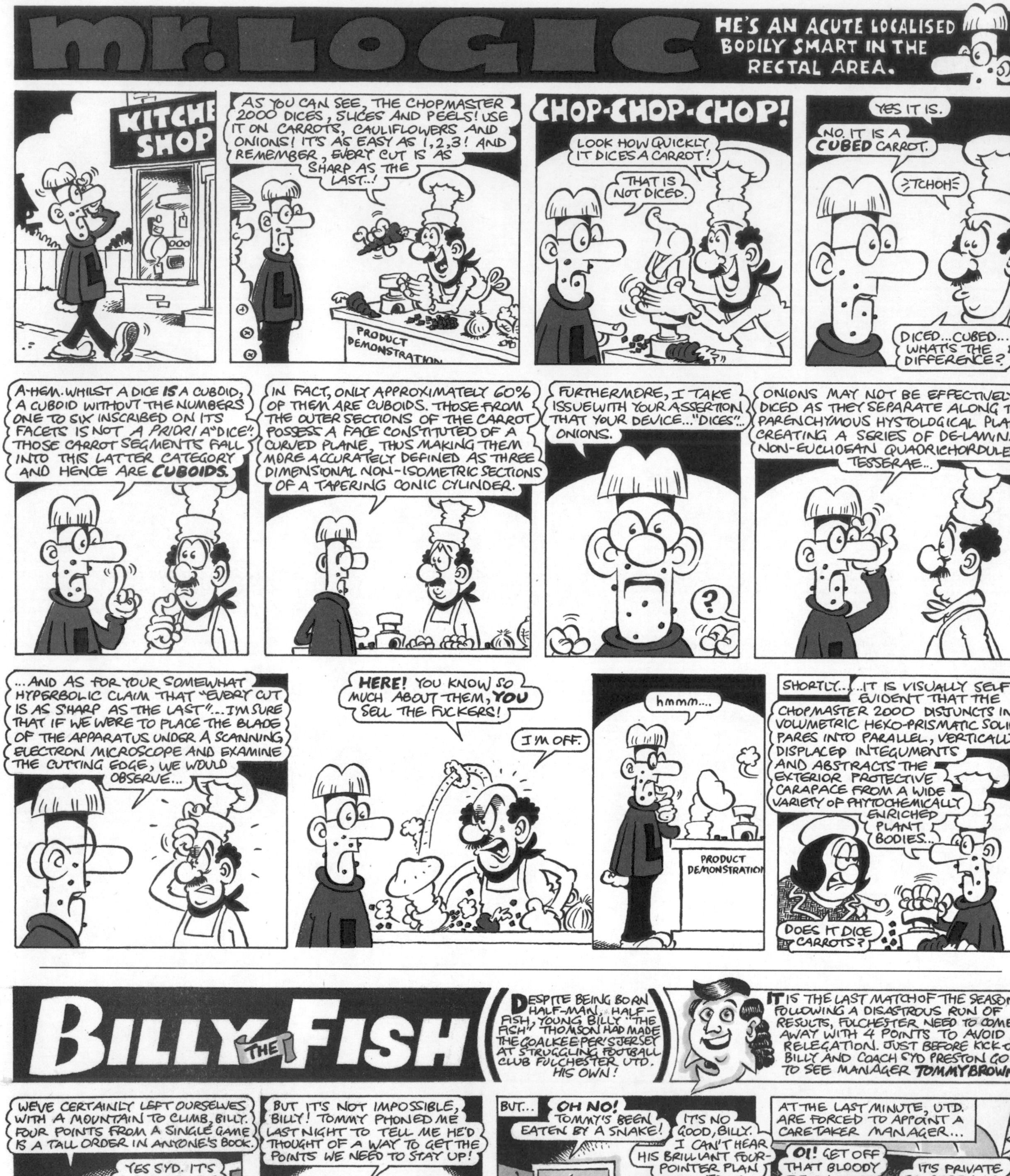
mr. LOGIC
HE'S AN ACUTE LOCALISED BODILY SMART IN THE RECTAL AREA.
hmmm.
KITCHE
SHOP
AS YOU CAN SEE, THE CHOPMASTER 2000 DICES, SLICES AND PEELS! USE IT ON CARROTS, CAULIFLOWERS AND ONIONS! IT'S AS EASY AS 1,2,3! AND REMEMBER, EVERY CUT IS AS SHARP AS THE LAST..!
PRODUCT DEMONSTRATION
CHOP-CHOP-CHOP!
LOOK HOW QUICKLY IT DICES A CARROT!
THAT IS NOT DICED.
YES IT IS.
NO. IT IS A CUBED CARROT.
TCHOH
DICED...CUBED... WHAT'S THE DIFFERENCE?
A-HEM. WHILST A DICE IS A CUBOID, A CUBOID WITHOUT THE NUMBERS ONE TO SIX INSCRIBED ON ITS FACETS IS NOT A PRIORI A "DICE". THOSE CARROT SEGMENTS FALL INTO THIS LATTER CATEGORY AND HENCE ARE CUBOIDS.
IN FACT, ONLY APPROXIMATELY 60% OF THEM ARE CUBOIDS. THOSE FROM THE OUTER SECTIONS OF THE CARROT POSSESS A FACE CONSTITUTED OF A CURVED PLANE, THUS MAKING THEM MORE ACCURATELY DEFINED AS THREE DIMENSIONAL NON-ISOMETRIC SECTIONS OF A TAPERING CONIC CYLINDER.
FURTHERMORE, I TAKE ISSUE WITH YOUR ASSERTION THAT YOUR DEVICE..."DICES"... ONIONS.
?
ONIONS MAY NOT BE EFFECTIVELY DICED AS THEY SEPARATE ALONG THEIR PARENCHYMOUS HYSTOLOGICAL PLANES, CREATING A SERIES OF DE-LAMINATED NON-EUCLIDEAN QUADRICHORDULENT TESSERAE...
...AND AS FOR YOUR SOMEWHAT HYPERBOLIC CLAIM THAT "EVERY CUT IS AS SHARP AS THE LAST"... I'M SURE THAT IF WE WERE TO PLACE THE BLADE OF THE APPARATUS UNDER A SCANNING ELECTRON MICROSCOPE AND EXAMINE THE CUTTING EDGE, WE WOULD OBSERVE...
HERE! YOU KNOW SO MUCH ABOUT THEM, YOU SELL THE FUCKERS!
I'M OFF.
hmmm....
PRODUCT DEMONSTRATION
SHORTLY...
...IT IS VISUALLY SELF-EVIDENT THAT THE CHOPMASTER 2000 DISJUNCTS INTO VOLUMETRIC HEXO-PRISMATIC SOLIDS, PARES INTO PARALLEL, VERTICALLY DISPLACED INTEGUMENTS AND ABSTRACTS THE EXTERIOR PROTECTIVE CARAPACE FROM A WIDE VARIETY OF PHYTOCHEMICALLY ENRICHED PLANT BODIES...
DOES IT DICE CARROTS?

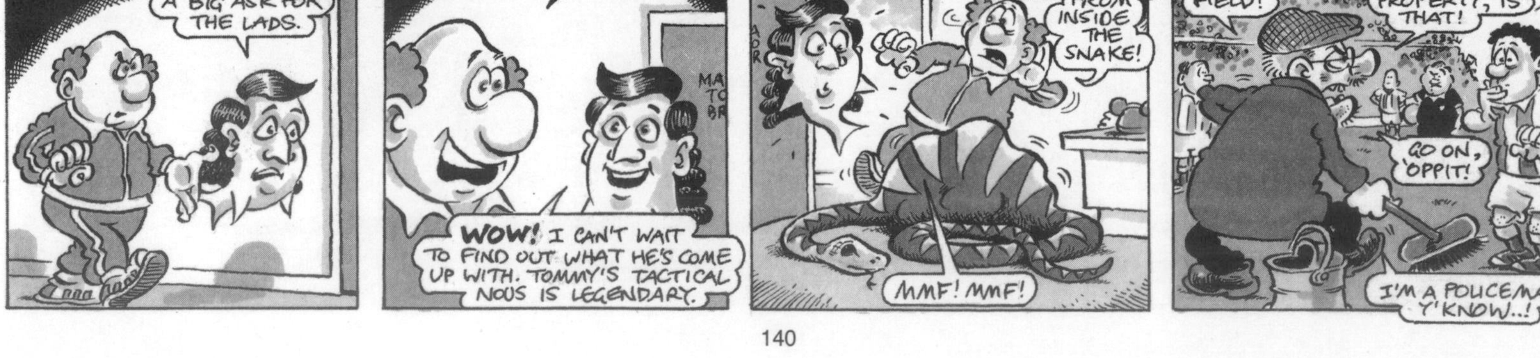
BILLY THE FISH
DESPITE BEING BORN HALF-MAN, HALF-FISH, YOUNG BILLY "THE FISH" THOMSON HAD MADE THE GOALKEEPER'S JERSEY AT STRUGGLING FOOTBALL CLUB FULCHESTER UTD. HIS OWN!
IT IS THE LAST MATCH OF THE SEASON. FOLLOWING A DISASTROUS RUN OF RESULTS, FULCHESTER NEED TO COME AWAY WITH 4 POINTS TO AVOID RELEGATION. JUST BEFORE KICK OFF, BILLY AND COACH SYD PRESTON GO TO SEE MANAGER TOMMY BROWN!
WE'VE CERTAINLY LEFT OURSELVES WITH A MOUNTAIN TO CLIMB, BILLY. FOUR POINTS FROM A SINGLE GAME IS A TALL ORDER IN ANYONE'S BOOK.
YES SYD. IT'S A BIG ASK FOR THE LADS.
BUT IT'S NOT IMPOSSIBLE, BILLY! TOMMY PHONED ME LAST NIGHT TO TELL ME HE'D THOUGHT OF A WAY TO GET THE POINTS WE NEED TO STAY UP!
WOW! I CAN'T WAIT TO FIND OUT WHAT HE'S COME UP WITH. TOMMY'S TACTICAL NOUS IS LEGENDARY.
BUT...
OH NO! TOMMY'S BEEN EATEN BY A SNAKE!
IT'S NO GOOD, BILLY. I CAN'T HEAR HIS BRILLIANT FOUR-POINTER PLAN FROM INSIDE THE SNAKE!
MMF! MMF!
AT THE LAST MINUTE, UTD. ARE FORCED TO APPOINT A CARETAKER MANAGER...
OI! GET OFF THAT BLOODY FIELD!
IT'S PRIVATE PROPERTY, IS THAT!
GO ON, 'OPPIT!
I'M A POLICEMAN, Y'KNOW..!

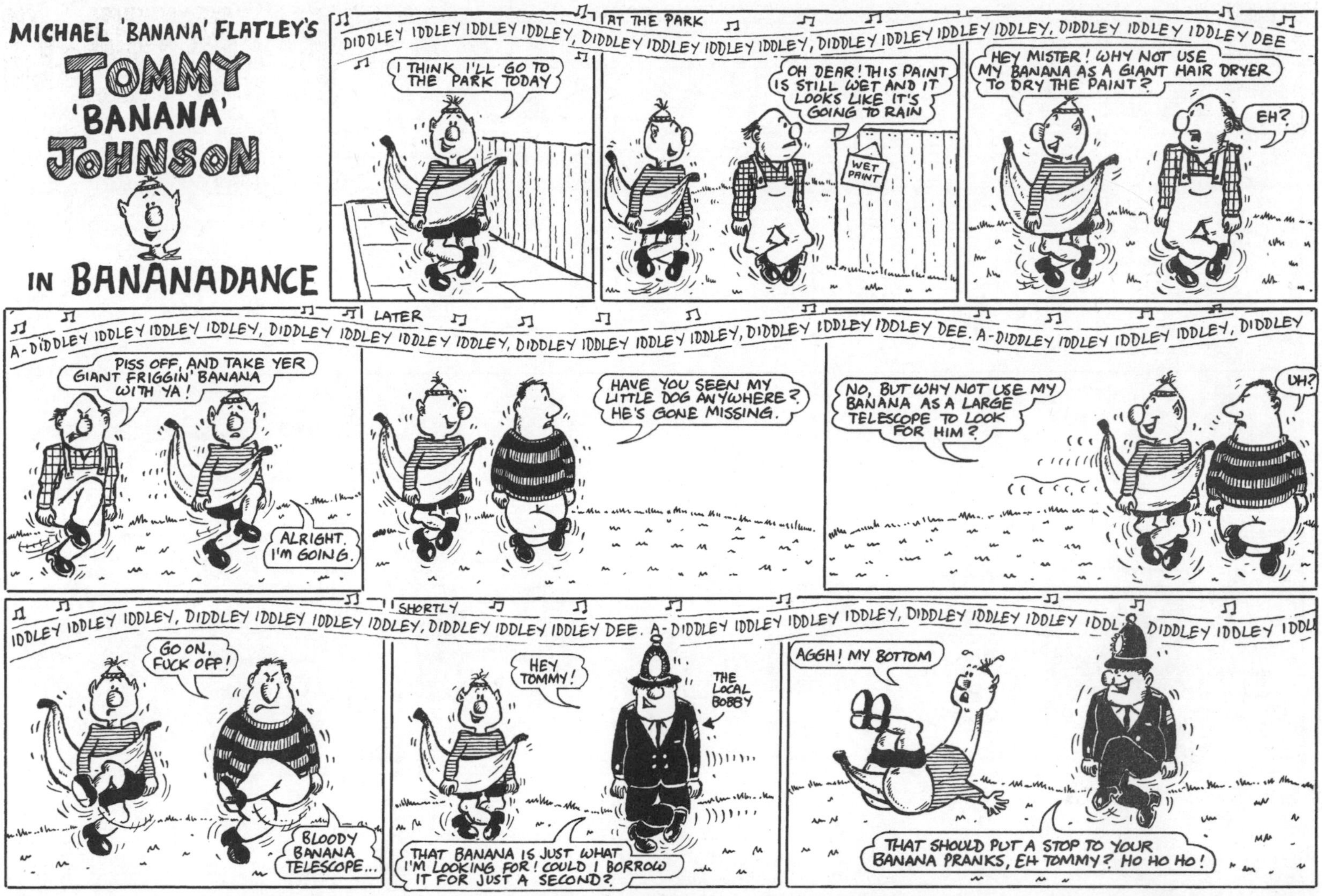
MICHAEL 'BANANA' FLATLEY'S
TOMMY 'BANANA' JOHNSON
IN BANANADANCE
DIDDLEY IDDLEY IDDLEY IDDLEY, DIDDLEY IDDLEY IDDLEY IDDLEY, DIDDLEY IDDLEY IDDLEY IDDLEY, DIDDLEY IDDLEY IDDLEY DEE
I THINK I'LL GO TO THE PARK TODAY
AT THE PARK
OH DEAR! THIS PAINT IS STILL WET AND IT LOOKS LIKE IT'S GOING TO RAIN
WET PAINT
HEY MISTER! WHY NOT USE MY BANANA AS A GIANT HAIR DRYER TO DRY THE PAINT?
EH?
A-DIDDLEY IDDLEY IDDLEY IDDLEY, DIDDLEY IDDLEY IDDLEY IDDLEY, DIDDLEY IDDLEY IDDLEY IDDLEY, DIDDLEY IDDLEY IDDLEY DEE. A-DIDDLEY IDDLEY IDDLEY IDDLEY, DIDDLEY
PISS OFF, AND TAKE YER GIANT FRIGGIN' BANANA WITH YA!
ALRIGHT. I'M GOING.
LATER
HAVE YOU SEEN MY LITTLE DOG ANYWHERE? HE'S GONE MISSING.
NO, BUT WHY NOT USE MY BANANA AS A LARGE TELESCOPE TO LOOK FOR HIM?
UH?
IDDLEY IDDLEY IDDLEY, DIDDLEY IDDLEY IDDLEY IDDLEY, DIDDLEY IDDLEY IDDLEY DEE. A-DIDDLEY IDDLEY IDDLEY IDDLEY, DIDDLEY IDDLEY IDDLEY IDDL DIDDLEY IDDLEY IDDL
GO ON, FUCK OFF!
BLOODY BANANA TELESCOPE...
SHORTLY
HEY TOMMY!
THE LOCAL BOBBY
THAT BANANA IS JUST WHAT I'M LOOKING FOR! COULD I BORROW IT FOR JUST A SECOND?
AGGH! MY BOTTOM
THAT SHOULD PUT A STOP TO YOUR BANANA PRANKS, EH TOMMY? HO HO HO!

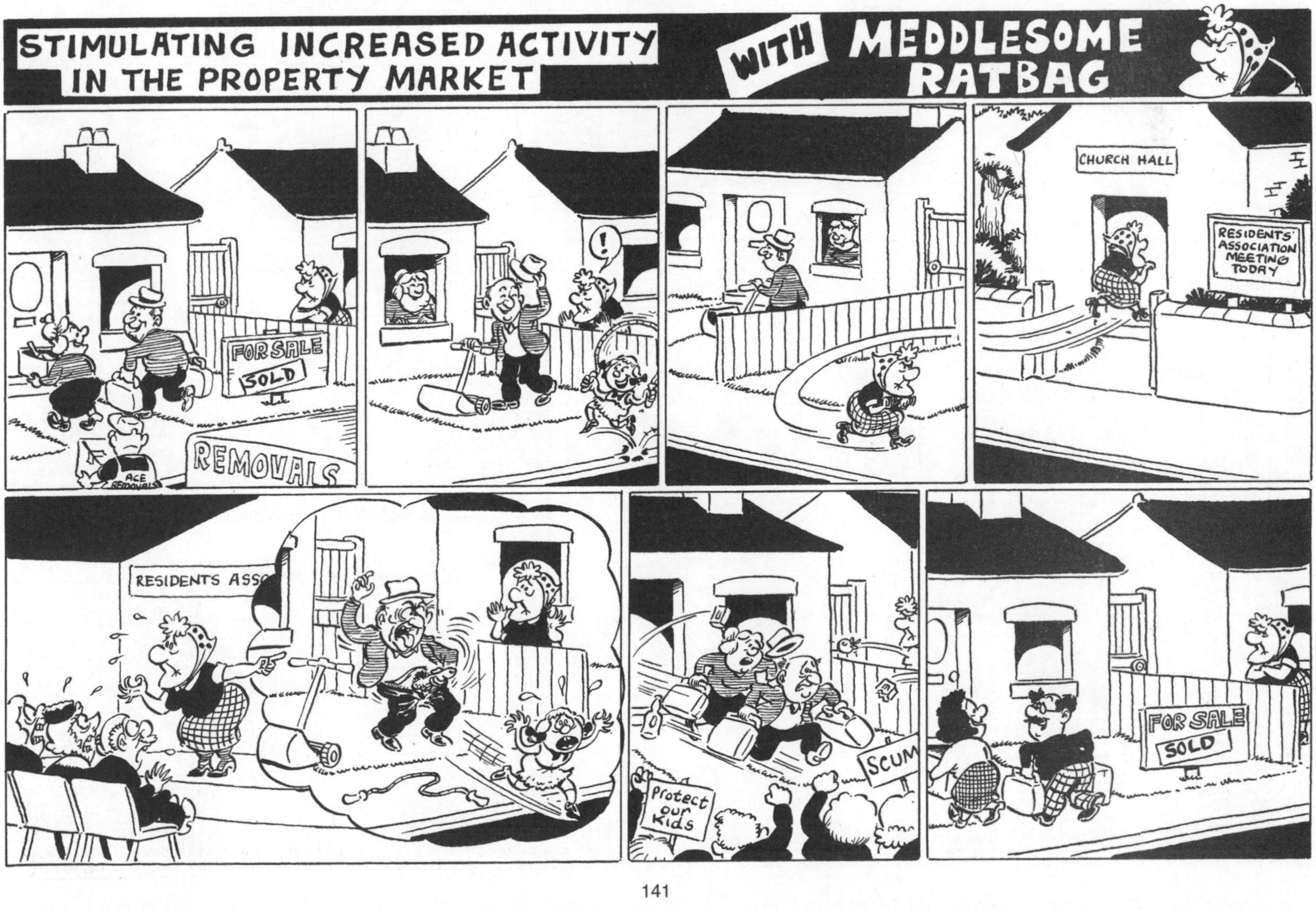
STIMULATING INCREASED ACTIVITY IN THE PROPERTY MARKET
WITH MEDDLESOME RATBAG
FOR SALE
SOLD
REMOVALS
!
CHURCH HALL
RESIDENTS' ASSOCIATION MEETING TODAY
RESIDENTS ASS
SCUM
Protect our Kids
FOR SALE
SOLD

FIRE-WALKING ALAN TURING

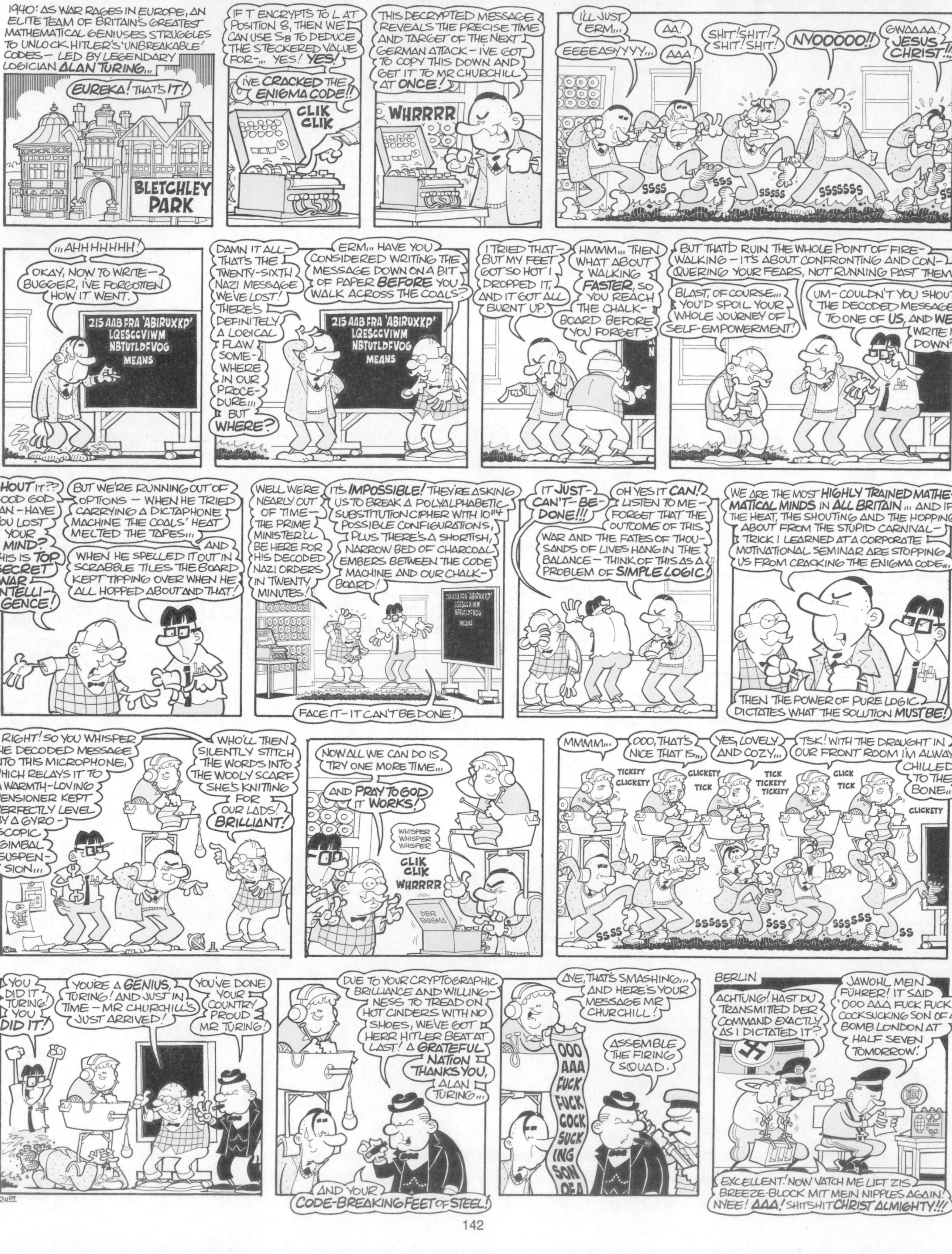
1940! AS WAR RAGES IN EUROPE, AN ELITE TEAM OF BRITAIN'S GREATEST MATHEMATICAL GENIUSES STRUGGLES TO UNLOCK HITLER'S 'UNBREAKABLE' CODES – LED BY LEGENDARY LOGICIAN ALAN TURING...
EUREKA! THAT'S IT!
BLETCHLEY PARK
IF T ENCRYPTS TO L AT POSITION 8, THEN WE CAN USE S8 TO DEDUCE THE STECKERED VALUE FOR–... YES! YES!
I'VE CRACKED THE ENIGMA CODE!!
CLIK CLIK
THIS DECRYPTED MESSAGE REVEALS THE PRECISE TIME AND TARGET OF THE NEXT GERMAN ATTACK – I'VE GOT TO COPY THIS DOWN AND GET IT TO MR CHURCHILL AT ONCE!
WHRRRR
I'LL JUST, ERM...
EEEEASYYYY...
AA!
AAA!
SHIT! SHIT! SHIT! SHIT!
NYOOOOO!!
GWAAAA! JESUS CHRIST!!!
SSSS
SSS
SSSSS
SSSSSSS
SS
...AHHHHHHH!
OKAY, NOW TO WRITE– BUGGER, I'VE FORGOTTEN HOW IT WENT.
215 AAB FRA 'ABIRUXKP' LQESCGVIWM NBTUTLDFVOG MEANS
DAMN IT ALL – THAT'S THE TWENTY-SIXTH NAZI MESSAGE WE'VE LOST! THERE'S DEFINITELY A LOGICAL FLAW SOMEWHERE IN OUR PROCEDURE... BUT WHERE?
ERM... HAVE YOU CONSIDERED WRITING THE MESSAGE DOWN ON A BIT OF PAPER BEFORE YOU WALK ACROSS THE COALS?
215 AAB FRA 'ABIRUXKP' LQESCGVIWM NBTUTLDFVOG MEANS
I TRIED THAT – BUT MY FEET GOT SO HOT I DROPPED IT, AND IT GOT ALL BURNT UP.
HMMM... THEN WHAT ABOUT WALKING FASTER, SO YOU REACH THE CHALKBOARD BEFORE YOU FORGET?
BUT THAT'D RUIN THE WHOLE POINT OF FIRE-WALKING – IT'S ABOUT CONFRONTING AND CONQUERING YOUR FEARS, NOT RUNNING PAST THEM!
BLAST, OF COURSE... YOU'D SPOIL YOUR WHOLE JOURNEY OF SELF-EMPOWERMENT!
UM– COULDN'T YOU SHOUT THE DECODED MESSAGE TO ONE OF US, AND WE WRITE IT DOWN?
SHOUT IT?? GOOD GOD MAN – HAVE YOU LOST YOUR MIND? THIS IS TOP SECRET WAR INTELLIGENCE!
BUT WE'RE RUNNING OUT OF OPTIONS – WHEN HE TRIED CARRYING A DICTAPHONE MACHINE THE COALS' HEAT MELTED THE TAPES...
AND WHEN HE SPELLED IT OUT IN SCRABBLE TILES THE BOARD KEPT TIPPING OVER WHEN HE ALL HOPPED ABOUT AND THAT!
WELL WE'RE NEARLY OUT OF TIME – THE PRIME MINISTER'LL BE HERE FOR HIS DECODED NAZI ORDERS IN TWENTY MINUTES!
IT'S IMPOSSIBLE! THEY'RE ASKING US TO BREAK A POLYALPHABETIC SUBSTITUTION CIPHER WITH 10^{114} POSSIBLE CONFIGURATIONS, PLUS THERE'S A SHORTISH, NARROW BED OF CHARCOAL EMBERS BETWEEN THE CODE MACHINE AND OUR CHALKBOARD!
215 AAB FRA 'ABIRUXKP' LQESCGVIWM NBTUTLDFVOG MEANS
FACE IT – IT CAN'T BE DONE!
IT JUST-CAN'T-BE-DONE!!!
OH YES IT CAN! LISTEN TO ME – FORGET THAT THE OUTCOME OF THIS WAR AND THE FATES OF THOUSANDS OF LIVES HANG IN THE BALANCE – THINK OF THIS AS A PROBLEM OF SIMPLE LOGIC!
WE ARE THE MOST HIGHLY TRAINED MATHEMATICAL MINDS IN ALL BRITAIN... AND IF THE HEAT, THE SHOUTING AND THE HOPPING ABOUT FROM THE STUPID CARNIVAL-TRICK I LEARNED AT A CORPORATE MOTIVATIONAL SEMINAR ARE STOPPING US FROM CRACKING THE ENIGMA CODE...
THEN THE POWER OF PURE LOGIC DICTATES WHAT THE SOLUTION MUST BE!
...RIGHT! SO YOU WHISPER THE DECODED MESSAGE INTO THIS MICROPHONE, WHICH RELAYS IT TO A WARMTH-LOVING PENSIONER KEPT PERFECTLY LEVEL BY A GYROSCOPIC GIMBAL SUSPENSION...
WHO'LL THEN SILENTLY STITCH THE WORDS INTO THE WOOLY SCARF SHE'S KNITTING FOR OUR LADS! BRILLIANT!
NOW ALL WE CAN DO IS TRY ONE MORE TIME...
AND PRAY TO GOD IT WORKS!
WHISPER WHISPER WHISPER
CLIK CLIK WHRRRR
DER ENIGMA
MMMM...
OOO, THAT'S NICE THAT IS...
YES, LOVELY AND COZY...
TSK! WITH THE DRAUGHT IN OUR FRONT ROOM I'M ALWAYS CHILLED TO THE BONE...
TICKETY CLICKETY
CLICKETY TICK
TICK TICKETY TICKETY
CLICK TICK
CLICKETY
SSSS
SSSSS
SSS
SSSSSS
SS
YOU DID IT TURING! YOU DID IT!
YOU'RE A GENIUS, TURING! AND JUST IN TIME – MR CHURCHILL'S JUST ARRIVED!
YOU'VE DONE YOUR COUNTRY PROUD MR TURING!
DUE TO YOUR CRYPTOGRAPHIC BRILLIANCE AND WILLINGNESS TO TREAD ON HOT CINDERS WITH NO SHOES, WE'VE GOT HERR HITLER BEAT AT LAST! A GRATEFUL NATION THANKS YOU, ALAN TURING...
AND YOUR CODE-BREAKING FEET OF STEEL!
AYE, THAT'S SMASHING... AND HERE'S YOUR MESSAGE MR CHURCHILL!
OOO AAA FUCK FUCK COCK SUCKING SON OF A
ASSEMBLE THE FIRING SQUAD.
BERLIN
ACHTUNG! HAST DU TRANSMITTED DER COMMAND EXACTLY AS I DICTATED IT?
JAWOHL MEIN FÜHRER! IT SAID 'OOO AAA FUCK FUCK COCKSUCKING SON OF A BOMB LONDON AT HALF SEVEN TOMORROW.'
EXCELLENT! NOW VATCH ME LIFT ZIS BREEZE-BLOCK MIT MEIN NIPPLES AGAIN! NYEE! AAA! SHITSHIT CHRIST ALMIGHTY!!!
RH09

LUVVIE DARLING
WILL EMOTE FOR FOOD
LUVVIE IS WORKING AS A CHILDREN'S ENTERTAINER...
RIGHT, SETTLE DOWN EVERYONE... BECAUSE WE'VE GOT A SURPRISE FOR YOU... A VERY SPECIAL TREAT..!
HOORAY!
...IT'S MISTER MUDDLES!!
HELLO THERE BOYS AND GURGLES!
DOH! ≡SPLUTTER!≡ DID I SAY BOYS AND GURGLES? I AM A SILLY OLD SAUSAGE! I MEANT BURPS AND GURGLES..!
HO HO!
HEE! HEE!
NOW... WHO LIKES BALLOONS..?
ME! ME! ME!
I LIKE BALLOONS TOO!
AW BLESS.
!?
WHAT DO YOU THINK YOU'RE DOING?
I WAS JUST BRINGING THE BIRTHDAY CAKE IN...
WHAT THE FUCK..? I OUGHT TO KICK YOUR FUCKING ASS!
I'M SORRY..?
NO! DON'T JUST BE SORRY. THINK FOR ONE FUCKING SECOND. WHAT THE FUCK ARE YOU DOING? ARE YOU PROFESSIONAL OR NOT? DO I FUCKING WALK AROUND AND...
WE WANT BALLOONS!
SHUT THE FUCK UP.
AM I GOING TO WALK AROUND AND SMASH YOUR FUCKING CAKE UP IN THE MIDDLE OF A PARTY? NO! SO WHY THE FUCK ARE YOU WALKING RIGHT THROUGH ≡A-TADA-TADA≡ LIKE THIS? WHAT THE FUCK IS IT WITH YOU?
WHAT DON'T YOU FUCKING UNDERSTAND? HEY! IT'S FUCKING DISTRACTING HAVING SOMEBODY WALKING UP BEHIND ME IN THE MIDDLE OF MY ACT... WHAT DON'T YOU GET ABOUT IT?
FUCK'S SAKE. YOU'RE AN AMATEUR!
YOU GOT SOMETHING TO SAY TO THIS PRICK? JESUS! I'M TRYING TO FUCKING DO BALLOON ANIMALS HERE AND I'M GOING WHY THE FUCK IS SHE WALKING IN THERE?!?
WHAT IS SHE DOING THERE? DO YOU FUCKING UNDERSTAND?
MY MIND IS NOT ON THE BALLOONS IF YOU'RE DOING THAT! STAY OUT THE FUCKING LIVING ROOM, FOR FUCK'S SAKE!
RIGHT, LET'S GO AGAIN... LET'S NOT TAKE A FUCKING MINUTE, LET'S GO AGAIN.
AND LET'S NOT HAVE YOU FUCKING WALKING IN... YOU'RE UNBELIEVABLE, UN-FUCKING-BELIEVABLE! I OUGHT TO FUCKING KICK YOUR FUCKING ASS..!
YOU DON'T FUCKING UNDERSTAND WHAT IT'S LIKE WORKING WITH ACTORS, THAT'S WHAT THAT IS..!
DO YOU WANT ME TO TRASH YOUR CAKE? DO YOU WANT ME TO FUCKING TRASH IT? YOU DO IT ONE MORE TIME AND I'LL WALK OUT OF THIS FUCKING PARTY. SERIOUSLY, YOU AND ME - WE'RE FUCKING DONE!
FUCKING PRICK.
NOW... WHO LIKES BALLOONS..?

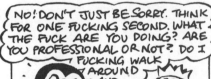

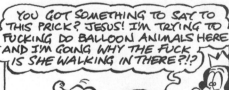

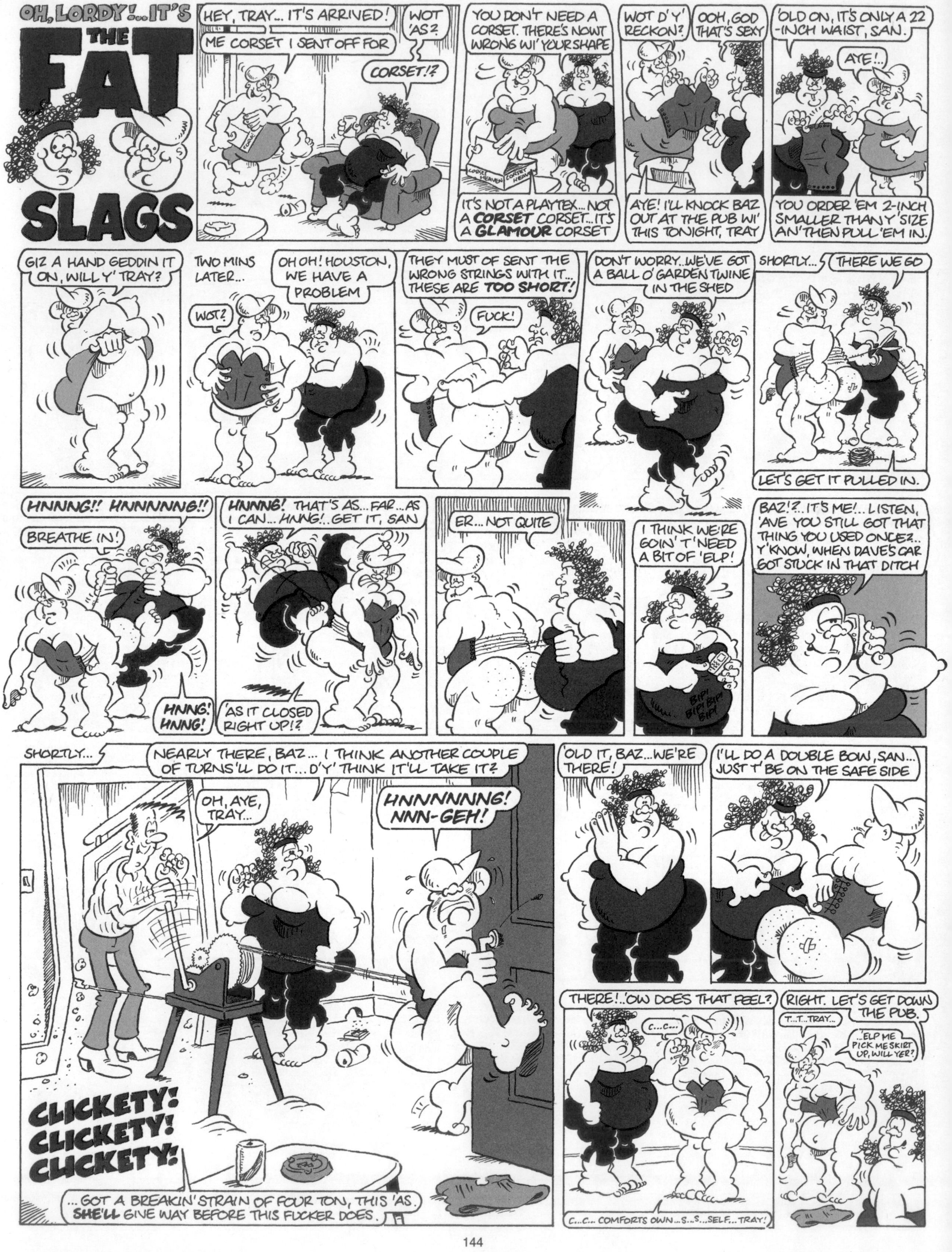
OH, LORDY!.. IT'S
THE FAT SLAGS
HEY, TRAY... IT'S ARRIVED!
ME CORSET I SENT OFF FOR
WOT 'AS?
CORSET!?
YOU DON'T NEED A CORSET. THERE'S NOWT WRONG WI' YOUR SHAPE
CORSET HEAVEN
IT'S NOT A PLAYTEX... NOT A **CORSET** CORSET... IT'S A **GLAMOUR** CORSET
WOT D'Y' RECKON?
OOH, GOD THAT'S SEXY
AYE! I'LL KNOCK BAZ OUT AT THE PUB WI' THIS TONIGHT, TRAY
'OLD ON, IT'S ONLY A 22-INCH WAIST, SAN.
AYE!...
YOU ORDER 'EM 2-INCH SMALLER THAN Y' SIZE AN' THEN PULL 'EM IN.
GIZ A HAND GEDDIN IT ON, WILL Y' TRAY?
TWO MINS LATER...
OH OH! HOUSTON, WE HAVE A PROBLEM
WOT?
THEY MUST OF SENT THE WRONG STRINGS WITH IT... THESE ARE **TOO SHORT!**
FUCK!
DON'T WORRY.. WE'VE GOT A BALL O' GARDEN TWINE IN THE SHED
SHORTLY...
THERE WE GO
LET'S GET IT PULLED IN.
HNNNG!! HNNNNNG!!
BREATHE IN!
HNNG! HNNG!
HNNNG! THAT'S AS... FAR... AS I CAN... HNNG!.. GET IT, SAN
'AS IT CLOSED RIGHT UP!?
ER... NOT QUITE
I THINK WE'RE GOIN' T' NEED A BIT OF 'ELP!
BIP! BIP! BIP! BIP!
BAZ!?.. IT'S ME!... LISTEN, 'AVE YOU STILL GOT THAT THING YOU USED ONCE?.. Y'KNOW, WHEN DAVE'S CAR GOT STUCK IN THAT DITCH
SHORTLY...
NEARLY THERE, BAZ... I THINK ANOTHER COUPLE OF TURNS'LL DO IT... D'Y' THINK IT'LL TAKE IT?
OH, AYE, TRAY...
HNNNNNNG! NNN-GEH!
CLICKETY! CLICKETY! CLICKETY!
...GOT A BREAKIN' STRAIN OF FOUR TON, THIS 'AS. **SHE'LL** GIVE WAY BEFORE THIS FUCKER DOES.
'OLD IT, BAZ... WE'RE THERE!
I'LL DO A DOUBLE BOW, SAN... JUST T' BE ON THE SAFE SIDE
THERE!..'OW DOES THAT FEEL?
C...C...
C...C... COMFORTS OWN...S..S...SELF... TRAY!
RIGHT. LET'S GET DOWN THE PUB.
T...T...TRAY...
...ELP ME PICK ME SKIRT UP, WILL YER?

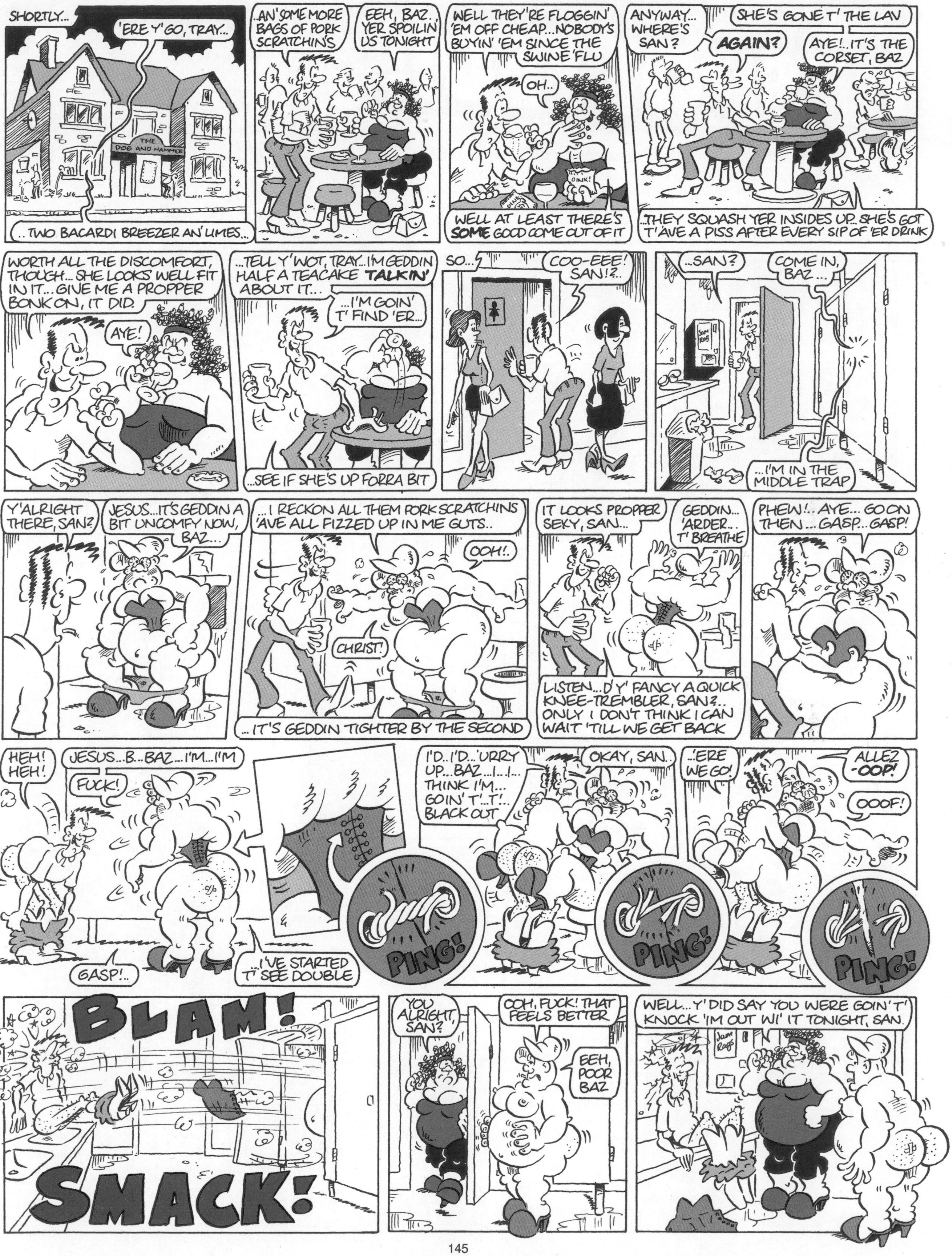
SHORTLY...
'ERE Y' GO, TRAY...
...TWO BACARDI BREEZER AN' LIMES...
THE DOG AND HAMMER
...AN' SOME MORE BAGS OF PORK SCRATCHIN'S
EEH, BAZ. YER SPOILIN' US TONIGHT
WELL THEY'RE FLOGGIN' 'EM OFF CHEAP... NOBODY'S BUYIN' 'EM SINCE THE SWINE 'FLU
OH..
OINK!
WELL AT LEAST THERE'S SOME GOOD COME OUT OF IT
ANYWAY... WHERE'S SAN?
SHE'S GONE T' THE LAV
AGAIN?
AYE!.. IT'S THE CORSET, BAZ
...THEY SQUASH YER INSIDES UP.. SHE'S GOT T' 'AVE A PISS AFTER EVERY SIP OF 'ER DRINK
WORTH ALL THE DISCOMFORT, THOUGH... SHE LOOKS WELL FIT IN IT... GIVE ME A PROPPER BONK ON, IT DID.
AYE!
...TELL Y' WOT, TRAY... I'M GEDDIN HALF A TEACAKE TALKIN' ABOUT IT...
...I'M GOIN' T' FIND 'ER...
...SEE IF SHE'S UP FORRA BIT
SO...
COO-EEE! SAN!?..
...SAN?
COME IN, BAZ...
...I'M IN THE MIDDLE TRAP
Y'ALRIGHT THERE, SAN?
JESUS... IT'S GEDDIN A BIT UNCOMFY NOW, BAZ...
...I RECKON ALL THEM PORK SCRATCHINS 'AVE ALL FIZZED UP IN ME GUTS..
OOH!..
CHRIST!
...IT'S GEDDIN TIGHTER BY THE SECOND
IT LOOKS PROPPER SEKY, SAN...
GEDDIN... 'ARDER... T' BREATHE
LISTEN... D'Y' FANCY A QUICK KNEE-TREMBLER, SAN?.. ONLY I DON'T THINK I CAN WAIT 'TILL WE GET BACK
PHEW!.. AYE... GO ON THEN... GASP... GASP!
HEH! HEH!
JESUS... B... BAZ... I'M... I'M
FUCK!
GASP!..
...I'VE STARTED T' SEE DOUBLE
PING!
I'D.. I'D... 'URRY UP... BAZ... I.. I.. THINK I'M... GOIN' T'.. T'.. BLACK OUT
OKAY, SAN.
PING!
...'ERE WE GO!
ALLEZ -OOP!
OOOF!
PING!
BLAM!
SMACK!
YOU ALRIGHT, SAN?
OOH, FUCK! THAT FEELS BETTER
EEH, POOR BAZ
WELL... Y' DID SAY YOU WERE GOIN' T' KNOCK 'IM OUT WI' IT TONIGHT, SAN.
Jam Rags

Our Paps have been out and about this week checking out the Despot Hotspots...

DESPOTTED!!

No Specs, Please. We're Cambodian!

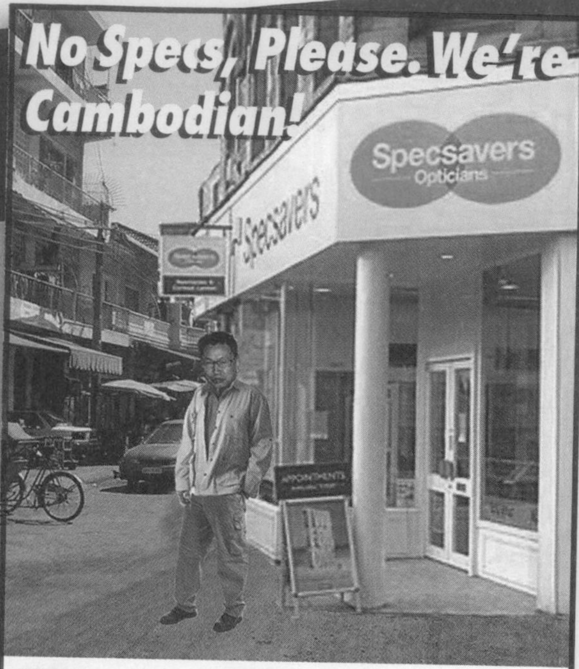

Specsavers
Opticians
Specsavers

Eye, eye! Who's this coming out of a Phnom Penh opticians after having his peepers tested? It's none other than hunky Khmer Rouge leader **POL POT**. And those sexy specs are sure to improve his *killing fields* of vision. But let's hope Potty Pol doesn't massacre himself when he clocks his decadent new lenses in the mirror!

What's that in your *Baghdad*? That's the question that **UDAY HUSSEIN** seems to be asking his old man, Iraqi despot, **SADDAM**, as they do a spot of sun bathing on the beach at Cleethorpes. And they've certainly picked a *Sunni* day for a bit of *Shia* relaxation. Lets's hope that the two unrepentant mass murderers have plenty of oil. *Sun oil*, that is!

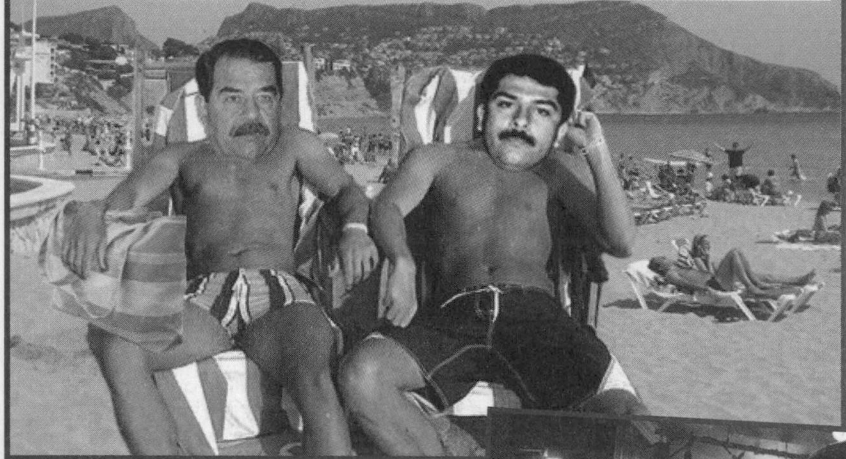

Bob's Your Uncle

Ballot-rigging bastard **SIR ROBERT MUGABE** joined the fun when his nephew Tristram Mugabe celebrated his 5th birthday at Harare's Hard Rock Cafe. And Uncle Bob helped the youngster snuff out the candles, just like he snuffed out the opposition during his recent successful election. Don't forget to make a wish, Tristram! And you too, Robert. *How about wishing for another 20 years of autocratic rule?!*

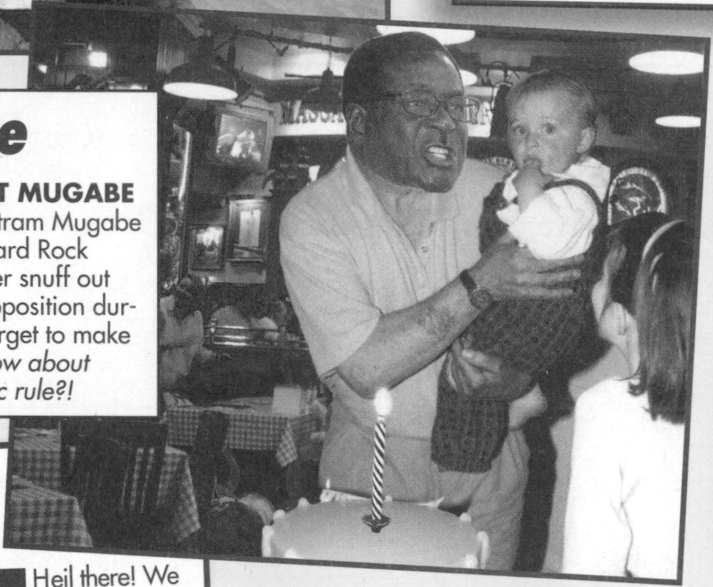

Kristallnacht on the Tiles!

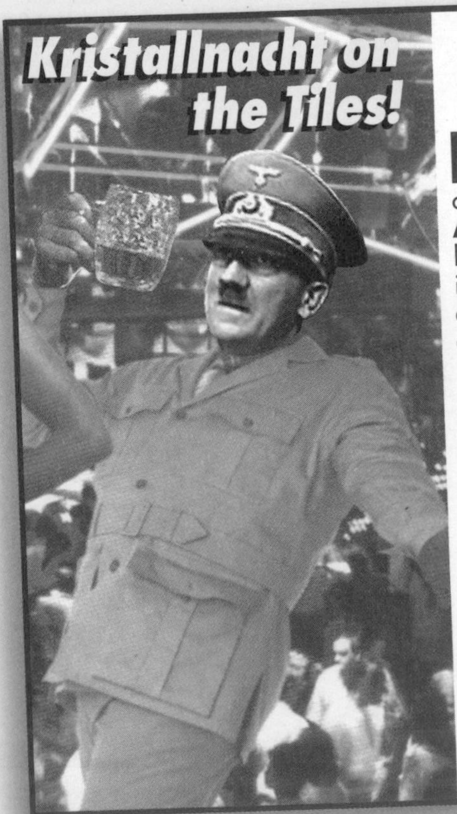

Heil there! We spotted genocidal megalomaniac **ADOLF HITLER** letting his *Herr* down in Spearmint Rhino earlier this week. And doesn't he look the *würst* for wear? Spies on the inside say the Führer spent the night getting *blitzed* with his Gestapo pals before leaving in a *Reich* old state at 3am. The dictator looked like he was heading for a hangover that would last a thousand years. *Maybe next time you should swastika to soft drinks eh, Adolf?*

Holey Joe! With the blood of 20 million on his hands, **JOSEPH STALIN** is the *crème de la Kremlin* of the ruthless tyrants. But he's certainly *gulagging* behind when it comes to dress sense. It looks like the Generalissimo has never had the iron out behind the iron curtain. *Perhaps you should spend less time repressing your dissidents and a bit more time pressing your fucking trousers, Joe!*

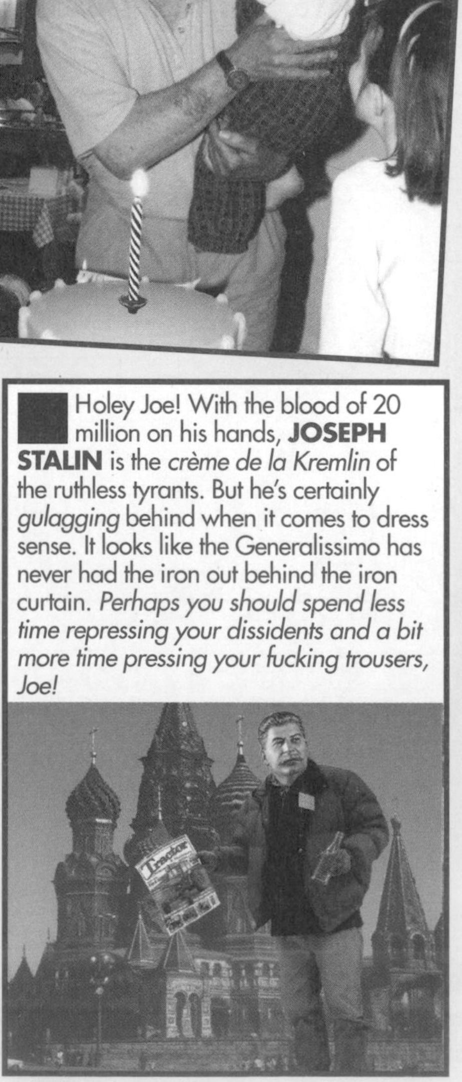

WHO! WHAT! WHERE!

Tyrants spotted out'n'about this week...

'Il Duce' **Benito Mussolini** *carrying his cat Mr Pookey out of a vet's surgery in Redditch...*

★★★★★★★★

Nicolae Ceausescu *and wife Dolly buying emulsion paint in a branch of Decor-8 in Gateshead...*

★★★★★★★★

North Korean eternal emperor **Kim il-Sung** *with a mystery blonde hiring a rowing boat in Pontefract Park...*

★★★★★★★★

Field Marshall **Dr Idi Amin**, *tucking into his Archbishop's liver on a picnic bench on Llandudno seafront...*

APOLOGY

In the last issue under the heading "Nick Nick! It's Chile Out", we printed a picture of comedian **Jim Davidson** leaving a restaurant with **General Augusto Pinochet**. The caption of the photograph implied that Mr Davidson had dined with the South American dictator. It has since been pointed out to us that Mr Davidson had been dining with his agent in the restaurant at another table, a fact which was not made apparent in the caption. We are happy to make clear that the Mr Davidson was not dining with, and indeed has never met Mr Pinochet. We would like to apologise to Mr Pinochet for any embarrassment caused by the publication of this article.

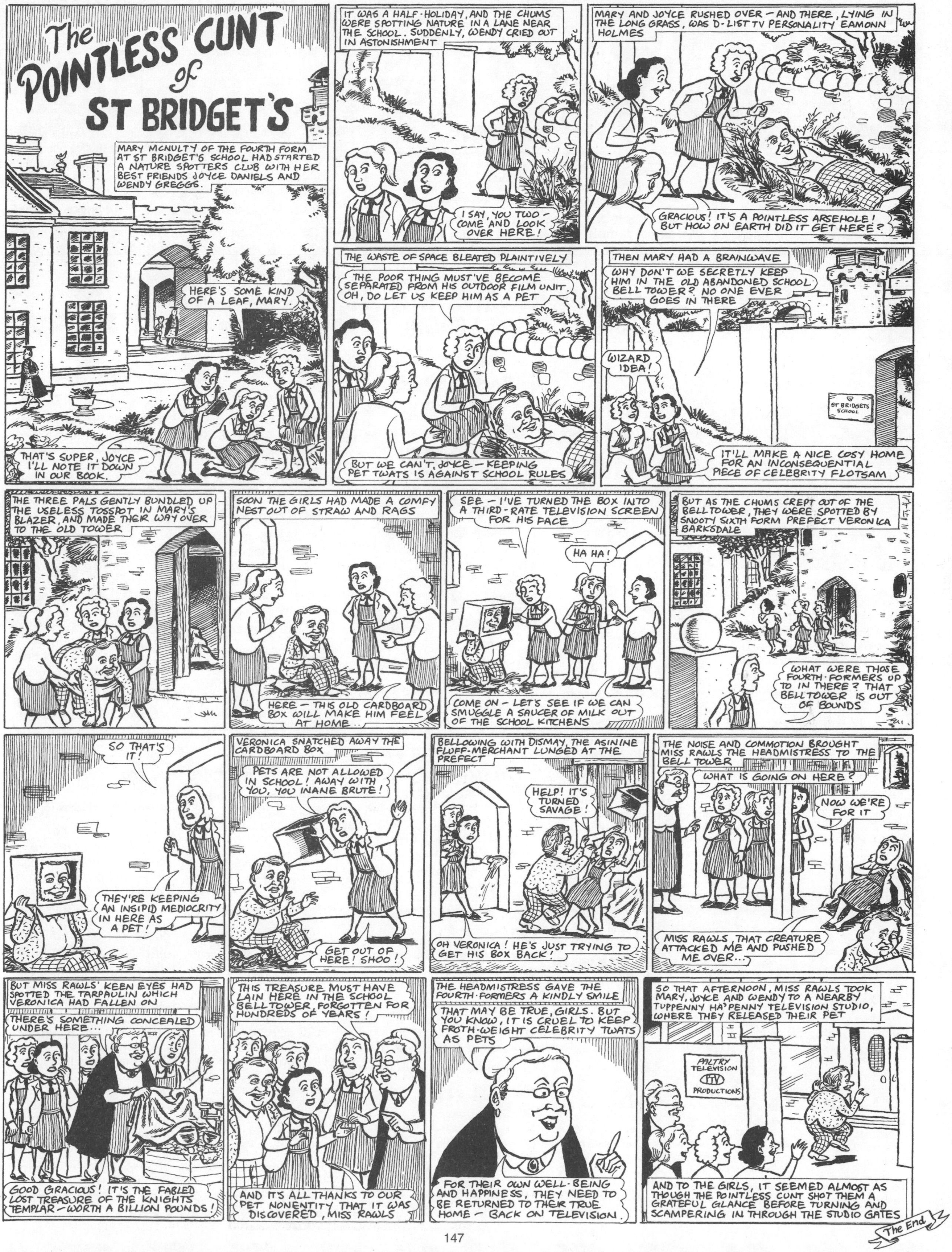

The Pointless Cunt of St Bridget's
MARY MCNULTY OF THE FOURTH FORM AT ST BRIDGET'S SCHOOL HAD STARTED A NATURE SPOTTERS CLUB WITH HER BEST FRIENDS JOYCE DANIELS AND WENDY GREGGS.
HERE'S SOME KIND OF A LEAF, MARY.
THAT'S SUPER, JOYCE - I'LL NOTE IT DOWN IN OUR BOOK.
IT WAS A HALF-HOLIDAY, AND THE CHUMS WERE SPOTTING NATURE IN A LANE NEAR THE SCHOOL. SUDDENLY, WENDY CRIED OUT IN ASTONISHMENT
I SAY, YOU TWO - COME AND LOOK OVER HERE!
MARY AND JOYCE RUSHED OVER - AND THERE, LYING IN THE LONG GRASS, WAS D-LIST TV PERSONALITY EAMONN HOLMES
GRACIOUS! IT'S A POINTLESS ARSEHOLE! BUT HOW ON EARTH DID IT GET HERE?
THE WASTE OF SPACE BLEATED PLAINTIVELY
THE POOR THING MUST'VE BECOME SEPARATED FROM HIS OUTDOOR FILM UNIT. OH, DO LET US KEEP HIM AS A PET
BUT WE CAN'T, JOYCE - KEEPING PET TWATS IS AGAINST SCHOOL RULES
THEN MARY HAD A BRAINWAVE
WHY DON'T WE SECRETLY KEEP HIM IN THE OLD ABANDONED SCHOOL BELL TOWER? NO ONE EVER GOES IN THERE
WIZARD IDEA!
ST BRIDGETS SCHOOL
IT'LL MAKE A NICE COSY HOME FOR AN INCONSEQUENTIAL PIECE OF CELEBRITY FLOTSAM
THE THREE PALS GENTLY BUNDLED UP THE USELESS TOSSPOT IN MARY'S BLAZER, AND MADE THEIR WAY OVER TO THE OLD TOWER
SOON THE GIRLS HAD MADE A COMFY NEST OUT OF STRAW AND RAGS
HERE - THIS OLD CARDBOARD BOX WILL MAKE HIM FEEL AT HOME...
SEE - I'VE TURNED THE BOX INTO A THIRD-RATE TELEVISION SCREEN FOR HIS FACE
HA HA!
COME ON - LET'S SEE IF WE CAN SMUGGLE A SAUCER OF MILK OUT OF THE SCHOOL KITCHENS
BUT AS THE CHUMS CREPT OUT OF THE BELL TOWER, THEY WERE SPOTTED BY SNOOTY SIXTH FORM PREFECT VERONICA BARKSDALE
WHAT WERE THOSE FOURTH-FORMERS UP TO IN THERE? THAT BELL TOWER IS OUT OF BOUNDS
SO THAT'S IT!
THEY'RE KEEPING AN INSIPID MEDIOCRITY IN HERE AS A PET!
VERONICA SNATCHED AWAY THE CARDBOARD BOX
PETS ARE NOT ALLOWED IN SCHOOL! AWAY WITH YOU, YOU INANE BRUTE!
GET OUT OF HERE! SHOO!
BELLOWING WITH DISMAY, THE ASININE FLUFF-MERCHANT LUNGED AT THE PREFECT
HELP! IT'S TURNED SAVAGE!
OH VERONICA! HE'S JUST TRYING TO GET HIS BOX BACK!
THE NOISE AND COMMOTION BROUGHT MISS RAWLS THE HEADMISTRESS TO THE BELL TOWER
WHAT IS GOING ON HERE?
NOW WE'RE FOR IT
MISS RAWLS, THAT CREATURE ATTACKED ME AND PUSHED ME OVER...
BUT MISS RAWLS' KEEN EYES HAD SPOTTED THE TARPAULIN WHICH VERONICA HAD FALLEN ON
THERE'S SOMETHING CONCEALED UNDER HERE...
GOOD GRACIOUS! IT'S THE FABLED LOST TREASURE OF THE KNIGHTS TEMPLAR - WORTH A BILLION POUNDS!
THIS TREASURE MUST HAVE LAIN HERE IN THE SCHOOL BELLTOWER, FORGOTTEN FOR HUNDREDS OF YEARS!
AND IT'S ALL THANKS TO OUR PET NONENTITY THAT IT WAS DISCOVERED, MISS RAWLS
THE HEADMISTRESS GAVE THE FOURTH-FORMERS A KINDLY SMILE
THAT MAY BE TRUE, GIRLS. BUT YOU KNOW, IT IS CRUEL TO KEEP FROTH-WEIGHT CELEBRITY TWATS AS PETS
FOR THEIR OWN WELL-BEING AND HAPPINESS, THEY NEED TO BE RETURNED TO THEIR TRUE HOME - BACK ON TELEVISION.
SO THAT AFTERNOON, MISS RAWLS TOOK MARY, JOYCE AND WENDY TO A NEARBY TUPPENNY HA'PENNY TELEVISION STUDIO, WHERE THEY RELEASED THEIR PET
PALTRY TELEVISION PTV PRODUCTIONS
AND TO THE GIRLS, IT SEEMED ALMOST AS THOUGH THE POINTLESS CUNT SHOT THEM A GRATEFUL GLANCE BEFORE TURNING AND SCAMPERING IN THROUGH THE STUDIO GATES
The End

LeTteRBoCKs

letters@viz.co.uk

WHY do police chiefs and FA spokesmen always tell us that football hooligans aren't real fans of the game? I support West Ham and love going to see them play as often as possible. Just because I like to attack passengers on the tube on the way to Upton Park and then hurl glass bottles and seats at visiting fans doesn't mean I enjoy the beautiful game any the less.

Victor Giraffe, e-mail

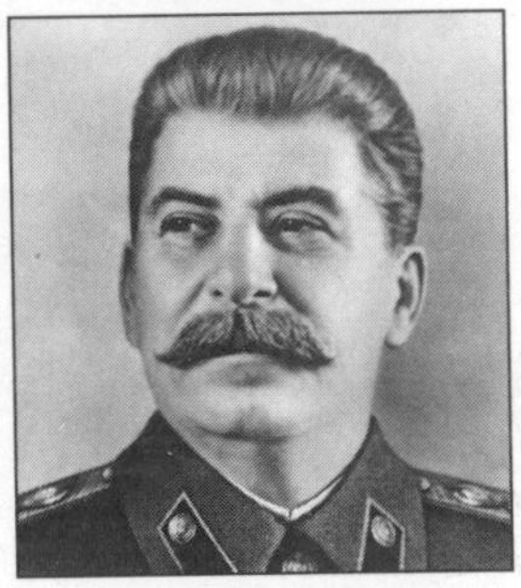

ACCORDING to Stalin's grandson, he was a really great bloke, and I suppose he knows more about Stalin than anybody. So I bet historians are feeling a bit silly now for making him out to be a right cunt.

W Wainhouse, e-mail

I CONSIDER myself a modern, cosmopolitan sort of guy, and have no problem buying Tampax for my wife. Although, apparently they're not a 'proper' present.

Dr Albans e-mail

STAR LETTER

WHY IS it that when your wife is pregnant, all her female friends come round, rub her tummy and say congratulations, yet none of them rub your cock and say 'well done.'

Stanley Prodworthy, e-mail

THE other day a sign on the road told me to 'Look Right', whilst on the other side of the road it was telling people to 'Look Left.' No wonder so many pedestrians get knocked over.

Frank Bramley, e-mail

VIZ COMIC, PO Box 656, North Shields, NE30 4XX

IN A recent opinion piece in the Daily Mail, A.N. Wilson wrote: "The trouble with a 'scientific' argument, of course, is that it is not made in the real world, but in a laboratory by an unimaginative academic relying solely on empirical facts." Bravo. It's about time someone took a stand against those who use empirical facts to come to a conclusion.

John Wednesbury, e-mail

RELIGIOUS people really get on my tit ends. When they die, we pay all that money for a funeral and they haven't even got the decency to come back as a ghost and tell us what the afterlife is like. They are never slow to bore the shit out of us when they are alive.

Matt McCann, e-mail

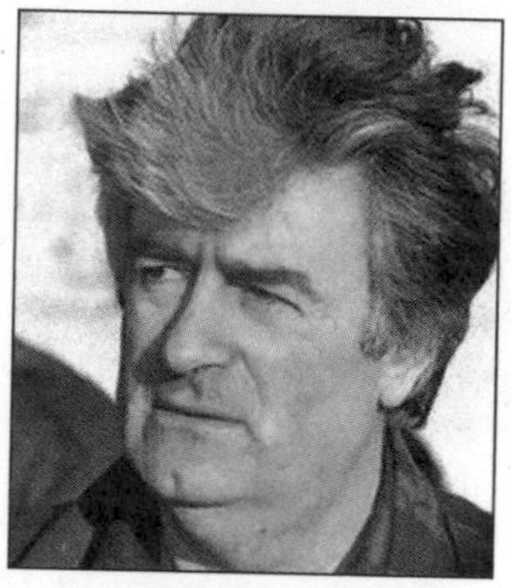

BEFORE they chuck Radovan Karadzic in prison for the rest of his life, do you think there's any chance he could play Father Ted in the long-awaited fourth series?

Cliff B, e-mail

"I AM an anti-Christ, I am an anarchist," wailed Johnny Rotten in the 70s. Now he's advertising butter. Come on, Mr Rotten, make your mind up. You can't be an anarchic anti-Christ and a butter salesman, the two things just don't go together.

Stuart Achilles, e-mail

I'M ALL for feminists burning their bras, but expecting me not to look at their nips whilst they're doing it is asking a bit too much, in my opinion.

Bill the Burger, e-mail

PEOPLE think that onions are the only vegetable that make you cry, but this is not true. My mate got hit in the face by a cabbage thrown from a car and she was in floods of tears.

Jack Daniels, e-mail

I MADE a nude lady out of keyboard symbols. Merry Christmas.

```
  /=-=\
  '|°.°|'
  /| o |\
 /(.)(.)\
 |  ) . ( |
 | ( V ) |
@|  |  | |@
    | | |
    | | |
   /_||_\
```

Jake Anna, M'brough

HAS anyone noticed how much smaller mobile phones are getting each year? What a rip off. I remember back in the 80s when you got a huge phone for your money, the size of a house brick and the charger weighed a ton. The manufacturers must be coining it in.

Henry Hamill, Arclid

TOP

LORRY drivers. Make time appear to stand still by attempting to overtake another lorry whilst taking care not to actually accelerate.

Errol Fudge, e-mail

MAKE your neighbours think that they live next door to Cliff Richard by stapling a rhino's scrotum to your neck and having a retired vicar move in with you.

Tam Dale, e-mail

SPECS wearers. Save money on alcohol, by simply drinking half as much, then taking your glasses off for the same pissed-up effect.

Rich, e-mail

ROOFERS. Try going up on the roof to inspect it, rather than standing at ground level next to me saying "it needs a lot of work done to it."

Mr Slater, e-mail

MOTORISTS. Keep a small black sponge in your car. If you get pulled over by the police for using your mobile phone whilst driving, you can grab it and claim you were just cleaning the side of your face.

Paul Joyce, Barnsley

SAVE money on window cleaning by covering your windows in clingfilm and removing it when dirty.

Lisa Stout, e-mail

FORMER 10cc member Lol Creme. When text messaging bad news, it is probably best not to add your name at the end as this may cause offence.

Stuart Penney, e-mail

WALLPAPER manufacturers. Measure the height of a average

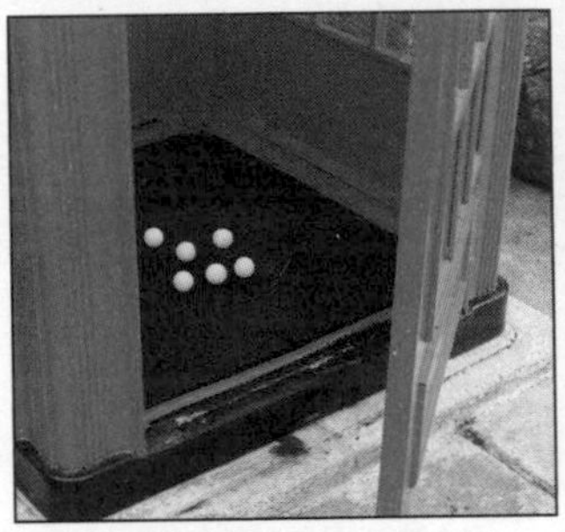

WHILST flicking through the Guinness Book of Records, I noticed that there was no entry for the greatest number of table tennis balls packed into a telephone box. So I claim the record with six and enclose photographic evidence of my record-breaking feat.

Adam Chamberlaine, e-mail

**If you can beat Mr Chamberlaine's record, then you're a kiosk-stuffing, ping-pong packing, phone-box-filling Record Breaker. Send us a picture as proof and we'll forward it to the ghosts of Ross and Norris McWhirter. And Roy Castle.*

I DON'T think people who believe in God should be allowed to be doctors. If I was being operated on by a surgeon, I wouldn't want them to think that it was no big deal if they balls the operation up as I'd be going to a better place. No wonder so many people die under the knife. The quicker the British Medical Association introduce an atheists only policy, the better.

Frank Dentressangle, Luton

The Late Ted Rogers's

3-2-1 XMAS QUIZ

"Solve the clue to find out what special festive present is hidden in Dusty Bin! Good luck!"

~ The late Ted Rogers

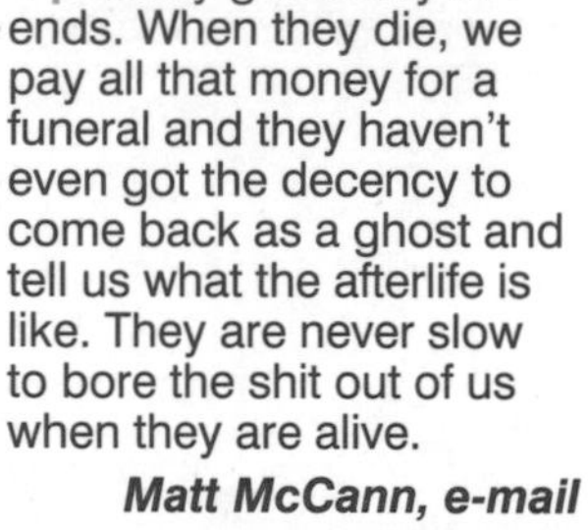

They're warm and they're snug and they fit on your feet,

They're inside your boots when you walk down the street,

Never alone - they're always a pair,

Darn them if they get a hole caused by wear!

Answer below:

Okay, so "they're warm and they're snug and they fit on your feet". Well what's warm and snug and fits on your feet? The answer might be shoes, and who has shoes? Well horses do. And something with an awful lot of horsepower is a shiny sportscar. "They're inside your boots when you walk down the street". Well, you get inside a car to drive it down the street, don't you, and a car has a boot. "Never alone - they're always a pair". Well two things make a pair, like the two seats in a high performance convertible. But a pair is also a fruit, and so is an apple. An apple, of course, has a "core", which is what people would say if they saw you driving down the road in a brand new Maserati. "Darn them if they get a hole caused by wear!" is the last line. Well "wear"ever you were headed, you'd have a "hole" lot of fun in your own sleek Italian supercar, wouldn't you. But as well as to abrade, the verb wear can also mean to put something on ... perhaps on your feet. That's right, it's a pair of socks.

sized living room, add 3 inches to the top and bottom and then multiply by 4. Then subtract 2 feet just to ensure the bastards can't get four lengths from each roll.

Tom Scott, e-mail

PARSNIP lovers. Save money by buying cheaper carrots and boiling them in water containing a little bleach.

James Turnip, e-mail

ANGLERS. Save money on expensive 20 foot long fishing rods by buying a 6 foot rod and sitting on the opposite bank of the canal.

P Watkinson, e-mail

NICK Griffin. After stating that you find the sight of two men kissing in public creepy, add that you find the sight of two women kissing highly erotic. That way you cannot be accused of homophobia.

Alasdair Henry, Newcastle

SKIERS. Carry a dog biscuit in your pocket. That way, in the event of an avalanche, the rescue dog will find you first.

J Tull, e-mail

AMATEUR winemakers. Pretend you tread your own grapes by standing in a bowl of purple rinse hair dye.

Dave Eccleston, Huyton

TORIES. Avoid wear and tear on your vocal chords when asked about poverty by simply shrugging your shoulders.

Hans Clap, e-mail

MAKE your own crunchy nut cornflakes by drizzling ordinary cornflakes with honey and sprinkling them with chopped almonds.

Tom Atow,e-mail

ROGER MELLIE
THE MAN ON THE TELLY
SAUNA
USED TOWELS
HI, TOM
HI, ROGER... HOW DID THE INTERVIEWING FOR THE RESEARCHER JOB GO?
WELL... I'M IN A BIT OF A QUANDRY ABOUT IT, TOM.
OH!?.. WHAT IS IT?
WELL, I HAD TWO CANDIDATES... ONE WAS THIS YOUNG LAD.. BAGS OF DRIVE AND EXPERIENCE...
SOUNDS GOOD
... PRESENTABLE, GREAT REFERENCES, THE LOT! COULD WALK INTO ANY JOB HE WANTED, TOM... EASY.
THE OTHER WAS THIS 19-YEAR OLD BIRD... THICK AS PIGSHIT AND BONE IDLE... BUT LEGS UP TO HER ARSE AND TITS LIKE SPACEHOPPERS.
ANY ADVICE, TOM?
WELL... I THINK IT'S OBVIOUS, ISN'T IT, ROGER?
NO...
...I MEAN... DO I TRY AND GET IN HER KNICKERS ON HER FIRST DAY AT WORK... OR DO I GIVE HER THE WEEK TO SETTLE IN?
...NO IT ISN'T, TOM... I REALLY DON'T KNOW WHAT TO DO...

✳ **I HAD** the misfortune of listening to a radio interview with Jay-Z the other day, during which he made several references to a 'God-given talent' that he had had bestowed upon him. Having listened to his music and found no clue as to what this talent is, I was wondering if any of your readers are able to tell me. Is he able to fart the alphabet or something?

Les, e-mail

✳ **WHY IS** it that, with all the millions he earns, Steven Gerrard still looks like he pays £6.50 for a haircut?

Nick, e-mail

✳ **I'VE JUST** read that Kelly Brook has denounced Ant and Dec for being two-faced. Well, how many faces does she expect them to have, the daft mare?

Johnny Pring, e-mail

✳ **THERE'S** a sign outside the Londis grocery store in Fleet Street which says 'Open 24 Hours Just for You.' I must admit that it's a huge gamble on their part, as I live in Surrey and only rarely pass through the area.

Christina Martin, e-mail

✳ **WHENEVER** that Autoglass advert comes on telly, I beam at my missus and sing 'Autoglass repair, Autoglass replace! Jism in your hair, jism on your face!' Does anyone want a broken Nintendo DS Lite?

Mr J Smith, e-mail

✳ **MY GOOD** mate Dave Russell from Cardiff drunkenly told me that he frequently thinks about men whilst masturbating, particularly Dec out of television's Ant and Dec. He telephoned me this morning and asked me to keep this information under my hat. Could any of your readers tell me what he meant by 'under my hat,' as it is not an expression I have come across before?

Les, e-mail

How to Enjoy a Family Festive Season

CHRISTMAS is a time for families. It's when we see our relations; we meet up with them to talk over past times and look forward to what next year will bring. Sometimes, it's the only chance we get to catch up with family members who live far away. They travel across the country to be with us at this most special time of year. The house is crowded and it's noisy with laughter and chatter. You can't hear the telly and there's probably somebody in your chair. To add insult to injury, you've got to spark up in your own fucking back yard because your spoilt nephew's got asthma.

You can't tell them all to simply piss off, because that would be rude, so what's the best way to stop them coming round in the first place? We went out on the streets to gather a few tips and wrinkles about keeping the family at bay during the festive season.

WHEN my elderly grandmother asks if she can come for Christmas, I tell her that she's welcome to stay, but since we will have a houseful of guests she'll have to sleep on the kitchen floor. Fortunately she suffers from crippling arthritis of the spine, so she invariably turns down my invitation.

Feliciano Bluewater, Surrey

I RING *up my relatives on Christmas Eve and tell them that the entire household has been laid low with a tummy bug. While I'm on the phone, my husband stands behind me making a farting noise with a bike pump with his thumb over the end, whilst my children empty tins of vegetable soup into a bucket.*

Felicity Carstairs, Roehampton

MY AGED mother lives on her own in a tower block, and she'd love to come to our house for Christmas Day. She's allergic to cats, so we usually buy a kitten around December 15th to keep her at bay. We put it in a sack and throw it in the river once the festivities are over.

Frank Hexagon, Reading

MY sister's got three children who I can't stand, so I took the precaution of indecently exposing myself near a school playground in order to get myself put on the Sex Offenders Register. The neighbours pushing dog dirt through my letterbox all year is a small price to pay for a nice quiet Christmas without my sister's horrible brats in the house.

Frank Crucible, Sheffield

MY 93-year-old mother lives in an old folks' home a couple of miles away. She looks forward all year to coming over to ours for Christmas dinner of turkey and all the trimmings with me, my wife and all her grandchildren. To prevent this, I phone her up on Christmas morning and tell her the car won't start. I've been doing this now since 1989, and it never fails because she can't remember what happened five minutes ago, never mind last year.

Fasbinder Glucose, Hull

EVERY December I announce to my family that I shan't be celebrating Christmas this year as I have turned Jewish. In case they demand evidence, I even have my foreskin chopped off. I keep it in a bag of peas in the freezer and get it sewn back on in January. It's a horrific and agonising ordeal to go through every year, but it's preferable to spending Christmas with my extended family. particularly my brother-in-law Reg, who is an utter cunt.

Fulton Suzuki, Yeovil

WHEN my relatives ask if they can come for Christmas, I adopt a sombre tone and tell them that there's nothing I'd like more, but unfortunately my husband is going into hospital for some tests on Christmas Eve. If they ask for any more details, I simply pretend to cry and tell them I don't want to talk about it.

Francine Gravy, Surbiton

WE turn out the lights hide behind the sofa when our relatives come round on Christmas Day, but they are very persistent and could stand on the step, knocking for hours. Consequently, we take everything we need to enjoy a lovely Christmas Day behind the sofa with us. The only concession we make is to remove the snaps from our crackers in case the noise alerts our unwanted visitors to our presence.

Freda Davitt, Huddersfield

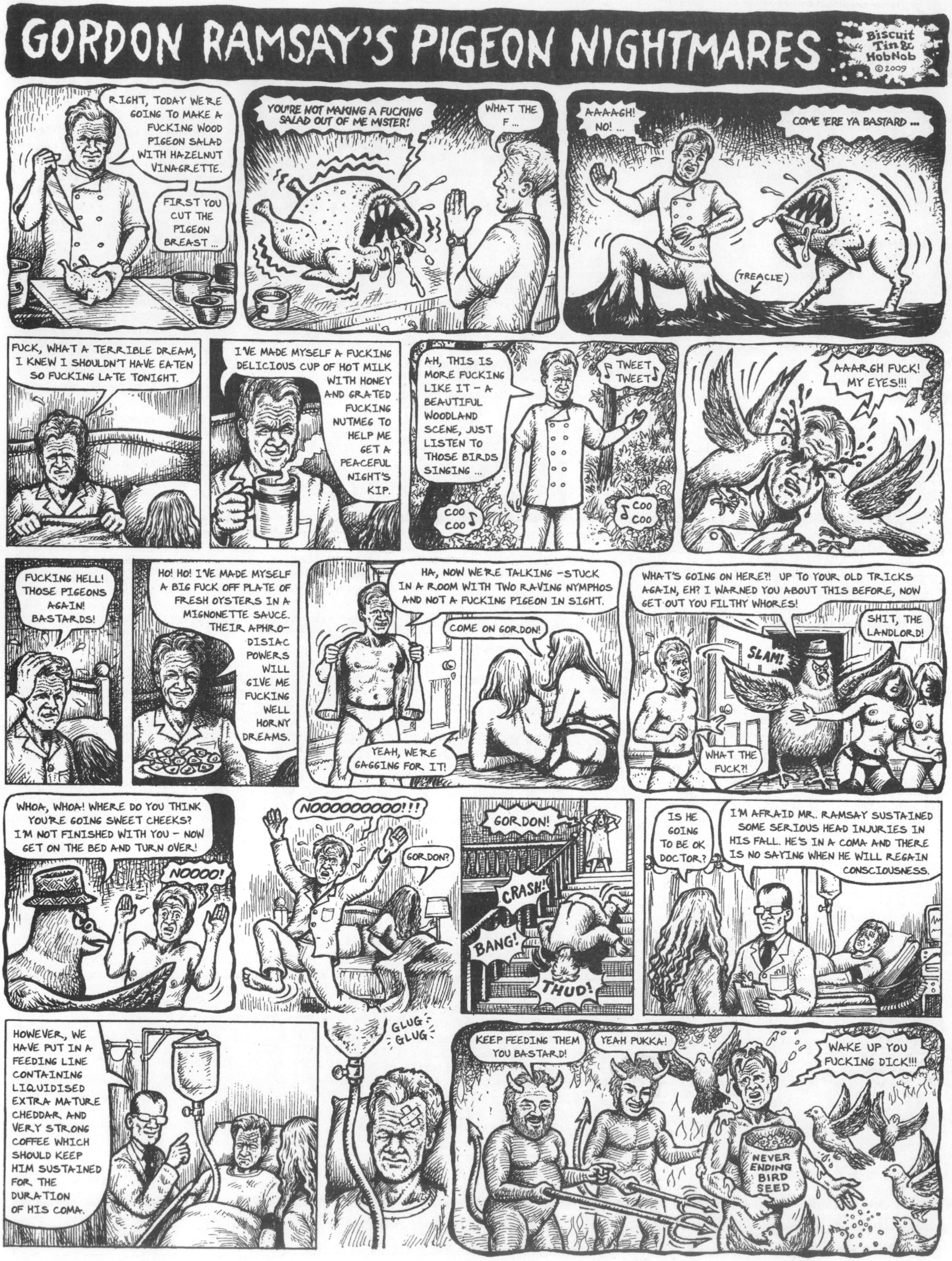
GORDON RAMSAY'S PIGEON NIGHTMARES
Biscuit Tin & HobNob ©2009
RIGHT, TODAY WE'RE GOING TO MAKE A FUCKING WOOD PIGEON SALAD WITH HAZELNUT VINAGRETTE.
FIRST YOU CUT THE PIGEON BREAST ...
YOU'RE NOT MAKING A FUCKING SALAD OUT OF ME MISTER!
WHAT THE F ...
AAAAGH! NO! ...
COME 'ERE YA BASTARD ...
(TREACLE)
FUCK, WHAT A TERRIBLE DREAM, I KNEW I SHOULDN'T HAVE EATEN SO FUCKING LATE TONIGHT.
I'VE MADE MYSELF A FUCKING DELICIOUS CUP OF HOT MILK WITH HONEY AND GRATED FUCKING NUTMEG TO HELP ME GET A PEACEFUL NIGHT'S KIP.
AH, THIS IS MORE FUCKING LIKE IT – A BEAUTIFUL WOODLAND SCENE, JUST LISTEN TO THOSE BIRDS SINGING ...
TWEET TWEET
COO COO
COO COO
AAARGH FUCK! MY EYES!!!
FUCKING HELL! THOSE PIGEONS AGAIN! BASTARDS!
HO! HO! I'VE MADE MYSELF A BIG FUCK OFF PLATE OF FRESH OYSTERS IN A MIGNONETTE SAUCE. THEIR APHRODISIAC POWERS WILL GIVE ME FUCKING WELL HORNY DREAMS.
HA, NOW WE'RE TALKING – STUCK IN A ROOM WITH TWO RAVING NYMPHOS AND NOT A FUCKING PIGEON IN SIGHT.
COME ON GORDON!
YEAH, WE'RE GAGGING FOR IT!
WHAT'S GOING ON HERE?! UP TO YOUR OLD TRICKS AGAIN, EH? I WARNED YOU ABOUT THIS BEFORE, NOW GET OUT YOU FILTHY WHORES!
SHIT, THE LANDLORD!
SLAM!
WHAT THE FUCK?!
WHOA, WHOA! WHERE DO YOU THINK YOU'RE GOING SWEET CHEEKS? I'M NOT FINISHED WITH YOU – NOW GET ON THE BED AND TURN OVER!
NOOOO!
NOOOOOOOOO!!!
GORDON?
GORDON!
CRASH!
BANG!
THUD!
IS HE GOING TO BE OK DOCTOR?
I'M AFRAID MR. RAMSAY SUSTAINED SOME SERIOUS HEAD INJURIES IN HIS FALL. HE'S IN A COMA AND THERE IS NO SAYING WHEN HE WILL REGAIN CONSCIOUSNESS.
HOWEVER, WE HAVE PUT IN A FEEDING LINE CONTAINING LIQUIDISED EXTRA MATURE CHEDDAR AND VERY STRONG COFFEE WHICH SHOULD KEEP HIM SUSTAINED FOR THE DURATION OF HIS COMA.
GLUG GLUG
KEEP FEEDING THEM YOU BASTARD!
YEAH PUKKA!
WAKE UP YOU FUCKING DICK!!!
NEVER ENDING BIRD SEED

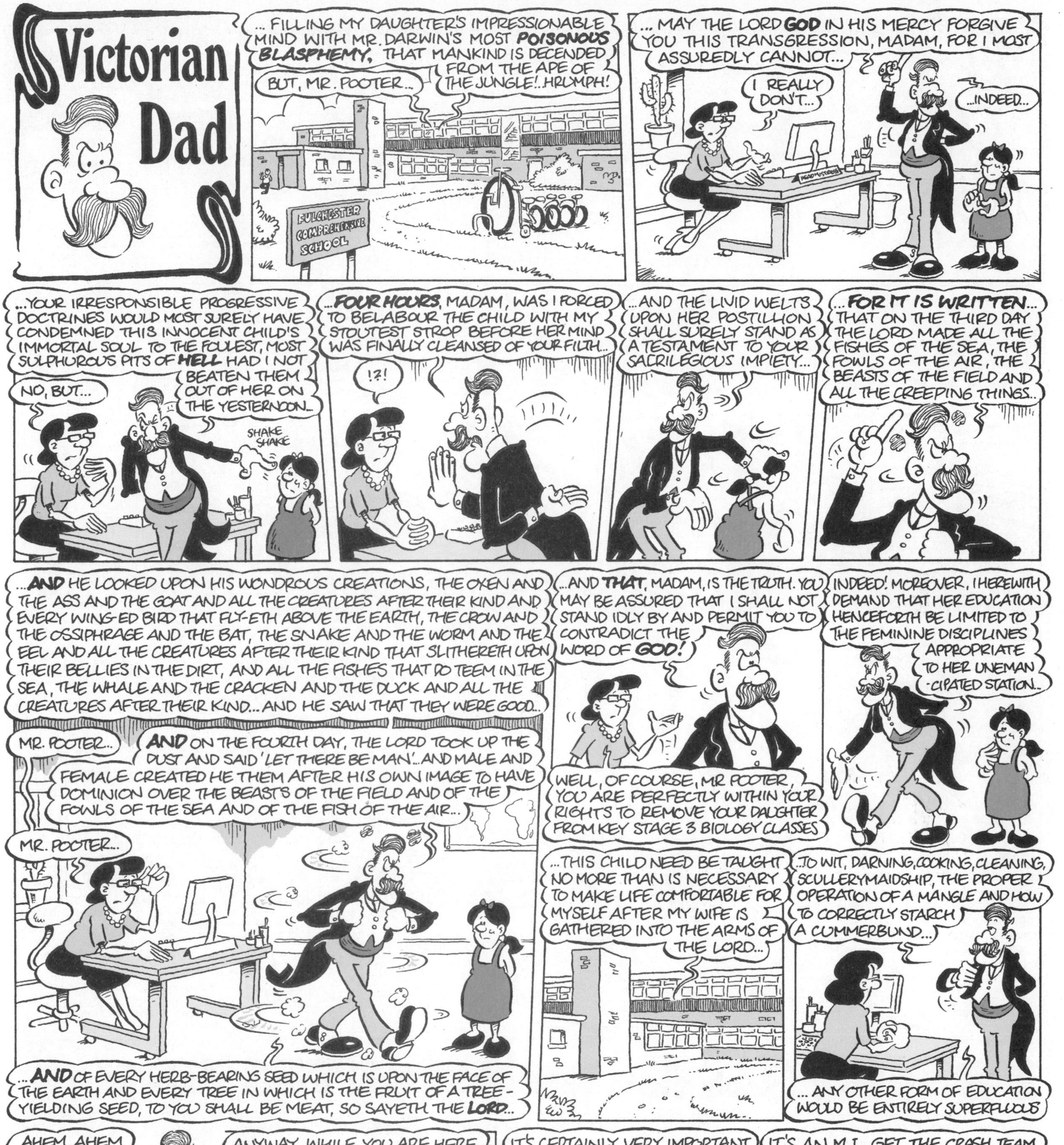
Victorian Dad
... FILLING MY DAUGHTER'S IMPRESSIONABLE MIND WITH MR. DARWIN'S MOST POISONOUS BLASPHEMY, THAT MANKIND IS DECENDED
BUT, MR. POOTER...
FROM THE APE OF THE JUNGLE!..HRUMPH!
FULCHESTER COMPREHENSIVE SCHOOL
... MAY THE LORD GOD IN HIS MERCY FORGIVE YOU THIS TRANSGRESSION, MADAM, FOR I MOST ASSUREDLY CANNOT...
I REALLY DON'T...
...INDEED...
...YOUR IRRESPONSIBLE PROGRESSIVE DOCTRINES WOULD MOST SURELY HAVE CONDEMNED THIS INNOCENT CHILD'S IMMORTAL SOUL TO THE FOULEST, MOST SULPHUROUS PITS OF HELL HAD I NOT
NO, BUT...
BEATEN THEM OUT OF HER ON THE YESTERNOON...
SHAKE SHAKE
...FOUR HOURS, MADAM, WAS I FORCED TO BELABOUR THE CHILD WITH MY STOUTEST STROP BEFORE HER MIND WAS FINALLY CLEANSED OF YOUR FILTH...
!?!
...AND THE LIVID WELTS UPON HER POSTILLION SHALL SURELY STAND AS A TESTAMENT TO YOUR SACRILEGIOUS IMPIETY...
...FOR IT IS WRITTEN... THAT ON THE THIRD DAY THE LORD MADE ALL THE FISHES OF THE SEA, THE FOWLS OF THE AIR, THE BEASTS OF THE FIELD AND ALL THE CREEPING THINGS...
...AND HE LOOKED UPON HIS WONDROUS CREATIONS, THE OXEN AND THE ASS AND THE GOAT AND ALL THE CREATURES AFTER THEIR KIND AND EVERY WING-ED BIRD THAT FLY-ETH ABOVE THE EARTH, THE CROW AND THE OSSIPHRAGE AND THE BAT, THE SNAKE AND THE WORM AND THE EEL AND ALL THE CREATURES AFTER THEIR KIND THAT SLITHERETH UPON THEIR BELLIES IN THE DIRT, AND ALL THE FISHES THAT DO TEEM IN THE SEA, THE WHALE AND THE CRACKEN AND THE DUCK AND ALL THE CREATURES AFTER THEIR KIND... AND HE SAW THAT THEY WERE GOOD...
MR. POOTER...
AND ON THE FOURTH DAY, THE LORD TOOK UP THE DUST AND SAID 'LET THERE BE MAN'...AND MALE AND FEMALE CREATED HE THEM AFTER HIS OWN IMAGE TO HAVE DOMINION OVER THE BEASTS OF THE FIELD AND OF THE FOWLS OF THE SEA AND OF THE FISH OF THE AIR...
MR. POOTER...
...AND OF EVERY HERB-BEARING SEED WHICH IS UPON THE FACE OF THE EARTH AND EVERY TREE IN WHICH IS THE FRUIT OF A TREE-YIELDING SEED, TO YOU SHALL BE MEAT, SO SAYETH THE LORD...
...AND THAT, MADAM, IS THE TRUTH. YOU MAY BE ASSURED THAT I SHALL NOT STAND IDLY BY AND PERMIT YOU TO CONTRADICT THE WORD OF GOD!
WELL, OF COURSE, MR POOTER, YOU ARE PERFECTLY WITHIN YOUR RIGHTS TO REMOVE YOUR DAUGHTER FROM KEY STAGE 3 BIOLOGY CLASSES
INDEED! MOREOVER, I HEREWITH DEMAND THAT HER EDUCATION HENCEFORTH BE LIMITED TO THE FEMININE DISCIPLINES
APPROPRIATE TO HER UNEMAN-CIPATED STATION...
...THIS CHILD NEED BE TAUGHT NO MORE THAN IS NECESSARY TO MAKE LIFE COMFORTABLE FOR MYSELF AFTER MY WIFE IS GATHERED INTO THE ARMS OF THE LORD...
...TO WIT, DARNING, COOKING, CLEANING, SCULLERYMAIDSHIP, THE PROPER OPERATION OF A MANGLE AND HOW TO CORRECTLY STARCH A CUMMERBUND...
... ANY OTHER FORM OF EDUCATION WOULD BE ENTIRELY SUPERFLUOUS
AHEM, AHEM AHEM.
HMM!
ANYWAY, WHILE YOU ARE HERE, HAVE YOU THOUGHT ABOUT WHETHER YOU'D LIKE YOUR DAUGHTER TO HAVE THE NEW CERVICAL CANCER VACCINE?
EGAD!!!
IT'S CERTAINLY VERY IMPORTANT THESE DAYS WITH GIRLS BECOMING SEXUALLY ACTIVE AT A YOUNGER AGE...
HNNG!
IT'S AN M.I...GET THE CRASH TEAM READY AT THE CARDIAC UNIT.
HNNG!...
QUICK!..APPLY A SULPHUR POLTICE SOAKED IN TINCTURE OF QUININE!

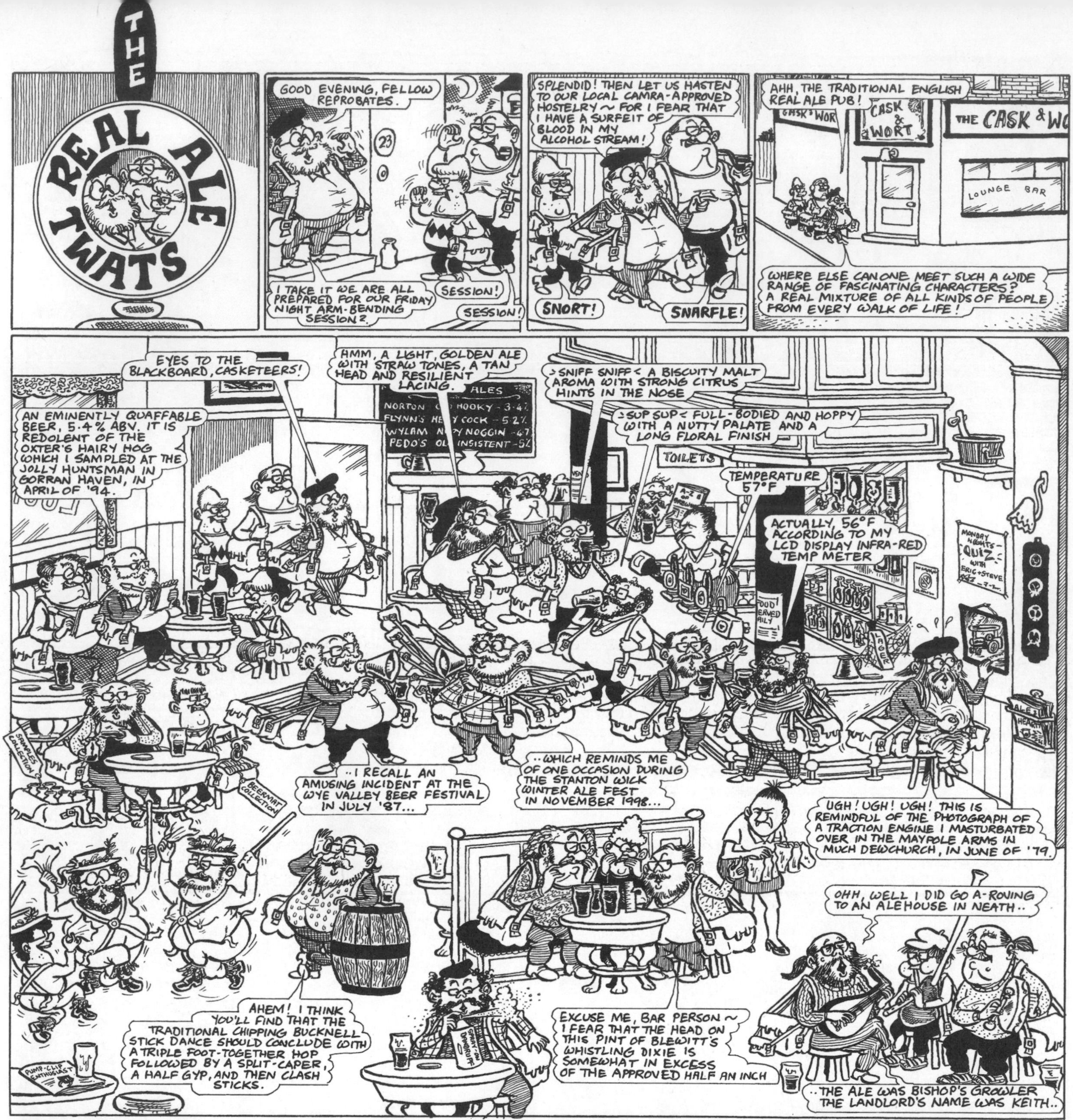
THE REAL ALE TWATS
GOOD EVENING, FELLOW REPROBATES.
23
I TAKE IT WE ARE ALL PREPARED FOR OUR FRIDAY NIGHT ARM-BENDING SESSION?.
SESSION!
SESSION!
SPLENDID! THEN LET US HASTEN TO OUR LOCAL CAMRA-APPROVED HOSTELRY ~ FOR I FEAR THAT I HAVE A SURFEIT OF BLOOD IN MY ALCOHOL STREAM!
SNORT!
SNARFLE!
AHH, THE TRADITIONAL ENGLISH REAL ALE PUB!
CASK & WORT
THE CASK & WO
LOUNGE BAR
WHERE ELSE CAN ONE MEET SUCH A WIDE RANGE OF FASCINATING CHARACTERS? A REAL MIXTURE OF ALL KINDS OF PEOPLE FROM EVERY WALK OF LIFE!
EYES TO THE BLACKBOARD, CASKETEERS!
HMM, A LIGHT, GOLDEN ALE WITH STRAW TONES, A TAN HEAD AND RESILIENT LACING.
>SNIFF SNIFF< A BISCUITY MALT AROMA WITH STRONG CITRUS HINTS IN THE NOSE
AN EMINENTLY QUAFFABLE BEER, 5.4% ABV. IT IS REDOLENT OF THE OXTER'S HAIRY HOG WHICH I SAMPLED AT THE JOLLY HUNTSMAN IN GORRAN HAVEN, IN APRIL OF '94.
>SUP SUP< FULL-BODIED AND HOPPY WITH A NUTTY PALATE AND A LONG FLORAL FINISH
TOILETS
TEMPERATURE 57°F
ACTUALLY, 56°F ACCORDING TO MY LCD DISPLAY INFRA-RED TEMP METER
..I RECALL AN AMUSING INCIDENT AT THE WYE VALLEY BEER FESTIVAL IN JULY '87...
..WHICH REMINDS ME OF ONE OCCASION DURING THE STANTON WICK WINTER ALE FEST IN NOVEMBER 1998...
UGH! UGH! UGH! THIS IS REMINDFUL OF THE PHOTOGRAPH OF A TRACTION ENGINE I MASTURBATED OVER IN THE MAYPOLE ARMS IN MUCH DEWCHURCH, IN JUNE OF '79.
OHH, WELL I DID GO A-ROVING TO AN ALEHOUSE IN NEATH..
AHEM! I THINK YOU'LL FIND THAT THE TRADITIONAL CHIPPING BUCKNELL STICK DANCE SHOULD CONCLUDE WITH A TRIPLE FOOT-TOGETHER HOP FOLLOWED BY A SPLIT-CAPER, A HALF GYP, AND THEN CLASH STICKS.
EXCUSE ME, BAR PERSON ~ I FEAR THAT THE HEAD ON THIS PINT OF BLEWITT'S WHISTLING DIXIE IS SOMEWHAT IN EXCESS OF THE APPROVED HALF AN INCH
..THE ALE WAS BISHOP'S GROWLER THE LANDLORD'S NAME WAS KEITH..

ROGER MELLIE - THE MAN ON THE TELLY

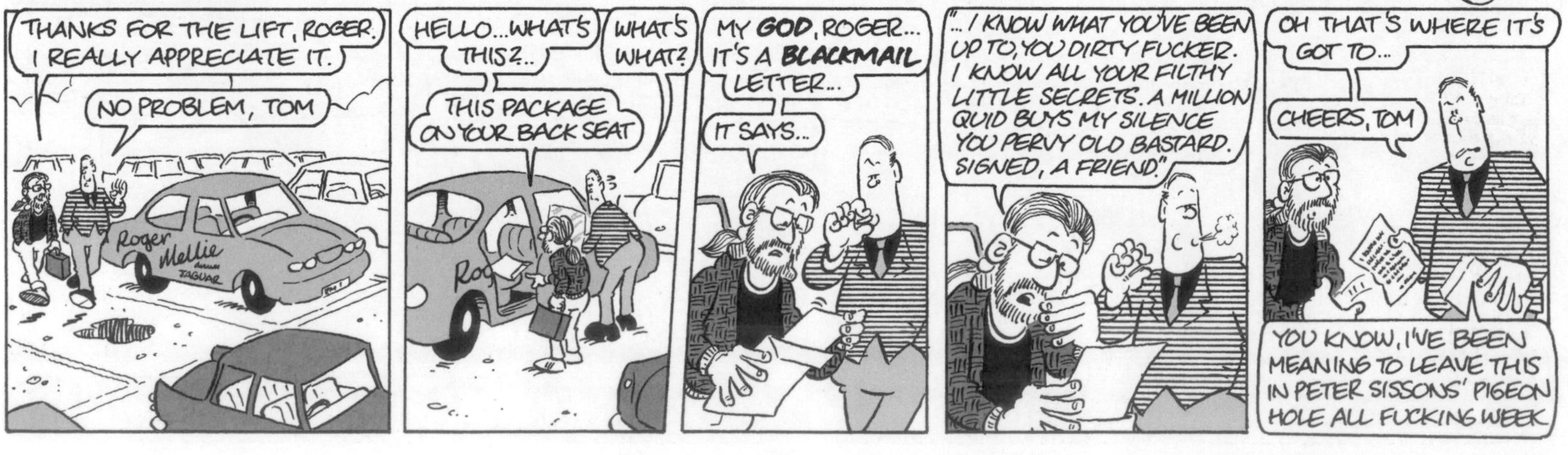
THANKS FOR THE LIFT, ROGER. I REALLY APPRECIATE IT.
NO PROBLEM, TOM
Roger Mellie
HELLO...WHAT'S THIS?..
WHAT'S WHAT?
THIS PACKAGE ON YOUR BACK SEAT
MY GOD, ROGER... IT'S A BLACKMAIL LETTER...
IT SAYS...
"...I KNOW WHAT YOU'VE BEEN UP TO, YOU DIRTY FUCKER. I KNOW ALL YOUR FILTHY LITTLE SECRETS. A MILLION QUID BUYS MY SILENCE YOU PERVY OLD BASTARD. SIGNED, A FRIEND."
OH THAT'S WHERE IT'S GOT TO...
CHEERS, TOM
YOU KNOW, I'VE BEEN MEANING TO LEAVE THIS IN PETER SISSONS' PIGEON HOLE ALL FUCKING WEEK

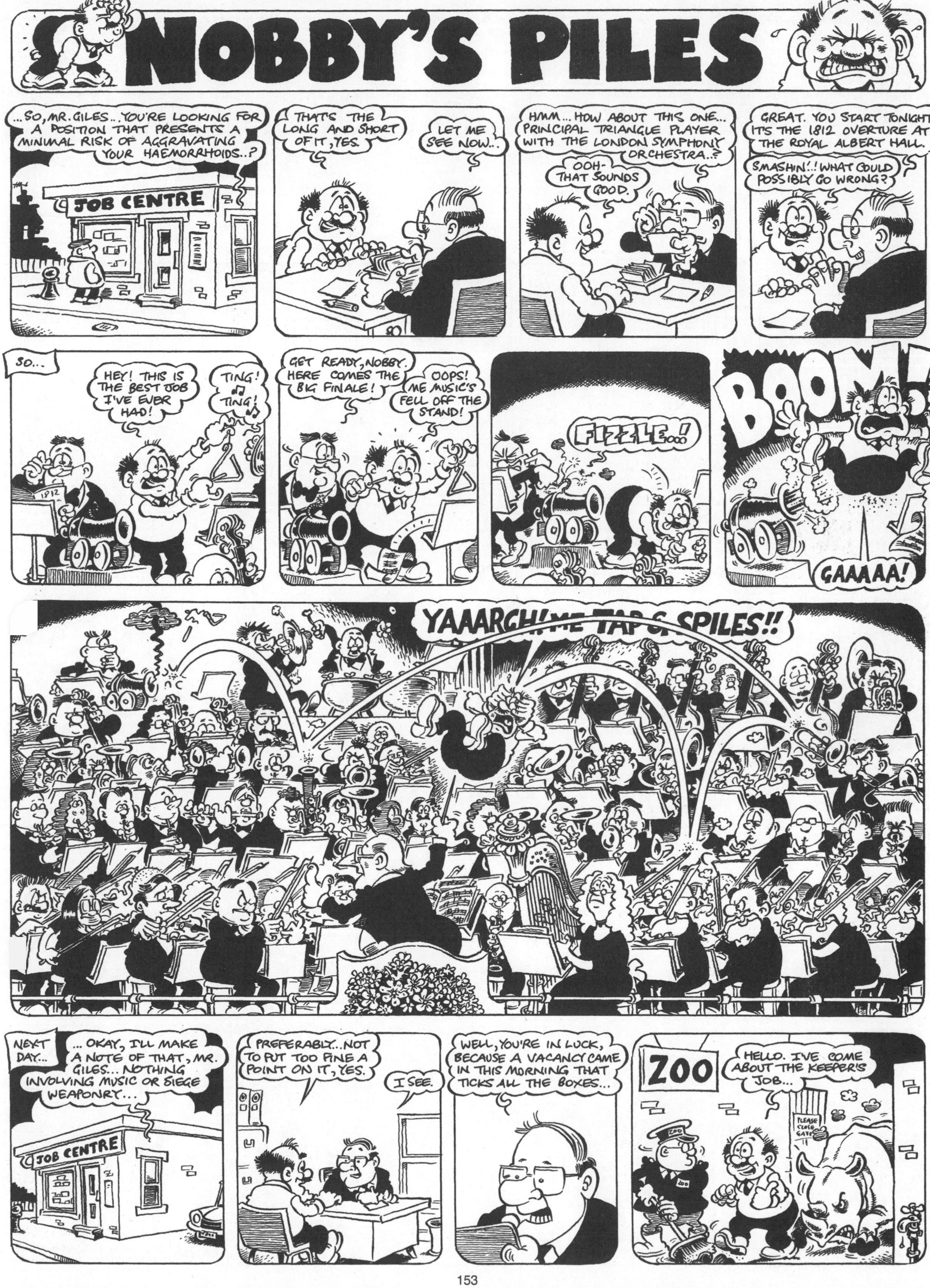
NOBBY'S PILES
...SO, MR. GILES... YOU'RE LOOKING FOR A POSITION THAT PRESENTS A MINIMAL RISK OF AGGRAVATING YOUR HAEMORRHOIDS...?
JOB CENTRE
THAT'S THE LONG AND SHORT OF IT, YES.
LET ME SEE NOW...
HMM... HOW ABOUT THIS ONE... PRINCIPAL TRIANGLE PLAYER WITH THE LONDON SYMPHONY ORCHESTRA...?
OOH-THAT SOUNDS GOOD.
GREAT. YOU START TONIGHT. IT'S THE 1812 OVERTURE AT THE ROYAL ALBERT HALL.
SMASHIN'..! WHAT COULD POSSIBLY GO WRONG?
SO...
HEY! THIS IS THE BEST JOB I'VE EVER HAD!
TING! TING!
1812
GET READY, NOBBY. HERE COMES THE BIG FINALE!
OOPS! ME MUSIC'S FELL OFF THE STAND!
FIZZLE...!
BOOM!
GAAAAA!
YAAARGH! ME TAP & SPILES!!
NEXT DAY...
...OKAY, I'LL MAKE A NOTE OF THAT, MR. GILES... NOTHING INVOLVING MUSIC OR SIEGE WEAPONRY...
JOB CENTRE
PREFERABLY... NOT TO PUT TOO FINE A POINT ON IT, YES.
I SEE.
WELL, YOU'RE IN LUCK, BECAUSE A VACANCY CAME IN THIS MORNING THAT TICKS ALL THE BOXES...
ZOO
HELLO. I'VE COME ABOUT THE KEEPER'S JOB...
PLEASE CLOSE GATE
ZOO

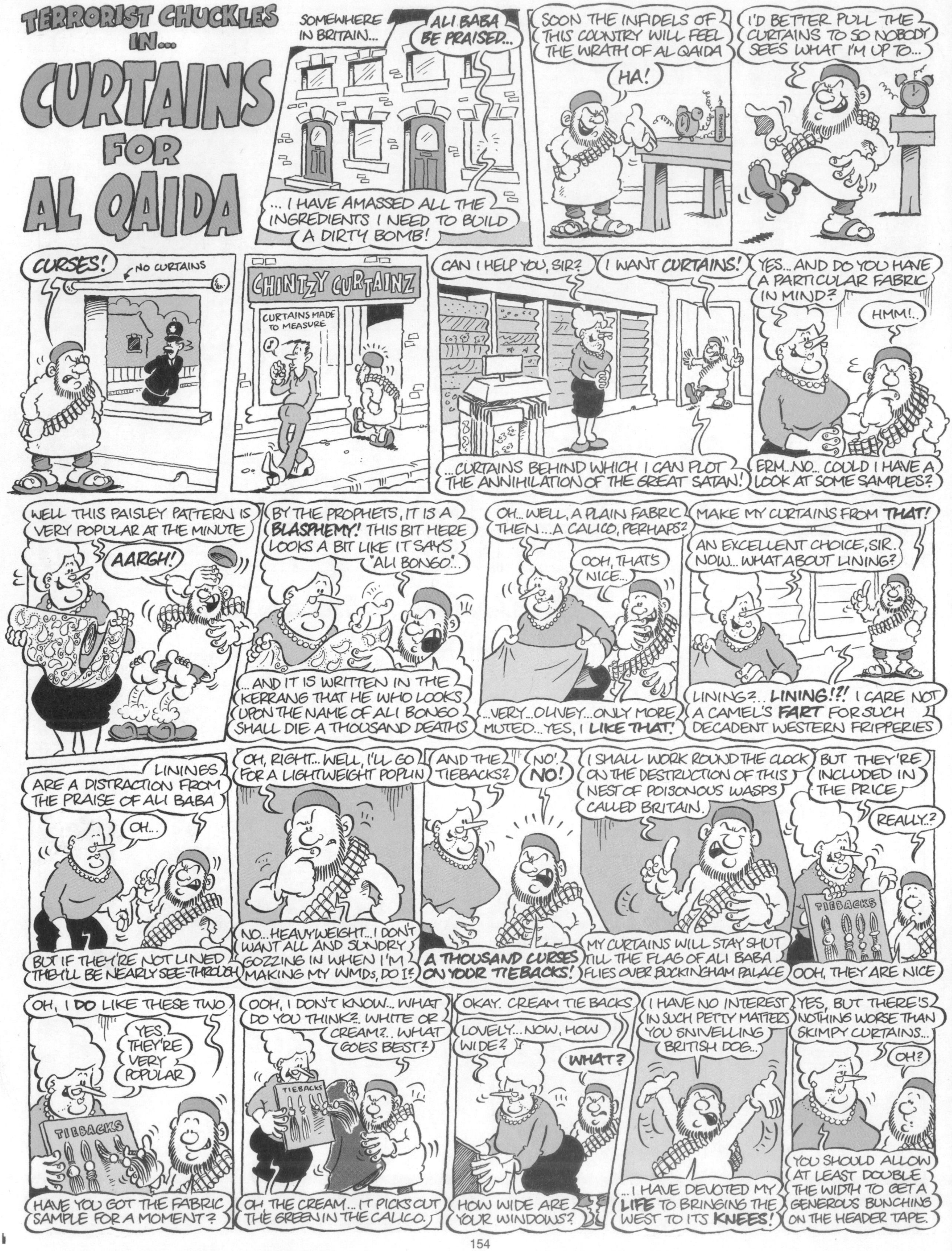
TERRORIST CHUCKLES IN...
CURTAINS FOR AL QAIDA
SOMEWHERE IN BRITAIN...
ALI BABA BE PRAISED...
...I HAVE AMASSED ALL THE INGREDIENTS I NEED TO BUILD A DIRTY BOMB!
SOON THE INFIDELS OF THIS COUNTRY WILL FEEL THE WRATH OF AL QAIDA
HA!
I'D BETTER PULL THE CURTAINS TO SO NOBODY SEES WHAT I'M UP TO...
CURSES!
NO CURTAINS
CHINTZY CURTAINZ
CURTAINS MADE TO MEASURE
CAN I HELP YOU, SIR?
I WANT CURTAINS!
...CURTAINS BEHIND WHICH I CAN PLOT THE ANNIHILATION OF THE GREAT SATAN!
YES... AND DO YOU HAVE A PARTICULAR FABRIC IN MIND?
HMM!..
ERM...NO... COULD I HAVE A LOOK AT SOME SAMPLES?
WELL THIS PAISLEY PATTERN IS VERY POPULAR AT THE MINUTE
AARGH!
BY THE PROPHETS, IT IS A BLASPHEMY! THIS BIT HERE LOOKS A BIT LIKE IT SAYS "ALI BONGO"...
...AND IT IS WRITTEN IN THE KERRANG THAT HE WHO LOOKS UPON THE NAME OF ALI BONGO SHALL DIE A THOUSAND DEATHS
OH... WELL, A PLAIN FABRIC THEN... A CALICO, PERHAPS?
OOH, THAT'S NICE...
...VERY... OLIVEY... ONLY MORE MUTED... YES, I LIKE THAT!
MAKE MY CURTAINS FROM THAT!
AN EXCELLENT CHOICE, SIR. NOW... WHAT ABOUT LINING?
LINING?... LINING!?! I CARE NOT A CAMEL'S FART FOR SUCH DECADENT WESTERN FRIPPERIES
LININGS ARE A DISTRACTION FROM THE PRAISE OF ALI BABA
OH...
BUT IF THEY'RE NOT LINED THEY'LL BE NEARLY SEE-THROUGH
OH, RIGHT... WELL, I'LL GO FOR A LIGHTWEIGHT POPLIN
NO... HEAVYWEIGHT... I DON'T WANT ALL AND SUNDRY GOZZING IN WHEN I'M MAKING MY WMDs, DO I?
AND THE TIEBACKS?
NO! NO!
A THOUSAND CURSES ON YOUR TIEBACKS!
I SHALL WORK ROUND THE CLOCK ON THE DESTRUCTION OF THIS NEST OF POISONOUS WASPS CALLED BRITAIN.
MY CURTAINS WILL STAY SHUT TILL THE FLAG OF ALI BABA FLIES OVER BUCKINGHAM PALACE
BUT THEY'RE INCLUDED IN THE PRICE
REALLY?
TIEBACKS
OOH, THEY ARE NICE
OH, I DO LIKE THESE TWO
YES. THEY'RE VERY POPULAR
TIEBACKS
HAVE YOU GOT THE FABRIC SAMPLE FOR A MOMENT?
OOH, I DON'T KNOW... WHAT DO YOU THINK?.. WHITE OR CREAM?.. WHAT GOES BEST?
TIEBACKS
OH THE CREAM... IT PICKS OUT THE GREEN IN THE CALICO.
OKAY. CREAM TIE BACKS
LOVELY... NOW, HOW WIDE?
WHAT?
HOW WIDE ARE YOUR WINDOWS?
I HAVE NO INTEREST IN SUCH PETTY MATTERS YOU SNIVELLING BRITISH DOG...
...I HAVE DEVOTED MY LIFE TO BRINGING THE WEST TO ITS KNEES!
YES, BUT THERE'S NOTHING WORSE THAN SKIMPY CURTAINS...
OH?
YOU SHOULD ALLOW AT LEAST DOUBLE THE WIDTH TO GET A GENEROUS BUNCHING ON THE HEADER TAPE.

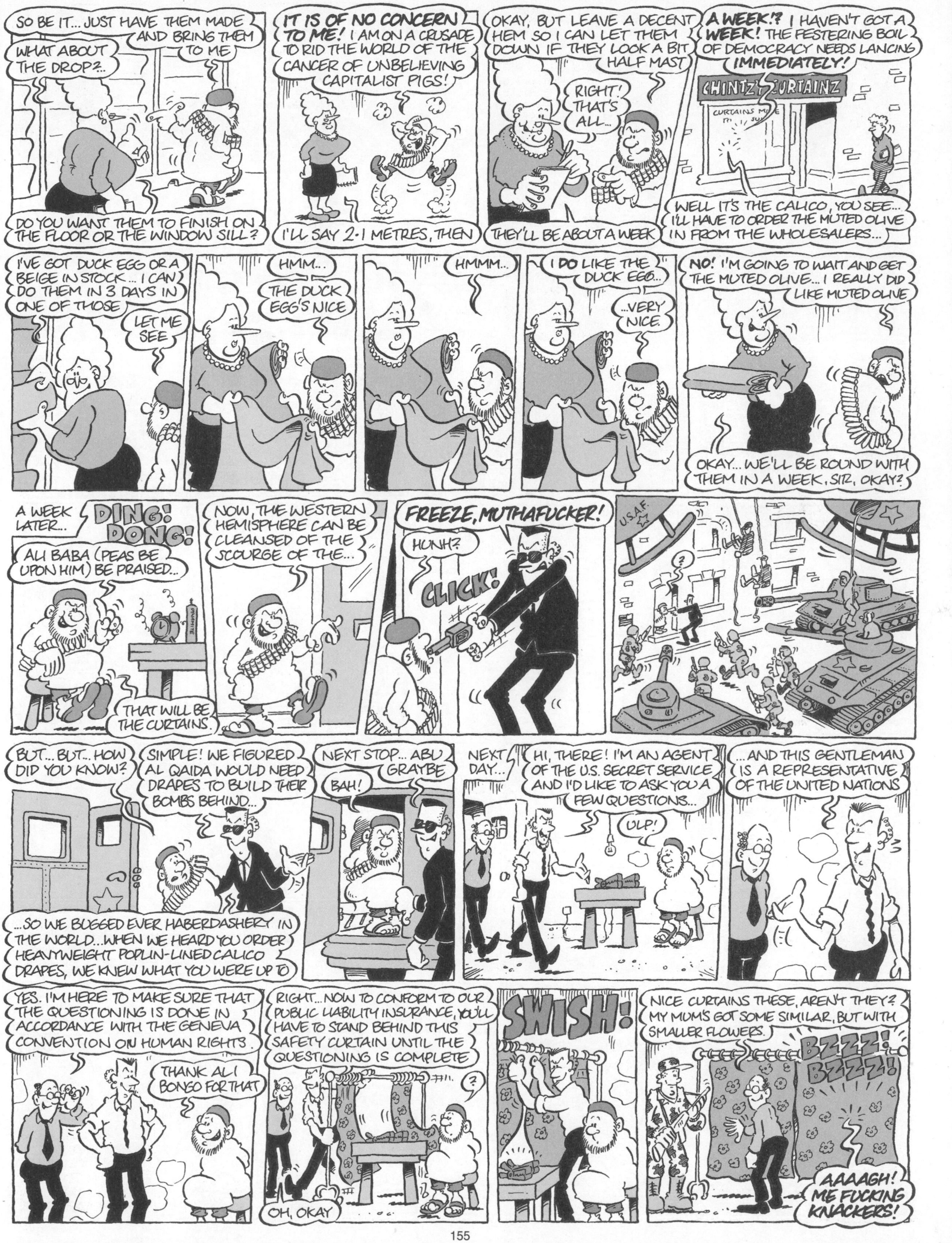
SO BE IT... JUST HAVE THEM MADE AND BRING THEM TO ME
WHAT ABOUT THE DROP?..
DO YOU WANT THEM TO FINISH ON THE FLOOR OR THE WINDOW SILL?
IT IS OF NO CONCERN TO ME! I AM ON A CRUSADE TO RID THE WORLD OF THE CANCER OF UNBELIEVING CAPITALIST PIGS!
I'LL SAY 2·1 METRES, THEN
OKAY, BUT LEAVE A DECENT HEM SO I CAN LET THEM DOWN IF THEY LOOK A BIT HALF MAST
RIGHT! THAT'S ALL...
THEY'LL BE ABOUT A WEEK
A WEEK!? I HAVEN'T GOT A WEEK! THE FESTERING BOIL OF DEMOCRACY NEEDS LANCING IMMEDIATELY!
CHINTZ CURTAINZ
WELL IT'S THE CALICO, YOU SEE... I'LL HAVE TO ORDER THE MUTED OLIVE IN FROM THE WHOLESALERS...
I'VE GOT DUCK EGG OR A BEIGE IN STOCK... I CAN DO THEM IN 3 DAYS IN ONE OF THOSE
LET ME SEE
HMM...
THE DUCK EGG'S NICE
HMMM...
I DO LIKE THE DUCK EGG...
...VERY NICE
NO! I'M GOING TO WAIT AND GET THE MUTED OLIVE... I REALLY DID LIKE MUTED OLIVE
OKAY... WE'LL BE ROUND WITH THEM IN A WEEK, SIR, OKAY?
A WEEK LATER...
DING! DONG!
ALI BABA (PEAS BE UPON HIM) BE PRAISED...
THAT WILL BE THE CURTAINS.
NOW, THE WESTERN HEMISPHERE CAN BE CLEANSED OF THE SCOURGE OF THE...
FREEZE, MUTHAFUCKER!
HUNH?
CLICK!
U.S.A.F.
BUT... BUT... HOW DID YOU KNOW?
SIMPLE! WE FIGURED AL QAIDA WOULD NEED DRAPES TO BUILD THEIR BOMBS BEHIND...
...SO WE BUGGED EVER HABERDASHERY IN THE WORLD... WHEN WE HEARD YOU ORDER HEAVYWEIGHT POPLIN-LINED CALICO DRAPES, WE KNEW WHAT YOU WERE UP TO
NEXT STOP... ABU GRAYBE
BAH!
NEXT DAY...
HI, THERE! I'M AN AGENT OF THE U.S. SECRET SERVICE AND I'D LIKE TO ASK YOU A FEW QUESTIONS...
ULP!
...AND THIS GENTLEMAN IS A REPRESENTATIVE OF THE UNITED NATIONS
YES. I'M HERE TO MAKE SURE THAT THE QUESTIONING IS DONE IN ACCORDANCE WITH THE GENEVA CONVENTION ON HUMAN RIGHTS.
THANK ALI BONGO FOR THAT
RIGHT... NOW TO CONFORM TO OUR PUBLIC LIABILITY INSURANCE, YOU'LL HAVE TO STAND BEHIND THIS SAFETY CURTAIN UNTIL THE QUESTIONING IS COMPLETE
?
OH, OKAY
SWISH!
NICE CURTAINS THESE, AREN'T THEY? MY MUM'S GOT SOME SIMILAR, BUT WITH SMALLER FLOWERS.
BZZZ! BZZZ!
AAAAGH! ME FUCKING KNACKERS!

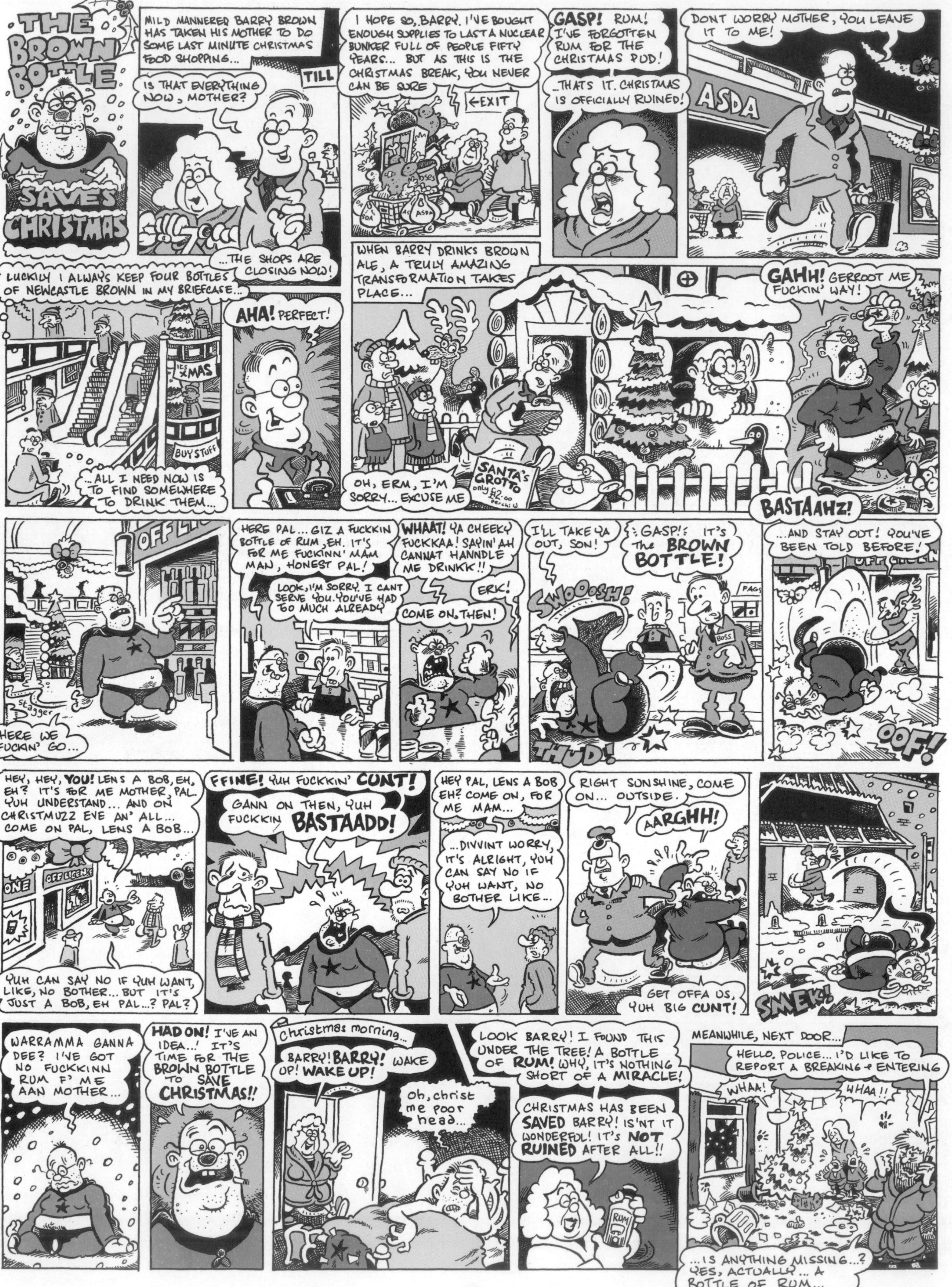
THE BROWN BOTTLE SAVES CHRISTMAS
MILD MANNERED BARRY BROWN HAS TAKEN HIS MOTHER TO DO SOME LAST MINUTE CHRISTMAS FOOD SHOPPING...
IS THAT EVERYTHING NOW, MOTHER?
TILL
...THE SHOPS ARE CLOSING NOW!
I HOPE SO, BARRY. I'VE BOUGHT ENOUGH SUPPLIES TO LAST A NUCLEAR BUNKER FULL OF PEOPLE FIFTY YEARS... BUT AS THIS IS THE CHRISTMAS BREAK, YOU NEVER CAN BE SURE
←EXIT
ASDA
GASP! RUM! I'VE FORGOTTEN RUM FOR THE CHRISTMAS PUD!
...THATS IT. CHRISTMAS IS OFFICIALLY RUINED!
DONT WORRY MOTHER, YOU LEAVE IT TO ME!
ASDA
LUCKILY I ALWAYS KEEP FOUR BOTTLES OF NEWCASTLE BROWN IN MY BRIEFCASE...
XMAS
BUY STUFF
...ALL I NEED NOW IS TO FIND SOMEWHERE TO DRINK THEM...
AHA! PERFECT!
WHEN BARRY DRINKS BROWN ALE, A TRULY AMAZING TRANSFORMATION TAKES PLACE...
OH, ERM, I'M SORRY... EXCUSE ME
SANTA'S GROTTO only £2.00
GAHH! GERROOT ME FUCKIN' WAY!
BASTAAHZ!
HERE WE FUCKIN' GO...
stagger
HERE PAL... GIZ A FUCKKIN BOTTLE OF RUM, EH. IT'S FOR ME FUCKINN' MAM MAN, HONEST PAL!
LOOK, I'M SORRY. I CANT SERVE YOU. YOU'VE HAD TOO MUCH ALREADY
WHAAT! YA CHEEKY FUCKKAA! SAYIN' AH CANNAT HANNDLE ME DRINKK!!
ERK!
COME ON, THEN!
I'LL TAKE YA OUT, SON!
GASP! IT'S THE BROWN BOTTLE!
SWOOOSH!
BOSS
THUD!
...AND STAY OUT! YOU'VE BEEN TOLD BEFORE!
OOF!
HEY, HEY, YOU! LENS A BOB, EH, EH? IT'S FOR ME MOTHER, PAL. YUH UNDERSTAND... AND ON CHRISTMUZZ EVE AN' ALL... COME ON PAL, LENS A BOB...
OFF LICENCE
YUH CAN SAY NO IF YUH WANT, LIKE, NO BOTHER... BUT IT'S JUST A BOB, EH PAL...? PAL?
FFINE! YUH FUCKKIN' CUNT!
GANN ON THEN, YUH FUCKKIN BASTAADD!
HEY PAL, LENS A BOB EH? COME ON, FOR ME MAM...
...DIVVINT WORRY, IT'S ALRIGHT, YUH CAN SAY NO IF YUH WANT, NO BOTHER LIKE...
RIGHT SUNSHINE, COME ON... OUTSIDE.
AARGHH!
GET OFFA US, YUH BIG CUNT!
SMEK!
WARRAMMA GANNA DEE? I'VE GOT NO FUCKKINN RUM F' ME AAN MOTHER...
HAD ON! I'VE AN IDEA...! IT'S TIME FOR THE BROWN BOTTLE TO SAVE CHRISTMAS!!
Christmas morning...
BARRY! BARRY! WAKE UP! WAKE UP!
Oh, christ me poor head...
LOOK BARRY! I FOUND THIS UNDER THE TREE! A BOTTLE OF RUM! WHY, IT'S NOTHING SHORT OF A MIRACLE!
CHRISTMAS HAS BEEN SAVED BARRY! ISN'T IT WONDERFUL! IT'S NOT RUINED AFTER ALL!!
RUM
MEANWHILE, NEXT DOOR...
HELLO, POLICE... I'D LIKE TO REPORT A BREAKING & ENTERING
WHAA!
WHAA!!
...IS ANYTHING MISSING...? YES, ACTUALLY... A BOTTLE OF RUM...

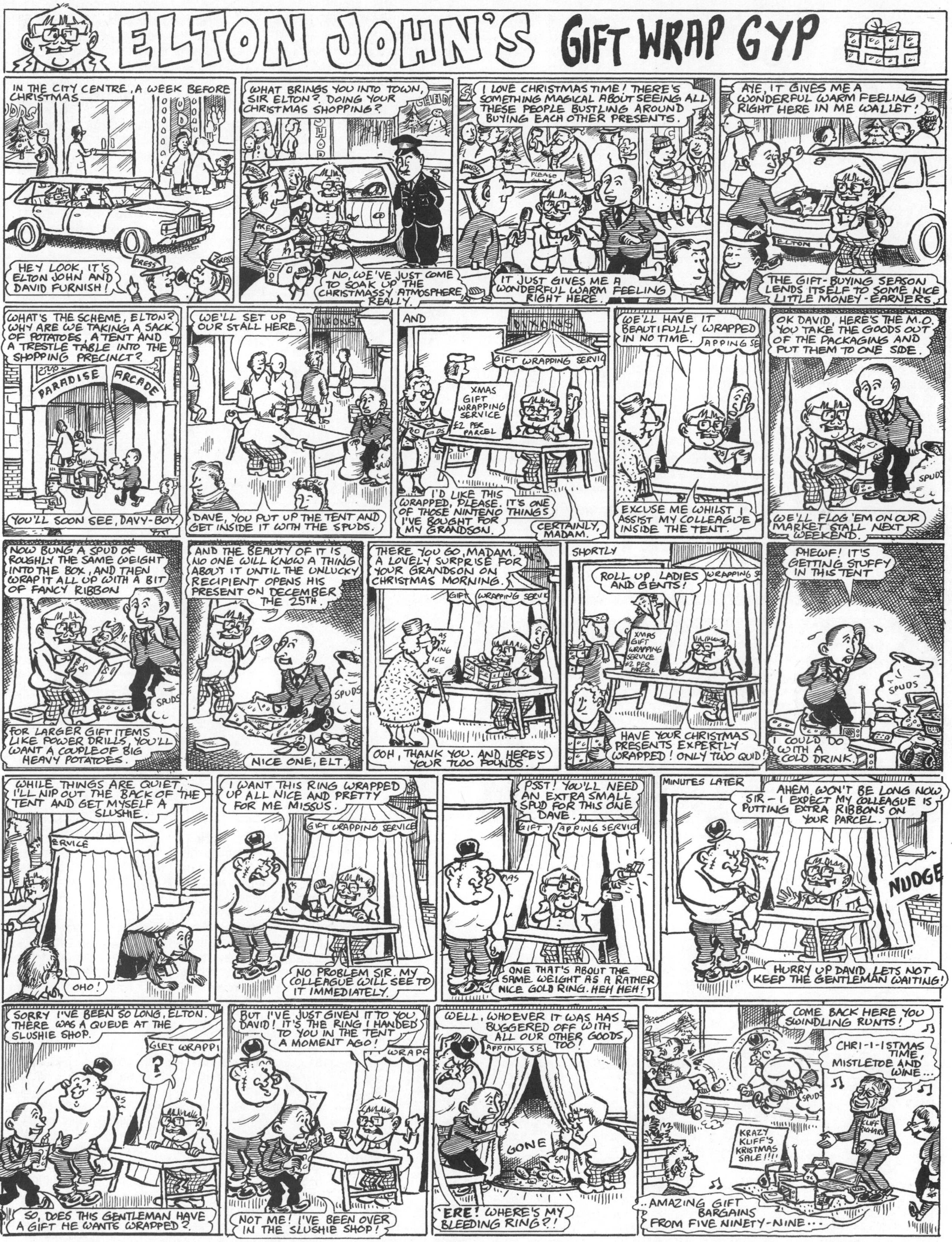
ELTON JOHN'S GIFT WRAP GYP
IN THE CITY CENTRE, A WEEK BEFORE CHRISTMAS...
HEY LOOK, IT'S ELTON JOHN AND DAVID FURNISH!
PRESS
WHAT BRINGS YOU INTO TOWN, SIR ELTON? DOING YOUR CHRISTMAS SHOPPING?
NO, WE'VE JUST COME TO SOAK UP THE CHRISTMASSY ATMOSPHERE, REALLY.
I LOVE CHRISTMAS TIME! THERE'S SOMETHING MAGICAL ABOUT SEEING ALL THESE PEOPLE BUSTLING AROUND BUYING EACH OTHER PRESENTS.
IT JUST GIVES ME A WONDERFUL WARM FEELING RIGHT HERE.
AYE, IT GIVES ME A WONDERFUL WARM FEELING RIGHT HERE IN ME WALLET!
THE GIFT-BUYING SEASON LENDS ITSELF TO SOME NICE LITTLE MONEY-EARNERS.
WHAT'S THE SCHEME, ELTON? WHY ARE WE TAKING A SACK OF POTATOES, A TENT AND A TRESTLE TABLE INTO THE SHOPPING PRECINCT?
PARADISE ARCADE
YOU'LL SOON SEE, DAVY-BOY.
WE'LL SET UP OUR STALL HERE.
DAVE, YOU PUT UP THE TENT AND GET INSIDE IT WITH THE SPUDS.
AND
GIFT WRAPPING SERVIC
XMAS GIFT WRAPPING SERVICE £2 PER PARCEL
I'D LIKE THIS WRAPPED, PLEASE. IT'S ONE OF THOSE NINTENO THINGS I'VE BOUGHT FOR MY GRANDSON.
CERTAINLY, MADAM.
WE'LL HAVE IT BEAUTIFULLY WRAPPED IN NO TIME.
EXCUSE ME WHILST I ASSIST MY COLLEAGUE INSIDE THE TENT.
OK DAVID, HERE'S THE M.O. YOU TAKE THE GOODS OUT OF THE PACKAGING AND PUT THEM TO ONE SIDE.
WE'LL FLOG 'EM ON OUR MARKET STALL NEXT WEEKEND.
SPUDS
NOW BUNG A SPUD OF ROUGHLY THE SAME WEIGHT INTO THE BOX, AND THEN WRAP IT ALL UP WITH A BIT OF FANCY RIBBON.
FOR LARGER GIFT ITEMS LIKE POWER DRILLS, YOU'LL WANT A COUPLE OF BIG HEAVY POTATOES.
AND THE BEAUTY OF IT IS NO ONE WILL KNOW A THING ABOUT IT UNTIL THE UNLUCKY RECIPIENT OPENS HIS PRESENT ON DECEMBER THE 25TH.
NICE ONE, ELT.
THERE YOU GO, MADAM. A LOVELY SURPRISE FOR YOUR GRANDSON ON CHRISTMAS MORNING.
OOH, THANK YOU. AND HERE'S YOUR TWO POUNDS.
SHORTLY
ROLL UP, LADIES AND GENTS!
HAVE YOUR CHRISTMAS PRESENTS EXPERTLY WRAPPED! ONLY TWO QUID!
PHEW! IT'S GETTING STUFFY IN THIS TENT.
I COULD DO WITH A COLD DRINK.
WHILE THINGS ARE QUIET, I'LL NIP OUT THE BACK OF THE TENT AND GET MYSELF A SLUSHIE.
OHO!
I WANT THIS RING WRAPPED UP ALL NICE AND PRETTY FOR ME MISSUS.
NO PROBLEM SIR. MY COLLEAGUE WILL SEE TO IT IMMEDIATELY.
PSST! YOU'LL NEED AN EXTRA SMALL SPUD FOR THIS ONE DAVE.
ONE THAT'S ABOUT THE SAME WEIGHT AS A RATHER NICE GOLD RING. HEH HEH!
MINUTES LATER
AHEM. WON'T BE LONG NOW, SIR - I EXPECT MY COLLEAGUE IS PUTTING EXTRA RIBBONS ON YOUR PARCEL.
NUDGE
HURRY UP DAVID, LETS NOT KEEP THE GENTLEMAN WAITING!
SORRY I'VE BEEN SO LONG, ELTON. THERE WAS A QUEUE AT THE SLUSHIE SHOP.
?
SO, DOES THIS GENTLEMAN HAVE A GIFT HE WANTS WRAPPED?
BUT I'VE JUST GIVEN IT TO YOU DAVID! IT'S THE RING I HANDED TO YOU IN THE TENT A MOMENT AGO!
NOT ME! I'VE BEEN OVER IN THE SLUSHIE SHOP!
WELL, WHOEVER IT WAS HAS BUGGERED OFF WITH ALL OUR OTHER GOODS, TOO!
GONE
'ERE! WHERE'S MY BLEEDING RING?!
COME BACK HERE YOU SWINDLING RUNTS!
CHRI-I-ISTMAS TIME, MISTLETOE AND WINE...
KRAZY KLIFF'S KRISTMAS SALE!!!
..AMAZING GIFT BARGAINS FROM FIVE NINETY-NINE...

STOP and THINK!

NOWADAYS WE ALL TAKE haemorrhoids for granted. The painfully swollen blood vessels which protrude from our anuses are as much a part of our modern lives as motor cars, microwave ovens and colour television sets. But have you ever stopped to think about the amazing ways in which these agonising and embarrassing objects have shaped human history? Let's take a slow, bow-legged stroll back through time, stopping along the way to wince, adjust our gussets and look at...

Haemorrhoids Through the Ages

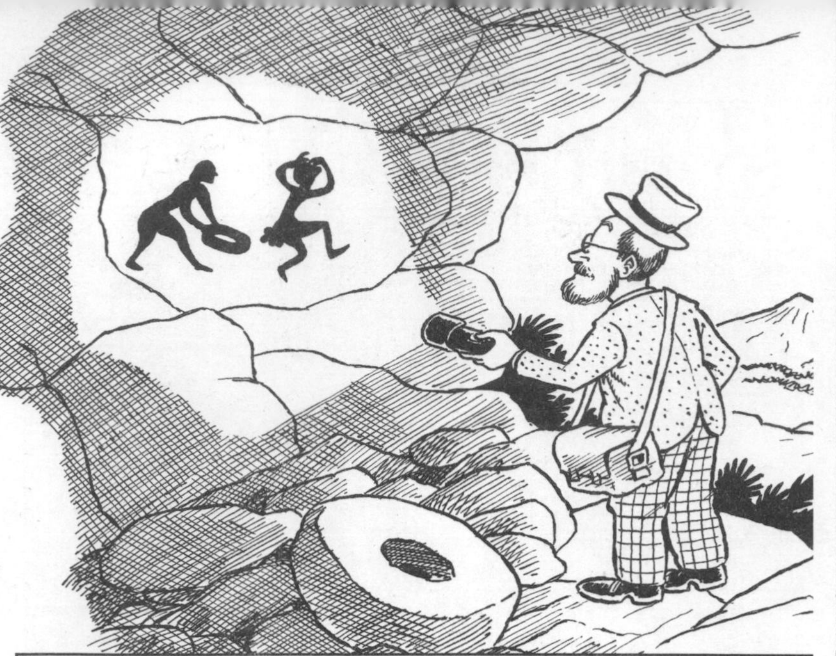

DOCTORS agree that haemorrhoids are caused by the weight of the gut bearing down on the rectum. This pressure causes blood vessels to swell and protrude through the anus. When primitive man first took the decision to come down from the trees and stand on his hind legs, Chalfonts were here to stay. Whilst excavating caves in France, archaeologists unearthed large, doughnut shaped rocks that at first were assumed to have been used for grinding corn. But following the discovery of cave paintings showing Neolithic hunter-gatherers suffering from enormous farmers, it is now believed that the artifacts are stone cushions, used to relieve the pressure on our ancestors' tender bum grapes.

CHRISTIANS believe that haemorrhoids are the Lord's way of testing our faith. According to the Bible, the first man to be afflicted with piles was the Old Testament prophet Job: "And the LORD spake unto Job in a loud voice saying, You are my beloved son that hath never foresaken me or taken my name upon your lips in vain. Yet still I know not whether your faith be true. And so it came to pass that the LORD did smite Job with the botch of Egypt and the span of his emerods was even unto one cubit and an half and the number thereof was multitude and mighty was the throbbing. And yet did Job still not take the LORD's name in vain, excepting just the once when the LORD didst place a hedgehog upon his litter and Job did sit upon it, crying out in a loud voice, saying, Jesus fucking wept! Me River Niles. And the LORD waxed exceeding wrathful, saying unto Job, A-ha! Just as I thought I have tested you and found your faith wanting. And Job was cast into the lowest pit of Hell for all eternity whereof demons and beelzebubs and imps poked him in the emerods with brillo pads and cactus trees and other pointy things and the number of the pointy things was legion. And great was the woe of Job."

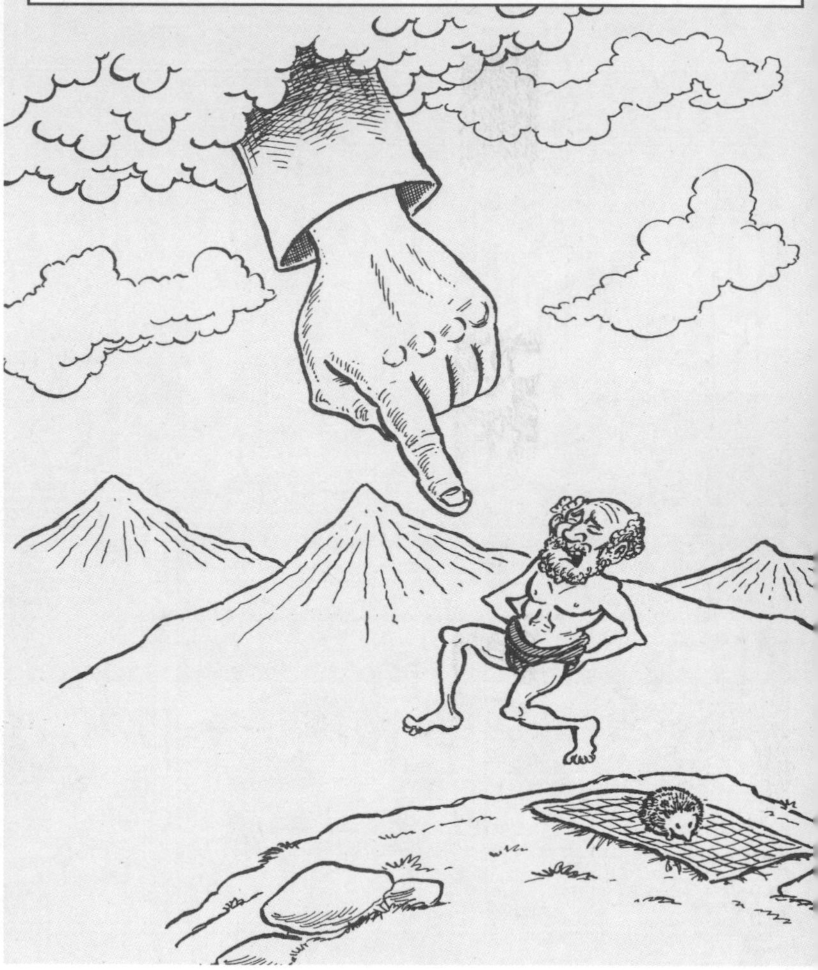

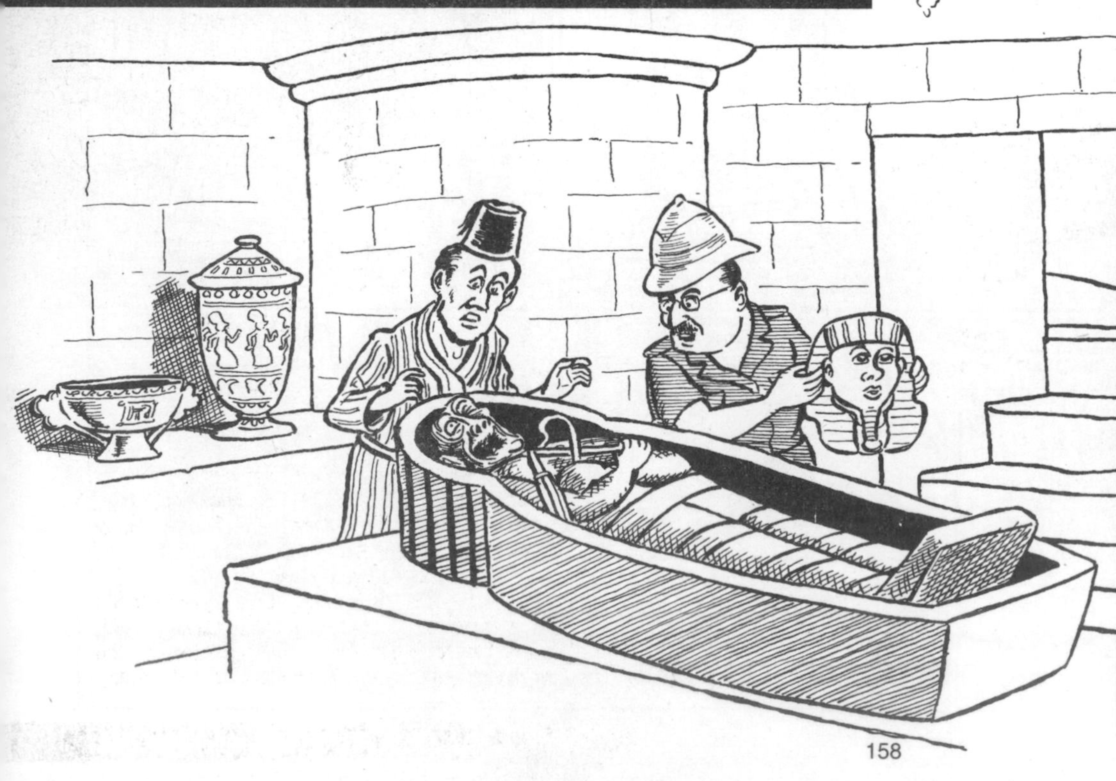

WHEN tomb raider Howard Carter removed the gold deathmask from the mummified remains of Tutunkhamun, he was met with a horrifying sight. For the late Pharaoh's face was contorted into a dreadful rictus of agony. Years of sitting on an onyx throne had caused the Boy King to develop the most excruciating Emma Freuds, a fact which was confirmed by examination of hieroglyphics on the walls of his tomb. Later, the mummified piles themselves were discovered in an ante-chamber, wrapped in bandages and stored in a canopic jar. They had been removed and preserved after the King's death so that his spirit could continue his agonies in the afterlife.

EVERY schoolboy knows how eighteenth century highwayman Dick Turpin famously rode his faithful steed Black Bess the 200 miles from London to York in a bid to escape the hangman's noose. What is less well known is that his marathon stint in the saddle brought down his galloping piles. Indeed, by the time he reached Stevenage, he was wincing so much that he was unable to open his eyes to see where he was going. When he finally got to his destination 11 hours later, Turpin was in such agony that he went straight to York police station where he confessed to all his crimes and begged to be executed.